The First of the Line

The First of the Line

The Avro Manchester Story

Robert Kirby
BSc (Hons), PhD, Dist.D.NE.

www.aviationbooks.org

About the Author

Following obtaining his doctorate at King's College, London, Bob Kirby has worked in the broad field of Oceanography. As a government researcher, he discovered and named a number of new phenomena in his field. Subsequently, as a consultant, he has invented and implemented a number of new and more advanced technologies for managing sediment in coastal waters, especially for the international port and shipping industry. In 2010 he was made a Distinguished Diplomate in Navigation Engineering by the prestigious American Society of Civil Engineers. Also, in that year he won the Telford Premium Award from the Institution of Civil Engineers in the UK.

He has maintained a lifelong interest in aviation, especially in the Second World War. From the early 1980s he took a particular interest in the under-researched Avro Manchester which, with relatively minor refinement, became the famous Lancaster. Following the publication of the first edition of his book on this aircraft in 1995, his continued studies have led to this new and definitive history.

Bob lives in Taunton, Somerset with his wife, Janette. They have two children and three grandchildren.

Originally published by Midland Publishing Limited in 1995 as *Avro Manchester – The Legend Behind the Lancaster*

Second edition published by Fonthill Media Limited in 2015.

This updated third edition first published in 2024 as *The First of the Line* by Aviation Books Ltd., CF47 8RY.

Copyright 2024 © Robert Kirby.

The right of Robert Kirby to be identified as Author of this work is asserted by him in accordance with the Copyright, Designs and Patents Act 1988.

Crown Copyright images and material are stored in microfiche and digital format by the National Archives. This material is reproduced under Open Licence v. 3.0.

All rights reserved. No part of this publication may be reproduced, stored in a retrieval system, transmitted in any form or by any means, electronic, mechanical, or photocopied, recorded or otherwise, without the written permission of the copyright owners.

This work has been researched, compiled and written by its author, who has made every effort to ensure the accuracy of the information contained in it. The author will not be liable for any damages caused, or alleged to be caused, by any information contained in this book. E. & O.E.

Every effort is made to trace the copyright holders of photographs and we apologise in advance for any unintentional omissions. These and other errors brought to our attention will be corrected in subsequent editions of this work.

A CIP catalogue reference for this book is available from the British Library.

ISBN 9781915335463

DEDICATION

Dedicated to the air and ground crews of RAF Bomber Command,
not forgetting my airborne cousins who flew, fought and survived -

Sidney Kirby, W/op Air, 44 Squadron 5 Group RAF Bomber Command
G. Alan Kirby, W/op Air, 150 Squadron 1 Group RAF Bomber Command
Dennis Kirby, Pilot, 880 Squadron Fleet Air Arm, HMS *Implacable*
Kenneth H. Kirby, Pilot, 294 Squadron RAF Coastal Command
and my uncle, Harold Beckett, TFU, later Blind Landing Experiment Unit, RAF Defford,
who inspired me.

Similarly, my cousins –
Steward Cecil Kirby, RN, who overcame his premonition on his last shore leave,
bravely rejoined his ship and was lost at sea when HMS *Gurkha* was torpedoed
and sunk off Sidi Barrani in the Mediterranean 17 January 1942. NKG.

and

Pte Leslie Kirby, Royal Army Medical Corps. who was cruelly abused by the Japanese
on the infamous Burma Railway.

Also, in memory of our Uncle Ces –

George Cecil Kirby, East Yorkshire Regiment, 9 January 1896 to 16 May 1917, KIA, NKG

Table of Contents

Foreword to First Edition 8
Foreword to Second Edition 11
Foreword to Third Edition 13
Acknowledgements for First Edition 14
Acknowledgements for Second Edition 15
Chapter One: A Difficult Birth 16
Chapter Two: Into Service 58
Chapter Three: First Operations 75
Chapter Four: Catastrophe 112
Chapter Five: A Faltering Return 153
Chapter Six: Against the Battlecruisers 223
Chapter Seven: New Tactics, New Owners 277
Chapter Eight: The Thousand Raids 301
Chapter Nine: Second Line Service 324
Chapter Ten: Reckoning 348
Appendix One: Manchester Evaders Reports 359
Appendix Two: Manchester Units 382
Appendix Three: Sortie and Despatch Statistics 386
Appendix Four: Aircraft Losses by Unit 390
Appendix Five: Individual Aircraft Histories 394
Bibliography 419

Foreword to First Edition

Wing Commander T. C. Weir DFC

It was March 1941 when, at last, Avro Manchesters began arriving at 61 Squadron. They came to us with great expectations and we gazed on them with awe and respect. No longer need we envy those squadrons that had been privileged to receive and operate their Manchesters before us. Needless to say, we felt some degree of inferiority. We had high hopes for the Manchester. Its size, bomb-carrying capacity, operating range, the enormous 2,000-hp Rolls-Royce Vulture engines, the huge airscrews were all very impressive to us who had been flying Handley Page Hampdens for so long. The luxury and sophistication of gun turrets provided a special feeling of protection from enemy attack.

Squadron conversion to the new aircraft was slow over the next three months. Training was periodically interrupted because Manchesters were being grounded for engine modifications. The Vulture engines were not standing up under normal training and intensive flying conditions. Engines were seizing up, dense fumes and white metal particles spewed from exhausts, and on occasion the failure of airscrews to feather, all contributed to a number of crashes and loss of life among Manchester squadrons during this period.

It was always a disappointment when the Manchesters were grounded although we knew it was for safety reasons, and only for a short time. Morale among the crews was maintained to a reasonable level by operating the few Hampdens we still had on strength in the squadron until the Manchesters returned to service. We had faith in each of the modifications and in the ability of our maintenance crews to make the aircraft safe for us. But there were disturbing stories circulating that height could not be maintained on one engine, and that crews had been forced to abandon their aircraft. Nevertheless, our desire to fly our Manchesters did not diminish. We were aware that a problem with the Vulture engine existed but, with supreme confidence, we believed that we could handle any situation. Besides, whatever the problem, it was always something that would happen to one of the other crews.

Some of our training flights involved intensive flying tests in which the engines were subjected to overload conditions, war load climbs and airscrew feathering. On one such flight I had on board a valuable cargo of thirteen aircrew members of the squadron, mostly pilots, to observe the tests. Suddenly, toward the end of the test, it happened. The port engine failed at about 1,000 feet 20 miles from base. Fortunately, the port airscrew feathered perfectly. Then followed a harrowing 20 minutes nursing the aircraft back to base, where we landed safely to the great relief of all on board. Rolls-Royce technicians were especially pleased to get a defective engine intact.

One of many Canadian aircrew in 5 Group, Wing Commander T. C. Weir DFC was a flight commander in 61 Squadron when the first Manchester was received. He became Commanding Officer on 5 September 1941, when Wing Commander G. E. Valentine was killed, and remained in command until June 1942, by which time 61 Squadron had relinquished their Manchesters (for Lancasters). (via Wing Commander T. C. Weir)

The Manchester responded lazily to the controls in the air. It had poor climbing ability because the Vultures were underpowered and inefficient for such a large aircraft, especially under bomb load conditions. Also, operating height over enemy territory was much lower than desired. However, we accepted these failings knowing we were delivering a much heavier bomb load than we had been accustomed to with our Hampdens.

Late in June 1941 the squadron carried out a few operational sorties in Manchesters but this period was short-lived. The Manchesters were grounded again and the squadron reverted to operating the Hampdens during the next three months. Manchester air time during this period consisted mostly of a limited number of intensive flying tests. This was a particularly difficult time for the squadron. There were two upheavals: first the squadron moved from Hemswell to North Luffenham, followed shortly afterwards to Woolfox Lodge. I was wounded one night by anti-aircraft fire, and while on sick leave was informed that our Squadron Commander, Wing Commander George Valentine, had gone missing on a Berlin trip in a Manchester, taking with him the station commander and several key station and squadron members. I was recalled immediately to take command of 61 Squadron. At this time, we did not seem to be a very effective part of the war effort. Morale was at a low level. In October 1941, when it seemed that the Vulture engine problems had been solved, flying hours on Manchesters increased, consisting mainly of training flights and conversion of more crews. Our confidence in the Manchester improved and, with the increasing activity, morale also began to improve.

We began to take part in operations again in December. The Manchester was capable of sustaining considerable flak and machine gun damage and still remaining under control in the air. Miraculously, many machines returned from operations severely damaged by enemy action. We were not always aware of the actual reason that some machines failed to return. Enemy action was usually considered the main reason but, in retrospect, it is possible that engine failure on a long, arduous flight could have contributed to losses.

Most pilots had their own favoured method of making their bombing run over the target. It was like believing in the benefit of a good luck charm. Some tried to follow closely an aircraft ahead, believing the first aircraft would get most of the attention from the flak gunners. Some glided, with reduced throttle, over the target. My plan was to study the pattern of flak concentration as I approached the target from some distance away, I imagined it was rhythmic with heavy and light concentrations, so I would time my run over the target as the flak concentration appeared to die down momentarily. Right or wrong, I convinced myself that these tactics were infallible.

Soon we began receiving additional Manchesters, exceeding our squadron establishment. These were transferred to us from other squadrons which were converting at that time to Lancasters. In addition, the squadron swelled with a heavy intake of newly graduated aircrews from Operational Training Units. The burden of converting these crews onto Manchesters rested with the squadron. Allocating flying time to such a large number of crews, and air time per serviceable aircraft required good organising ability by the two flight commanders, Squadron Leaders Paape and West. These two officers had provided long, efficient service in the squadron, and their operational tours were stretching out. I was hoping they would soon complete their lengthy tours and go on well-deserved rest periods. We had several good, experienced officers who could be recommended to take their places. In addition, the demand for flying hours put a great strain on our maintenance personnel to keep serviceability of aircraft at a high level for both operational and training duties.

In March 1942 we started conversion to Lancasters and April saw the last of the Manchesters in 61 Squadron. It had been thirteen months alternating between optimism and frustration; a difficult time for any commander to maintain squadron morale, especially among aircrews.

I had a young Canadian air gunner in my crew who often provided a little lift for me. He would poke his head through my office doorway to ask if we were flying on operations that night. If the answer was 'No', I could clearly hear him muttering as he turned away, 'Ah, heck!'

That completes the story of the Manchester during its period of service in 61 squadron. It is sad to relate that the Manchester did not make its way into greatness, but it did leave its mark. Perhaps its most notable claim to fame is that its weaknesses gave birth to the magnificent Avro Lancaster.

Dr Kirby has studied the Avro Manchester and the Rolls-Royce Vulture engine for many years. He researched manufacturer's records, RAF records, and all Manchester equipped squadrons in 5 Group, Bomber Command, gaining a thorough knowledge and understanding of the service history of the Manchester. Dr Kirby has been instrumental in awakening the memories of former members of aircrews, and in doing so has brought some interesting and exciting stories to light. Of special note, he had brought some aircrew members into contact with each other after so many years. In particular, in at least one case, one crew member found another whom he believed had not survived the war.

Hidden for 50 years, this gem is from a small batch of photographs taken at Waddington on 17 July 1941 by Sir Cecil Beaton. Five unknown aircrew members from 207 Squadron pose with L7378 EM-A. This evocative picture serves as a fine tribute to all Manchester aircrews. Cecil Beaton, (Courtesy of Sotherby's, London)

Foreword to Second Edition

In respect of official records of the development and service history of the aircraft, two files were devoted to the Manchester. These are 627801/37 which related to the period 1936 to 1939 and AVIA15/2323 for 1939 to 1942. Regrettably, 627801/37 was destroyed in the late 1940s, fortunately not before Professor Lindhoff had made a brief summary for the Ministry of Supply. AVIA15/2323 remains available in the National Archives in Kew. The situation with respect to the aircraft and engine manufacturer is little better. Most Avro drawings and records related to the Manchester were destroyed in a fire at Chadderton in 1959, whilst the drawings and documentation related to the Rolls-Royce Vulture were disposed of by an over-zealous manager in recent years. Records of A&AEE trials at Boscombe Down remain in place and have been consulted, but regrettably the archives of the Catapult & Arrested Landing Department of RAE Farnborough were transferred when that department moved out to RAE Bedford in the 1950s. When Bedford closed the trail went cold. Operational records in the various unit Form 540 and 541s are complete, although skeletal, at Kew. Complementary Luftwaffe records were destroyed or are difficult to gain access to.

Twenty years have passed since the first edition was published in 1995. In that time a wide variety of additional material has emerged and the manner in which World War II aviation history is approached has advanced. As the number of Manchester survivors have dwindled, we have shifted from spoken to written history, whilst the passing of that generation is yielding a number of formerly unknown archives and photographs. Furthermore, the researcher's task is now greatly eased by distillations in a number of key reference books and much readier interchange via the internet between researchers in the UK, France, Belgium, Holland, Germany and elsewhere has become routine.

The first edition has now been extended and corrected using these several routes and gaps have been filled. The account of early aircraft development has benefitted from information taken from diaries kept by A. V. Roe's test pilots. A former RAE employee engaged in accelerated take-off and arrested-landing trials helped make the chapter on Second Line Service more authoritative. Inevitable gaps in operational experiences throughout this history have often been filled with recently emerged participant's accounts, offering a more rounded product. Additional German night fighter combat reports are occasionally available and incorporated. This new rendering is accompanied by further fresh illustrations.

The early war years remain difficult to write about with any degree of intimacy. Many aircrews died in the Manchester era or in later war service. This is compounded by photography and record-keeping being formally frowned upon in the early war years with a view to avoiding giving inadvertent military assistance to any potential invading forces.

A number of aircraft, the Mosquito, Spitfire, Mustang and others, sprang more or less fully formed off the drawing board. Many others, such as the Lerwick, Botha, Blackburn B.20, even the Battle, on which high hopes were initially pinned, were flops. This history deals with what became our 'war-winning bomber' – the Manchester/Lancaster. This aircraft had a prolonged and difficult gestation and in its early life a myriad problems bedevilled it. The account deals with a stream of constant development and improvement between 1936 and 1943, which only found its ultimate expression with the Lancaster prototype's first flight in January 1941 and its commencement of front-line operations early in 1942.

Over this period, to name but a single theme, the wings, designed to span 72 feet, first emerged at 80 feet and proved to be woefully inadequate. The operational Manchester benefitted from a further extension to 90 feet 1 inch. A 95-feet stretch was stillborn and the definitive four engine 'Manchester III', renamed the Lancaster, flew with wings spanning 102 feet. The heart of the Manchester problem lay with its under-developed Rolls-Royce engines. The company are to be congratulated on the account they provide here of the intrinsic problems implicit in trying to fight a war using an untried power plant, meanwhile struggling with the most fundamental of design issues. This is just one manifestation of the desperate situation Britain found itself in from the outbreak of war in September 1939.

A reader will be forcibly struck with the many difficulties encountered by Bomber Command trying to operate this aircraft with any success between its delivery to a first line unit in November 1940 and its eventual withdrawal in late June 1942. The main justifications for persisting with the type were the critical stage of the war, coupled with the greater success of A. V. Roe than its rivals in building and delivering the type. In spite of the most determined efforts of its crews, what they could achieve was often modest in the extreme. Due to four grounding periods when serious engine problems were investigated, the aircraft endured a stop-start initial ten-month introduction to front line service. The latter part of this, in mid-summer 1941, coincided with the lowest point of the war for both the Manchester and RAF Bomber Command. From this time onward things slowly and almost perceptibly got better. For the aircraft, engine reliability improved, snags were ironed out, more squadrons were equipped, new navigation and target-finding devices began, belatedly, to come on-stream. These several sources improved confidence and capability, as indicated by the still unrefined success of the March 1942 raids on the Baltic ports of Lubeck and Rostock and, most notably, the precision low-level attack on Billancourt. The aircraft just hung on to be involved in the three iconic '1000 Bomber' raids of May/June 1942. By 1943 Manchesters were still actively training 5 Group crews at HCU and OTUs.

Perhaps the best accolade with which to reward all contributors' efforts is the perspective that in May 1943, only ten and a half months after Manchesters were relegated to training, many of the same crews in the definitive four-engined version, still lacking air superiority, mounted what still remains the most audacious and successful precision attack in darkness ever made - the dams raid. Soon afterwards precision bombing at night became routine and using Tallboy and Grand Slam bombs, Lancasters pierced and destroyed the *Tirpitz* from high altitude in daylight, along with other pinpointed targets such as the Saumur Tunnel, Antheor Viaduct, U-boat pens and the V3 site at Mimoyecques. Only Lancasters proved capable of carrying the full range of weaponry which evolved.

In addition to improving accuracy, numerical strength progressed inexorably, Lancasters being joined by their partner types in Bomber Command. It is sobering to reflect that the US Strategic Bombing Survey in its Cologne Field Report compiled with others immediately after the war recognised that the frequency of attacks and severity of damage led the city administration to stop repairing damaged buildings by December 1943. Money as a medium of exchange became limited to a smaller sector of the economy and by October 1944 fire-fighting had terminated. Second tour ex-Manchester aircrew found a situation almost unrecognisable to that in their early operational experience. Nevertheless, the ferocity of the defence and industrial output was maintained until a very late stage.

Over an 18-month period 202 Manchesters using 538 Vulture engines managed just 1,264 operational sorties ranging widely in nature. Overlapping with this, eventually the 7,377 Lancasters built flew around 156,000 wartime sorties, dropping 608,612 tons of bombs.

Whereas we still lack authoritative histories of more numerically-abundant early British bomber types such as the Whitley, Battle, and even to some extent the Wellington, the rationale justifying attention given here to a 'minor type' is the unbroken development link between the Manchester and its successors.

There are many books about the Lancaster, as well as multiple biographies and autobiographies written by Lancaster crew members. This is the only account that deals adequately with the initial challenges in trying to use this 'engine test bed' simultaneously as an operational bomber. It makes clear why it was militarily a wise decision to persist. A further initial attraction to a researcher was that, though used in only small numbers and solely in the European Theatre, much of such little as had already been published about the aircraft, its engines and career was woefully inaccurate.

What emerges above all is the immensity of the efforts made by A. V. Roe, Rolls-Royce, Air and Ground crew of Bomber Command - all flowing from the ultimate wisdom under extreme pressure from the likes of Wilfred Freeman at D. Tech D. This department, and substantially Freeman himself, deserves the credit for, amongst other types, the unarmed wooden Mosquito, the Packard-built Merlin in the P-51 Mustang and the decision explained here under pressure not to cancel Manchester production in favour of HP Halifax's, but to use the existing jigs to shift more swiftly and efficiently to its four-engine sibling.

Following publication, it is intended to donate the research material upon which this book is based to the A. V. Roe Heritage Centre at Woodford.

Foreword to Third Edition

The book title alludes to the fact that constructors drawings for parts for the Manchester were also used to build subsequent Avro heavy aircraft, the Lancaster, Lincoln, York and Shackleton. The author is pleased to say that all prime research material assembled in the course of preparing this book is now lodged in perpetuity at Avro Heritage Centre, Woodford, Cheshire.

As far as the author is aware there is no complete Rolls-Royce Vulture engine in existence. Over the 82 years since Manchester's last fought operationally, no complete example has been found.

It emerges now that a substantially complete Manchester has been tracked down. On the night of 25/26.3.1942 Manchester L7390 ZN-? of 106 Squadron, flown by F/L RJ Dunlop-Mackenzie, was shot down at 22.28 inward bound to the enemy coast by Oblt Ludwig Becker of 6/NJG2. The aircraft fell with bomb load intact upside down on the thick ice of the Dutch Ijsselmeer off Kornwerderand and, W of Makkum. The body of F/L Dunlop-Mackenzie floated free, was recovered and buried at Harlingen. Those of F/O Cann, Sgt Burrows, Sgt Hill, F/S Welham, Sgt Mc Donald, and Sgt Stewart are believed still to be in the aircraft.

Dr. Robert Kirby and his wife now live in Liverpool.

Acknowledgements for First Edition

Much of this book is based on personal recollections and experiences of former servicemen. My research has extended beyond the United Kingdom to Australia, Canada, New Zealand, South Africa and the USA. Without exception they responded to my questions with patience and, where independent checking was possible, with commendable understatement of their experiences. If I have done them justice my main objective will be fulfilled. It is invidious to single out individuals but it is necessary to acknowledge the late Jim M. Duncan, and Jim A. Taylor (ex-207 Squadron) who motivated and encouraged my early researches. I also thank Canadians 'Mike' W. J. Lewis (ex-207 Squadron) and Bill H. Shorrock and T. C. 'Cam' Weir (ex-61 Squdron) for their assistance, friendship and hospitality.

The author has received guidance, encouragement and information from a large number of organisations and individuals: Richard Bateman, David Birch, Roy Bonser, Michael J. F. Bowyer, Chaz Bowyer, W. 'Bill' R. Chorley, Andrew Clarke, Mrs Margaret Dove, Sid Finn, John Foreman, Peter Green, Peter Hall, Mr and Mrs Alec Harvey-Bailey (jnr), Charles Hawes, Harry Holmes, George A. Jenks, Mr and Mrs Bob Howell, Ray E. Leach, Francis K. Mason, Geoff Page, Simon Parry, Bryan Philpott, Bruce Robertson and Ray Sturtivant. The following historical co-workers overseas: Denmark: Birger Hansen; Belgium: Jacques de Vos, Peter Loncke; German: Herbert Scholl, Eric Nonnenmacher, Horst Diener, Horst Amberg, Gebhard Aders, H. Frhr. von Friesen, Heinrich Griese; Netherlands: Gerry Zwanenberg, Ab Jensen, Chris Timmer, J. G. T. Hans de Haan, Co Marschalkerweerd.

Squadron Associations: 49, Tom Gatfield; 50 and 61, Eddie Davidson, Doug McKinnon and Skip Welford; 83, Ron Low and Frank Harper; 106, Des Richards; and 207, committee and members.

Thanks are due to the following institutions: Aeroplane and Armament Experimental Establishment, Boscombe Down (now the Aircraft and Armament Evaluation Establishment); Aerospace Publishing, publishers of *World Air Power Journal* and *Wings of Fame*; Air Historical Branch, Whitehall; British Aerospace; Dept of Health & Social Security, Newcastle; Imperial War Museum, Lambeth; Peronnel Management Centre, Innsworth; Postmaster General's Office, Crawley; Prisoners of War Association; Public Record Office (now National Archieves), Kew; Rolls-Royce; Royal Aircraft Establishment, Farnborough (later the Royal Aerospace Establishment and now part of the Defence Research Agency); Royal Air Force Escaping Society; Royal Air Force Museum, Hendon.

The original manuscript was typed by Mrs Janet A Edis. Much of the photography was undertaken by Alain Lockyer. Computer discs were translated by Tim M Buckley.

Many individuals, too numerous to thank individually, provided photographic materials. Their contributions are credited in the captions. I am indebted to them all.

Robert Kirby
Taunton, Somerset
August, 1995

Acknowledgements for Second Edition

In addition to extensive new research undertaken by the author, this new edition is given balance from summarising short extracts from a number of earlier accounts – notably Brickhill & Pan Books, Bushby & Ian Allan, Garbett & Goulding, also Ian Allan, Clegg & Aero Books, Hellwinkell and Pen & Sword Books, Hinchliffe & Cerberus, Walker & Spearman, a number of privately published works (by Harrison, Holyoak & Rope), as well as unpublished private papers from the Bayley & Hall families. In addition, journals written by Ken Houghton & loaned by his nephew, Tony Sherwin, and by John Justin McCarthy provided via the Dwight Blok family have been referred to.

The author is especially pleased to acknowledge the contributions from European aviation historians – notably Gildas Saouzanet and Claude Hélias in France, Wim Govaerts in Belgium, Rene Metz and Dr Theo Boiten in Holland, and also close colleagues in Germany – Andreas Metzmacher, Karsten Schulze, Peter Reinhardt and Tina Delavre (née Lent), together with Max Thimmig in Sweden.

Here in the UK, a written account of accelerated take-and arrested-landing trials on the Manchester aircraft has been provided by Geoffrey Cooper, an ex-employee of RAE Farnborough.

Sincere thanks are offered to the committee of the 207 Squadron Association for their encouragement, as well as for their sponsorship of the Woodcock cover illustration. Similarly, to Frank Haslam (Jnr). Over the twenty years separating the first and this definitive edition many family members of Manchester aircrew & fellow historians have supported the author with their interest and information. The source of all illustrative material used has been attributed and the hope is expressed that other correspondents will forgive the author if they are not all named.

Mrs Janet Edis has spent many hours upgrading this editon from the initial 1995 text. Alan Hornsey digitised all the photographs for this edition and Mrs Annie Makepeace compiled some of the drawings. My enduring thanks to all.

Robert Kirby
February 2015

Chapter One: A Difficult Birth

Avro's Type 679 Manchester was a disappointment and a failure in service. As such it ranks in obscurity alongside other early war British types such as the Blackburn Botha, Boulton Paul Defiant, Fairey Battle, Saunders-Roe Lerwick and Vickers Warwick – aircraft specified and developed during the same 1930s' desperate race to re-arm. However, to place the Avro design in the same category as these five is both harsh and unjustified. Largely due to the efforts of the Avro chief designer, Roy Chadwick, the Avro Type 679 Manchester was a triple triumph. Firstly, for its innovative aeronautical design, secondly for engineering, because Chadwick not only designed and built the aircraft but also many of the lathes and machines on which it was constructed, and thirdly, and as importantly, as it employed a break-down construction which represented a major advance in mass production techniques which put it streets ahead of its rivals. This technique not only produced huge benefits in terms of subcontracting and dispersing production, but in speeding repair and returning to service damaged or 'weary' examples.

At a very advanced stage in the continuous development programme, Avro wisely changed the Manchester's name to the Lancaster. The Battle, Botha, Defiant, Lerwick and Warwick went no further but the Manchester evolved into a new form. Aircrew morale was restored, and a legend was born.

Chadwick not only designed and built the Manchester, and out of it the Type 683 Lancaster, but went on to design the Type 685 York, the Type 694 Lincoln and the Type 696 Shackleton – all types that were directly descended from the Manchester and the thinking that it embodied. Each was a success story in its own right. Unlike any other bomber design of the Second World War, a dynasty stemmed from the Manchester.

The advanced nature of the design and the extent to which so many of the Manchester's systems and roles represented major steps into the unknown tend to be lost in the type's problematical service history. The type helped to refine the role of the strategic bomber. Paralleling this are the development history and problems arising from the design of its new and, for the time, extraordinarily powerful Rolls-Royce Vulture engines. In this connection the Manchester was unique in being the only aircraft to employ the Vulture on operations.

Model of the Avro Type 679 submitted with the Company's tender to specification P13/36 in late February 1937. (G. A. Jenks collection)

Arising from the under-developed nature of the latter the Manchester might justifiably lay claim to being the only British engine test bed to undertake 1,264 sorties over occupied Europe!

However, the initial phase of the Manchester story belongs to the bureaucrats and Air Ministry officials, to Rolls-Royce, and to Avro staff. Hindsight allows the many blind alleys and mistakes during the development to be highlighted clearly, but all three were striving to bring to reality a heavy strategic bomber, something which simply did not exist prior to that time. Nobody in that era of galloping technological change knew where the limits lay and what such a bomber could or could not accomplish. As initially specified the Manchester had a variety of roles and requirements. Amongst these were the capability of being catapulted from an airfield, a role envisaging torpedo bombing with a multiple load and dive bombing from an angle of 60 degrees.

In the end two major problems led to the abandonment of the Manchester. Firstly, it was a victim of its 1936 twin-engine specification and the two under-developed Rolls-Royce Vultures, and secondly it became weighed down by an unsupportable middle-age spread. Other recurring themes are the multitude of difficulties which bedevilled the project and the oscillation in the ascendancy of the Manchester in comparison to the design of the Handley Page Halifax and Short Stirling. Starting as the leading contender, the Manchester fell behind and became poorly regarded to the point where it was on the brink of cancellation in favour of the Halifax. Saved by a few visionaries it was regarded as worthy of continuation only on grounds that it was cheaper and faster to progress than to switch wholly to the Halifax. Only later, when transformed into the Lancaster, did it achieve its true ascendancy over the Halifax and Stirling. A final aspect of this initial phase which runs through the entire history of the type is the Herculean efforts, on an almost continuous basis, by the principal participants and their staffs.

During the mid-1930s the concept of a bomber with a really long range and heavy bomb load was still evolving and in the summer of 1936 the Air Staff formulated operational requirements for a new heavy bomber. This was

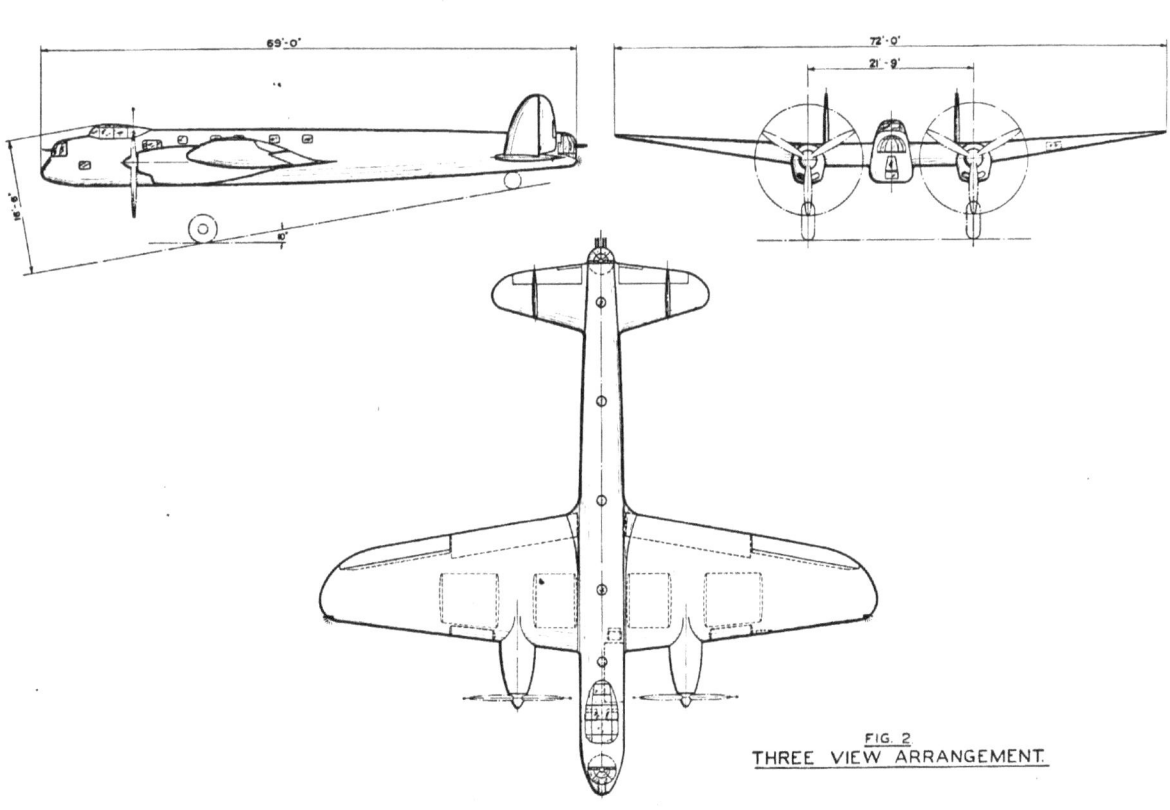

Three view general arrangement of the P13/36, dated January 1937 that appeared in the tender document. Note the format of the tailplane, fins and rudders. (G. A. Jenks collection)

later to be issued as Specification P13/36 to which the Manchester would be designed. At this time the Air Staff were formulating Expansion Programme 'F' and were influenced by three criteria:

1. Most important was a requirement for a substantial striking force of heavy bombers
2. Every enterprise was hampered by financial constraints
3. In view of limitations imposed by 2. (above), every aircraft was required to have as great an offensive capability as possible

Whilst Specification P13/36 was still being appraised it was calculated that the aircraft would be the operational equivalent of three Fairey Battles in range, speed and bomb load. This estimate went partway towards satisfying criterias 1. and 2., and in an endeavour to satisfy 3. it was hoped to combine in the new bomber the roles of torpedo carrier, general reconnaissance and general purposes aircraft. Fortunately for P13/36 these alternative roles were never allowed to spoil the design. The requirements were approved by the Chief of the Air Staff in August 1936 and represented a big improvement over the bomber specification issued only one year previously, the B1/35, which was to emerge eventually as the Warwick. In itself this is a mark of the pace of technical development in the 1930s.

B1/35 and P13/36 compared:

Spec.	Cruising Speed	Max. Range	Max. Bomb Load
B1/35	230 mph at 15,000 feet	2,000 miles with 2,000 lb	4,000 lb with 1,000 mile range
P13/36	275mph at 15,000 feet	3,000 miles with 3,000 lb	8,000 lb with 2,000 mile range

The all-up weight of the P13/36 was to be approximately the same as the B1/35, but the former was envisaged to be a good deal smaller and faster. The heaviest bomb load or longest range could be realised by catapult take-off, for no engine then being developed was powerful enough to meet the needs of a twin-engined type to this requirement without this advantage.

Operational requirements were sent in advance of formal specification on 24 August 1936 to six firms – A. V. Roe, Boulton Paul, Bristol, Handley Page, Short Brothers and Vickers. The final specification was approved by the Director of Technical Development in Septeember 1936 and when this was issued by Contracts Branch in November 1936 copies were also sent to Fairey and Hawker.

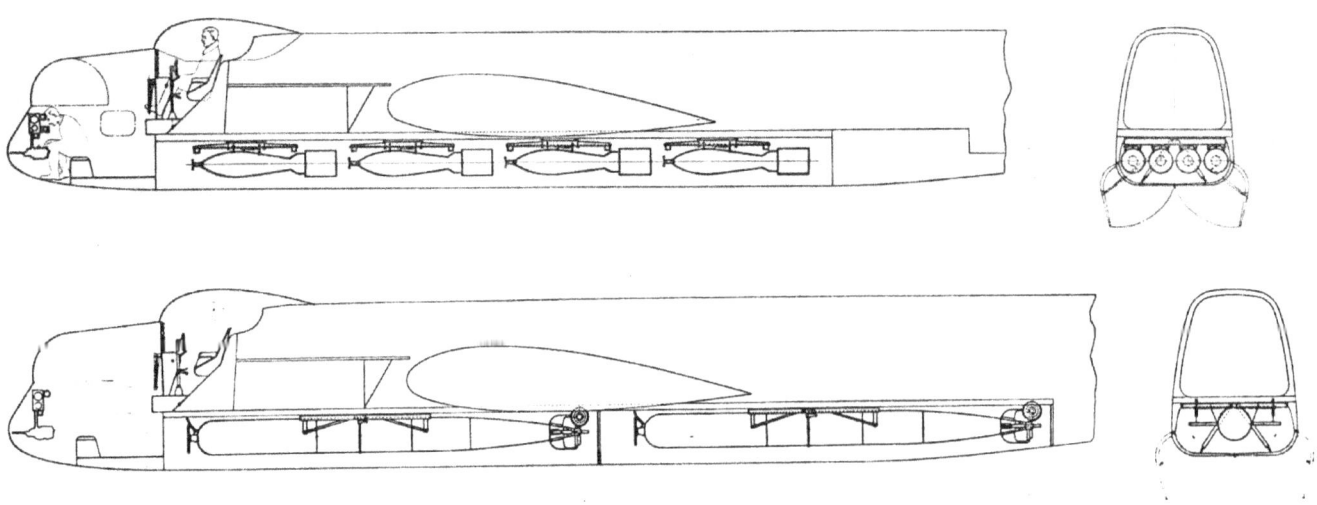

Diagrams taken from the P13/36 tender document showing how the bomb bay could take up to sixteen bombs or two 18-inch torpedoes. (G. A. Jenks collection)

The specification represented a major challenge to Avro, who were then working on the wooden framed, later welded steel tube, and canvas covered Anson. P13/36 called for an all metal, stressed skin twin-engined bomber of 45,000 lb all-up weight powered by two of the new 1,700 Rolls-Royce Vulture liquid cooled, twenty-four cylinder engines. The successful competitor would need to achieve a speed of not less than 275 mph at 15,000 feet on two-thirds power. Its service ceiling was to be 28,000 feet. In the event of one engine becoming unserviceable the aircraft needed to be able to fly and maintain height at 10,000 feet. Bearing in mind restrictions at existing airfields, the aircraft had to be capable of taking off within 500 yards with a 1,000-lb bomb load and fuel for 1,000 miles or 700 yards with a 3,000-lb load and fuel for 2,000 miles. The size of existing airfields was partly behind the requirement for an accelerated take-off capability, carrying the maximum bomb load of 8,000 lb with a range of 2,000 miles. Also envisaged in this same requirement though, was the need to carry the heaviest bomb load over the longest distance.

A multiple role was envisaged for the aircraft. The bomber must be able to operate in the strategic role, involving the longer range but more modest bomb load, or alternatively as a short range, tactical bomber with a heavy bomb load. In the latter role the aircraft must, for reasons of accuracy of bomb delivery and its own security, be capable of diving at angles up to 60 degrees. Indeed, the loads required had to be even more diverse, envisaging as a further option two 18-inch torpedoes to be carried internally. Since these weapons were each 18 feet 3 inches long this implied an extraordinarily long bomb bay. A final option envisaged the carriage of sixteen fully armed troops, with no bomb load. This was a daunting specification for the period. To fly the aircraft, a crew of four was called for, whilst the latest power-operated turrets, mounting twin guns in the nose and quadruple guns in the tail, were required.

In particular the specification stressed that good all-round visibility was required for the pilot, together with excellent manoeuvring characteristics at high speed. Emphasis was placed upon designing, constructing and testing all the aircraft's services at the greatest possible speed. Amongst other requirements was suitability for easy quantity production and certain restrictions on overall sizes and those of major components. The central span and longest fuselage section must not exceed 35 feet, with other wing and fuselage sections limited to 22 feet. The latter restrictions were imposed by the existing RAF vehicles, buildings and packing cases in which the aircraft or its components might be transported or housed.

Urged on by Roy Dobson, Avro's Managing Director, Roy Chadwick, the Chief Designer, immediately set to work every designer and draughtsman who could be spared. So many new things had to be evaluated and designed, but by late February 1937 the Design Tender to P13/36 was ready and within a few days submitted to the Air Ministry. The tender was accompanied by a large number of detailed drawings and included a scale model of the aircraft. The Avro Type 679 envisaged a rather diminutive 'Medium' mid-winged monoplane with, as yet, little resemblance to the final Type 679 Manchester which emerged.

The demanding specification could only be met by the employment of the most advanced design characteristics. All metal construction, including a light alloy monocoque fuselage built-up on a frame-work of hoops and stringers was to be employed, with flush riveted skin. The performance was to be achieved by employing the smallest possible size and highest safe wing loading, together with special attention to surface smoothness, in overall design but also in skin finish, and the use of cellulose lacquer paint to minimise drag. In addition to its small size, the use of the new and advanced constant speed, fully feathering airscrews was planned. Furthermore, all three of the undercarriage legs and wheels were to be fully retractable and enclosed by doors. Extensive use of hydraulic power was envisaged to control flaps, bomb doors and the fully feathering propellers but also to drive the heavily armed gun turrets. The aircraft spanned a mere 72 feet. The wing was of twin main spar construction and had an equal taper on leading and trailing edges, but an asymmetrical curve to the tip, which left the maximum span close to the leading edge. The tail had a similar planform and was surmounted by inset fins rising from the upper surface only.

The narrative within the tender informed the Air Ministry that the requirements of the bombing task had dictated the basic design, but the general reconnaissance and general purposes requirements had also been catered for. The problem of exploiting the alternatives between long range and very heavy bomb load, made possible by catapulting, had been accommodated by a simple design in which all the bombs were carried in the fuselage and all fuel and oil in the wings.

The cavernous bomb bay extended for two-thirds of the fuselage's length and it was this requirement that had necessitated the mid-wing design. In respect of the bomb carrying capacity the tender outlined that the 8,000-lb requirement had been accommodated in a considerable number of alternatives. In the case of the 2,000-lb bombs, six of which could be lifted, making a total of 12,000 lb, the specification had been improved on by a large

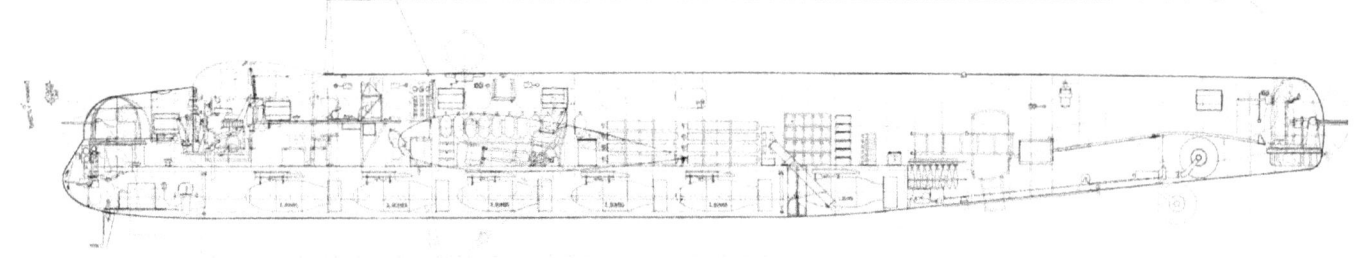

P13/36 tender drawing showing interior details. The all-encompassing specification is apparent in the rear fuselage where the originally-requested message pick-up hook can be seen in stowed position immediately forward of the retractable tail wheel. (G. A. Jenks collection)

margin. Even with 12,000 lb of bombs, catapulting permitted a range of 1,000 miles to be attained. Avro stated the view that the bomb provisioning was one of the best attributes of the design.

The small size and careful attention to clean lines was expected to result in a high cruising speed of 294 mph at 15,000 feet and a corresponding maximum speed of 341 mph. The company announced it had developed a rapid and effective method of flush riveting which would form the countersink in the plating and head the rivet in one operation. The skin of the aircraft would thus be flush riveted in its entirety.

In order to ensure adequate space and freedom of movement for the crew, three mock ups of the front fuselage had been constructed and evaluated at the Newton Heath works. The four man crew included pilot, navigator, and wireless operator accommodated in close proximity and a bomb-aimer gunner. A sound-proofed rest room equipped with two couches or reclining chairs was planned in the centre section for two additional crew members, who could relieve the duty crew during long flights. Nash and Thompson gun turrets were incorporated in the nose and tail as required by the specification, but in addition, space was provided for a retractable mid-under turret if considered necessary.

The high speed had been attained by employing a high wing loading. This in turn had raised the problem of which trailing edge flaps should be used. These were planned to double as dive brakes and for this reason, to withstand the heavy loads imposed on them and their operating mechanism, split trailing-edge flaps were recommended.

The tender then gave a general description and performance estimate, parts of which are reproduced below. The figures merit attention because in them can be seen unmistakably the seeds of the ultimate failure of the type. Whilst the output of the twin Vulture engines was correctly specified within a few horse-power, the weight would increase disproportionately, leaving the aircraft fatally underpowered.

Avro Type 679 Design Tender:
Principal dimensions:
Span	72 feet 0 inches
Length	69 feet 0 inches
Height	16 feet 6 inches
Wheel track	21 feet 9 inches
Wing area (gross)	930 square feet
Tail area	165 square feet
Fin and rudder area	70 square feet

Weight estimate:
Structure	10,150 lb
Power units	7,120 lb
Empty weight	17,270 lb

Gross weight of aircraft: – normal load range 1,000 miles, bomb load 1,000 lb
Weight empty	17,270 lb
Fixed military load	1,353 lb
Removable military load (incl. four crew)	2,820 lb
Fuel (562 gallons)	4,330 lb
Oil (30 gallons)	270 lb
Total gross weight	26,043 lb

Gross weight of aircraft: – overload range 2,000 miles, bomb load 8,000 lb
Weight empty	17,270 lb
Fixed military load	1,353 lb
Removable military load (incl. six crew)	10,464 lb
Fuel (1,068 gallons)	8,240 lb
Oil (50 gallons)	450 lb
Total gross weight	37,777 lb

(Two intermediate loads were also presented.)

Engines	Two Rolls-Royce Vultures
Engine Power, Max.	1,710 bhp at 3,000 rpm at 15,000 feet
Max. Climb	1,680 bhp at 2,850 rpm at 13,500 feet
Take-off	1,480 bhp at 3,000 rpm at sea level

Performance with Normal Load – Level speed
Max. Speed	at sea level	266 mph
	at 5,000 feet	290 mph
	at 10,000 feet	315 mph
	at 15,000 feet	341 mph
	at 20,000 feet	331 mph
	at 25,000 feet	306 mph

Cruising speed at two-thirds max. power at 2,600 rpm
	at sea level	231 mph
	at 5,000 feet	252 mph
	at 10,000 feet	273 mph
	at 15,000 feet	294 mph
	at 20,000 feet	282 mph
	at 25,000 feet	263 mph
Take-off, still air	without flap	305 yards

	with 30 degrees flap	245 yards
	with 60 degrees flap	225 yards
Distance to clear 50-feet obstacle		
	without flap	415 yards
	wth 30 degrees flap	365 yards
	with 60 degrees flap	345 yards
Landing run with brakes and flaps		250 yards
Service ceiling		31,400 feet
Absolute ceiling		32,400 feet
Wing loading (on gross area)		28 lb psf

Performance on one engine – Level speed
  Max. speed at sea level   185 mph
  Climb rate at sea level   512 feet/min
  Service ceiling   19,300 feet
  Absolute ceiling   20,600 feet

Performance with maximum overload was specified and only diminished by about 8 to 11 mph across the range of height and power.

Take-off with maximum overload if catapult not used

Take-off run in still air with	no flap	775 yards
	30-degrees flap	615 yards
	60-degrees flap	550 yards
Distance from rest to clear 50-feet obstancle with		
	No flap	1,085 yards
	30-degrees flaps	935 yards
	60-degrees flaps	880 yards

Performance with maximum overload
  Climb rate at sea level   1,050 feet/min
  Time to 5,000 feet   5.02 min
  Service ceiling   24,250 feet
  Absolute ceiling   25,400 feet
  Wing loading (on gross wing area)   40.60 lb psf
  Engine loading (on max. Power)   11.05 lb bhp

Left: One of three wooden mock ups built or evaluated at Avro's Newton Heath works to test crew positions and freedom of movement. Right: Head on view shows front turret and bomb-aimer's position. (G. A. Jenks collection)

Differences in cockpit framing indicate another of the wooden mock ups at Newton Heath. Note the 'collar' being worn by the pilot. (G. A. Jenks collection)

With assurances of good stability and responsiveness to the controls in all axes, having been tested on the company's Anson, and a projected speed which would leave the Hawker Hurricane, still two years away, standing and prove a good match even for the sleeker Supermarine Spitfire, the tender went on its way. If the proposed aircraft lived up to expectations it looked as if Avro would have a world beater on its hands. At the tender design conference in February 1937 all the designs were analysed and first and second places went to Avro and Handley Page respectively.

On 30 April 1937, just eight weeks after tenders had been submitted, the Air Ministry informed the winning companies their tender was successful. Two prototypes of each of the Type 679 and HP56 aircraft were required. The race was on in earnest. There was intense pressure from the Air Ministry to foreshorten the timescale of development as well as competition between Avros and Handley Page and Shorts, who had a contract to develop the larger 55,000-lb all-up weight, four-engined heavy bomber to specification B12/36 on the same timescale.

Avros immediately launched into the design and development work required. During the design stage the appearance of the aircraft changed. The inset fins were replaced by end plate fins, whilst the original 72-feet span was increased to 80 feet 2 inches. Wind tunnel models show the outline of the aircraft at this time and the Manchester look is clearly already apparent.

Whilst Avros were overjoyed that they had been successful and had beaten such well established designers of large aircraft as Fairey, Handley Page, Shorts and Vickers, it is as well to pause for sober reflection. Although the Type 679 had won the tender competition and was hence initially the favourite, Chadwick's relative inexperience had led to unwarranted optimism in a number of respects. Whilst the timescale from receipt of an instruction to proceed and the first flight was pegged at twelve months, it actually took twenty one months. Whereas emphasis had been placed on speed and a calculated maximum of 341 mph at 15,000 feet with normal load, 265 mph was to be closer to the eventual mark. At various stages the wing was to be stretched twice by a significant 18 feet, tailplane span was to increase by 5 feet and the fin design was to change several times and bedevil the design. Furthermore and fatally, weight was to escalate dramatically.

In addition to his great skill, Chadwick was a realist and later, with those he knew he could trust, quite open. When the problems with the Manchester became apparent and the need to switch to the Merlin evident, Chadwick told Air Vice Marshal Wilfred Freeman and the Director and Deputy Directors of Technical Development, W. Farren and N. E. Rowe, that it was his inexperience in designing large all-metal aircraft of the rigidity demanded by the specification which had led, in part, to the aircraft coming out overweight. All this was in the future because, however advanced the aircraft was, it would only perform as well as its engines permitted. Here too, although in common with a number of other new types, the Manchester would be breaking new ground.

During the early 1930s it had steadily become apparent at Rolls-Royce that the Air Ministry would soon be launching specifications for larger aircraft for which the power available from existing engines would be inadequate. To anticipate this, in September 1935 Rolls commenced the design of a bigger engine. One factor which is likely to have influenced the design is that it would have to run on 87 octane petrol. At this stage only the United States had 100 octane fuels and arising from the neutrality act it was anticipated that this might not be available in the event of war.

Top: Wind tunnel model of the Type 679. The design has evolved to embrace the end plate fins and rudders and the bomb aimer's 'blister' in the lower nose. (G. A. Jenks collection) Bottom: Recruiting and Training Programme model of the P13/36, dated March 1938. (via Peter Green)

Considering what sort of engine this might be, it was recognised that it was desirable to keep within the bore sizes on which the company had experience. Cylinder size would thus be controlled by the desired bore/stroke ratio. Increased capacity over existing engines had to come from increasing the number of cylinders. A. G. Elliott, the Chief Designer, may have considered V16 or V24 engines as well as H and X pattern cylinder layouts, but eventually opted for the X24 cylinder concept having four banks of six cylinders. Moreover, the bore of five inches and stroke of five and a half inches chosen permitted the frontal area to be kept to a minimum.

Rolls' policy in engine design was to build on existing and known technology, keeping innovatory aspects in each design few at a time. This led to a design based on the existing Kestrel and the Peregrine which had evolved from it. The same bore and stroke was chosen with the two V crankcases placed back to back driving a single crankshaft. The angle between the blocks was to be 90 degrees, giving a swept volume of 2,590 cubic inches. The cylinder and piston design were similar to the Kestrel but here the similarity ended. The light alloy crankcase was new, the two halves being located by shallow tongue and groove dowels at each main bearing panel, of which there would be seven.

The crankshaft had six throws on the seven bearings and whereas Royce, in his earlier Eagle X16 pattern engine, had tackled the connecting rod problem by using two pairs of fork and blade rods on a common crankpin and thus staggered the cylinders, Elliott opted for a 'star-rod' design, with a master and three articulated rods. The implication of this was of four pistons and cylinders per bearing and herein lay an intrinsic defect of the design. The star-rod concept implied some variation in cylinder stroke, whilst the chosen design of the rods was complex, one articulated rod was located on the master and the other two were in the cap, giving a split line for the big end at an angle to the master rod. To close the con-rods around the bearing thus required two long and two very short bolts. This design concept too was untried and provided a further Achilles' heel. The loadings of the four con-rods were such that a high brinell nickel-chrome steel, probably S65, was used for the bolts. This was a major departure from Rolls-Royce experience, since all their 'V' engines used a more ductile 3.5% nickel steel for their con-rod bolts, giving a tensile strength approaching 55 tons.

The engine was to have a two-speed supercharger of the Farman pattern, adapted by Rolls-Royce and similar to those previously used by the company. The supercharger downdraft intake was adapted from the Peregrine, except for the outlets to the two trunk pipes. The reduction gear was of a lay-shaft design and was also new. The cylinders would each have four valves operated by an overhead cam-shaft and two sparking plugs. Each engine consequently had 48 plugs and each Manchester 96!

Design and construction proceeded during 1936 and 1937, with the first engine being test run on the bench on 1 September 1937. In the first year of development testing over 860 hours running were completed with the engine reaching its design power of about 1,750 hp. By this time the engine was at the heart of a number of new aircraft designs. However, development did not proceed without problems. Possibly the main development problems involved crankcase distortion and main bearing reliability. In view of the resulting delays and Rolls-Royce's increasing importance to the future war effort, with its Merlin, Griffon, Exe and Peregrine engines, Vulture development did not get the highest priority within the company.

In the original Vulture design the two crankcase halves were secured by diagonal bolts and with the somewhat small dowels it was easy to distort the crankcase assembly as the nuts were tightened. The main bearing materials in general use then were lead bronze with 1% tin and a similar material with 0.5% silver. The 1% tin lead bronze had good mechanical properties but was prone to seize if there were any breakdown in lubrication. The 0.5% silver lead bronze had good bearing properties but tended to crack just above the bond with the steel shell causing the surface to break up. The crankcase distortion was tackled by replacing the existing dowels with large 'cheese' dowels on either side of the main bearing bore in the crankcase panels. This enabled production engines to be built without excessive distortion.

Concern was also expressed about the cylinder top-end condition. With the single piece block, deterioration in this top joint would allow a coolant leak into the cylinder or a gas leak into the cooling system. Saddle studs were introduced in the Vulture in an effort to maintain the seal at this point. The rest of the engine seemed to work reasonably well during development, although the coil ignition as originally proposed was abandoned in favour of magneto ignition. This also gave rise to problems later.

Meanwhile, although design work was still in an early stage, Avros received a great stimulus with an order, to the modified Air Ministry Specification 19/37, for 200 of the Type 679, now named 'Manchester'. The contract, No.648770/37/C4(c) arrived on 1 July 1937. A very large scale logistics exercise was required, involving hiring and training designers and engineers. Planning for production also had to be organised and scheduled; parts had to be designed and assembled, materials ordered, tools designed, built and bought, sub-contractors appointed and the factory floor space extended. Planning and preparation took so much time that the first metal was not cut until mid-1938. In addition to the thousands of drawings, the myriad of structural items had to go through rigorous strength tests.

By mid-1937 preparations were well underway. Various options for constructing the spar system and bulkheads were evaluated in co-operation with High Duty Alloys Ltd. Structural demands eventually necessitated using the type of spar extrusions recommended by the latter firm and then cutting a length of appropriate section diagonally to produce two tapering booms, later machined to leave the precise amount of metal proportionate to the load as it diminished towards the wing tips. Such machining required a large and expensive apparatus. The only such machine known to Dobson was a Kendal & Gent Plano-Miller. However, Dobson was contemptuous of this and instructed his works manager, Jack Green, to contact the well-known wood working machinery company Wadkins and give them a specification. The resulting tool was a great advance, working the metal five times faster than the old Plano-Miller. This, as with everything, was designed to facilitate mass production. Chadwick's involvement not only concerned these factory machine tool designs, but later such standard equipment as bomb carriers and gun installations. His involvement truly reached every facet of the design.

By early 1938 doubts had arisen concerning the development of the Rolls-Royce Vulture and alternative power plants were considered. Not only were there problems with the engine itself, but doubt arose as to the production capacity of the Rolls parent factory. The Air Ministry, accordingly, directed Handley Page to reconfigure their HP56 to take four Merlin engines on a stretched wing. The new design was redesignated as the HP57 and ultimately became the Halifax. Human perversity being what it is, Sir Frederick Handley Page complained vehemently over the delays induced by forcing him to redesign for the four-Merlin configuration. Later, as Vulture delays proliferated, Dobson and Chadwick of Avro were to complain equally strongly when Air Ministry initially refused to consider switching to four Merlins on the Manchester. As a consequence the Manchester was left as the sole successful contender to specification P13/36.

The pace of development was such that numerous meetings were required with Air Ministry and RAF officials and suppliers at London, Derby, High Duty Alloys and George Dowty, etc. Thus, during 1937 and early 1938 emphasis was on designing and building machine tools, jigs, making drawings and refinements to the design. A number of milestones en route were as follows:

Manchester Design Milestones:

18 March 1937	Advisory design conference
26 April 1937	Preliminary examination of mock up of front fuselage
4 May 1937	Final mock up conference
1 July 1937	First production order off the drawing board
4 August 1937	Decision that the first prototype will have Bristol Hercules engines and the second Rolls-Royce Vultures
26 August 1937	Torpedo requirement cancelled
4 July 1938	Catapult requirement cancelled
11 August 1938	Dive bombing requirement cancelled

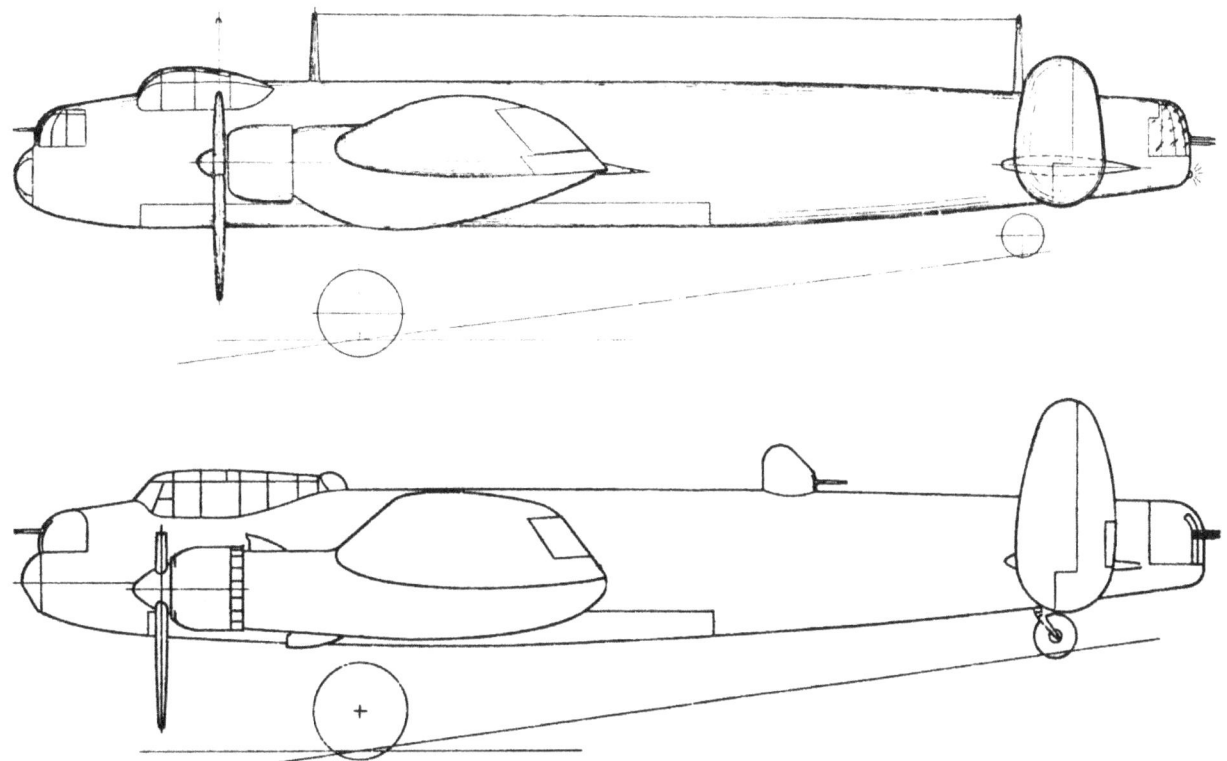

Engine options were almost constantly being considered. Top view shows Drawing No.A1491 dated 29 April 1937 to 27 January 1938 showing the Type 679 with Bristol Hercules radials. Lower view is A1605, dated 25 August 1941 and the Manchester II Bristol Centaurus radial installation. (via Chaz Bowyer)

Taking these in chronological order, it would seem that two mock-up noses were scrapped before final approval for the crew disposition was given. The principal change was replacement of the prone bomb aiming position by a seated and later, a kneeling one. The proposal to adopt the Bristol Hercules was merely a stop-gap to enable flying experience to be gained with the first prototype.

Vulture development was already lagging in mid-1937, but even so with the Hercules at this time outputting only 1,350 hp it is unlikely the Manchester would have got airborne with such units. As its role evolved, and also arising from the extreme pressures which were building up for the bomber to reach the production line, it is notable that the ancillary roles were progressively laid to one side. In addition to the extra design work entailed, Coastal Command had assessed the Manchester and decided it would be too large, too unmanoeuvrable and unsuited to control in a dive to accomplish torpedo attacks safely.

A year later the catapulting and dive bombing requirements were cancelled. By this time the design had been frozen and the great additional strength and weight demanded by these two requirements was an intrinsic part of the design. It had originally been agreed that catapult launching facilities in the aircraft were to be designed by Avro in collaboration with the Royal Aircraft Establishment (RAE). By May 1938 Avro had proposals agreed for the structural integrity of the airframe, and the catapult strong points. Some two months later, when the option was cancelled, the first twenty aircraft on the production line were already too advanced to take account of the weight saving offered. Whether this requirement was ever designed out of the aircraft has not been established. Despite the importance of reducing weight Chadwick estimated it would lead to a 6 to 9-month delay and £50,000 extra cost in jigs and tools.

Indeed, the first prototype was employed on accelerated take-off trials as distinct from catapulting, and the dive-bombing requirement re-emerged for a short period in April 1940. It was finally cancelled only when the 60 degree angle considered essential for bombing accuracy was judged unattainable. Of all ancillary requirements it was the troop carrying which persisted longest, not abandoned until 30 January 1940.

These are three major items of design to provide examples, but in fact during 1937 and 1938 the design changes were too numerous to list. Undoubtedly the most far-reaching was the decision to set aside the catapult requirement. Together with the changes in requirement, the cumulative effect of the extra design and constructional effort must have retarded progress on the two prototypes very considerably and in turn adversely affected production. The work load on Chadwick and his staff must have been ferocious and, reading between the lines, the patience of a saint must have been an essential requirement in dealing with some Air Ministry and RAF requests.

A typical, if rather extreme, example is the letter Avro received from the Air Ministry dated 17 January 1938 under the heading 'Duplicate Engine Policy'. It informed Chadwick: 'In future it will be a fundamental policy of Air Ministry that all aircraft will be specifically designed to take alternative types of engine'. The P13/36 design for the Hercules and Vulture now had to be capable of conversion to either the Napier Sabre or Bristol Centaurus within 48 hours. In a classic of bureaucracy the writer concluded: 'I do not wish to be informed of the difficulties to be overcome!' Another requirement, stemming this time from concerns over the availability of light alloys, targeted the Manchester specifically. All firms were to consider alternatives to light alloys including steel, reinforced synthetic resins, plywood, pigmented cellulose acetate sheet and laminated paper. The Manchester was highlighted as its design was at the critical stage when substitutions might be made.

Requirements piled on requirements at fever pitch. The Director of Repair insisted on additional design effort in a number of areas, including the requirement that fuel tanks, not only be removable but interchangeable. Avro designed the aircraft to accept standard bomb hoisting carriers, but Air Ministry later changed the requirement again so that Avro had to redesign and stress a large part of the cabin floor once more. Avro's own bomb carriers offered better flexibility and were eventually adopted. A misunderstanding in respect of take-off loads necessitated larger undercarriage members, which in turn entailed redesign of the stowage space in the engine nacelles.

These few individual changes must be anticipated to have multiplied up through the entire design, providing a glimpse of just what a massive undertaking the Manchester was. Of the multitude of changes, perhaps the most visually obvious, as described, were the replacement of the inset fins by elliptical fins and rudders at the ends of the tailplane and the extension of the wing span from 72 feet to 80 feet 2 inches. The latter modification is particularly significant in that, bearing in mind the marginal take-off and flying performance necessitating further wing extension, even with Vultures rather than Hercules engines installed it seems unlikely that with the original wing the aircraft would have left the ground at all. Later, on reflection, it was considered that the delays in getting the Manchester into production stemmed sequentially from the initial need to design and build machines on which the aircraft itself was in turn built, then from the multitudinous changes in design and finally due to the problems incurred with the Rolls-Royce Vulture engines.

At the end of 1938 'Expansion Programme L' projected the acquisition of 3,500 medium and heavy bombers for the RAF, 1,500 to be Manchesters. To achieve this, the Manchester Production Group was established involving not only Avro but also Armstrong Whitworth, Fairey and Metropolitan-Vickers (known as Metrovick). A second batch of 200 Manchesters was ordered from Avro, 100 from Metrovick in 1939 and plans made to bring Armstrong Whitworth at Coventry and Fairey at Manchester into the production group. Orders for 300 Manchesters were placed with each of these companies in late 1939 or 1940. Part of these seem to have been as outlined in the table below. Eventually they emerged as Lancasters.

Manchester Production Group initial orders were:

Serials	Quantity	Contractor	Date
R4525 to R4744	150	Fairey Aviation	September 1939
R5273 to R5477	150	Armstrong Whitworth	September 1939
R5482 to R5763	200	A. V. Roe	September 1939
W1280 to W1498	150	Armstrong Whitworth	December 1939
W4102 to W4700	450	A. V. Roe	January 1940

In early 1939 a visiting team from the Directorate of Aeronautical Inspectors had carried out a preliminary critical report on the suitability of the two prototypes, L7246 and L7247, then under assembly, for quantity production. They declared themselves to be generally satisfied and were especially impressed on account of the limited previous experience at Avros in all-metal aircraft construction.

Separately, as 1938 had progressed, the Air Ministry also began to give increasingly urgent thought to the defensive armament to be carried by its three new heavy bombers. Historians and analysts have frequently criticised RAF Bomber Command for sticking to the small calibre 0.303in gun, power operated turrets, whilst heavy calibre cannon were ranged against them by opposing German fighters. In fact the Air Ministry Directorate of Armament Development (DArmD) was to carry out a long and intensive development programme to equip RAF bombers with two 20-mm power operated cannon turrets.

After months of planning on 15 May 1939 a design conference was held at the Air Ministry to draw up a specification from which the Nash and Thompson Company would design and build the installations. Space mock ups based on a 48-inches diameter ring had already been constructed. The concept involved very large diameter, low drag cannon-armed turrets located close to the centre of gravity of such aircraft in mid-upper and mid-lower positions. At this time development of the Manchester was more advanced than its two rivals and the type was chosen for the long term development of such turrets. On 6 April 1939 Mr W. S. Farren had written to the Director General of Research and Development setting out the concept. The requirement was considered at this time of such high priority that four of the Manchesters, numbers ten, fourteen, eighteen and twenty-two were to be requisitioned from the production line for the development. The task was a major one, involving not only redesign and streamlined fairing of the nose and tail positions, but also a probable swelling around the centre fuselage station to accept a variety of development turrets up to 10 feet in diameter!

At a meeting on 21 September 1939 held at Avro, Chadwick informed the assembled Air Ministry and turret manufacturers' representatives that the revised Manchester fuselage, designated Mk.2, was largely designed, other than for turret specifications from the various manufacturers. Avro would manufacture a belly bulge capable of taking the largest of the three turrets and would install a standard diameter ring in the special fuselage to take the largest turret. The other two manufacturers would have to supply adapter rings with their turrets to fit this standard ring. The three turret manufacturers involved offered different alternatives.

Nash and Thompson had designed the 90-inches ring, enlarged from the earlier 48-inches upper and lower turrets with either 37 to 40-mm or 20-mm guns. Boulton and Paul proposed 78-inches ring upper and lower, four Hispano cannon turrets and Bristol a 96¼-inches ring, four Hispano upper and lower turrets. The latter two turrets were also scheduled for installation in a new bomber to specification B1/39.

Avro were to be responsible for any necessary fairings and a 30-hp Scott air-cooled engine was to be installed in the fuselage to drive the turrets. In each case the mid-under gunner would be able to abandon the aircraft without entering the fuselage. Avros were also to provide a rest position and oxygen point for the gun loader adjacent to the upper and lower turrets.

The problems of realising such powerful turrets were prodigious. Each 20-mm gun weighed 110 lb and just two 60-round magazines weighed 132 lb. The estimated total weight of a turret, less ammunition, gunner or accessories was at least 500 lb. Such weight considerations suggested a reduction to a single 20-mm Hispano cannon, but the rate of fire achievable would then be inadequate.

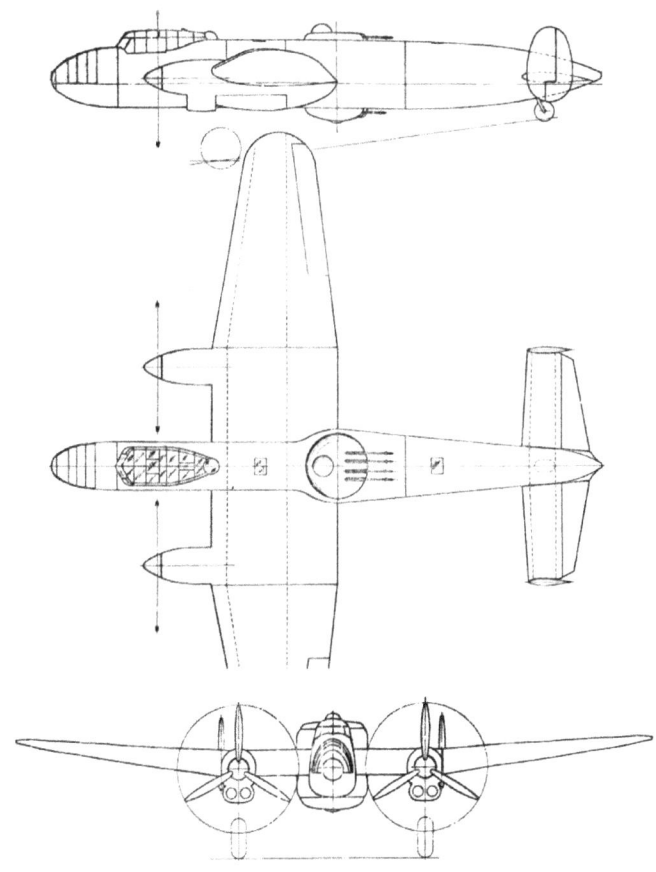

Side, top and front views of the Manchester armament development aircraft. This is Drawing No.1528, dated 29 August 1939, showing upper and under Boulton Paul turrets each with four cannons. Note the bulbous effect to the mid-fuselage. (via Chaz Bowyer)

The earlier meeting on 15 May 1939 had considered ammunition supplies. 30 or 60-round magazines were available, with the 60-round desirable for daylight work or sustained gagements. The turret would need to carry four 60-round drums with an approximate weight of 224 lb. A further ten 60-round drums of reserve ammunition were required and increased the weight by a further 560 Ib. The 20-mm Hispano Suiza was naturally much larger than the 0.303-inches Browning. It had a length of 8 feet 2½ inches. At least 5 feet 6 inches would protrude from any turret and, in addition to the drag, problems with barrel whip would be encountered. One palliative was to shorten the barrel length, but then problems with excessive muzzle flash blinding the gunner were encountered. It was discovered that Anti-Aircraft (AA) Command had secured exclusive access to scarce supplies of flashless propellant. The power requirements were stated to be 2-hp for two 20-mm, greater than the Manchester had available. A further limitation was that depressing the guns below the horizontal on the beam was found to present serious design and structural problems.

Throughout this period manhandling the heavy ammunition drums in aircraft taking any evasive action proved a severe limitation. As initially formulated, Nash and Thompson informed the meeting that to reload it would be essential to align the turret fore and aft, train the guns vertically and use a mechanically powered drive to disconnect the expended and reconnect the next 30- or 60-round drum. These requirements were not attainable in a Manchester. Later belt feeding for larger calibre guns was developed, but the higher gun, ammunition and power unit weight requirements precluded multiple turret installations aft of the Manchester centre of gravity. The problems proved insuperable.

In spite of this, the need persisted and was revisited a year later. Air Vice-Marshal Robert Saundby of Bomber Command Headquarters and one of the leading proponents of heavy cannon turrets, summarised the main problems in a letter to Air Vice-Marshal J. Slessor of 5 Group Headquarters as late as May 1941. These were:

1. A reduced rate of fire compared to the 0.303-inch, although the sighting accuracy was equal
2. The excessive weight of adequate ammunition supply and its bulkier stowage
3. These considerations necessitated both the turrets and stowage of spare ammunition being close to the centre of gravity (cg) of the aircraft. Tail installation was hence precluded
4. The absorption of the recoil stresses added greatly to the aircraft structural weight
5. The increased drag of the exposed barrel, or barrels, required much greater horse power for traversing or elevating
6. Throughout this era, severe difficulties were experienced with handling and reloading the heavy cylindrical magazines, whilst belt feeding for cannon was not available until 1941

When Lord Beaverbrook shelved all further development work on the B1/39 'Ideal Bomber' and F11/37 turret fighter projects, work on 20-mm turrets was also suspended. Nevertheless, as operational experience with the Manchester was gained, serious efforts to substantially increase the defensive armament re-emerged in May/June, above, and October/November 1941 particularly.

So, the development programme came to nothing and it was not until the very late stages of the war that even the twin 0.5-inches calibre turret was available for rear defence – long after the Manchester had passed into oblivion. Clearly, what was lacking was not the vision, but rather the technology to implement it.

Construction of the Manchester prototypes proceeded during late 1938 and early 1939, but all this time Vulture development had been falling steadily behind. The problems with crankcase distortion during construction and a welter of other problems had limited even bench running. After first rescheduling the HP56 to take four Merlins, which Avros initially did not object to because it allowed them to leap ahead in the unofficial race, serious consideration was given to switching to either Napier Sabre or Bristol Centaurus engines in the Manchester. Nacelle design apparently reached an advanced stage, but since neither engine was as advanced as the Vulture, neither offered realistic options. It was already clear to Chadwick that at the pace the Manchester was evolving and with the number of changes imposed upon the company undiminished, modifications would have to be incorporated into aircraft on the assembly line as and when they became finalised.

First prototype L7246 with main and tail wheels well lashed and weighed down during its initial engine runs at Ringway on 26 June 1939. Note that the spinners, propellers and turret fairings remain in aluminium finish. (British Aerospace)

Whilst the two prototype Manchesters began to come together rapidly as 1939 advanced, it became obvious that a delay would arise due to the late delivery of the Rolls-Royce Vulture engines, which would, moreover, end up more than a ton per pair heavier than originally envisaged. The first prototype, L7246, had 80-feet 2-inches span wings, the 28-feet span tail and twin end plate fins.

Early in 1939 flight test engines had finally become available for evaluation on the Hawker Henley test beds. The engine in the first Henley, K5115, suffered the problem of insufficient coolant flow, leading to aeration, which was thought to have been cured by fitting a larger capacity header tank in the aircraft. However, the problem subsequently recurred on several occasions in the Manchester. The second Vulture Henley, L3302, suffered another of the typical lubrication problems with the engine, namely a fall in oil pressure with altitude, accompanied by excessive oil aeration. The aircraft later force-landed on the beach at Borth, Wales when a con-rod broke. Soon, too, engines were released for the Vickers B1/35 Warwick and the Manchester. Chadwick is recorded asserting that only 1,630 to 1,650 hp was available from the Vultures at this stage in their development.

L7246 had finally come together at Ringway in April 1939, by which time weight had risen alarmingly. Historian Peter Clegg has had access to the diaries of Avro chief Test Pilot, Captain H. A. 'Sam' Brown. On 23 June 1939 Brown had L7246 jacked up on trestles to try out the flaps and undercarriage retraction system. On Monday 26 June at Ringway he performed the first engine runs, finding the Vultures started easily and ran 'fairly satisfactorily'. This must have given rise to false optimism. The weather was unseasonably cold and wet and Brown was to find himself carrying out tests throughout weeks at any time of the day when weather permitted.

His diary for early July 1939 itemises:

Sunday 2 July	Hydraulics still giving a lot of trouble
Sunday 9 July	Spent most of the day at Ringway. Machine damaged in the evening when hydraulic accumulator blew up. One or two people saturated in oil. Roy Dobson furious and very unreasonable with all staff
Tuesday 11 July	Manchester repaired. Hydraulics working better
Tuesday 18 July	Ringway in afternoon for taxiing trials on the Manchester. Rained heavily, ground lousy. Could not do much with (aircraft) due to it skidding on wet surface. In spite of a high level effort, a combination of extremely wet weather and a multitude of serviceability issues prevented much progress
Friday 21 July	Ringway in the morning. Good runs and two short hops in the Manchester. In the evening did three more. Rolls-Royce reps. with me. Very satisfactory

L7246 was made ready for its first flight on Monday 24 July 1939. Avro staff and the various Air Ministry officials seconded to the company had by now been living with the project for approaching three years. This, combined with the variety of novel and complex systems in the aircraft, led to an unusually heightened tension as preparation for the initial test was completed. Chief test pilot, 'Sam' Brown, accompanied by assistant Bill Thorn and two engineers boarded the aircraft, watched not only by Dobson, Chadwick and other senior staff but small knots of workers all round the airfield. L7246 looked unusually smooth and clean with it's faired over front and rear turret positions as it taxied to the end of the runway and began a protracted take-off run. The aircraft roared into the sky and disappeared from view. In the absence of any radio link those on the ground were left in suspense until its return and safe landing a mere seventeen minutes later. As it taxied in 'Sam' Brown offered a quick thumbs up to Dobson and Chadwick, but after the engines were shut down there was clearly much to discuss and of a more than superficial nature.

For this day Brown records:

Monday 24 July	Maiden flight of L7246. Weather very indifferent in morning, temporary improvement afternoon, wind changed and weather deteriorated later. Took to the air at 18.30 hours with Bill (Thorn). Everything went off fairly well

In fact, the hydraulic pump shafts had broken and rudder control was very inadequate. Both engines had run very hot and Brown had to nurse and watch these closely. More directly relevant to Chadwick, however, was that even lightly loaded, the take-off had been unusually protracted and the climb rate disappointingly below that initially specified. Indeed performance in this respect was sufficiently marginal that a substantial increase in wing area was obviously essential. A major redesign effort was necessary. Furthermore, lack of directional stability indicated that tail fin area had also been seriously underestimated. A top speed of 265 mph was recorded, way below that initially forecast. The original all-metal elevators were also considered unsatisfactory. Investigations revealed that the elevator shape, hinge point and construction were all wanting and work was put in progress to redesign a new metal framed elevator with fabric covering.

Two days later Brown records:

Wednesday 26 July	To Ringway to fly Manchester but found hydraulic pump had packed up

There seemed an inevitable absence of coincidence between good flying weather and aircraft serviceability. Clearly, as opposed to nearing the end of the design phase, Avro had a great deal of rethinking to do. Much of this can have been no surprise to Chadwick, although the extent to which the aircraft had underperformed must have been worrying. Chadwick must also have been conscious of the fundamental dilemma facing the design. Over the three year period the fixed military load had escalated sharply, as had structural weight. In contrast,

L7246 being towed out immediately prior to its first flight at Ringway. The date is c. 29 July 1939. Note what appear to be two lights, as opposed to a perspex window, beneath the bomb aimer's blister, the painted turret fairings, and the lack of fin flashes. (British Aerospace)

L7246 after towing out for its first flight. The tow rope is still attached to the main wheels. A ring bolt and escape hatch, soon to be obstructed by the addition of a centre fin, are located in the upper rear fuselage. (British Aerospace)

Rolls-Royce Vulture. (Rolls-Royce)

A Manchester main spar showing the undercarriage mounts and a bare Vulture on the engine bearers. (British Aerospace)

not only had power availability in the Vulture not kept pace with the weight escalation, it did not as yet meet its initial design power output.

Chadwick's dilemma was that to improve flying performance it was now estimated that a further span increase to 90 feet 1 inch and enlarged tail surfaces were required. This in turn meant even greater weight. Moreover, much of the military load, including the turrets, had yet to be installed.

On the plus side, in general the aircraft had handled quite well and good flying characteristics and well co-ordinated controls were later to become an acknowledged feature of the Manchester and Lancaster. For the moment Chadwick and Dobson had more serious and immediate problems to deal with. These were the related ones of continued lack of progress with Vulture development and power output, coupled with the steady and apparently inexorable weight increase. Indeed these two problems were to continue to bedevil the aircraft throughout its service life.

Consideration of longer term options must have become more sharply focused in Chadwick's mind from this time onwards. It was never possible to judge quite how close Rolls-Royce were to fully overcoming the Vulture problems and the company were naturally optimistic, at least publicly, on prospects. The Sabre and Centaurus options were serious possibilities, if only in view of the limitations of the Vulture. Possibly around this time Chadwick began to seriously explore a more radical enlargement to four engines. Certainly, as the more pessimistic prospects emerging from Avro became known, Bomber Command preference began steadily to swing in favour of the second placed design in the tender competition, the Handley Page Halifax.

From this time onwards, Avros continued to struggle to maintain a flight test and development programme, frustrated by long periods of unserviceability due to engine problems. Rolls-Royce too at this stage were investing a massive manpower effort in Vulture development, which was still at the heart of a number of vital aircraft programmes, not least amongst which were the Hawker Tornado fighter and the Manchester.

'Sam' Brown's records continue:

Tuesday 14 August	35-min flight in the Manchester. Hot weather, poor visibility. For third time running a quill shaft on the hydraulic pump broke
Wednesday 17 August	Fourth (1 hour 5 min) flight. Made trim and hydraulic tests in the air. On touching down and applying brakes starboard wheel brakes failed inducing a most violent skid. Quill shaft broke again
Wednesday 30 August	Fifth flight. Spent 40 min on taxiing and ground handling tests, then bad swing on take-off and in flight violent vibrations from Rotol propellers. Machine not at all satisfactory. After landing hydraulics found to be full of foreign matter - suspect mixing of oil with glycol
Saturday 2 September	Attempted sixth flight at Ringway. Trouble with Constant Speed Units and could not fly aircraft. Taxiing only. de Havilland man does not seem to know his job
Sunday 3 September	Another (seventh) attempt, but props went into coarse pitch for no reason. Fed up. Will not attempt to fly aircraft again until thorough investigation has been carried out

Avro's giant step forward into new techniques, as represented in the Manchester, was further complicated by a range of other problems, of which the most serious seem to have been hydraulic failures in the aircraft. On 27 September 1939, after L7246 had been grounded for a month due to hydraulic and engine problems, 'Sam' Brown records in his diary:

September 27th 1939	Eighth attempt. 43-min flight in fairly good weather. Propellers badly adjusted and hydraulic pumps failed

On this occasion a quill shaft failed in the port engine, incapacitating the hydraulic system. At this time flexible hydraulic pipes were installed in a number of places in an effort to overcome the hydraulic failures, which perpetually occurred in flight and not on the ground. Pressure fluctuations were suspected to be the cause, but finally vibrations in the air were found to be the origin. At Boscombe Down, the A&AEE (Aeroplane & Armament Experimental Establishment) were standing by to evaluate the aircraft, but clearly it was far from ready.

These diversions cannot have helped Chadwick in the autumn of 1939 as Avros struggled to come to terms with the range of fundamental problems still besetting the design.

'Sam' Brown's tribulations 'at the sharp end' testing the prototype continued:

Sunday 11 October	Ninth flight. 45 min. On Ringway approach the port Vulture blew up, with the crankshaft fracturing and disintegrating pistons and con rods poking through the crankcase

Fortunately the Graviner fire extinguisher worked, but Brown had still to deal with the resulting powerful asymmetric thrust and severe yaw. He force-landed across the airfield. In his diary he wrote: 'Had rather a shaky time getting her down'.

In the course of replacing the engine, both propellers were changed to Hydramatic units in an attempt to solve problems with the Rotol props.

The diary further records:

Sunday 18 October	Tenth flight. 55 min. Very difficult to control

[Author's comment: If Brown ventured such a comment how would service pilots ever cope?]

Friday 23 October	Eleventh flight. First trouble-free flight. Climbed to 17,000 feet and carried out level speed trials

By late 1939 Chadwick finally believed reliability in the Vultures, the hydraulic system and the aircraft in general was improved sufficiently for L7246, still unarmed and with short span wings and the small, twin fin tail to proceed on to its next major hurdle, at A&AEE. Time was to reveal a major contrast between Avro's expectations and unfolding events.

Again from Brown's diary:

Wednesday 15 November	1 hour 25 min with a Professor Shaw from Rolls-Royce on board L7246

Brown carried out vibration tests whilst airborne, arising from the installation of more powerful Vulture engines. Afterwards they sat down with Dobson and two others to discuss the status of the Vulture.

In anticipation of delivery to Boscombe Down, on 25 November 1939 Captain 'Sam' Brown carried out a final test flight in L7246 from Woodford. The aircraft was loaded to 32,500 lb. His report praises the good and simple take-off performance, requiring only the advancement of the starboard throttle ahead of the port to counteract the swing to starboard. Aileron and rudder control was assessed as light and effective at all speeds, although the elevator was acknowledged as somewhat heavy, especially at high speeds. The machine was reported both laterally and directionally stable although fore and aft stability was questionable. Brown concluded that the Manchester was easy to handle and had no vices whatever, apart from the easily controlled tendency to swing on take-off.

On Tuesday 28 November Brown and Thorn set out for Boscombe Down at around lunchtime. After only ten minutes in the air, and whilst passing Stoke on Trent on the port side, both engines stopped. At their low altitude and with the high sink rate of the aircraft, their feverish efforts failed to find an explanation. Brown was able to lower the undercarriage and side slip into open parkland by Charnes Hall outside Wetwood village in central Staffordshire about eight miles east of Market Drayton. Once the aircraft stopped and they got out the only visible damage was twisting of the horn balances on the rudders and a quick check soon revealed that the petrol cocks had been inadvertently set to 'Reserve' instead of 'Main tanks'. Importantly, and in spite of their embarrassment, they were unhurt and the precious prototype virtually undamaged.

A Rolls-Royce Vulture with all ancillary services installed, but with cowlings removed. Almost certainly this is the prototype, L7246; note the aluminium finish to the propeller and the spinner. (British Aerospace)

On 30 November, after a take-off strip had been checked for obstructions and rolled flat under orders from Jack Green, the Avro Works Engineer, a ditch in-filled and the Hall's owner had reluctantly agreed to sacrificing a few prize mature tree specimens from his parkland, Sam Brown arrived to fly L7246 back to Ringway. By this time the wind had shifted and was blowing strongly at an angle to the prepared strip. 'Nods and winks' about the importance of this new and secret aircraft to the war effort persuaded the by now even more crestfallen owner and head gardener into felling a few more majestic trees. At about 14.00 hours Brown lifted off safely and was soon back on home ground, where the necessary minor repairs were completed by the next day. At Boscombe, Avro had made arrangements to increase the vertical tail surface area, first with an unusually shaped shark-fin mounted on the centre rear fuselage, but within a few days by a larger, more oval shaped fin, more in keeping with the general contours of the aircraft.

From 'Sam' Brown's diary:

Sunday 3 December	Following rapid repairs and much longer waiting for suitable weather, dive tests and recovery at design speeds
Sunday 10 December	Following another week of bad weather, Ringway-Boscombe Down for service trials. 162 miles in 44 min in bright sunny weather

On Tuesday 12 December and through every day to Tuesday 19th, other than for a brief period on the 14th, the weather prevented any other than short familiarisation flights and the Type Trials could not be got under way. For Monday 18 December Brown's diary records: 'Another lousy day. Weather hopeless'.

Finally, on Wednesday 20th with better weather, Collins, of A&AEE, got airborne with a view to commencing the long-delayed type testing. However, first he encountered hydraulic problems and then separate difficulties with bomb door operation. To crown it all, he was attacked by over-zealous RAF fighters at 6,000 feet over the Downs, necessitating violent manoeuvring to avoid them. He had a lucky escape.

On Saturday 23rd A&AEE finally commenced a series of tests to evaluate take-off performance at various weights. These were brought to a sudden halt when the port Vulture failed. Height could not be maintained on the remaining engine and the prototype force-landed wheels up in a field near the aerodrome, the co-pilot being showered through the broken plexiglas nose by a hail of soil and cabbages. Avro engineers recovered the aircraft to Boscombe Down.

Examination of the defective engine disclosed that a complete internal failure had occurred, with two con-rods protruding from the crankcase. Evidently the Manchester problems were far from solved and the aircraft was dismantled and returned to Woodford. It seemed wise to defer further testing and risk to the sole prototype until the serious engine and airframe problems had been attended to. The A&AEE had accomplished enough trials flying to at least provide a brief report and this provided a stark contrast with that of the Avro chief test pilot only two weeks earlier.

Initial trials in L7246 were carried out at weights of 34,000 lb and 40,000 lb. On take-off the elevators were very heavy and excessive force was required to raise the tail and then to unstick the aeroplane. At 40,000 lb the take-off performance was most unsatisfactory. The aircraft took 580 yards to take-off and had only reached 20 feet after 1,070 yards so that the distance required to clear a 50-feet screen could not be obtained. Take-off performance was considered one of the most unsatisfactory aspects. Whereas the ailerons were light and effective at all speeds, the rudder only became effective at speeds in excess of 100 mph. The elevators were too heavy and ineffective below 100 mph and at over 260 mph in the dive. In view of the instability of the aircraft throughout the speed range, it was considered that a larger tailplane was necessary.

The first armed Manchester, second prototype, L7247, with interim 'shark' fin fitted. This was soon replaced by the definitive centre fin. Yellow underside and fuselage roundel are rendered black by the Orthochromatic film. Note the rear FN4A turret trained fully to port and the lowered mid-under FN21A. (G. A. Jenks collection)

Two views of the prototype after its forced landing near Boscombe Down on 23 December 1939. Evidently the port engine was stopped at the time of landing. (via R. C. B. Ashworth)

The aircraft would maintain height on one engine at 3,000 feet at a load of 32,400 lb but not at 40,000 lb. On approach and landing, lowering the undercarriage produced nose heaviness and the flaps, tail heaviness. The tail heaviness became greater with increase in engine power on approach and it was difficult to hold the aircraft in a glide. Approach with full flap and little engine was straightforward until the aircraft was flared prior to touch down, when the elevator became very heavy indeed. As a result a controlled landing was considered virtually impossible. The general conclusion seems to have been that serious problems had still to be overcome in the Manchester.

Brown returned to Woodford in order to fulfil his obligations to testing other types coming off the production lines. All in all precious little useful flying had been accomplished in six months and no significant type testing essential prior to the aircraft being accepted for RAF service.

Bill Thorn, 'Sam' Brown's deputy, has left less extensive records than 'Sam' himself, but Peter Clegg has also drawn on material on Thorn's flying career with Avro's. From this it is clear that he also had his own full share of problems testing early Manchesters, including the Charnes Hall pilot error incident. Bill is 'credited' with having had at least seven Vulture engine failures or forced landings on these aircraft, doubtless most in the company of 'Sam'. (Avro lost their records in a fire at Chadderton, as noted). Support for these assertions comes from interviews with Chadwick carried out by Professor Michael E. W. Postan and Mr R. Lubbock in 1944, now held in the National Archives in Kew.

Chadwick explained that: 'flight trials on the Manchester prototype had been protracted and difficult owing to terrible powerplant problems which persisted during the second half of 1939 and 1940. One Vulture after another had blown up and been completely destroyed, until half a dozen had been consumed over this period. Rolls-Royce had never been able to input anything like the effort into Vulture development as was contributed to the even more important Merlin programme'.

These facts point clearly not only to the roots of the Manchester problem but also to the eventual solution. Whilst the test pilot's attention was naturally focussed on the one complete Manchester, since mid 1939, Avro had continued airframe construction at a quickening pace. With the first prototype back at Ringway, opportunity for repair was coupled with installation of new Vultures having a higher power output. By 5 March 1940 'Sam' Brown was at Ringway looking over the second prototype, L7247, which was coming together including the fitting of the Frazer Nash nose, and mid-under and rear gun turrets. Engineers were test operating these in the hangar. In the first three days of April the Air Ministry held a 37-man conference on the Manchester programme. In order to be well briefed for this, 'Sam' again inspected L7247 which had many modifications and new equipment installed. All new systems on this aircraft, together with further ones on later aircraft, were discussed, ending at 19.00 hours on the third day. One focus was to agree installations in order to render it suited to type testing of coming production Manchesters. The entire programme had the highest priority in view of the critical situation in the 9-months old war, coupled with the importance of Britain's strategic bomber offensive to future prosecution of the war. In this case both the airframe and engine were untried. The feverish pace of Manchester development continued, but its focus shifted. Whilst pressing Rolls-Royce as hard as was possible to come up with solutions to the serious engine problems, stress was imposed on Avros in two directions, towards reducing weight and improving aerodynamic performance.

In February and March 1940 correspondence passed repeatedly between Norman E Rowe, the Deputy Director of Technical Development, and Roy Chadwick in connection with a major revision in Manchester design with a view to substantially cutting the all-up weight of the aircraft. Only a major weight-saving was considered capable of rescuing the flagging fortunes of the aircraft. In reviewing the situation in May 1940, Director General of Research and Development reported to the Air Ministry Directorate of Planning that since February 1939 the equipped weight of the Manchester had increased by 4,485 lb, whilst a further 550 lb was about to be added. As unassisted take-off was not assured at weights in excess of 45,000 lb, this steady escalation in equipment had to be pegged back and indeed reduced if any significant bomb carrying capability was to be retained.

L7246 at Boscombe Down, probably in December 1939, with definitive form of centre fin. Note that the propellers and spinners have been painted, the under-wing serials deleted and under-wing roundels applied. (A&AEE Boscombe Down HA447-2)

Chadwick immediately set to work. Little could be achieved on the initial twenty aircraft, which were already at an advanced stage of construction, but by various radical changes, mainly a reduction in the gauge of metal used in the aircraft skin, a substantial improvement was achieved. On 24 April Rowe wrote to Chadwick congratulating him on the 1,550-lb total weight saving proposed and instructing him to set these in hand immediately. These further alterations, and others soon to follow to the design and equipment of the aircraft, would ultimately require Avro to restress the aircraft six times. However, despite his efforts in this direction, Chadwick was now engrossed in a more radical and revolutionary solution.

In spite of the unsatisfactory nature of the stage of Vulture development and perhaps in view of the service urgency, in January 1940 Rolls-Royce had commenced full scale engine production. By 6 May the company appeared to have overcome their problems to a large extent and an Air Ministry minute reports that the maximum rpm available for take-off had increased to 3,200 and Rolls were now satisfied that these latest engines would behave satisfactorily. Time was to be a harsh judge of this ill-placed confidence.

Bitter experience had undermined any confidence at Avro and from March 1940 the design team began to press harder for the adoption of the four-engined solution to the Manchester dilemma. On 18 April 1940 Chadwick wrote to the Air Ministry setting out his proposed mark numbers for the various Manchester subtypes then under active development, ending with the Manchester III powered by four Merlins and with the rider: 'This type will probably be given another name later'.

The reality of the Manchester's position was only too apparent. Having started as the leading contender and achieving most of its development milestones earlier than its two rivals it now looked a very poor second compared to the Halifax. It was all too evident that the Manchester, with its two Vultures and all-up weight of 45,000 lb, would not compare with the four-Merlin Halifax, which at this stage was designed to operate at 50,000 lb. Worse was to follow. By the summer of 1940 Vulture development and production, and the technical position of the Manchester itself, were such that the whole future of the type was in jeopardy. Yet delivery of the first pre-production aircraft had still to be made! For the rest of the year, and especially during the critical discussion period of autumn 1940, the Halifax would become the yardstick by which the Manchester and, more importantly, the four-Merlin Manchester III, would be judged. Thus, even before it reached RAF service, much of 1940 was to be a crisis period for the design. Although Manchester production would outpace that of the Halifax, only much later, from early 1942, would the design regain its ascendancy over the Halifax and indeed achieve its true and deserved superiority.

The Manchester's immense bomb bay, also showing the extended FN21A turret. The flat bottomed inner surface of the early bomb doors, which proved unable to close around the 4,000-lb 'Cookie', is evident. (British Aerospace)

In spring 1940, Chadwick and Avro's design staff were, for the moment, fully occupied with more immediate issues. In the shorter term the dominating weight problems had been tackled with the proposed crash weight reduction programme, whereas in the longer term Chadwick hoped to eradicate these completely by switching to the four-Merlin configuration.

Weight was only one of the Manchester's problems. Equally serious were the take-off, climb, single-engined and general flying characteristics. In order to improve the first three, plans were well advanced to stretch the span of the outer wings to 90 feet 1 inch. This was achieved by leaving the centre section to outboard of the engines unchanged, but then machining new main spars to the required length and spacing the ribs at wider centres along the wing. This was the second such extension from the initial design span of 72 feet and would become the standard for the entire Manchester force. Using the same basic idea, Chadwick gained permission for a further tip extension to 95 feet on 24 April 1940 and used the same idea a fourth time to finally stretch the wing to 102 feet, the final production form of the Manchester III.

As the winter of 1939/40 progressed towards spring an intense level of effort by Avros continued to refine the airframe and by Rolls-Royce to overcome snags with the Vultures. Naturally, Sam Brown only became involved when these multitudinous streams of effort came together for testing. On 5 March 1940 he checked over the turret installations coming together in the second prototype and visited the adjacent first prototype undergoing repairs after its forced landing and being fitted with all the agreed new systems including Vultures of increased power. Take-off power was raised from 3,000 to 3,200 rpm and available boost reduced.

His diary records:

26 March	Went over the Mk.2 Manchester with Fred Rowarth from Boscombe Down

Production airframes were by now also coming together quickly. The first of the new, more powerful Vultures was run in L7246 on 11 April, initiating the countdown to its return to the trials programme.

Brown's diary itemises:

16 April	L7246	Hydraulic tests. One or two small snags
17 April	L7246	Late afternoon. Ground testing new Vultures. Unsatisfactory – very difficult to throttle down to low rpm
18 April		Met Chadwick. Agreed Rolls must improve throttling of motors
19 April	L7246	Aircraft not ready. Ran engines but unsatisfactory
23 April	L7246	Aircraft ready by about 13.00 hours. Got airborne. 40 mins. Everything fairly satisfactory

This was hardly a ringing endorsement after such prolonged and intensive effort.

25 April	L7246	Thirty min. Had trouble with the propeller pitch mechanism. Clearly fed-up, he announced "he wouldn't fly it again until de Havillands sorted the problem"
26 April	L7246.	In spite of his frustration, airborne twenty-five minutes. Propellers still very unsatisfactory
Sunday 28 April	L7246.	Take-off 11.30 hours. Pitch mechanism better but still wanting adjustment and later in the afternoon with Mr James of Rolls-Royce and Mr Gilmore of de Havillands. Take-off 15.00 hours. Five min after take-off the starboard Vulture packed up. Staggered back to Woodford and force-landed with great difficulty
1 May	L7246	Top Rolls-Royce executives arrived Woodford to seek explanation for engine failure. (Brown's second and the aircraft's third - author). Already suspect oil starvation to front main bearing. Air Ministry very concerned. Both engines will be replaced
6 May	L7246	Woodford-Ringway. Engineers in Experimental Flight Test hangar to change de Havilland back to Rotol propellers again
7 May	L7246	15 min test curtailed by bad weather. Rotols no better, switched back to de Havillands overnight

9 & 10 May	L7246	1 hour 40 min and 20 min. Satisfactory
11 May	L7246	50 mins. Aircraft loaded to 37,500 lb. Dead calm conditions, all went 'quite well'

Following further trouble-free tests at this weight on 12 May, Brown decided L7246 was safe enough to return to A&AEE at Boscombe Down for them to continue the much delayed type-testing. Bill Thorn made the delivery on Tuesday 14 May. At this stage the 80-feet long wings and short span tail were retained, as they were initially on the second prototype, L7247. Opportunity was, however, taken to improve the longitudinal stability of L7247 as rapidly as possible. As an interim measure, and by way of obtaining design information, two small ancillary 'park bench' control surfaces were mounted on struts beneath the elevators of L7247. These rendered the elevator control more effective and reduced control column loads. A more permanent and radical solution involved scrapping the 28-feet metal tailplanes and elevators entirely and replacing them with a new 33-feet metal tailplane and steel-framed, fabric covered elevator. This increased tailplane area by 20% whilst the root and tip chords were unchanged. To improve elevator effectiveness the hinge was set back by 24% at the same time. Whilst all this was going on, plans were confirmed to fit all production Manchesters with the enlarged third fin located on the top rear fuselage. In this configuration the Manchester would be further tested and ultimately go to war.

Around this time plans were finalised to incorporate the large twin gun Fraser Nash FN21A 'low drag' mid-under turret. This naturally went a significant way towards nullifying any weight saving gained by Chadwick in pursuit of improved take-off, climb and single-engined performance. The total weight of the FN21A was 608 lb so whether this is the 550-lb item complained of by Tedder in May 1940 is uncertain.

It is hard to believe that in the summer of 1940, with production so advanced and the RAF set to receive the aircraft for service, virtually no type-testing of any significance had been accomplished at the A&AEE at Boscombe Down. With handling and performance trials of only the most perfunctory nature carried out and a range of urgent modifications in prospect, pressure was extreme to get some testing of the Manchester carried out. Accordingly, in May 1940, still without turrets, with 80-feet wings and 28-feet tail and the same elevators but now with take-off power conditions altered to 3,200 rpm and +6 lb psi boost, L7246 was returned to Boscombe Down for the vital take-off trials. These immediately confirmed that, even with more powerful engines, take-off, climb and single engine performance were all unacceptable and the 90-feet wing was essential. In addition, longitudinal stability was so inferior that a longer span tail was essential for the twenty-first and subsequent Manchesters.

Magnificent shot of the second prototype, L7247, apparently prior to first engine runs. The nose FN5 turret is shown to advantage. Wingspan 80 feet, Tailspan 28 feet. Note the 'bench seat' ancillary elevators. (207 Squadron archives)

Trials Programme, Boscombe Down, Spring 1940:

15 May	L7246 with A&AEE crew loaded to 37,500 lb
16 May	L7246 with A&AEE crew loaded to 40,000 lb take-off tests
17 May	L7246 with A&AEE crew loaded to 43,000 lb series of air tests
19 May	L7246 'Charlie' Sleigh of A&AEE undertook series of climbs and dives at 44,000 lb all-up weight

These perfunctory tests were then considered adequate for the purpose and at the end of the afternoon 'Sam' and Bill returned L7246 to Ringway, arriving at 18.33 hours to be greeted by Roy Chadwick, who immediately took them for a drink. After a saga lasting five months, the prototype had at long last finally completed its handling trials and been accepted. The sense of relief must have been palpable.

The above chronological minutii are all that remain to us, but in scale of intensity of effort must be envisaged to have multiplied up through the entire A. V. Roe and Rolls-Royce companies, through various departments of the Air Ministry, and the RAF.

By 20 May 'Sam' Brown was shifting his focus onto the second prototype, L7247, which was now almost ready for flight. On Thursday 22 May Roy Dobson called all Avro staff together to tell them that production of all aircraft types, the Manchester and Anson but also the subcontracted Blenheims, was to be immediately and dramatically increased. This may have been an urgent response to the German invasion of the Low Countries on 20 May, but whatever the trigger it represented a sudden intensification of effort. As May slipped into June, development of L7246 and L7247 continued, still with the by now familiar Vulture, propeller and hydraulic problems. The former still included throttle setting tests.

In late June Brown and Thorn redelivered both prototypes back to Boscombe Down – L7246, now, finally, with 90-feet 2-inches span wings, for 'vibration and other tests' and L7247 for armament trials. L7247 was also allocated to A&AEE in late June 1940 for urgent armament trials. It still had the original 80-feet wing and 28-feet tail but had the interim auxiliary aerofoil balance beneath the elevators to lighten control forces. Ground trials loading all specified combinations of bombs were carried out, with good results, other than for a number of superficial and readily rectified complaints. In the final design the bomb aimer knelt on a specially provided cushion beneath the front turret. The complaint was made that the front turret could not be manned simultaneously with the bomb aiming station. Furthermore, a large collecting box and chute for spent cartridges largely blocked the view for the bomb aimer and had to be removed and stowed to permit access to the bombsight. It was recommended that this be replaced by permanent, less obstructive canvas chutes with cartridge containers either side and behind the bomb aimer, and that both crew must be able to carry

Experimental FN4 with early 'D' shaped cupola rotated to port, showing positions for the four 0.303-inch Browning guns. (Crown Copyright 10123(B))

Two views of mock up Manchester rear fuselage hung inverted from the roof of the 24-feet wind tunnel at the Royal Aircraft Establishment to evaluate aero-dynamic behaviour of, Top: the FN20 Stirling type cupola. This was never adopted. (Crown Copyright 31848). Bottom: mock up rear fuselage and circular cupola, July 1940. (Crown Copyright 32000)

out their duties immediately and simultaneously. Even better were the results of bombing trials. In the air low level bombing trials from 1,000 feet produced a very high accuracy with a mean error of eight bombs of 24 yards. This was attributed to the Manchester being such a steady bombing platform.

Meanwhile, in early July 1940 Brown and Thorn began test-flying the first four production Manchesters – L7276 to L7279. It seemed that they were at last underway. L7276 went to Boscombe Down for its acceptance trials on 19 July. Further tests were made on L7246 in July and August 1940 with the 90-feet wing and with the new elevator design, although these still spanned the original 28 feet. Take-offs were repeated at +6 lb psi and +9 lb psi boost. The 90 feet span, combined with greater power, had clearly resulted in a considerable improvement in performance and operating safety margins. Control loads on the elevators were also greatly reduced with significant improvement in general handling.

Preliminary results of the turret trials at A&AEE had proven problematical, especially regarding the rear turret installation. Clearly, the Manchester was one aircraft which would not be 'right first time'. As originally specified, the first batch of Manchesters was to have the FN4 tail turret with a specially designed, metal-framed and perspex cupola streamlined into the rear fuselage lines. The second and subsequent batches would have the later, more advanced, FN20 turret with servo ammunition feed. In a later departure and attempt at standardisation in aircraft turret armament, it was decided to adopt a 'mean' cupola with a circular section in plan view. This standard turret would equip not only Manchesters but also Stirlings, Short Sunderlands and Vickers Wellingtons. Unfortunately, the circular cupola was oversize on the Manchester and in full scale mock up wind tunnel tests produced drag increases of 7 to 11 lb or more. The additional weight and drag of the FN20 led Avros, already acutely concerned in respect of the escalating weight, to protest. The timing of the installation of the FN20 with circular cupola was steadily put back during 1940 and eventually the cupola was abandoned on the Manchester and later on the Lancaster.

Initial flight trials with the FN4 with D-shaped cupola on L7247 and later L7278 had alarming consequences. In the first tests on L7247, turret rotation in level flight at 232 mph led to vibration and buffeting in the rear

Close up of the FN4 four gun rear turret in L7247. In this state, the aircraft is as initially delivered, with the 28-feet span tail, no diagonal chamfer on the inner edge of the elevators and lacking the flared deflector on the extreme rear fuselage. Chronic vibration problems were experienced with this configuration. (via Chaz Bowyer)

fuselage, which was readily detected in the pilot's controls. The vibration led to hesitation in the speed of turret rotation. Even worse, when a further trial involving a dive to 280 mph and rotation of the FN4 was repeated, a violent and uncontrollable trim change in the Manchester was induced. Rotation in one direction led to a nose down pitching, which could not be corrected using the controls until the turret rotated back fore and aft. Rotation in the opposite direction induced a violent nose-up attitude followed by a stall. Turret rotation became jerky in both modes. At this speed, as rotation continued, vibration of the turret and buffeting became steadily more violent and transmitted itself to the entire rear fuselage, especially from the tail spar aft. Nash and Thompson representatives became sufficiently scared that, fearing a complete structural failure of the aircraft, they called for the test to be terminated.

In a similar trial a few days later a rigger stationed in the rear fuselage encountered actual jamming of the turret at two points in its rotation and jerky rotation between. Accompanying the savage vibration he noted the fuselage itself twisting with the imposed stresses. The trial was again abandoned and a landing made at Boscombe Down.

Examination proved that the port elevator aerodynamic balance had collapsed, the complete structure supporting the turret was loose and the entire cupola could be rocked from side to side and made to touch the fuselage sides! The rear of the aircraft had been close to total disintegration. A series of countersunk screws and nuts fastening the curved cover to the fuselage end and the turret mounting had come loose.

RAE Farnborough examined the problem, which they immediately suspected had the same source as similar effects encountered on the Lerwick and Sunderland. The wind tunnel tests took account of the fact that the Manchester elevators were in close proximity to the turret and the violent nose down pitching was due to the rapid development of a region of high pressure above the elevator and in front of the protruding turret shoulder, forcing the elevator downwards. Dr J Seddon, who carried out the wind tunnel tests, was unable to induce the nose up pitching, possibly because of the absence of prop wash in his model tests. These would be present on the full-scale aircraft, however.

Possible cures included:

1. Fitting deflectors to the fuselage ahead of the turret to smooth the airflow over the turret on rotation
2. Cutting a wedge from the inboard edge of the elevator where the high pressure region was concentrated
3. Moving the tailplane forward or downward from the disturbed region

Thus informed, considerable restressing and beefing-up of the Manchester was undertaken. The rear fuselage was lengthened and the rear turret located six inches further aft, obviating the need to move the tailplane forward.

Three quarter rear view of L7247 in the green/brown/yellow camouflage. (G. A. Jenks collection)

A wedge-shaped section was cut from each inboard elevator and deflectors fitted to the extreme rear fuselage to flare it out in front of the turret. The countersunk screws and nuts in the curved turret housing were replaced by rivets, the nuts having become slackened by vibration. Hoop and transverse stiffeners were fitted within the curved turret housing. Finally, struts were fitted between the lugs on the turret mounting and the fuselage sides, to eliminate lateral rocking of the turret. With these modifications the FN4 was refitted and the trials programme resumed. At all airspeeds and turret rotation speeds vibration and buffeting were eliminated and the turret turned smoothly and evenly.

The next trials programme at Boscombe Down provided both a major milestone in performance and a warning of things to come. On or close to 23 August, the first production Manchester, L7276, arrived to carry out the long delayed type testing to its 45,000-lb design weight. The aircraft was fitted with the production 90-feet wings and two Vulture II engines modified to the latest standard, with power output increased to 1,850 hp and a two speed supercharger. The 28-feet span tail was retained because the new 33-feet tail had only just been tested and would only be introduced in production from the twenty-first aircraft onwards. However, the latest elevator modification, albeit at 28 feet, was incorporated.

It is worth pausing to review the findings of the testing of L7276. With the new engines operating at 3,200 rpm and +9 lb-psi boost, L7276 took off at the maximum all-up weight of 45,000 lb in 660 yards and cleared a 50-feet screen in 1,175 yards, a great improvement on L7246 in the initial condition. Landing run was 845 yards. The aircraft attained a maximum speed of 261 mph at 17,000 feet and a ceiling of 22,100 feet. A range of 1,700 miles with 8,000 lb of bombs and 1,000 miles with the maximum load of 11,000 lb was achieved. Best climbing indicated airspeed at 45,000 lb was 135 mph.

Nett and gross wing loadings were 43.5-lb psf and 40-lb psf respectively. L7246's maximum all-up weight was disposed as follows.

Tare weight	29,360 lb
Typical Service Load	3,070 lb
Fuel and Bombs	12,570 lb
Fully Loaded Weight	45,000 lb

Comparative views of the FN21A 'low drag' mid-under turret in extended and retracted positions. Heath Robinson would have been immensely proud, but in mitigation it was one of the very earliest attempts at a powered mid-under installation. Note the vertical stowage of the gun barrels. (British Aerospace)

The extensive report evaluated many aspects of the operation of the aircraft. Ground handling was reported as good and straightforward. Take-off, climb and single engine performance were still indifferent but now within acceptable limits. Handling qualities in the air were found to be good and controls light and effective. Night flying characteristics and view from the cockpit were all excellent and a great compliment to Chadwick. In many respects the docile Manchester was to be likened by crews to a big Anson, quite a commendation for a heavy aircraft.

Of the very few problems amongst the many pages, the engine noise at the pilot's seat was found to be very high and accompanied by 'drumming' with the result that fatigue set in after flying for two to three hours. At the nearby navigator's and wireless operator's stations noise levels reduced by about a third. The control column was too high, causing difficulties in seeing the instruments and the aircraft leaked in a number of places, notably the front and rear turrets, radio mast and position and the top escape hatches. Front and rear turret operation was now considered satisfactory with latest changes incorporated, but the mid-under FN21A was a quite shocking affair.

A&AEE produced evaluations of Manchester gun turrets on 31 July 1940, 21 August 1940 and finally on 11 January 1941, and it was these which finally buried the FN21A. The clear view areas were at best restricted. Rotation through 360 degrees was possible, but downward search angles were limited to thirty to eighty degrees. In practice oil from the leaking bomb door rams perpetually smeared the perspex so that the gunner could see very little. During firing, an additional crew member had to be stationed in the fuselage looking through the fuselage windows and directing the gunner to the danger area! Worse still, the 'low drag' notation attached by the manufacturers was a distinct misnomer. During initial tests at 220 mph, lowering the turret resulted in a speed loss of sixteen mph, a speed reduction sufficiently major that the crew would be forgiven for believing the aircraft had stopped in mid-air. Subsequent modifications to the footwells rpeduced this speed loss, but other, equally serious, problems were manifest. During firing whilst the turret was trained on the beam, the forward of the two guns frequently ceased firing due to links and empty cases blowing back into the gun body and fouling the breech block. The balancing fin was of insufficient size and interfered with rotation at high speed, whilst the two retractable footwells distorted on rotation.

Finally, it was not found possible to effect retraction at normal cruising speeds. The turret jammed on the port side and it was necessary for three crewmen to lift very strenuously to raise it back into the aircraft! The port turret ram was ineffective. It was clear the turret was far more of a hindrance than an asset and the findings of the tests merely served to reinforce the decision promulgated on 1 July 1940 to delete the FN21A from production Manchesters.

A warning in the A&AEE report, if such were needed by Rolls-Royce and Avro, was contained in the recorded maximum oil inlet temperatures. The port engine had hovered at 85 degrees centigrade and the starboard at 83 degrees centigrade against a permissible maximum of 90 degrees centigrade for half an hour only!

With the problems seemingly overcome, Brown delivered the first production Manchester, L7276, to 27 MU at Shawbury, where it was to receive its full service fit prior to delivery in early November 1940 to 207 Squadron. In early October 'Sam' Brown air-tested L7277 which had been given two new, up-rated Vulture II engines. In addition to lack of confidence in the engines, another regrettable spate of seemingly insuperable problems with the early hydraulic systems resurfaced. At a time when air-testing new production machines for delivery should have been the priority, instead they were inundated by an intense period of development and testing to try and rectify these still unsolved problems. In this evolutionary phase, on 12 September, L7276, left by Brown at A&AEE for service trials, experienced a near disaster. An A&AEE test pilot was carrying 7,000 lb of practice bombs when an engine failed on take-off, the aircraft crashing back within the aerodrome boundary with its under-carriage still partly retracted. The bombs detached themselves and fell onto the closed bomb bay doors, leading to recovery difficulties. The Manchester was damaged sufficiently for it to need dismantling and returning to Woodford by road for repair. Whatever progress Rolls had made, it was clear there was still a way to go.

Rolls-Royce were getting desperate to get to the bottom of engine seizure in the Vulture and in early September 1940 Brown carried out repeated tests on modified oil tank and oil system installations on L7277, the second production machine. He carried out further tests of oil installation modifications in L7278 at about the same time.

Finally in the trials programme, the elevator appendages had proved unsatisfactory, but the new steel frame and fabric-covered elevator which replaced it had both nose balance and inset geared balance tabs. These new elevators resulted in a great improvement in control at both low and high speeds, including in the dive. L7247 returned to Boscombe Down in September for the first tests with the new 33-feet tail and redesigned elevator, and with the standard triple fin tail. A further significant improvement in longitudinal stability with the new tail was found. Also evaluated at the same time was the strengthened rear turret housing. It is evident that even with the severely limited flying programme attained, Chadwick was coming close to ironing out the aerodynamic problems with the design. Had engine availability and reliability been at all reasonable, it seems inevitable this satisfactory situation would have been accomplished much earlier. No one could possibly have appreciated at the time that, whilst these airframe problems were close to solution, the mechanical problems with the new aircraft, especially the hydraulic system and the engine problems, had barely been recognised, even at this advanced stage.

In October, as Manchesters came off the production line, 'Sam' Brown and his test pilot colleagues immediately flew them over to Ringway where the latest modifications were incorporated by the Experimental Department sited there. During this month the flight test team needed to input a big effort to address the welter of joint failures in the hydraulic pipework serving the three turrets and general aircraft services system. By early November, when 207 Squadron was scheduled to be completely equipped, only five production aircraft had left the factory, though by the end of the month L7294 had emerged making a total of nineteen altogether.

A ground engineer in the Flight Testing Department at Avro summed up the engine and hydraulic problems at this time:

'We used to listen to Manchesters taking off from Woodford. If the whine of the propellers in fine pitch continued beyond 1,000 feet and hadn't changed into coarse – sure enough there'd be a "bang" as the unit went, and the engine packed up. As for the hydraulics, every time a Manchester started up there'd be one or more "bangs" and oil would squirt out of the pipe couplings. Even when we'd cleared a Manchester for flight, we could never guarantee that next time it started there wouldn't be the same problems! The oil coolers burst regularly, too. One day I fitted six successive oil coolers to one Manchester and they all burst'.

Two views of second prototype, L7247, with FN21A mid-under turret lowered. Orthochromatic film renders lower colour black. (R. C. B. Ashworth/G. A. Jenks)

At times before 1940 closed, most of the completed Manchesters seemed to be standing idle around Woodford's perimeter tracks awaiting engine, propeller or hydraulic modifications. It was not a happy time and morale among the workers was not high.

Whilst these many changes were being specified, designed, built, incorporated and tested, pressure from Bomber Command was becoming even more insistent in respect of its need for the aircraft. It was to this end that as far back as 27 May 1940 the Director General of Research and Development, Air Vice-Marshal Arthur Tedder, authorised Avro to delete certain essential items of operational equipment from the first production batch of twenty aircraft, then at an advanced stage of construction at Woodford. The Air Ministry had taken this step with a view to hastening the introduction of the first batch, with the intention of using these as bombing and gunnery training aircraft so that crews could become familiar with the new type. As a temporary expedient, it had been decided that only one in three of these first twenty aircraft should be completely equipped and a list of twenty-two small items to be deleted was handed to Avro on 28 May 1940. The action was thus unrelated to the weight reduction programme then in progress and furthermore recognised that the aircraft would need later retrospective modification. Resignedly, Chadwick concurred with this latest edict.

When the impact of each of these new changes filtered through to Avro it was accepted that the first twenty aircraft were already too advanced for the long span tailplane to be incorporated on the production line and it would need to be a retrofitted item. Deliveries and installations of FN21A mid-under turrets had barely got underway when, on 1 July 1940, a further Air Ministry instruction was received to have the recently introduced FN21As on the Manchester and Halifax deleted and replaced by two hand-held Browning or Vickers gas operated guns in this lower position.

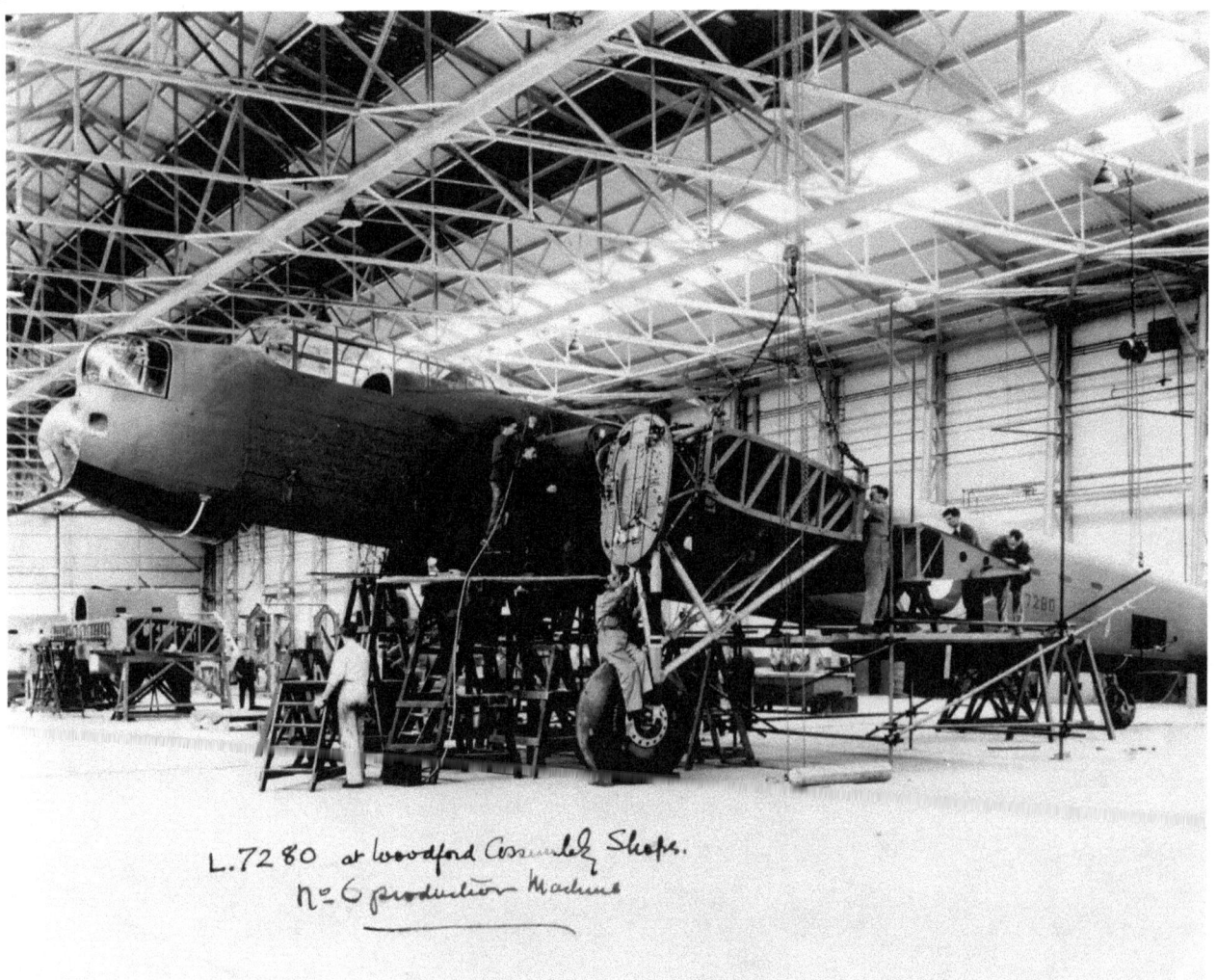

Sixth production Manchester, L7280, coming together rapidly at Woodford, mid-1940. It is fitted with the mid-under FN21A turret. Note early marking scheme. (British Aerospace)

Delivered to Boscombe Down on 25 October 1940, with the very latest modifications to its Vulture II engines, L7277 was soon grounded due to aeration and frothing of its lubricant system. An urgent enquiry laid the blame on the oil pump on this occasion. (RAF Museum P6298)

On the other hand, trial installations of the FN7A mid-upper turrets in the Stirling, Manchester and Halifax were to proceed. More than 100 of these had become available following the cancellation of the Blackburn Botha. Pending the final decision on the FN7A, hand-held beam mounted guns were to be provided.

Accordingly and patiently, Chadwick instructed that no more FN21As were to be installed, although between nine and eleven from the initial batch of twenty already had these incorporated. Indeed, the saga of Manchester defensive armament was far from over. This recently scheduled, mid-under, handheld gun installation was objected to by the RAF in that it obstructed the vacant mid-under position which now needed to be retained as an escape hatch. Chadwick obligingly designed Avro's own retractable, mid-under, hand-held installation. All this effort eventually came to nothing for in service the FN21As were soon removed and subsequent aircraft delivered until March 1941 had no mid-positioned armament of any kind.

Soon L7277 and L7281 arrived at Boscombe Down for further trials, but in September and October 1940 the focus began to swing away from A&AEE and to Bomber Command itself, where urgent preparations for introducing the aircraft to service were being made. Despite many of his short term problems with the Manchester being overcome by the recent spate of modifications and trials, Chadwick remained deeply sceptical of the Vulture and the autumn was to provide the ultimate decision in respect of the long term future of the type.

Indeed, much more than scepticism over the Vulture was worrying Dobson and Chadwick at this time. On 28 August, Air Vice-Marshal Charles Portal had advised the Air Staff that henceforth, as a matter of policy, all the Command's heavy bombers were to have four engines. With the future of their twin-engined brainchild already looking bleak, this policy decision turned the Manchester into an anachronism overnight and before it had even reached service. There were many things about the Manchester that 5 Group aircrews would never know. In retrospect one can only observe that this was just as well. Now it was crystal clear to Avros that the only long term future for the aircraft was the four-Merlin Manchester III, or Lancaster.

In an unexpected diversion on 9 September 1940, Bomber Command called a conference to review the inadequacies of the Manchester arising from the many essential items omitted from the first twenty machines. In an unnecessary show of petulance, Portal wrote to Saundby that the aircraft was deemed 'completely useless' for operations. Sight had apparently been lost that it was the Ministry itself which had authorised the deletions a mere three months earlier! Certainly at this stage Portal was no friend of the Manchester. The situation was made worse because Squadron Leader Hyde, Commanding Officer designate of the first Manchester squadron, had been invited as an observer. Chadwick's deep well of diplomacy must have been severely tested. It was agreed that retrospective fitting would be carried out at the earliest convenient date and that, meanwhile, deliveries should continue.

Much more serious was that on 6 October 1940 Rolls-Royce commenced delivery to Avro of what, once again, it hoped would be the final and definitive version of the Vulture II with all development problems allegedly cured. This was clearly not to be the case when, within a few days, L7277 was found to persistently throw large quantities of oil from the crankcase breather of one of its Vultures at high rpm. A hurriedly convened meeting on 19 October 1940 learned from Rolls-Royce that the oil loss was caused by frothing, the cause of which the company had tracked down in the last few days to a defect in the oil pump. The problem was in all probability cured and no delay would ensue on this account.

Whilst production of Manchesters proceeded apace at Woodford, and was now well underway at nearby Metropolitan Vickers, Dobson and Chadwick's sternest test, possibly of their entire careers, was at hand. With squadron service imminent, the long term future of the project hung by a thread. Powerful forces such as Lord Beaverbrook, the Minister for Aircraft Production (MAP), and others, encouraged in no small measure by Sir Frederick Handley Page, were determined to cancel the aircraft and switch the factory space created to Halifax production.

In MAP and Bomber Command the expectation was that the Halifax would be a superior aircraft and that the Manchester III would never match it in performance. At this time the Halifax was expected to operate at an all-up weight of 57,000 lb. Mr Farren, the Director of Technical Development, reported to Patrick Hennesey, Beaverbrook's deputy at MAP, that the Manchester development, the Lancaster, could not operate at this all-up weight and would never quite catch up on the Halifax. Hennesey did not readily accept this view, even though Sir Wilfred Freeman had also expressed similar reservations. On 15 November Mr Rowe, the Deputy Director of

Avro workers cluster around an early Manchester in the final assembly shop at Woodford in 1940. (G. A. Jenks)

Technical Development, went to Manchester and returned satisfied that Chadwick could indeed produce a 55,000 to 57,000-lb capability from the development.

Furthermore, on 19 November 1940 Farren reported again to Hennesey that the change in all-up weight was a big job, but nothing like as big as the change from Manchester to Halifax production. He judged that the two types would eventually be equally acceptable to the Air Staff. It was safe to plan for production of whichever type was most convenient.

Those two weeks in November were the climax of the debate over the future of the Manchester/ Lancaster and ended in victory for Mr Hennesey and those directing Lancaster production at Avro. At no time was it ever suggested that the Lancaster might be better, indeed the aircraft had yet to fly, merely that it would be no worse than the Halifax.

What seems to have swung the argument is the assurance that the aircraft would merely be quicker into production with the many existing jigs and tools already common to the Manchester. That the production techniques developed by Avros were infinitely better than those at Handley Page never seems to have crossed anyone's mind, or if it did it was never recorded.

Although the records appear to reveal Hennesey as an open-minded individual susceptible to rational argument, Chadwick himself, in 1944, was to be adamant in crediting Sir Wilfred Freeman with the vision to push ahead with the Lancaster, whilst Hennesey was of no material assistance. No doubt what is most important in all this is that, whoever deserves the credit and whatever the reasons dictating it at the time, history shows that the right decision was made. Clearly it was a close run thing and it would still be a long time before the Avro development of P13/36 would be reinstated in the minds of Air Ministry and Bomber Command as the better design.

With the Manchester poised to enter service it is appropriate to consider its progress beside that of its contemporaries, the Handley Page Halifax and the Short Stirling. Their developments and chronology are virtually coincident.

Manchester, Halifax and Stirling compared:

	Avro 679 Manchester	HP57 Halifax	Short S.29 Stirling
Specification	P13/36	P13/36	B12/36
Issue date	24.8.36	24.8.36	24.8.36
Prototypes	2	2 (as HP.56)	2
Ordered	30.4.37	30.4.37	30.4.37(?)
First flight	25.7.39	25.11.39	14.5.39
First del. to RAF	6.11.40	13.11.40	2.7.40
First operation	24/25.2.41	10/11.3.41	10/11.2.41

Despite the many and variable trials and tribulations of achieving the transition from first specification to their operational baptism, the chronological histories of the three aircraft had run remarkably in parallel. At this stage the many intrinsic advantages to the Avro airframe had not become manifest.

Comparison with a near-contemporary American bomber, the Martin B-26 Marauder, is also instructive. While the Manchester specification was issued in 1936 and that to which the Marauder was designed as late as January 1939, the two appeared in service at a similar time. Manchester operations and delivery of the first four Marauders to the USMC both took place in February 1941. The two aircraft had comparable engine power in the two Rolls-Royce Vulture engines at 1,780 hp each and the Pratt & Whitney R-2400 Double Wasp at 1,850 hp apiece.

As initially designed, operating weights were also similar at 26,043 lb for the Manchester and 27,200 lb for the Marauder. Here the similarities end and these statistics hold the key to the respective failure and success of the two types in service. Whereas the Vulture was underdeveloped and unreliable, the Double Wasp was not only developed and thoroughly reliable, but a robust radial.

The contrast in the aircraft is even starker. Whereas the Marauder was a comparatively diminutive aircraft with an initial span of 65 feet and length of 56 feet, the Manchester was much larger, spanning 90 feet 1 inch and having a length of 69 feet 4¼ inches. In keeping with their size the Marauder initially operated at an all-up weight of only 27,200 lb, whereas the RAF were soon attempting to operate the Manchester at 45,000 lb. Even when latterly some semblance of reliability was available in the Vulture, the Manchester thus had a weight penalty approaching 18,000 lb in comparison to its lighter near-contemporary.

Amongst the serving aircrews there was an impatience and excitement at the prospect of the introduction of the three new 'secret' types. The RAF had decided to allocate the Stirling to 3 Group, the Halifax to 4 Group and the

Manchester to 5 Group. Whilst 3 and 4 Groups elected to make the transition to service by equipping existing operational units, 5 Group chose to create a new unit, 207 Squadron, to achieve the transition.

5 Group aircrews knew little of the new aircraft, but from that which filtered out they were eager at the prospect of a change in their fortunes. They had been operating Handley Page Hampdens, aircraft with a span of 69 feet, length of 53 feet, and maximum bomb load of 4,000 lb at 1,200 mile range, with manual gun positions, no propeller feathering mechanism and extremely cramped crew positions for four.

To ease and speed the transition to service 5 Group was prepared to attach the aircrews allocated to the new 207 Squadron to A&AEE so that they could make the earliest possible start on learning the complexities of these large, new and sophisticated aircraft. So many new systems had to be learned. In comparison to the Hampden, the six-man crew of the Manchester had comparatively luxurious accommodation, there were two pilots and aircrew could readily change positions in flight.

The Vulture engines, with their 16-feet diameter propellers, were considered so powerful that it was judged unsafe for personnel or vehicles to pass behind aircraft whilst these monsters were being run up on test. After a Commer pick-up truck had allegedly been blown over whilst passing behind a Manchester during engine tests, a new regulation was promulgated that a prohibited entry area, staked out with red flags, must be established for fifty yards behind each of the powerful new behemoths! Crews were no doubt taken by this impression of barely suppressed power.

Noel C. Hyde, who was operational with 44 Squadron flying Hampdens from Waddington, was sent for by Air Vice-Marshal 'Bert' Harris at Headquarters, 5 Group at Grantham in late August 1940. Ushered in, the Air Officer Commanding (AOC) informed Hyde that he had been chosen to reform 207 Squadron, at that time absorbed into 12 Operational Training Unit (OTU) at Waddington with the new heavy bomber. Hyde promptly went off on attachment to A&AEE at Boscombe Down in order to learn everything he could about the Manchester aircraft. He began familiarisation flying on 1 September 1940 in the first production aircraft, L7276.

Test and development flying continued from Boscombe Down at a pace dictated by the many serviceability problems and modifications needed by the aircraft and during the same period Hyde was also busy seeking out experienced captains who would be sufficiently proficient to bring the new aircraft up to an operational status. He was fortunate in that a number of pre-war pilots were completing their first operational tours on Hampdens at this time. The first he acquired was Flying Officer Johnny Siebert, an excellent Australian pilot, who had been in Hyde's flight on 44 Squadron. With the assistance of Avro flight personnel, Rolls-Royce engineers and their own crews, Hyde and Siebert began regular handling flights on the second prototype, L7247, in early September. On 9 September 1940, Hyde took L7247 from Boscombe to Grantham. With him in the aircraft were Johnnie Siebert, Freddie Rowarth the chief engineer at A&AEE, and two crew members. The purpose of the flight was to allow the AOC of 5 Group, Harris, to inspect the aircraft. RAF aircrews rapidly found themselves drawn into the development programme of the aircraft, testing L7277 with a modified petrol pump on 17 September 1940. Frequent flights to the Avro factory at Woodford to discuss the progress of development and to the all grass airfield at Waddington commenced.

However, all was not frantic activity. Sergeant Eddy Edmonds, an air gunner, remembers the long periods of inactivity when the aircraft were grounded for engine or airframe modification. Then they would report to the duty officer early in the morning and in the absence of any requirements wander across to the aircraft, where their activities were confined to sitting in their future crew positions trying to familiarise themselves with their new surroundings.

The Rolls-Royce Vulture engines were still far from satisfactory. On 24 September 1940 Hyde flew L7247 to Ringway. Whilst they were there it was decided to ground all the Manchesters in the flight test programme until a minor engine modification was carried out. In September 1940 a breakdown in coolant flow to two banks of cylinders in the Vulture-powered Vickers Warwick K8178 led the Rolls-Royce test pilot, Reg Kirlew, to make an emergency landing at the small grass airfield at Burnaston, on the outskirts of Derby, when an engine overheated and caught fire, the cylinder blocks themselves burning like Thermite. Subsequently the Warwick was re-engined, first with Pratt & Whitney Double Wasp and later with Bristol Centaurus engines. K8178 was the only Vulture powered version.

The coolant problems were not easy to track down because they were not replicated in all Vulture engines simultaneously. Whilst Manchester production got into its stride in late 1940 and plans for the introduction of the aircraft to RAF service were hurriedly progressed, a Rolls-Royce minute dated September 1940 seemed finally to come to grips with one of the elusive coolant problems. Overheating arose, it was decided, when the coolant became contaminated by small amounts of oil, which coated the internal coolant passages and provided insulation. The coating prevented the coolant from picking up the heat from the cylinder liners.

Finding the source of the oil was difficult to establish but it possibly had an external source, as opposed to one within the engine itself. This line of enquiry seems to have arisen by analogy with experience with the Merlin. Early Merlins used 100% ethylene glycol cooling and no problems had arisen, whereas overheating began to show itself in certain engines when the coolant was changed to a 30% glycol/pressurised water mixture. Skilful detective work showed that the manufacturing process left small quantities of oil in the coolant passages. 100% ethylene glycol dissolved the oil films whereas the 30% mixture did not.

The problems with the Merlin were cured by employing a sodium metasilicate flush of the cooling system prior to test. It is possible that the Vulture problems were alleviated in this way too. Whilst the exclusion of the oil from the coolant system alleviated the coolant problem to some extent the operating temperatures were still unacceptably high, especially in local hot spots. These not only put strain on these areas but also had a deleterious effect on oil temperatures and thus pressures.

Presumably as a consequence of the grounding, Hyde did not fly in another Manchester until 25 October 1940. In the meantime he was busy hunting more experienced flight crews and in the intervening period acquired Squadron Leader Charles Kydd, destined to be one of the giants of the Manchester period, and his crew. Within a few days another highly experienced captain, Flying Officer Peter Burton-Gyles, and his crew joined the unit working up at Boscombe Down. This was the state of play at the end of October 1940 when the first Manchester deliveries to 207 Squadron and RAF service commenced. After the protracted development, the great range of problems encountered and overcome, and the advanced nature of the new technologies intrinsic to the design, there might have been reason to expect a bright future for the aircraft.

The reality would prove more brutal.

Chapter Two: Into Service

207 Squadron was reformed at Waddington on 1 November 1940 as part of 5 Group Bomber Command to introduce the Avro Manchester Mk.1 into RAF service. As of that date the squadron had no aircraft allocated to it. A note in the Operational Record Book (ORB) reads as follows: 'Several Officers and NCOs have been attached to A&AEE Boscombe Down to gain experience of these aircraft. Owing to engine unserviceability very little flying has been done, but maintenance personnel have gained useful experience'.

No one could have realised at the time what a prophetic judgement on the subsequent flying career of the Manchester these few words were to be. On 6 November L7279, the squadron's first aircraft, was collected from 6 Maintenance Unit (MU) Brize Norton and flown to Boscombe Down. On the 8th Squadron Leader 'Hettie' Hyde, Squadron Leader Kydd and Pilot Officer McCabe, the Engineering Officer, flew L7279 to Waddington for the first time and all squadron personnel were moved by air and rail to join them – some 75 airmen of all trades. That very night, coincidentally, Waddington was bombed by a German intruder with no damage to L7279. On the 10th the squadron's second aircraft, L7278, was collected from 27 MU Shawbury.

In the meantime, more air and ground crews were arriving at a rapid rate and the NCOs trained at the A&AEE began passing on their knowledge to the new recruits – Acting Flight Lieutenant D. J. Dereck French, Flying Officer F. E. 'Frankie' Eustace DFC, Flying Officer W. J. 'Mike' Lewis DFC.

A note in the 207 Squadron ORB for 12 November specifies that representatives of Rolls-Royce had arrived to carry out urgent modifications to the aircraft cooling system.

Eight days later, on the 20th, the book records little flying had been accomplished due to the need for engine modifications, whilst next day orders were received that L7278 and L7279 were to fly intensively until 500 hours had been achieved on both aircraft to test modifications which had been incorporated.

Leading up to this spate of activity, Rolls-Royce had run to earth another problem with the cooling system. The Vulture had two coolant pumps, each serving two banks of cylinders independently from the other. Airlocks within the cylinder blocks caused poor distribution of the coolant. It was discovered that the air-locks arose by cavitation within the pump which centrifuged the water. Air accumulated progressively in the pump and in exceptional circumstances built-up to such an extent that the coolant could no longer pass through it. Rapid seizure of the engine followed. The airlocks were eliminated by the fitting of a balance pipe linking the two pumps. This permitted one pump to feed the other two banks of cylinders if required and at a stroke eliminated the airlocks and hot spots.

Rolls-Royce records indicate that the first balance pipe modification was incorporated into L7279, 207 Squadron's first Manchester, and flown on 20 November 1940. It seems likely that both L7279 and L7278 were so fitted and that this refinement was the one to be proved during the intensive flying programme. This modification did turn out to rectify the deficiency and at the same time reduced oil temperatures to some extent. 207 Squadron were later to lose a Manchester at Perranporth in May. Rolls-Royce themselves lost their own trials aircraft at Tern Hill in June 1941 due to coolant problems and in that crash the test pilot lost his life. Possibly these later defects had a different origin.

A photograph of L7279 taken soon after delivery shows the general configuration of these first aircraft. They were the triple finned Mk.1 variety with 28-feet span tailplanes. Compared to the prototype aircraft, the colour scheme had already changed - the demarcation line between the brown and green shadow-shaded upper surface and the night black underside was moved to a position half way up the fuselage sides, the actual separation line being straight. With an establishment of only one flight and eight aircraft the initial two machines soon received code letters: L7278 EM-A, L7279 EM-B. The letters were painted grey and serials soon repainted grey on the squadron. Fuselage roundels were type A1.

The most notable feature of L7278 and L7279, as initially delivered, was that they had the original Frazer-Nash FN21A retractable 'dustbin' mid-under turret. In July 1940 a policy decision had been made to delete the FN21A after the tenth airframe on the production line, but available records variously state that nine, ten or eleven aircraft were actually fitted.

Both the Rolls-Royce Vulture engines and the Manchester airframes had a range of novel features being introduced to service aircraft for the first time. These items were as new and untried as the aircraft itself and many were to prove sources of unserviceability in the future.

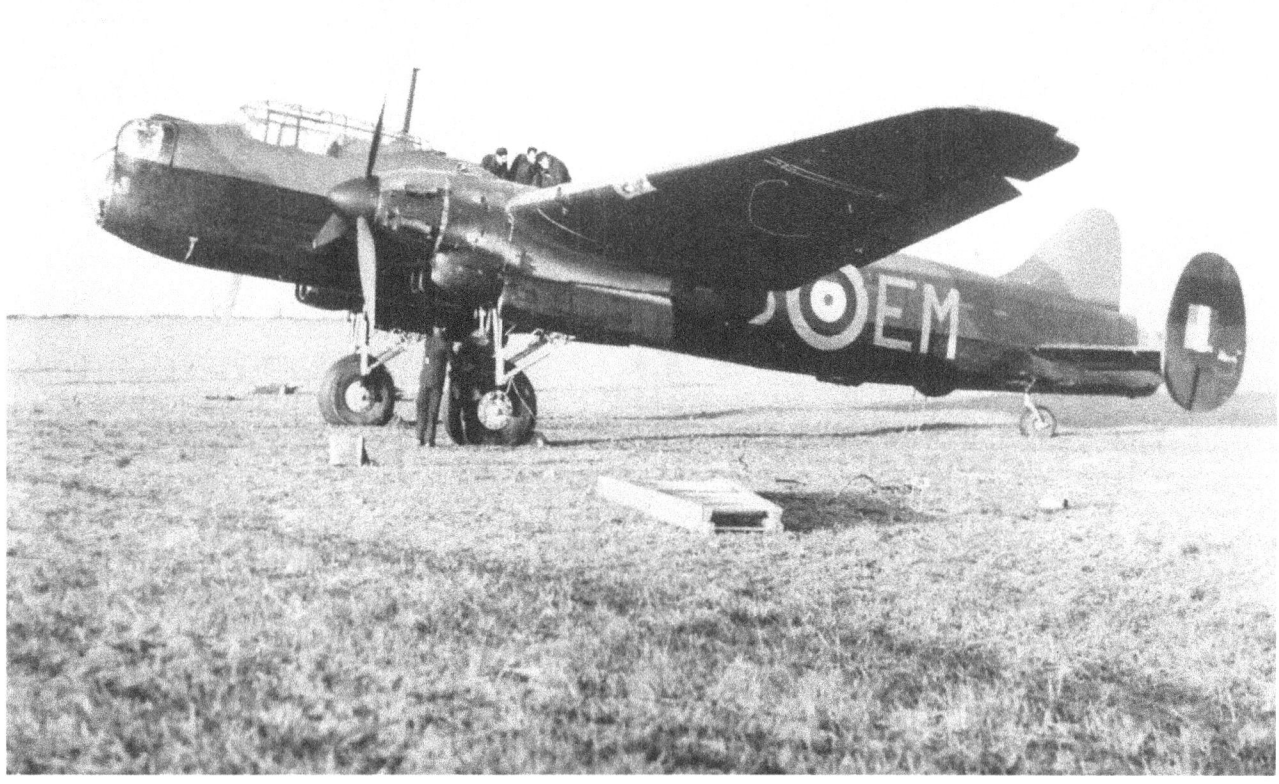

207 Squadron's first Manchester, L7279 EM-B, photographed at Waddington soon after its delivery. It carries the initial camouflage scheme, grey codes and a red serial behind the code letter 'M'. The FN21A mid-under turret is retracted. L7279 undertook a single operation before being relegated to training duties. (207 Squadron archives)

For example, the initial Manchesters had no cabin heating system, although it was intended to install one in later aircraft. In the meantime crews were each issued with the Irvin electrically heated trousers, jackets, gloves and boots. These had electrical leads joining with a master lead which plugged into a socket at each crew station. During service training and development flying, carried out from November onwards, the suits were also evaluated and found seriously wanting. Crews constantly experienced shorts and burn-outs, especially in the boots and gloves and as a result they regularly flew five or six hour test flights at 15,000 feet with nothing to warm them whatsoever.

These initial aircraft had an untried method of joining their long runs of hydraulic piping together, called Ermeto couplings which replaced the earlier Aircraft General Spares (AGS) couplings. In the latter the pipe ends were belled out to accept a metal 'olive', the assembly then being clamped together by male and female nuts and locked in place with wire. Ermeto couplings, once made, could not be undone and did not require wire locking, hence speeding up production of airframes. The couplings had been tested under workshop conditions, but the vibrations in the airframes when flying led to frequent fracturing of the hydraulic pipes at the Ermeto joints. Since many of the services in the Manchester were hydraulically operated, this presented frequent problems.

Another deficiency indicative of the desperate urgency with which the aircraft was introduced was that these early aircraft, possibly the first twenty, had no engine driven air compressors. These were necessary to maintain the air pressure in the pneumatic wheel brakes at the required level. Therefore, in these aircraft the ground crews had the task of topping up the air bottles after every two landings to maintain the pressure. By the end of November only twenty-five hours of flying had been accomplished. However, with the allocation of L7283 and L7284 to the squadron the aircraft strength had risen to four Manchesters.

A disservice to the war effort was provided by non-flying personnel at about this time. On 24 November 1940 when Flying Officer Siebert, Flight Lieutenant French and crew were again participating in the intensive flight test programme, they were briefed to carry out an endurance test in L7279. The test required them to fly at ceiling height of approx. 17,000 feet between turning points at Waddington, Trowbridge, Shrewsbury, Gainsborough and Northallerton in Yorkshire. The crew was supplemented by two army officers. After almost three hours of monotonous flying, with fuel running low at the end of the northern leg, French decided to terminate the test, break cloud and return to Waddington. Everything was calm on board, the wireless operator and one of the army officers were playing noughts and crosses, when they had the misfortune to emerge directly over Linton-on-Ouse airfield, where a German air raid was in progress. They immediately came under intense anti-aircraft fire from the airfield defences and by a rare chance one of the first shells burst close-by, tearing off part of the wing tip.

Feverish activity ensued whilst evasive action was taken and Siebert fired off a volley of colours of the day, accompanied by unprintable remarks regarding the aircraft recognition capabilities of the anti-aircraft crews. Various suggestions were made including landing and taking issue with the belligerents, but good sense prevailed and the aircraft returned safely to Waddington.

A gunner getting acquainted with the FN4 rear turret in one of 207 Squadron's first Manchesters. (207 Squadron archives)

Whilst 207 Squadron pilots began their earliest tentative flight trials with the Manchester, back at Ringway on 27 November a new Manchester, L7292, gave a pilot inexperienced on the type a virtuoso performance of the full range of problems it was to inflict on aircrews over the next three years. A ferry pilot and skeleton crew collected L7292 at the Woodford works. Very soon after take-off an Ermeto hydraulic coupling behind the pilot's seat failed. A dense and fierce mist of fluid then sprayed into the cockpit as the aircraft began to climb away, temporarily blinding the pilot. The entire contents of the system sprayed over the pilot and crew, the inside of the perspex canopy and all the flight instruments.

No sooner had the spray begun to die away than the starboard engine ran away. The revs rose to 3,600-rpm and the engine noise reached a deafening howl as the propeller feathering mechanism failed, sending the airscrew into the fully fine position. The drenched, shocked and deafened pilot was unable to obtain any response from the constant speed unit, and neither would the starboard engine respond to movements of the throttle lever. Miraculously, the pilot kept the aircraft level, meanwhile heading with desperate urgency for Ringway and an emergency landing.

En route the pilot deliberated whether he should shut down the overheating and racing starboard engine by switching off its fuel supply, but recognised that such action would leave him in a worse situation, with a dead engine and windmilling propeller. The engine continued to race uncontrollably for nine minutes until it finally seized on finals for Ringway, where a safe wheels-down landing was effected. No damage to the aircraft or occupants was reportedly occasioned, although one Vulture was wrecked. The pilot no doubt departed hence, a nervous wreck in urgent need of de-greasing solvents and a clean pair of underpants!

The accident report stresses that clear thought by the pilot was impeded by his unfamiliarity with this new type of aircraft, the unexpected drenching from the Ermeto failure and the extremely high noise level, which made it very difficult for him to pass any instructions for the operation of the emergency flap and undercarriage system to the other crew members.

Investigation proved that the cause of the high revs was a failure of the Hallite washer joining the constant speed unit to the engine. This denied pressure oil to the pitch mechanism such that the blades remained against the fine pitch stop. de Havilland were asked to undertake a modification to prevent a recurrence, but feathering failures were to plague the Manchester for much of its life. The Ermeto problem was already appreciated it appears because the report merely re-emphasises the urgency of replacing it with the tried and tested AGS system.

During December flight testing and development flying continued, two aircraft, L7280 and L7286, and additional personnel joined the squadron. The problems being experienced with the new systems in the aircraft, especially with the engines, were sufficiently serious and intractable that a meeting to consider them was held at Waddington on 9 December 1940, attended by the new Air Officer Commanding (AOC) of 5 Group, Air Vice-Marshal N. H. Bottomley, and Sir Robert Renwick of the Ministry of Aircraft Production (MAP). They discussed the modifications and additional equipment which would be essential before the Manchester could become operationally fit.

Worrying as the underdeveloped state of the Manchester and the serious hydraulic problems were, the over-riding problem was that it was so grossly underpowered. When the squadron received their first aircraft they were flown at a maximum all-up weight of 45,000 lb. The aircraft was powered by two 1,760-hp Vultures. Indeed the Manchester was the largest British twin-engined aircraft of the war and therein lay its Achilles heel.

Subsequent to the 9 December meeting agreement was reached on the essential modifications needed by all Manchesters and on further intensive flight trials. As has been described, desperate measures had been required

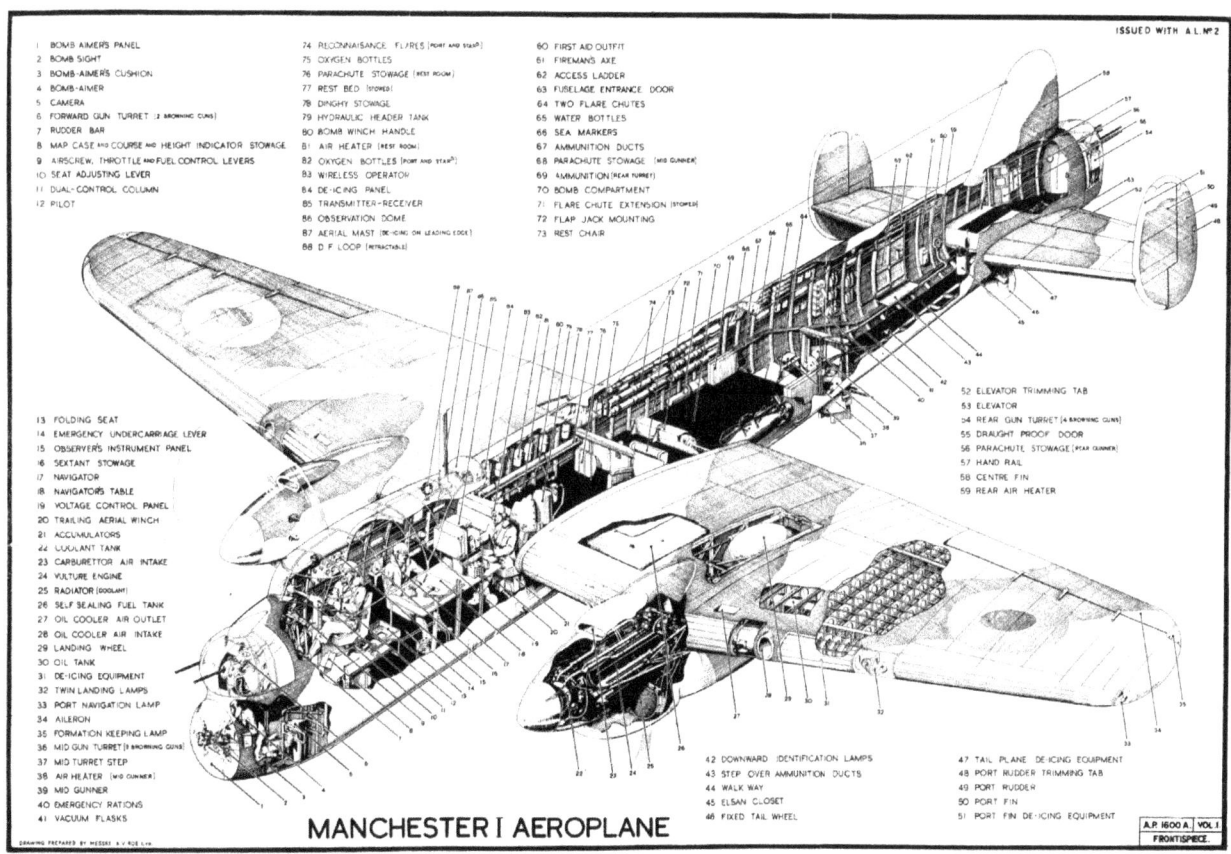

Illustration from frontispiece of Air Publication AP1600A Volume 1 - The Manchester Aeroplane. The cutaway shows an aircraft with 80-feet wings, 28-feet tail and a mid-under turret, appropriate only to the second prototype.

to get the Manchester into service and requirements were changing on an almost daily basis. Many deletions had been permitted in order to get the first batch of 20 into service and at that moment on the production line aircraft were still being fitted with the original 28-feet span tailplane. These aircraft were not considered operationally fit by Bomber Command and a long and indeed ever-lengthening list of modifications was demanded.

As of this date a Bomber Command letter lists:

Manchester In Service Modifications:
Items which are recent or new requirements considered essential by the Command:
Resin Lights
Improvement in fuel content determination
Deletion of under turret and provision of escape hatch in same position
Strengthen W/op table
Reposition W/op key
Reposition three 24-volt accumulators
Neutralising unit repositioning
Separation of aerials for TR9f and R1082
New carriers for 2,000-lb AP bombs, 1,800-lb CP and mines
Modification to accommodate 1,000-lb bomb in 500-lb carriers

Items considered desirable by Command:
Glycol spray for bomb aimer's panel
Wiper for bomb aimer's panel
Anti-dazzle plate for landing lamp

Items discussed at meeting with Command at Manchester on 22 October 1940:
Cabin heating OR Electrically heated clothing (Gloves and boots provided for first 38 aircraft. 39th and subsequent aircraft to have cabin heating system)
Armour plate & draught proof bulkhead (Retrofit)
Barrage Balloon Cutters (Retrofit)
Exhaust flame dampers
Curtain at navigator's table
Perspex blister at navigator's station
Distant reading compass (51st and subsequent aircraft)
Hot and cold air intake
Bomb aiming panel, increased downward vision
Provision of extra fire extinguishers
First aid box
Fuel jettison system (Installation ready for 21st aircraft)
Increased vision for rear turret (Nash & Thompson) modification ready for test

Other Items:
Oxygen and intercom for nose turret
Wireless mast de-icer, also wings and tail
Fitting IFF R3003
Introduction of H type 1000 generator
Automatic controls Mk.IV (Impractical on first twenty aircraft)
F24 camera stowage (Impractical on first twenty aircraft)
Marconi T1154 - R1155 (Impractical on first twenty aircraft)
Lorenz Blind Approach equipment (Investigate to see if can be fitted)

The twenty-sixth aircraft is expected in mid-January 1941 and will have all operational requirements, including cabin heating [note discrepancy with list - Author]. It is intended to withdraw the early aircraft and modify them at Avros or Maintenance Units.

Comments about the status of the Stirling and Halifax were also included. Eight Manchesters had so far reached 207 Squadron, whereas only two Halifaxes had reached 35 Squadron. The letter recorded that these two had completed very little flying due to tail wheel problems, but that Bomber Command considered that it may turn out to be the best of the three aircraft operationally. It was agreed that 207 Squadron would receive the twenty-first and subsequent machines, and L7296, the twenty-first production airframe, became the first with the 33-feet span triple fin tail and all current operational equipment. Avro had tested this example satisfactorily on 18 December.

An itemised list of Avro Works Modifications from this period details:

119	Wing tips 90-feet span - all aircraft
108	Large tailplane – twenty-first and subsequent (and retrofit to earlier batch)
11	Self-sealing petrol and oil tanks - all aircraft
45	Barrage Balloon Protection – twenty-first and subsequent aircraft
13	Armour protection for crew
93	Armour plate bulkhead at Former No.8 – twenty-first and subsequent aircraft
121	Bulletproof glass
?	Twin beam guns pending
?	Under gun mount pending
?	Cabin heating (being designed)
86	Oxygen regulator
80	Regulator restrainer
70	Wiring for bomb aiming panel
35	Heated panel for bomb aimer
75	Heated boots and gloves
?	Autopilot – twenty-first and subsequent aircraft
?	Bombsight CSBS Mk.9A
106	R3003 IFF
85	T1154 & R1155 W/T
110	1000 Watt Generator
24	Lorenz beam approach equipment - all aircraft
83	Mixing box – twenty-first and subsequent aircraft
116	Aerial feeder
30	Airscrew de-icer
32	Tail de-icer
33	W/T mast de-icer

Headquarter's Bomber Command also required 207 Squadron to intensively fly six aircraft until 500 hours on each had been completed. The following aircraft were selected: L7278, L7279, L7280, L7283, L7284 and L7286. Take-off, climb, all-up weight, and single engine performance were all to be evaluated. However, it was already clear that the desired increase in power was unlikely to be forthcoming.

The intensive test flying programme commenced, but fairly soon one aircraft was in trouble. One morning the squadron's first crew, that of Flying Officer Johnny Siebert, were allocated the task of testing the single engine performance of L7286 from Waddington. The four or five crew members were supplemented by two or three soldiers from the airfield defence force along for a joy ride. Over Lincoln at about 7,000 feet the captain and second pilot, all former Handley Page Hampden aircrew with no previous experience of feathering airscrews, finding single engine flying rather tame and tedious, decided for the hell of it to feather the other airscrew and glide. It was certainly a novel experience for them and seemed fun.

When the aircraft was down to 3,000 to 4,000 feet the crew initiated the procedure to unfeather the propellers and restart the engines. Regrettably, the feathering mechanism had failed, either because of flat batteries or jammed solenoid valves, and neither propeller could be unfeathered, despite increasingly feverish efforts. At the gliding angle of a Manchester the ground was approaching rapidly and Siebert called for everyone to assume their crash positions at the rear of the aircraft.

There was no large field ahead but without power they had no options. The pilot made his approach, lowered the flaps and undercarriage and touched down in a ploughed field. Before their forward speed had decreased significantly, and with the tail still up, the River Witham appeared across their path. In desperation Siebert hauled back on the stick, jumped the river and pulled up in another ploughed field beyond, near the Bardney sugar beet factory. With considerable sighs of relief the crew climbed out to take stock of the damage. This turned out to be confined to the loss of the long trailing aerial, which was wound fully out at the time of the incident.

Other arrivals, quickly on the scene, were the village police force and a couple of armed farmers, who had initially mistaken the Manchester for a German aircraft. The Wireless Operator, Sergeant Jim Taylor, called Waddington on the radio and they were collected by a vehicle sent out from the airfield. The impact of the incident on the army passengers was not recorded! On 22 December 1940 after the greater proportion of the fuel had been drained, the ground had firmed up with the frost, and with the wind in the right quarter the Commanding Officer, Squadron Leader Hyde, flew the Manchester out solo and returned safely to Waddington some fifteen minutes later. The only disciplinary action resulting from this misadventure was that Jim Taylor received a bill from the RAF for the loss of the trailing aerial.

Meanwhile, Flight Lieutenant Dereck French experienced one of the first serious hydraulic problems in 207 Squadron. On 19 December French, Burton-Gyles and three crew took off in L7280 on a local test flight. Immediately after the wheels left the ground the pipe carrying hydraulic oil to the port engine radiator shutters burst, spraying the fluid onto the hot exhaust pipe. The engine burst into flames. French aborted the test and completed the shortest possible full circuit, landing back at Waddington some fifteen minutes later with the port engine still blazing. Fire engines were already standing by as the aircraft rolled to a halt and the flames were quickly extinguished with little further damage to the airframe. It had been a narrow escape.

Whilst production at Woodford began to get into a rhythm, aircraft deliveries seemed on the point of a major boost with the coming on stream of the Metropolitan Vickers assembly line. Construction had commenced earlier in 1940 and the first deliveries were scheduled before the year end. The Metrovick factory at Trafford Park in Manchester had no adjacent airfield and it was intended that completed broken down major components would be moved to Woodford for final assembly and flight testing alongside Avro built machines. It was agreed that Metrovick's first Manchester, R5768, should undergo a test assembly at the factory as a one-off operation to ensure that everything fitted, prior to disassembly and final completion at Woodford. R5768 eventually came together on 21 December 1940 to the satisfaction of management and workforce and was photographed inside the factory next day. On the night of 23 December, a German air raid by KG1, led by pathfinding Heinkel He111s from KG100, attacked Manchester. By coincidence, or otherwise, the Metrovick factory was heavily bombed and the assembled R5768 and components for the next twelve in line (R5769 to R5780) were destroyed or damaged beyond repair, along with essential jigs and tools - a cruel setback at such a crucial moment.

Following building repairs Metrovick production soon resumed. The serial numbers R5768 to R5780 were reallocated to the next aircraft on the production line, but it was three months later, on 31 March, before the new R5768 was assembled at Woodford. The Germans had provided a lesson in strategic bombing and R5768 became the only Manchester to appear twice as a complete aircraft.

On 31 December the Air Ministry Overseer, Resident Technical Officer and Chief Designer of A. V. Roe arrived for a conference on Manchester modifications and equipment. The Group and Station Engineer Officers also attended. The squadron strength at the end of the year had risen to eleven Manchesters. These were probably: L7278, L7279, L7280, L7282, L7283, L7284, L7286, L7288, L7290, L7291 and L7292.

Instead of accomplishing 500 hours of intensive flying on its six aircraft by the last day of the year, 207 Squadron had achieved a mere seventy-eight hours on all aircraft for the whole month of December. The low flying hours did not reflect a lack of effort, however, since Avro, Rolls-Royce and the squadron air and ground crews were working at an intense pace.

The winter of 1940/1941 was one of the coldest on record and the Manchester was presenting the 207 Squadron ground crews with quite desperate problems as a result of the early stage of its development. Pilot Officer McCabe and his colleagues did, however, discover that they had cause to be grateful for two features of the Rolls-Royce Vulture. The engine turned out to be one of the easiest piston engines of all time to start in cold weather, which was one factor to be grateful for when the ground crews of 44 Squadron at Waddington were struggling with the Bristol Pegasus engines of their Hampdens. Also, when the Rolls-Royce Vultures were running they were as smooth as a turbine, unlike the highly tuned, but by comparison rough, Merlin from the same stable.

Former Sergeant Bill Buck recalls one take-off early in the Manchester work-up period, when a young Rolls-Royce development engineer was on board to monitor engine performance. By a not unusual coincidence one engine began streaming smoke as they accelerated on their take-off run. With no apparent power loss, but increasing trepidation amongst the crew, the take-off was completed. Suspecting that the smoking engine might pack up at any moment Buck tackled the engineer and asked, with commendable understatement, whether the presence of such volumes of smoke was altogether safe and normal. The engineer replied with disarming reassurance that there was no need for concern and that the smoke was perfectly normal for an engine at this stage of development. Buck was not taken in by a single word and speculated on whether the engineer would be so relaxed had the smoke materialised with him on board over Berlin instead of the airspace around Waddington.

The Vulture problems became no better during January 1941. Whilst the flight testing and training continued at a hectic pace, slowed only by the fight to keep the Manchesters airworthy, no major failure had occurred so far to a Vulture engine whilst airborne. This changed when, at about this time, Flying Officer Frankie Eustace had an engine fail at the most crucial period, on take-off. In these circumstances the pilot had to be either extremely fortunate or capable, preferably both, to avoid a crash. Control became critical and the golden rule said at all costs maintain the heading and under no circumstances turn into the 'dead' engine. On this occasion Frankie Eustace feathered the dead engine but then committed the cardinal sin of turning back to the airfield. Generally an aircraft at this stage could be expected to spin in and crash, but on this occasion Eustace got away with his mistake and managed a successful downwind landing back at Waddington.

After this providential escape the Manchester was towed in from the airfield and parked outside the flight office. A number of pilots, including Frankie Eustace and 'Mike' Lewis, were relaxing in the flight office when the Manchester was towed in. The aircraft had the first of the de Havilland fully feathering propellers. The pilots sat around digesting the good fortune of Eustace's survival. As 'Mike' Lewis recalls: 'one of the assembled group suddenly noticed that the propeller of the seized engine was unfeathered'.

Thinking that the unfeathering had been done by a ground crew member whilst their attention was diverted, they continued their discussion. However, a few moments later someone else noticed that the propeller was feathered again. To a man they leapt up and, forming a posse, sought out the engineering officer immediately. Together they inspected the aircraft and found to their surprise that nobody had been near or had entered the aircraft since it was towed in. A technical inspection revealed that the feathering solenoid had stuck closed and that as long as the battery lasted the propeller would have continued to feather and unfeather itself.

So the aircraft not only had engine but also propeller troubles. What if this had occurred some distance from base? Emergency calls to de Havilland resulted in a party of engineers from the company arriving and disconnecting the feathering circuits until such time as they devised a solenoid which would not stick closed. Regrettably this was not to be the last of the propeller feathering problems to be encountered by the squadron.

Whilst the development flying progressed and decisions were made to implement the modification programme specified on 15 December, preparations for operational flying continued in parallel. On 6 January 1941 the ORB notes a detachment was being formed at Driffield to speed air firing training.
On 21 January 1941 the AOC, Air Vice-Marshal Bottomley, visited the station to discuss the possibility of the squadron undertaking restricted operational flying and it was agreed that this should be implemented. By the 24th the initial plans were prepared and the AOC 5 Group was informed that the squadron would try to have four aircraft and crews fit for operations on February 14th. The ORB noted that six aircraft and crews were being prepared.

During this period Manchesters continued to arrive at Waddington from various maintenance units, including 6 MU Brize Norton, 27 MU Shawbury and 46 MU at Lossiemouth. Subsequent to the first few Manchesters received by the squadron with the FN21A mid-under turret, the next aircraft had no mid-positioned armament of any kind fitted: these were destined to be the aircraft with which the first tentative operations were flown, despite the undertakings of 9 December 1940 which promised that the later, operationally fit aircraft were to be issued to the squadron for these initial operations.

These early aircraft maintained the colour scheme of the first aircraft to be received by the squadron in having the upper and lower surface colours meeting in a straight line mid-way up the fuselage side. The well known photographs of L7284 EM-D and L7288 EM-H show such Manchesters to good advantage and were probably taken very early in 1941. The loss of the weight of the mid-positioned turret offered a marginal improvement in performance of these aircraft. The last Manchester to be received by the squadron with no mid-position turrets is unknown but the rest of the batch at least up to and including L7302, some twenty or twenty-one aircraft, were delivered without any mid-position armament.

Two views showing, Top: test assembly of the first Metropolitan Vickers Manchester, R5768, on 21 December 1940 at Trafford Park. Two nights later R5768, together with major components of the next twelve in line, were destroyed in an air raid. Bottom: very rare photograph showing wrecked fuselage sub-assemblies from the initial production batch, R5769 to R5780, lying outside the Metrovick factory at Trafford Park soon after the German air raid of 23 December 1940. (Both via G. A. Jenks)

On 25 January 1941 an Avro working party arrived at Waddington to carry out the agreed modifications to the Manchesters, which were to be done at the rate of five aircraft per week and require the aircraft to be housed in the hangar. Fourteen to be modified at Waddington, a further nine awaiting delivery at Woodford and four still at the MUs.

Mr Burke of the Ministry of Aircraft Production (MAP) visited the station to discuss the situation with respect to modifications and equipment for the aircraft to make them operationally fit. Several very desirable modifications, such as the fitting of autopilots, balloon cable cutters etc. would not be included.

Second Aircraftman Norman Rushton, a member of 207 Squadron's ground crew in the Maintenance 'M' Flight, recalls that another necessary modification carried out on some aircraft was the fitting of self-sealing fuel tanks in place of the original unprotected tanks. Possibly this related to the first few pre-production aircraft which were originally envisaged as test, development and crew conversion trainers. To facilitate this modification the lower mainplane skin was detached to allow the tanks to be removed. Three ground crew then raised the new self-sealing tanks into place, bracing these upwards into the space whilst the rest of the team fastened the metal retaining straps and tightened them with turnbuckles. Finally the wing skin was pop-riveted back in place.

The FN21A turrets were removed by the squadron armourers and airframe fitters working with the Avro party, the circular holes being infilled with a neat removable hatch. Norman Rushton remembers constructing these from wood. They were of the correct depth to span the gap between the floor and the outer skin of the aircraft, being flat on the top and curved to blend with the fuselage contours beneath. The hatches were closed by an interior spring-loaded bolt and had a ring handle and cable to lift them clear in an emergency.

Installation of the cabin heating system was not such a simple matter. A square hole was cut in each wing leading edge between the fuselage and engine cowling inboard of which a radiator was located. A duct was run directly from the engine to this radiator conducting coolant through the radiator and returning it to the engine cooling radiators located beneath the engine nacelle. Air introduced through the leading edge intake was led through this radiator and thence straight into the aircraft in the wing root, one to each side of the fuselage.

On test it was found that both ducts projected a terrific blast of hot air directly at the radio operator at his seat on the port side just in front of the main spar. Thus, after trials and further complaints from the aircrew a thin steel deflector plate was fitted over each inlet to distribute the heat laterally to some extent. However, there was no internal ducting to direct the heat forward to the front turret and bomb-aiming position or towards the rear for the tail gunner. Consequently, although the centre section became reasonably warm there was no significant benefit at the extremities of the aircraft.

On 30 January the Senior Air Staff Officer (SASO) of Headquarters 5 Group, Group Captain A. P. Richie, visited Waddington to discuss the status of the training, the modification programme and the establishment of the squadron. Meanwhile the Avro working parties continued the intensive modification programme. The fourteen Manchesters at Waddington were: L7278, L7279, L7280, L7282, L7283, L7284, L7286, L7288, L7290, L7291, L7292, L7294, L7298, L7299.

During early February 1941 the number of pilots and aircraft continued to increase rapidly. On the 11th seven modified Manchesters were allotted to the squadron. The precise date of delivery is uncertain but the aircraft possibly included L7300 and certainly included L7302, L7303 and L7304.

By this time a decision had been taken to form a new 97 Manchester squadron, from 'B' Flight of 207 Squadron. The new squadron was to utilise aircraft from the original batch of twenty which, despite the modification programme, would still not be considered suitable for operations. 207 Squadron was to operate the newer, better-equipped aircraft from subsequent batches. For the moment aircraft and personnel continued to arrive at Waddington, where the Avro working party and squadron ground crews continued their intensive modification programme. Optimism for the Manchester was still running at a high level. Sir Robert Renwick had estimated that the Manchesters in 5 Group would be fully modified to current operational status by 1 March 1941.

By then Avro would have similarly modified a further twenty-five aircraft prior to delivery and produced a further twelve to current status. If this was realised, both 207 and 97 Squadrons would have their eighteen initial establishment plus one in reserve and a further thirty-four fully operational Manchesters would be available.

L7282 EM-J, one of the initial batch of pre-production, non-operationally fit aircraft, at Waddington c. January 1941, in the early paint scheme with mid-under FN21A turret retracted. The outer profile of the original bomb doors is well displayed. (RAF Museum P022535)

Starboard, three quarter rear view of pre-production L7282 EM-J c. March 1941 at Waddington. White horizontal stripe in front of background hedge is either snow or handiwork of the censor. (Andrew Jackson)

L7288 EM-H at Waddington with squadron codes over-printing the serial. Note trestle in place around the starboard Vulture. The FN21A mid-under turret was never fitted to this aircraft. (207 Squadron archives)

A 'press ganged' scratch crew assembled in front of L7288 EM-H, c. December 1940 to January 1941. Left to right: Flying Officer Peter Burton-Gyles (captain); Sergeant J. A. Taylor (wireless operator); unknown; Sergeant Hudson, (observer); Sergeant J. Scott (wireless operator/air gunner). The aircraft joined 207 Squadron on 7 December 1940, and passed to 97 Squadron on 26 February 1941. (207 Squadron archives)

L7288 EM-H at Waddington. Photograph must have been taken pre-February 1941 because the aircraft lacks the lower bomb aimer's window, balloon cable cutters, cabin heater intakes and cockpit side blister. Engine covers are off the starboard Vulture. (207 Squadron archives)

An internal Avro Minute records the items involved and progress of the modification programme:

Manchester Modification State, January/February 1941:

Item	Status
Mine Carriers	All
Wireless R3003	All
Cabin Heating	L7311 onward
Armour Plate	L7300 onward
Flame Dampers	All
Resin Lights	All
Lorenz	All
Heated bomb aiming panel	All
Perspex blisters	All
Remove FN21A	First nine aircraft
Completed by 23 January	L7288, L7284, L7292, L7294, L7286, L7300, L7282, L7299
Completed by 21 February	L7279, L7298
Completed by 28 February	L7278, L7280, L7283, L7290, L7291

Wireless operator Sergeant J. A. Taylor and wireless operator/air gunner Sergeant J. Scott pose at the radio position in L7288, 207 Squadron. (207 Squadron Archives)

Avro production was to have reached three per week by this time and plans were laid to form a new squadron or re-equip an existing Hampden unit. 61 Squadron was eventually chosen, but events were to overtake these optimistic plans. On 14 February 1941, despite the allocation of the new aircraft to the squadron, the ORB records that the four operationally fit aircraft promised to the AOC fourteen days previously were still not available.

On 15 February 207 Squadron at last had six operationally fit crews and aircraft. No operations were required, so the crews undertook night cross-country training in the Manchesters. That same day more experienced pilots, Pilot Officers W. G. Gardiner DFC, W. S. Herring DFM and Flying Officer G. R. Taylor DFC, arrived on posting from a spell as instructors at 16 Operational Training Unit (OTU), Upper Heyford.

207 Squadron was poised for operations against the Third Reich. The RAF's intention of providing a core of experienced and high calibre aircrews to introduce the Manchester into service, as intimated by newly-promoted Wing Commander 'Hettie' Hyde, had been implemented. Regrettably it was to prove a much more intractable task to achieve the transition of the Manchester to a successful service aircraft.

Although the transition had proved far from routine, up to this date there had been no significant accidents. There was still a good deal of enthusiasm for the aircraft. By comparison with the Hampdens most aircrew were accustomed to, the Manchester was a much larger and very advanced aircraft.

At the time of their introduction to operations the aircraft standardised on a crew of six – a first and second pilot, an observer (navigator), who also aimed the bombs and manned the front gun turret, two wireless operators/air gunners (W/op AG) and a rear gunner. The captain was invariably an experienced second tour officer, whilst the second pilots were freshly trained sergeant pilots straight from Hampden OTUs. Having gained Manchester and operational experience under the direction of the captain it was envisaged that these second pilots would then go on to form their own crews. Part of the second pilot's duty was to monitor the engine instruments.

At this time the trade of navigator did not exist and neither was a front gunner, bomb aimer or flight engineer carried. Similarly, the 1st W/op was a second tour man and the 2nd W/op AG was a new boy completing his training on operations before transferring to a crew in his own right. The 2nd W/op AG occupied the mid-upper FN7A, soon to be introduced. In those aircraft which continued to operate without the mid-upper turret, the 2nd W/op AG occupied the front turret.

The Vulture engines were rated at 1,760 hp each. The aircraft had an empty weight of 29,432 lb, a mean weight of 41,315 lb and a maximum loaded weight of up to 45,000 lb. A maximum bomb load of 10,350 lb could be lifted but more usually 8,000 lb or 6,000 lb of bombs were carried. With an 8,000 lb load the range was 1,630 miles. On trials a top speed of 265-mph at 17,000 feet was recorded. The best cruising speed was 185 mph at 15,000 feet. Take-off performance was marginal, supposedly requiring a 1,300 yards run to clear a 50-feet obstacle in calm conditions. In practice a fully loaded Manchester was unlikely to clear 6 feet at 1,400 yards in warm weather, whilst the average landing run was 1,050 yards.

By this time 'Mike' Lewis had a large number of flying hours in Manchesters, including the testing and development work done on the squadron, the training of the less experienced second pilots allocated to the unit and the preparation for operations. Lewis recalls the Manchester as an exceedingly stable 'bombing platform'. The triple-finned Mk.1 was especially stable laterally. Once the aircraft had settled onto the desired heading it would hold it until the cows came home, almost as if an automatic pilot was engaged. In comparison, Lewis later found its offspring, the Lancaster, was less stable in that, even with the most precise flying from the pilot, the nose continually described a gentle rotary motion in the sky. This spiralling motion must have been the bane of bomb aimers.

The ailerons of the Manchester were also very light and responsive. Lewis found that the aileron feel became lighter as speed increased in a dive. At an indicated airspeed (IAS) of about 250 mph in a dive the aircraft could be rocked up to thirty to forty-five degrees either side of horizontal using only one finger of each hand on the control column. In comparison the Lancaster with the same ailerons and a very similar wing plan was much heavier, the weight increasing progressively as speed built-up.

In contrast, the elevators of the Manchester Mk.1 with short span tail were extremely heavy. When the aircraft was trimmed to fly straight and level this had some virtue but it was unsatisfactory for carrying out evasive manoeuvres and when engaged on circuits and landings. Receiving dual instruction on the early Mk.1 was a physically demanding task for the trainee pilot. Quite excessive force was necessary to raise and lower the nose, to the extent that pilots rapidly exhausted their physical resources. Pilots under instruction found that three take-offs and landings was the limit they could achieve at one session and this was rarely sufficient to accomplish a complete check out of a new pilot. Lewis found he could speed the task of converting new pilots onto the type by carrying two trainees on each flight. When one pilot had carried out three circuits and landings he changed seats with the other trainee until he had recovered his strength.

Another experienced pilot of the time, Flying Officer 'Junior' Gardiner, was to survive the war, with 267 hours on Manchesters with 207 Squadron and a further seventy hours in subsequent training units. On completion of his second tour on 28 October, he had flown twenty-seven Manchester and four Hampden sorties – the highest number of Manchester missions by an aircraft captain. In the course of his service he flew sixty-two of the 202 Manchesters built from L7279 (the fourth production) to L7485 (one of the last). He may have made the last ever Manchester flight when, on 12 October 1943, he flew L7307 from Swinderby to Syerston to become the 'dummy fuselage' for 5 Lancaster Finishing School. He never experienced an engine failure with 207 Squadron, a fact he attributed (rightly or wrongly) to his handling technique. All this was very much in future when, after an hour's dual with Flight Lieutenant Dereck French and a brief check flight in the company of Wing Commander 'Hetty' Hyde, along with two other pilots and a circuit and landing each, they were considered fully operational.

In common with the initial response of other former Hampden captains, Flying Officer Gardiner was impressed with many aspects of the new aircraft – from its huge spinners in which a hip bath could be taken, to its four gun rear turret which seemed infinitely preferable to the two mid-upper Vickers Gas Operated machine guns (VGOs) in the Hampden, and the huge bomb bay. However, once they began taking it into the air a host of issues manifest themselves. Not only Rolls-Royce but also Avro representatives danced constantly in attendance. Gardiner recalled a test in an early pre-production aircraft with 28-feet span tail. In inclement weather, along with Bill Thorne of Avros, he was to familiarise himself with the Beam Approach System at Waddington. Thorne declared himself favourably impressed and expressed a desire for such a system at Woodford, where his chief concern on returning to base was to avoid 'making a hole in the Pennines'. However, as they descended into the murk Thorne became increasingly agitated. This intensified when Gardiner selected full flap on approach with the aircraft still close to full load. Gardiner's level of concentration was such as to preclude asking the reason for this until, once safely on the ground, Thorne explained that with the short span tail there was insufficient down elevator control to counteract the tendency of the nose to rise in the event of a fully loaded overshoot with full flap. No one at Boscombe Down had mentioned this and it was never mentioned in "Pilots' Notes" – the matter being rectified with the 33-feet span tail.

Flying the classic corkscrew evasive manoeuvre in the early Mk.1 for any length of time was very demanding on the pilot. If rapid changes of flight direction or height were needed in the event of a fighter attack they learnt to use a combination of gentle corkscrew with simultaneous use of flying and engine controls.

For the moment, pilots satisfied themselves in regard to the flying characteristics of the aircraft, which proved generally adequate, whereas their major concern centred around the engines. Being so seriously underpowered was a major limitation on performance, and reliability was at best marginal.

By late February 1941, about the time they first operated, many Manchesters underwent a further and hasty field modification to their colour scheme. The demarcation between the upper surface colours and the black undersides was raised again, this time to the top of the fuselage. On the tailplane, wings and cowlings the actual junction was a straight line. In contrast, on the fuselage top decking the junction was wavy. The central fin was coloured black to match the twin endplate fin and rudder assemblies.

Colour schemes differed slightly from aircraft to aircraft. Generally the wavy black underside colour swept up to the leading edge of the central fin leaving the whole of the rear fuselage black. Although having a black central fin, at least two aircraft, L7309 and L7319, had the wavy demarcation on the fuselage all the way through to the rear turret. On these aircraft the unit codes, the individual aircraft letters, and the serials were grey. This colour scheme remained unchanged until September 1941.

On 18 February 1941 Squadron Leader R. D. Stubbs arrived from 144 Squadron, Hemswell, with a view to assuming command of 'B' Flight of 207 Squadron. The ORB for this day also noted that Squadron Leader D. F. Balsdon arrived on attachment at Waddington from Headquarters 3 Group to gain experience on Manchesters. He was to command the reformed 97 Squadron scheduled to be based at Coningsby. 207 Squadron was to transfer the necessary aircraft, aircrews ('B' Flight) and maintenance personnel to form the nucleus of the new unit.

To this end, aircrews continued to assemble at Waddington for training. On 20 February 1941 Flying Officers Paape DFC and Ayton, Flying Officers Blakeman and Romans, all experienced and decorated second tour pilots, arrived. The squadron's work-up to operations, embracing many aspects, continued at a feverish pace. On the 22nd it was noted that four new aircraft were collected from Woodford: L7310, L7311, L7312 and L7313. L7313 was the first squadron Manchester to be fitted with the FN7A mid-upper turret, but on a visit on the 24th the Director of Technical Development (DTD) Inspector noted that this remained unserviceable as the firing cut out cams had yet to be fitted.

By now the airfield at Waddington had become so crowded that nine aircraft were dispersed to nearby Coleby. At the same time it was arranged for the squadron air firing detachment to be recalled from Driffield. To ease and speed the training, Headquarters 5 Group had agreed to the allocation of two Fairey Battle target tugs to Waddington so that air firing training could continue at the nearby Wainfleet Ranges. Meanwhile, the intensive night flying training, bombing and operational preparation continued. The milestone of the squadron's and the Manchester's first operation was at hand. Whilst the squadron was poised expectantly to carry out its first operation the contrast between this anticipation and their true predicament was stark. A decision to abandon the Manchester had been made in November 1940 and the Lancaster prototype had flown in January 1941. Before they flew their first operation their aircraft was already obsolete. 207 Squadron and the 5 Group units in its wake were about to endure almost a year and a half of operations with, thankfully unbeknown to them, no significant prospect that the problems would be sorted out. Unwittingly, they were the victims of the grave and desperate position the Allies were in. Every aeroplane was needed, even if it was of doubtful serviceability.

Flying Officer Peter Burton-Gyles in the captain's seat of L7288, 'unknown' in second pilot's seat and W/op AG Sergeant J. 'Scotty' Scott in an unaccustomed place by the navigator's table. (207 Squadron archives)

Chapter Three: First Operations

On 24 February 1941 the Command was briefed for an attack on a *Hipper* class cruiser known to be tied up in Brest. Some thirty aircraft from 3 Group, 25 Handley Page Hampdens, six Manchesters from 5 Group and some Coastal Command aircraft were involved.

Whereas up to May 1940 French naval forces on the Atlantic coast had accomplished nothing positive of an offensive or defensive nature, their ships, mainly, to the everlasting regret of the Allies, turning to port and their doom in the Mediterranean, rather than turning to starboard and their salvation in British waters, shore-based military forces had accomplished a great deal in denying facilities to the enemy. The new German Naval Commander, Brittany, Vizeadmiral Lothar von Arnauld de la Perière, arrived in the port of Brest on 21 June 1940 and recorded gloomily in his war diary:

Oil tanks at Brest, gunned by the British, are burning. No ships in the harbour. In the naval arsenal the scene is chaotic. Inestimable quantities of material damaged and wrecked. Guns found for the most part ruined. Severe damage to all kinds of installation. Many sunken vessels, cranes. Everywhere great disorder.

French naval demolition squads had been hard at work. Not a single dock was useable. Quay installations and the arsenal river were blocked by sunken shipping.

Naval installations at St-Nazaire, La Rochelle, Lorient and Brest offered German forces great potential to carry the offensive to the British in the Atlantic without the need to run the gauntlet through the English Channel or northabout around Scotland. Brest offered the best potential for surface ships and U-boats even though it lay within easy range of British aircraft. Great efforts were immediately made to return the inlet to operational use. By the end of July 1940 Brest still had only one serviceable dry dock in the merchant harbour, not the naval base, its cranes only capable of light loads. A battleship couldn't be accommodated here. In the entire naval arsenal not one crane was working and it was still impossible to forecast when other dock installations would be serviceable. By October a berth for a battleship at Flotilla Quay in the warship harbour and two berths in the neighbouring dry docks were available: their maximum size would accommodate *Scharnhorst* and *Gneisenau* but not *Bismarck* or *Tirpitz*. The latter could only be accepted in the Normandy Lock at St-Nazaire, later the scene of the dramatic 'Cambeltown' attack. Refuelling facilities still relied on moored tankers, judged vulnerable to air attack. There was, similarly, an acute shortage of trained manpower.

The heavy cruiser *Admiral Hipper* broke out through the Denmark Strait in December 1940, but experienced engine problems which necessitated taking emergency refuge in Brest. This provided the first stern test as to whether the base could repair as well as protect her from the RAF. On 4 January 1941 *Hipper* was photographed in dry dock, triggering 175 RAF bombing sorties though without serious damage to the vessel. Flak defences had meantime improved and a large smoke screen facility was envisaged. On 1 February the repaired *Hipper* sallied forth into the Atlantic, finding a convoy and sinking seven British merchant ships before returning to the dry dock in the mercantile harbour on 14 February. Whilst entering this dock the cruiser severely damaged a propeller after hitting a sunken barge in the harbour basin. Repair facilities in Brest couldn't handle this and as there were no suitable new propellers anywhere in France, a new one had to be brought, in wartime, from Kiel in the extreme north of Germany to the extreme west of France. Thus disabled, opportunity was taken to overhaul the cruiser's range-finding optics, but this had to be done by Carl Zeiss at Jena. Neither task was complete by the end of February 1941, by which time *Scharnhorst* and *Gneisenau* were in the North Atlantic.

At this time Brest deployed eighteen heavy anti-aircraft and coastal defence and thirteen light anti-aircraft and coastal batteries, but still only one of the two great naval dry docks was operational. So, whilst the potential may have been very real, the actual was currently less than the worst fears of British Naval Intelligence. For Bomber Command and its new heavy bomber types, including the Manchester, raids on Brest were to figure largely in the next year often without much readily apparent to show for it. Modern analysis indicates an outcome more positive than generally appreciated at the time.

For 207 Squadron's memorable first operation of the war there was a state of high excitement. In addition to squadron personnel, high ranking officers from 5 Group and distinguished Avro and Rolls-Royce guests were invited to witness the operational debut of their protégé - the Manchester. The aircraft were mainly from the original batch delivered to the squadron. They lacked mid-upper turrets, still had the 28-feet span tailplane and

Mk.1 L7288 EM-H of 207 Squadron at Waddington, c. Jan./Feb. 1941. (207 Squadron archives)

saw only limited operational flying. Bomb loads consisted of twelve 500-lb semi-armour-piercing bombs, except for L7300 which, for some reason, only carried eleven.

Crews operationally fit at this time were those of Flight Lieutenant Dereck French, Squadron Leader Charles Kydd, Flying Officers Johnnie Siebert, Peter Burton-Gyles, Frankie Eustace and 'Mike' Lewis. Typically of the man, Wing Commander 'Hettie' Hyde was not going to miss this first operation. Not having his own crew, he 'borrowed' French's crew for the occasion, leaving the dejected Flight Lieutenant behind. 'Hettie' was to earn his unit's undivided respect by being the only Commanding Officer in the squadron to fly Manchesters regularly on operations during the 18- month period it operated them. He was a very experienced pilot and had a tremendous rapport with both his air and ground crews. French remained on the ground to play host to the distinguished visitors, retaining vivid memories of the unit's first operational sortie. It was a bad night with poor visibility, storms, snow lying on the ground and still falling.

Operational Debut, Brest - February 24th 1941:

Serial	Code	Squadron	Captain
L7300	EM-*	207	Wg Cdr N. C. Hyde
L7288	EM-*	207	Sqn Ldr L. C. J. F. Kydd
L7279	EM-*	207	Fg Off. J. A. Siebert
L7284	EM-*	207	Fg Off. P. R. Burton-Gyles
L7286	EM-*	207	Fg Off. F. E. Eustace
L7294	EM-*	207	Fg Off. W. J. Lewis

*In this and subsequent raid tables, an asterisk indicates that the individual aircraft code has not been confirmed

The aircraft took off at closely spaced intervals between 18.35 and 18.50 hours. Four aircraft recorded a take-off time of 18.40 hours. The aircraft made their way individually to the target area, as was the procedure at this stage of the war, there was no 'forming up'.

In L7284 the second pilot, Sergeant Les Syrett, received his first surprise soon after take-off. Having completed his post take-off checks, established their designated course and reached a height of 1,500 feet, Flying Officer 'BG' Burton-Gyles turned to Syrett and, indicating the controls, called: 'It's all yours, call me when you reach the target'. With this he slipped out of the pilot's seat and steadied the controls whilst Syrett took his place. Syrett had expected to undertake maybe half a dozen trips before he was allowed to do more than relieve the pilot for short spells during the safer and more routine legs of the flight. Yet here he was, only a few minutes into the flight on his first operation, in command of a fully loaded Manchester.

Syrett climbed to the briefed flying height and set a new course with mixed feelings of excitement and apprehension. The feeling was heightened by the fact that 'BG' had already disappeared aft. These early Manchesters had no second pilot's seat and consequently the captain could only stand beside him and observe. This indeed was Syrett's normal crew position. While Syrett felt some trepidation at his responsibilities, 'BG' felt none. For four months he had been training and flying with this crew. During the time he had watched each one closely and progressively gave the newcomers more to do as their ability and confidence developed. On their long endurance and test flights 'BG' had increasingly encouraged Syrett to do the flying. He would not have been sitting there if 'BG' had harboured any doubts. The outward flight was uneventful and as they approached Brest Syrett called 'BG' telling him the target was dead ahead.

The squadron Operational Record Book (ORB) records all aircraft as making individual 'high level' bombing attacks, although the debriefing reports show that in general the height reached was around 10,000 feet. Wing Commander Hyde reached 15,000 feet, some 4,000 feet higher than the next Manchester. Over the target area and to the north, south and west the aircraft encountered searchlights, light and heavy flak, but night fighters were not in evidence.

As Burton-Gyles took L7284 across Brest, Sergeant Syrett had his second great surprise of the night. 'BG' was flying at his favourite height of 8,000 feet and the flak, particularly the lighter guns which were firing mainly tracer, seemed so dense to the newcomer that he could not imagine them completing the attack without being hit. Syrett had expected the captain to put the nose down a little, traverse the target area as rapidly as possible, dump the bombs and go.

Not Peter Burton-Gyles. He circled the target, trying to establish the best direction of approach for his bomb run. Having satisfied himself on the location of the target and the best approach, he next did a dummy run across the area. All this time the flak was hammering away around them and 'BG' and the experienced crew members with him appeared to be completely unperturbed.

Burton-Gyles then made two further attacks during which, on the instructions of the observer, Sergeant Houghton, in the bomb aiming position, they released a stick of six bombs on each run. The reason for this was to prevent the Germans calculating the bomb load of the new bomber. Owing to a design fault, the bomb aimer could not observe the fall of bombs and thus Syrett was ordered to look down through the starboard blister in the cockpit. Syrett found he could see the weapons falling away for some time because of the sky being brightly illuminated by searchlights and flak.

With the attack completed, Houghton tried to close the bomb doors. At this point a second problem with the design became apparent, because, as a result of a flak hit or a leak, the hydraulics had failed and the bomb doors could not be closed. 'BG' turned for home and once clear of the target area handed control over to Syrett. He ordered: 'Take over and call me when you reach base'. Syrett regained the seat and began setting his new course, checking time and the fuel situation. To his surprise and concern he found they had been over the target for exactly 40 minutes.

This was a bit disturbing because the maximum bomb load and short range of the target had meant them not carrying a full fuel load. In addition to the time spent over the target, Syrett had to contend with the additional drag of the open bomb doors.

All six Manchesters bombed what they believed to be the target: two dropped the bombs in two separate runs of six bombs per stick. Further problems with the attack force, which were to prove more intractable than the observation of the fall of bombs, manifested themselves during the return flight. L7300, Hyde's aircraft, developed a serious hydraulic leak, which resulted in a film of hydraulic fluid spreading over the windscreen. As a result he had to complete his return flying almost blind. Before the situation deteriorated further he wisely decided to make a precautionary landing, which was successfully accomplished at Boscombe Down at 22.55 hours. Frankie Eustace diverted to Middle Wallop for unexplained reasons. The four remaining aircraft flew on to Waddington where Johnnie Siebert landed at 23.45 hours before the assembled VIPs. 'Mike' Lewis touched down at 23.55 hours followed by Charles Kydd 35 minutes later at 00.30 hours.

Meanwhile L7284 was plodding back across England under the control of Les Syrett. Although delayed by the drag of the enormous bomb bay, the fuel situation appeared to be marginal but sufficient. They arrived last of all in the circuit at Waddington where control was returned to Burton-Gyles for the landing. Entering the circuit,

Manchester Mk.1 L7284 EM-D during a photocall in February 1941. Tailspan 28 feet, but it is uncertain whether the FN21A mid-under turret was ever fitted to this aircraft. L7284 was, in many respects, not operationally fit when it participated in the first operation on 24 February 1941. It never operated again, passing to 61 Squadron in mid-April. (207 Squadron archives)

'BG' called the control tower and obtained permission to land. Below, the various dignitaries assembled for the occasion strained to catch sight of the approaching aircraft. At this point the seriousness of the hydraulic leak became apparent when they were unable to lower the undercarriage.

Following the failure over Brest this had not been unexpected and was not a cause for concern because the emergency pneumatic system to lower and lock the legs was available as a back up. When directed at the appropriate time, Syrett operated the emergency system. To their dismay the undercarriage warning lights showed green on the port side and red on the starboard. The starboard undercarriage leg had failed to lock down. Aborting the landing approach, 'BG' overflew the control tower where a visual check confirmed that this was not a check light failure but the starboard leg was indeed stubbornly retracted. 'BG' tried everything possible to get the remaining leg down, but without success. Avro's Chief Designer, Roy Chadwick, was one of the invited guests and he established radio contact with the aircraft, making a further series of suggestions as to how the reluctant undercarriage might be released. These options were exhausted in turn and eventually with the fuel situation critical and the engines faltering, 'BG' informed the tower of his intention to make a one wheel landing. The crew were sent to crash stations. The rear gunner, 'Eddy' Edmonds, left his turret and sat on the floor with his back to the mainspar, facing aft.

They descended towards the snow-covered grass runway at about thirty degrees to it. As they crossed the perimeter and entered the flare path funnels 'BG' turned into line with the runway and dropped the port wing as low as possible. Flaring out with the left wing low they touched down onto the port main wheel and tail wheel simultaneously. 'BG' fought with rudders and ailerons to keep them straight and gave full left aileron to keep the starboard wing up. At a critical speed he trod on the brakes and the right wing descended gently onto the ground. By this time the speed had dropped away to such an extent that they merely slewed round to starboard, coming to rest facing across the runway. Damage was confined to the bomb doors, starboard wing tip and propeller.

Nobody was hurt and the aircraft was repaired within a few days. It had been a magnificent landing. L7284 was the first Manchester to be damaged in the course of operational flying.

As well as the damage to L7284 there was an embarrassing sidelight to the incident. Examination proved that the reason for the failure of the emergency undercarriage system was due to its incorrect assembly by the Avro working party.

A tragic perspective on this first operation is that of the six captains involved, four were eventually killed and the other two became prisoners of war. Of the second pilots, Sergeant Pendrill was killed, Syrett badly injured, and Hugh Morgan, John Nunn, and Robson were taken prisoner. The fate of Sergeant Rowlands has not so far been established.

With Roy Chadwick on this occasion was Sandy Jacks, the Avro Chief Inspector. Both had maintained a close liaison with the squadron, in particular Jacks was a frequent visitor to Waddington. Chadwick had flown to Waddington in an Anson and both Avro employees stayed on the station overnight. Next morning bad weather grounded the Anson and Chadwick and Jacks travelled back to Woodford by car. The two discussed the events of the previous night during their journey. They knew they had an urgent problem on their hands. The hydraulic failures they had witnessed were serious but surmountable and the crews' reaction at debriefing was generally enthusiastic. Jacks recalled that some of the Manchesters had suffered superficial flak damage, although this is not reported in the ORB. What was clear was that the aircraft were not able to climb above the light and medium flak. Whether all the crews had deliberately chosen to bomb from such a low height cannot be ascertained, but this seems unlikely. Chadwick voiced his worries to Jacks: 'If they are in the flak now they will be no good a year from now, even if the engine power can be increased'. Chadwick's concern was centred on the Vulture engines: even if their reliability could be improved they would still not be capable of providing the Manchester with a satisfactory operational ceiling. The German flak gunners would slaughter them.

As a result of the first operation Avro's rushed ahead with fabrication of the perspex insert to the lower fuselage immediately behind the bomb aiming bubble. Along with other urgent modifications this was incorporated at

Another view of L7284, showing the effectiveness of the camouflage on the starboard wing against the wintry Lincolnshire countryside. (207 Squadron archives)

Waddington by the hard pressed Avro working parties. On 25 February 1941 the 207 Squadron ORB records the formal establishment of 97 Squadron at Waddington and that it was planned to transfer sufficient aircraft and crews to form a flight of eight aircraft as a nucleus.

The following day five Manchesters were detailed for night bombing operations to Cologne. For this raid the five Manchesters were to join 72 aircraft from 2 and 3 Groups, whilst 5 Group provided nine Hampdens from Hemswell, and ten each from Scampton and Lindholme. The target was the industrial centre of Cologne and the bomb load of each aircraft twelve 500-lb general purpose (GP) bombs. The aircraft took off in a group between 19.10 and 19.15 hours.

Cologne – 26 February 1941:

Serial	Code	Squadron	Captain
L7300	EM-*	207	Flt Lt D. J. French
L7292	EM-*	207	Fg Off. J. A. Siebert
L7288	EM-*	207	Fg Off. P. R. Burton-Gyles
L7286	EM-*	207	Fg Off. F. E. Eustace
L7294	EM-*	207	Fg Off. W. J. Lewis

*Individual codes unknown – not recorded in the ORB

Three aircraft believed they had located the target area, each making two separate runs and bombing from heights between 8,000 feet and 13,000 feet for five of the six runs. In L7288 Les Syrett had again taken over from Burton-Gyles soon after take-off. This operation was to be a more severe test for him than the last, involving as it did several hours flying over occupied territory, including German airspace itself. On reaching the target 'BG' took over and, looking ahead and below, the crew could see fires burning everywhere and bombs from other aircraft exploding every few seconds. Surprisingly, there was no sign of flak, searchlights or fighters. All this indicated they were really over a decoy target, but a careful check appeared to confirm they were indeed over Cologne. The first stick of bombs was duly released with no response whatever from the ground below.

Remaining unconvinced of their precise target, 'BG' turned away and, having withdrawn to a suitable position, turned back and dived on the target to have a closer look. The observer in the nose, Ken Houghton, and the rear gunner, 'Eddy' Edmonds, were told to stand by and, satisfied that this appeared to be a built-up area, 'BG' levelled out at 2,000 feet over the designated aiming point and ordered Houghton to release the bomb load. Taking advantage of their proximity to the ground, Edmonds blazed away with his four Brownings for good measure.

By this time the rear gunners had cut a kite-shaped clear-vision panel in the perspex between the guns. As soon as he ceased firing, Edmonds stood up in his turret and stuck his head through the panel to have a look at the effects of the attack on the built-up area below. Unbeknown to him, as he stretched forward his intercom plug came out, isolating him from the rest of the crew. When 'BG' called each crew station in turn there was consequently no response from the rear turret. As Edmonds sat down and plugged in his intercom connection again he was startled when the turret doors suddenly burst open as a crew member arrived to check whether he was still around.

There can be little doubt that, along with the other operational captains in 207 Squadron, Burton-Gyles fully appreciated by this stage the unreliability of the Vulture engines and the degree to which they were underpowered. Many Manchesters on test proved to be unable to maintain height on one engine. Even when lightly loaded, carefully trimmed and with the throttle of the remaining engine fully advanced, many still sank, some at a more alarming rate than others. To take the risk of diving to a low altitude over enemy territory, as 'BG' did and other Manchester captains were to do subsequently, was to court certain disaster in the event of an engine failure. The fact that they were prepared to go to such lengths to ensure their bombs were laid on target, in full awareness of the risks, speaks volumes for the enthusiasm and 'press on' spirit of the aircrews, operating against almost insuperable odds in their Manchesters. Almost before L7288 had crossed the town and whilst still at 2,000 feet, 'BG' called on Syrett standing beside him to change seats. Having done so, Syrett wasted no time in climbing to a respectable height and heading for home.

The remaining two aircraft in the operation both experienced equipment failures, necessitating early returns. Close to the enemy coast Frankie Eustace, in L7286, experienced a serious drop in oil pressure in the port engine, a common Vulture problem at this time. He diverted to Flushing, dropping his bomb load in two sticks from 10,000 feet and 9,000 feet before returning safely to Waddington at 22.10 hours. In L7294 'Mike' Lewis was even more unfortunate. A serious hydraulic failure developed within an hour of take-off. The bombs were jettisoned in the North Sea and the aircraft returned to Waddington, effecting a safe landing at 21.10 hours. Bomber Command records indicate 353 high explosive (HE) and 15,060 incendiaries dropped from the 106 aircraft which bombed. The German archivist in Cologne reported only ten HE and ninety incendiaries actually fell within the city limits.

Meanwhile, on 27 February 1941 the actual transfer of 'B' Flight, 207 Squadron to form the cadre of 97 Squadron took place. The aircraft involved comprised: L7282, L7283, L7290, L7291, L7292, L7294, L7298 and L7299. The twelve officers transferred to provide a nucleus of trained crews were: Squadron Leader R. D. Stubbs DFC; Flight Lieutenants G. O. L. Bird DFC and J. S. Sherwood, Flying Officers F. E. Eustace DFC, W. J. Lewis DFC, M. J. C. Harwood DFC and Pilot Officers R. S. Ayton DFM, H. S. Blakeman DFM, W. A. Brown, Observers F. G. Reid and A. A. Morgan, and Gunner J. Trueman.

Flying Officer Peter Burton-Gyles (hatted) and crew being debriefed at Waddington following an operation. (207 Squadron archives)

On that day 97 Squadron nominally had three Manchesters available for operations although the unit would not have been able to sustain any intensive pressure in this regard. Established initially on a single flight basis, three Manchesters were in the maintenance hangar having their bomb compartments modified by Avro whilst the remaining two aircraft were dispersed at Coleby awaiting modifications. The aircraft in any case still lacked many essential refinements. Fully trained crews were heavily engaged test flying aircraft and collecting new ones. Fresh crews were arriving and required training. By early March the Squadron still did not have an engineer or armaments officer and the aircraft were plagued with many minor problems, mostly to the hydraulic systems.

On 10 March 1941 the pressure on Waddington eased somewhat when 97 Squadron personnel moved out to Coningsby. Here the grass airfield was flooded and boggy, precluding transfer of the aircraft. Eventually aircraft were flown in between 15 and 18 March but by the 27th all had become bogged down after further heavy rain, preventing any air activity for some days.

Although limited operational flying with this initial batch of aircraft was undertaken by 97 Squadron, as with 207 Squadron, they lacked mid-upper turrets and various other refinements and most retained the 28-feet span tail. Later batches of more operationally fit Manchesters were collected in dribs and drabs as they became available.

An indication of the feverish pace of activity for the squadrons during this work-up period was that on 1 March 1941 two complete aircrews and fifteen maintenance personnel were attached to 207 Squadron from 61 Squadron

Full flap. A 97 Squadron Manchester Mk.1 a few seconds from touch down at Coningsby. Possible blooming spring flowers amongst the barbed wire in foreground. (Tomlinson collection, Imperial War Museum HU42454)

at Hemswell for this unit to gain experience on the Manchester. The crews were those of Flying Officer Geoff Hall and Pilot Officer Peter Casement and their training began in earnest next day. 97 Squadron was to pass on its pre-production aircraft to this unit in turn during March so that conversion could begin.

This rapid expansion of the Manchester force concealed an impending crisis of catastrophic proportion – engines! At this stage it was merely the case that Rolls-Royce were unable to maintain even the output to satisfy production of this one type. Avro had set up frequent internal Manchester production meetings. In February 1941 they recorded the position as critical, with Avro themselves nine Vultures short and Metrovick four short of the promised output. By 17 March the shortfall had risen to ten for Avro and six for Metrovick. The situation was soon to worsen and threaten the aircraft's entire future.

On 2 March 1941, Johnnie Siebert with his crew in L7303 and maintenance personnel was detached to the Air Fighting Development Unit at Duxford for trials. By this time serious serviceability problems with the remaining Manchesters, especially with the hydraulic systems and the oil cooling system of the engines, had reduced the available Manchesters to a minimum. For 207 Squadron's third operation on 3 March only two aircraft could be raised for another attack on a *Hipper* class cruiser at Brest. The main operation for the night was a force of seventy-one aircraft dispatched to Cologne. The two squadron aircraft joined five others in a diversionary raid to the French port.

Brest – 3 March 1941:

Serial	Code	Squadron	Captain
L7302	EM-R	207	Flt Lt D. J. French
L7313	EM-C	207	Fg Off. P. R. Burton-Gyles

Scene at Coningsby. A pre-production Manchester Mk.1 of 97 Squadron in early colour scheme taxies past L7291 being bombed-up. Part constructed hangar behind. (Tomlinson collection, Imperial War Museum HU42460)

Both aircraft carried eleven 500-lb semi-armour-piercing (SAP) bombs, but although they remained serviceable they were unable to locate the target, owing to low cloud over the continent. The crews were aware of the general locality of the target owing to the intense flak coming up through the cloud layer. However, aiming SAP bombs on pinpoint targets such as ships was out of the question in such circumstances.

As captain of L7313 EM-C, Peter Burton-Gyles had elected to allow Les Syrett to fly the entire operation, changing seats as they waited on the runway for the green light from the Aldis lamp. The outward trip had been uneventful, but target location proved impossible. Turning aside from the immediate target area and over the sea they did a climb from low level, establishing that the cloud base was well below 1,000 feet and extended to well above their ceiling. There was no possibility of bombing in such conditions without danger to the French civilian population in the neighbourhood. Accordingly, with the weather extremely bad and no secondary target specified, they aborted the operation and turned towards England.

In L7302 EM-R Dereck French, with a total crew of only five, had been flying for over an hour on instruments. As he approached the target area the weather deteriorated further with a series of violent thunder storms and much lightning. In what he estimated to be the target area, L7302 was struck by lightning, which hit the fuselage near to the identification, friend or foe (IFF) set. To ensure its security in the event of a forced landing in enemy territory the IFF was fitted with a small Thermite explosive charge which could be detonated by pressing the appropriate button. The lightning strike exploded the charge, destroying the set, blowing a jagged hole in the side of the aircraft. Inspection by torchlight revealed a small heap of molten metal on the fuselage floor beneath the site.

In these extreme conditions it was impossible to locate the target and French decided there was a better chance of regaining base without the bomb load. Having crossed the French coast he jettisoned the load 'safe'. In the bad weather conditions he found the aircraft easier to handle, eventually landing back at base 5 hours 45 min after take-off.

On reaching base, Syrett assumed Burton-Gyles would wish to land the aircraft as the full bomb load remained on board. However, 'BG' stood beside him in the second pilot's position and supervised Syrett making the landing himself. 'BG' advised on the timing of the lowering of the flaps and undercarriage, the engine revolutions and propeller settings and continued to encourage his protégé all the way into a smooth landing. As soon as this was effected, 'BG' nipped into the pilot's seat and taxied the aircraft to its dispersal.

By this time an experienced pilot with approaching 1,000 hours flying and a tour on Hampdens behind him, French was well equipped to make the decision to jettison the bombs in the interests of saving the aircraft and its crew. He was accordingly outraged to be 'carpeted' next morning by an insensitive Station Commander who abused him for 'throwing away bombs to the value of his annual salary'. French could hardly believe his ears. Incredulously he tried to explain that in terrible weather, jettisoning the bombs had possibly made the difference between saving and losing the aircraft. He rapidly recognised that reason and commonsense was not one of that officer's strong points.

On 4 March Sir Robert Renwick, Group Captain Anderson and Mr Rosenberg of the Ministry of Aircraft Production (MAP) visited 207 Squadron to discuss the Manchester's hydraulic system. At the meeting, confirmation was given of the decision to scrap the Ermeto-type hydraulic joint and if possible to retrospectively modify the existing aircraft. In the meantime, the squadron would have to carry on with the existing system. A further problem, stemming from the defective hydraulic system, was capable of solution. Oil from the persistent leaks was also found to be affecting the undercarriage micro-switches, whose operation provided the visual cockpit indication that the main wheels were locked in position. Hydraulic oil penetrated the micro-switches causing them to malfunction and preventing the green indicator lights from illuminating when the undercarriage was lowered. Therefore the pilot was not aware whether the hydraulic fluid in the retraction system of the undercart had leaked away, or whether the wheels were locked but the micro-switches were simply not operating.

Only a few days before, on 28 February 1941, perhaps as a direct consequence of these difficulties, Sergeant Harwood had the misfortune to have the undercarriage on L7312 collapse on a normal landing at Waddington. There were no casualties. An answer was required urgently. Lockheed engineers were called in to advise on the hydraulic systems, whilst a staff member from Pye Ltd went to Manchester to advise Avro on the micro-switches. The short term solution devised was to integrate the press button of the switches within an oilskin diaphragm sealed into the sides of the switch.

At the same time, a system of testing the integrity of the switches was devised. This involved a bicycle pump mounted on a board connected through tubes to a suction pad, while a connection went to a large glass 'U' tube. If pumping air through a hole drilled in the case raised the level of red ink in the tube and then held steady, then the switch was airtight. The hole was finally plugged with whalebone and sealed with resin. These modified micro-switches made it possible to distinguish true hydraulic failures from micro-switch failures once more.

Early March 1941 was a period of continued, almost non-stop pressure on the ground crews. Serviceability of the Manchesters continued to be poor despite their most urgent endeavours. Modification to the existing aircraft continued. In the meantime small numbers of serviceable Manchesters were detailed for operations which were invariably called off.

On 6 March 1941 a 207 Squadron Manchester was prepared for an attack on Brest, which was later cancelled. On the 8th three aircraft were prepared for an attack on the oil refinery at Gelsenkirchen, but the operation was cancelled at 17.00 hours owing to bad weather. Finally on the 11th four aircraft were detailed for a raid on Kiel. The weather caused this operation to be abandoned also.

By now the original crews knew each other very well. Wing Commander Hyde had already earned the respect of air and ground crews alike. Introducing a new aircraft to operations was a demanding task at the best of times. The almost insurmountable number of technical problems, both large and small must have made the situation doubly difficult. To these problems was added the continual need to train new aircrews, as well as lose existing experienced crews to the squadrons designated for conversion. At this period 207 Squadron was an experimental and test unit, a conversion unit and an operational squadron all rolled into one. On the few occasions when these pressures allowed Hyde to get away he could be seen in the mess. He was renowned for his liking for pink gins, which he invariably ordered in threes. A typical posture was to be deep in conversation, a glass in each hand and the third at the ready in the crook of his elbow.

Manchester Mk.1 L7291 of 97 Squadron being bombed up. Serial number aft of entry door. Black underside colour has been raised and meets upper scheme in wavy line extending to rear turret. (Tomlinson collection, Imperial War Museum HU42459)

Squadron commanders in Bomber Command were not established with a personal crew as they were not supposed to fly regularly on operations. By this stage, Hyde had almost as many hours on Manchesters as anyone and when he felt the need to gain experience of flying the aircraft on operations he took the simple expedient of 'borrowing' a crew.

During their detachment to Duxford for fighter affiliation duties, Johnnie Siebert and his crew had another little adventure. Arriving at their dispersal point one morning from their briefing they could find no sign of their maintenance personnel. Siebert and the other three crew members, Fomison (observer), Taylor (wireless operator) and Gurnell (rear gunner) were impatient to be on their way and decided they could pre-flight L7303 themselves. They removed the covers, ran the checks and, priming the engines with the low-geared manual handles provided, started them with self-starter and internal batteries. All the instrument readings rose to normal levels and with no more ado they removed the chocks and taxied out. L7303 was carrying a full dummy bomb load. They lined up on the live runway and received a 'green' from the control tower.

Siebert advanced the throttles and soon they were belting down the runway. The pilot concentrated on keeping the aircraft straight, the tail came up and the boundary fence was approaching fast. Siebert glanced at the airspeed indicator to judge precisely the moment of lift-off – no airspeed! Consternation ensued. They lifted off and Johnnie kept the aircraft down to build up flying speed. A quick glance confirmed their worst fears – the cover was still on the pitot head.

A landing back at Duxford was considered unwise and they agreed to make for Newmarket with its longer runway. En route, construction work in progress at another airfield, Waterbeach, drew their attention. What was also apparent was that, save for the construction workers, the airfield was unoccupied. Following their failure to

L7382 OF-J of 97 Squadron airborne from Coningsby. White of fin flash has been darkened. (Tomlinson collection, Imperial War Museum HU42452)

carry out the pre-flight checks correctly, Waterbeach apparently offered an opportunity to save face. They could land unobserved, remove the pitot head cover and take off again so nobody would be aware of their error.

The decision to land was endorsed by those on board and Siebert made a wide circuit before lining them up with the long, deserted runway. The approach was difficult without an airspeed indicator and as a precaution against the fatal stall Siebert kept the speed well up. Everything went smoothly until at the moment of their high speed touch down they suddenly realised that the runway was coated with loose gravel. They careered down the strip in their overloaded condition with the brakes having little effect in checking their progress. The aircraft overshot the runway and charged on through an unoccupied perimeter gunpost. In passing, the spinning propellers picked up many strands of barbed wire and the coils flew everywhere before they tangled themselves tightly around the propeller bosses. A truck was sent to retrieve the shamefaced crew and L7303 was later recovered with only minor damage.

207 Squadron undertook an uneventful operation to Hamburg with four aircraft on 12/13 March 1941. With continued favourable weather Bomber Command maintained its offensive on Hamburg the very next night. This operation was to prove far more eventful. 207 Squadron was called on to provide two Manchesters, but managed to produce five, including L7313 EM-C, possibly still the only aircraft on the squadron with a mid-upper turret, and L7278 EM-A. The latter was one of the earlier batch not passed on to 97 Squadron. Squadron Leader Kydd, Flight Lieutenant French and Flight Sergeant Harwood and their crews were to operate for the second consecutive night and were joined by Wing Commander Hyde and Flying Officer Matthews.

Hamburg – 13/14 March 1941:

Serial	Code	Squadron	Captain
L7313	EM-C	207	Fg Off. H. V. Matthews
L7310	EM-H	207	Sqn Ldr C. J. F. Kydd
L7303	EM-P	207	Wg Cdr C. N. Hyde
L7302	EM-R	207	Flt Lt D. J. French
L7278	EM-A	207	FS F. B. Harwood

The aircraft again carried ten 500-lb GP bomb loads and although no take-off times are noted in the ORB it is believed that they assembled for take-off around 20.00 hours. Four aircraft took off safely, but the fifth, L7313 EM-C piloted by Matthews, burst its tailwheel tyre due to undercarriage leg shimmy whilst taxiing. Take-off times were not rigidly controlled during this period and it was decided to replace the tail wheel out on the aerodrome, a task which took about thirty minutes.

Matthews restarted the engines, taxied to the take-off point and, having received a 'green' from the control truck Aldis, set off in pursuit of his colleagues. Activity on the flarepath had been detected by a lurking intruder. A Junkers JU88A-2 or 'A-4, possibly coded 'R4+NL' of 1/NJG2 at Gilze-Rijen in Holland and crewed by Feldwebel Hans Hahn (pilot). Unteroffizier Ernst Meissler (wireless operator) and Uffz. Helmut Scheidt (engineer) were patrolling the Lincolnshire airfields. Undetected, though misidentifying his target as a Blenheim, Fw. Hahn timed his attack to coincide with the moment the Manchester became airborne and was at its most vulnerable. The crew never had a chance and L7313 was riddled with cannon and machine gun fire soon after crossing the airfield boundary.

The noise of the firing and low flying combat brought many people rushing to their windows on the airfield and in the town of Lincoln. The wife of Sergeant Jim Bryce, a wireless operator under training and serving with 207 Squadron, saw the blazing Manchester pass low over the roof tops closely followed by the JU88. The scene was also witnessed by Flight Sergeant John Wells from the window of the aircrew quarters on the airfield at Waddington. He saw the navigation lights of L7313 as it took off, the sudden sharp brilliant lines of tracer from the fighter and the glare from the crash as the aircraft hit the ground behind trees.

L7313 crashed at Whisby some five miles west of Waddington and continued to burn on the ground, part of the bomb load exploding. Flying Officer Matthews, Sergeants Redgrave, Welch and Hemingway were killed outright. Flight Sergeants W. A. W. Cox, the wireless operator, and Marsden were thrown clear, but received multiple injuries. They were taken to Lincoln hospital where Marsden later died. Bill Cox survived although with the loss of a leg.

The remaining aircraft attacked the Blohm und Voss shipyards at Hamburg in fine weather and returned safely. The entire raid caused 119 fires, including one in a timber yard. The casualty list, giving 51 killed and 139 injured, was the heaviest in the city to date. 207 Squadron had suffered its first loss and the whole unit was stunned to have seen the savagery and finality with which death could strike right on their own doorstep.

Incensed by the loss of their comrades, Wing Commander Hyde and Squadron Leader Kydd conspired with the Squadron Intelligence Officer, who believed he knew where the intruders were based. It was agreed to arm two aircraft and each put in a spare trip to retaliate. The prospect of using a Manchester as a night intruder may seem incongruous now and the existence of the aircraft was still being kept secret from the Germans at this time. Fortunately good sense prevailed and the beat-up never took place. Flying Officer Matthews and Sergeants Redgrave and Welch were buried at Waddington Parish Church on 18 March 1941.

For some reason all previous Manchester histories have wrongly identified this first operational Manchester loss as L7319. Why this should have occurred is unknown since the ORB, Air Historical Branch aircraft record cards and the records of the War Graves Commission are quite clear that L7313 EM-C was the aircraft concerned. Indeed L7319 EM-X went on to have a long and active career before being struck off charge on 1 January 1943.

On 18 March Flying Officer Geoff Hall went to 46 Maintenance Unit (MU) at Lossiemouth to collect 61 Squadron's first Manchester, L7307, and deliver it to Hemswell. Back at Hemswell the entire squadron crowded round to inspect the aircraft, from which great things were expected. In order to safeguard the few valuable aircraft becoming available, only crews having more than 100 operational hours on Hampdens were allowed to fly Manchesters at night. Within days and to further conserve the operationally fit aircraft, L7276, L7292 and L7294 from the pre-production batch were allocated as crew trainers. L7315, L7387 and L7388 came later in anticipation of operational flying. Geoff Hall was at an advanced stage in his first tour on Hampdens with 106 Squdron when he was tasked with becoming the Manchester conversion pilot on 61 Squadron. He eventually flew more than 200 hours on the aircraft commenting ruefully that he completed his tour, though mainly by reverting to Hampdens. Later in 1943 he flew a second tour, again in 61 Squadron on Lancasters. His Manchester service extended from March 1941 to April 1942 including secondments to 207 Squadron and 25 OTU during which he completed a single Manchester operation. On another occasion a serious coolant leak before take-off led to the sortie being abandoned. A further sortie was aborted when the radiator temperature went off the clock some thirty minutes after take-off. No-one could know then what a difficult time 61 Squadron faced. On 22 March Geoff wrote to his parents:

'I took Wing Commander Valentine up for dual instruction this afternoon (in L7307) and had a hectic time. It was rather a bumpy day, but after I had done a couple of demonstration circuits and landings, the Winco took over. His first landing was quite good, but then the wind changed through ninety degrees, and he approached to land dead across wind. However, he saw it in time, and made another circuit, but came in very high and fast. Having completely boobed, he said: 'You've got her!' and left it for me to sort out. By applying full flap and brakes I just stopped it short of the hedge, feeling very relieved. We were both pouring with sweat after the effort. Still, it was a bad day for visibility, so we'll excuse him'.

Two days later, on 20 March 1941, 207 Squadron suffered its second Manchester loss, again on operations. The squadron produced three aircraft which joined twenty-one Armstrong Whitworth Whitleys for a minor operation to the Lorient submarine base in France. Take-off was arranged for 18.50 hours but delayed by Group until 02.00 hours.

Lorient – 20 March 1941:

Serial	Code	Squadron	Captain
L7310	EM-H	207	Sqn Ldr C. J. F. Kydd
L7302	EM-R	207	Flt Lt D. J. French
L7278	EM-A	207	FS F. B. J. Harwood

A closely guarded secret was that the squadron took two observers from the still neutral USA on the operation. The two US Navy servicemen attended the briefing and Commander McDonnell accompanied Kydd, whilst Lieutenant Commander Wannamaker flew in L7302 with French. The reason for US Navy, rather than Army Air Force personnel being involved may have been to do with the target. Both American servicemen flew in full US Naval uniform and several mused at the consequences if either had been killed over occupied Europe or captured.

The bomb loads were ten 500-lb SAP bombs intended for the concrete U-boat pens. As usual, the take-off of the heavily loaded Manchesters was a very marginal affair. Harwood took the aircraft to the extreme end of the airfield and took off over the hangars and administrative buildings. L7278 had by this time been shorn of its mid-under FN21A turret and so the second wireless operator/air gunner, Sergeant Aitken, flew in the front turret. No mid-upper turret was fitted. Owing to the continued engine problems the observer, Flight Sergeant Roy Holland, had been given extra duty of watching the oil pressure gauges mounted on the starboard side of the fuselage, adjacent to the navigator's position, but directly behind his seat.

The night was dark and moonless such that as the crew settled down to their routines they had only the altimeter to reveal how painfully slowly the Manchester was gaining height. The route ahead involved flying south to the English Channel and on into occupied France. After only thirty minutes flying Holland, on one of his periodic checks, was startled to see a major drop in oil pressure on the port engine accompanied by rough running, which he reported immediately to the captain. Whilst the two pilots debated whether to return, the rough running of the engine disappeared. Half a minute later the rough running recommenced, temperature rose off the dial and the engine caught fire. The aircraft had struggled to a mere 1,200 feet by this time and as soon as the engine failed began to lose height rapidly. Quick action was required to avert a certain catastrophe and Harwood ordered the crew to bale out whilst he held the machine steady.

The rear gunner, Hallam, left his turret and baled out from the rear entry door on the starboard side. Aitken, from the front turret, was the first to leave the escape hatch in the bomb aimer's position, followed in succession by Holland. The second pilot, Sergeant Birch, was helping Harwood maintain the aircraft on an even keel as Holland passed him. By the time Holland had collected his parachute stowed near the hatch, clipped it on and jumped, Birch was right behind and escaped directly after him. Aware of the extremely close proximity of the ground, Holland pulled his ripcord the instant he vacated the hatch. He felt a tremendous jerk as the parachute opened and immediately afterwards hit the ground in the middle of a ploughed field.

In the aircraft the wireless operator, Sergeant Hogg, had remained to try and assist Flight Sergeant Harwood with the forced landing. There was no prospect that the captain could have escaped from such a low level and there had been no time to drop the bomb load safe. The fire had by this time spread and the whole port wing was alight. In the total pitch darkness Harwood had no choice but to land blind with no knowledge of the terrain ahead. Regrettably the landscape was heavily wooded and the port wing hit two large trees causing the aircraft to slew round and crash in the adjacent field. L7278 continued to burn and several bombs exploded. The two crew members remaining in the aircraft were killed. Birch and Aitken were later found dead and it appeared they had been unable to open their parachutes before impact with the ground. Only Holland and Hallam survived.

To his surprise Holland found that he was completely unhurt and stood up to release his parachute. About half a mile away he saw the flames from the crashed Manchester and heard the first of the bombs detonate. In the distance, a farmhouse was just visible in the intense darkness and he made his way there. Transport was obtained and he was taken to nearby Cottesmore, where he spent the night in the sick bay alongside Hallam. They returned to Waddington next day. L7278 had crashed just west of the A1, one and a half miles east of Wymondham in Leicestershire and five miles north-west of Cottesmore. (This crash has previously been incorrectly reported as occurring on return from the operation and at Wymondham in Norfolk.)

The port engine had been flung clear in the crash and initial examination revealed it to have two holes in the crankcase where broken con-rods had hit it. Subsequent investigation showed the cause of the failure of the port engine to be a break up of the 0.5% silver main engine bearing. 207 Squadron had lost its second Manchester.

The remaining two aircraft claimed to have located the target area and both dropped their bomb loads at the estimated time of arrival through cloud from only 10,000 feet in two separate sticks. On the second run over the presumed target area the navigator in French's aircraft, Sergeant Wells, inadvertently knocked off the fusing switches at the last moment before the second stick was released with the result that the remaining three 500-lb SAPs fell away safe.

Since all the aircrew positions were occupied, Wannamaker, the US Navy observer in French's aircraft, had to stand for the whole flight other than on take-off and landing. Near the target he had tapped Wells on the shoulder and asked what the fireworks were. 'Flak' came the reply. Following their safe return the American had remarked: 'Good Show', whether in relief at getting his feet safely back on the ground or in praise of the operation is uncertain. What the observers learned can't have been a great deal, but at least they had survived the experience.

207 Squadron personnel were shocked at another loss so soon after that of Flying Officer Matthews and bitter that it was the result of engine failure, not enemy action. Another blow fell soon after. On 27 March the squadron was called upon to provide four of the thirty-nine aircraft raised by Bomber Command for operations to Dusseldorf. The Manchesters were still plagued with a host of problems of which lack of power and persistent bearing and crankshaft failures in the engines were merely the worst.

Dusseldorf – 27 March 1941:

Serial	Code	Squadron	Captain
L7311	EM-F	207	Sqn Ldr C. J. F. Kydd
L7302	EM-R	207	Fg Off. D. A. A. Romans
L7303	EM-P	207	Flt Lt J. A. Sierbert
L7318	EM-K	207	Fg Off. A. M. Paape

'Mike' Lewis remembers what a heart stopping experience a take-off in a fully loaded Manchester could be with an occasion reminiscent of 27 March and of many others, when he watched other pilots fighting to become airborne. Dave Romans and the other pilots were using the long runway to the north-east. Having reached the extremity of the available runway, Romans began his take-off run. The run seemed interminable with even the tail reluctant to rise. Eventually, and with little runway remaining, the Manchester unstuck, but it continued to sit there in a more or less three-point attitude showing no inclination whatever to climb, even to the height of the airfield boundary hedge. With great presence of mind and skill, when he came within 100 to 200 feet of the hedge, Romans rammed the stick hard forward, causing the aircraft to drop its wheels onto the ground and bounce. At full power Romans hauled back on the stick once more to hold the aircraft at the top of the bounce, cleared the hedge by a whisker and was then able to raise the undercarriage and climb laboriously away!

Lewis observed that even on the longest take-off run (north-east to south-west) he considered things going normally for a Manchester take-off if he passed the Lorenz hut with his port wing tip just above the hut obstruction light. Off the south-western end of this runway some three and a half miles distant lay the small country church of Coleby. The normal climbing performance when fully loaded was such that they expected to pass over this church at little over 100 feet with the wheels and flaps up. Little wonder that the ground staff in their quarters also awaited each departure with bated breath, never quite being certain when they might expect a Manchester to lose power and join them in the building.

On the night of 27 March the four Manchester crews briefed for the Dusseldorf raid were seen off at around 19.30 hours by Group Captain Boothman, the new station Commanding Officer. As the crews climbed into the lorry which took them to their dispersed aircraft his parting words were to Johnnie Siebert's observer, Sergeant George Fomison, who was wryly advised: 'to be sure to pick out a nice, fat maternity hospital in Dusseldorf as his aiming point'. This was a sarcastic jibe at 'Lord Haw Haw', who was claiming in propaganda broadcasts at that time that the RAF only bombed hospitals and non-military targets. In other ways this was ironic since Bomber Command at this time would most dearly have loved the ability to exercise any degree of selectivity over the targets it bombed!

Soon after take-off Flying Officer Paape DFC in L7318 EM-K experienced a major drop in oil pressure in one of the Vultures, which necessitated an early return. The aircraft landed back at Waddington with its bomb load intact before the engine failed and caught fire. The remaining three aircraft located Dusseldorf without undue difficulty. Kydd and Romans dropped four 1,000-lb GP and 420 4-lb incendiaries from 10,000 feet and 7,500 feet respectively, each in two approaches to the target area.

At around 22.30 hours. Siebert bombed the target, making two approaches and dropping a stick of bombs on each run. Very intense flak was encountered in the target area, as was to be expected in 'Happy Valley'. One flak shell burst sufficiently close to the aircraft to jolt the starboard wing up in the air. After the shock, level flight was resumed and course set for the return. The crew speculated as to whether they had merely experienced a near miss or whether any damage had occurred on the starboard side. All instruments were giving expected readings.

As they approached the searchlight belt over the Dutch border the flak died down and fighter attacks were expected, a careful lookout was maintained. Suddenly, the starboard engine began to smoke and lost power. The propeller was promptly feathered and the engine shut down. L7303 EM-P immediately began to lose height and within a few seconds the port engine, which had been advanced to full power in an attempt to maintain height, started to lose thrust too. The, by now, notorious Vulture engines were proving inadequate to the task.

Johnnie Siebert was heard to call that he could not hold the aircraft up any longer and the Manchester fell into a sideslip to port, nose down but still under some semblance of control. In the wireless operator's position Jim Taylor slammed the key of his wireless set over to transmit and, without waiting for the fifteen seconds necessary for the set to warm up, began transmitting their position to base. As he did this he suddenly noticed air-to-air tracer passing the aircraft on the port side.

The crippled Manchester had been intercepted by a Messerschmitt Bf110 night fighter of III/NJGI from Eindhoven in Holland, piloted by Oberfeldwebel Herzog. The time was 23.30 hours. Herzog had already shot down a Whitley of 78 Squadron at 23.05 hours although in his combat reports he was to identify both of the aircraft he attacked as Wellingtons.

Taylor was temporarily cut off from the intercom as he transmitted and missed the captain's first order to abandon. The starboard engine had by this time caught fire and a hydraulic failure was experienced. Neither of these was an unusual experience in Manchesters at this time and there is no absolute certainty that Herzog's fire actually hit the aircraft to cause further damage.

Jim Taylor was then firmly slapped on the shoulder as the second wireless operator/air gunner, Sergeant McDougal, hastened forward from his position in the mid-upper turret to the escape hatch in the nose, struggling into his parachute as he went. Taylor slipped the clip over his Morse key to clamp it on 'transmit', ripped out his intercom lead and oxygen connection and followed McDougal.

By this time the triple-finned aircraft was side-slipping viciously, diving steeply and one engine was racing. The hydraulic failure had severed the power to the rear turret and the main undercarriage had flopped down. As Taylor dived through the hatch he was closely followed by Pete Gurnell, the rear gunner, who, without power to his turret had also been unable to rotate it by hand. McDougal had elected to hasten forward to the lower escape hatch despite his proximity to the rear entry door. On leaving the rear turret, Pete Gurnell looked for the quickest way out. Having reached the crew entry door he wrenched the handle intending to bale out from there. To his dismay the handle came away in his hand and he later decided that in his haste to escape he had probably twisted it the wrong way.

The starboard main wheel narrowly missed Taylor and Gurnell as the aircraft side-slipped over them. They were the last crew members out alive. It is likely that the gallant captain escaped the same way but was hit by the main wheel. His body was located next day in a depression which testified to the force of the impact. His parachute was unopened.

As the surviving five aircrew floated down on their parachutes the abandoned aircraft dived away beneath them, an engine still racing, and crashed on a farmhouse at Bakel north-east of Helmond and near Eindhoven. Oberfeldwebel Herzog had attacked the Manchester from below and as he broke away he observed the survivors' parachutes in the glow of the searchlights. He then dropped or fired a flare, which burst beneath the descending airmen. In its light they could see that they were falling into an area of open water. Taylor and Gurnell were feverishly blowing up their Mae Wests when they splashed down into four inches of water overlying a further two feet of mud. Taylor sprained an ankle in the landing and after disposing of his 'chute waded alone for about an hour before reaching firm ground and eventually a village. Here he was taken in by the residents of the local cafe, given first aid and fed before being sent on his way with the name of a contact in the Dutch underground movement in Eindhoven. He was spotted early next morning, arrested by a patrol and taken to the nearby Eindhoven airfield where he was reunited with the survivors of his crew and those of a Wellington shot down nearby.

By a strange coincidence, in the early hours of the morning one of the two pigeons carried by L7303 arrived back in its loft in the very street in Lincoln where Taylor's girlfriend of the time, later his wife, then lived. How the pigeon escaped will never be known.

At Eindhoven the crew met Herzog who described to them his combat with their 'Wellington'. Many knowing glances were exchanged amongst the crew as they knew that no Manchester had previously fallen in occupied territory. Following this meeting Taylor and Robson had the tragic task of identifying the body of their pilot brought in by the Germans. They were later kept in solitary confinement, deprived of cigarettes and interrogated for almost three days.

By then the Germans must have inspected the wreckage of the aircraft and in the absence of any of the distinctive geodetic structure perhaps began to suspect that they had shot down a new type of aircraft and not a Wellington. The airmen were threatened with a firing squad if they did not talk and quizzed closely about the names of the Dutch citizens who aided them. Throughout the ordeal they managed to stick to their story of wading through the swamp all night and not meeting any of the local population.

207 Squadron had lost its third Manchester and L7303 became the first to fall in enemy territory. It is likely that the aircraft was sufficiently fragmented in the crash that the Germans learned little from it. L7303 was lost to a combination of flak damage, engine failure and fighter attack, although the aircraft was clearly already doomed when Herzog came upon it. A postscript to this sad event is that Johnie Seibert was the first Allied serviceman to be buried in Eindhoven cemetery. Every year on their liberation day the grateful Dutch population still hold their remembrance service and put flowers on this grave.

Following night flying tests, on the afternoon of 30 March 1941 207 Squadron produced four aircraft to attack the *Scharnhorst* and *Gneisenau* at Brest. These had put into the port on 22 March. An engine breakdown on *Scharnhorst* had forced its commander to curtail his intensions. *Gneisenau* went into the one functioning dry dock in the warship harbour, whilst *Scharnhorst* berthed at the Flotilla Quay. Apart from these engine repairs, an exchange of all boiler superheaters was needed, together with a new installation of banks of torpedo tubes. Superheaters supplied very hot, dry steam to drive the propulsion turbines. All aircraft located the target, where two sticks each of six 500-lb SAP bombs were dropped from heights ranging from 15,000 to 9,500 feet. Three aircraft claimed that their bombs hit the dock whilst the crew of EM-J were unable to observe the result of their attack.

Brest – 30 March 1941:

Serial	Code	Squadron	Captain
L7302	EM-R	207	Flt Lt D. J. French
L7319	EM-X	207	Fg Off. D. A. A. Romans
L7309	EM-J	207	Fg Off. A. M. Paape
L7311	EM-F	207	Plt Off. W. G. Gardiner

Paape and crew had a frightening experience on arriving back in the vicinity of Waddington. The controllers refused to light the flarepath due to a reported prowling intruder. The tower advised Paape to divert to Digby, where a landing was successfully accomplished. Afterwards, whilst unwinding in the mess, they received a severe shock when one of the station Bristol Beaufighter pilots came over. Having established that they were a recently arrived Manchester crew he told them he had just landed from an operational patrol immediately behind them and had come within a whisker of shooting them down. Keyed up from the chase for intruders he had completed his circuit to land and lined up on finals directly behind this strange and indistinct shape ahead. As the Manchester had throttled back the Vultures produced showers of sparks, which streamed out behind in a trail and rushed back towards the Beaufighter. For several seconds the pilot had misidentified the sparks as tracer from an intruder. Only in the last fraction of a second before he attacked the aircraft ahead did the pilot correct his identification. It was a stark demonstration to the crew of L7309 that they were never safe until they had landed and vacated their aircraft.

March had been a difficult month for 207 Squadron. Three Manchesters had been lost on operations with many crew members killed or taken prisoner, serviceability continued to be poor with a wide range of serious problems, of which those with the Rolls-Royce Vultures were the worst. Things were soon to take a significantly greater turn for the worse. In March one flight of 61 Squadron had begun to work up on the Manchester to join 207 and 97 Squadrons. Events were to prevent 61 Squadron flying its first operation in the Manchester until late June.

The 19th Manchester production meeting on 31 March itemised delays in Vulture delivery as the major stumbling block, whilst the loss of L7278 on operations was to herald a desperate crisis for Rolls-Royce and the Vulture. Evidently the engine was far from being safe to fly let alone operate over Germany. Paradoxically it is reported that the Vulture II was type-tested at 2,010 hp and +9 lb boost on 100 octane fuel for the first time during March. Moreover, R5768, the first Metrovick Manchester, was finally complete. In the event, again dictated by the impending engine crisis, R5768 did not reach the RAF until a year later on 18 April 1942.

April 1941 began with 207 Squadron continuing its operations at a feverish pace in the hope of bottling up the German Navy in the European ports. On the 4th five Manchesters were prepared for another attack on the battlecruisers at Brest.

Brest – 4 April 1941:

Serial	Code	Squadron	Captain
L7314	EM-T	207	Fg Off. D. E. Pinchbeck
L7317	EM-C	207	Flt Lt P. R. Burton-Gyles
L7313	EM-F	207	Fg Off. A. M. Paape
L7319	EM-X	207	Fg Off. D. A. A. Romans
L7302	EM-R	207	Fg Off. W. G. Gardiner

Serious technical problems continued. L7314 failed to take-off owing to engine trouble, whilst in L7311 Paape had to turn back after eleven minutes with hydraulic trouble, landing back at Waddington with the bomb load intact. Each Manchester carried three 2,000-lb SAP bombs with the intention of making a precision attack on the ships themselves. Brest was located and attacked in good visibility. The three remaining aircraft which reached the target bombed from between 8,000 and 11,000 feet. Burton-Gyles and Gardiner believed their bombs fell in the dock area but the crew of Romans' aircraft were unable to observe the results of their attack.

Returning crews claimed a direct hit on one of the German cruisers. German records which have become available show that one bomb fell in the flooded dry dock in which *Gneisenau* was lying but failed to explode. Bombs also fell on the Continental Hotel in Brest just as the evening meal was being served. Several German naval officers from both *Scharnhorst* and *Gneisenau* were killed.

By this time *Gneisenau* had been in the dock in the warship harbour for eleven days with the gate shut but, of necessity, had remained afloat. The Kriegsmarine yard lacked vital machine tools, and the pumps to empty the dry dock remained inoperative. After the raid a small capacity, portable pump was rigged, but when the dock was finally dry an unexploded armour-piercing bomb was discovered below *Gneisenau's* bow and the dock had to be reflooded, the vessel towed out and secured to a mooring buoy. At this time Brest lacked any torpedo nets to protect a moored vessel and she was soon spotted by British reconnaissance aircraft. On 6 April, Flying Officer Kenneth Campbell of 22 Squadron, operating out of St Eval, carried out an ultra-low level torpedo attack in a Bristol Beaufort which resulted in a direct hit. The damage was sufficiently serious that it took six months to repair the ship. Met with a vast array of anti-aircraft fire from all quarters, the Beaufort was destroyed in the raid. Campbell was awarded a posthumous Victoria Cross. Responding to these early reverses, Admiral Raeder flagged this as 'an unlucky break', stating that: 'in view of the decisive operational and strategic significance of the French Atlantic coast, Brest would remain the fleet's base no matter what'.

Eric Burton, a World War I pilot with a permanent service commission, had been promoted to Group Captain in October 1940 and posted to Command RAF Hemswell in Lincolnshire, then home to two Bomber Command squadrons. On 6 April 1941 his log book records a test flight for an unidentified new Manchester piloted by Wing Commander Valentine, the 61 Squadron Commanding Officer. After a one hour flight, he records: 'A grand aeroplane!' His view was doubtless soon to change. Even his next flight on 24 April, again with Valentine, records: 'returning with hydraulic leak'.

207 Squadron returned to Brest on 6 April for a follow up precision attack on the enemy cruisers. In reality the chances of finding and hitting such small targets with the equipment available and at night without perfect conditions and an element of luck were minuscule, and on this occasion the target was found to be blanketed in 10/10ths cloud. There would have been more chance of finding a needle in a haystack. Bomber Command had still to learn its hardest lessons. It was nonetheless an eventful operation. Following night flying tests, four Manchesters were serviceable. Once more, each of the aircraft carried three 2,000-lb APs.

Brest – 6 April 1941:

Serial	Code	Squadron	Captain
L7322	EM-B	207	Flt Lt P.R. Burton-Gyles
L7311	EM-E	207	Fg Off. W. J. Lewis
L7310	EM-H	207	Fg Off. A. M. Paape
L7314	EM-T	207	Fg Off. D. E. Pinchbeck

'Mike' Lewis' description of his experiences provides the best insight into the difficulties experienced trying to employ such an under-developed aircraft on operations:

'During the early days of April I formed up a new crew, composed of Flying Officer Nunn as my co-pilot, Pilot Officer Sheen as navigator, Sergeants Riddell as wireless operator, Roberts as the second wireless operator/air gunner and McPhail as my rear gunner. However, with that crew I carried out only one operation – that being a bombing raid on 6 April to Brest.

Three quite separate technical problems manifest themselves during this operation to Brest. The first of these was the on-going problem we were having at this time with the hydraulic system. We regularly had hydraulic leaks and hydraulic line failures, which we found out could be mainly attributed to the fact that all the joints, especially the ninety degree joints in the hydraulic lines, were built without any 'olives'. These joints did not always hold under the 400 and 600 lb psi pressure on the hydraulic system and we had hydraulic failures. When we had these failures we realised we had a second problem and that was that we could not get the bomb doors open. To correct this Avro drilled holes in the lower portion of the bomb door jacks and inserted pins in these holes, which were connected by a wire to a loop or bracket on the front of the bomb bay. The theory was that if we experienced a hydraulic failure, by pulling on the wire we would remove the pins, thereby causing the oil in the lower portion of the bomb door jacks to leak out. The weight of the oil on the upper part of the jacks would then crack the bomb doors and once they were open the slipstream would pull them all the way.

The operation to Brest introduced us to a third problem, which had not previously occurred. This was the seal on the control for the radiator flaps. The control was a two position rotary switch by which the pilot could either select the flaps to fully open or to the automatic position, where the position of the flap was controlled by the temperature in the radiator. We found very early in operations that in the trail or automatic position the undercarriage would not retract completely as the undercarriage doors caught on the radiator flap. Hence, all take-offs and landings had to be carried out with the radiator flap in the fully open position.

Back to the matter of the radiator control. As I was taking off that night, I pulled up the undercarriage after lift-off, the undercarriage retracted and it was a characteristic of the hydraulic system that it operated normally at 400-lb psi. The correct mode of operation was that after the undercarriage completed its retraction the pumps continued to build up pressure until they reached 600 lbs, at which time a relief valve cut in and the system went back to idle at 400 lb. This night, when the pressure had reached the point of probably about 500 lb, the seal on the engineer's panel which controlled the radiator flaps burst and the pumps sprayed the whole contents of the hydraulic system into the cockpit, squirting it all over the entire crew and the area forward of the main spar and there was not a thing we could do about it. I might say that that was one take-off that was certainly blind, even my instrument panel was completely covered by a film of oil to the extent that I could not clearly read the instruments.

Despite having lost the use of the complete hydraulic system and with those crew members in the cockpit area soaked in hydraulic oil we continued with the operation on the understanding that on reaching Brest, instead of opening the bomb doors hydraulically we could initiate the famous Avro manual 'pull-the-wire' system and open the bomb doors. So on reaching the target we pulled the pins and the wires and we pulled and we pulled and we shook the airplane and in no way could we get the bomb doors open. We had on board three 2,000-lb AP bombs and there was no way we could get rid of them. So, after about half an hour in the target area, during which we failed to get the bomb doors open, we turned around and headed back for Waddington.

About half way across the English Channel the bomb doors came open. By this stage we did not have enough gasoline left to turn around and return to Brest and drop the bombs and then get back home again, so I decided the best thing to do was just take the aircraft home as it was. This we did with the three 2,000-lb bombs dangling in the open bomb bay. We avoided all cities and towns en route and we were able to return to base and carry out a safe landing at Waddington.

So, the emergency bomb door opening system did not work, but furthermore, we found out a more fundamental weakness in the hydraulic system of the aircraft. The seal that let go on the control panel on the starboard side of the aircraft, that is the control that operated the radiator flaps, was made of pressed paper. It only stood to reason that after a short period of operation that pressed paper seal was going to fail, as it did in my case, and empty the whole contents of the hydraulic system into the aircraft. So, once again, emergency modifications were made and all the paper seals were removed and proper seals replaced them.

It is impossible to recall the proper sequence, dates, etc. of all the modifications etc. that were made to the airplane, but eventually all of the joints in the hydraulic system were replaced with proper joints containing 'olives', good seals were placed in all the hydraulic system, but they never did modify that radiator flap to the point that it could be left in the automatic position at take-off and still permit the undercarriage doors to open and close'.

As with 'Mike' Lewis, when the other three 207 Squadron aircraft reached what they estimated to be the target area they found it completely obscured by cloud. Indeed Brest itself was only vaguely detectable from the flak coming up through the solid overcast. They stooged around until, despairing of finding a hole in the cloud, both 'Pappy' Paape and Derek Pinchbeck dropped an armour piercing bomb in the general area of the flak concentration. Later, for good measure, Paape dropped the remaining two, this time having the satisfaction of seeing the glow of a fire through the cloud as some consolation for his efforts.

Meanwhile, in L7322, Les Syrett had flown to the target area where Peter Burton-Gyles changed places with him. They had been briefed to be as accurate as possible because near misses would do no harm to the two battlecruisers. There was 10/10ths cloud and the target was only detectable from the flak bursts and occasional bomb flashes beneath the cloud layer. Using these as a guide the crew released the first stick of AP bombs, but this was too much 'faith and blind hope' to suit the likes of 'BG'. Roy Holland, the observer that night, explained the obvious, that he could not bomb what he could not see. As with their first operation to Brest, 'BG' withdrew to a safer distance to formulate an alternative plan.

Off to seaward from the flak barrage they descended to discover the cloud base, finding it at 2,000 feet. Below this height the searchlight concentration was intense and dazzling and 'BG' quickly popped back into the enveloping murk.

As they climbed back up to 8,000 feet 'BG' decided on a diving attack. He advised the crew that he would be giving them one chance and one only. The observer, second pilot and captain would have to operate as a well trained team. Holland was instructed to set 2,000 feet and 200 mph on his bomb sight and Syrett was to stand beside the captain calling out the height and speed as they descended. Having reached 8,000 feet 'BG' pointed the aircraft at the colourful commotion and entered a shallow dive. Holland was poised in the bomb aimer's position and 'BG' concentrated on maintaining their heading, hoping he would not have to hunt for the ships once they emerged. Their speed built-up as they descended and it soon exceeded 200 mph, showing no sign of easing the rate of increase. Syrett called: 'Skip, we're diving too fast, you'll never slow down to 200 at this rate'. 'BG' replied: 'It can't be helped', so Syrett kept calling out their height and speed as they descended. As they

L7319 EM-X of 207 Squadron on 25 March 1941, possibly at the Air Fighting Development Unit. The early straight line camouflage demarcation has already been raised. The wavy separation runs through to the rear turret. L7319 was one of the longest serving and most successful Manchesters. It flew thirty-one operations with three Manchester squadrons and continued in use at 1654 Conversion Unit until February 1943. (via R. J. Edmonds)

broke cloud at 2,000 feet they flew straight into the glare of what seemed like fifty searchlights just waiting for them.

'BG' headed for the ships whilst Syrett called to the observer: 'Any moment now we will be at 1,500 feet and doing 300 plus. Can you cope?' Holland responded instantly: 'Do what I can, hold it level Skip, right, more right, too much, left a bit, hold it, steady, bombs gone'. By this time they were below 1,000 feet and had to climb hard to regain the sanctuary of the cloud. Syrett marked the fall of bombs and thought they had achieved at least one direct hit, although other crew members believed they had probably overshot.

Sergeant Syrett then flew back to Waddington, where Peter Burton-Gyles made a safe landing. On disembarking the crew observed to their amazement that their dive onto the ships at Brest had resulted in the fabric covering being stripped completely from their central fin to leave the fragile skeleton exposed. For his skill and determination 'BG' was awarded a bar to his DFC. However, the sortie was futile. In the unlikely event that the ships had been hit, armour piercing bombs needed to fall at least 7,000 feet to reach a speed at which they would penetrate armour. To many of the aircrews it must have seemed that even when they were, by input of the most determined efforts, able to overcome the almost insuperable problems of operating their Manchesters, that Bomber Command was squandering their efforts to very little effect. Nevertheless the endeavours of the aircrew were undiminished. Many young men were beginning to feel that they were not just fighting the Germans, but Avro, Rolls-Royce and the whole dumb Air Force. Such was their spirit at this time that they actually expected to win.

Next day and unbeknown to the crews, Avro's had their regular production meeting. Three new Vulture engines were out of commission at Woodford due to carburettor trouble. Avro listed their requirement as two Vultures per day until the 24th of the month whilst Metrovick were desperate for six engines immediately. The bottleneck was becoming more accentuated. The intensive pace of flying continued and a day later, on 8 April 1941, 207 Squadron made available the largest number of Manchesters yet achieved, joining a force of 229 aircraft for an operation to the shipyards at Kiel. Each Manchester carried a load of four 1,000-lb GP and 240 4-lb incendiaries.

As 207 Squadron were undertaking their largest operation to date, 97 Squadron embarked on its first Manchester operation from Coningsby, also to Kiel. Although aircraft from batches beyond the first twenty airframes were beginning to arrive at Coningsby the earlier aircraft, chiefly with the experienced crews posted in from 207 Squadron were mainly preferred. Each aircraft is recorded as carrying a load of twelve 1,000-lb GP and 840 4-lb incendiaries but it is more likely that the GPs were 500 pounders.

Kiel – 97 Squadron's Debut, 8 April 1941:

Serial	Code	Squadron	Captain
L7290	OF-*	97	Flt Lt G. O. L Bird
L7291	OF*	97	Fg Off. J. S. Sherwood
L7308	OF*	97	FS G. E. A. Pendrill
L7294	OF*	97	Plt Off. H S Blakeman
L7302	EM-R	207	Wg Cdr N. C. Hyde
L7300	EM-S	207	Flt Lt G. R. Taylor
L7309	EM-J	207	Fg Off. W. J. Lewis
L7314	EM-Y	207	Fg Off. D. E. Pinchbeck
L7319	EM-X	207	Fg Off. D. A. A. Romans
L7317	EM-C	207	Plt Off. W. G. Gardiner
L7322	EM-B	207	Plt Off. W. S. Herring
L7310	EM-H	207	Sqn Ldr C. J. F. Kydd

Insisting on keeping abreast with operating problems, Wing Commander 'Hettie' Hyde had again borrowed Dereck French's crew, although they had been 'headless' for a few days after French was posted to 97 Squadron. Hyde had with him Flying Officer H. T. Morgan (second pilot), Sergeants J. Wells (observer), W. Buck (wireless operator), D. Budden (second wireless operator/air gunner), and L. 'Lofty' Hedges (rear gunner). L7302 had no mid-positioned turret so Budden occupied the front one.

The eight 207 Squadron and four 97 Squadron aircraft took off in good weather between 21.00 and 22.00 hours. Hugh Morgan remembers the outward crossing of the North Sea in full moonlight all the way. Crossing the enemy coast just north of Kiel Bay the East Frisian Islands provided a beautiful sight – black on a silver sea. Their route then took them along Kiel Bay to approach the dockyards themselves. The aircraft was possibly flying as high as 17,000 feet. They had no trouble on the outward flight and there seemed to be nothing going on ahead over Kiel as they approached. Probably they were one of the first aircraft to arrive on target. This happy situation changed dramatically as soon as they began their final run into the outskirts of Kiel, when they were suddenly illuminated and coned by what seemed like fifty searchlights. Flak promptly began bursting and Hyde took desperate evasive action, throwing the cumbersome Manchester around as if it were a light aircraft. They were, however, unable to escape the merciless beams.

Fortunately, most of the heavy flak burst behind the aircraft, possibly because of the speed built-up on approach and during the evasive action, although a few bursts looking as big as houses came close enough to buffet the aircraft and they were also troubled by tracer from smaller calibre flak guns, fragments from which penetrated the fuselage. Blinded by searchlights, unable to identify the target or escape the groping fingers, there was no alternative so Hyde called the navigator in the bomb aimer's position to get rid of the bomb load, holding L7302 straight and level for a few seconds until they tumbled away into the night. Hyde then pushed the nose down, speed built-up rapidly and they were soon out of range of the lights and enveloped once more in the protective darkness.

Hyde turned the aircraft onto the planned return flight course. Turning away north from the bay, they headed towards Flensburg with the intention of turning west again and overflying the narrowest part of Schleswig Holstein. Things had calmed down and none of the cockpit instruments showed any sign of damage to the systems of the aircraft. They were halfway across the narrow neck of Schleswig south of Flensburg when Morgan next turned to check the engine instruments mounted on the starboard side behind the observer's chair. The starboard glycol temperature gauge was way above normal, but his attention was drawn from this immediately by the sight of the starboard engine. The exhaust ports and all other thin pieces of the starboard engine nacelle were glowing with a dull red heat. Turning swiftly he tapped Hyde on the shoulder but, within seconds, flames had burst out of the engine.

Hyde immediately feathered the starboard propeller, turned off the fuel supply and pressed the extinguisher button. If the extinguisher worked at all it had no effect and soon flames were streaming out fifty yards behind the wing trailing edge and showing signs of spreading. It was difficult to gauge how long the flames might take to reach the starboard wing tank, but on account of the fire remaining undiminished Hyde soon had no alternative but to order the crew to bale out.

Later they were to be thankful that they did not have to come down in Kiel in the midst of a raid and that the engine should choose to catch fire fifty miles away directly over the narrow part of Schleswig Holstein. There was no sign of enemy activity and they believed the fire to be a delayed effect of flak damage resulting in an oil or glycol leak. For the moment there was feverish activity as the crew hurried to vacate the aircraft. John Wells recalls that for no apparent reason when his turn came to bale out of the front hatch he chose to throw his helmet through ahead of him.

Morgan put on his breast type parachute and was third or fourth in line to reach the hatch. He straddled the opening and was helped out by a shove in the behind from the next in line – no time to think of the 14,000 feet of nothing between him and the ground. Outside it was still bright moonlight with unlimited visibility and, having checked the altimeter, Morgan decided there was height enough in hand to free-fall clear of the aircraft. Having made the decision partly out of curiosity, he found the sensation rather pleasant. Consequently, he held on for quite a while, perhaps until 10,000 feet, before he felt it must be time to check whether the parachute would actually work. It did. Pulling the ripcord produced an explosion of white silk in front of his face followed by a tremendous jerk and there he was – apparently stationary in space. A few searchlights were playing some distance off and occasional flak bursts were in evidence over Flensburg.

Back in the aircraft Hyde was more at ease once the crew were safely out. He waited at the controls, hanging on with bated breath on the off chance that by some miracle the fire would die out of its own accord. He had more experience of flying the Manchester solo than perhaps any other pilot and might just get back on the remaining engine. However, the fire showed no sign of abating and so within a short while he followed the crew down into Schleswig Holstein.

With Hyde out of the aircraft it was now out of control. Morgan could hear the sound of the engines and it was coming closer. He looked around and saw it above him in a spiral dive trailing a banner of flames like a comet. With the engines making a loud rising and falling 'wow-oo-wow-oo-wow-oo' the aircraft swooped close beside him. Another interesting experience! Morgan continued to watch as the Manchester picked up speed and soon hit the ground below him with a tremendous bang. The flaming wreckage spread out in pieces over an acre or two of ground. Clearly the Germans would not make much out of that.

Above, Morgan could see the cluster of parachutes from the rest of the crew, from whom he was separated because of his free fall. Hyde, too, was separated from the rest as a consequence of his later escape from the aircraft. Buck, Budden, Wells and Hedges landed within a few seconds of each other in a village. Morgan touched down gently in a ploughed field some distance away, whilst Hyde landed with a bump in a frosty field even further away from the main group. He made off and remained at liberty for two days and nights during which time he walked into Flensburg under cover of darkness. He had hatched a plan to stow away on a Swedish ship he hoped to find moored in the port and so make good his escape. No such luck. Police spotted him in the town whilst he was trying to locate the port area and he was arrested and taken first to the local Luftwaffe station.

Morgan, too, started to walk north hoping to reach Denmark and establish contact with the resistance network. He navigated by the pole star. Within a few hours of starting the journey he was confronted by a canal: some way off was a bridge. He was dressed only in his thin black flying overalls complete with Cambridge University Air Squadron badge. The bridge beckoned. He approached with what he thought was extreme caution and waited: it seemed unmanned. He was almost across when, with sudden shock, he became aware of an armed sentry motionless in the shadows watching his every move. Bluff seemed to be the only remaining option and he approached what proved to be a middle-aged Private armed with a rifle. 'Guten Abend' called out Morgan with a cheery wave. 'Komm', replied the sentry.

Taken first to some guardroom or police station, he was surprised to be handed over to the Luftwaffe and driven by them to the officers' mess of the night fighter squadron based at Flensburg. He was ushered into the ante-room where a number of young officers crowded around him and plied him with Sekt (German champagne), meanwhile trying to persuade him that one of their night fighters had shot them down, not the flak. They were charming and it was all very 'Beau Geste' and unreal. He slept comfortably in one of their guest rooms, his real life as a Prisoner of War (POW) only beginning the next day when he was reunited with the main group of his fellow crew members. They had had an entirely different experience. John Wells watched the buildings of the village as he drifted down towards them and was unable to avoid landing heavily on the sloping roof of a farm building. The parachute collapsed and before he could obtain a safe handhold he slid down and off the roof, landing softly but with mixed fortune in a pile of manure.

Having had a hardly silent and unannounced arrival he decided to knock at a nearby farmhouse door. The door opened. Raising his eyebrows he asked in his best English: 'Is this Denmark?' The man in the doorway fixed him with a hostile stare: there was no sign of being welcomed across the threshold in the first glance. *'Nein, Deutschland'* came the reply. Still the penny didn't drop. Wells was a young and not much travelled airman with no European experience and had no idea where Deutschland was. There was certainly no sign of a welcome, so he turned away and wandered off in confusion.

A hue and cry had obviously been raised and he was soon rounded up by an armed soldier. The soldier gestured to him and made it clear that he was to pick up his parachute and march ahead down the lane away from the village. Within a short while Wells decided not to carry the parachute and threw it into the ditch alongside. The escort became a little excited and indicated he should retrieve it. Wells stood his ground. The soldier pointed to him: 'Officer?' Wells drew himself up to his full height and replied in a loud voice: 'Non-Commissioned Officer'.

This seemed to settle the dispute and the guard thereupon sent for a young boy, who appeared on a bicycle with a pannier on the front. The boy retrieved the 'chute and, putting it on the pannier, marched along behind them to the local school hall. Here he was reunited with Buck, Budden and Hedges, one of whom handed Wells back his flying helmet, which he had picked up in a nearby lane. Eventually the crew were reunited in the Dulag Luft interrogation camp before Hyde departed for the officers' camp.

Following the early bird Hyde, the rest of the squadron aircraft located Kiel in their turn. They bombed from heights ranging from 12,000 to 14,000 feet, with the exception of Dave Romans who came down to an almost suicidal 3,500 feet before releasing his bombs. All crews found the visibility nearly unlimited, but later crews, including Romans, had difficulty identifying the target and observing the results of their attack as the dock area became obcured by smoke.

L7309 was one of the early Manchesters lacking any mid-positioned armament. Lewis was flying his first operation with the crew and, in the absence of a mid-upper turret, that night Bill Wetherill was flying in the front turret. Amongst the crews and the RAF's intelligence community there was a belief at this time that most of the German flak batteries were directed by sound locators and 'Mike' Lewis had been busy thinking up a new idea to try to fox these predictors. His tactic was to climb as high as possible upwind of the target, whereupon he

Wing Commander Noel 'Hettie' Hyde (second left) photographed in a prisoner of war camp. He failed to return from the Kiel raid of 8 April 1941. (207 Squadron archives)

would pull back the throttles to full idle and set the propellers to fully coarse pitch and then glide more or less silently down across the target to avoid detection by the 'sound locators', releasing the bomb load at 9,000 to 10,000 feet. Lewis had tried out the idea locally in the skies around Waddington and decided to test the new technique that night: it didn't work!

It was a beautiful clear night and having reached a location just south-east of the target they did a wind finding triangle at 15,000 feet. The observer, Frank Belfitt, confirmed a south-east wind, which he had previously calculated from observations made en route to the target. Thus prepared, at about seven to eight miles south-east of Kiel, Lewis went into the planned attack. Everything went according to plan until they got down to about 11,000 feet and were almost directly over the target when they realised that the wind at low altitude was from the north-west and their ground speed was becoming very low. They carried on and had just released the bombs at about 9,000 feet when the searchlights suddenly homed onto them and locked on. Attempting to climb out of the danger proved fruitless and the flak began to rise and burst close around them. The defences of Kiel were well prepared and had other, more efficient, location devices by this time.

The only way out before the flak pinpointed them fatally was to dive down the searchlight beams and with this in mind Lewis called the front gunner, Bill Wetherill, and told him to stand by to shoot out the lights. Thus prepared, Lewis stuffed the nose down and went for the deck. As he did so, Wetherill blazed away at the blinding sources of the beams, being successful in dowsing more than one of their tormentors, before the guns jammed. Flak continued to rise and Wetherill, now unoccupied, was feeling very exposed in the front turret. He obtained permission to vacate the turret and in an instant appeared in the cockpit to sit in the parachute rack behind the pilot's armoured seat, facing aft. As the descent continued the unattended front turret swung slowly on to the beam, setting up an increasing buffeting as it did so. Wetherill had to return to the turret and traverse it to the fore and aft position and then lock it. Never having flown in this position, Wetherill had not appreciated the necessity for such action.

As they finally escaped the beams and pulled out of the dive, Wetherill returned to his station behind the pilot's seat. As he did so he glanced out of the cockpit window just in time to see an 88-mm flak shell pass straight through the starboard wing tip, tearing upwards large sections of the wing skin before carrying on up to explode perhaps 10,000 to 12,000 feet above them.

It was a lucky escape, but the torn and twisted upper wing skin was now standing straight up and forming a 'dive brake', resulting in a serious disturbance of the airflow over the right aileron. The aileron was induced to flap uncontrollably by the turbulent air flow. Lewis and the second pilot, Sergeant Brailsford, were hard pressed to hold the wildly flailing control column, whilst the aircraft was vibrating so badly that Lewis feared for a structural failure of the airframe.

Looking down, Wetherill saw they were now so low that in the bright moonlight he could make out, not only farmhouses and treetops, but signposts. Eventually Lewis and Brailsford managed to lift the shuddering Manchester to 300 feet, at which point they inadvertently overflew a fully alerted German airfield. Light flak from the airfield defence force was soon bursting around them. Lewis could do no more than return rapidly to treetop level and no further damage occurred.

The vibration in the airframe had continued unabated and both pilots were rapidly losing the remaining strength in their arms. Shortly afterwards, however, the force of the airflow on the upstanding section of wing skin bent it back over itself until it came to lie flat over the surface behind. The vibration suddenly died away almost completely and the pilots were then able to recover their strength and take turns flying the aircraft back across the North Sea.

They returned at low level and landed back at Waddington. Needless to say the tactic of a silent diving approach was abandoned. On reflection the crew were able to tease Wetherill over the speed with which he had moved from the turret to get the substantial armour plate of the pilot's seat between himself and the flak. He countered by remarking that he hadn't joined to see flak shells coming through the wings or for a guided tour of the byways of Northern Germany. It was obvious they had had a lucky escape. In comparison, 97 Squadron crews had a gentler introduction to Manchester operations. The good visibility made target identification easy and Sherwood identified Kiel from the fires whilst still 60 miles distant. Blakeman had the misfortune to have his incendiaries hang up.

So the remaining Manchesters came home to Waddington and Coningsby. Next morning the news of the loss of Wing Commander Hyde swept through 207 Squadron. All were devastated at the loss of their popular Commanding Officer, who had done more than anyone to bring the Manchester into operational service. As a temporary measure, Squadron Leader Charles Kydd was given command of the squadron until Bomber Command decided upon a replacement.

Although even the Intelligence Units were not aware of it, this was one of the most successful raids of the early night bombing campaign. The attack had lasted for nearly five hours and towards the end the town's electricity supply broke down completely. Many fires were started and the local brigade had to call in reinforcements from all the surrounding areas. Bomb damage was focused on the Eastern Dock Area with the Deutsche Werkes and Germania Werkes prevented from building U-boats for several days. Naval, industrial and civilian damage was widespread and eighty-eight Germans were killed and 184 injured in the attack.

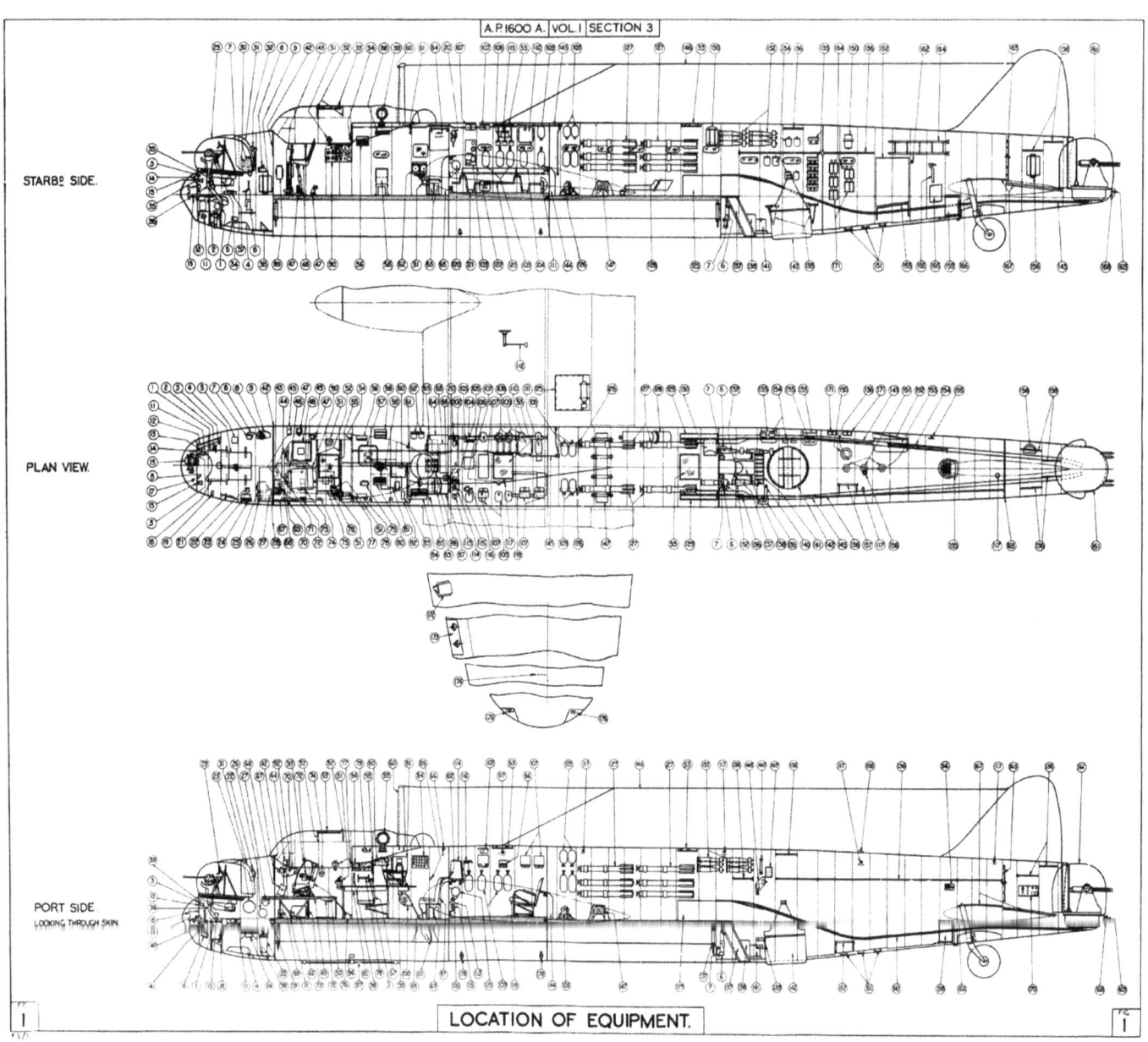

Another illustration from Avro Manchester, Air Publication AP1600A (Fig.1). It provides a good insight into the location of the complex array of fittings inside a Manchester Mk.1. The second prototype or a pre-production aircraft with mid-under turret is illustrated

Key:
1. Bomb aimer's support
2. Tail drift sight
3. Dimmer switch
4. Door and cushions
5. Immersion switch
6. Recuperator
7. Oil filter
8. Aldis signal lamp and stowage
9. Front gunner's parachute stowage
10. Not annotated
11. Stowage for bomb firing switch and bomb sight lead
12. Automatic distributor and bomb selector switch panel
13. Cockpit lamp
14. Headlamp
15. Automatic bomb sight
16. Bomb sight control panel
17. Steering control (auto controls)
18. Target map case
19. Turn regulator (auto controls)
20. Fire extinguisher
21. Bomb aimer's port instrument panel
22. Rudder servo (auto controls)
23. Elevator and rudder gyro (auto controls)
24. Gyro azimuth
25. Camera F24
26. Aileron gyro (auto controls)
27. Elevator servo (auto controls)
28. Camera motor
29. Front gun turret
30. Inspection lamp and lead stowage
31. Draught screen
32. Stowage for dual control rudder pedals
33. Inertia switch (fire extinguisher)
34. Gravity switch (fire extinguisher)
35. Bomb aimer's writing pad and pencil stowage
36. Empty cartridge chute
37. Tail drift sight stowage
38. Bomb aimer's foot ramp
39. Suppressor
40. Course setting bomb sight
41. Azimuth bracket
42. Pilot's instrument panel
43. Junction box (blind approach)
44. Control column and dual control handwheel
45. Flying control locking gear stowage
46. Main receiver (blind approach)
47. Stowage for 0.2 compass brackets
48. 2nd pilot's folding seat
49. Pilot's floor
50. Pilot's seat
51. 0.2 compass positions
52. Sun blinds
53. Emergency exit

54. 2nd pilot's oxygen socket
55. Not annotated
56. Oxygen regulator panel
57. Navigator's swivelling seat
58. Sextant stowage
59. DF loop aerial
60. Aerial mast
61. Navigator's oxygen socket
62. Voltage regulators
63. Accumulator stowage
64. Electrical services panel
65. Step and cover at front spar
66. Upward firing Very pistol mounting
67. Automatic control panel
68. Map case and course and height indicator stowage
69. Rotary transformer (blind approach)
70. Pilot's oxygen socket
71. Aileron servo (auto controls)
72. Control unit (blind approach)
73. Signal receiver (blind approach)
74. Undercarriage warning buzzer
75. Observer's tip up seat
76. Emergency hand pump
77. Observer's oxygen socket
78. Navigator's pencil tray
79. Height and speed computer stowage
80. Douglas protractor and course and speed calculator stowage
81. Wireless apparatus and equipment
82. Navigator and wireless operator's table
83. Wireless operator's instrument panel
84. Wireless receiver coil stowage
85. Wireless operator's oxygen socket
86. Wireless transmitter coil stowage
87. Wireless operator's seat
88. Very pistol cartridge stowage
89. Junction box
90. Observer's instrument panel
91. Rheostat
92. Pilot's bomb firing switch
93. Sutton harness (pilot's)
94. Navigator's instrument panel
95. Navigator's table lamp
96. Terminal block (blind approach)
97. Dipole aerial (blind approach)
98. Navigator's torch
99. Wireless operator's drawer
100. Winch aerial
101. Fairing for winch aerial fairlead
102. Very pistol stowage
103. De-icing services panel
104. Rest bed
105. Hydraulic accumulator
106. Aerial lead-in insulator
107. Flying rations

During the afternoon, amidst the continued training and test flying still in progress, the squadron prepared one aircraft for operations. This involved L7319 EM-X captained by Flight Lieutenant Burton-Gyles. The target was the Vagesack shipyard downstream from Bremen on the River Weser. The operation was unusual in the respect that only one aircraft was made available and joined eight other aircraft from other units in a diversionary raid. The operation was also unusual in that the aircraft carried a chest of packaged tea with instructions that the route should involve overflying Leeuwarden and Groningen in Holland where the tea was to be dropped in small packages. The bomb load is reported in the ORB to have been made up of four 1,000-lb GPs and 420 4-lb incendiaries.

'Eddy' Edmonds, the rear gunner that night, suggests the aircraft carried a 4,000-lb high capacity (HC) bomb and was allocated the Vagesack target to attack as a lone aircraft under cover of a larger attack being carried out up-river. The purpose of the solo effort was suggested to be to permit subsequent damage assessments to be made in the absence of the complication of bomb damage caused by other aircraft. However, the ORB notes a normal bomb load and it is unlikely L7319 was modified to carry a 4,000-lb 'Cookie' at this time. The eighty-strong main force aircraft attacked Berlin.

En route to the target Les Syrett was given the job of dispatching the tea down the flare chute. On paper it should have been a simple and easily accomplished task. In the rear fuselage by the flare chute were stowed two plywood tea chests bound by the usual metal strips. Taking the aircraft's crash axe Syrett prized off the metal bands and opened the chests. In the dark and cramped conditions this took quite a time. Inside he found a large number of tightly packed paper packages each containing about four ounces of tea.

After circling so that Syrett could gain access to the provisions, 'BG' then made his first run over Leeuwarden. On receiving the call to start discharging Syrett removed the cover from the 'chute' and thrust in the first handful of packets. These promptly flew back in the blast of outside air into the face of the dispatcher before bursting on the fuselage roof and spraying loose tea everywhere. They never trained aircrews for this humanitarian operation.

Manchester captain Flying Officer W. J. 'Mike' Lewis, framed in the flak hole made in the starboard wingtip of L7309 EM-J of 207 Squadron during operations to Kiel on 8/9 April 1941. The wingtip was replaced next day at Waddington. (W. Wetherill)

By experiment, Syrett found that if he rammed in a handful of bags and clapped the cover straight back onto the chute he could prevent the blowback. After waiting a few seconds to ensure the bags had been discharged he could re-open the cover and push in more bags. The operation was laborious in the extreme and despite circling for a prolonged period Syrett had only discharged half a chest full by the time 'BG' calculated they must continue their main mission to Vagesack.

Whilst the tea was being dispatched the aircraft must have been a sitting target for any prowling night fighter. Only the weakness of the German night fighter defences, possibly coupled with the fact that other RAF bombers were concentrating their attention elsewhere, led to the aircraft being able to undertake the humanitarian element of the sortie. Later in the war such a task would never have been contemplated. It will never be known if any of the tea packets cleared the aircraft without being ripped to tatters, or if any were recovered by the oppressed Dutch population for whom they were intended.

Syrett opened the second chest to save time later. They encountered no serious opposition over the target, which was bombed from 10,000 feet. The bombs were estimated to have fallen a quarter mile short of the target. The remainder of the tea was dropped on the return leg and the aircraft landed safely back at Waddington 5 hours 35 min after take-off. Les Syrett had alternated between flying the big bomber and throwing the tea bags about. It was sometimes a strange war.

During daylight on 10 April 1941, 61 Squadron experienced at first hand one of the more terminal problems the Manchesters were liable to. Flying Officer Geoff Hall, together with the commanding officer, Wing Commander Valentine and ten crew, took off from Hemswell in L7307 for air firing practice. Immediately after lift-off and whilst still at maximum power, the starboard engine blew up in a spectacular way and caught fire. Hall immediately went for the feathering button and fire extinguisher, but neither had any effect. The failure was sufficiently complete that flying con-rods and pistons had destroyed the feathering and extinguisher lines. Hall managed to achieve a complete circuit and landed back at base, hotly pursued by the fire engine, which managed to contain the fire.

On 10/11 April 1941 97 Squadron dispatched its second Manchester operation when five were allocated to the usual target at Brest. Again, all five aircraft remained serviceable and reached the primary target.

Brest – 10/11 April 1941:

Serial	Code	Squadron	Captain
L7323	OF*	97	Sqn Ldr R. D. Stubbs
L7294	OF*	97	Flt Lt J. S. Sherwood
L7308	OF*	97	Fg Off. C. P. D. Price
L7292	OF*	97	Flt Lt D. J. French
L7298	OF*	97	Fg Off. F. E. Eustace

On this night Bomber Command inflicted further heavy damage on *Gneisenau*. Back in its dry dock, the battleship was hit by four heavy bombs, killing seventy-five of its crew, injuring many others, including a large number of cadets who had only just joined. The forward switching and computing centre for the vessel's flak defences, the forward electric compass installation, the galley, messes and bakery, as well as large areas of the accommodation deck, were seriously damaged. Amongst the dead were all the ship's cooks and, as all the galleys were destroyed, the hundreds of crewmen had to be fed from field kitchens ashore. After its serial misfortunes in short order in early April, perhaps this is when the ship first attracted its title 'Unlucky' *Gneisenau* in the German navy. She had become a 'bomb magnet'. The incident called into question again the wisdom of keeping Brest as its Atlantic capital fleet base. Raeder responded that; 'circumstances at Brest were equivalent to those at the home ports of Wilhelmshaven and Kiel', ruling out any relocation of the ships and merely requesting an upgrade of air defences.

Gneisenau's set backs further emphasised the inadequacies at Brest naval base where, due to qualified labour being in such short supply, the crew had to remove some engine parts and five sections of the starboard propeller shaft so these could be sent to Krupps at Essen. Aboard *Scharnhorst* Kriegsmarine Yard staff had begun removing tubing, fittings and boiler covers to retube the superheaters as this could not be coped with at the French naval arsenal.

The only incident which upset an otherwise uneventful operation for the 97 Squadron aircraft occurred soon after 02.00 hours when Sherwood's aircraft was attacked without warning by an intruder as it approached to land at Coningsby. The first attack was wide of the mark. Sherwood immediately took evasive action and raised the flaps and undercarriage. The control tower diverted them to a nearby beacon which they orbited for some time before returning to land undamaged. Next day many machine gun and cannon shell cases which had fallen from the intruder's ejectors were picked up on the airfield.

By the time 207 Squadron was called upon to operate again on 12 April 1941, it could produce six aircraft for a further attack on the *Scharnhorst* and *Gneisenau* in Brest. The attack force numbered 66 RAF bombers. The aircraft concerned were:

Brest – 12 April 1941:

Serial	Code	Squadron	Captain
L7317	EM-C	207	Flt Lt P. R. Burton-Gyles
L7309	EM-J	207	Fg Off. J. L. Nunn
L7322	EM-B	207	Plt Off. W. S. Herring
L7311	EM-F	207	Flt Lt G. R. Taylor
L7314	EM-T	207	Fg Off. D. F. Pinchbeck
L7319	EM-X	207	Plt Off. W. G. Gardiner

Each aircraft carried a load of ten 500-lb SAP bombs. The operation got off to a bad start for the Manchesters as Flying Officer Pinchbeck returned to Waddington after only thirty minutes due to another hydraulic leak, this time in L7314. Over the continent dense cloud cover was encountered and all aircraft experienced difficulty in finding the target. Locating what was believed to be the general target area 'Dicky' Taylor was making his bomb run when a hydraulic failure occurred in his aircraft, L7311. This resulted in the bombs being jettisoned on the approach, although Taylor later estimated them to have fallen in the target area. Whether the hydraulic failure caused the bombs to be released automatically, or whether the failure was of a type similar to that experienced by 'Mike' Lewis on take-off a few days previously, making jettisoning of the load prudent, is not known.

Gardiner gave up any hope of locating the target after a prolonged search and returned to Waddington with bomb load intact. Herring and Nunn dropped their bombs through cloud from 10,000 and 12,000 feet respectively being unable to observe any result, whilst 'BG' came down to 7,000 feet and claimed to have made two visual attacks on the target. The first of these was estimated to have straddled the *Gneisenau* and the second to have fallen in the target area. All in all, it was not a successful raid and only thirty-seven aircraft claimed to have attacked the target area.

In view of the failure to resolve the extreme difficulties being experienced with the Rolls-Royce Vulture engines, next day (13 April 1941) the Air Ministry announced that all Manchesters were to be grounded forthwith pending investigation of the bearing trouble in the engines. Following earlier failures, Rolls-Royce engineers had descended on Waddington and found many of the Vulture engines had faulty main bearings. By the 13th, a sufficient number had been isolated that work began on all 207, 97 and 61 Squadron aircraft to permit rectification of this major defect.

The engine bearings had been suspect for some considerable time and it seems likely Rolls-Royce were following several separate lines of enquiry at the time, all of which led back ultimately to damage to the bearings themselves. Previous investigations had focused in two particular areas – namely the suitability of the metal alloy from which the bearings were turned and the oil system in the aircraft. Taking these two problems in turn, it was recognised that the original 1% tin lead-bronze bearings tended to break up – a problem exacerbated by the unrelated problems of low oil-pressure. At some stage the standard bearings were replaced by 0.5% silver lead-bronze bearings, but this proved not to be much better and led to several failures. For example, the Rolls-Royce's Defect Investigation Department specifically attributed the L7278's crash on 20/21 March 1941 to a failure of this material.

Arising from this and earlier failures, the metallurgists at Rolls had embarked upon a research programme to discover a suitable alternative. Eventually a LA4-type material containing 4% silver alloyed with the lead-bronze was developed and seemed to offer promising prospects. A batch of bearings sufficient to equip a large number of engines was produced, the first of which, numbers thirty and seventy-eight, were made ready and installed in L7295, the Rolls-Royce development aircraft.

In addition to the use of the new LA4 material, the opportunity was taken to turn the bearings slightly undersize, the gap between bearing and crankshaft being reduced from 0.0047 inches to the range 0.0030 to 0.0035 inches. The purpose of the reduced gap was to promote an increase in oil pressure in the region, lack of which was believed to have seriously increased the bearing problems.

The level of urgency was such that Rolls-Royce immediately commenced installation of the new bearings purely on the result of bench testing. L7295 was about to start its initial flight testing exactly at the time of the April grounding. The aircraft was set to accumulate 120 hours flying in as short a time as possible.

The test flying was curtailed after 112½ hours when the port engine developed a leak, lost its coolant in the air and overheated. Reg Kirlew, the test pilot, landed the aircraft successfully and both engines were removed and returned to Derby for inspection. L7295 later had the engines reinstalled but had only completed a further seven hours before the overheating and engine fire which this time killed Kirlew.

Sir Robert Renwick, Group Captain Roberts and Mr Fielding visited 5 Group on 19 April to arrange the replacement of defective engines in all group Manchesters. Avros and Rolls-Royce delivery schedules, already seriously behind, were put further adrift. A Rolls-Royce Minute of 28 April specified:

Two LA4 engines, numbers 360 and 206, have been delivered to Avro's and these are being fitted to L7393, which is being prepared for dispatch to 207 Squadron. Fourteen LA4 engines have been delivered to 207 Squadron: numbers 44, 240, 250, 356, 358, 362, 364, 366, 368, 370, 372, 374, 382 and 390. Two LA4 engines have been delivered to A&AEE for L7373, numbers 352 and 386.

The engines probably arrived at Waddington on or before 14 April and engine replacement and flight testing began. Arising from the bench running of the LA4-type bearings and the results of the inspection of Vulture numbers 30 and 78, confidence was building at Derby that a successful material had been found. Eventually the Vulture was to be the only engine to utilise the LA4-type bearing materials.

In April 1941, Rolls-Royce's major attention, at least as far as it was perceived and communicated to the RAF, was focused not so much on the bearing material itself but elsewhere in the engine, namely upon its oil system. The oil system was subject to a number of inadequacies, which were difficult to isolate one from another, but it is likely that a major step towards rectifying these was accomplished during the April groundings.

The oil system inadequacies had become familiar to all Manchester crews and included a pronounced tendency for oil pressure to decline with altitude, accompanied by critically high and fluctuating oil temperatures and in extreme cases, failures of oil supply to the big end bearings. In exceptional circumstances the oil pressure would suddenly fall to zero at altitude leading to overheating, engine failure and fire. Such sudden pressure drops were traced to air-locking of the scavenge pumps by an accumulation of bubbles.

Mk1 L7380 EM-W at Waddington with a revised but still interim colour scheme. The demarcation between upper and lower camouflage is raised to the upper fuselage decking but, anticipating a later version, is straight. By September 1941 the join had been over-sprayed wavy. Unit codes are now ahead of the roundel on the port side and very pale grey. Serial is red. Delivered on 13 April 1941 it undertook five sorties before it failed to return with Flight Lieutenant W. J. 'Mike' Lewis on 7/8 September 1941. (207 Squadron archives)

Overcoming these problems involved a prolonged effort and was not made easier by the fact that both Rolls-Royce and Avro systems were involved. Not only did a natural tendency arise for both companies to blame the other for problems, but suspicion at times fell on the RAF ground crews and their maintenance procedures.

It has not been possible to establish the precise sequence and timing of the recognition of the problems and the development of solutions. The reason for the declining and low oil pressure with altitude was traced to air entering the oil system. The source of the air proved difficult to track down and turned out to arise in several unrelated ways. The first source was eventually traced to shrinkage of a fibre washer in the oil pump suction union. Shrinkage allowed the connection to become loose and air to be drawn in. Aerated oil is a very poor lubricant and a contemporary report concluded that this was most probably the cause of the fall in oil pressure in Vulture engines in Manchesters on operations. Avro implemented an immediate and simple solution - the replacement of the fibre washer with a soft aluminium one.

At about the same time it came to light that Avro's had deleted the extension suction pipe in the oil tanks of the first fifty-six aircraft because of a lack of the necessary castings. As a consequence, frothy oil from the top of the oil tanks, instead of de-aired oil from lower levels of the tanks, tended to be drawn off. Rolls-Royce recommended that all such affected oil tanks should be immediately modified and on 24 April the Manchesters were grounded completely to permit the oil tanks to be removed for this to be accomplished.

The aeration problem was only one of the major problems with the oil system of the engine. In the Vulture system, oil was fed to the main bearing journals on the crankshaft and from there it passed through drilled passages to the big-end bearings. Failures of the main bearings had arisen, it was suspected, due to oil starvation. Centrifugal forces generated by the crankshaft led to air collecting in the main bearing journals, displacing the oil. The risk of big-end failure was consequently greatly increased.

At the same time as the LA4 bearing material was being developed, consideration was given to increasing the oil flow and pressure to the big-end bearings. It was thought that this might be achieved by grooving of some kind. Various forms of grooved bearings were experimented with, including partial grooving, shallow continuous grooves, and deep narrow grooves. Experiments showed that the deep narrow continuous grooves supplied the greatest quantity of oil and hence provided the best lubrication. These trials may have been concluded in early 1941. It seems likely that the new LA4 bearings incorporated the deep narrow continuous grooves and were built with their clearance reduced to the range 0.0030 to 0.0035 inches.

Aeration, failure of oil supply to the main bearings, inadequate oil pressure, excessive oil temperature – all these aspects of the oil system had taken many months to recognise and, it was hoped, put right. The twenty-second Manchester production meeting on 26 April noted that Rolls-Royce and Avro were supervising the engine changing programme. Notwithstanding these unscheduled diversions, Avro had delivered five Manchesters, L7390 to L7394, in the last seven days and in addition three Metrovick aircraft were at various stages of assembly at Woodford.

Amongst all this engineering mayhem the squadrons were standing-by, waiting to resume operations to Germany. Nothing provides so stark a reminder of the desperation of Britain's plight in early 1941 than this placing of an aircraft at so early a stage in its development in the very front line of Bomber Command. Such knowledge as can be assembled today makes the endeavours of the aircrews that much more worthy of respect.

With this wide range of modifications confidence was high that the major problems were finally resolved. Sadly, even at this late stage, it proved not to be the case. The oil system itself, despite its extensive reworking, still continued to be subject to a range of problems. In July Avro were to attempt a radical solution to this, which had disastrous side effects on the already marginal climbing and flying characteristics of the aircraft. Coolant problems and con-rod bolt problems were still to be recognised and overcome, whilst serious propeller malfunctions remained to be isolated and remedied. All this mercifully was unknown to 5 Group and the aircrews as they began testing their modified Manchesters in April 1941.

Whilst the Manchester was grounded for engine changes and incorporation of modifications, advantage was taken to carry forward other improvements and the suspect paper seals in the hydraulic system were replaced. The Ermeto coupling had also proved unsatisfactory. It may be that the Ermeto couplings were replaced at this time by the older, proven, AGS system. It was now agreed that in the interests of quick production wire locking of all the AGS joints would be dispensed with. Retrospective action was not taken on the earlier aircraft, which were either not used on operations or perhaps returned to Avro or the Maintenance Units for replacement of the hydraulic piping.

The precise timescale over which these modifications to the hydraulic system were carried out is not clear, but by the late summer the greasy-floored Manchester was becoming a thing of the past. One memory of such aircraft relates to Peter Burton-Gyles and his pet terrier, which invariably accompanied him on training flights. Jim Duncan, his wireless operator, recalled that one day the dog took up its usual station on its haunches alongside 'BG's seat in a particularly oily Manchester. As they started up and taxied out the dog stayed put but as the aircraft accelerated for take-off the friction between dog fur and oily floor was suddenly overcome with the result that the startled dog, still in upright position, slid aft, latterly accompanied by much scrabbling of feet, until it came to an abrupt halt with its rump against the main spar!

In respect of the "serious propeller malfunctions" referred to above, Rolls-Royce sought to harness the maximum power offered by the big Vulture engine by employing a particularly large diameter propeller, of either de Havilland or Rotol design. This had a diameter of 16 feet (Lancaster 13 feet). Bearman (2021) has shown for Manchesters that the tip blade speeds of these at Max Revs was such that they exceeded the speed of sound, thus inducing a shock wave, causing a "mini sonic boom" and hence prop vibration, which absorbed large amounts of energy. This caused R-R and Bomber Command pilots to reduce maximum RPM on Vultures from 3,200 to 2,850-a counter-intuitive step, which actually improved performance-hence this was a limiting factor.

A second limiting constant newly discovered in propeller development was induced by the compressibility of air, being named "Mach tuck". Avro and Rolls later recognised and minimised the effect of this factor once the effective thickness of prop blades was significantly reduced-as put into practice in the Nash Kelvinator paddle-blade propellers used later in Lancasters. This emerged from knowledge of laminar-flow theory. It was never applied to Manchester propellers. So neither the effects of propeller shock waves, nor compressibility had been drawn into 1940-41 propeller design.Bearman(2021). Interestingly,perhaps, the Germans experienced the same serious problems with their big Daimler Benz DB606 engine and 16 foot diameter propeller on the Heinkel He 177 bomber,as later,would the Americans.

Whilst these more fundamental problems of the engines and hydraulic system were keeping the aircraft away from operational commitments, other developments and testing continued apace. As early as 10 April 1941 the Air Officer Commanding 5 Group and Wing Commander Butler had visited Waddington to inspect the 4,000-lb bomb installation in one of the first 207 Squadron aircraft to be equipped to carry this new bomb – the thin cased, high capacity 'Cookie'. The aircraft, L7379, was destined to have a very short lifespan. On 13 April 1941 the ORB notes that aircraft (numbers and identities undefined - author) with special bomb racks for 4,000-lb bombs were collected from Woodford. It is almost certain that L7377, L7378 and L7380 were these aircraft, followed two days later by L7381.

When these aircraft reached the squadron a bomb stowage problem was immediately manifest. With the bomb installed the doors would not quite close. The reason for this was that the doors were absolutely flat along the bottom of the aircraft on their inner surfaces and the circumference of the bomb was just enough to bear on this flat bottomed section, preventing them closing snuggly into the belly of the aircraft. To overcome this, a section of each door was cut out. This cut out section was further modified by having a wedge-shaped piece on the centre line on the inside all along the door cut away and a flat piece of Alclad skin was then inserted into each door. Finally this cut-out section was hinged back in place in the aperture in the bomb door. An air deflector or streamlined combing was added at the front and rear of the bomb doors which were now held shut by lengths of heavy duty elastic cord. To load the 'Cookie' the doors had to be forced open against the tension of the elastic and clamped. Then the bomb was winched into position on the bomb hook, following which the doors were allowed to close around it, being finally held with a pin.

When the bomb was to be dropped the doors were no longer opened from within the aircraft. Instead the bomb was simply released in the normal way by the bomb aimer, whereupon it fell onto the hinged door inserts, which sprung open with the weight of the bomb and allowed it to fall free from the aircraft. Immediately the tension in the rubber cords would pull the inserted bomb door panels closed. On test and later in operational use it was found that the slipstream would sometimes prevent these inserts in the main doors from closing simultaneously. This whole procedure produced a weird series of noises and sensations in the aircraft. Firstly, there was the jolt and bang of the 'Cookie' falling on the bomb door inserts, followed by a shudder in the airframe as the inserts were forced open and finally by two bumps as each door was pulled closed individually by the heavy rubber cords. 207 Squadron operated with this 'Heath Robinson' modification for some time before Avro came up with the curved bomb doors which closed around the bomb and eventually became standard on the Manchester and later the Lancaster.

Whilst work on these problems was in progress, on 15 April 1941 Group Captain Boothman AFC, the Station Commanding Officer at Waddington, carried out a test on a Manchester's mid-upper turret. Crews had complained that rotation of the mid-upper turrets installed on their latest batch of aircraft caused a severe tail flutter to be set up in the canvas-covered central fin. The vibration was sufficiently severe that for a time 97 Squadron operated its Manchesters at Coningsby with the mid-upper turret unarmed. The early installations of the FN7A allowed the unit to protect high out of the fuselage and it may have been these aircraft too which lacked the fairing around the turret. It is possible that some mid-upper turret installations were actually undertaken retrospectively on squadron aircraft at Waddington and perhaps it was these early installations which gave the greatest trouble.

The tests, undertaken by John Boothman as second pilot, involved L7321, with Flight Lieutenant (as he had become) Burton-Gyles as pilot and 'Eddy' Edmonds in the mid-upper turret. The object of the test was to investigate the effects of the turret on the fin at various speeds. 'BG' climbed to altitude and put the aircraft into a dive, maintaining a steady speed. Edmonds then had to rotate the mid-upper onto the beam and check what was happening to the centre fin. The procedure was repeated at progressive increments of speed until, at around 320 knots and with the turret abeam, the fin started to deform.

The unit thus obtained some information about the safe operating envelope of the mid-upper turret. Later aircraft had the FN7A set lower in the fuselage and surrounded by a streamlined fairing, which decreased, but never eliminated, the vibration set up in the central fin by rotation. Nevertheless, Manchesters continued to shed the canvas coverings to their central fins and return, gingerly at first, to Waddington and Coningsby with just the flimsy metal framework left in place. On more than one occasion the disturbance to the airflow actually caused an aircraft to shed the entire centre fin in flight. Despite initial great alarm it was found that the aircraft remained controllable. Flight Lieutenant French of 97 Squadron had found that the mid-upper turrets also decreased the sensitivity of the rudder control such that it became impossible to make a turn with the certain knowledge that the aircraft would end up on the desired bearing.

During operations the pilot would always know in advance when his mid-upper gunner was ready to test his weapons since the turret would first be traversed until the guns were directed on the beam. As the FN7A turret rotated, it disturbed the airflow across the central fin to such a marked degree that a perceptible tremor ran through the airframe and was even detectable in a small rocking pressure of the control column in the pilot's hands.

The unsatisfactory situation with the mid-upper turrets continued to alarm 5 Group. Trials were hurriedly set up with the test aircraft, L7320, at Boscombe Down. Tests showed that when the FN7A 'Botha' turret was rotated, buffeting was so serious that the centre fin of the aircraft was very largely destroyed. A number of problems had been chasing each other around, so to speak. When inadequate lateral stability dictated the fitting of the third fin it did so at the expense of the only other emergency exit in the rear fuselage upper decking. Only the removal of the FN21A mid-under turret had made an aperture available for an escape hatch. Absence of mid-positioned armament then led to installation of the FN7A mid-upper turret, whose rotation in turn compromised the centre fin itself. Furthermore the centre fin limited the field of fire of the FN7A. Given more time Avros might have progressed more rapidly to the twin 'Lancaster' tail fin configuration. Time was one thing Avros did not have.

Bomber Command had completely lost patience and on 30 April 1941 issued an edict stating that: 'they either wanted mid-uppers which worked or no turret at all'. Whilst Avro cast around for a solution, an instruction, Avro Mod 243, called for the removal of all mid-upper FN7A turrets from Manchesters. The weary Avro work parties and squadron ground crew buckled down to yet another desperately urgent task. Avros were considering two options – either a strengthening of the fin or a change of turret, but in the intervening period out they had to come. A number of pilots viewed this with some satisfaction: anything to decrease the weight and ease the strain on the underpowered aircraft was a bonus.

As with the experienced Lewis and others, 'Junior' Gardiner had rapidly become aware of the marginal nature of the performance of the Manchester, being similarly conscious of the critical situation in the event of an engine being put out of service. When further changes were imposed, the additional weight of the mid-upper turret and its gunner, the wider span tail plus the increased drag arising from flame damping exhaust shrouds he, too, felt the need to act. For preference he adopted L7300 EM-S which never had a mid-upper turret fitted and did everything he could to keep it for himself.

The various serviceability problems resulted in spells of frantic activity interspersed with long periods of boredom. During one of the latter, when local flying was permitted, Gardiner and crew took off on a low level practice sortie to the nearby Wainfleet Range carrying sand-filled 500-lb bombs. By some mischance, when on one run the weapon released behaved erratically, bouncing before sliding into a nearby farmyard where it buried itself under the manure heap, they chose not to report it. They considered some things were best left unsaid.

On 15 April 1941 207 Squadron also passed on three of its older aircraft to 61 Squadron, in line to be the third Manchester unit. L7279, L7281 and L7304 were collected and flown to Hemswell.

During spring 1941 the pressure for improvements in Manchester armament at squadron and group level intensified. It is clear that Air Vice-Marshal Jack Slessor at 5 Group Headquarters in Grantham was one of the major driving forces and that he had the active support of Air Vice-Marshal Saundby at Bomber Command Headquarters in High Wycombe. 5 Group had been let down by the Directorate of Armament Development (DArmD) in the defensive armament for the Hampden. In desperation they had turned to two local British firms in their area – British Manufacturing and Research Company (MARC) of Grantham and Messrs Rose Brothers of Gainsborough. Mr Kendall, the managing director of British MARC, and Mr Rose had got together and quickly built the electrically operated, but hand held, RB3 installation for two Vickers Gas Operated 0.303in machine guns. These had greatly improved rear defence in the Hampden. Now faced with the limitations of the defunct FN21A and the obsolete FN7A, 5 Group turned once more to these unofficial saviours.

On 26 and 29 April Wing Commander Butler of 5 Group guided Mr Rose and a British MARC representative around a 207 Squadron Manchester at Waddington. They recommended a radical solution in which the FN7A would be scrapped and replaced by twin handheld, but electrically traversed, 0.5-inches Hispano cannon with shortened barrels and a belt-feed system. 5 Group sent these recommendations to a receptive Saundby at High Wycombe with a request to proceed. DArmD, who had been informed as a courtesy, replied sourly and obstructively that a shortened 0.5-inch cannon did not exist, nor could it be belt fed and, in any case, their own extensive experimentation proved that only hydraulic power was adequate to such a task. Slessor responded by pointing out that the short barrelled 0.5-inches Hispano cannon was already operational in Coastal Command Anson and Bristol Beaufort aircraft for anti-submarine and E-boat operations! A belt-feed system for cannon had recently been tested successfully on the Hurricane II wing at Air Fighting Development Unit Martlesham Heath and the RB3 mounting was giving excellent service! In a phrase that demonstrates 5 Group's ambitions for the strategic bomber, Slessor stressed: 'We must get these big heavies onto day work as soon as possible and we want the heavier metal for that'.

In the short term 0.5-inch guns in power turrets were not likely to be available. As an interim measure a power assisted and lighter twin 0.5-inches installation on a more robust scarf ring was proposed. The installation was to be enclosed in a perspex and metal cupola which would project no more than eighteen inches into the slipstream and rotate through the rearward arc as the guns themselves traversed. Belt feeding was to be incorporated in order to maintain an adequate continuous defence without the awkward drum feeds with their intrinsic defenceless periods whilst reloading was in progress. When the time came to progress this development, 5 Group requested the damaged fuselage section from Squadron Leader Mackintosh's Perranporth crash on the 18 May (see later). The undamaged upper section would be ideal for Rose and Kendall to play with.

Slessor acknowledged that this course of action would be very unorthodox but pointed out that Rose and Kendall had agreed to provide all materials and labour free of charge. He quoted the precedent of the RB3 as an example of previous achievements. Quite what became of these proposals is unclear because the 0.5-inches Hispano installation never materialised in the Manchester. The squadron engineering officer, Flight Lieutenant Eric McCabe, and fitter gun armourer, Sergeant Hodgkinson, both recall assisting in some trials with 0.5-inches Hispano cannon but in respect of the rear turret.

In 97 Squadron, concern had been focused on the continuing inability to man and operate the FN5A nose turret when the bomb aimer was kneeling at this sight, a factor which was of much greater significance with 5 Group anxious to use Manchesters for daylight operations. By late May, as a temporary field modification, 97 Squadron had lowered the bomb sight mountings of all squadron Manchesters by 2½ inches and at the same time dispensed with the cumbersome shell case collector chute and boxes. Thus modified, the FN5A could operate whilst the Manchester was on the bomb run. The hot empty shell cases fell on the bomb aimer's back and littered the bomb compartment, but 97 Squadron considered this a minor inconvenience compared to the benefit gained.

During this period the roles of 207 and 97 Squadrons as test and development, or guinea pig, units were well to the fore. Manchesters were declared airworthy again and on 1 May 1941 three of 207 Squadron's aircraft were prepared for operations to Hamburg, which were later cancelled due to the weather. A period of intensive, but still extremely frustrating, activity was about to commence.

Almost as if it were a token to mark this return to operations, on 3 May Bomber Command notified Avro of the third change in camouflage markings consistent with the field modifications to the colour scheme which had been introduced on the squadrons in late February. The divide between the upper and lower colours was to be moved to the top of the fuselage decking and the straight separation changed to a wavy one. Any unmodified service aircraft were to be repainted on the squadrons as opportunity permitted.

207 Squadron armourers, Spooner, left, and Smith pose in front of a 207 Squadron Manchester. Behind are a 44 Squadron Handley Page Hampden and a Fairey Swordfish. The latter was used by the Navy to bring the naval armourer to fuse sea mines. Only the Hampdens carried mines at this time. Photograph probably taken between February and 15 April 1941. (E. B. Spooner)

Chapter Four: Catastrophe

For the first time, the Manchester was destined to carry the new 4,000-lb high capacity (HC) bombs operationally. On 2 May 1941 three aircraft from 207 Squadron were serviceable for a raid on Hamburg, in two of which the bomb bays were to carry 'Cookies'. These joined the force of ninety-five aircraft dispatched.

Hamburg with the first 'Cookies' – 2 May 1941:

Serial	Code	Squadron	Captain
L7377	EM-G	207	Sqn Ldr C. J. F. Kydd
L7317	EM-C	207	Fg Off. D. A. A. Romans
L7379	EM-T	207	Fg Off. D. E. Pinchbeck

The three aircraft took off at intervals during the course of the evening. The crew of L7379 were a little excited knowing that the mission was on, but that on return they were all going on leave. The observer, Sergeant S. E. Panton, was flying with the crew for the first time having returned from leave to find that his own crew, that of Pilot Officer Gardiner, were on a course at Cottesmore. At briefing they were issued with the standard warning – all gun turrets were to be manned on take-off, over target and on landing. Also a close watch had to be maintained on engine oil pressure. If the pressure fell into the red area they were to return.

At this time one of Bomber Command's philosophies was still to extend the duration of the attack in an attempt to keep the German workforce from their beds. Accordingly, L7379 was the second aircraft to take off, departing with its 4,000-lb 'Cookie' at around 22.00 hours Panton gave Pinchbeck a course for the 'gate' on the English coast near Skegness. There was to be the usual strict wireless silence until the aircraft crossed the enemy coast on the way back home, with the exception of all Manchesters. These aircraft were required to broadcast their call sign every hour. This was part of the investigation set up to establish whether Manchesters were being lost due to engine failure or enemy action. The other standing instruction to the wireless operators at this time was that in the event of their aircraft having to go down over enemy territory they were to broadcast their position and one of three coded words for 'flak', 'fighters', or 'engines' to indicate the cause of their demise. One source claims that there is only one example of such a message ever being received and that said 'engines'. This claim has not been substantiated. It was clear that, along with the crews, the Command was acutely sensitive to the reliability of the Vulture engines.

At the briefing, Sergeant W. M. McGregor, the wireless operator in L7379, had been given a list of German beacon stations operating for the use of their own aircraft and submarines. To assist Panton, McGregor tuned in to them in turn and kept taking direction finding (D/F) bearings to provide the observer with running fixes and so pinpoint their position all the way across the North Sea. The flow of slips of paper with station name and position continued. Panton also monitored the oil pressure regularly and although it fluctuated during the crossing it did not fall to danger point.

They were behind time but decided to press on. Suddenly McGregor was surprised to see and feel the effects of flak bursting around them at a time when he thought they should be still well out to sea. He stood up and glanced at Panton's chart and saw they were over the island of Heligoland. From this inadvertent pinpoint they set course for the mouth of the River Elbe. This too was a surprise as McGregor had expected them to make a landfall to the north near Flensburg and then turn south to come down on Hamburg through the 'back door'. The banks of the Elbe were heavily industrialised and thus protected by a corridor of flak guns – this was the 'front door'. On their approach to the target along the Elbe they were consequently detected by the defences and received their close attention, taking quite a number of near misses from flak in the process. Fortunately they remained undetected by the searchlights. They found the weather at the target to be fair with ground haze and extreme darkness making it difficult to identify the aiming point.

Panton went forward to the bomb aiming position. The flak was increasing in intensity as they reached the outskirts of Hamburg. Suddenly all the searchlights lit up and L7379 was coned and held in the beams. The flak continued to rise and became increasingly accurate. Panton felt a shudder of at least one hit from the fire. As they steadied on the bombing run close to 01.00 hours and at 12,000 feet another flak hit was received and the aircraft immediately lifted as it rid itself of the 4,000-lb 'Cookie', toggled away by Panton. Almost as soon as this happened and before he could leave the bomb aiming position a sliver of flak came through the perspex dome of the bomb aiming position, hit the bombing panel and splintered it.

As Panton began to return to his navigating position he was shocked to see that the port engine was on fire, with flames streaming back from the cowling. Pinchbeck operated the Graviner extinguisher and feathered the propeller, whereupon the fire in the port engine seemed to abate to some extent.

Pinchbeck turned the aircraft away to the north in an attempt to clear the target area and pick up a course for home. Already they were losing height. The remaining Vulture was not proving adequate to the task. The pilot called Panton to say he could not get the aircraft round onto its new westerly course for home, to which Panton replied that in that case they would end up in the Shetlands. At this moment the starboard engine too burst into flames, with fire already creeping along the leading edge of the wing towards the fuselage. Pinchbeck gave the inevitable order to bale out; fortunately no one had been wounded.

Unaware of what was happening up front, when the flak slowly died down McGregor had started to set up his transmitter and receiver and to reel out the trailing aerial. He would then be ready to transmit a message to 5 Group saying L7379 had bombed the primary target and was crossing the enemy coast on the way home. Sergeant A. S. Duncan, the second wireless operator/air gunner, was standing in the walkway behind the navigator's seat with his head in the perspex bubble on the starboard side looking down on Hamburg. At this moment McGregor was on the wireless, not the intercom, and Duncan, who had been moving around the aircraft, was not plugged into the intercom either. Suddenly Duncan turned round and started kicking McGregor's boot to attract attention. He was shouting. McGregor tried to lip read as he spoke but the only word he could make out was 'fire'.

Thinking Duncan was getting excited about the fires of Hamburg down below them, and being an 'old stager' himself, McGregor thought he would have seen it all before and so didn't even bother looking out. The flak had more or less stopped and he continued reeling out what remained of the trailing aerial in preparation for transmitting his message. Turning next to his radio equipment he finished setting it up. Having completed this task, he looked round the partition in his compartment to get a time from Panton for crossing the enemy coast. He was dumbfounded to see Pinchbeck, alone in the aircraft, struggling in his seat.

Following the order to bale out, which McGregor had missed, Panton proceeded immediately to the forward escape hatch. Releasing the hatch, he held it for a moment before pitching it out and watching it tumble end over end in the slipstream as it dropped away. He tightened his parachute harness and waited for the rest of the crew. When he saw Lee, the second pilot, leave his seat he sat on the edge of the hatch and dropped free, the first crew member to leave. He was quickly followed by Lee and then Duncan. When McGregor saw Pinchbeck was alone the realisation of their predicament and the fact that he should clearly be long gone was naturally instantaneous. Discarding his helmet he put on his parachute and moved forward to the now vacant second pilot's position. Entering the cockpit area he noticed for the first time the starboard wing well ablaze - his first intimation of the cause of the rest of the crews' hasty exit.

Reaching the second pilot's position, McGregor saw that the skipper had not fastened his parachute harness and his right hand lap strap had fallen between the flap and undercarriage levers. Instead of turning the harness and lifting it out of the narrow gap the preoccupied and desperate pilot was tugging frantically at the strap, which was jamming across the gap.

McGregor reached over and took the stick in his hands, holding the descending Manchester on an even keel and allowing the pilot to use both hands to release the buckle of his harness and get it securely fastened. What McGregor did not notice at the time was that Pinchbeck was flying in an observer-type parachute harness due to the fact that his own 'chute was being repacked. Instead of sitting on his pilot-type 'chute, Pinchbeck had placed a cushion in the bucket seat of the aircraft. Obviously Pinchbeck did not realise what lay ahead for him, for as soon as his harness was fastened up tight he gave McGregor the thumbs up. With the starboard wing burning furiously and the port engine still alight the risk of an explosion appeared imminent and the wireless operator wanted no further encouragement! Turning round, he dived from the step to the second pilot's position, head first, straight through the open forward escape hatch after his three colleagues.

As he dived through the hatch one visual image burned itself into his brain. Turning his head, he had seen an observer-type parachute in the camera hatch. He pulled his rip-cord as soon as he vacated the aircraft and the canopy jerked open, leaving him swinging suspended beneath. As the aircraft passed above him he had noted that the undercarriage was in the down position and that the aircraft was carrying full flap. These factors, added to the loss of the engines, no doubt contributed to the extremely rapid sink rate.

On the way down McGregor dwelt on which crew member he presumed must have jumped from the forward hatch without a parachute. He could not imagine Lee, Panton or Duncan having done so and to salve his conscience he decided it must probably have been left in the aircraft from a previous flight. He judged this would be unusual, but not impossible.

Back in the aircraft, Pinchbeck and the rear gunner, Sergeant C. N. Barron, had still not escaped, although neither knew that the other was still on board. When Barron got the order to bale out he found the hydraulic supply to the rear turret had failed and he was unable to traverse the turret. Reaching inside the aircraft he took his parachute and spent some time clipping it to his chest. Outside he could see the flames streaming back from the blazing wing and expected the aircraft to explode at any moment.

Barron then tried to traverse the turret manually with the emergency system. The rate of turn seemed painfully slow and before he had achieved the ninety degree traverse on to the beam to allow him to tumble out backwards he changed his mind. In his desperation it seemed the rear door offered a quicker exit route. Traversing the turret back to the fore and aft position he accordingly scrambled out and rushed forward to the rear entry door on the starboard side. He pulled the handle and threw all his weight onto the rear door but it appeared to be completely jammed.

With time passing and his anxiety rising with every passing second, he abandoned this course of action and returned once more to the turret. Once inside he began the painfully slow business of traversing it onto the beam. Despite what seemed to be his most feverish activity, no doubt by this time with every second seeming like a year, he was unable to swing the turret at a speed which appeared to provide him any early prospect of escape. Once more he changed his mind, surely by chopping off the handle of the rear door with the fire axe he could force it open and effect a rapid exit. He could not recollect any sign that the door was distorted or damaged.

Squadron Leader Charles Kydd, 'A' Flight Commander and Commanding Officer of 207 Squadron, after Wing Commander Hyde failed to return on 8/9 April 1941. Kydd died following the crash of L7310 on 21 June 1941. (207 Squadron archives)

Traversing the turret back to the fore and aft position again he hurled himself back along the fuselage a second time. He grabbed the fire axe but as he did so he was immediately thrown to the floor and held there by tremendous G forces. The immediate thought which came to him was that he was too late and that with the pilot finally vacating the aircraft it had commenced its final uncontrollable plunge to destruction. He could do nothing more than wait for the final impact.

Meanwhile, up in the cockpit following McGregor's escape, Pinchbeck's next move was to reach behind himself to the parachute storage position behind his seat, where he had placed his parachute. This was difficult to achieve since he had to release the stick to turn around and reach into the stowage rack. The aircraft was either not fitted with an autopilot or alternatively it was not working. Eventually reaching the rack, Pinchbeck discovered, to his abject horror, that it was empty. Subsequently it transpired that Duncan, who had been moving around the aircraft taking his parachute with him, had gone into the nose compartment and put his parachute in the camera hatch whilst he busied himself with another task. On returning to the main deck he left his 'chute behind and, on receiving the order to bale out, did not appreciate that the pilot was using the unusual observer-type parachute and harness. Accordingly, he had mistaken the one in the stowage rack behind the pilot's seat for his own and in his haste grabbed it, buckled it on and went.

Derek Pinchbeck now realised where Duncan's 'chute was, presumably being able to see it lying there from his position in the cockpit. His only chance seemed to be to release the controls and rush forward and grab it before the aircraft went out of control. Unbeknown to Pinchbeck, however, L7379 had on full flap and the undercarriage was down. Consequently as soon as he released the controls and moved towards the forward compartment the Manchester put its nose down and went into an almost vertical dive.

More than one unsuccessful attempt was made to leave the controls with, unknown to him, rear gunner Barron bouncing around in the tail section. Finally, Pinchbeck made a last desperate attempt and succeeded in getting hold of the 'chute, however the aircraft had by this time entered a vertical power dive, pinning them both down. It was clear to Pinchbeck that he was not going to be able to clip on the parachute and climb down against the G forces to the forward hatch and bale out.

The aircraft had by this time lost a great deal of height and little time appeared to be left if he was to save himself. Pinchbeck dropped the parachute and forced himself, with an almost superhuman effort, back to his seat. Desperate measures were called for and so, placing his feet on the instrument panel, he linked his forearms around the stick and heaved. Slowly his straining began to have some effect and he finally managed to recover the aircraft onto an even keel at about 2,000 feet. He knew then that alone he would have no other opinion but to carry out a forced landing in the dark in open country.

Back in the rear fuselage, Barron could hardly believe his deliverance. Acting automatically he jumped up, chopped the lock from the rear door with a few axe blows and jumped out. He had no idea of the altitude and it's likely the Manchester was down to 1,000 feet or less when he baled out. Pulling the ripcord immediately, the parachute blossomed above him and he was suffused in a mixture of immense relief and embarrassment. In his panic to escape he had been trying to force the door outwards whilst actually it was designed, as he well knew, to open inwards. All in all it had been a lucky escape for him.

Up front, Pinchbeck prepared himself for the forced landing, the wing was still ablaze, it was completely dark outside and he had no idea of what lay ahead in his path. He had no power and a rapid sink rate and so no opportunity of choosing his land-fall. It would be first and final. Still unaware that the undercarriage was down he anticipated a belly landing. The aircraft sank lower until it was only fifteen to twenty feet above the ground. This was it. Suddenly ahead, directly in his path, and his first sight of ground, a farmhouse loomed up in the darkness. He was almost on to it before it became distinguishable. This must be it, death was staring him in the face once more and this time he could do nothing. At this point chance took a hand and the subsequent few seconds passed with no one other than fate in control.

Instead of hitting the farmhouse or descending on to its belly, at its high sink rate the main under-carriage wheels chose this moment to meet the ground hard. The aircraft still had plenty of speed and a high bounce ensued which lifted the Manchester clean over the farmhouse without disturbing a slate. On the second touchdown, fortunately on open ground behind the house, the undercarriage collapsed and L7379 descended onto its belly, skidding along for some distance before stopping.

Pinchbeck was practically unhurt and immediately climbed out of the upper escape hatch in the cockpit canopy, jumped down and raced away from the still blazing aircraft. He had covered about 150 yards when the petrol tanks exploded destroying what remained of the wreck.

Instead of being the last Pinchbeck turned out to be the first to find his feet on the ground, followed soon afterwards by Barron. Panton, who was first out, was able to glimpse the aircraft towing a banner of fire as it plunged earthwards. He had escaped from quite a high level, perhaps 10,000 feet and eventually landed at Stade at 03.15 hours.

McGregor, too, heard the noise of the Manchester's remaining engine as it flew over him in his parachute. There was no flak or noise other than the wind in the rigging lines. He was absolutely freezing as the only outer flying clothes he was wearing at his overheated station were flying boots. He heard the aircraft go into a vertical dive and then a minute or two later a loud explosion as the petrol tanks ignited on the ground. He landed safely in a ploughed field and as it would soon be dawn he found a wood, stuffed his parachute, Mae West and harness into a rabbit hole and hid in some bracken along the edge of the wood nearby. L7379 had crashed at the village of Bremervorde over thirty miles due west of Hamburg.

Ahead of L7379, Flying Officer Romans dropped four 1,000-lb general purpose (GP) and seven small bomb carriers (SBC) containing 420 4-lb incendiaries from 12,000 feet. The bombs were not seen to burst but the incendiaries straddled the docks. Romans' aircraft, L7317, was also hit by flak, but managed to reach Waddington and land safely.

Meanwhile Squadron Leader Kydd had been briefed to make a dawn sortie to Hamburg. Following the night's heavy raid it was intended to keep the weary defenders on their toes by triggering the early warning radar, sounding the air raid siren and raising the city-dwellers from the beds they had so recently returned to. Take-off time was 23.10 hours. This was to be an operation calling for all Charles Kydd's unrivalled qualities of leadership and coolness.

Following an extremely dark night the rising dawn still presented target identification problems due to a persistent ground haze over the city. The observer, Pilot Officer Sheen, now in the bomb aiming position, searched desperately for the aiming point as they held a steady course at 15,000 feet on their bomb run. The defences were well and truly roused and the flak was intense. It seemed as if every gun in Hamburg was concentrating on this lone Manchester. The wireless operator, 'Scotty' Scott, was sweating profusely at Kydd's dedication and praying second by second for the cry of 'bombs away'. The incantations over the intercom as Sheen conned

L7309 EM-J of 207 Squadron back from the wars again, this time with its tail feathers shredded. The crew fought a prolonged engagement with two Messerschmitt Bf110s and sustained damage to the tailplane, fins, fuselage, wings, fuel tanks and undercarriage doors, entailing some 360 skin perforations en route to Berlin, 10/11 May 1941. Squadron Leader Kydd made a successful early return. (via E. McCabe)

Kydd towards the aiming point appeared to come from one totally detached from the hell all round them.

Suddenly Sheen called: 'I think we're overshooting'. Kydd calmly replied: 'Alright, we'll go round again'. Scott's hopes were dashed. Kydd turned and made a second bombing run through what Scott recalled as the heaviest anti-aircraft fire he had ever experienced. Kydd never flinched or deviated from his determination to fly straight and level. The 4,000-lb 'Cookie' fell away on Aiming Point 'B'. As the short night lifted, Kydd dived away from the seething, thoroughly roused, target and finally escaped the jolting flak. Descending to ground level to take advantage of the last vestiges of twilight, Kydd hedge-hopped across Germany towards the coast.

In addition to the flak defences the Luftwaffe were also thoroughly alerted. As Kydd concentrated on following the terrain a few feet beneath, the gunners and lookouts could clearly see the day fighters overhead quartering the sky in a desperate search for them. They escaped detection and crossed the coast without further incident, reaching Waddington at 05.10 hours. They never came cooler or more efficient than Charles Kydd. The Hamburg Authorities in their own report noted 26 fires, thirteen of them large. Three people were killed and sixteen injured.

From the aircraft which failed to return, L7379, the whole crew, especially Pinchbeck and Barron, had had a quite shocking experience and were lucky to have all escaped with their lives. The degree to which engine failure contributed to the loss of L7379 is impossible to judge. At least the port engine appears to have been set on fire by flak and the aircraft was clearly losing height even before the starboard engine took light. A third Manchester had now fallen in occupied Europe but as yet the Germans had been left with precious little on the ground.

Back at Waddington, three 207 Squadron aircraft were required for operations the very next day, 3 May 1941. Two were briefed to attack Cologne with 4,000-lb HC bombs and the third was to go to Brest to keep up the pressure on the *Scharnhorst* and *Gneisenau*, carrying three 2,000-lb armour- piercing (AP) bombs. This night, Bomber Command split its forces, allocating 101 aircraft to Cologne and a further thirty-three to Brest.

Cologne and Brest – 3 May 1941:

Serial	Code	Squadron	Captain
L7377	EM-G	207	Fg Off. W. J. Lewis
L7378	EM-A	207	Fg Off. A. M. Paape
L7316	EM-U	207	Plt Off. W. G. Gardiner*

* Aircraft designated to Brest

Lewis and Paape attacked Cologne with their 4,000-lb bombs. Lewis attacked from 12,000 feet and observed his bomb bursting near the aiming point. Subsequent to releasing the bomb, Lewis dived on the target to give the gunners a chance to suppress the town defences. The wireless operator/air gunner, Sergeant Jim Duncan (not to be confused with A. S. Duncan who was on board L7379 during the horrific sortie of 2 May), records in his logbook that they overflew the target area at 2,000 feet and the gunners blazed away at searchlights, flak batteries and the empty streets. Such an action was not uncommon, but the more remarkable in that none of the Manchester crews doubted the certain outcome of losing an engine at that height over Germany. Paape dropped his 'Cookie' from 7,000 feet but was unable to see this explode. Similarly, Gardiner dropped his three 2,000-lb AP bombs in his attack on Brest but was unable to ascertain any effect. Heavy cloud had led to problems for the Cologne force and from the aircraft dispatched only eight to ten bombs fell within city limits, causing minor damage and casualties.

207 Squadron had operated on virtually every night in May and on the $9^{th}/10^{th}$ were called upon again. This time four aircraft were made ready, of which one was allocated to Mannheim, whilst the remaining three were detailed to attack 'The Big City', Berlin, for the first time in the Manchester's history. The tactical plan involved numerous aircraft attacking Mannheim with a diversion to Berlin by five bombers. It was by far the deepest penetration so far and no mean return journey for an underpowered aircraft with such unreliable and underdeveloped engines. Three experienced captains were to attack Berlin, whilst the new 'B' Flight commander, Flying Officer T. C. Murray, took on Mannheim.

Berlin, the first 'Big City' raid – 9/10 May 1941:

Serial	Code	Squadron	Captain
L7309	EM-J	207	Flt Lt P. R. Burton-Gyles
L7381	EM-R	207	Fg Off. T. C. Murray
L7316	EM-U	207	Plt Off. W. S. Herring
L7393	EM-V	207	Flt Lt G. R. Taylor

Murray had an uneventful mission to Mannheim where the 4,000-lb bomb was dropped in the target area from 17,000 feet. The flash of the explosion was readily distinguished and large fires reported. Local records document that a large number of buildings of all types were destroyed or damaged, 64 persons were killed and 122 injured.

From the Berlin force, Taylor's aircraft, L7393, returned after an hour with wireless transmitter failure, an unusual fault in the midst of so many engine and hydraulic problems. Herring and crew in L7316 were heading eastwards over the North Sea towards the enemy coast and had reached 10,000 feet when they were intercepted at 23.20 hours by a night fighter, identified as a Messerschmitt Bf110. After a brief encounter the '110 was claimed shot down by the rear gunner, Sergeant 'Tiny' Hallam, and L7316 was able to proceed, apparently undamaged. Flashes of other bombs exploding were observed in the target area and L7316 released six 1,000-lb bombs on the aiming point. The aircraft was hit by heavy flak and, although it is not recorded, it is likely that the damage occurred in the target area. The flak must have missed the vital parts and the delicate engines because L7316 was able to return safely to Waddington.

Burton-Gyles also reached Berlin in L7309 and his six 1,000-lb GP load was dropped in the target area from 18,000 feet. The following night, 10/11 May, 207 Squadron was again called for a follow up raid to Berlin. In its turn, 97 Squadron raised four Manchesters. In all, 119 aircraft were dispatched to Hamburg with the Berlin force numbering twenty-three. Only two aircraft were available from 207 Squadron, L7316 missing out perhaps due to the flak damage it incurred the previous night. Major R A Holmes of the Anti-Aircraft Liaison with 5 Group accompanied Kydd as an observer. He was to have an eventful night, although not at the hands of the flak batteries.

Berlin – 10/11 May 1941:

Serial	Code	Squadron	Captain
L7383	OF-*	97	Plt Off. H. S. Blakeman
L7374	OF-*	97	Fg Off. F. E. Eustace
L7323	OF-*	97	Plt Off. R. S. Ayton
L7324	OF-*	97	Flt Lt G. O. L. Bird
L7309	EM-J	207	Sqn Ldr C. J. F. Kydd
L7393	EM-V	207	Fg Off. D. A. A. Romans

* Individual codes unknown - not recorded in the ORB

It was a clear, moonlight night. Frankie Eustace of 97 Squadron experienced a series of serviceability problems and eventually diverted to Borkum. German night fighters were very active. Soon after crossing the enemy coast and whilst flying at 17,000 feet between Rensburg and Husum in Schleswig Holstein L7309 was intercepted by two Bf110 night fighters, apparently operating as a pair. At the moment of interception Kydd and Flying Officer Nunn were flying the aircraft, Pilot Officer Sheen was at the navigator's table, Sergeant Scott was manning the front turret, whilst the second wireless operator/air gunner, Sergeant Linklater, was on the radio and Sergeant Oliver was vigilant in the rear turret. As soon as the interceptors were spotted Linklater climbed up into the astrodome to observe the proceedings. In the action which followed Kydd was blind to the attacks and depended entirely on instructions from behind, whilst Oliver was fully occupied trying to repulse attacks and keep an eye on two Bf110s at once. Consequently, Linklater fell naturally into the role of attack co-ordinator.

He commenced a running commentary on the ranges and manoeuvres of the attackers. As they closed in, he instructed Kydd when and in which direction to break and the pilot began to throw the over-loaded bomber around the sky in a spirited fashion, losing height all the while. Scott could do little but sit and wait, listen and watch in trepidation as the tracer fire periodically flew past him. It was a desperate battle for the ultimate stakes. After two passes one of the fighters made a mistake, allowing Oliver to get in a telling shot. The aircraft dived away, apparently out of control. Oliver claimed this aircraft destroyed. Linklater was getting excited; although his commentary remained unbroken it was frequently interspersed with expletives, pronounced with the greatest emphasis: 'Bugger Me!', he shouted: 'Jesus Christ!'.

The second Bf110 carried out seven separate attacks, throughout which Kydd's evasive manoeuvres persisted with undiminished vigour. Despite this, the enemy pilot knew his stuff and on each approach the Manchester staggered under the impact of cannon and machine gun hits. They were hit in the tailplanes, fins, fuselage, wings and undercarriage doors. Kydd continually monitored the engine instruments. So far the vulnerable engines and vital services remained miraculously intact, but there was a serious fuel leak in the port wing tank.

Finally, Oliver was able to draw a bead and the fighter was seen to disengage immediately. Oliver claimed this as a probable. Later they were to learn that the entire episode had been seen by other British aircraft in the vicinity, who confirmed that this interceptor crashed, apparently into the sea.

As they slipped away into the night the crew of L7309 found that the combat had extended down to low altitude and as they took stock of the situation they found every system apparently serviceable, but there was an all pervading smell of aviation spirit. The petrol gauges indicated a rapid loss of fuel and in the circumstances Kydd had no alternative but to abort the operation and make an early return.

On arrival back at base he made a normal approach but found the aircraft virtually without elevator control. Consequently when he flared for landing the aircraft flew more or less straight on into the ground, making what for him was an unusually heavy landing. The six 1,000-lb GP bomb load was still intact. Inspection on the ground showed that the canvas covering on the central fin shredded by the fire from the night fighter had been all but torn off by the slipstream. The fabric was largely torn from the elevator accounting for the heavy landing. In the circumstances they marvelled that Oliver had escaped without a scratch. The self-sealing in the two tanks had worked to some extent, staunching the main leaks sufficiently for the Manchester to race back to base before they became dry completely.

Next day the airframe fitters counted some 360 perforations to the skin of the aircraft. Following their debriefing, Sergeant Oliver was awarded the DFC whilst Sergeant Linklater received the DFM, the citation eulogising the 'brilliant commentary' which had been a major contribution to their success.

Two 97 Squadron crews, L7388 and L7324, were also intercepted, this time by Junkers JU88 night fighters en route to the target. Both Blakeman and Bird managed to evade the attacks and went on to bomb Berlin successfully, as did Herring.

The night was to provide the first loss for 97 Squadron and the first of three consecutive encounters with the cold, pitiless North Sea. Earlier in the day the 'A' Flight Commander, Squadron Leader Ronnie Stubbs, had carried out a night

From inside an FN4A rear turret such as this, Sergeant Oliver of 207 Squadron claimed two Messerschmitt Bf110s on the night of 10/11 May 1941. (via Aerospace Publishing)

flying test in his personal aircraft, L7323 OF-A. Its performance, especially the power available from the two Vultures, was below normal and Stubbs had reservations about Pilot Officer Ayton taking it to Berlin, especially since this would be Ayton's first Manchester operation.

The crew of six consisted of Paddy Ayton (captain), Sergeants Jack Chantler (second pilot), 'Jock' Bryce (observer), Bill Sykes (wireless operator), Bob Anderson (rear gunner), and Dennis Harvey (front gunner), the latter on his first ever operation. At briefing the crews were given the German parliament buildings, the Reichstag, as their aiming point. The bomb load consisted of six 1,000-lb GPs with twelve hours delayed action fuses. For the first time the bombs were to have small rockets attached which would erupt on impact, permitting the fall of bombs to be observed. The course to be followed in and out was the same northerly route via the Baltic.

Normally at his station at the navigator's table, 'Jock' Bryce wore only his uniform tunic, as the blast of hot air from either side of the fuselage to his left was terrific. Some quirk this Saturday night made Bryce break his usual routine and don not only a white polo neck sweater but also his outer flying suit and flying boots. When all the

Few photographs of Manchesters serving with 97 Squadron have come to light, so this view of OF-Z is a particular delight. There are two candidates for the identity of this machine: L7474 was OF-Z, but close scrutiny suggests this may be L7424 (no previously known code) lost with Flying Officer Little on 12/13 August 1941. (Wells via Vincent/Merrick)

preparations, drawing Mae West and parachute, completing pre-flight log and checking his charts, were complete he and the crews climbed aboard the tenders and were driven to the aircraft.

At the dispersal L7323 was waiting, bomb doors still agape. Their ground crew, with several WAAF girls along to see them off, had chalked messages on the bombs. Bryce looked up at the load they were to carry to Berlin for the squadron's first visit. 'Ow's this for size Adolf?' said one. 'Up yer Jacksie, Goebbels' read another. Bryce's scan also took in the novelty of the rockets mounted on the bombs. The girls wished them good luck and a safe return and their presence led to them overlooking their ritual pee on the tail wheel.

In the failing light the Manchesters started up and taxied out into line, snaking to the north end of Coningsby airfield. Last in line, Paddy Ayton's crew watched the Manchesters on their headlong southerly run, each lifting off when some two thirds of the way down the grass runway. Ayton swung 'A-Apple' onto the grass runway and gunned the engines. The run seemed interminable and the aircraft had only just begun to lighten when they passed the two-thirds marker. Slowly the wheels unstuck, but 'A-Apple' immediately sank back and bounced. The bounces became further apart as the boundary hedge approached. Ayton was committed and still L7323 steadfastly refused to rise. The crew would never forget streaking over the boundary hedge just as their undercarriage began to retract.

A sea of shocked civilian faces zipped past just below eye level. At Waddington the local population were accustomed to aircraft departing for operations, but Coningsby was a new station and half the population of Boston and neighbouring villages had turned out to cheer them on. Had they known the identity of the target their encouragement would have been more enthusiastic still. Adrenalin continued to flow as L7323 clipped and carried away a radio aerial from a cottage roof.

Ayton commenced a tentative climbing shallow turn to port onto course and with the setting sun now behind they made out their three comrades ahead and already way above. Despite rpm and air speed being as recommended and with the flaps still down, L7323 'A-Apple' was a ground bird and steadfastly refused to rise. Slowly and almost imperceptibly, however, the aircraft did begin to lift and at midnight, as they passed

Heligoland on the port beam, they had achieved 7,000 feet. A full moon rose, illuminating the night sky, its brightness unsettling for an overloaded bomber whose main defence was its invisibility in the dark sky. As they kept a vigilant lookout the two pilots and front gunner all cried out in unison: 'Vapour trails'. These appeared momentarily and persisted for short intervals before fading again as different air masses were traversed. L7323 had reached 10,000 feet and could be coaxed no higher on its existing fuel and bomb load.

Jim Bryce, the observer, was taking a running series of bearings from Radio Hilversum and plotting these against compass bearings as they map read across the coast of occupied Europe. The visibility was virtually unlimited making him doubt his calculations from time to time. Soon after crossing the coast they altered course for Potsdam. Approaching the western suburbs of Berlin they were behind on the estimated time of arrival but relieved to have escaped any interference by searchlights, flak or fighters. Now the lights and flak began to rise – alarming because there was neither mist nor cloud to disguise it. Their lowly height had the consolation that most of the flak was bursting above them.

The great distance at which landmarks were perceptible was still causing Bryce concern, but suddenly Dennis Harvey, the front gunner, spotted a lake ahead, by which Bryce was able to establish that they were 5 miles to the west of the proposed track. Ayton swung east and made for the final turning point. Occasional vapour trails were still evident over the target; they had not been singled out by the defences and were only a few minutes late.

Turning onto the final leg, Bryce descended to the bomb aimer's position, set the flying height, wind speed and direction and other inputs. The city beneath was laid out like a map and the front gunner and Bryce, with their eyes not glued to the bomb sight, began quartering the suburbs for a sighting of Templehof aerodrome. The searchlight and flak activity had become intense and the crew were keyed up during this crucial run up. Everyone leapt when the rear gunner shouted suddenly over the intercom: 'Holy Christ! Are we that big?' An urgent query from the pilot: 'What's the matter?' 'A bloody big Manchester just cut across our tail', replied the gunner. 'That's alright then, just keep quiet!' said Ayton, restoring calm and concentration on board.

In the final few seconds an industrial haze made map reading difficult, a distinctive north-west to south-east highway gave a pinpoint but the Reichstag had not been located and Bryce gave a; 'Left, left, steady' to the pilot before pressing the button.

The automatic sight was moving fast, an indication that the bombs would undershoot the aiming point. The aircraft jolted and bucked as the bombs fell away in a neat stick over about ten seconds. Following the release, Bryce immediately called: 'Bombs gone, close bomb doors, course 330 compass'. After the short delay Anderson saw the rockets explode with orange flashes at the point of impact 10,000 feet below.

Their briefed course led them on a north-westerly heading out towards the Baltic and a return flight mainly over water. After a few minutes on this heading Ayton requested a new and more direct course pretty much due west back to Coningsby. On this return leg they soon picked up the distinctive outline of the Elbe, and as they continued, searchlights and flak defences sprang up to the north-west as a second Bomber Command attack on the port of Hamburg developed. To avoid meeting the attacking force head on, Bryce suggested a further south-westerly diversion to pick up a familiar pinpoint over a lake west of Hanover.

With the lake in view the return flight was uneventful until the second pilot, Chantler, up in the mid-upper turret, watching for night fighters, called to report oil flowing back from the starboard nacelle across the wing upper surface. Bryce checked the oil and temperature gauges on the starboard Vulture, which were still normal and then looked out to see the heavy flow rippling in the slipstream. Immediately rechecking the engine instruments Bryce was dismayed to see that within those few seconds the oil pressure had dropped and the temperature had risen off the dial. Before he could alert the pilot there was a tremendous explosion in the engine and flames shot out to be carried behind like a fiery comet. Anderson noted these extended aft of his position at least two aircraft lengths. Ayton immediately hit the extinguisher button. Fortunately the fire died rapidly. The feathering mechanism had also remained undamaged, permitting the propeller blades to be turned edge-on to the airflow.

An interesting sidelight was that, arising probably from the vibration problems in the centre fin induced by rotating the mid-upper turrets, L7323 was flying this night with the turret unarmed, the squadron ground crew had not had time to remove it in accordance with Bomber Command instructions.

Despite the immediate emergency receding, their situation was unpromising, the airspeed dropped to 110 mph and from their height of 10,000 feet they began a steady and inexorable descent. Bryce gave Ayton a course to the nearest point on the English coast at Cromer. A slight consolation arising from the sudden course change and loss in speed and height was that fresh bursts of flak began to explode above and to the right on their previous course.

There was initially little concern, by common consent they agreed that without the bomb load and with much of the fuel gone, as they descended the denser air would progressively provide more lift and they would make it. Ayton trimmed the aircraft so that it would lose the least height possible, all removable equipment, save for one Browning and 100 rounds in the rear turret was jettisoned, but their descent continued. They crossed the Dutch-German border and continued out over the Zuider Zee and thence the North Sea. Speed dropped almost to the stall and the aircraft kept yawing towards the dead engine. Ayton was fighting for every foot of altitude. They could have done without the dead weight of the useless FN7A turret. They continued westward in this manner for about fifteen minutes: the rev counter on the remaining port Vulture had packed up and the boost reading was steady at +3 lb.

When the altimeter reading reached 50 feet, Ayton threw caution to the winds and rammed the throttle lever through the gate. The boost reading fell to -0.5 lb and the glycol immediately began boiling out of the breather like frothing milk. The options exhausted, L7323 was set to descend right into the sea.

They were low enough to determine that the sea was fairly smooth and unbroken by white caps. Ayton was fully occupied and it was Chantler, the second pilot, who called the front and rear gunners to the mid-section. Bryce went to the rest seat and strapped in whilst Chantler joined the gunners. Sykes, the wireless operator, was stationed behind the pilot with instructions to link his arms around him at the moment of impact.

Ayton dropped the flaps and cut the throttle, raising the nose as he did so, 'A-Apple's' tail made contact and rose again so that the next contact was nose down, accompanied by a violent deceleration. Bryce jack-knifed forwards across the lap strap and banged his head violently against the armour plated doors ahead. Coming round in a daze from the parachute rack by the rear spar and had been thrown violently forward by the impact, injuring his ribs. Ayton was also pitched forward, breaking an ankle and losing his boot in the process.

The aircraft settled quickly, but each man took up his assigned role. Ayton was soon standing in the escape hatch in the cockpit roof directing the release and inflation of the dinghy; astern the second wireless operator/air gunner was releasing the pigeons. Bryce called to the wireless operator in the cockpit to retrieve his navigation satchel which he had stuffed with maps, Very pistol and cartridges in anticipation of the ditching. However, it was immediately obvious that the satchel was already underwater and the Manchester was settling quickly. Ayton just had time to recover his parachute from the rack to use as a sail. A small wave broke across the mainplane and washed the slowly inflating dinghy into the sea. It was time to leave.

The crew scrambled out and hauled the dinghy alongside by its static line. They embarked, easing the groaning rear gunner in on top last of all. The next shock was the sudden appreciation that nobody knew how to release the static line or had given any thought till now to a knife. Here a minor and highly opportune miracle manifest itself because, when Bill Sykes thrust his hands into the Irvin jacket he had borrowed for the flight, he found a penknife placed there by its more thoughtful owner. With this they cast the dinghy adrift and were well clear when L7323 sank seven minutes after ditching close to 52°30'N 4°15'E, 22 miles west of Bergen am Zee at 04.10 hours.

Next day Wing Commander Balsdon and Squadron Leader Stubbs carried out air sea rescue searches for Paddy Ayton and his crew, but they were searching well to the north along the briefed return route. Despite Sykes' best efforts, their SOS message was not received and it's likely the radio was unserviceable. Having ditched early on Sunday morning, 13 May, they remained at sea for four and a half days until they were seen and picked up by a group of small Dutch trawlers at about 18.30 hours on Thursday 17 May and were landed early on Friday back at Ijmuiden and captivity.

In the long running battle with the Luftwaffe, the night had more or less belonged to the Manchesters. 97 Squadron crews had evaded their assailants and gone on to complete their operations, whilst Sergeant Oliver of 207 Squadron had claimed two night fighters shot down.

Again, on 12 May 1941, 5 Group called on 207 Squadron to operate its Manchesters. Squadron Leader Kydd was still acting commanding officer and the pace of operations remained feverish. Three aircraft were prepared for an operation to Mannheim. In the event it was an unsuccessful operation even by the Manchester's standards. L7310 failed to take off due to unspecified unserviceability at the last moment.

Mannheim – 12 May 1941:

Serial	Code	Squadron	Captain
L7310	EM-H	207	Unknown
L7322	EM-B	207	Fg Off. W. J. Lewis
L7316	EM-U	207	Fg Off. T. Murray

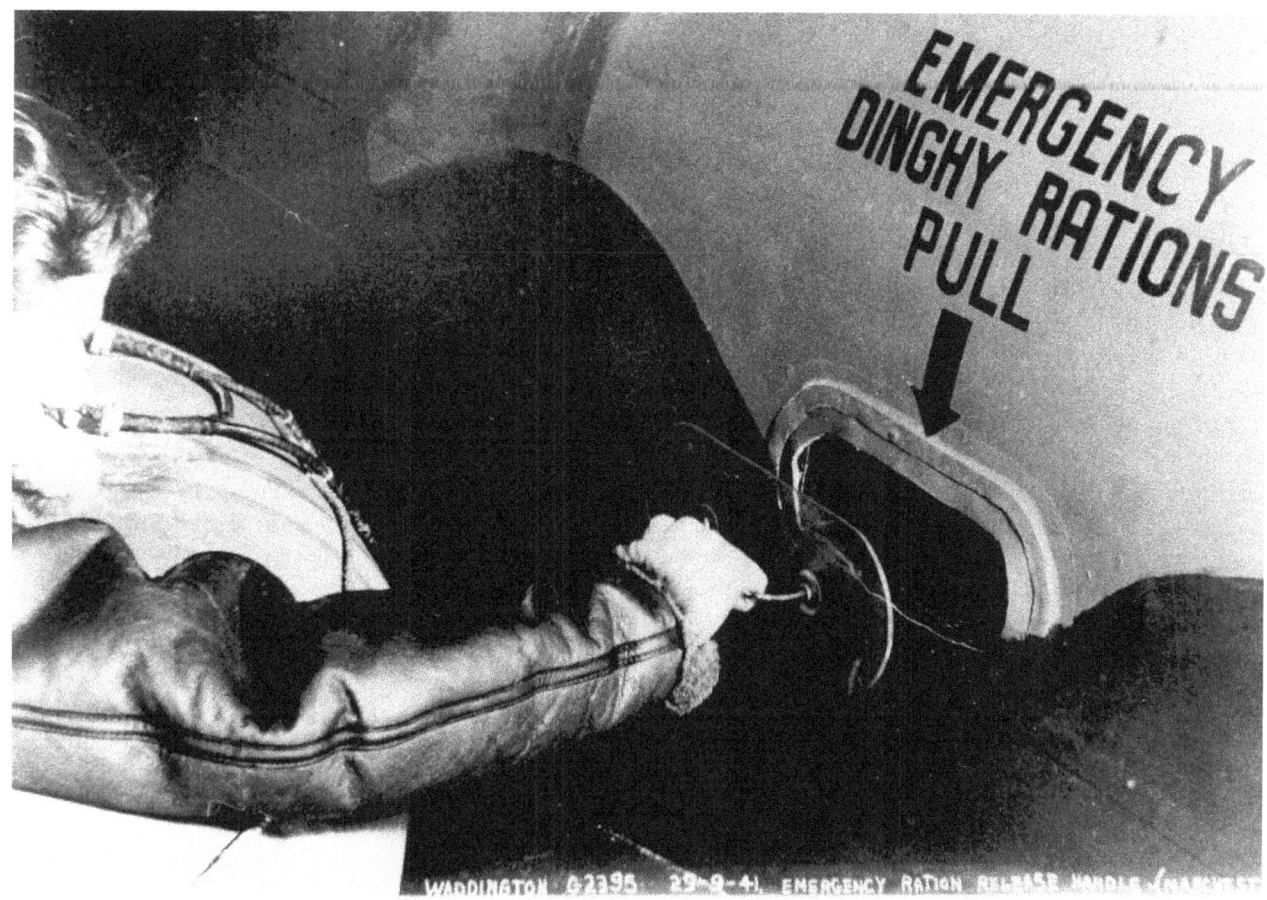

A 207 Squadron Manchester showing Emergency Ration Release Handle. 29 September 1941. Aircrew member is in a dinghy resting on the wing root. (E. McCabe)

In L7316 Flying Officer Murray and crew had serious navigational problems partly due to thick ground haze over the Ruhr. Instead they diverted to Cologne where an aiming point (AP) was attacked from 16,000 feet with six 1,000-lb GPs. These were seen to explode slightly north of the AP. Immediately prior to their arrival the crew witnessed and reported an enormous flash three miles east of the town. In L7322, a Manchester stripped of its FN7A, 'Mike' Lewis experienced another of the engine problems which plagued the squadron, as he relates:

On 12 May I acquired a new aircraft, L7322, which as far as I was concerned, was the best Manchester I ever flew, and it became pretty well my personal aircraft until I completed my tour. However, it had its teething problems. On this night we set out for a raid on Mannheim, but by the time we got well south of Cologne, the starboard engine oil temperature rose to the danger mark, the pressure dropped and I was forced to drop my bomb load from 16,000 feet on my alternate target, which was the railway station at Koblenz, and return to base. The arrival back at base was far more hair-raising than the operational trip in and out over enemy territory. We arrived back at base still with low oil pressure and the temperature in the starboard engine nearly off the clock, to find an intruder in the circuit. The flying control officer at Waddington refused to put on any lights whatsoever whereby I could carry out a landing. The wind was in the east that night, which necessitated coming around to the west and turning over the village of Waddington, the airfield married quarters and landing towards the east.

Of course, of all the things that had to happen, the local air defence corps on the airfield operating one of their searchlights decided to illuminate me and having done so sat with the light on me for a considerable time, naturally providing a nice target for the intruder as well as blinding me. I could only get rid of the thing by firing off the colour of the day, which was a most undesirable act as the intruder would obviously see it and could possibly copy it.

I did a very tight circuit and used no lights until I arrived over the boundary of the airfield, at which time I turned on the landing lights and put L7322 down. As soon as I landed I turned the lights off again. I had no sooner accomplished this and was still braking on my landing run when the intruder laid down a stick of four bombs, about 400 yards to my starboard side and parallel with my heading. We ended up taxiing to our dispersal using flashlights to find our way through the hedges. The searchlight crew were persona non grata for some time.

Of the 105 aircraft dispatched no more than ten dropped their bombs within the city limits causing light damage and few casualties. However, ninety-two soldiers were killed in Cologne when a bomb hit their barracks.

On 13 and 14 May 207 Squadron was allowed a brief respite from operations. The only major flying reported by 207 Squadron on the 13th was that Flight Lieutenant Burton-Gyles visited the de Havilland factory at Hatfield to procure new washers for the constant speed units in the propellers of the aircraft. The precise reason for the change being necessary is not made clear but at about this date Flying Officer Nunn had a bad experience whilst engaged on a training flight in L7377 when the constant speed unit in one engine packed up. The engine promptly over-reved itself and on trying to feather the propeller Nunn found it moving instead to the fully fine position, resulting in excessive drag on one side. Fortunately Scampton was spotted just within reach and an emergency forced landing was successfully accomplished between the hangars. This was another serious fault with the aircraft, which further lowered the crews' confidence in the Manchesters.

On 15 May 207 Squadron found four Manchesters available and 97 Squadron a further four for a repeat operation to Berlin. Only fourteen aircraft were detailed for this diversion to Berlin, whilst 101 aircraft raided Hanover. It was to prove the last operation for some weeks and was a disaster for the two squadrons. Some hundreds of personnel had spent thousands of hours to get just these eight aircraft serviceable.

Berlin – 15 May 1941:

Serial	Code	Squadron	Captain
L7324	OF-*	97	Flt Lt G. O. L. Bird
L7306	OF-*	97	Fg Off. J. S. Sherwood
L7374	OF-*	97	Fg Off. C. P. D. Price
L7383	OF-*	97	Fg Off. H. S. Blakeman
L7322	EM-B	207	Flt Lt P. R. Burton-Gyles
L7321	EM-D	207	Fg Off. J. L. Nunn
L7393	EM-V	207	Flt Lt G. R. Taylor
L7316	EM-U	207	Fg Off. W. G. Gardiner

Following their take-off the first casualty was with 207 Squadron. Flying Officer Nunn, in L7321, encountered engine trouble necessitating an early return after only 95 min flying. When some 150 miles out, Flying Officer Price in L7374 lost power in his starboard engine, necessitating the bomb load being jettisoned. Fortunately he was able to return to Coningsby still nursing the failing starboard Vulture.

Flight Lieutenant Bird was less fortunate. Several radio messages were received from the aircraft, the last an SOS message from a position about twenty miles off Borkum in the Frisian Isles timed at 23.00 hours. The message told its own story: 'Starboard engine cut and the other giving trouble. Changing to Heston, please tell them'. The message was passed on and the squadron remained optimistic, but the hopes were misplaced. Bird and his crew were never heard of again and are presumed to have drowned in the North Sea, their final moments never to be established.

Next, as they laboured eastwards dragging L7393 up to the best altitude they could achieve, Flight Lieutenant Taylor and crew became sufficiently concerned about the high fuel consumption that they finally abandoned the attempt to reach the primary target and diverted to Hanover, where they dropped their six 1,000-lb bombs, but did not observe any of them to burst.

Most frustrating of all, in L7322 Burton-Gyles, having lugged his six 1,000-lb bombs all the way to Berlin, found the bomb doors jammed. Despite all his manoeuvres they would not budge. They had to be happy with jettisoning one package of 'NICKELS' (propaganda leaflets) over Berlin before carrying the whole bomb load back to Waddington.

With nearly three months experience, Gardiner had now become familiar with the performance of his aeroplane. Like the others, he found it now took off readily at 47,000-lb all-up weight on 1,800 hp from each Vulture at +9 lb boost and 2,850 rpm from the 1,500 yards of grass at Waddington. It seemed reluctant to edge much above 10,000 feet on lean mixture and this was more marked on warm nights. In our modern days of steep climbs to operating altitudes it is sobering to reflect that when heading south-east for the Dutch coast even with constant coaxing they could expect no more than 7,000 to 8,000 feet by the appointed time to cross the enemy coast.

Stuck with an aircraft he defined as 'big, black and, when climbing, slow', Gardiner elected to nurse his engines using full throttle for take-off only. His preferred policy on operations was high and fast with little regard for fuel consumption. In L7316 EM-U on this night he was able to use these tactics to the full in what he came to regard as his best Manchester sortie. With him in the aircraft he had Sergeant Keartland, a Rhodesian second pilot under training, Sergeant Smith as Observer, and Sergeant Humphries as rear gunner, together with Sergeants Jones and Wain. Gardiner describes Keartland as 'a rather strange looking figure whose grey flying overalls were spattered with paint of assorted colours'. 'It happened that when night flying on Hampdens at Cottesmore he had swung on landing and gone through the wooden hut just off the airfield that was used as the paint and dope store, splashing these on the aircraft and himself. Arising from his providential escape, Keartland came to regard his multicoloured overalls as lucky'.

The rear gunner, Sergeant Humphries, was remembered as a 'cool little chap'. To the best of the captain's knowledge, he never came forward of the aircraft entrance door. He would climb the ladder into the aircraft, turn left to his turret, where he remained until they landed and taxied to dispersal. On another occasion too, Sergeant Humphries reported by intercom that his turret had jammed at about 45 degrees to the fore and aft position. Knowing full well that his turret was thus disabled and neither could he escape in an emergency, Gardiner enquired how he was. Humphries told him to press on, staying put until landing. He was never seen on the station except for NFTs and for briefing when some instinct told him to be present. He was eager to fly and never complained even when a panel was cut out of the perspex of his turret directly in front of him permitting a clear vision through what was often otherwise a thin smear of hydraulic oil. Without his heated suit, he would have had a very cold ride at 15,000 feet.

Arising from the poor climbing performance alluded to above, on this night Gardiner chose his take off time and route, electing a long sea crossing of 300 miles to Denmark, thus offering ample opportunity for a long weak-mixture climb to altitude with few hostile distractions. Nursing the twin Vultures as they climbed imperceptibly, they crossed the enemy coast at what was considered a safe height, before switching to a new course to a pinpoint 60 miles north-west of Berlin, from where they headed south-east to the target, lifting L7316 up to 16,000 feet for the final approach. The weather was fine and clear with a good moon making navigation easy. Sergeant Smith moved to the nose and map read to the city which they could see clearly in the moonlight. The Aiming Point itself was not distinguishable due to ground haze, but their six 1,000-lb GPs were dropped in the north of the city, together with three quarters of their remaining 'NICKELS', the first fistfuls having been jettisoned over Hanover.

The return was similarly uneventful, other than for concerns over fuel consumption on the 1350 statute mile operation. With L7316 lightened of its bomb load and much of its fuel, and with height in hand, Gardiner lowered the nose slightly, air speed built-up to an indicated 170 mph, the Manchester was at its best, the Vultures settled at 1800 rpm, with the huge propellers turning slowly and efficiently. They touched down at Waddington after seven hours fifty minutes in the air.

During the return flight other Manchesters ran into a severe electrical storm. For Flight Sergeant Bob Fletcher, the second pilot to Flight Lieutenant Sherwood in L7306, it was his first experience of St Elmo's fire. The leading edges of the mainplanes and other areas glowed as if red hot. Fork lightning danced from the propellers and gun barrels. Suddenly the static which had built-up discharged with a terrific flash, temporarily blinding the entire crew After what seemed an eternity the eyesight started to return and the two pilots slowly began to discern the instruments. The only damage was to the radio set which was put out of commission. Eventually they landed back at Coningsby almost on dry tanks after 7¼ hours in the air. Sherwood and Blakeman completed their operations but without observing any results.

The whole raid was a dismal failure. Of the eight Manchesters dispatched, only three bombed Berlin, the remaining five having serviceability problems of varying degrees of seriousness.In tying up so many trained servicemen it was difficult to see at this time that the Manchester was not more of a help to Germans and a hindrance to the British. Despite being in service for almost seven and a half months the aircraft were of extremely limited usefulness and plagued by a multitude of most serious operational short-comings.

Sergeant Harwood, possibly Flight Lieutenant Siebert, Flying Officer Ayton and now Flight Lieutenant Bird, all experienced second tour pilots, had all been lost in a few weeks due to engine failures. Despite the adoption of LA4 bearings it was clear that other equally serious problems remained to be cured. It had to stop.

On 16 May 1941 three aircraft were detailed by 207 Squadron for a raid on Hamburg, which was mercifully cancelled at 20.30 hours. On the 17th, orders were once more received that Manchesters were to be withdrawn from operations for a second time, whilst intensive investigations were carried out to try to overcome the engine problems. Intensive test flights at full load were to begin immediately on a few selected aircraft.

On the 18th, a sunny and clear late spring day, Squadron Leader Mackintosh embarked upon one of the earliest flights of this intensive test programme. L7393 was loaded with a full dummy bomb and fuel load and was to fly a three-legged cross country at maximum height to test the engines under the most arduous conditions. The route involved turning points at Land's End and the Isle of Man, starting and finishing at Waddington. The flight crew of six was supplemented by two or three additional aircrew along for a joy ride. No second pilot was carried. The aircraft climbed to a height of 16,000 feet and the leg down to Land's End passed without incident.

Mackintosh turned north and set course across the Celtic Sea en route to the Isle of Man. They had reached perhaps thirty miles along this track, mid-way between Land's End and the Welsh coast, when a sudden rise in glycol temperature was noticed in the starboard Vulture. The engine rapidly overheated and caught fire. Mackintosh immediately turned off the fuel supply to the engine, feathered the propeller and hit the Graviner button. To their intense relief the fire died down and went out. Their plight was still acute because the bomber was heavily laden and its power reduced by half. L7393 began to lose height rapidly and Mackintosh executed a quick turn to port. A crew member went down into the nose to release the bomb load and decrease the all-up weight.

The rate of descent was appreciably diminished but Mackintosh immediately set course for the nearest airfield, the small grass strip at Perranporth, only just large enough for its resident Spitfires. A radio call alerted the airfield and the ambulance and fire engine were deployed in anticipation of their arrival. Their inexorable descent continued and Perranporth could clearly be seen ahead. As they approached, Mackintosh suddenly became aware that they were unlikely to clear the towering cliffs above which Perranporth was perched. He immediately commenced a flat turn to port whilst the crew rapidly dismantled the guns from the three turrets, ditching them and their ammunition from the various hatches. At the same time the bulk of the remaining fuel load was jettisoned. As they completed the turn Mackintosh headed in to Perranporth. There was no beach visible along the coast to either side. It was Perranporth or bust.

L7393 was now able to maintain its height and in a very flat circuit at low speed Mackintosh dragged the aircraft into its final approach. The flaps were only lowered partially to avoid increasing the descent rate and they crossed the cliff top with only a few feet in hand. Having touched down they rapidly gobbled up the available open space and it became clear they would not stop within the airfield boundary. Accordingly, Mackintosh raised the undercarriage and dropped the aircraft on its belly in an attempt to stop. Earth, turf and sparks flew around them as they skidded first through the boundary hedge, crossed a road and went through another hedge into an adjacent field. After slithering a further 50 to 100 yards, their forward motion was diminished when the port wing hit a parked lorry and they slewed to the left before finally grinding to a halt.

The aircraft was still more or less intact but severely battered. By good fortune it did not catch fire and the crew, although badly shaken, were able to scramble out. Sergeant Nisbet was the only member with a significant injury, the rest being superficial and they were able to make their way to the ambulance which had come to a halt by the newly created gap in the hedge.

L7393 was a write-off and L7280, flown by Flight Lieutenant Taylor, carrying Mr Walker and Mr Nicholson of Rolls-Royce, was sent to Perranporth to make an early investigation of the faulty engine. It was decided that the starboard engine should be transported by road to the Rolls-Royce factory at Derby, where a complete strip down and detailed investigation could proceed.

Despite the almost terminal nature of the Vulture problems, Manchester production was proceeding apace. In the week up to 5 May 1941 L7395, L7396, L7386 and L7398 were built, whilst R5770, R5771 and R5772 were in an advanced stage of assembly or delivered. By the 19th, deliveries in the previous week had included L7401, L7402, L7415, L7416 and L7417, whilst components for R5773 were arriving at the assembly shop at Ringway.

However, it was clear Rolls-Royce were beginning to come to terms with yet another potentially fatal engine problem, even though only a little over two weeks had elapsed since the Manchester was returned to operations. Participants at the twenty-fifth production meeting were advised that not only were Rolls-Royce thirty-one engines behind on their agreed Vulture delivery schedule, but also that serious delays were being incurred by another new programme to change every Vulture engine. Indications were that Rolls-Royce engineers, like the Avro workforce and the aircrews making Herculean efforts, had pinpointed and thought they had devised a solution for yet another Vulture problem. What was desperately needed now was a breathing space to manufacture

Manchester Mk.1 L7393 EM-V of 207 Squadron following its forced-landing at Perranporth on 18 May 1941. The starboard Vulture failed and Squadron Leader Mackintosh had raised the undercarriage attempting to stop. The aircraft burst through hedges, crossed a road and slewed round in the next field having hit a parked lorry with the port wing. (Peter Green collection)

modified parts and then yet again strip and rebuild every Vulture. Small wonder delivery schedules had slipped. For the immediate future no time was to be allocated. Miraculous though it may seem, other departments involved with the Manchester had made some progress and on 20 May, as stated above, all units received formal authority to increase the take off weight of the Manchester to 47,000 lb.

On 21 May Wing Commander K Purdon Lewis finally took command of 207 Squadron from the acting Commanding Officer, Squadron Leader Kydd, and that very day all aircraft were held on the ground so that the oil filters could be examined and for the removal of the viscosity valves from the engines. It was established that every oil filter was unserviceable, being between 0.25 and 0.375 inches too short. The following day Kydd flew to Avro's Woodford factory and returned with 86 serviceable oil filters for immediate installation. Clearly, this was an Avro rather than a Rolls-Royce component. These filters and the viscosity valves were installed over the next day or so in all 207 and 97 Squadron aircraft and between the 23rd and the 25th all aircraft did war load climbs. This was a different and parallel problem clearly not requiring engine removal.

Despite the fact that Manchesters were officially grounded, in the next couple of days the urgency of the war situation necessitated all serviceable aircraft being kept available for immediate take-off with a load of ten 500-lb semi-armour-piercing (SAP) bombs. The *Bismarck* and the *Prinz Eugen* were out in the Atlantic and every possible aircraft was required to cover all conceivable contingencies. Fortunately the Manchesters were not required and on the afternoon of the 27th they were stood down completely.

On 29 May 1941, in pursuit of the pressing engine problems, Wing Commander Lewis, Flight Lieutenant McCabe and the 'resident' Rolls representative at Waddington visited the Rolls-Royce factory at Derby to inspect the engine of L7393, which had meanwhile been taken apart by the engineers. No definite reason for the failure seemed to be established at this stage and the party returned still with no satisfactory diagnosis of the problem.

The Manchester allocated to Rolls-Royce for engine investigations had itself crashed on 26 May in similar circumstances to L7393. Reg Kirlew, the Rolls-Royce test pilot, had already survived several emergency landings following Vulture failures in the Manchester. At 14.20 hours on the 26th the starboard engine of L7295 caught fire and Kirlew attempted to land the aircraft at Tern Hill instead of simply abandoning the valuable test-bed with the evidence. One mile north of Tern Hill they ran out of altitude, the starboard wing and engine were torn off and thrown clear on impact with a large tree and the remainder of the aircraft burnt out. The pilot died and his three compatriots in the aircraft were injured.

Fortunately the vital damaged starboard engine remained for Rolls-Royce engineers to carry out their meticulous forensic examination. This showed that a similar failure to the one at Perranporth had occurred. By now four Manchesters had crashed due to engine failure in May alone. Those of Paddy Ayton and 'Golly' Bird of 97 Squadron were lost in the North Sea but the Vultures from Mackintosh's and Kirlew's aircraft were available. In a fifth Manchester, that of Derek Pinchbeck, an engine failure was the contributory factor in the loss.

With the Manchesters still grounded, a conference was held on 31 May to consider the engine failures. The Rolls-Royce engineers concluded that the primary cause was the oil system and that the engine fires were secondary and resulting from overheating, which was considered to be most likely due to the DTD (Director of Technical Development specification) 1094 oil used as a lubricant tending to gum up the pistons, leading to partial seizures and coolant leaks.

During a more prolonged investigation Rolls-Royce eventually discovered that the real reason was that oil was leaving the scavenge pump contaminated by air bubbles which, with the standard aircraft system, did not disengage from the oil once it reached the main oil tanks. The restriction caused by the actual viscosity element of the viscosity valve was also found to promote aeration by further breaking up the air bubbles into smaller ones. The function of this valve was to bypass oil when it was cold so that it kept circulating through the engine until it warmed, when its flow was diverted through the oil coolers located in the wing leading edge, outboard of the engines.

The aeration leading to oil-pressure reductions, oil temperature rises and ultimately air-locking of the scavenge pumps was tackled in a range of ways. Firstly and importantly the oil pump was recognised as not being large enough. Rolls-Royce discovered that by replacing the existing Roloid gears with new Rolls gears the flow rate was improved by 50%. This required some opening up of the casings, the new gears featuring large tooth spaces and short pitch contacts to benefit capacity but having only marginally greater diameter than the Roloid units.

Secondly, the aircraft oil scavenge line was re-engineered. A Vokes filter was installed before the oil cooler, whilst the original viscosity valve, with its aeration creating constriction, was replaced by a simple spring-loaded relief valve allowing freer passage of the oil.

The filter eliminated much of the aeration, evidently by causing the smaller bubbles passing through the filter felt to aggregate into larger bubbles, which were more easily disengaged from the oil once it reached the tank. Oil pressure was also substantially increased. After this prolonged investigation some of the more disconcerting attributes of the Vulture were overcome.

In addition to the crisis at 5 Group caused by the Manchester grounding, which had placed in abeyance the entire Manchester re-equipment programme, Avros now had a crisis of a different nature. The combination of shortfall in Vulture deliveries together with the current serviceability problem led to completed aircraft accumulating at the Woodford and Ringway factories to such an extent that both space considerations and the ever present threat of German attack were causing acute anxiety. Yet without serviceable engines, how could the aircraft be dispersed?

Following agreement on 31 May and despite its gross inefficiency, the course of action eventually taken proved the best option. A small batch of special 'slave' engines modified to the latest, but still interim, Rolls-Royce standard were installed into the waiting aircraft in turn, permitting them to be more widely dispersed to such localities as Cranage and Tollerton. There the engines were removed and returned to Avro to permit other Manchesters to be steadily and slowly dispersed into storage. In only four short months the optimism of 5 Group and the aircrews for their new Manchesters had been dashed in a dramatic manner.

On 1 June another Vulture on a 207 Squadron Manchester failed in the air. Flight Lieutenant Peter Burton-Gyles was gliding down from bombing height after a test flight in L7317 when a coolant leak in one engine led to overheating. He landed at Waddington before the engine finally seized. This was another permutation on the engine problems and investigation on this aspect was intensified, whilst the other problems were still under examination.

Next morning yet another engine failure occurred, this time of a terminal nature. After starting L7318 at Waddington a con-rod went through the sump on the port engine, which then proceeded to catch fire. A large piece of the con-rod assembly buried itself in the ground between the fortuitously placed feet of Rex Nicholson, the resident Rolls-Royce representative. Fortunately quick action with an extinguisher saved the aircraft. This time a big-end bolt failure was suspected. Yet another fundamental Vulture problem was beginning to be appreciated.

Elsewhere on the aerodrome at Waddington and in the presence of Rolls-Royce engineers, eight gallons of coolant were added to the suspect starboard engine of L7317, which had overheated the day before, and the coolant system then pressure tested. Extensive leaks were manifest at the bottom of the guard tubes and water drained from the sump. Unfortunately at the same period the thermostatic overflow valves fitted in the coolant header tanks of the Vultures also began to misbehave, the valve sticking in the open position and resulting in coolant being lost. In extreme cases engines would seize up.

Problems seemed to be occurring at a more rapid rate than they could be investigated. It was a very depressing situation, with no indication that a realisation of the underlying problems had been isolated, or that effective action was being taken. Propellers, cooling, oil filters, oil and possible big-end failures – the engine problems seemed never ending.

Although the aircraft were still 'grounded', much test flying of modified Manchesters was still required. To give the crews something else to do whilst trundling around the sky for hours on end, Bomber Command found two liaison exercises with the ground defences for them to participate in.

It seemed that Anti-Aircraft Command had become concerned that enemy aircraft may have been able to evade detection by feathering their propellers and gliding down on their targets. Whether it was in the belief that the bombers could simply evade the outdated sound locators, or alternatively that the new ground-to-air radars then coming into use for directing the anti-aircraft batteries onto their targets would thus become less effective, is not altogether established.

207 Squadron was instructed to undertake a series of dummy silent approach attacks on Nottingham. This city had apparently been chosen as it was one of the first areas in central England to be issued with radar-guided guns. Consequently, on 4 June, Flight Lieutenant Burton-Gyles, Flight Sergeants Syrett and Houghton, accompanied by the squadron engineering officer, Flight Lieutenant Eric McCabe, and Mr Hook, undertook the first silent approach attack on the city in Manchester Mk.1 L7377. The attack procedure involved climbing as high as the Manchester would reach, generally 18,000 to 19,000 feet, upwind of the target. The aircraft then headed for the city, the engines were stopped, both propellers feathered, the stick pushed forward and the aircraft was to glide down across the 'target'.

In itself this was a hardly appropriate procedure in a Manchester, in that all the instruments were power-driven off the engines, so that once these were shut down the blind flying instruments ceased operation. Uppermost in the minds of the Manchester crews was whether, having glided across the target to 20 miles beyond, there would be enough power left in the aircraft batteries to unfeather the propellers after such a lengthy time stopped.

On the 4th 'BG' glided down towards Nottingham, simulated a bomb run at 12,000 feet culminating in Ken Houghton dropping a photoflash whose ignition was recorded on the ground, and carried on beyond the target to below 8,000 feet. At 6,000 feet he initiated the procedure to unfeather the propellers and restart the engines. The starboard engine started, but the propeller of the port Vulture steadfastly refused to unfeather. The aircraft would not maintain height on the one engine and it was clear they would not reach Waddington. They began looking for a very large field and, as they got even lower, any size of field. At this moment they came within sight of the flying training school at Harlaxton. Unannounced and with precious little height in hand they dumped the undercarriage and flaps and lobbed in over the hedge, crosswind. As they touched down Syrett saw several Airspeed Oxfords on their take-off runs crossing their paths from left to right. The Oxfords were on a collision course, but as they accelerated and the Manchester slowed the trainers passed under the nose, missing them by a mere 50 feet. The crew breathed a sigh of relief at this close shave.

Inspection showed that a failure of the Gaco washer in the propeller feathering mechanism had caused the problem. This was an oil sealing washer fitted inside the propeller. When this ruptured, oil was prevented from reaching the right side of the operating mechanism which altered the pitch of the propeller. The silent approach trials went on until 12 June. Flying Officer Lewis and others participated in them, each being ever more nervous over the chance of a propeller feathering failure.

At this time the German blitz was in full swing and desperate measures were being considered to combat the ever more accurate bombing. For the moment there was little that could be done to distract the German bomb aimers once the target finding radio beams were laid on. One of the precautions that Anti-Aircraft Command was considering at this time was large-scale smoke screens over British cities and other military targets, the idea being that once the authorities identified which target the beams were laid over they could ignite a large smoke making operation up-wind of the city and completely blanket the city with smoke.

To test the idea smoke screens were set up over several selected areas and on 10 and 12 June 'Mike' Lewis and other pilots carried out smoke screen recces over these areas. Quite how obscuring the target area would have made the target less visible to the radio beams is unclear, possibly it was hoped to obscure fires from incendiary bombs released by the pathfinders which the less experienced crews could otherwise home in on.

Manchester Mk.1 of 207 Squadron at West Raynham on 6 June 1941 for inspection of examples of RAF aircraft by Prime Minister, Winston Churchill. Aircraft captain, at extreme right and half cut off, was Squadron Leader Charles Kydd. Crew, from the left: Nunn, Oliver, Goldstraw, Scott, Linklater plus three groundcrew. Note the retention of the old style, mid-fuselage, colour separation. Aircrew logbooks list this aircraft as L7310 or L7322. (207 Squadron archives)

After this intensive series of trials the crews flew down to Hendon on 16 June for a conference at the Air Ministry regarding the effectiveness of the smoke screens and the silent approach attacks on Nottingham. The smoke screens were destined not to be implemented and presumably the Anti-Aircraft Command proved able to detect the Manchesters. The aircrews were no doubt most relieved that they were never required to employ the silent approach technique in an offensive fashion over occupied Europe. Lewis was no doubt able to give first hand experiences of the results of using similar techniques over Kiel.

On 16 June the Manchesters, which had only been allowed to carry out very limited flying, were completely grounded for modifications to the coolant, cabin heating systems and the thermostatic over-flow valves. Another suite of engine problems was being overcome but major difficulties still remained. Following the series of engine fires leading to the forced landings at Perranporth, Tern Hill and elsewhere, and a prolonged enquiry into their causes, entailing a number of false leads, the source was finally appreciated.

The sequence of failure was believed to stem from a combination of poor distribution of coolant through the cylinder blocks, exacerbated at times by leaks of coolant from a gland on the water pump. Overheating of the areas not adequately supplied with coolant led to piston seizure, followed fractionally later by con-rod failure. Very often prior to the seizure the cylinder liners got so hot that the liner-to-head seal was destroyed. The water/glycol coolant then entered the cylinder and produced the white smoke from the exhaust manifold so characteristic of this type of failure.

In the case of the Perranporth and Tern Hill crashes the con-rod failures were rapidly followed by engine fire which, in the case of the Tern Hill aircraft, was sufficiently intense for the aluminium cylinder block to flare and burn. To further improve coolant distribution locally within the crankcase it was also deemed necessary to fit baffles between the cylinder liners. These distributed the coolant more evenly within the cylinder blocks, especially around the sparking plugs and exhaust port areas. An internal baffle system was developed and tested but never incorporated into production engines.

At this same period in mid-June 1941 the opportunity was taken to modify the thermostatic valves in the coolant system. Leaks, lack of balancing pipes between the upper and lower banks of cylinders, uneven distribution and suspect thermostatic valves had all contributed to the severe cooling problems, the various inadequacies being difficult to isolate and overcome.

Mid-June also represented a low point in the fortunes of the Manchester with worse to come, until the eventual, but by no means ideal, solution to the Vulture problems in early August. Perhaps surprisingly, the situation with respect to Handley Page Halifax and Short Stirling availability at this moment was worse. In Air Marshal Linnell's second weekly report on progress in clearing troubles with service aircraft on the 18th, a review undertaken two days earlier revealed that only sixteen Halifaxes and fourteen Stirlings were available for operations. In contrast, three squadrons of Manchesters, numbers unspecified, were available. On their return to operations a few days later, 207, 97 and 61 Squadrons raised eighteen serviceable Manchesters.

By 11 July preserved records of the complete engine changing programme then found necessary lists the total completed Manchesters at 94, disposed as follows:

Location	Number	Location	Number
Waddington	20	Burtonwood	2
Coningsby	12	Woodford	14
Hemswell	9	Ringway	9
Finningley	7	Bracebridge Heath	4
Boscombe Down	2	Cranage	7
Brize Norton	2	Tollerton	6

Avro had done well to achieve such an output in view of the many setbacks. Had Rolls-Royce had the capacity to overcome the Vulture problems, Bomber Command would have had a Manchester force of four to five squadrons at its disposal by this time. The host of engine modifications and constant attempts at improvement created a bottleneck in component supply. Availability of Vulture spares was always a major problem, but with the spate of changes it became acute. Obtaining items through normal Rolls-Royce channels and Air Ministry bureaucracy would have introduced an unacceptable delay and it is here, to his eternal credit, that the Rolls-Royce Service Engineer at Waddington, Rex Nicholson, became a key man in the Manchester serviceability story.

Being the Rolls-Royce rep. at the sharp end must have been an unenviable task, requiring a deep well of tact and diplomacy. The company had obviously chosen wisely. Nicholson had identified closely with the aircrew from the beginning. One of his offices in Waddington's hangars became a veritable treasure trove of the latest spares, unobtainable through the RAF stores procedure. He maintained the stock by regular visits to the Derby and Ilkeston Rolls-Royce factories, mostly in the dead of night, where various colleagues supported his clandestine activities in acquiring factory-fresh spares straight out of the back door of the company. As he has acknowledged, in any other circumstances he would have been charged with theft on a large scale.

The myth arose amongst the Engineering Officers of 207, 97 and 61 Squadrons that Nicholson had the power to perform miracles of no less magnitude than that of the loaves and fishes. This unorthodox short-circuiting of the spares supply route significantly eased some of the more critical shortages and gave the units at least a fighting chance of mounting operations on a limited scale.

By 20 June 1941, with modifications completed, the aircraft were air-tested during the day and declared available for operations once more. Nobody was to know, but 207 Squadron was facing one of the bitterest and most tragic days in the 18-month period it was to operate Manchesters, with the Germans no more than waiting in the wings.

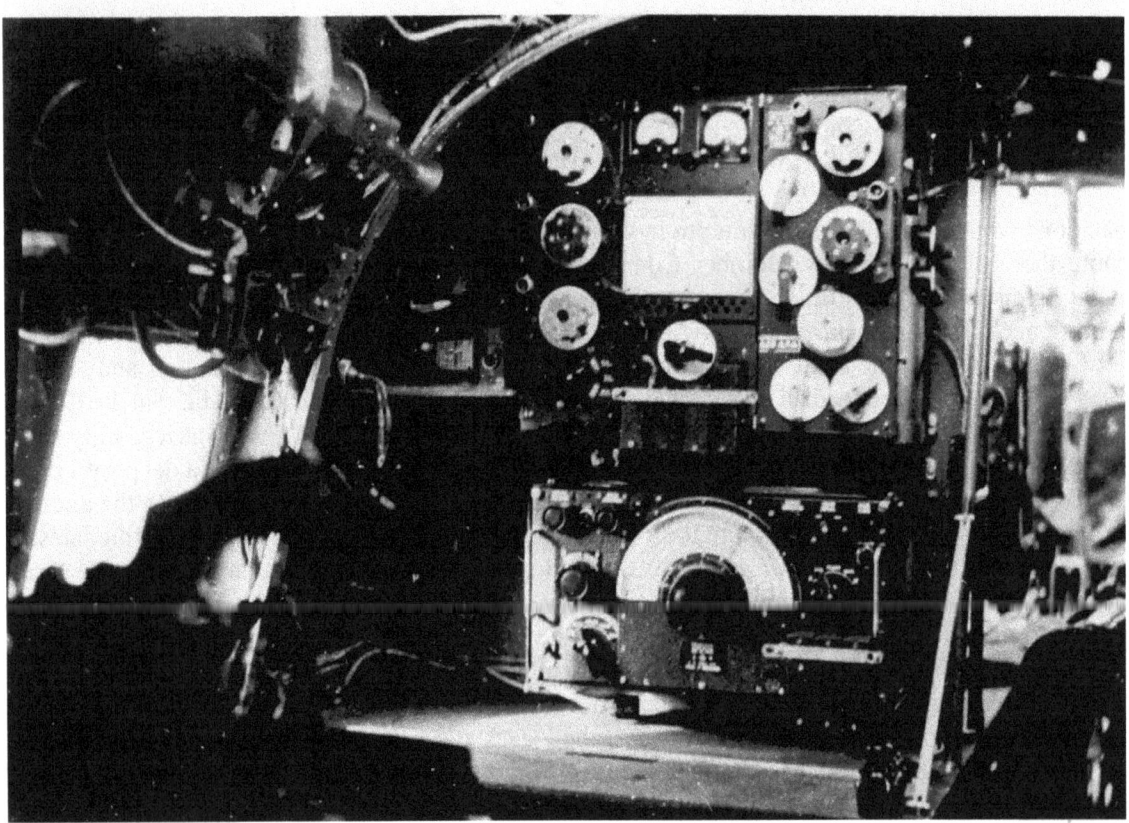

*Top: Looking forward inside the cockpit of a 61 Squadron Manchester. The second pilot's seat is stowed.
Bottom: Radio position of Manchester Mk.1 R5786 of 61 Squadron. (both L. Boot)*

Sergeant Les Syrett had already undertaken a number of operations with the experienced captains in the squadron – Flight Lieutenant Burton-Gyles, Squadron Leader Kydd and Flying Officer Nunn. The crew under training included Sergeants Jim Duncan, at that time a second wireless operator, 'Scotty' Scott, observer Ken Houghton, and rear gunner 'Eddy' Edmonds. On 21 June Kydd was due to give Syrett his final dual check out. Syrett had asked the crew if they would be willing to operate with him if he was accepted and checked out as a first pilot. They agreed and during the morning Syrett visited the flight office asking if they would accompany him on the check out. It was a hectic morning as it was already known that a maximum effort would be required from 207 and 97 Squadrons on their return to operations and that 61 Squadron was to undertake its first Manchester operation. Preparations for night flying tests, with the multitude of tasks this entailed, were in progress.

Several of the crew were missing, but Syrett buttonholed 'Eddy' Edmonds, who was living in Lincoln at the time and had already arranged to go home to lunch. He agreed that if Syrett could delay the test, then after lunch he would rustle up the crew and they would accompany him during the afternoon. It would be their first ever flight with Syrett as captain. Thus agreed, they went their separate ways to make their plans.

Unfortunately it was not to be. 'Scotty' Scott had made himself scarce earlier in the day, having been forewarned that a gas mask practice was to be held. Such practices entailed wearing the masks for an hour whilst carrying out normal duties. Scott abhorred such practices and, accordingly, was skulking in his room. He was not essential to the air test.

Kydd was perhaps unable to delay the test until later in the afternoon so at 13.00 hours his 'own' aircraft, Manchester L7310, was made ready for the check. In addition to the two pilots, only the wireless operator, Sergeant Arnott, accompanied them.

Night flying tests were already in progress at Waddington and one of Kydd's closest friends, Flying Officer 'Pappy' Paape, a New Zealander, was already in the air carrying out the necessary check of all the systems in L7322. Sergeant Bill Wetherill acted as wireless operator on that test.

The radio was switched so that the crews could talk to each other as well as to the watch tower, and Paape and his crew could both see L7310 lining up for take-off and hear the patter between Kydd and the flying control officer. Syrett was strapped in the left hand pilot's seat, Kydd was standing in the second pilot's position, and Arnott was at the wireless operator's station.

They commenced their take-off run towards the south, parallel to the Sleaford Road, on the east side of Waddington aerodrome. The take-off took the aircraft between the old First World War hangars on the south side of the airfield and the bomb dump. L7310 became airborne about in line with the hangars and the bomb dump and had achieved perhaps 150 feet above the boundary when the port engine failed. The problem was the usual, terminal one of complete disintegration, through causes not at that time established, which resulted in a piston coming right out through the side of the crankcase.

It was the single most critical moment of the whole flight. The port airscrew was immediately feathered. Paape saw a wisp of smoke and heard the clipped voice of Kydd: 'Returning to base, engine failure'. Everyone looked on with bated breath as L7310 fought a battle for precious speed and height. Syrett had ten degrees of flap on and had retracted the undercart, but as the aircraft was only five mph above stalling speed he could neither take off the flap nor lower the wheels or even change course. The aircraft was descending almost as fast as it was going forward. Within seconds, Paape and all in radio contact heard Kydd's final transmission: 'Losing height, have to go down'. In helpless frustration Paape called into the radio: 'Be careful, Charles'. It was not to be. L7310 had run out of options.

Syrett headed for a field which was guarded by a row of trees directly in his path. Unable to increase speed or climb to clear the trees, he called to the other two to brace themselves. The aircraft flew into and through the trees, stalling as it did so. It crashed heavily into the field beyond, where its forward motion was further checked by a grassy bank. The deceleration forces and impact were tremendous. They were on the east side of the Sleaford Road at Dunston Pillar. Syrett did not lose consciousness but immediately after the impact saw that his left arm was broken, as it was bent the wrong way at the elbow. He found he could move his right arm and used it to move his left arm, cradling it in his lap. Only what seemed seconds after the impact an ambulance came tearing across the field. It had apparently been on the nearby road and, seeing the crash, the crew simply turned in through the open gate. Miraculously the aircraft had not caught fire, but their situation was dire. Syrett felt very weak and detached and could hear Arnott yelling for morphia. There was no sound from Kydd.

Two soldiers managed to climb in through a hole in the nose. Syrett instructed them to get the other two out first and give them morphia. Having extracted Kydd and Arnott, the rescuers returned for Syrett. Even after forty-five years Syrett could recall his precise directions: 'My left arm's broken, something else too I think. I can't move. Undo these harness straps. No, don't take them right off. Take hold of each end and carry me out. Use it as a stretcher. Careful please I feel very fragile somehow'. Syrett was grievously injured, in deep shock, and his responses were detached and automatic and not logically worked out in any way. He recalls asking how the others were and was told they were OK, as was he. Paape had landed immediately but was, like the rest, totally unable to help.

The three were loaded in the ambulance. Syrett has no further recollections beyond this until he came round in hospital with an army officer scrutinising his identity disc. The officer asked his home address and Syrett was able to give it. Suddenly, realising why it was required, Syrett shouted at the departing officer that he would break his neck if he sent any alarming telegrams to his home.

Syrett had the feeling Kydd and Arnott were in the beds beside him, but within hours an ambulance arrived to move him from Bracebridge Heath to the larger Raunceby Hospital 40 miles away. Sadly Kydd and Arnott were beyond help and died shortly afterwards. The whole squadron was shocked and depressed by the incident. Squadron Leader Kydd, the 'A' Flight Commander, was one of the most capable and experienced pilots in 207 Squadron and had been the main force in keeping the unit together when Wing Commander Hyde was lost. Liked and greatly respected by everyone, there was never enough of his sort around.

The incident also showed how random and blind the hand of fate was: a chance arrangement, unthinkingly made, saved 'Eddy' Edmonds and others in the crew. The most inconsequential and commonplace decisions in wartime could spell the difference between life and a horrifying death. The crew mourned and grieved the loss of their comrades and at the same time felt overwhelming bitterness and frustration at the waste and pointlessness of war.

Meanwhile on 21 June despite the apparent evidence that the previous month of groundings had done little or nothing to cure the serious problems with the Vulture engines, preparations for their return to operations continued at Waddington, Coningsby and Hemswell, As a concession, 5 Group had given them only a shallow penetration attack on shipping and the docks at Boulogne on the occupied coast of France. A total of eighteen Manchesters were allocated to Boulogne, by far the largest force assembled to date, and ten Wellingtons were to raid Dunkirk. Meanwhile, the main force bombers were divided, 68 being allocated to Cologne and 56 to Dusseldorf.

It was to be 207 Squadron's twenty-forth operation with Manchesters, originally employing eight aircraft. With good reason the eighth, L7310 with Pilot Officer Syrett, was the one missing when the Manchesters lined up. By now 61 Squadron had had some Manchesters on strength for almost four months and had witnessed their problems with increasing trepidation. Nevertheless a rising sense of expectation was apparent at Hemswell as six were prepared. Wing Commander Valentine, the commanding officer, and Squadron Leader Weir, the flight commander, had made themselves available.

Boulogne, the largest yet – 21 June 1941:

Serial	Code	Squadron	Captain
L7387	QR-	61	Wg Cdr G. E. Valentine
L7388	QR-	61	Sqn Ldr T. C. Weir
L7389	QR-	61	Fg Off. M. Parry
L7307	QR-	61	Fg Off. G. Hall
L7304	QR-	61	Fg Off. K. G. Webb
L7315	QR-	61	Flt Lt J. L. Riley
L7308	OF-	97	Sqn Ldr R. D. Stubbs
L7325	OF-	97	Flt Lt J. S. Sherman
L7324	OF-	97	Flt Lt D. J. French
L7382	OF-	97	Fg Off. F. E. Eustace

L7383	OF-	97	Plt Off. H. S. Blakeman
L7316	EM-U	207	Fg Off. D. A. A. Romans
L7322	EM-B	207	Fg Off. A. M. Paape
L7378	EM-A	207	Fg Off. J. L. Nunn
L7311	EM-F	207	Fg Off. W. M. R. Smith
L7321	EM-D	207	Fg Off. W. J. Lewis
L7312	EM-L	207	Flt Lt R. W. Reynolds
L7314	EM-Y	207	Fg Off. J. D. G. Withers

On this occasion each 61 Squadron aircraft was limited to a 7,500-lb load of 500-lb GP bombs. In keeping with their excitement, Flying Officer Parry had his port rev counter go unserviceable on starting engines, but elected to keep quiet about it and press on regardless.

207 Squadron's Manchesters were loaded with twelve 500-lb GP bombs and headed individually towards their target. The route was south past the west side of London before turning south-eastwards to Boulogne. The operation began to go amiss from an early stage. Flying Officer Withers was outward bound on track at around 6,000 feet. German intruders were active over Lincolnshire and one, which was being tracked by the Lincolnshire Air Observer Corps, by chance followed a course overlapping that of L7314.

10 Group Fighter Command had scrambled a number of night fighters, including airborne interception radar equipped Bristol Beaufighters from 25 Squadron at Wittering, to counter the threat posed by the German intruders. The controller at 10 Group was homing one of these aircraft along the presumed track of the intruder and when the two tracks crossed the Beaufighter was mistakenly homed onto the track of L7314.

It appeared that in addition to this mischance another was to contribute to the events of the next few minutes. 5 Group's operations plan for that night, giving times and routes etc. had gone via Bomber Command to Fighter Command, arriving at 10 Group Headquarters just at the time of the change of controllers. The new controller had received the operations plan, but it had become covered by other papers on his desk and the details within it had not therefore been extracted and placed on the operations board. Consequently he had no information before him to indicate the presence of friendly aircraft at the vital location.

Accordingly, the controller homed the fighter onto the 'hostile' until, in the darkness, the pilot was able to obtain a visual on the aircraft ahead. Squadron personnel believe that what happened next was that the Beaufighter pilot identified the aircraft as an RAF bomber and relayed this to the controller, who was unwilling to accept this identification. Cautiously the Beaufighter moved closer, recognising roundel markings and RAF squadron codes in pale letters on the fuselage. The bomber crew had also seen the attacker for they fired off the correct colours of the day. This was passed to the ground station, where the controller still insisted the aircraft to be hostile and instructed the pilot to complete the interception and shoot the aircraft down.

Although in two minds, the Beaufighter pilot dropped back before finally closing in again beneath the Manchester, still flying slowly and straight and level, and giving it a burst with the fixed forward cannon and machine guns. Mr L A Pack, then a farmer's boy from Crow Hill Farm, Irthlingborough, a small settlement east of Northampton, witnessed the combat from his parents' bedroom window and reports: 'The most northerly site at which debris, shards of perspex, from the Manchester were discovered was the next day in fields at Crow Hill Farm. Later an airman's glove and perspex dome were found in the same field. These perhaps hint at damage in the cockpit area blowing out a navigator's glove and the observation dome? Further unidentified debris was picked up in the playground of College Street School in Irthlingborough itself. A second burst of fire maybe from a further attack was seen by observers on the ground as Withers overflew Chester House on the A45 road north of Irchester, leading to the Manchester catching fire. Withers had no time to jettison bombs or fuel and none of the crew escaped by parachute. The Captain then accomplished an exemplary belly landing in a field at Lovett's Farm south-east of Wollaston at about 01.55 hours. Several crew members began scrambling from the burning wreck but unfortunately part of the bomb load exploded and no-one survived. The Beaufighter crew, Pilot Officers Smith and Lusty, were later Court Marshalled.

Next day only traces of five separate bodies and the identity disc of Sergeant James, the second pilot, could be found in the burnt out wreckage. It was a tragic mistake which should never have happened and for which safeguards were in operation, yet under the stress of war such human errors were likely. Flying Officer Withers and crew had had only about 20 minutes of operational flying experience on their second tour before being so brutally and mistakenly cut down.

Further on down the track, 207 Squadron's contribution was dogged by other unforced errors. As Flying Officer Mike Smith in L7311 approached the south coast, his front gunner inadvertently pulled his parachute ripcord. The silk spilled out all over the bomb aimer's station and billowed back into the pilot's cockpit in the many draughts streaming into the aircraft. The lower escape hatch was blocked by silk and rigging and there was the chance of the controls becoming fouled and jammed by the wayward cords and material. Wisely, Smith aborted the operation and returned to Waddington with the bomb load intact.

Over the target there was some interference from flak and searchlights but the remaining 207, 97 and 61 Squadron aircraft carried out the planned attack. On return, Flying Officer Romans diverted to Biggin Hill where the starboard engine suddenly caught fire as he was landing. The fire was fortunately extinguished, whether by Graviner or the station fire service is not recorded, before any serious damage was done to the aircraft or crew. On examination next morning the fire was found to be caused by the 'banjo' fitting for the petrol gauge on the engine coming loose with the result that petrol dripped onto the hot exhaust pipes.

Flight Lieutenant J. S. Sherwood (later more famous for his miraculous survival after being shot down in Lancaster L7573 OF-K in the daylight raid on Augsburg on 17 April 1942) had been allocated L7325 OF-C of 97 Squadron. His second pilot was Sergeant Bob Fletcher. Not named in the unit ORB for the sortie was the 5 Group Engineering Officer, Squadron Leader John W. Bayley, who chose to accompany this crew by way of gaining first hand experience of Vulture performance with these latest modifications.

John Bayley died some years ago but, amazingly, a written record of his recollections of that same operation has been preserved by his family. He was to obtain operating experience in more ways than one. He says:

We took off from Coningsby at 22.59 hours and headed south towards Boulogne. By the time we arrived at the south coast of England we had only reached 12,000 feet and had to circle back over England to gain an extra 4,000 feet to reach our bombing height of 16,000 feet.

(Unlike other aircraft, L7325's crew seem to have had no difficulty identifying their target and the Manchester turned for home – author).

Somewhere north of the Thames a Defiant night fighter (from Wittering) picked us up and shadowed us, tucked in tight beneath us. The pilot reported to his controller that he had intercepted a twin-engined bomber and suspected it was a Heinkel III because he could see four exhaust flames. It seems Fighter Command had not been told that the Manchesters were back on operations, however the pilot was told not to attack but to continue shadowing.

As we approached Coningsby the Captain lowered the nose to make his landing approach, a change in flying attitude that the Defiant pilot interpreted as the commencement of a bombing run by an intruder. The Defiant gunner accordingly raked the entire length of the fuselage of our aircraft with gunfire. At the time I was sitting on the edge of the Navigator's table immediately behind the pilot and was startled to see bright sparks shooting up between my legs and the pilot's back. In my ignorance I thought that one of the wireless sets below the table had short-circuited or something.

The pilot realised that it was gunfire and, not being able to see the Defiant below us, and assuming it was AA fire from the ground, ordered the recognition signal for the day to be fired. This was a two coloured Very flare, the colours of which were changed throughout the 24 hour period.

The attack took place at 03.15 hours. Unfortunately it later transpired that the colours of the day had changed at 03.00 hours and we fired those appropriate for the earlier time. Seeing the incorrect signal the Defiant crew were even more convinced we were about to attack Coningsby and opened fire, seriously damaging both of our engines. Fortunately the hydraulic pressure in the aircraft systems remained sufficiently high for us to make a direct approach to the airfield and a very shaky but safe landing.

The second pilot, Sergeant Bob Fletcher, goes on to report:

It was a wise precaution because the damage incurred immediately began to manifest itself. One engine failed as we approached the end of the landing run and clouds of steam were rising from the pierced coolant system of the other Vulture. Fluid was squirting from nicks in the hydraulic lines. In the circumstances we were very fortunate to have reached Coningsby at all on two failing engines and to have lowered the flaps and undercart with the remainder of the hydraulic pressure still in the system. We had no alternative but to stop on the flare path and shut down the remaining engine, whose temperature had rapidly risen above the danger level. A tractor came to tow us back to dispersal. Next day we counted over 200 holes in the aircraft.

On 24 June 1941 a number of photographs were taken of L7325 OF-C in the course of its repair at Coningsby. These have never seen the light of day until now, having been discovered by John Bayley's family in his effects following his death.

The Defiant crew were also Court Marshalled and Sherwood and his crew were called to Wittering to give evidence. It was here that they learnt the night fighter crew's side of the story. It had been a clear night over the United Kingdom and the patrolling aircraft had been warned that German intruders had already dropped bombs in several localities. The crew had detected a large aircraft and managed to infiltrate themselves directly beneath it without being seen. Whilst doing this they had called up their ground controller to enquire if any friendly aircraft were in the vicinity. On receiving a negative, they immediately opened fire, riddling the centre section of L7325. On seeing the colours of the day fired they broke off the attack and rechecked with the controller who belatedly recognised the aircraft as friendly. The Defiant's crew got off with a severe reprimand as it was considered that the main fault lay with the ground controller.

The remaining aircraft returned to Waddington, Coningsby, and Hemswell landing between 0420 and 05.35 hours. When the events of the last 24 hours filtered back, a mood of deep gloom and depression, mixed with intense frustration and anger settled on the squadrons. They had reached perhaps the lowest ebb in the whole difficult period over which they operated the Manchester. At least 61 Squadron crews had completed their first operation without any of the incidents which had marred the return of the two senior squadrons.

On the night of 23/24 June seven aircraft were detailed from 207 Squadron taking off between 23.28 and 23.50 hours, and five from 61 Squadron taking off between 23.14 and 23.25 hours for operations to Dusseldorf. 'B' Flight of 61 Squadron also dispatched five Handley Page Hampdens.

Dusseldorf – 23/24 June 1941:

Serial	Code	Squadron	Captain
L7387	QR-*	61	Wg Cdr G. E. Valentine
L7388	QR-*	61	Sqn Ldr T. C. Weir
L7389	QR-*	61	Fg Off. M. Parry
L7304	QR-*	61	Fg Off. K. G. Webb
L7315	QR-*	61	Flt Lt J. L. Riley
L7311	EM-F	207	Fg Off. W. M. R. Smith
L7378	EM-A	207	Fg Off. J. L. Nunn
L7381	EM-R	207	Fg Off. W. G. Gardiner
L7322	EM-B	207	Plt Off. W. S. Herring
L7380	EM-W	207	Plt Off. A. W. Hills
L7319	EM-X	207	Fg Off. T. C. Murray

* Individual codes unknown - not recorded in the ORB.

Port and Starboard rear quarter views of Manchester L7325 OF-C of 97 Squadron at Coningsby on 24 June 1941 following the 'friendly fire' engagement with a Defiant. Straps hanging down beneath both inner wings were to hold the fuel tanks in place. The FN7A mid-upper turret is unarmed and has no fairing. The white of the national colours has been darkened. Some skin tears are chalk ringed. (Bayley family)

Superb and earliest known photograph of a 61 Squadron Manchester Mk.1 flying from Hemswell. Partly obscured serial of QR-H could signify a pre-production aircraft, L7281, L7284 or L7294. Paint mismatch on starboard wing might imply L7284 which suffered wing damage with 207 Squadron on 24 February 1941. Note absence of FN7A turret fairing and three pale patches, one ahead of starboard tailplane root and two inboard of each wing roundel. Photograph likely taken during intensive engine trials in July 1941. It went to Avro SAS on 14 July 1941. (via John Stretton and Andy Thomas)

Nick to coolant pipe in port Vulture of L7325, 24 June 1941. (Bayley family)

This night the usual severe lack of power for take-off was exaggerated even more by the high summer temperatures. Fortunately, all became airborne safely. These high temperatures led to overheating, power and performance losses and consequently the Manchesters were barely able to climb.

As a result of the overheating and the recent continued engine failures the pilots were naturally unwilling to 'cane' the engines for fear of further seizures. They avoided using full boost and 3,200 revs in the hope of nursing their aircraft to a height safe enough to permit a return to base from occupied Europe in the event of an engine failure. The deaths of the crews lost in the preceding months were too vivid and real to permit any other course.

Despite his best endeavours, Flying Officer Mike Smith was unable to lift L7311 above 7,000 feet even though he had been airborne for ninety minutes. It would be suicidal to attack Dusseldorf from such a height and the chances of getting far if an overheated engine did finally fail were remote. Reluctantly, but wisely, he unloaded his six 1,000-lb GPs and 180 4-lb incendiaries on the airfield at Flushing. Three other 207 Squadron Manchesters encountered the same problem to a serious extent. In L7319 Flying Officer Thos Murray defied instructions and operated his Vultures at high revs and with low boost having ascertained with experience that the engine ran more smoothly set up this way. He nursed his aircraft across the North Sea but after being airborne for more than an hour had still reached only 7,000 to 8,000 feet with the coolant and oil temperatures in both Vultures off the clock in the red! On crossing the enemy held coast of Holland he sought out the aerodrome at Haamstede where he released a 1,000-lb GP to lighten the load on the straining motors. Coolant and oil temperatures eased and Murray was gradually able to con L7319 up to a safer height for the penetration into Germany where the remaining bombs were dropped in the target area. Flying Officer Herring, having used up some fuel, finally reached 10,000 feet by the time he was in the target area.

Reports from only one 61 Squadron aircraft are available but, as with the initial operation, all returned safely. Flight Lieutenant Riley was unable to locate either the primary or any last resort target and brought his bombs

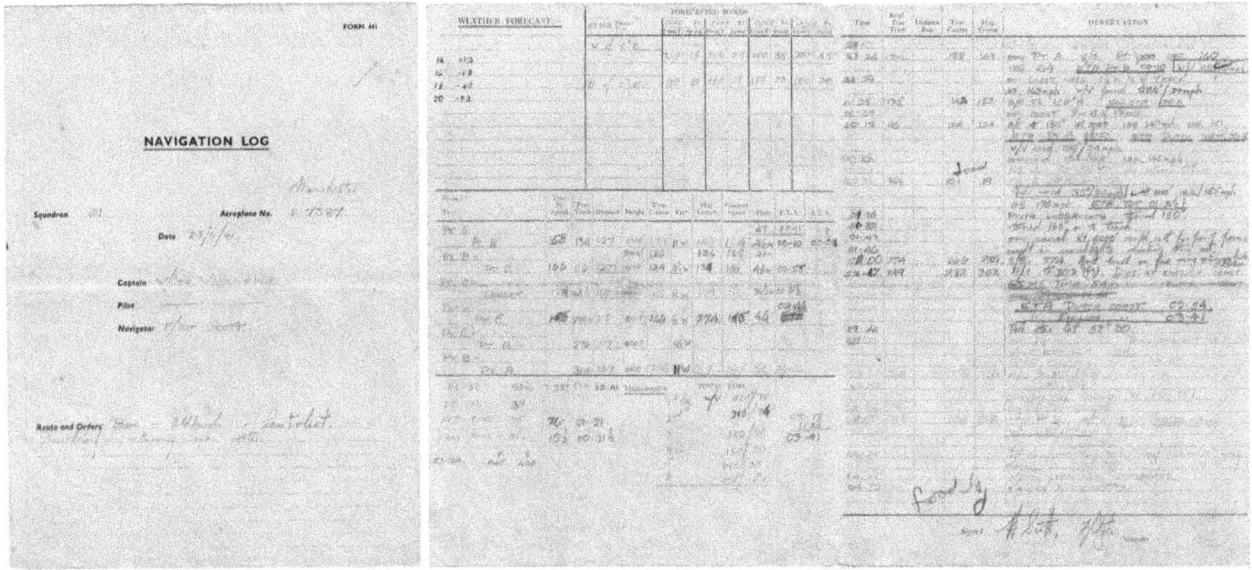

The Navigation Log (Form 441) reproduced here was completed by Flight Sergeant H. Scott, during an Operation which routed Hemswell - Aldburgh - Santollet - Dusseldorf, returning same route in L7387, on the night of 23/24 June 1941. The aircraft captain was Wing Commander G. E. Valentine, the 61 Squadron Commanding Officer. Although there is no mention of engine trouble on this occasion, there was certainly drama. At 01.43 hours the log reveals: 'Height 4,000 feet, could not pin-point position, caught in searchlights, shooting them out' and at 02.00 hours. it indicates 'S/C [set course] 274. Front turret on fire, using extinguishers'. The ticks and 'good log' comments are the work of Flight Lieutenant A. B. Harrison, the 61 Squadron navigation leader, confirming that Bomber Command was doing its best, with methods then available, to achieve quality control on its operational flying. Ten weeks later both Wing Commander Valentine and Flight Lieutenant Harrison were lost with all on board L7388 when shot down over Berlin on the night of 2/3 September. The height profile for this entire operation - Hemswell-Dusseldorf and return - noted in column five of the centre page, ranged between 4,000 and 8,000 feet. This, juxtaposed to such severe engine problems, requires no further explanation. (Author's collection)

back to Hemswell. Those reaching Dusseldorf returned to base between 03.50 and 05.18 hours. 207 and 97 Squadrons returned to Dusseldorf again the next night.

On the 26th, 207 and 97 Squadrons, joined by 61 Squadron on its third operation, were off again, this time to Kiel, along with fifty-one aircraft to Cologne, and forty-four to Dusseldorf. Again, eighteen aircraft were involved. The eighth aircraft assigned to the operation from 207 Squadron burst a tail wheel tyre taxiing for take-off and consequently was left behind when the remaining group departed in a bunch between 23.10 and 23.25 hours.

German night fighters had become very active in the approaches to the German coastline at this time, possibly aided by ground radar tracking. 61 Squadron sustained its first operational casualty when L7304, piloted by Flying Officer Webb, crashed near the North Sea coast at Brunsbuttel at a locality given in German records as Marne/Holstein (Adolf Hitler Koeg) in Germany. They were a victim of Oberleutnant Walter Fenske of 3/NJG1, being brought down at 01.31 hours. There were no survivors.

About an hour after take-off, Coningsby received a desperate message from the wireless operator of Flying Officer Frankie Eustace's L7374, to the effect that the rear gunner, Sergeant McLaren had been killed by enemy fire. No further transmissions were received and it is known that the aircraft later crashed on the coast at Süderkoog in the German Frisian Isles with the loss of the seven man crew. One body was found washed up at nearby Westerhever. Frankie's aircraft was claimed at 01.46 hours also by Oberleutnant Walter Fenske of 3/NJG1 based at Schleswig

Kiel – 26 June 1941:

Serial	Code	Squadron	Captain
L7387	QR-*	61	Wg Cdr G. E. Valentine
L7388	QR-*	61	Sqn Ldr T. C. Weir
L7389	QR-*	61	Fg Off. G. Hall
L7304	QR-*	61	Fg Off. K. G. Webb
L7315	QR-*	61	Flt Lt J. A. Stewart
L7423	OF-*	97	Sqn Ldr R. D. Stubbs
L7424	OF-*	97	Flt Lt D. J. French
L7375	OF-*	97	Fg Off. J. A. Little
L7374	OF-*	97	Fg Off. F. E. Eustace
L7383	OF-*	97	Plt Off. H. S. Blakeman
L7382	OF-*	97	FS D. H. Rowlands
L7378	EM-A	207	Fg Off. J. L. Nunn
L7381	EM-R	207	Fg Off. W. G. Gardiner
L7319	EM-X	207	Fg Off. T. C. Murray
L7317	EM-C	207	Flt Lt G. R. Taylor

* Individual codes unknown - not recorded in the ORB.

An anxious Coningsby awaited the return of the Manchesters and when it became undeniable that Frankie Eustace was the latest victim, many 5 Group aircrews were deeply saddened. Frankie was well known to many in 5 Group, who recalled the night he was over the North Sea returning from Ops in a Hampden when the windscreen suddenly shattered and flew back into his face following a bird strike. Having no goggles, he flew for the remainder of the flight with the wind blasting straight into his face. His eyes looked like two raw hamburgers for a week after the incident. A great character, New Zealander Frankie was engaged to be married. Frankie's beautiful golden Cocker spaniel, 'Jill', was given to his grieving fiancé and his friends tried desperately to put this latest loss behind them.

Sergeant Rowlands was attacked by a Bf110 night fighter approaching the enemy coast approximately thirty miles west of Tonning. The aircraft was hit in several places and one crew member, Sergeant Harvey, received a slight head wound. By excellent co-ordination and effective fire control the crew were able to damage the attacker. Smoke was seen issuing from the enemy fighter which broke off the attack. L7382 then carried on and successfully bombed Kiel. At its attacking height of 14,000 to 15,000 feet, Flying Officer Little's aircraft, L7375, was heavily engaged by flak. The aircraft was hit in many places but sustained no serious damage and returned to base.

Aircraft had no difficulty locating the target and the reports indicate the attacking aircraft reached heights ranging between 13,000 to 16,000 feet. None of the reports indicate any problem with climbing, perhaps because the air temperature had decreased. On the 26th, the attack was wide of the mark as the authorities reported slight damage and no casualties.

Despite the occasional faltering morale arising from losses such as Flying Officer Eustace, spirits were generally high and it was necessary to curb the exuberance of individual crew members, who from time to time smuggled on board large quantities of house bricks or empty beer bottles. The bricks were reputed to be very effective when they fell in built-up areas, whilst the tumbling bottles produced a scream or wail like a siren as they fell. Despite the personal interest this gave to individual crew members themselves, efforts had to be made to moderate the practice because the Manchesters were already so overloaded on take-off.

Following this operation, on 28 June, 207 and 97 Squadrons received orders to commence daylight formation practice, including both formation bombing and gunnery practice. The objective of the training was to prepare them for participation in a major daylight operation against the *Gneisenau* in Brest and the *Scharnhorst* in La Pallice. In the event the attack took place on 24 July 1941 involving RAF Boeing (Flying) Fortresses, Hampdens, Wellingtons and Halifaxes. Although the *Gneisenau* was not damaged, the *Scharnhorst* was hit by five AP bombs, three of which went straight through the ship. It was incapacitated for four months.

Finally, on 29/30 June, 207 Squadron took part in its last operation for this period. Eight aircraft were detailed for a raid on Hamburg, joining a diversionary force which totalled twenty-eight aircraft. The main raid went to Bremen, with 106 aircraft. In the event, only six Manchesters took off since one burst a tail wheel tyre taxiing out, the third time such a problem had occurred, whilst another developed electrical trouble which could not be cured in time for the aircraft to participate. It was to be another eventful operation for the squadron, although, as with so many times before, the Germans had no part to play in the difficulties experienced. Two aircraft carried 4,000 lb HC bombs whilst the remainder carried five 1,000-lb GPs. They took off between 23.00 and 23.26 hours.

Hamburg – 29/30 June 1941:

Serial	Code	Squadron	Captain
L7319	EM-X	207	Flt Lt T. C. Murray
L7316	EM-U	207	Plt Off. A. W. Hills
L7321	EM-D	207	Fg Off. W. J. Lewis
L7381	EM-R	207	Fg Off. W. G. Gardiner
L7322	EM-B	207	Flt Lt R. W. Reynolds
L7373	EM-T	207	Plt Off. H. G. Keartland

Of the six aircraft despatched, one, L7316 EM-U, flown by Pilot Officer Bill Hills, with Pilot Officer Bowes-Cavanagh (second pilot), Sergeants Glenn (observer), Smith (first wireless operator), van Puyenbroek (front gunner) and Spindler (rear gunner), was gaining height painfully slowly as usual as they crossed the North Sea en route to the target. By the time they had reached a position 40 miles north of Terschelling they had still only reached 5,000 feet.

Suddenly, Bowes-Cavanagh gestured with his hand towards the starboard engine and called Hills on the intercom: 'Do you see what I see?' Craning his neck and looking across the second pilot, Hills saw that the starboard engine was on fire. The flames were already shooting back over the engine nacelle and upper surface of the mainplane.

The nervous tension rose to fever pitch; things had to, and did, happen quickly. 'Jettison bombs' called Hills and the navigator, Glenn, rushed forward to the bomb aiming position in the nose to rid them of the load, which would otherwise rapidly bring them down to ditch in the sea on the one remaining engine. Before further action was initiated though, the most immediate problem was the fire.

Hills called: 'Feather starboard propeller', at the same time reaching out to cover the port propeller feathering switch to prevent it being inadvertently pressed in the dimly lit cockpit. His action was both seen and misinterpreted by an agitated Bowes-Cavanagh, who immediately reached across and knocked Hills' hand away, calling: 'Not that one'. Bowes-Cavanagh then feathered the starboard propeller, stopped the engine, and pressed the fire extinguisher. The propeller feathered and began to windmill slowly and at about the same time they felt the pronounced lift as the bombs fell away safe from the open bays.

'Parachutes' shouted Bowes-Cavanagh on the intercom, beginning to leave his seat. Obviously he was convinced that the fire was not going to be extinguished and that perhaps only seconds remained before the wing spar burnt through.

'No, you fool' called Hills, 'it's a bloody long swim from here'. Bowes-Cavanagh resumed his seat, Glenn closed the bomb doors and both pilots continued to watch the burning engine. In accordance with standing orders related to action in the event of engine failure, Charles 'Smudger' Smith, the wireless operator, hurried to send the specially abbreviated code which had been worked out so that Group could be informed of the reason for an aircraft going down. The aircraft began to lose height but within a short period they were relieved to see the fire first die down and then go out altogether. Hills immediately began a gentle turn to port into the live engine and requested a course for the nearest point on the English coast.

Whilst Glenn worked out the best course Hills trimmed the aircraft to conserve every precious foot of altitude. Despite his best efforts the aircraft continued to lose height. The urgency of the initial emergency was over, but the tension remained high and the crew sat with bated breath as the Manchester descended almost imperceptibly towards the English coast. After many minutes flying, a comparison of height and distance travelled made it clear that, provided the port engine maintained power, there was a chance that the coast would be reached before they ran out of airspace.

The Manchester could only make 120 knots on one engine and was now flying into a headwind. It was a long and tense flight, the only conversation being the regular checking of height loss versus distance remaining. Eventually the British coast appeared ahead, but another difficult decision now faced Hills. The aircraft was continuing to lose height despite everything he did to trim the aircraft and use the best engine settings. They were already below 2,000 feet and could not be sure they would reach base. Hills knew that 1,000 feet, which they would soon be down to, was a crucial height at which they must either be within certain contact with an airfield otherwise he would have to bale the crew out. If he waited until they were lower there was a strong chance they would not all escape from the aircraft in time.

Hills informed the crew that he was going to restart the starboard engine in the hope of gaining more altitude. This was risky: normally an engine which had been on fire would never be restarted because the chances of the

An anonymous Manchester of 207 Squadron awaits its bomb load at a grass dispersal. (Unknown provenance, via J. Simpson)

fire flaring up again were so high. Hills judged that if the crew were all ready to jump there was no significant additional risk, for at their present sink-rate they would all be in their parachutes within a few minutes anyway.

Having prepared the crew, the restart procedure was initiated. To their mingled surprise and relief the engine restarted and did not catch fire. Advancing the starboard throttle up to that of the port engine, Hills was then able to climb for the first time since the fire. Keeping a careful eye on the starboard Vulture, they climbed to a safe height, at which point he then throttled back. Immediately, and for no apparent reason, the starboard engine stopped and subsequently resisted all attempts to restart it a second time. Nevertheless, the engine had done what was required of it and they now had precious altitude in hand. Hills feathered the dead starboard engine, and having called Waddington to tell them he was coming in on one, carried out a safe landing back at base. In respect of this incident the squadron Operational Record Book notes: 'Left, inner, starboard engine manifold was found to have a large hole through which flames played on the engine cowling'.

A second aircraft, L7322 EM-B, captained by Flight Lieutenant Reynolds, reached the target area where the crew found, as so often happened in the Manchester, that a hydraulic leak had developed which prevented the bomb doors opening. Despite their best efforts they were unable to open the doors manually and they reluctantly and disconsolately returned to Waddington with all of the bombs still on board.

The remaining four aircraft eventually fought their way up to altitudes between 14,000 to 16,000 feet to drop their bombs on the target area. They returned to Waddington and landed between 04.30 and 05.30 hours on 30 June. The part played by these four cannot be ascertained but Hamburg reports chronicle much damage on this small raid, with eight killed and 115 injured. A large fire destroyed a big stockpile of rice in a food store. Three bombers were shot down by night fighters over the town, the crash of one of these possibly caused the fire in the rice store.

On 30 June the Manchesters were grounded yet again. They had been operational for only eight days since the previous 4½ weeks grounding. This time they were off operations for five weeks but the final serious problem with the filter was cured to the extent that was possible. Problems with the Vulture were so varied and multifaceted that they overlapped in time. Whilst the cooling problems had finally begun to be solved, a new and equally serious defect had started to make its presence felt.

First of all the engine from Squadron Leader Kydd's aircraft was inspected and the failure which led to this crash found to be a 'red herring' in the search for the continued Vulture problems, although a no less fatal one. A loose tappet nut had led to a valve blockage and then in turn induced a complete engine failure. In direct line with the spate of most recent accidents, the port engine of L7318 of 207 Squadron, which failed during ground running on 2 June 1941, had been received and inspected by the Defect Investigation Department of Rolls-Royce at Derby. Initial inspection suggested that the two short big-end bolts had sheared.

On 29 June L7315 of 61 Squadron had an uncontrollable engine fire causing the crew to bale out near Grantham. The aircraft crashed and was written off, killing the pilot, Pilot Officer C. G. Colborne. This fire was also tied to the same con-rod bolts failing. Next, L7389 QR-J of 61 Squadron had an engine fire in the air and force-landed in a wheat field near Fowlmere. There were no casualties on this occasion. This engine failure too was traced to a similar con-rod bolt failure.

Following such bolt failures the unrestrained con-rods would then flail around, break loose and smash through the crankcase, sometimes almost severing the engine in two. Even worse, such catastrophic damage frequently destroyed the propeller feathering line, with the result that the dead engine's propeller could not be feathered. The drag from the windmilling blades, plus the loss of 50% of the total engine power, was too much and the remaining engine could not keep the aircraft airborne. Following the 30 June grounding it was decided that four aircraft each from 61, 97 and 207 Squadrons were to carry out intensive flying to investigate the problem.

Manchester L7427 of 97 Squadron force-landed on or before 3 July 1941. No-one was injured but con-rod bolt failure was to blame. By the 6th the number of aircraft had been reduced to one per unit to fly until 240 hours had been achieved on all engines.

During June, the Defect Investigation Department of Rolls-Royce had become aware that the cause of the bolt failures was uneven and, in some cases, excessive tightening of the bolts. Lovesay, the Chief Development Engineer, had the bolt loads at maximum rpm recalculated, which showed them to be higher than was thought.

Meanwhile, the engines of every Manchester had to be removed once again and returned to Rolls-Royce, who were to issue replacement engines with new con-rod bolts which were now to be tightened to a lower and carefully monitored value to ensure the precise degree of stretch required to give adequate bolt tension.

A second contributory factor to bolt failures was considered to be a conflict between the saw-tooth location in the master con-rod and cap, and the fitting diameter of the bolts. The powerful control of the saw-teeth tended to

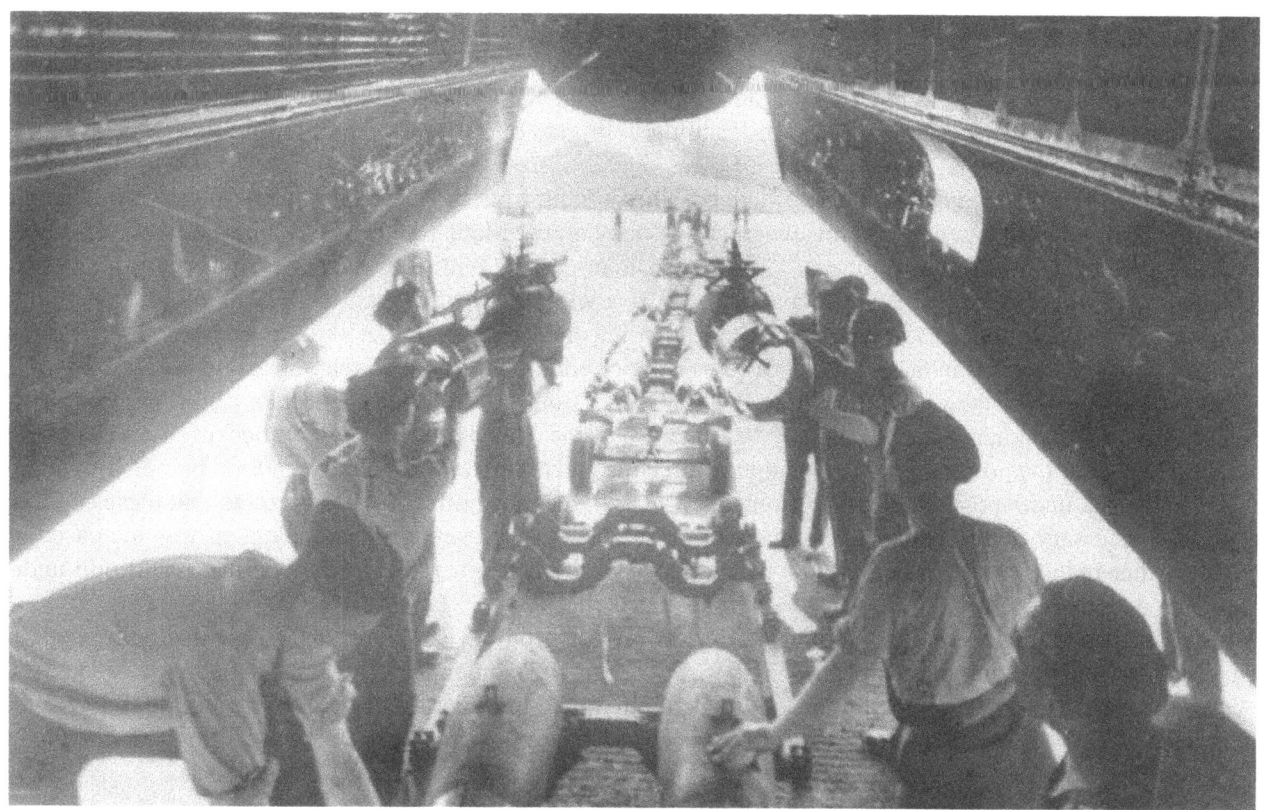
Unusual shot from inside the bomb bay during bombing-up. (P. Beauchamp)

dog-leg the connecting rod bolts, affecting their tension. Rolls-Royce rectified this as Modification No.44 and it was to be the modification following which the engines finally became reliable.

A contributory factor to the excessive strain on the single bearing imposed by the four con-rods was the high loading at 3,200 rpm. Accordingly, as part of Mod. No.44 and to protect the short con-rod bolts, the maximum rpm was reduced to 2,850, giving the suggestion of de-rating. At the same time, however, the boost pressure was increased to 9 lb, effectively restoring take-off power, so the de-rating referred only to rpm and not to power. The combination of modified tightening techniques, relieved fitting diameters and reduced rpm produced a reliable operation at overhaul lives initially of 120 hours, subsequently rising to 180 hours. An added bonus to this change was that the engine actually operated better at this rating and gave a little more power and shorter take-off run.

During June, whilst Rolls-Royce strove so doggedly to track down the range of serious defects still popping up in the Vulture, Avro had opportunity to consolidate their efforts. By the 10th all FN7A mid-upper turrets had been shorn from service aircraft, whilst consideration was given to overcoming the rotation/vibration interaction of the turret and centre fin. By the 27th all the options had been evaluated. Both Bomber Command and Avro had recognised that the centre fin could not be strengthened and the only option was to bring in the final tail modification, the deletion of the three fins and their replacement with two new 'Lancaster' end-plate fins and rudders of larger area. This was Avro Mod No.390. The only drawback was that this modification would not be available until mid-July at the earliest. It was agreed to bring this modification in at the earliest moment on the production line and also provide additional sets to retrofit existing aircraft as and when possible.

Accordingly, permission was given to refit the FN7A, but to restrict its arc of traverse. The principle reason for re-introducing the FN7A was that it offered the only beam defence for the aircraft. Ground crews and armourers set-to once again. Notwithstanding this instruction, some Manchesters which had never had this item fitted continued without it (eg. L7300), others which had been temporarily stripped had the item reinstated and yet others, like L7309 which had not previously carried the turret, now had it installed. Aircrew preference and pressure of other modifications and normal routine maintenance seem to have influenced the situation.

At the 27th Manchester production meeting on 9 June 1941, the number of aircraft completed and the serious state of the engine delivery and modification programme were stressed. By the next meeting, on 14 June, Manchesters L7427 to L7430 had been completed, whilst R5772 to R5774 were being erected. The firm were thirty-two engines short for new construction and the state of flux in respect of the engine modification was causing further disruption. On the 18th A M Linnell reported that Rolls-Royce were ninety-six Vultures behind the initially projected schedule but some good news was that the company had promised eighteen modified engines per week for the next three weeks. The running to ground of the con-rod bolt failure further delayed this programme.

In the meantime, during late May and June and possibly arising from the increasing threat of the German night fighter force, Bomber Command was reviewing crew policy on the Manchester. By 27 June a decision had been made to raise the complement by one to make seven man crews. Within days the policy was promulgated, requiring every turret to be permanently manned, whilst a wireless operator had to be continuously on watch. There were to be two pilots, an observer to do the navigating and bomb aiming, a wireless operator/gunner in the radio position and a second in the front gun turret. Two air gunners were to man the dorsal and rear turrets.

This was in line with the planned refitting of the FN7A 'Botha' turret, but conceivably more lay behind it. Possibly Bomber Command was still hoping to make use of the Manchester in daylight because Avro had been asked to reconsider the possibility of designing a retractable and hand-held gun mounting for a pair of Brownings in the vacant mid-under position. In an apparent conflict with the new policy it was suggested that these could be manned as necessary by the first wireless operator/air gunner. In the event crew complement was increased by one, to further reduce the already marginal performance of the beleaguered aircraft. The hand-held mid-under assembly never materialised, which was probably just as well.

Engines incorporating Mod. No.44 were received at Waddington on 12/13 July 1941, one each day, for 207 Squadron's intensive flying Manchester, L7419. 97 Squadron contributed L7425 and 61 Squadron L7388.

At the same time as the aircraft was grounded, Avro attempted to effect a further modification to improve the persistent problem with oil cooling in the Vulture. The modification was to the oil cooler ducting and involved a

Night fighter's eye view of the elegant proportions of the Allies' largest twin-engined bomber. It is not possible to distinguish the Mk.1 and Mk.1A from this aspect. (J. Simpson)

technique for improving airflow through the system. This entailed placing a lip in front of the exit duct on the upper surface of the wing, outboard of the engine. The purpose of the lip was to increase the air flow through the system and increase cooling.

From 17 July onwards, three crews in each of the three squadrons were taken off operations for a week to take turns to fly five hours each day in their designated aircraft, each trip included a climb to 17,000 feet at +6 boost and 2,850 rpm. In the meantime, again anticipating success, from the 19th onwards the installation of new engines in all squadron Manchesters commenced.

By the 19th Rolls-Royce had delivered sixteen Vultures to Waddington, eleven incorporating both LA4 bearings and a Mod. No.44 con-rod assembly. Sixteen were delivered to Coningsby by the 26th, eighteen more for 207 Squadron at Waddington by 2 August, together with twelve for 25 Operational Training Unit at Finningley. Finally, four were delivered to Hemswell for the Manchester Flight of 61 Squadron by 9 August. To permit this flow rate the squadrons had to return Vultures from their aircraft at a rate of four a day from 16 July.

On 28 July the engines of L7419, having flown 120½ hours in nine days, were removed and dispatched to Rolls-Royce for dismantling and investigation. The engines of the 97 Squadron aircraft were similarly sent away. After feverish stripping and inspection they were reassembled and the fleet of Manchester aircraft in 5 Group were declared fit for operations once more.

Nobody could have known it at the time, but Mod. No.44 was to prove the final key to the Vulture becoming a reasonably reliable engine. Further problems were to occur, especially a spate of propeller feathering failures, but these were not Rolls-Royce problems. In respect of the Avro cooling lip modification, the effect was by no means as satisfactory, as will be apparent later. So, in mid-summer, the Manchesters returned to operations.

Up to this time the engine had experienced four major and a host of minor problems. The major problems involved the bearings, the oil system, the coolant system and the con-rod bolts. Not only the bearings themselves, but also the other three problems had a direct effect upon the bearings, with the result that failures of quite different origins led to similar types of damage to the engine.

A major associated consequence already alluded to, which greatly exacerbated even these very terminal failures, was that on occasions the liberated con-rods would sever the line to the feathering mechanism leaving the dead engine windmilling at fine pitch, greatly increasing the drag.

During this grounding, between the end of June and 7 August, different contingency plans were made for the aircrews. With the Manchesters stood down, they were to be temporarily seconded to nearby Hampden squadrons to carry on operating. Later the squadrons were temporarily issued with a number of Hampdens and carried on operating using these aircraft for a while. What was in fact a retrograde step must have seemed like a deliverance.

In June 1941 New Zealander Flying Officer 'Pappy' Paape had been posted to 61 Squadron to assist them working up their Manchesters to operational status. Paape did not survive the war. Flying Officer Dave Romans, the Canadian, was posted on, having participated in his last operation with 207 Squadron on 21 June. Romans was killed soon afterwards (on 8 September 1941) flying an RAF Fortress I in daylight with 90 Squadron, when he was attacked by two Messerschmitt Bf109 fighters and crashed in Norway.

Despite not being able to do anything about the fundamental underpowering of the Manchester, there was some glimmer of hope that engine reliability would at last be improved from the catastrophic low experienced between 13 April and 7 August. In almost four months 207 Squadron's Manchesters had attempted a mere sixty-one operational Manchester sorties whilst 97 and 61 Squadrons had attempted thirty-eight and sixteen respectively.

Many crews were feeling that just to get the aircraft in the air deserved a medal. Yet during the seven months 207 Squadron had flown its Manchesters the crews had received precious little recognition in the form of decorations. In contrast, the Stirlings and Halifaxes were going from strength to strength in both day and night operations and their crews were the 'glamour boys' of Bomber Command. As usual with human endeavour, recognition, praise and awards went hand in hand with achievement and no honour attended determination, application and effort. Many directly involved felt it took considerably more courage and bravery to fly over occupied Europe in their Manchesters than in either of the four-engined 'heavies'. The crews were distinguished from the rest of the aircrews of Bomber Command by their continual operation in a totally unreliable aircraft.

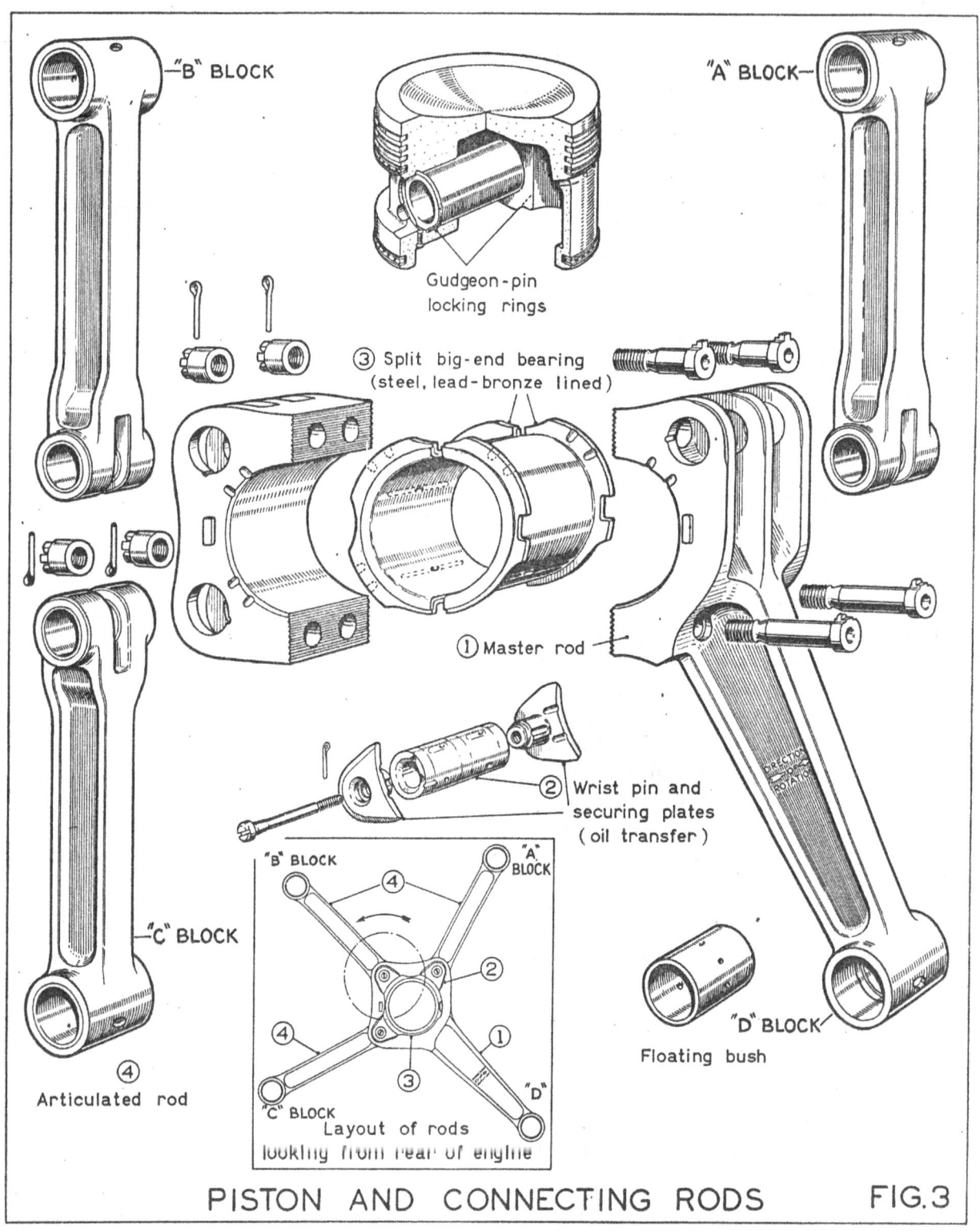

Heart of the Vulture's problems, the main big-end bearing and star rod design. The diagonal split line between the master rod and cap and the unequal length con-rod bolts are shown to advantage. (Taken from AP.1801A, Volume I, Rolls-Royce Vulture)

Compared to watching the oil temperature and pressure continually fluctuating and rising so close to, and at times past, the danger mark, the dangers presented by the Germans often seemed modest and certainly short-lived in proportion. There was little in wartime to compare with the sweet torture of perpetually speculating on which system was going to fail first. Perhaps the nearest comparable situation was the crews in the Atlantic convoys spending days at a time wondering with every beat of the engines whether a German torpedo was coming through the ships plates to join them. The crews of the Manchester squadrons were the forgotten airmen, feeling the RAF was as ashamed of them as it was embarrassed and humiliated by the continual disappointments they had encountered with the aircraft in their charge.

By this time 5 Group had drastically revised its schedule for re-equipping its squadrons with Manchesters. After 97 Squadron received its first Manchesters on 27 February 1941 and 61 Squadron its initial complement early in March, no further squadrons had been converted. Indeed 61 Squadron never had more than ten Manchesters on strength until October. 207, 97 and 61 Squadrons had spent much of their time grounded and non-effective. The remaining 5 Group squadrons soldiered on with their obsolescent Hampdens. A decision had long ago been made to transfer all Manchester orders to Lancasters.

With Manchesters returning to operations, Avro could concentrate on the remaining aircraft on order as well as tooling up for Lancaster production. For Rolls-Royce, effort on the Vulture was soon to terminate almost completely. In the case of the groundings, 207 Squadron engineering personnel in particular had put in a magnificent effort. Wilfred Freeman, Vice-Chief of the Air Staff at the Air Ministry, had recognised the tremendous dedication of the squadron, writing to Air Vice-Marshal Jack Slessor the Air Officer Commanding 5 Group on 1 August 1941 to commend him on the 249 hours twenty-five minutes of flying the Manchesters of the three squadrons had achieved in such a short period of time. In turn, Slessor passed on these commendations to Group Captain Boothman, the officer commanding RAF Waddington, who conveyed these commendations, coupled with his own praise and thanks to Wing Commander Purdon Lewis, adding the rider that the main bouquet was due to Eric McCabe and his engineers, as their aircraft had achieved 120 hours of the total 249 flown.

The Manchester crews could not have realised that the period June and July 1941 also represented one of the all time low points in the fortunes of the whole of Bomber Command. Before war commenced the Air Staff had calculated that the average expected bomb aiming error in daylight would be 300 yards. By 1940 this was, in some unexplained manner, transformed into an expectation for night bombing too: a pious hope.

During 1940, photoreconnaissance showed little evidence of damage to targets reportedly heavily attacked. Similarly, reports filtering back from occupied Europe were at odds with the claims of returning bomber crews. There was apparently a gulf between what Bomber Command was achieving and that which a superficial assessment and the propaganda it led to claimed. Quite how large was the gulf would soon be made clear.

By April 1941 Air Staff studies for night bombing revised the average aiming error for moonlight from 300 yards up to 1,000 yards. An Air Staff directive of 9 July 1941 indicated that this implied that precision targets, such as transportation systems and the oil industry, could thus be attacked on a quarter of the nights of any month, with large working class and industrial areas allocated for the remaining three quarters of any month.

Throughout the winter of 1940/1941 and on into spring 1941, Prime Minister Winston Churchill had followed the progress of the bombing offensive. He was aware of its shortcomings, especially in its inability to do effective damage even against the invasion barges in the channel ports. Lord Cherwell (Professor Lindeman), Churchill's scientific advisor, shared his concern. To allow an independent and objective assessment of the problem, Lindeman had arranged for cameras to be made available for installation in RAF night bombers. By use of a photoflash dropped with the bomb load and timed to ignite at the instant the shutter in the camera opened, the intention was to photograph the ground in the area where the bombs had fallen. Subsequent photo interpretation was used to identify the spot and relate this position to the designated aiming point.

An intensive bombing survey campaign using this technique was mounted in June and July 1941, and the resulting material generated passed to Lindeman's secretary, D. M. B. Butt. Having analysed the data, Butt published his results in early August 1941 in what became known as 'The Butt Report'. Its findings were devastating. Butt had analysed the photographs from 6,105 sorties undertaken mainly to the French ports and the Ruhr area of Germany. He found that close to a third of sorties dispatched had failed to attack the designated primary. He therefore concentrated his analyses on the two thirds which reported they had attacked the primary target. Dividing these sorties by target area, he found that only one third of sorties to French coastal targets came within five miles of the aiming point. Against targets in the Ruhr the statistics were even worse, with only a tenth of sorties claiming to have hit the primary actually plotted within five miles of the aiming point. Reduced to easier terms, of every 100 aircraft dispatched only twenty-two bombed within five miles on French targets and a mere six-point-six over the Ruhr.

The report had an immediate effect upon Churchill and an initially incredulous Air Staff. The implication was that for deeper penetration operations the statistics may be even worse, although the persistent industrial smog blanketing the Ruhr was a significant factor in the difficulty of identifying such targets.

Divided up using different criteria, Butt showed that on moonlight nights two crews in five came within five miles of the aiming point whereas on moonless nights the ratio fell to one in fifteen. At the very moment when perceptive airmen, aware of the intensified German night fighter capability, already foresaw the end of bombing operations in bright moonlight, the Butt Report found their capability for moonless nights to be negligible. Submission of the Butt Report thus signalled the low water mark in the fortunes of Bomber Command.

When Professor Blackett, writing on 18 February 1942, made his assessment of Bomber Command's achievements in terms of German casualties, he reported that during the entire previous year the British bomber force had been killing Germans at about the same rate that the German defences were killing highly trained British aircrew. It was a dismal outcome for all the efforts.

For the first time it was starkly clear that Bomber Command had not yet reached the stage of having a bomb aiming problem, as the over-riding navigation problem prevented the aircraft reaching the target area in the first place. The report was to lead Air Vice-Marshal Saunders, the Senior Air Staff Officer of Bomber Command, to equate the bombing effort with 'exporting bombs in the general direction of Germany'.

As a result of this, although Bomber Command specified particular buildings as the aiming points to crews in the future, from then onwards it was tacitly understood that most were merely carting bombs to the surrounding suburbs. The area bombing policy was taking shape.

Although the Butt Report concentrated minds admirably on the total inadequacy of astro-navigation, dead reckoning and radio beacons, in one respect salvation was at hand, albeit at some distance. By coincidence, the first of Bomber Command's target finding aids, GEE, was under trial in August 1941. Regrettably for Bomber Command, navigational deficiencies were not the only factor impeding its effectiveness.

The British bombs of this period were both defective and inefficient, with the result that when they did go off they did very little harm. The range of GPs, which were the principal weapons of the RAF at this time were badly designed. When dropped they were likely to bury themselves in the ground, with the result that much of the blast went harmlessly upwards rather than outwards. It was also found that these bombs had a casing far too thick, with a casing to charge ratio of 27% compared to 50% for the bombs currently in use by the Germans. Much of the explosive force was consequently used in blowing the case apart. Even worse than this, throughout 1941, and on into 1942 and 1943 the proportions of dud British high explosive bombs remained steady at 25%.

Many of these deficiencies were progressively becoming apparent and being overcome. Indeed, from as early as March 1941 the thin-cased, high capacity 4,000-lb blast bomb – the so-called 'Cookie' or 'Dangerous Dustbin'- was already coming into service. However, one further deficiency of staggering proportions was to remain overlooked until as late as September 1943. Only during the planning of British defences against the threat of the German 'V' weapons did it finally come to light that the explosives used by the Germans were 80% more efficient than those used in British bombs. This was the more appalling when it was appreciated that virtually all concerned, other than the Air Ministry, was aware of this fact.

In the inquiry which followed it emerged that in April 1940 the Ministry of Supply, Armament Research Department in Sevenoaks, had proposed a programme of testing aluminised explosives. The programme was turned down due to an aluminium shortage. However, despite this the Navy was well aware of the value of aluminium as an explosive enhancer, using this in the Torpex in torpedoes and the Minol in depth charges. Following these revelations the first aluminised explosive-filled bombs finally reached operational squadrons on 4 December 1943. It was a galling failure of basic communications.

As far as the immediate situation in August 1941 was concerned, Churchill was in despair: 'I find it an awful thought that three quarters of our bombs go astray. If only we could make it half and half we would have doubled our bombing power'. Despite these setbacks, Churchill remained undaunted. He had not promised or expected quick solutions.

Mercifully unaware of these doubts and deficiencies, the squadrons were about to emerge from the longest period of grounding of the Manchester since its service introduction. They had more than their fair share of problems within their own microcosm. For the moment there was some optimism that Rolls-Royce had finally grasped the nettle as far as the problems with the Vulture were concerned. With LA4 bearings and correctly tensioned con-rod bolts to Mod 44, the aircrews were all set to give the Manchester another chance.

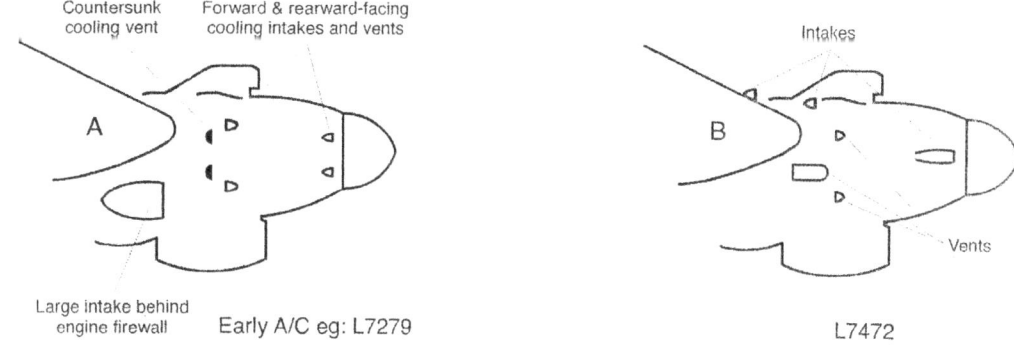
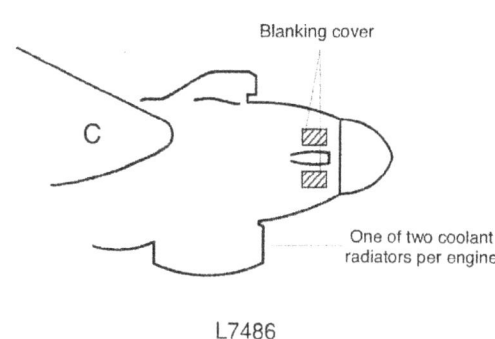
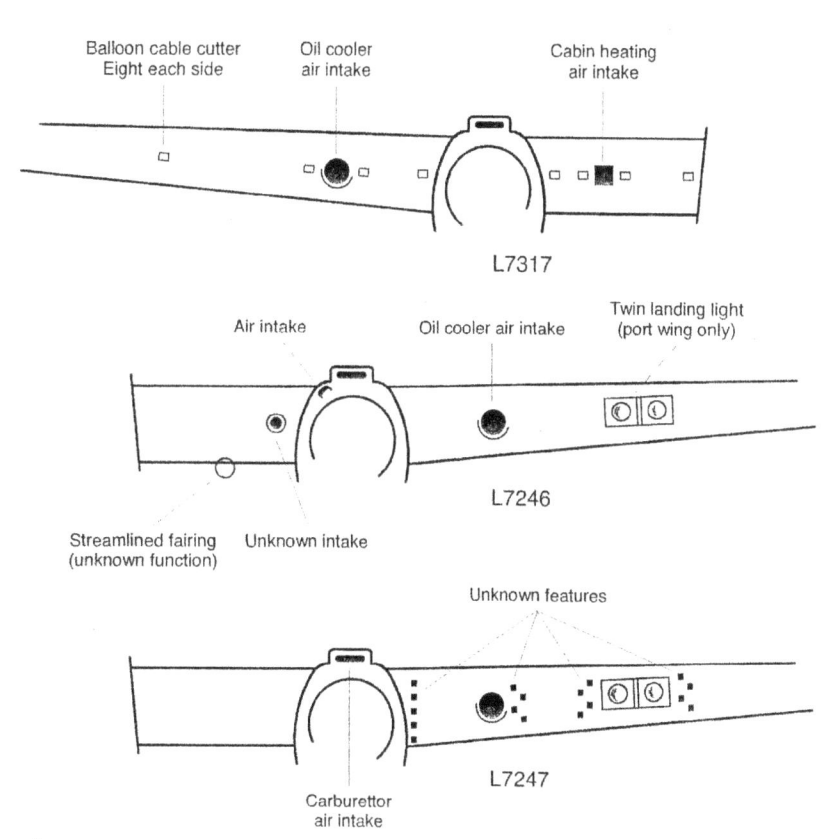

Vulture Sketch (A) – Nacelle as on L7279. Four small forward and rearward-facing intakes and vents probably provide cooling air directly to the spark plug area. This zone would be very hot, especially with a twenty-four cylinder engine, leading to risk of melting the plug lead harness. Similarly, a great deal of heat radiation in this area would emanate from the exhausts which were covered by the cowling, except for the protruding fishtail. The black toned half moon orifices interpreted as depressions in the cowling are vents to expel engine bay heat and fumes. The large intake on the nacelle side under the wing leading edge is sited behind the engine firewall, thus it has been speculated to be an airframe, rather than engine service feature.

Sketch (B) – Nacelle as on L7472. Larger and extra, smaller forward and rearward-facing intakes and vents show a modification in the spark plug/exhaust area to admit greater cooling airflow. Small forward-facing intakes deleted in favour of single, larger area intake to increase cooling airflow between cylinder banks. The rear-facing, less draggy, small vents have been retained to supplement the single, enlarged rear-facing vent.

Sketch (C) – Nacelle as on L7486 etc. Blanking covers at location of original smaller intakes.

Sketch – Starboard wing leading edge as on L7317. Inboard square intake cabin heating. Outboard round intake oil cooler. Streamlined intake on engine top supplies air for carburettor. Eight small square ballon cable cutters.

Sketch – Port wing leading edge as on First Prototype L7246. Oil cooler inlet and landing light outboard. Three features inboard: small intake on upper cowling forward of and adjacent to central carburettor air intake, function unknown. Guess this might be to provide cooling air to a Heywood air compressor driven from rear of the upper camshaft. Unknown streamlined fairing beneath wing centre section. Unknown intake in inboard leading edge.

Sketch – Port wing leading edge as on L7247 – features of unknown purpose. (G. A. Warrener, 1996)

Information from Rolls-Royce Heritage Trust who suggest that perhaps an Air Publication (AP) for the Vulture powerplant was never produced. APs for the Manchester aircraft and Vulture engine were produced (Manchester powerplant was the responsibility of Avro).

Chapter Five: A Faltering Return

Bomber Command wasted no time. On 7 August 1941 the Avro Manchester was declared fit for operations once more and on that very day 207 Squadron was called upon to join in a planned raid by 106 aircraft to Essen. Three Manchesters and seven unit Handley Page Hampdens were given the Krupp works itself as their aiming point. Each Manchester carried five 1,000-lb general purpose (GP) bombs and sixty 4-lb incendiaries. Take-off was 00.40 to 01.00 hours.

Essen – 7 August 1941:

Serial	Code	Squadron	Captain
L7381	EM-K	207	Fg Off. W. M. R. Smith
L7422	EM-V	207	Flt Lt W. J. Lewis
L7373	EM-T	207	Flt Lt T. C. Murray

Once in the air, there was some confidence that Vulture engine reliability was improved in the Manchesters. Yet this was the very day on which yet another problem became manifest. The aircraft experienced tail flutter in various degrees of severity. Flight Lieutenant Murray in L7373 experienced severe tail flutter on the outward flight which forced him to abandon the attempt to reach Essen and instead attack the first 'SEMO' he located. A SEMO was one of the Command's euphemisms to cover its inability to find and pinpoint precise targets. The acronym stood for Self-Evident Military Objective – how this could be established in the cloudy, smog-laden darkness over the Ruhr was not made clear. The bombs dropped by Murray were believed to have fallen on Duisburg. Flak batteries engaged the aircraft whilst it was on its bombing run and it finally landed back at 06.00 hours.

L7381 and L7422 encountered severe static and icing conditions en route to the target. A ground haze over Essen prevented precise target location, but both dropped five 1,000-lb GPs and sixty 4-lb incendiaries, which were estimated to have fallen in the general target area. A large fire was seen near Essen.

Flying Officer Smith's aircraft iced up badly on the return flight, but he managed to land back at 04.45 hours. All the Hampdens also returned safely. Following this operation the Hampdens were withdrawn from 207 Squadron. Unlike the Manchesters, they had not encountered any serviceability problems and none were lost on operations with the squadron. Consistent with the cloud and industrial haze, Essen reported a light raid with only thirty-nine high explosive and 200 incendiaries falling in the town. There were no casualties. For the moment both 97 and 61 Squadrons continued with one Manchester and one Hampden flight.

Until this time aircraft losses in the squadrons were mainly due to flak. Despite the concern felt in the Command over Manchester losses on operations due to engine failure, only the aircraft of Sergeant Harwood, Pilot Officer Ayton and Flight Lieutenant Bird had been lost solely due to this cause. German flak defences were already very efficient and few aircrews had encountered German night fighters in combat. Although RAF Fighter Command had been operating aircraft interception (AI) airborne radar equipped night fighters since July 1940, their German equivalents were lagging behind in this area. The German night fighter force was still relatively small at this stage of the war, having approximately 170 serviceable aircraft.

This was a situation which was soon to change, as the Manchester squadrons were to find to their cost during August. On the 12th Bomber Command laid on a deep penetration raid to Berlin and 207 Squadron was called to provide six Manchesters with 97 Squadron offering three more. The total force was seventy aircraft to Berlin, seventy-eight to Hanover and thirty-six to Magdeburg.

Berlin – 12 August 1941:

Serial	Code	Squadron	Captain
L7306	OF-	97	Sgt D. H. Rowlands
L7383	OF-	97	Fg Off. H. S. Blakeman
L7424	OF-	97	Fg Off. J. Little
L7422	EM-V	207	Flt Lt W. J. Lewis
L7373	EM-T	207	Plt Off. A. W. Hills
L7316	EM-U	207	Plt Off. H. G. Keartland
L7380	EM-W	207	Fg Off. W. G. Gardiner*

| L7381 | EM-R | 207 | Fg Off. W. M. R. Smith |
| L7377 | EM-G | 207 | Sqn Ldr G. R. Taylor |

*with Wing Commander Purdon-Lewis as second pilot

When the crew lists were posted at Waddington, Sergeant Bill Wetherill found himself listed to fly as wireless operator with Squadron Leader Dickie Taylor. Initially a member of Flying Officer Paape's crew until the latter was posted in June, Wetherill had flown several operations in July in Hampdens with Squadron Leader Taylor. This would be their first operation together in Manchesters and an enlarged crew would be required. The nucleus of the crew was Taylor (pilot), Sergeants Beattie (observer), McPhail (rear gunner), Wetherill (wireless operator) and Sergeant Nottidge second pilot. Sergeant G. R. Birt was listed as the second wireless operator/air gunner.

As the preparations advanced, Wetherill was approached by a wireless operator he did not know. The newcomer introduced himself as Bob Birt and remarked that he was down to fly with Taylor as the second wireless operator/gunner. On grounds that he was senior to Wetherill, he proposed he should be first wireless operator/gunner and occupy the radio position, whilst Wetherill should take his place in the mid-upper turret and be on hand to take the coffee round to the various crew positions from time to time. Wetherill countered by pointing out that he was already the 'regular' in the crew. This little difficulty was resolved in gentlemanly fashion when the two agreed the best way out of the dilemma was a compromise in which Wetherill would be first operator/gunner on the way to the target and, having cleared the target area, they would swap so that Birt could be the same for the return flight.

Neither was to know, but this agreement was to be the first of three occasions during the next twelve hours when Wetherill's life was to be saved by pure chance. From one of the other crews, the captain, Flight Lieutenant 'Mike' Lewis was to recall this as one of the saddest days of his life. Consistent with the deeper penetration, the take-off time was commensurately earlier than for the Ruhr operations. Pilot Officers Hills and Keartland, and Flying Officers Gardiner and Smith took off very close to 21.30 hours, and it is likely that Flight Lieutenant Lewis was last away at 21.35 hours. Manchesters from 97 Squadron took off from Coningsby between 21.02 and 21.11 hours. On account of the anticipated fuel consumption, most pilots chose a route to the north of the Ruhr via a more or less direct line from Waddington to Berlin. It was a beautifully clear night with absolutely unlimited visibility.

Flying Officer W. Mike R. Smith and Flight Lieutenant W. J. 'Mike' Lewis, close friends and pilots with 207 Squadron, in front of the mess at Waddington. Mike Smith was killed on his fiftieth Op on 12/13 August 1941 and 'Mike' Lewis failed to return from an operation on 7/8 September 1941, becoming a prisoner of war. (W. J. Lewis)

As the nine Manchesters headed eastwards across the North Sea one aircraft was already in trouble. Gardiner was discovering that despite his most determined efforts, L7380 was quite unable to climb to a reasonable flying height, added to which excessive tail flutter was experienced. L7380 was one of the Manchesters with the poorest

Left: 207 Squadron 'A' Flight commander, Acting Squadron Leader G. R. 'Dicky' Taylor, who was killed on his forty-seventh Op, to Berlin, on 12/13 August 1941. (via M. B. Taylor) Right: Sergeant W. 'Bill' Wetherill, sole survivor from L7377 EM-G. (via Wetherill family)

performance. With no alternative, Gardiner diverted to nearby Emden and dropped his bombs on the port area and landed back safely at Waddington at 02.50 hours.

As they crossed the enemy coast crews could already see, flicking across the sky miles ahead, the fingers of the lights in the searchlight belt over Holland, like gigantic cobwebs reaching out to trap them. In a foretaste of what was soon to follow, another Manchester, L7306 of 97 Squadron piloted by Sergeant Rowlands, was intercepted by an unidentified night fighter over Holland. The alert gunners fortunately spotted the interceptor as it closed and L7306 nipped smartly into nearby cloud. The same aircraft was spotted on the starboard quarter three to four minutes later, but Rowlands slipped away to port and no further attack materialised.

Bringing up the rear of the phalanx after crossing the Dutch coast, 'Mike' Lewis was concentrating on the airspace ahead, whilst the gunners kept a sharp look out for other aircraft in their designated sectors of sky. There was no protective cloud to blanket them by the time 207 Squadron reached the area and fighter attacks had to be expected.

Suddenly, directly ahead, he registered a stream of tracer fired between one aircraft and another. This was immediately followed by a large, distinctive, pinkish-centred flash of a 'Cookie' exploding in a bomber and then the awful brilliant yellow flare of the aircraft's fuel tanks exploding. The disintegrating, shattered wreck tumbled earthwards, shedding blazing fragments until it fell below Lewis' line of vision under the nose.

He had witnessed the instantaneous destruction of an RAF bomber caught naked by a German night fighter. The awful sight was imprinted in his memory and on return he learned that his best friend, Mike Smith, just 21-years and a few days old, had been killed on his fiftieth operation over occupied Europe, together with his entire crew. His enquiries on return led him to believe that he had almost certainly witnessed his friend's death, but only recently has the evidence been assembled to prove the truth of this supposition.

L7381 had fallen to one of the most experienced German night fighter aces of the time, Oberleutnant Ludwig Becker. Becker was doubly famous, being credited as the first German night fighter pilot to obtain a victory with the AN ground radar guidance system back on 16 October 1940. The action in which he obtained his second 'first' had come only three days before he shot down Mike Smith. Following his successes in 1940, Becker pulled some strings and arranged to be transferred to Berlin-Werneuchen, the German experimental night fighter centre. Here he did much of the development flying on the 'Liechtenstein' airborne interception system. Many German night fighter pilots were bitterly opposed to this equipment when it was first issued to operational units. Its serviceability was poor, and its weight and the drag of its cumbersome external aerial array significantly impaired the already marginal speed advantage of the makeshift night fighters then in use. These radar-equipped aircraft were thus commonly left on the ground while the crews, not experienced in the use of the radar, preferred their earlier, more manoeuvrable aircraft.

This situation persisted for quite some time in mid-1941, but when Becker was posted to a front line unit, IV/NJG1 at Leeuwarden in Holland, in July 1941, the situation changed dramatically. Becker and his radar operator, Feldwebel Staub, were so competent and experienced with the 'Liechtenstein' equipment that very soon the other crews had christened Becker the 'Nachtjagd-professor'.

On the night of 8/9 August he took off from Leeuwarden in a Dornier Do215 equipped with 'Liechtenstein'. With him were Feldwebel Staub as wireless and radar operator and Obergefreiter Wilhelm Gaensler as air gunner. Shortly after midnight, with the aid of the Seeburg plotting system and 'FREYA' ground radar station, he was guided onto the tail of an incoming RAF bomber. At a range of a few kilometres they detected the raider on their 'Liechtenstein' set and Staub was able to direct Becker close enough to obtain a visual sighting. Becker fired at the gently weaving bomber and Vickers Wellington T2625 GR-B of 301 Squadron crashed near Bunde just across the German border, the first ever airborne radar victory by a German night fighter. L7381 EM-R was the second German airborne radar assisted victory of the war.

A copy of the combat report submitted by Becker following this action has survived. In translation it reads:

On 12 August 1941 I took off at 23.20 hours in Do215 G9 +OM for night operations in the vicinity of Leeuwarden. (The crew were Becker, Staub and Gaensler). I was guided by means of the Seeburg table (controller Leutnant Maier) and picked up the target on 'Liechtenstein' radar at a height of 4,700 m and at a distance of 2,500 m and at 01.25 hours. I distinguished high in front of us the enemy aircraft, a type unknown to me. I attacked from down and behind, one single attack, firing several bursts of fire. My burst of fire went exactly through the centre of the fuselage. Target disappeared downwards into clouds and I could not observe how the aircraft crashed on the ground. The aircraft, an Avro Manchester, was found with numerous hits by machine gun and cannon near Slochteren [east of the town of Groningen] by the Aircraft Recovery Commando from Leeuwarden. I landed at 02.02 hours at Leeuwarden'.

Confirmation of the destruction was obtained from Oberfeldwebel Reinthal who was flying over Schiermonnikoog with Leutnant Gehring at that time. He observed the firing and its result and recorded it at 01.25 hours. The 'Liechtenstein' radar in Becker's Do215 became unserviceable at the end of September and it was well into 1942 before the next airborne radar-assisted kill was achieved.

Local reports say that the Manchester exploded with the bomb load and the enormous load of petrol. Burning pieces came down behind the Apostolic Church at Froombosch near Kolham and a real rain of fire from the petrol fell on the land. All around lay the bodies of the six airmen. Flying Officer W. M. R. Smith from Knebworth, Hertfordshire, was found in a ditch, still sitting in his seat. One other airman had come down in a stubble field, making in it the impression of his body. The six airmen were buried on the afternoon of 14 August 1941 in the cemetery near the Hoofdweg at Kolham. In 1951 they were reburied at the Central Allied Cemetery at Holten in the Province of Overijssel. There can be no doubt that none of the six knew what had hit them.

As an Oberleutnant, Becker went on to claim forty-four victories, rising to the rank of Hauptmann and Staffelkapitän of NJG1. His life was squandered for no benefit when he died with Oberfeldwebel Staub at his side on 26 February 1943 during his first daylight operation over the North Sea. The 'Nachtjagd-professor' had no familiarity with the tactics required to attack massed American bomber formations.

Perhaps the most surprising factor of the Do215 versus Manchester combat is that although neither of the crews involved survived the war such a complete record of the incident from eye witnesses and combat reports on both sides could be assembled more than 50 years later.

Oblt. Ludwig Becker of IV/NJGI at Leeuwarden in Holland, who shot down the Luftwaffe's first airborne radar-guided victim of the war on 8/9 August 1941. On 12/13 August Flying Officer W. M. R. Smith's Manchester became the second such victory. There were no survivors. (via Theo Boiten)

Following the return of Flying Officer Gardiner and the loss of Flying Officer Smith, the seven remaining Manchesters continued their mission to Berlin, cloaked in the anonymity of darkness. En route over Hanover Sergeant Rowlands was heavily engaged by flak and released his bombs on that city to enable him to escape the barrage. On locating the target area Lewis, Keartland, Hills and Blakeman all received a hot reception from the flak defences. Lewis dropped his five 1,000-lb GPs on the west side of Berlin, observing three fires on the ground caused by earlier bombers. Keartland unloaded his five 1,000-lb GPs north-east of the aiming point. Hills carried a 4,000-lb high capacity (HC) and 240 4-lb incendiaries and also found the searchlights very accurate on his bombing run. For five minutes he was coned by approximately thirty searchlights. He eventually evaded the beams and his 4,000-lb bomb, dropped through the 207 Squadron-designed bomb aperture in the bays, fell on the north side of the city. Flying Officer Blakeman dived to bomb a fire in the position his observer calculated Berlin to be.

Meanwhile, Squadron Leader Taylor was also approaching the target area at about 12,000 feet. Other than a brief encounter with searchlights and flak in the defensive belt at the Dutch coast their outward flight had been uneventful. Each of the experienced captains had their own philosophy for survival on operations, developed from the lessons of their first tours. Taylor had explained this to Sergeant Wetherill during their preparations for previous flights. He believed that when caught by accurate flak barrages the best course of action was to fly absolutely straight and level. Statistically, he claimed, the aircraft was just as likely to jink into a flak burst as away from one.

Perhaps his was an appropriate philosophy for the early days of the war when the threat of night fighter interception was relatively remote and radar predicted flak was in its infancy. The Achilles' heel of this approach to anti-aircraft fire was soon to become manifest.

Bill Wetherill's most vivid memory is of their approach to the target area. The searchlights seemed more numerous, active and dangerous than ever before. They appeared to be working in groups and in close co-ordination with the heavy flak batteries. The flak guns were also working in unison, throwing up box barrages into the apex of those searchlights which had located and held a bomber.

On the bomb run Taylor continued to hold L7377 straight and level whilst 'Tam' Beattie in the bomb aimer's position coned them towards their designated aiming point. Their load was a single 4,000-lb HC 'Cookie', which Beattie duly dropped on what was believed to be the aiming point. The aircraft was equipped with the modified bomb doors which Wetherill recalls as being canvas covered and they all felt the bump as the bomb fell on the doors, prising them open, followed immediately by the reverberation as the aperture sprang closed once more. Beattie left the bomb aiming position and made his way back to his navigator's seat, hooking up his intercom.

Suddenly they were illuminated by a searchlight, joined in rapid succession by others. They were coned and held by the mercilessly bright beams. It almost appeared to Wetherill that the release of the bomb was a signal which activated the lights. Within a few seconds an intense and co-ordinated flak barrage opened up on them. Wetherill felt the concussion of the first burst, not one but a number of shells exploding together in a small area of sky. Beattie called on the intercom that the first burst was well ahead and above the aircraft.

Contemporary German propaganda photograph of the tail of Squadron Leader Taylor's aircraft down amongst the buildings in the suburbs of Berlin on 13 August 1941. (via Karsten Schulz and Peter Reinhardt)

Taylor continued to fly his steady course and at intervals of several seconds further barrages exploded. It became apparent that although the gunners had initially over-estimated their speed they were gradually getting closer with each burst. Then a burst jolted them from such a close distance ahead and above that they immediately flew through the smoke, smelling the distinctive acrid cordite which had yet to disperse. They waited with bated breath, still held like a fly at the centre of a spider's web, but the next burst was even closer, immediately above the nose inducing a tremendous shock and shudder in the aircraft. A shower of splintered perspex flew from shrapnel penetrating the cockpit canopy.

In the absence of any call Wetherill could not be certain what damage had been caused. Consequently he left his radio position and moved forward into the cockpit. Dicky Taylor had been hit in the wrist by a flak splinter which had severed an artery. 'Tam' Beattie was already standing between the pilots and Wetherill could see that he was trying to fasten a temporary tourniquet above the spurting artery to staunch the flow of blood, whilst Sergeant Nottidge had taken over control and was flying the aircraft.

Wetherill offered assistance but received an assurance from Beattie that he could cope. Further bursts of flak continued to buffet the airframe but at this stage Wetherill could discern no further damage. Beattie, an experienced and senior observer, had taken control of the situation, as he continued to work on Taylor's wound. At the same time he was calmly directing the inexperienced Nottidge in a series of evasive manoeuvres in an attempt to escape the clinging lights.

Wetherill returned to his position and stood watching for any evidence that they might be shaking off the flak, to no avail. The next group of shells burst with a loud explosion and concussion beneath, which shook the aircraft again. With the blast the armour plate doors behind Wetherill's seat, providing access aft, burst open. Turning, Wetherill saw to his horror that the whole of the inside of the fuselage aft of his position was already a raging inferno.

The size and intensity of the conflagration immediately after the shells had burst surprised Wetherill. This was no small fire, but already an enveloping blowtorch of flame. He could only surmise that perhaps the flak had set off the flares stored immediately beneath Bob Birt, trapping him in his position in the mid-upper turret. The rapidity with which they had been engaged by the flak gunners had prevented Birt and Wetherill effecting their agreed exchange of crew stations.

This one look down the 'blowlamp' of the rear fuselage convinced Wetherill that the aircraft was doomed and that his only hope of survival was to escape from the aircraft a quickly as possible. He grabbed and fitted his observer's chest-type parachute and made to move to the forward escape hatch beneath the nose. To his dismay he found his exit completely blocked by the three aircrew struggling in the cockpit. In desperation he flung off his leather flying helmet, pulled open the armoured doors, and tried to force a way to the rear entry door instead. He was met by a veritable ball of fire which set his hair smouldering. By now the fire was spreading to the wings and the flames began to shoot forward through the armoured doors into the cockpit area. There could, it seemed to Wetherill, be but a few seconds remaining to effect an escape.

Returning to the cockpit area, he found it deserted. Fortunately the aircraft was still flying straight and level in a gentle dive, perhaps under control of the autopilot. By this time Taylor, Nottidge and Beattie were crouched around the forward escape hatch but were still not getting out. Beattie was still tending to the tourniquet on Taylor's wrist, effectively blocking Wetherill's escape. The whole airframe was hot and fire was licking at Wetherill who, without his leather flying suit, was already beginning to burn.

The only possible escape from a certain and horrific death in the blazing coffin of L7377 seemed to be the starboard cockpit window. In desperation Wetherill grabbed the catch and slid it backwards. A searing pain shot through his hands as he found the catch so hot his flesh stuck to it. Ripping his hand away and leaving the skin behind, he pushed the chest-type 'chute through the narrow opening. By now the fire was shooting into the cockpit area, forcing him into frenzied activity in an attempt to escape it. He stuck his head through the aperture then worked his shoulders through one at a time. Heaving himself outward, his feet left the cockpit floor and he was out of the aircraft almost to his waist.

Having momentarily escaped the worst of the fire a sudden chilling fear gripped him when he noticed for the first time the starboard propeller still turning at maximum revolutions some 18in. behind his right shoulder. Any further progress in this direction and he would inevitably fall directly into the arc of the airscrew and certain death. He must retreat, despite the advancing fire. In his last desperate lunge through the cockpit window he had lost the purchase of his feet on the cockpit floor. Indeed, in blind panic he discovered that he could now no longer move forward or back into the aircraft but was stuck tight in the window.

The fire had by now reached Wetherill's legs and he felt them burning but continued his frenzied efforts to get back into the cockpit, his mind focused on the forward escape hatch which must, surely, by now be vacant. Shock and exhaustion combined to weaken him and he was trapped, totally unable to help himself. His face a few inches from the spinning propeller blade tips, his legs burning: he was a helpless victim of fate. He fainted. Fate took a hand in an incredible fashion, for his next memory is one of feeling very sick and dizzy whilst tumbling over and over through the air as he fell. His immediate thought was quite obtuse. A few nights earlier he had had his first experience of drinking too much, with the attendant detached stupor of finding all about him spinning. Determining later never to do it ever again he was now irrationally angry to find himself in the same state.

Cold reality quickly dawned on him: the only possibility was that the flames had finally reached the fuel tanks, exploded the aircraft and thrown him clear. This was his second escape from death during the operation. Wetherill raised his hands, which were skinned from the wrist down, and took the D-ring in his grasp. Despite excruciating pain he pulled the ripcord and to his relief the parachute blossomed unburnt above him. The whole action, from illumination to hanging in his parachute, seemed an eternity, although in truth it is likely to have occupied only two minutes or so.

Following the last gentle dive of L7377 and his own free fall, Wetherill found himself still quite high, perhaps 10,000 feet. He became aware of material flapping in his face. Despite his burns he could discern it to be the two legs of his battledress trousers. Whilst trapped in the cockpit these had completely burnt through all the way down the back to leave the fronts as loose strips of cloth, as soon as he was hanging upright in his harness they rose up into his face. One flying boot was missing and on the way down he kicked off the other. Overhead he could hear the raid still in progress and see the searchlights quartering the sky for their next quarry. Soon he could see the ground, and as the features grew nearer and larger, realised he was heading for an area of trees. Unable to use his burnt hands he reached up vainly with an elbow to try and shorten the suspension cords and steer the parachute to one side. He succeeded merely in inducing a violent swing and fearing it might collapse, left it to its own devices. Thus he was unable to prevent himself from crashing through a large tree at Gross-Beeren Teltow, on the southern outskirts of Berlin.

The parachute stuck high in the tree and Wetherill was left swinging in the air still suspended some distance from the ground. Looking down he saw he was in the top of a hedge bordering a lane. He reached up for the quick release buckle of the parachute at his waist. Despite exerting as much force as the pain in his hands would allow, he was unable to turn it. His full weight was on the buckle and he had no strength left in his hands. After several attempts he gave up, slumped exhausted in the harness, and waited to be found. Above he could still hear aircraft engines, bombs exploding and the flak.

After only a few minutes he heard and then saw people out searching for him with torches. His descent had obviously been witnessed from below. They progressed along the lane beside him but could not find him. In shock and pain from his burns, realising the urgency with which he needed medical attention, he abandoned all prospect of escape and called out to the search party in his best schoolboy German. They stopped. 'Wo sind Sie?' ['Where are you?'] 'In dem baum' [In the tree'] replied Wetherill. Shining their torches aloft they soon located him. A group reached up and took hold of him. With an unceremonious tug they pulled him down from the tree, parachute and all. Seeing the seriousness of his burns the party realised he was unable to undo his parachute buckle and removed the parachute for him.

Subsequent memories are fragmentary and incomplete and it seems that Wetherill lost consciousness from time to time during the next few days. As he drifted between oblivion and reality some vivid memories remain. He came round as the search party tried to get him on this feet. There were a number of them, including one middle-aged man in a Sturm Abteilung (SA), [the 'Storm Trooper' brownshirt uniform] and a teenage boy of about sixteen years of age. As they were escorting him along the lane he overheard and understood that they were discussing where best to take him. Suddenly the 'Brownshirt' stopped the procession and, drawing a gun, spoke to the rest of the party: 'Uberlassen Sie ihn mir. Ich erledige ihn um die ecke'. ['Leave him to me. I will take him round the corner']. His eyes dropped illustratively to the Luger. Wetherill understood only too well what was being proposed.

To his surprise and immense relief the teenage boy immediately intervened on his behalf, standing between airman and 'Brownshirt'' and condemning the adult in strident tones. The rest of the party sided with the teenager and so, humbled and thwarted, the 'Brownshirt' backed down and holstered his gun. Wetherill could breathe again. An adolescent and enemy stranger had just saved his life, and in the middle of an air raid at that. Not having exchanged places with the mid-upper gunner, being blown clear of the doomed aircraft and now saved from murder, this was the third life-saving moment since the Manchester had been caught in the searchlights. Turning, the boy spoke in English: 'You will be safe when some military come', he smiled reassuringly.

After a short walk they reached what Wetherill took to be an underground first aid post or air raid shelter. There nurses appeared and cut off what remained of his trousers. They bathed his burns, which extended down the whole length of the backs of both legs and bandaged them. His badly burnt hands were also dressed and loosely bandaged. His face was less severely burnt and therefore left uncovered. Wetherill fainted again and has confused memories of being laid down on what he took to be a pile of sawdust. Many people, each it seemed in a different style military uniform, came to look down at him, shaking their heads and clicking their tongues at his condition.

Sometime later it became apparent that another wounded airman had been brought in and Wetherill was asked if he could identify the newcomer. Although the man was badly burned and his features were unrecognisable, with a start Wetherill suddenly recognised an unburnt section of Fair Isle pullover on the chest of the person lying before him. It was McPhail, the rear gunner. Doug McPhail was a short, stocky chap with red hair and a distinctive handlebar moustache. The hair and moustache were gone now and the features puffed up and distorted by the fire so that only the sweater gave a clue to his identity.

Wetherill never discovered how McPhail managed to vacate the aircraft, since the crew believed he was sufficiently wide in his flying suit to have difficulty falling out of the turret doors during ground practices. From German research we now know that the spinning and burning rear fuselage section fell towards an occupied property, veering aside at the last minute onto the farm buildings opposite. Fire-fighting teams were soon on site, a team member being a local resident, Herr Ribbecke. Together they extinguished the fire and removed from his separated rear turret a grievously injured and badly burnt Sergeant McPhail. He was conveyed to hospital. Nearby, in the middle of the Bahnhofstrasse, the body of another airman, presumed to be that of Sergeant Birt, was lying. Shortly afterwards a German officer arrived in an Opel and took custody of Wetherill. McPhail stayed behind since his first aid was still not completed.

Wetherill accompanied the officer alone, whilst the initial treatment of McPhail's grievous burns continued. In the back of the Opel the officer addressed Wetherill, his English impeccable: 'I'm sorry, old boy, that it had to be my flak battery that shot you down'. Wetherill speculated on just how sorry the officer was, but managed to reply diplomatically: 'Well never mind, thus are the fortunes of war'.

Wetherill was taken first to a German Military Hospital where his burns could be properly treated. He had the great good fortune to be attended by an extremely considerate and sympathetic German doctor, who apologised profusely for the necessity of causing him pain and discomfort. All the bandages on his legs and hands were removed, the wounds cleaned and redressed, and the strips of hanging skin picked or cut off.

Owing to his lapses of consciousness the timescale is uncertain, but Wetherill believed he remained in the hospital all that night.

His next recollection is of travelling in a military ambulance over the cobbled streets of Berlin to a French POW hospital somewhere in or near the city. This was a very uncomfortable journey as the bumpiness of the ride aggravated his wounds and caused great pain, such that before he had arrived he had lost consciousness once more. The main wards were taken up by wounded and sick French POWs and he was put in a small room as he was the only English person in the hospital.

At some stage McPhail was brought into the ward beside him. McPhail was not only severely burned but also deeply traumatised by his experience. In the main he was conscious, although far from lucid, and fought all attempts to give him the medication he so desperately needed. The attendants tried to attach McPhail to a saline drip but he resisted. Wetherill tried to reason with him, but McPhail continued to toss and turn until the drip came out of his arm.

McPhail clearly recognised Wetherill, calling out: 'They're trying to kill us Bill' and 'Don't let them do this to us'. Wetherill tried to reason with McPhail: 'No Mac, they're French, they're trying to help us', but it was to no avail and McPhail died later that day.

Wetherill, too, was seriously burned and continued to experience periods of lucidity interspersed with losses of consciousness. Under the devoted care of the French doctors and nurses he slowly began to improve. One nurse told him later he was the one not expected to pull through. The treatment of such severe burns was virtually an unknown area of medicine. When he was sufficiently recovered the doctors began their attempts at skin grafts on his burns, although by no means were all of those attempted successful and his injuries would require very prolonged hospitalisation.

Photograph of Mary Skepper, Bob Birt's girlfriend, taken off his body by the Germans, given to Bill Wetherill and later, in Stalag 8B, handed on to Bob's friend Jim Taylor. Note scorching at top of the photograph. (via Jim Taylor)

With time he became more mobile and eventually quite well acquainted with the German officer-in-charge, Statfeldwebel Salmon. When Wetherill became well enough to be mobile, Salmon would allow him into his room to listen to the BBC, although he always returned before the news was due and switched off the set. From time to time Salmon would also give him a tot of Schnapps to drink and showed him many kindnesses without ever forgetting that they must, unfortunately, remain enemies.

One day, during the early part of his convalescence, a Luftwaffe officer arrived at the hospital to interrogate Wetherill. He had a sheaf of papers with details the Germans had gleaned already about their aircraft. Looking over the German's shoulder, Wetherill could read under aircraft type the words 'Manchester' and under captain 'Squadron Leader Taylor'. The officer asked many questions which Wetherill was unwilling to answer, amongst the most important and a question he kept returning to was: 'How many engines did your aircraft have? Two or four?' The wreckage must have been very scattered, but clearly the Germans were perplexed, believing such a big aeroplane should really have required four engines. Up to this time the Germans had only had the opportunity to examine the wreckage of Siebert, Hyde, Pinchbeck, Little, Smith and Taylor's Manchesters and in every case the aircraft were almost totally destroyed.

When the German was unable to obtain the answers he wanted, Wetherill eventually felt able to ask him what had become of the rest of his crew. The interrogator told him that Taylor, Nottidge and Beattie had all drowned in the lakes around the city of Berlin. It has not been possible to corroborate from any source what Wetherill was told, but if there is any truth at all in the information it would perhaps imply that the three did successfully parachute from the front hatch before the aircraft disintegrated. Since all three were wearing their Mae Wests and the water temperatures in August must have been relatively high, it would seem surprising if all had drowned as the German claimed.

The Germans had also found the body of Bob Birt. From his body they took two photographs, both burnt at the edges, of Birt with a girlfriend sitting in the gateway of a field on his motorcycle. The interrogator told Wetherill that Birt was also dead and gave him the photographs for safekeeping.

Wetherill remained in hospital for more than five months before being sent to Stalag 8B POW camp near Breslau in January 1942. His wounds were far from healed and he very quickly went back to the camp hospital. In Stalag 8B he met Jim Taylor, the wireless operator from Johnny Siebert's crew.

Taylor had been a good friend of Bob Birt so Wetherill offered him the scorched and burnt photographs. Taylor took the photographs and carried them amongst his personal possessions all through his time in POW camps. With him they survived harsh winters in Stalag Luft 3 in Upper Silesia where the inmates had no heating and ice from the prisoners' breath built-up to six inches on the inside walls of the barracks. They survived a forced march right across northern Germany before the advancing Russians in the winter of 1944/1945 and more than 50 years later were still kept in his wallet.

Wetherill still required further hospital treatment and in 1943 he finally went before a neutral Red Cross medical board. On the panel were a German military doctor, a British (POW) doctor and a Red Cross doctor, who jointly considered the medical condition of wounded prisoners with a view to repatriating those whose medical condition warranted it. In October 1943 Wetherill was repatriated to Sweden and on to England via a hospital ship. So, returning to the events of 12 August, 207 Squadron had lost their 'A' Flight Commander, Squadron Leader Taylor, on his 47th operation.

From the 97 Squadron force L7424 OF-Z? with Flying Officer J. A. Little and crew failed to return. Consistent with the date, the Vultures in this aircraft would have boasted both LA4 bearings and con-rod bolts correctly tensioned to Mod. No.44. A brief account of this loss has emerged from Sergeant Lloyd G. Robinson, wireless operator/air gunner, in recent years. Little lifted off from Coningsby at 21.02 hours and it is evident that this aircraft reached Berlin and bombed its target. Doubtless in doing so they, as with Squadron Leader Taylor, encountered the flak defences protecting the city. On the return flight the port engine caught fire. It is not known whether a shrapnel fragment may have damaged a vital component. The crew faced an identical problem to those experienced by Pilot Officer 'Kipper' Herring and Flight Lieutenant 'Mike' Lewis and their crews on 7/8 September in their raids on Berlin. It is not known what action, if any, was taken to lighten the aircraft, but frantic steps were certainly made to transfer fuel from the port to the starboard wing tank. In the panic the fuel valve lever broke. They were uncertain of their position but doubtless willing L7424 to cover the intervening miles. Signals were sent out at 01.35 and 02.22 hours requesting fixes. Regrettably, Flying Officer Little was unable to keep the aircraft airborne. They believed they had made it over the border into Dutch airspace, where there might be some prospect of a friendly reception on the ground. At 02.28 hours Robinson clamped his morse key and was ordered to be the first out. This act is recalled as the most frightening moment of his life and, in baling out of

L7424, in his own words: 'he left the last piece of England behind'. The entire crew escaped by parachute, their aircraft crashing in a ball of flames and rousing the neighbourhood. On landing, Robinson sprained his ankle but soon encountered fellow crew member Sergeant Scott RNZAF caught up in a tree by his 'chute, badly injured. Robinson and a German farmer together hauled Scott down from the tree and the crew were reunited in the local police cells, Sergeant Scott having been carried there strapped to a ladder on an army vehicle. They were at Nordhorn-Schuthorf in Germany contemplating the next four years in captivity.

The remaining Manchesters of the Berlin force made their way back to Waddington and Coningsby and landed safely. They had been badly mauled by the flak defences over the 'Big City'. More seriously, although unknown to them, a new and potent force had been deployed effectively against them for the first time. With Flying Officer Smith having been brought down by a radar-equipped night fighter, the aircrews which came after him would have good reason in future to be more fearful of the radar equipped night fighter than the flak defences, which in the main were to prove a threat only over the immediate target area. Of the seventy-strong Berlin force, only thirty-two aircraft had bombed Berlin. Nine aircraft – three Manchesters, three Wellingtons, two Halifaxes and a Stirling – were lost.

Following a raid on Magdeburg, on 6 August 207 and 97 Squadrons were called on to participate in a raid on Dusseldorf. 207 Squadron sent two aircraft to Dusseldorf and two new crews undertook a shallow penetration raid on Ostend to gain experience. 97 Squadron supplied four aircraft – Flying Officer Gardiner and Pilot Officer Keartland were to take-off from Waddington close to 23.00 hours, whilst the 97 Squadron force took off between 22.47 and 22.56 hours.

Dusseldorf/Ostend* - 16 August 1941:

Serial	Code	Squadron	Captain
L7423	OF-	97	FS D. H. Rowlands
L7306	OF-	97	Flt Lt C. P. D. Price
L7383	OF-F	97	Fg Off. H. S. Blakeman
L7384	OF-	97	Flt Lt J. L. Nunn
L7432	EM-Z	207	Fg Off. W. G. Gardiner
L7311	EM-F	207	Plt Off. H. G. Keartland
L7380	EM-W	207	Plt Off. T. R. Gilderthorp*
L7422	EM-V	207	Plt Off. P. C. Birch*

Nothing seemed to go right in Keartland's aircraft from the very start of the operation. Out on the grass airfield at Waddington it was raining very heavily. The deluge was sufficiently severe that Keartland completely overlooked his usually unvarying custom of 'watering' the tail wheel before boarding. This practical preparation for a long flight had, for many crews, become steeped in tradition and superstition. To miss any part of the routine which had 'protected' them before was regarded as a bad omen.

When engines were started, Keartland found that it was impossible to run them to full power without the aircraft dancing and sliding uncontrollably across the grass. Consequently, L7311 was taxied from the grass dispersal onto the nearby Sleaford main road, holding up the Lincoln-Sleaford bus. Here the brakes were applied and the engines tested to satisfaction. They finally took off through the rain at about 23.15 hours.

Pilot Officers Birch and Gilderthorp took off at 01.40 and 01.46 hours respectively. Peter Birch located Ostend docks and dropped two 1,000-lb GPs from 14,000 feet, which were estimated to have fallen on a jetty west of the dock. Unfortunately the remaining two 1,000-pounders hung up and despite vigorous manoeuvring it proved impossible to jettison them. Birch returned to Waddington at 04.45 hours. Gilderthorp was unable to identify Ostend but eventually found another port to bomb which was subsequently identified as Terneuzen on the River Scheldt. He landed at 05.00 hours.

The six Manchesters of the Dusseldorf force were well ahead. In L7311 the crew's concentration level rose a notch as they crossed the enemy coast inward bound for Dusseldorf. They had dragged L7311 up to 15,000 feet but now one of the engines was dropping revolutions. The two pilots, Keartland and Ross, discussed the situation over the intercom. Bill Hart, the rear gunner, recalls that since the performance did not appear to be deteriorating any further and Dusseldorf was a relatively shallow penetration target, Keartland had decided to press on.

Their next objective was to traverse the searchlight belt stretching across eastern Holland without being detected. They appeared to be close to achieving this and had reached a position near to the Dutch/German border, only some 20 minutes flying time from the target, when they were suddenly illuminated 'by the blue searchlight'. All the other searching fingers of light nearby immediately converged on them. With a full bomb load and still carrying the bulk of the fuel load, Keartland was unable to effect any violent evasive action. They were well and truly coned and held by the lights.

In the rear turret Hart was completely blinded by the glare and could give no warning when, at 02.05 hours, only shortly after they were located, they were shocked to see and feel cannon and machine gun bullets strike the aircraft. Holes appeared in the perspex turret close to Bill Hart and he was lucky to survive. In the few hectic seconds of the attack he was scarcely aware of what was happening to him. Still the attacker was unseen, but the closing speed of the fighter on the overloaded and underpowered Manchester was such that he overshot the lumbering bomber. In doing so, the fighter entered the glare of the lights surrounding the Manchester, allowing the snap identification. Hart believed his attacker to be a single-engined Messerschmitt Bf109. He was a sitting target almost in the rear gunner's sights and Hart immediately pressed the triggers, at the same time operating the turret slewing controls. Nothing happened. The initial attack had severely damaged the aircraft, knocking out all the hydraulic systems and silencing the turret armament, the port engine was set on fire and the flying controls damaged.

Hart lost sight of the fighter as he checked the reason for the turret malfunction, but shortly received a warning on the intercom that the fighter was making another attack on the port quarter. Hart traversed the turret by hand towards the port quarter. As he did so, he fired a short burst. The object was to check whether the first failure to fire was due to a round jamming the guns or alternatively to the hydraulic failure. The short burst was not directed at the fighter and did nothing to deflect it from a second short accurate burst of fire, which this time caused hits in the front fuselage, slightly wounding the second pilot, Sergeant Ross.

Despite his injuries, Ross was the first to regain his faculties, ramming forward the stick and diving the Manchester until it evaded the searchlights. Enquiries have now ascertained that the attacker was the German ace and commander of Stab1/NJG1, Hauptmann Werner Streib based at Stade and possibly flying a Messerschmitt Bf110. He was to become one of the Luftwaffe's top aces and attain a high wartime rank, surviving the war with a tally of sixty-five victories in the night skies of Europe. This was his twentieth.

Hart was still unaware of the damage up front and now had time to call the pilot on the intercom, which was, fortunately, still functioning. There was no reply to the first call, the two pilots no doubt having their hands full, and Hart called again. In the front turret, Sergeant Ball had seen little of the attacks and had not been hit. Ross managed to recover from the headlong dive and found they had evaded both the lights and the night fighter. Everything told them that L7311 was doomed. Sergeant Eddie Ball was enveloped in acrid smoke and glycol in the pitch darkness. The port engine was on fire and the flames were spreading. 'Sorry chaps, you will have to bale out', called the second pilot.

Discovering the seriousness of the situation, Hart began to prepare to abandon the aircraft, noticing for the first time as he did so that his left arm and left side of his body seemed numb and useless. His actions thus restricted, he opened the doors in his turret and reached into the fuselage stowage rack for his parachute. Clipping the 'chute onto his chest harness, he locked on the right clip but was totally unable to fasten the left. A parachute course had taught him that baling out with one clip fastened should be quite safe, as the rigging lines were linked together guaranteeing a safe and full deployment of the silk. Thus prepared, Hart traversed the turret onto the beam, again one handed.

After what seemed an age, the turret appeared to have traversed far enough for him to fall out of the aircraft. He leant his full weight backwards only to discover, to his dismay, that the doors, so recently opened for him to collect his parachute were now jammed. In desperation he braced his feet in the turret and exerted all the force he could muster on the doors, which burst open allowing him to somersault free.

Hart pulled the ripcord and received a severe jolt as the parachute blossomed above him. For the first time in the hectic encounter with the night fighter, which had probably lasted less than a minute, he had time to collect his thoughts. His left arm still hung down uselessly and he realised that he had, indeed, been wounded. He could feel blood trickling down his back inside his flying suit. It later transpired he had stopped both a cannon shell splinter and a machine gun bullet, although how these had reached his back when he was sitting facing the gunfire from the fighter is not clear. They may have been ricochets and lost much of their momentum before hitting him.

Meanwhile, Sergeants Curry, Wappet and Ball, the navigator, wireless operator and front gunners respectively, had great difficulty in escaping from the lower hatch in the nose. Ball's parachute had only just deployed when he hit the ground, damaging the base of his spine. A few fields ahead, the Manchester, still with the bomb load aboard, blew up on impact. L7311, lying shattered at Kruchten, over the German border, must have provided little information for the Germans.

Owing to the darkness, Hart was unable to see the ground and made a heavy landing amongst bushes he could barely discern. Partly paralysed and in great pain, he dragged his parachute over himself and settled down to await daybreak, assess the seriousness of his wounds and get his bearings. Unbeknown to him, he had landed at Roermond in eastern Holland.

That night the crew of L7384 of 97 Squadron comprised Flight Lieutenant J. L. Nunn (captain), Sergeants Ratcliffe (second pilot) and Wood (observer), Flight Sergeant Ashmore (wireless operator), Sergeant Currie (front gunner), Flight Sergeant Williams (rear gunner) and Sergeant Smith (mid-upper gunner). The night remained hot and sultry even at the take-off time close to midnight. Nunn recalled that even with a load of only six 1,000-lb GPs his take-off from Coningsby was a marginal and unnerving experience.

The aircraft had climbed painfully slowly in the thin air as they headed out over the North Sea at full throttle. As they approached the coast of occupied Europe they were still below 10,000 feet and Nunn toyed with the idea of jettisoning one or two of the bombs safe into the sea, so they would be able to climb to a safer height before crossing the searchlight belt. He decided to keep the bombs on board, a decision he would later regret, but one which probably had little effect on the events which followed.

By the time they reached 'The Belt' in eastern Belgium he had still only hauled the Manchester up to 11,000 feet. On approaching the searchlights, Nunn began corkscrewing the aircraft. Despite his exertions he was trapped in the beams and illuminated. His efforts to escape the cone became more desperate, but to no avail. At 01.52 hours they were attacked by the prowling Bf110 night fighter of Oberleutnant Hermann Reese of 2/NJG1 which seriously damaged the Manchester with the first burst of fire. The starboard engine caught fire and the hydraulics were damaged. The undercarriage dropped down, slowing their speed further and making evasion even more difficult.

Nunn feathered the starboard propeller and pressed the fire extinguisher button. Despite the serious damage caused in the first pass the night fighter continued to press home his attack and the next burst of fire caused further destruction, including wounding the front gunner, Sergeant Currie.

It was obvious that the Manchester was doomed. They were descending quickly and there was little time to spare. Nunn ordered the crew to bale out. The second pilot, observer, wireless operator and mid-upper gunner baled out, the rear gunner also jumped, but his body was found later. It is likely his parachute had failed. The remaining four were taken prisoner.

Nunn was in a dilemma. He was alone in the crippled Manchester with his front gunner, who was too badly wounded to escape. To bale out meant leaving Currie to certain death. They were within a few thousand feet of the ground and would soon be too low to bale out anyway. The Graviner system seemed to have worked as the fire in the starboard engine died down and appeared to have gone out. At least something in the shattered aircraft worked.

The dying fire helped Nunn to decide to try and save Currie's life by force landing the Manchester. It was a pitch black night with only the stars visible and Nunn could make out no details whatever on the ground. Other than knowing that most of eastern Belgium was fairly flat he would be landing totally blind, with some of the hydraulics shot away and carrying 6,000 lb of bombs plus most of the fuel load. Nunn maintained his resolve. On the remaining port engine the Manchester sank very quickly so that it was soon too low for Nunn to bale out even if he had changed his mind. His responsibilities to his crew remained uppermost.

Nunn pumped furiously on the emergency flap handle as they descended, but it was not possible to judge whether the flaps had extended at all. In any case the emergency system took a lot of pumping to fully lower the flaps and on his own with the aircraft to control, there was insufficient time. Still, the ground beneath was invisible.

At 100 feet on the altimeter, still blind to what lay in their path, Nunn throttled back the port engine and pulled back on the stick. The Manchester sank onto the ground in an area of small fields and trees. The dangling undercarriage collapsed and the careering aircraft smashed through several hedges and trees. A large branch smashed the cockpit perspex and then the aircraft ground to a halt. The bomb load, which Nunn had not had the opportunity to jettison, was not fused and remained intact. Nunn was severely shaken around in the impact and deceleration of the landing.

When they finally stopped his first thoughts were of the possibly holed and ruptured fuel tanks and whether the fire in the starboard engine was out or might flare up again. He was shocked and in pain himself, but his immediate thought was for Currie, his front gunner. He struggled forward to the turret and with great difficulty extricated

Left: Flight Lieutenant John L. Nunn, whose bravery in staying in control of his aircraft on the night of 16 August 1941 didn't emerge until nearly fifty years later in correspondence with the author. Right: Flight Sergeant Peter Williams, rear gunner to Flight Lieutenant John Nunn. His parachute failed to open when he baled out of R7384. (Both Wim Govaerts)

the wounded man. Dragging him up to the cockpit, he hauled the gunner through the broken cockpit canopy. Despite the pitch blackness the aircraft appeared to have survived the ordeal quite well. It was on an even keel, the wings were still in place and it was more or less in one piece. Nunn thinks he lowered Currie the short distance to the ground and followed himself. He laboriously dragged the gunner to a safe distance from the wreck in the expectation that the bomb load would soon detonate, or leaking fuel on the hot engines must soon set the aircraft on fire. They had landed some sixteen km west of Maastricht, five km north-west of Maeseyk in Belgium, at about 01.00 hours on 17 August 1941.

This last effort was all Nunn could achieve and he collapsed beside the wounded gunner. Later, he was to discover that amongst his many injuries were breaks to both his arms. In the circumstances his achievement in extricating Currie showed loyalty and fortitude of the highest order. Currie was much more seriously wounded. Hit in the chest, a bullet had punctured his lung. As a result of their injuries and the exertion of escaping from the aircraft they could go no further. They lay there until next morning when they were discovered by Belgian children. Soon the Germans arrived.

They were taken to Maastricht hospital, which was full, so they had to be transferred to another one nearby. Sadly, Currie died from his wounds the next day. His death cannot detract from the devotion shown by Nunn, who risked his own life in the force landing in an attempt to save his disabled gunner.

In L7422 Flying Officer Gardiner soldiered on to Dusseldorf, where five 1,000-lb GPs and three small bomb carriers (SBCs) of incendiaries were dropped in the town centre. The searchlight and flak defences were intense but the aircraft escaped damage and returned safely to Waddington at 03.50 hours on 17 August. From 97 Squadron, Flight Lieutenant Blakeman's aircraft was repeatedly hit by flak as it traversed the searchlight belt on the outward leg, but bombed the estimated target and returned safely to Coningsby.

During this period in mid-August 1941 cooling the over-taxed Vultures was still a problem and operating oil temperatures were commonly too high for safety. A means of improving the situation had been the lip fitted on the wing upper surface alluded to earlier. This relatively small modification was to have an unforeseen, but dramatic, effect on the aerodynamic efficiency of the aircraft. At this time the aircraft experienced severe tail flutter when climbing with a full bomb load. This time it was the whole tailplane and not just the central fin which was affected.

On 25 August 207 Squadron offered seven Manchesters and 97 Squadron two for an operation planned on Mannheim. It was to be a night of high nervous tension and desperate endeavour on behalf of the beleaguered aircrews but, as so often with the Manchester, it was one which produced only the most negligible achievement in military terms. Following briefing, the crews were taken out to their aircraft, the engines and all system checks were carried out preparatory to take-off. At this stage two 207 Squadron Manchesters became unserviceable, one with yet another burst tail wheel tyre, the other with a bad oil leak.

Mannheim – 25 August 1941:

Serial	Code	Squadron	Captain
L7308	OF-	97	Flt Lt C. P. D. Price
L7306	OF-	97	Sgt T. J. Mycock
L7300	EM-S	207	Fg Off. W. G. Gardiner
L7378	EM-A	207	Plt Off. L. A. Paskell
L7316	EM-U	207	Plt Off. W. S. Herring
L7317	EM-C	207	Flt Lt W. J. Lewis
L7432	EM-S	207	Plt Off. P. C. Birch

The aircraft took off between 20.00 and 21.00 hours. The take-offs themselves were unusually protracted, even for the Manchester, and once airborne the most extreme flying difficulties were experienced in several machines. The aircraft seemed more than usually unwilling to climb.

Flying Officer Gardiner gives an account of a controversial sortie in his 'personal Manchester', L7300 EM-S, to Mannheim on this night. By this time he was very familiar with it, though haunting every aircrew member, along with concerns over serviceability, weather, flak and fighters, was the constant fear of being branded LMF (Lack of Moral Fibre). Gardiner writes: 'For some reason I couldn't fathom at the time, the aeroplane behaved very badly. I couldn't get it to climb or cruise at anything like its normal speed. The tail was fluttering and I couldn't get it to climb above 8,000 feet'. After two hours in the air, Gardiner reluctantly abandoned his operation, dumped his bombs and returned to base, landing at 23.23 hours. Pilot Officer Len Paskell experienced similar difficulties and dropped his bomb load on Dunkirk docks before returning to base at 00.04 hours. In addition, Pilot Officer Herring in L7316 experienced tail flutter, whilst in L7432 the climbing performance was so marginal and the engines overheating so severely that Pilot Officer Birch had no alternative but to jettison a 1,000-lb bomb to ease the strain. At the estimated time of arrival for the target, a break in the cloud below L7432 revealed no sign of it, so Birch eventually dumped the load on an unidentified searchlight concentration.

As the remaining crews continued their eastward flight over the continent, the weather deteriorated rapidly. All these aircraft encountered 10/10ths cloud, sleet, rain, icing and electrical storms, making flying conditions extremely uncomfortable. Flight Lieutenant Lewis was unable to locate Mannheim owing to the extreme weather but dropped four 1,000-lb GPs and 180 4-lb incendiaries on an urban area, later tentatively identified as St Goarshausen. Only Herring claimed to have dropped five 1,000-lb and 180 4-lb incendiaries on the town centre at Mannheim. Sergeant Tommy Mycock had to abort owing to a hydraulic failure but reported his engines running well.

Flight Lieutenant Price was unable to locate the main post office at Mannheim owing to the same cloud cover but estimated his bombs to have fallen in the southern sector of the town. He reported his aircraft behaved perfectly. It remains uncertain whether the 97 Squadron aircraft had the lip fitted to the oil cooling system.

On return, the 207 Squadron crews complained of the truly awful flying performance they had endured with their aircraft. On 27 August Mike Lewis, who had encountered the least problems, was delegated to carry out an altitude test on Herring's aircraft, L7316. There was some suspicion in high places that the crews were exaggerating the poor performance and using it as an excuse not to press home their attacks. Mike Lewis had been Acting Commanding Officer for the week, standing in for Group Captain Boothman who was on leave. Wing Commander K. P. Lewis became station Commanding Officer in turn.

Following the fuss that had been raised, the test crew consisted of Group Captain Lewis Roberts, an Avro test pilot, 'Bill' Thorn, Gardiner and Lewis. Having made an early return, Flight Officer Gardiner was the centre of the gravest suspicion. He was also required to test L7300. L7316 had a full bomb load to simulate the conditions experienced and was found to have a pitiful flying performance. Approaching 14,000 feet the aircraft stalled completely with a tremendous flutter in the starboard wing and tailplane. Gardiner lifted L7300 to 16,000 feet. Initially the tests seemed inconclusive and Gardiner and others remained under suspicion for showing insufficient resolve and 'starting a hare' for no good reason. After the test flight a senior non-commissioned officer ground crew approached Gardiner separately to say that the static line in the bomb aimer's station of L7300 had been found to be disconnected. Gardiner and the non-commissioned officer deduced from this that earth loops in the aircraft had caused a major error in the pilot's flying instruments and this was the cause of the degradation in performance. In the absence of a rigorous diagnosis any number of irrational theories was put forward. However, further testing and evidence led to the conclusion that the tail buffeting was caused by climbing the aircraft too near the stall and that the best climbing speed was 150 mph at 2,850 rpm and +6 boost. A second and separate problem was that the new lips fitted over the oil cooler outlets, whilst improving oil cooling to a limited extent, induced a breakdown in the airflow over the upper wing surface, causing turbulence and a significant loss of lift. The loss of lift was felt to have the greatest effect on those aircraft additionally burdened by a mid-upper turret. Thus, they had identified another major performance defect which had been created in attempting to solve an earlier problem.

The modifications to the oil cooling system were quickly dispensed with and these extreme climbing and tail flutter problems were overcome. Later trials with L7320 at the Aeroplane & Armament Experimental Establishment confirmed this diagnosis. It was found that by using 10 degree flap on the climb tail flutter could be substantially reduced, but this did little to ease the degradation in take-off performance. The cooling lips were found to be located in the worst possible place and shed 'dirty', turbulent air which impinged directly onto the fin/tailplane junction inducing the vibration. Remedial action had already been taken on the squadrons.

Although the number of aircraft available for operations remained small, the demands on 207 Squadron continued to be high. For the night of 31 August/1 September 1941 the command asked for four Manchesters to participate. On this occasion the engineering side managed to make six aircraft serviceable. These joined a total of 103 aircraft dispatched to Cologne.

Cologne – 31 August/1 September 1941:

Serial	Code	Squadron	Captain
L7419	EM-K	207	Plt Off. A. W. Hills
L7312	EM-L	207	Fg Off. W. G. Gardiner
L7373	EM-T	207	Plt Off. W. S. Herring
L7316	EM-U	207	Plt Off. T. R. Gilderthorp
L7422	EM-V	207	Plt Off. P. C. Birch
L7321	EM D	207	Plt Off. L. F. Kneil

The aircraft took off close to 20.30 hours and made their separate ways towards Cologne. Soon after entering enemy airspace over Holland, L7422 was detected by a Messerschmitt Bf110 night fighter. It attacked, seriously damaging the Manchester in the tailplane, blowing great holes in the elevators and making sixty-three separate holes in the rear turret, knocking out its hydraulic traversing mechanism. The fuselage and cockpit perspex were also holed. Miraculously there were no casualties, but as Pilot Officer Birch took evasive action the damage to the elevators resulted in loss of control and the bomber plunged earthward.

Birch eventually righted the aircraft sufficiently for the bomb load to be jettisoned, but control difficulties remained severe. They were near Roermond in Holland. Almost immediately the second pilot, on his first operation and apparently unnerved by his experience, switched on the aircraft's navigation lights, left his seat and baled out of the aircraft via the crew entry door. The lights were soon extinguished and it became clear that as a consequence of the violence of the manoeuvres, assisted perhaps by the return fire of the rear gunner, Sergeant Shadbolt, the night fighter had been shaken off.

Although the aileron and rudder controls remained operative, the airflow was acting alternately on the partly detached upper and lower coverings of the shattered elevators. Still cabled through to the cockpit, this was causing the control column to thrash backwards and forwards uncontrollably. The Manchester was climbing and diving in response to the movements of the damaged elevators. Eventually, Peter Birch established that he could reduce and control the switch-backing by means of the tail trimming wheel. Marginally in control, Birch flew L7422 back to Waddington and achieved a safe landing. Previous histories have reported L7422 as crashing on 1 September 1941, whereas the aircraft survived this encounter, only to be written off in a forced landing on 26 October 1941. L7422 was a triple-finned Manchester Mk.1 but it is possible that, following the severe damage to the tail, it was one of the aircraft modified to Mk.1A configuration by the retrospective fitting of the larger end plate fins.

Meanwhile, L7316 EM-U, captained by the Australian Pilot Officer T. R. Gilderthorp, continued struggling for extra height as it ploughed on across Holland. Gilderthorp had been on the high seas en route to England to join the RAF when war was declared. This was the third operation of his first tour. L7316 had reached 7,000 to 8,000 feet as it entered German airspace when it was suddenly illuminated by searchlights. They were immediately trapped in what they thought to be a heavy and accurate flak barrage. With the bomb load still on board and before any significant evasive manoeuvres could be undertaken, the Manchester was hit by a burst of gun fire and immediately caught fire. The shells almost certainly ruptured the wing fuel tanks and shrapnel fragments penetrated the fuselage, one wounding the pilot in the back.

There was obviously no prospect of saving the aircraft, which quickly became a raging inferno. Gilderthorp and the observer, Sergeant Leonard C. Parker, baled out from the front hatch before the flames reached them. Wounded and unable to see the ground approaching, Gilderthorp was unprepared for the severity of the impact and, on landing, suffered further serious injury, including a broken pelvis. He was rendered unconscious and consequently has no recollection of where he fell or how he was located and taken to hospital. It was several days before he recovered consciousness and many weeks before he was strong enough to be passed on to the POW camp. Parker also survived the descent and was captured. L7316, with the remaining crew members, fell at Oberkruechen near Cologne, at 23.39 hours.

Meanwhile, L7316 EM-U, captained by the Australian Pilot Officer T. R. Gilderthorp, continued struggling for extra height as it ploughed on across Holland. Gilderthorp had been on the high seas en route to England to join the RAF when war was declared. This was the third operation of his first tour. L7316 had reached 7,000 to 8,000 feet as it entered German airspace when it was suddenly illuminated by searchlights. They were immediately trapped in what they thought to be a heavy and accurate flak barrage. With the bomb load still on board and before any significant evasive manoeuvres could be undertaken, the Manchester was hit by a burst of gun fire and immediately caught fire. The shells almost certainly ruptured the wing fuel tanks and shrapnel fragments penetrated the fuselage, one wounding the pilot in the back.

There was obviously no prospect of saving the aircraft, which quickly became a raging inferno. Gilderthorp and the observer, Sergeant Leonard C. Parker, baled out from the front hatch before the flames reached them. Wounded and unable to see the ground approaching, Gilderthorp was unprepared for the severity of the impact and, on landing, suffered further serious injury, including a broken pelvis. He was rendered unconscious and consequently has no recollection of where he fell or how he was located and taken to hospital. It was several days before he recovered consciousness and many weeks before he was strong enough to be passed on to the POW camp. Parker also survived the descent and was captured. L7316, with the remaining crew members, fell at Oberkruechen near Cologne, at 23.39 hours.

Whereas L7316 had been overwhelmed in what was clearly an unexpected and devastating attack, it now transpires this was due to a classical night fighter stalk rather than a flak hit. Oberleutnant Wolfgang Thimmig of 2/NJG1, with his wireless operator FW Steckemetz, had been ordered to patrol night fighter boxes 8C and 9A in their Bf110. Thimmig's combat report has survived. He records:

We climbed through a 10/10 layer of cloud, although breaks appeared later in the patrol. At 23.30 hours the ground controller advised me of enemy aircraft entering my area. Shortly afterwards I spotted a bomber captured briefly by a searchlight beam. I turned towards it and was able to pick it up in the darkness ahead. I made my approach from directly behind, closing to within fifty to thirty metres before opening fire at 23.35 hours.

(It is likely that Thimmig dived below the path of the Manchester before pulling the nose up and firing as L7316 passed through his sights – author).

Top; A close shave for Flying Officer Peter Birch and his crew in Manchester Mk.1 L7422 EM-V of 207 Squadron following a night fighter attack over the Netherlands en route to Cologne on 31 August 1941. Cockpit perspex was perforated. Bottom: Tail unit damage. Birch maintained marginal control and landed back at Waddington. (Both J. M. Duncan)

The rear gunner had not seen me and there was no return fire. I made three attacks hitting the intruder on each occasion. Thick oily flames streamed back from both his engines and he plunged downwards. At 23.39 hours I saw an explosion on the ground through cloud as the enemy aircraft, a Handley Page Hampden, exploded. It crashed at Oberkrüchen, south-west of Waldniel.

Subsequent examination revealed that Thimmig fired 690 machine gun and ninety-six cannon shell rounds in the engagement - his sixth victory. The remaining four aircraft successfully bombed Cologne before returning to Waddington, where Pilot Officer Hills landed back at 01.37 hours on 1 September 1941. The heavy cloud cover had again protected Cologne and only a few bombs fell in the city, killing one civilian. The remaining loads dispatched from the 103 aircraft must have been spread over open country and other built-up areas.

That day a conference on crew training on Manchesters was held at the 5 Group Headquarters attended by the commanding officers of 207, 97 and 61 Squadrons – Wing Commanders K. Purdon Lewis, D. F. Balsdon and G. E. Valentine respectively. It was agreed that 'A' Flight of 207 Squadron would remain operational, whilst 'B' Flight would be withdrawn to concentrate on crew training. The 207 Squadron Operational Record Book (ORB) records that, as of this date, the squadron had eight Manchester captains and ten under training. 5 Group had guaranteed that 207 Squadron would continue to have priority over other units regarding the supply of new aircraft and crews.

The final and definitive version of the Manchester, the twin finned Mk.1A had started to leave the production lines, being held in readiness at the maintenance units (MUs) for delivery to the squadrons. During August 61 Squadron had only managed one air-sea rescue sortie and one bombing raid with their aircraft. A large influx of Manchesters was expected now that the engine problems seemed to be overcome and to cater for this 'A' Flight of 97 Squadron was stood down to train crews of 'B' Flight.

On 2 September 1941 207 Squadron received orders for a raid on a railway station in Berlin. Four aircraft were serviceable and carried out night flying tests, but unfortunately one developed engine trouble as it prepared to take-off and was withdrawn. The aircraft took off between 20.55 and 21.26 hours. 61 Squadron also produced an aircraft, flown by the commanding officer.

Central figures from group photograph of 61 Squadron. Left in peaked cap is Squadron Leader 'Cam' Weir with right, in forage cap and hands clasped, Wing Commander George E. Valentine. (via John 'Val' Valentine)

Berlin – 2/3 September 1941:

Serial	Code	Squadron	Captain
L7388	QR-*	61	Wg Cdr G. E. Valentine
L7373	EM-T	207	Plt Off. W. S. Herring
L7300	EM-S	207	Plt Off. A. W. Hills
L7378	EM-A	207	Plt Off. L. A. Paskell

On the way out across the North Sea, Pilot Officer Hills flew over unbroken cloud at 9,000 feet. Pilot Officer Herring reported seeing several groups of German night fighters flying in formation, one group having five and another seven aircraft involved.

All three Manchesters from 207 Squadron reached Berlin but failed to locate the railway station owing to haze and cloud. Each of them elected to drop their bombs on the urban area as a secondary target. All found the searchlights and flak defences active and accurate as they ran up to drop their bomb loads.

Herring estimated his 4,000-lb HC and 120 4-lb incendiaries fell in the city centre from 17,000 feet. Hills experienced an intense flak barrage and dropped his five 1,000-lb GPs on the city centre from 16,000 feet. Paskell was able to see his 4,000-lb 'Cookie' burst after it was dropped from 15,500 feet but saw no details owing to the haze. His aircraft was peppered by shrapnel from near misses, fortunately without being hit in a vital place.

By 2 September, and in spite of not being obliged to fly operationally, Wing Commander George Valentine had flown more Manchester sorties than any other 61 Squadron Captain. By a rare fluke of chance, the Navigation Logs of his observer, Sergeant H. A. Scott, for his first three of these have survived. On his first operation to Boulogne on 21/22 June Valentine bombed the target in a dive starting at as little as 8,000 feet and releasing his load before pulling out at a lowly 5,000 feet. The next night he had been frustrated when at 4,000 feet over

Dusseldorf hydraulic failure caused the bomb doors to remain closed and he brought his bombs back. On 26th/27th he attacked Kiel from 10,000 feet. On 14/15 August, in an attack aimed at the railway junction at Magdeburg, his Manchester, L7388, bombed the target from a lowly 1,500 feet. On this occasion all five other Manchesters from 61 Squadron returned early, their crews complaining of excessive flames from their engine exhausts rendering their aircraft readily visible to prowling night fighters. It was evident that morale in the unit, still with a flight operating its reliable but obsolescent Hampdens, was exceptionally fragile.

Immediately afterwards 61 Squadron moved to North Luffenham, taking a few days to settle in. As an experienced Second Tour Captain and Commanding Officer of the unit, for its next Manchester operation Valentine decided to mount a high profile morale-boosting raid on Berlin to demonstrate the newly proven reliability of the aircraft. He took with him the Station Commander from North Luffenham, Group Captain Barrett, as a passenger, with Flight Lieutenant Harrison the Squadron Navigation Leader, and Flying Officer Duckworth, the unit Gunnery Leader. No doubt, too, Valentine intended to follow his, by now, usual practice of making a low level penetration prior to climbing to a safe height to bomb the Schlisiger Railway Station in Berlin.

A routine radio transmission was received at 23.38 hours, thirty minutes before the briefed time over target. At 01.25 hours European Time the aircraft was engaged by Flakbaterie I/321 and brought down in Berlin-Bonsdorf, the Schönfeld district, killing the entire crew. A set of seventeen photographs taken by German recovery squads on 3 September of the shattered remains of L7388 has emerged.

The crew still lie together in the Commonwealth War Cemetery in Charlottenburg. Following this loss orders were issued that Station and Squadron Commanders were not allowed to fly operations without special permission. 61 Squadron's Manchester flight was dispersed for a while and several crew members seconded to 207 and 97 Squadrons.

In his exceptionally risky style of carrying the war to Germany, with its utmost bravery, George Valentine gave his life and that of his crew desperately trying to bring 61 Squadron up to fully operational status and a peak of efficiency. The result was the reverse of his intention. Valentine was only 20 years from the stoicism and unimaginable slaughter of the First World War. The determination he showed may have been strongly influenced by this earlier conflict.

At the time Squadron Leader 'Cam' Weir was lying in Raunceby Hospital. On his latest Hampden operation he had made his bombing run through an intense flak barrage. Struggling to maintain straight and level flight in the bucking bomber, he failed to carry out his regular procedure of pulling his flying goggles down from his forehead to protect his eyes. A flak shell burst immediately above and ahead of the nose showering shrapnel down onto his windscreen, shattering it and sending thousands of shards from the armoured glass into his face and eyes, blinding him. Incredibly, he maintained control, the navigator coming forward to become his eyes, reading the flying instruments out loud to enable Weir to continue flying. In this manner they accomplished the multi-hour return journey, even effecting a safe landing back at base. As soon as news of Valentine's loss reached the Squadron, Weir was discharged and given the unenviable task of working the unit up to operational status. It was another three months, on 7/8 December, before the unit got itself back to first line service.

On the return flight from Berlin, Herring saw seven more night fighters patrolling Hamburg but managed to elude them, whilst Hills received a rousing send off from the flak defences at Bremerhaven. As L7378 was crossing the North Sea a crew member observed a light on the water flashing 'SOS'. They carried out a brief search of the area, but failed to find its source and finally landed back at Cottesmore at 05.08 hours due to fuel shortage. The remaining two aircraft had reached Waddington an hour earlier.

As a consequence of the policy change on training, between 2 September and 20 October 207 Squadron returned to being the only operational Manchester squadron. Owing to the various postponements and cancellations the next operation, on 7 September 1941, became the second successive return to Berlin. A total of 197 aircraft were sent to the city with a further fifty-one aircraft diverted to Kiel. Six Manchesters of 207 Squadron stood by for the operation, which was allocated the main telephone exchange in Berlin as its aiming point. As so often was the case, two Manchesters failed to take-off owing to mechanical failure.

Top & Bottom: Two views of centre section and port wing of Manchester Mk.1 L7388 lying upside down in open ground at Berlin-Bonsdorf on 3 September 1941 being inspected by members of the flak battery which brought it down. The bomb doors are open. Large hydraulic ram in foreground may be the flap accuator. (Unknown German serviceman)

Top: 3 September 1941. Detached starboard wing of L7388 lying right way up with rear section of smashed Vulture engine and distinctive engine cowling. Bottom, Tail assembly of L7388 showing effects of fire. (Unknown German serviceman)

Berlin – 7/8 September 1941:

Serial	Code	Squadron	Captain
L7380	EM-W	207	Flt Lt W. J. Lewis
L7432	EM-Z	207	Plt Off. W. S. Herring
L7419	EM-Y	207	Fg Off. W. G. Gardiner
L7378	EM-A	207	Plt Off. L. A. Paskell

By this time, 'Mike' Lewis had completed his second tour and was scheduled to remain at Waddington to be posted to 44 Squadron as their conversion pilot to the Avro Lancaster. 44 Squadron were to receive the first prototype, BT308/G, on 16 September. (The /G suffix was an indication that the aircraft must be guarded at all times). When the operation was called the Squadron Commanding Officer sought out Lewis and asked him to put in just one more operation. It was a fateful decision. The aircraft Lewis was allocated became unserviceable prior to the night flying test and he had already been obliged to take the reserve. He had carried out a night flying test on L7380 during the afternoon and viewed the aircraft with some trepidation. During the air test he had stopped the engines in turn and discovered that even without a bomb load the aircraft would not maintain height on a single engine. It was, he recalls: 'a clunker amongst clunkers'.

The first three Manchesters took off between 21.35 and 21.40 hours. Lewis taxied L7380 around to the take-off point, joining a queue of aircraft. Ahead, poised at the Chance Light, was a 44 Squadron Hampden already lined up for take-off, with a second waiting to line up as soon as the first was airborne. They were taking off towards the north-east and Lewis watched the Hampden begin to roll on its take-off run. It became airborne, but for some reason the pilot lost control and it piled straight into the ground immediately across the Sleaford road. The bomb load and fuel exploded with a fearful detonation. No radio call of any kind came from the doomed aircraft to hint at its fate. As this aircraft had started its take-off run the second Hampden had lined up on the active runway. The pilot received a 'green' from the control caravan but sat there apparently frozen in the horror of what had unfolded in front of his eyes.

Stuck behind, Lewis was absolutely champing at the bit. With his engines getting hotter and hotter take-off could not be delayed, so he got on the radio and in no uncertain terms told the Hampden pilot to either take-off or move aside, he simply could not wait. With the urgency conveyed by this call, the Hampden pilot finally plucked up the courage and made his own take-off run. Lewis swung L7380 onto the runway as soon as the Hampden was rolling and commenced his protracted take-off run. It was even more heart-stopping than usual for none of them knew whether the whole of the crashed Hampden's bomb load had detonated or not. L7380 rose slowly and reluctantly, with Lewis raising the under-carriage as they passed over the Hampden's burning wreckage.

Lewis headed for 'The Gate' near Skegness, his usual exit point when crossing the English coast outward bound. He climbed up through a low deck of stratus cloud which was topped at about 3,000 feet and levelled out at 8,000 feet. Each aircraft proceeded separately along a route chosen by its captain. In order to lessen the risks of traversing the searchlight belt in Holland twice, Lewis elected to take a flight path across the North Sea to hit the German coast just north of the River Elbe almost due west of Kiel. From that point he intended to change course towards the south-east, heading directly for Berlin. Such a track would have taken L7380 about mid-way between Kiel and Hamburg and thus, for the most part, clear of the flak defences of those cities, as well as north of such other major defended city areas as Magdeburg, lying directly west of Berlin. The more northerly route avoided not only the Dutch searchlight belt but also the adjacent flak defences of the Ruhr valley and beyond.

Lewis had decided to complete the crossing of the North Sea maintaining a height of 8,000 feet until within striking distance of the north German coast. By this time, he would have burned off almost two hours of fuel, lightening the aircraft's all-up weight to an extent where he was hopeful they could climb to perhaps 14,000 to 15,000 feet – the most he could expect from the aircraft without overheating the engines.

Having left the English coast and heading out over the sea, the crew settled into a well-established routine. The gunners called in turn asking permission to test their guns. Lewis felt the discernible tremor in the airframe as Warrant Officer Hall traversed the mid-upper turret onto the beam before his short test burst.

With the experience of his two previous tours, Lewis had developed his philosophy for operational flying. This was applicable to a situation in which the aircraft carried a second pilot who did not have a duplicate set of instruments. Thus, Lewis maintained that if he himself became incapacitated the first thing was for the crew to extricate him so the second pilot could take over his position. With this in mind, Lewis had his friend in Lincoln (who owned a furniture store) fashion him a comfortable rubber and material covered cushion of the exact proportions to fit into the bucket seat of the aircraft. Instead of the seat pack parachute, he wore an observer-type harness and carried a chest pack-type parachute in the stowage position behind his seat.

When the aircraft reached cruising altitude Lewis adopted the custom of undoing his seat strap safety harness so, if necessary, he could easily be removed from his seat in the darkness. At the same time the co-pilot and navigator would swing up the armour plate, giving protection from the rear to the pilot's head and shoulders. On this flight, when Lewis dropped his safety harness, the co-pilot and navigator, for reasons they could not identify in the darkened cockpit, had great difficulty pushing the armoured plate the last part of the way and eventually had to use considerable force. However, the seat back was finally raised and could be locked in place. The reason for the difficulty was to become apparent a little while later.

The outward flight towards the German coast was uneventful other than that it suddenly dawned on them that they must have picked up a much stronger tail wind than the Met. forecasters had predicted, as they were reaching the enemy coast earlier than expected. Lewis therefore initiated a climb and soon L7380 was slogging up as fast as it could on full climbing power and travelling not much more than 110 mph indicated air-speed.

They had reached an altitude of approximately 13,000 feet and were still over the sea at a locality a few kilometres west of Tönning in Schleswig Holstein. The time was close to 22.00 hours GMT when 'Dusty' Miller, the rear gunner, suddenly called: 'night fighter astern!' The fighter concerned is now known to have been that of Feldwebel Siegfried Ney of 4/NJG1 in a Bf110 and the combat was timed at 00.10 hours on 8 September.

At the low speed Lewis was flying there was no possibility of any evasive action, but an instinctive and fortuitous presence of mind caused him to slam the stick hard forward. Simultaneously with the call they received a burst of tracer, combined machine gun and cannon fire, which hit the port wing in and around the port engine. The aircraft immediately sank like a stone and the nose dropped. No sooner was this action initiated then a second burst of machine gun and cannon fire soared over them, exactly in the position they had occupied moments earlier.

The fighter had approached from seven o'clock high and in the split second of its approach 'Dusty' Miller had drawn a bead on the closing night fighter and opened fire. The twin-engined aircraft was over-shooting and as the Manchester disappeared under his nose he broke away above and to port coming, as he did so, within the mid-upper gunner, Charles Hall's, field of fire at a range of only fifty to 100 feet. Miller also fired in the direction of the fighter before it broke away and lost contact completely.

Whilst the gunners kept a sharp lookout lest the fighter should return, Lewis took stock of their situation. Miraculously the aircraft had not caught fire under the hail of tracer bullets. Lewis could vaguely discern the many hits they had taken in the port wing and engine cowling. All engine functions appeared normal but the fuel gauges indicated a serious leak in the port fuel tank. It did not appear that any fire from the fighter had entered the fuselage and there were consequently no injuries. As a result of the seriousness of the fuel leak, Lewis recognised that it was hopeless going on towards the primary target, Berlin. He accordingly diverted south to Wilhelmshaven, dropped his 4,000 lb 'Cookie' and incendiaries on the town and had the navigator work out a course for Waddington.

A radio message was transmitted saying they had been attacked by a night fighter and were returning to base. Somehow the position passed with this message became garbled so that the squadron believed the attack to have taken place fifty miles from Berlin whereas, in reality, they had barely crossed the coast. L7380 was now heading westwards again over the North Sea at 8,000 feet. By this time the fuel had virtually stopped leaking from the wing tank, indicating that the self-sealing mechanism of the tank had eventually worked and staunched the flow.

Suddenly Lewis and Sergeant Powell, the second pilot, noticed that the port engine temperature was rising rapidly. Lewis took a quick look and saw that the whole engine and thin parts of the engine cowling were glowing red hot. By the time he had shut the engine down and feathered the propeller it had become white hot and would probably have seized and caught fire if left a few seconds longer.

After their lucky escapes from the night fighter and from fire when the engine almost seized, the fight to keep L7380 airborne now began in earnest. A last radio message was received at Waddington, timed fifteen minutes later than the first, saying that the port engine was smoking. Lewis set the starboard engine up on maximum power. He was grateful that the port tank had stopped leaking as they would obviously need every pint of fuel they could save if they were going to keep the aircraft airborne and reach the UK flying now into the wind. Relieved of the bombs and part of the fuel load and supported by the denser air at low level, Lewis was determined to make an all out effort. It would be touch and go, as he recalled: 'with the starboard engine wide open they were going to chew up an awful lot of gas to reach even East Anglia'.

Lewis immediately turned on the cross-feed to the port tank and shut off the starboard tank to draw the fuel out of the port wing and cut down the dead weight on the port side. The Manchester had started to lose height at a fairly rapid rate following the engine failure but Lewis had actually encouraged this. Below them was the layer of stratus and they felt like sitting ducks up at 8,000 feet on one engine.

Lewis intended to let down slowly until they were immediately above the layer of cloud. Here he reasoned at least they would be safe from attack from below and the gunners could keep a sharp look out in the lighter areas of sky above, if only they could maintain that flying height. They descended to about 5,000 feet, at which altitude they were within easy reach of the sanctuary of the protective layer of cloud. Unfortunately, despite Lewis' best efforts to trim the aircraft and the use of maximum power on the starboard Vulture, L7380 continued to sink. Slowly they descended into the cloud tops and on down through the cloud layer on instruments until they eventually emerged to see the dark waters of the North Sea beneath. Still the aircraft was showing no sign of maintaining altitude and it began to look certain that within a very short timescale they would have to ditch.

At this point, when they were down to perhaps 1,000 feet, Lewis decided that, since they would inevitably end up in the water if they maintained their present heading, it would be better to put the aircraft down somewhere on a beach rather than well out to sea where there was the serious risk of losing lives. Thus resigned to not reaching the UK he turned off course to the south until he hit the coast of the Frisian Isles, from which he had been slowly diverging. Having located the coast he again turned westwards keeping the aircraft just offshore. The starboard engine remained at maximum power but still the inexorable loss of height continued.

They were now below 500 feet and slowly sank on down towards 300 feet. At this height the aircraft began to give the first signs that it might hold altitude and there was suddenly the faintest glimmer of hope that they might remain airborne. The aircraft would fly straight and level for ten seconds or more and then drop a few feet and so on. Unfortunately these downward steps 'on the stairs' continued until Lewis could see by the beach off the port wing tip that they were practically in the water. Lewis deemed that this point, whilst they were flying along an open beach rather than crossing the open stretches of water between the islands, was as good a place as any to set them down. To carry out the forced landing Lewis needed to be strapped in again and here the problem with the armour plate head protection became apparent, for when Sergeant Powell tried to pass Lewis the safety harness they discovered that the shoulder straps were still over the back of the seat and now jammed by the raised head protection. It was these which had led to the difficulty in raising the plate. To the pilot's dismay the straps were jammed and he was unable to fasten his safety harness. Recognising the problem, Powell and Warrant Officer Macleod, the observer, tried to pull the pins to lower the armoured plate and release the straps, but it was so tightly jammed they were unable to free it. Time was short and a certain amount of confusion arose. As an emergency alternative Lewis had the co-pilot stand behind his seat and grab him by the shoulders to help reduce the impact. To the rear, 'Dusty' Miller misunderstood their instructions to take up crash landing positions and, thinking they were about to crash, opened the rear side entry door and made to jump out. Mid-upper gunner, Charles Hall, also climbing down from this turret to take up his crash position, just had time to grab Miller, pull him back and slam the door.

As Hall settled in position with the aircraft down to about 25 feet, Lewis pulled back the throttle to idle, dumped full flap and carried out a belly landing on the water about 100 feet out from the water line. There was a terrific shock from the impact, the deceleration from which being sufficiently minor that Powell managed to maintain his hold on Lewis. Immediately there was a second, more severe impact, when the aircraft struck the beach below the water, stoving in the bomb aiming perspex dome and bringing them to a shuddering halt. Lewis was catapulted from the Powell's grasp into the windscreen. A mighty wave of sea water gushed in through the crumpled nose section, rose up beneath the instrument panel and struck Lewis with full force at virtually the same moment he hit the windscreen. The massive tidal wave no doubt saved Lewis from possible serious injury. He received a severe bang on his head, was rendered semi-conscious, yet still functioned.

To the rear Miller was not yet settled in the crash position and was thrown violently forwards, breaking a small bone in his right hand. At the same time the circular hatch over the former dustbin turret position burst inwards atop a fountain of sea water.

The crew then scrambled to vacate the fuselage in case the aircraft sank. On climbing out of the escape hatches they found to their relief that L7380 had settled down in about 6 feet of water, facing west south west and lying parallel to the beach. Lewis' next real conscious memory is of coming-to sitting in the escape hatch in the cockpit roof, his feet dangling inside and calling to the crew: 'Is everyone out OK?' He was somewhat chastened by the impatience of the response to the query: 'Christ, Skipper, that's the third time you've asked us that - we are all OK!'

They began to collect themselves and their thoughts. The time was approximately 01.00 BST. Looking around there was no indication that their spectacular arrival had attracted any attention. They agreed to take their time and return into the aircraft, finding the interior flooded to knee depth on the flight deck. Having collected the fire axes from their stowage positions they commenced a thorough and systematic destruction of anything and everything which could possibly interest the Germans. They chopped the instrument panel to pieces, the engine instrument panel on the starboard side, the navigation equipment, the radio, the gun sights etc. They pressed the self-destruct buttons on the confidential items like the bomb sight and identification, friend or foe (IFF) gear but

L7380 EM-W of 207 Squadron on the beach at Ameland, Frisian Islands. German work party waiting for the tide to recede. Note that the port propeller is missing. This is the wing and engine damaged by the night fighter. (Rene Metz)

found they had already detonated and then proceeded to demolish these with the axes too. The two wireless operators, Kingston and Hall, between them ate all the night's coded signals they had been issued with at briefing. Although printed on rice paper these were still more than a mouthful!

Having done a thorough job, they decided to make for the shore. Suddenly they heard a hiss and turned to see the dinghy appear from its stowage in the starboard wing root. As it inflated it flopped obstinately upside down into the water by the wing trailing edge. After a struggle this was righted and towed round to the port side. They then walked to the port wingtip and dropped into the sea, which was here only three to four feet deep. This was of great relief to Lewis, a life-long non-swimmer.

In a group they waded to the shore, pushing the dinghy ahead of them, where a sudden and frightening thought struck Lewis. During 1941, Commando raids by British troops had started in earnest. It came to his mind that surely these exposed beaches on the seaward side of

L7380 EM-W on Ameland beach, probably on the earliest tide on 8 September 1941 before being scoured into the beach. Damaged port fin possibly stained with oil from the Vulture engine. (Rene Metz)

the Frisians must be mined. He held back the crew in shallow water and set off alone up the beach, with a great deal of trepidation, instructing them on leaving that if he made it to dry land they were to follow him in single file stepping in his footsteps. In the event there were no mines and they all made it onto the main part of the island without incident.

There was still no sign of life. They started walking along the beach heading westwards, trying to establish their location and before long found themselves heading back eastwards. This confirmed to them that they were on an island, which was in fact, unknown to them, Ameland. Shortly afterwards they found a large lifeboat at least twenty-five feet long mounted on a cradle consisting of a half-track bogie with wagon wheels at the front, obviously designed for launching by a team of horses. Inspection showed it to be equipped with a mast, engine and fuel. They went through the boat from stem to stern and finding a bottle with a small amount of rum remaining, shared it between them.

They found boards and poles and, working as a team, tried to lever the boat seawards in the hope of sailing it away. They continued to work all night without moving the heavy boat by as much as a fraction. As the dawn rose they saw beyond, at a short distance, a village with a wharf but no sign of other boats they might use. They decided not to involve the local Dutch population for fear of bringing the wrath of the German occupying forces down upon the civilian population. It was a wise decision, for as it turned out there was no way the local people could have helped them to get off the island. At around 09.00 hours a German soldier appeared over the dunes. He raised his rifle and shouted to them to raise their arms. Covering them, he called out to others nearby and they were rapidly surrounded and captured.

At more or less the same time that 'Mike' Lewis was setting L7380 down on the beach at Ameland the remainder of the Berlin force reached the target area. Flying Officer 'Junior' Gardiner observed a large fire started by preceding aircraft and dropped his four 1,000-lb GP bombs on Aiming Point 'A' from 18,000 feet, starting a small fire. Searchlights and flak were as fierce as ever and although Gardiner was not singled out for attack he did see another bomber caught by the lights weaving desperately to escape. At one point this aircraft was seen to fire on a sister aircraft, fortunately with no discernible effect.

As Pilot Officer 'Len' Paskell guided L7328 onto the target at 17,000 feet he was in turn trapped and illuminated by the searchlights. More and more lights converged on his aircraft until the crew estimated that twenty-five to thirty from all over the city were involved. The heavy flak batteries began to get their range and despite vigorous evasive action the aircraft was hit fifteen times, rendering the hydraulics and turrets unserviceable. The crew eventually slipped away into the protective cloak of darkness and returned home, fortunately without being detected by the patrolling night fighters. The results of their efforts could not be observed due to smoke from fires burning near the aiming point.

Flying Officer 'Kipper' Herring and crew had followed a route north-east to a point close to Flensburg and then dog-legged across the Baltic to Berlin, entering German airspace between Lubeck and Rostock. En route to the target they observed and successfully evaded patrolling night fighters on five occasions. As they approached the target area they had reached 18,000 feet. The defences were thoroughly alerted and intense flak and searchlight activity was evident. As they held a steady course on the bombing run they were trapped in a large searchlight cone and shrapnel from near misses began to pepper the aircraft. Four 1,000-lb GPs were released and seen to straddle the target. As the observer closed the bomb doors, and Herring prepared to recommence violent evasive action, the aircraft was suddenly hit by a flak burst. Most seriously hit was the port Vulture, which began to lose coolant rapidly. In quick succession four more flak hits shook the Manchester.

In desperation, Herring put the aircraft into a dive to escape the barrage. As the engine temperature rose he had no alternative but to shut it down and feather the propeller. Unknown to them other damage had occurred, not the least of which was that the bursts had activated the dinghy release. The life raft had inflated and floated down to join the mayhem below. Loss of the port engine meant that the hydraulic supply was also rendered unserviceable, incapacitating all three turrets.

As soon as Herring felt them to be clear of the barrage he pulled out, fortunately they had sustained no further damage. As they levelled out they were relieved to find all the flak bursting several thousand feet higher. In fact they had sustained more than thirty flak hits in the wings and fuselage. The port flank had taken the brunt, with the engine dead and three holes in the wing tank. Fortunately the self-sealing around the tank worked and the fuel loss was contained. Their immediate situation had stabilised but the long term prospect of a single engine return from such a distant target as Berlin was remote. Herring was determined to give it his best shot and a hurried discussion took place. Offered the option of baling out or co-operating in the attempted return, the crew chorused in unison: 'We're staying with you, Skipper'.

A serviceman trying Charles Hall's mid-upper turret for size. (Rene Metz)

Work parties return to the wreck of L7380 and remove the guns. Note how the wavy colour demarcation is over-sprayed on a sharp and straight factory finish. In the foreground the serviceman is using an oxy-acetylene burner. (via G. J. Zwanenburg)

Top: Second Pilot Sergeant Sam Powell and bottom, W/op AG Sergeant Charles Hall, photographed by the Germans at Nes, the ferry harbour on Ameland on 8 September 1941. (Rene Metz)

Left: Wilfred Stanley 'Kipper' Herring sketched six months after his memorable single-engine return from Berlin. By this time he had risen in rank to Squadron Leader. (G. R. Herring) Right: Sergeant M. A. 'Mad Max' Riddell, one of the giants of 5 Group Bomber Command, who provided the account of the single engine return of L7432 EM-Z on 8 September 1941. (M. A. Riddell)

As they vacated the target area L7432 began to lose height slowly. Whilst Herring set up the aircraft to fly straight and level and minimise the height loss, the observer, Sergeant Smith, laid out a course in a direct line across the most heavily defended areas of Germany. The wireless operator, Sergeant Riddell, was equally occupied. He transmitted the usual 'Q' code group for duty carried out and that they had encountered heavy defensive action. A coded damage status report followed. He continued listening out for Bomber Command broadcasts of weather conditions during the return flight and began taking bearings to assist the navigation on the homeward leg.

Their predicament, in a Manchester reduced to a single engine and with its defensive armament totally disabled, deep in enemy territory, was precarious in the extreme. Whilst the pilots, observer and wireless operator were fully occupied, the two gunners were relieved from their defensive responsibilities. However, L7432 was continuing to lose height and the two were set to work stripping out and jettisoning everything they could get loose from the airframe to decrease their all-up weight. This had to be accomplished rapidly but with the minimum of movement within the aircraft so as not to upset the delicate trim. Every foot of altitude was precious and once lost could not be recovered. First Sergeant Everett jettisoned the bombsight, the twin Brownings and all the ammunition from the front turret through the forward escape hatch.

'Tiny' Hallam, the rear gunner, opened the rear hatch and the crew members now formed a human chain passing first the readily dismountable items. The remaining six Brownings from the rear and mid-upper turrets and all their ammunition were dumped. The oxygen bottles, flares etc all went and next the crew set to with fire axes removing parts of the airframe, including even the armoured doors between the cockpit area and the rear fuselage. Despite the critical nature of their situation there was still time for light-hearted banter, Hallam ribbing Smith to the effect that the latter would be missing his date with his girlfriend yet again. This was a crack at Smith having become serious over a local girl to the extent that he moaned loudly every time his scheduled dates were interfered with by unscheduled changes in plan.

Their height was now down to 5,000 feet and with the reduction in weight, Herring found L7432 could now maintain this altitude. They were fortunate in evading detection by the defences as they approached the Dutch searchlight belt and Riddell allowed himself to be buoyed up by the prospect that they might at least reach the North Sea with the chance of ditching and being picked up by the air-sea rescue service. Nobody had any idea that the dinghy had been lost. As they crossed the searchlight belt Herring managed to take careful, but spirited, evasive action to avoid detection by the probing beams. The controls started to become sluggish and Herring realised the aircraft was icing up and they were forced lower still.

Eventually the enemy coast was reached and the long laborious crossing of the North Sea began. The crew could barely believe that the starboard Vulture would continue to keep them aloft for so long, but stagger along they did. L7432 was really a unique Manchester.

After a five hour return flight, in the first light of dawn and on the last dregs of fuel the aircraft reached West Raynham. Having used the emergency system to blow down the undercart, 'Kipper' approached the airfield still carrying opposite rudder to counteract the loss of the port engine. He kept the port wing high to minimise the forces on the damaged side of the aircraft and lined up on the grass beside the active runway. Such a cautious approach proved wise when, having touched down on the starboard wheel first, speed was lost before the port wheel was allowed to touch the runway. Unbeknown to the pilot the port tyre was flat, with the result that they swung round sharply to the left, although without further damage to the aircraft. The time was 06.00 hours. It was a truly magnificent feat of airmanship and an even more miraculous landing.

When the crew shut down the starboard engine, opened the doors and got out to inspect the aircraft, they found to their amazement that the dinghy, which for some hours they had expected to use, was missing. According to some reports a 1,000-lb GP bomb was found to be hung up in the bomb bay, but this has not been confirmed. It was exactly a month since the final spate of engine mods and few could doubt that despite this crews' determination, engine unreliability prior to this time would probably have prevented such prolonged full throttle operation. L7432 must have looked a wreck, but it was a popular aircraft and following repair returned to the squadron. Herring christened his mount 'London Pride' and it became much sought after by fellow crews. It was later to experience another engine failure, but once more carry its crew back to a safe landing.

Maxwell Alexander Dick Riddell was already a notable character on 207 Squadron. Having completed a Hampden tour, he proved himself over and over again to be irrepressible. Not content to fly his briefed operations, on his off duty days when the Squadron was operating he was regularly to be found hanging around the crew room on the off chance of a Wireless Operation/Air Gunner dropping out at the last minute. In this way he hoped to scrounge extra sorties. Soon, and from his initials, fellow aircrew were calling him 'Mad Max'. His role as a talisman was further emphasised when, prior to operations, new aircrew members insisted on clapping him on the shoulder saying: 'Good Luck, Max'. In response to his mystified requests of his friends, they laughingly replied that his superstitious fellows believed that by touching him they picked up his luck. As they explained: 'They know you'll always come back, Max'. Indeed, Max Riddell went on to fly more or less continuously from 1939 to 1945, completing more than ninety operations.

Gardiner and Paskell had returned to Waddington at 05.00 and 05.20 hours respectively. After the raid, 137 crews reported attacking Berlin in clear weather and many buildings were damaged in the Lichtenberg and Pankow districts to the east and north of the centre; thirty-six civilians were killed and 212 injured. On the squadron there was dismay at the loss of 'Mike' Lewis and crew but joy and wonder at the near miraculous return of 'Kipper' Herring and his crew.

Within a few days Kipper's crew were invited to the Avro factory at Woodford to be feted by the firm. They had dinner with the Managing Director, Mr Roy Dobson, and Chief Designer, Roy Chadwick, which included, as one was to recall later, the best tomato soup he had ever tasted. Each member was presented with a silver cigarette case to commemorate their achievement. Such was the reputation of the Manchester and the limitations of its military achievements that simply to get one home was an occasion worth celebrating. This fact could not detract in any way from the magnificent feat of airmanship 'Kipper' Herring and his crew achieved.

From early September things had begun, imperceptibly, to improve. Groundings were at an end, serviceability was improving, 61 Squadron had temporarily relinquished its Manchesters, 97 Squadron had reverted to training, and 'B' Flight of 207 Squadron was working up to operational status again. On 10 September another development was manifest for the first time when 207 Squadron took delivery of it's and the RAF's first twin-finned Mk.1A Manchesters, when L7483 and L7484 were received at Waddington. L7483 was the 133rd not the twenty-first Mk.1A airframe as all previous histories claim.

With the arrival of these aircraft the Manchester experienced its fourth and final change in colour scheme. The wavy line demarcation between the upper and lower surfaces was replaced by a simpler, straight line. Despite the removal of the central fin, the straight line demarcation continued to sweep up over the fuselage top as if the central fin was still in place.

Also on 10 September 5 Manchesters, including Flying Officer Gardiner and crew in L7309 EM-O were briefed to attack Turin in Italy. They were to extend their range by staging through Wattisham in Norfolk, reaching there late in the afternoon. On landing they found it was a small grass airfield with trees on the boundary of the longest run. Briefed to refuel and take-off at dusk, they were concerned as to whether their aircraft could clear the trees with a full load. As it happened, the commanding officer, Wing Commander K P Lewis, had flown down in a spare aeroplane with no bombs, a light fuel load, and with a number of ground crew, Lewis immediately undertook a trial take-off which was sufficiently marginal that a fully loaded take-off was clearly impossible. The crews stayed the night, returning to Waddington next day without refuelling.

In an unusual interlude on 11 September 207 Squadron entertained a Russian military mission at Waddington. Colonel Fedrovi, a Russian test pilot, and Major Shvetsov, the Air Attaché as interpreter, were given a 45 minute demonstration flight in Manchester L7319 by Flying Officer Geoff Hall, on secondment from 61 Squadron. The evaluation included fighter affiliation with a Boulton Paul Defiant and Colonel Fedrovi had by this time taken the controls. The Russian put the wind up Hall on more than one occasion with unconventional manoeuvres during this close encounter. It steadily became apparent the visitor was a very competent pilot and Hall had little alternative but to sit back and try to keep calm. After the aircraft disengaged they returned safely to Waddington where the Russians departed following hearty handshakes and lunch in the mess.

The underlying purpose of the visit is uncertain, but it is tempting to suggest that some especially imaginative 'bod' at the Air Ministry had devised the ideal solution to the Manchester problem – give them to the Russians! Our Russian Allies accepted everything offered to them, often with bad grace. Palming them off with Manchesters would have been a master stroke. Alas it was not to be!

Official photograph of one of 207 Squadron's first Mk.1As, L7483 EM-H, at Waddington, c. September/October 1941. Later coded EM-O, this aircraft was written-off after a forced landing at Martlesham Heath by Squadron Leader K. H. P. Beauchamp. The crew named it 'Hobson's Choice' – a fitting description of their own situation. (Author's collection).

Imposing shot, probably of Mk.1A L7483 now EM-O at Waddington, September/October 1941. (Author's collection)

One of 207 Squadron's first Manchester Mk.1As, L7486, caught on a brief air test from Waddington soon after delivery in early September 1941. L7486 was dispatched nineteen times as EM-P and EM-B. (J. Simpson)

On Sunday 11 September another Australian pilot, Flight Sergeant W. G. (George) Hawes, arrived at Waddington to fly Manchesters. His first operation was on 12 October to Huls and he completed twelve more by 12 March 1942 before converting to Lancasters. George became firm friends with fellow Antipodean, John McCarthy, as well as with one of a pair of New Zealand twins in Bomber Command, Geoff Allen (and Ralph, his brother), together with Canadian gunners Bob Bestel and Bill Blair and navigator Jack Leahy. George's letters home were kept by his family and subsequently privately published by his niece, Denise Rope, under the title *'For The Duration'*. In the letters at one time George jokes he should start with 'Dear Folks and Censor' nothing material in respect of his service flying emerges though, providing good accounts of his off-duty life. In the grim slaughter that was the bomber war, all these 207 Squadron aircrew were to be killed, George Hawes and John McCarthy on the same night in July 1942.

On 12 September 1941, three more Mk.1As arrived at Waddington – L7485, L7486, and L7487. The boys from 'B' Flight of 207 Squadron congregated in front of one of the new Mk.1As within two or three days and had their photographs taken. The new aircraft were allocated directly to them. 5 Group's commitment to giving the squadron priority regarding the supply of aircraft was being adhered to.

By mid-September the bulk of the Vulture problems were cured up to a point. Mod. No.44 was being applied to all Vultures in turn by Rolls-Royce and the re-engineered motors finally delivered to Avro for the engineless Manchesters standing idle and forlorn at Cranage, Woodford and Ringway. It seems that the last Avro-built Manchester was completed in late September 1941, whilst Woodford were to complete the last Metrovick aircraft in about November, before switching to Lancasters. At last the equipping of the remainder of 5 Group with Manchesters, albeit now as a stopgap measure, could be considered.

The reduction in rpm from 3,200 to 2,850 reluctantly agreed to by Rolls-Royce was of great significance in terms of Vulture development and its future potential. It signified the acceptance by the engine designer that it was his star-rod design which was placing an ultimate ceiling on power output in the engine. Opinion within Rolls-Royce was later to be virtually unanimous that it was the star-rod design which killed the Vulture. Only a further major redesign could provide a con-rod configuration capable of absorbing continual increments of power, as opposed to the pegging back represented by reduced con-rod bolt loading.

In late 1941, when the power output from the Merlin was going up in leaps and bounds, the Vulture was operating at the extreme limit it could be stretched to at that stage of its development. By this time only the Manchester was powered by the Vulture and even if the engine had been fully developed and reliable, the Manchester would still have remained underpowered and seriously at risk in the event of one engine failing. As far back as November 1940 it had been recognised that the four-Merlin Manchester lll, the Lancaster, offered the way forward.

At this stage Rolls-Royce's own assessment of the Vulture was that, to emulate the Merlin and take the first step on the ladder to greater power, the Vulture needed three things: a redesigned con-rod assembly; a two piece cylinder block; a two stage blower. A Rolls-Royce director and confidant of Lord Hives, Mr R. W. Harvey-Bailey (Senior), had produced a redesign of the star-rod assembly in the Vulture as a private venture. This reached the model stage and was apparently highly regarded in respect of its innovative design. The redesign envisaged a big-end cap carrying three rods and a union with the fork of the master rod in the same plane as the rod, avoiding the troublesome diagonal junction in the existing star-rod. The low ductility, high brinell con-rod bolts were to be replaced by four long bolts in the steel more commonly used for this purpose by Rolls-Royce metallurgists. These, too, were oriented in the same plane as the master rod.

Pilots of 'B' Flight 207 Squadron, Waddington, posed in front of one of their new Manchester Mk.1As in early September 1941. Left to right: Warrant Officer K. A. King (unit unknown), Flight Lieutenant Geoffrey Hall (seconded from 61 Squadron), Flying Officer John de Lacey Wooldridge, Pilot Officer Gordon Crump (killed 15 September 1941), Flying Officer David A. Green, Pilot Officer John C. L. Ruck-Keene (killed in action 20/21 October 1941), Pilot Officer B. Derek Bowes-Cavanagh (killed in action 12/13 October 1941) and Pilot Officer George R. Bayley (killed in action 8/9 January 1942). (207 Squadron Archives. Crown copyright CH3893)

Power output at altitude was restricted by the two-speed supercharger and the need for a two-speed, two-stage supercharger another essential requirement. Had these three developments come to fruition then possibly the Vulture would have outperformed the Napier Sabre and gone on to a bright future. In September the brutal truths of the Vulture situation were all too obvious to Rolls-Royce personnel. Eventually Lovell felt sufficiently confident to raise take-off power back up to +9 lb psi boost and 3,000 rpm. This was a mere drop in the ocean.

Roy Chadwick was relentless in pressing Rolls-Royce to increase take-off power still further. He had enquired whether power could be raised further to 3,200 rpm, which would give +11 lb psi boost. Rolls reflected that this was not covered by type test approval and was already too much for the con-rod assembly.

Moreover, Chadwick had pressed for further increases, mentioning revolutions as high as 3,400 rpm. Rolls-Royce commented that at 3,000 rpm the Vulture was already using the maximum power obtainable as the engine was full throttle at +9 lb psi. They pointed out that Boscombe Down had shown that 3,200 rpm at +9 lb psi boost gave no measurable improvement in take-off. The difference between Roy Chadwick's hopes and the reality was stark. In the end wartime expediency killed the Vulture just as that same expediency had thrust it forward into the limelight in 1940, well ahead of its designated time. It was about this time that the decision was made to cancel any further development. The Vulture had reached the end and when the decision to abandon the engine went around the Rolls-Royce factory at Derby, the only reaction was a loud and almost universal sigh of relief from all sides.

At this time anyone who was the least bit superstitious would have been excused for believing the Vulture and indeed the Manchester was irretrievably jinxed. As if to strengthen such views an epidemic of propeller feathering mechanism failures now burgeoned in the squadrons. Rolls-Royce compiled a record of these failures with a view to isolating a common cause. The list, dated 17 November, no doubt included failures over much of 1941 as well as those of recent date. The Rolls-Royce report concluded that the constant speed unit and feathering system had been the cause of the trouble. The airscrew itself appeared satisfactory. A large proportion of the forced landings would not have happened had it not been for a fundamental defect in every Manchester installation, causing the airscrew to lock in fine pitch.

Manchester Propeller Feathering Failures – 17 November 1941:

Serial	Operator	Pilot	Date
L7375	97 Squadron	Blakeman	28.09.41

Written off in forced-landing near Coningsby. Pressure cut-out switch did not work when feathering, so airscrew unfeathered again to fine pitch stops, and remained there owing to defect referred to above.

L7308	97 Squadron	Blakeman	28.10.41

Written off in forced-landing near Coningsby. Airscrew feathered itself on take-off, due to defect in constant speed unit. (Aircraft Record Cards indicate aircraft reincarnated at some stage – Author)

L7520	61 Squadron	Searby	02.11.41

Written off in forced-landing Roxton, Beds. Port engine cut in flight and airscrew could not be feathered so that aircraft could not maintain height.

L7280	207 Squadron?	Eustace?	-

Landed downwind at Waddington aerodrome. Airscrew feathered itself on take-off due to defect in constant speed unit.

L7465	97 Squadron	-	-

Vulture No.548. Went to fine pitch stops after unfeathering at Coningsby. Four con-rods broken.

R5782	207 Squadron	-	11.11.41

Vulture No.166. Went into fine pitch after unfeathering. Engine returned to works after over-reving. No damage done.

L7286?	207 Squadron	Burton-Gyles?	04.06.41?

Force-landed in field near Waddington. Airscrews could not be unfeathered after a silent approach test.

L7320	A&AEE	-	-

Airscrew feathered itself and then went to the fine pitch stops on take-off. Solenoid switch was stuck. Collided with wireless mast and force-landed at Boscombe Down.

L7282	97 Squadron?	-	-

Force-landed on Waddington aerodrome. Port airscrew would not unfeather after feathering test.

L7292	-	-	27.11.40

Force-landed on Woodford aerodrome. Airscrew went to fine pitch on take-off due to failure of constant speed unit washer. Con-rod broken.

L7322 - - -

Force-landed on Waddington aerodrome. Same as above. Over-revving did not damage engine.

L7377   207 Squadron   Nunn   05.41

Force-landed between the hangars at Scampton. The airscrew feathered itself in flight, and then went to the fine pitch stops due to a short in the electronics.

Flight Sergeant Stan Harrison RAAF was experiencing his 'type conversion' onto the Manchester with an air experience flight with Flying Officer 'Ginger' Blakeman in L7375 OF-B on the first listed incident. In his book *A Bomber Command Survivor*, he explains:

On 20 September my flight commander on 16 OTU Upper Heyford informed me I was shortly to be posted for a second operational tour in 5 Group, joining 97 Squadron at Coningsby. The thought that I must endure a further thirty operational missions was depressing, even more so in Manchesters for their unenviable reputation for unreliability was widely feared. On 28 September Flying Officer Blakeman took me aloft. Cloud base was a bare 1,200 feet and this doubtless influenced 'Ginger' to demonstrate the feathering and single engine performance at a lowly 1,100 feet. Having done this, the blade feathering mechanism allowed these to rotate until they reached full fine pitch, offering maximum resistance and making an efficient air brake. In spite of 'Ginger's' strenuous efforts to unfeather the propeller we descended rapidly towards the fortunately flat open Lincolnshire countryside, force-landing with a resounding, ear-piercing, sliding crunch as the nose, bomb bay and lower fuselage crumpled. We stopped quickly as a massive shower of earth, stones and general debris erupted through the shattered nose. We were shocked but unhurt on noticing with surprise back along our track the enormous and very deep ditch over which we had skated as we arrived semi-stalled.

The subsequent investigation report stated: Propeller unfeathered itself spontaneously, went to fine pitch stops and stuck. Engine promptly over-revved itself and the drag on one side caused an immediate forced landing to be made at East Sibsey near Boston, writing off the aircraft.

My feelings towards the Manchester were not improved, though I calmed down somewhat a few days later when our Flight Commander, Squadron Leader 'Flap' Sherwood demonstrated the same manoeuvre successfully from a safer height.

Miraculously nobody was killed in any of these incidents, but they can have done little to bolster confidence in the Vulture or the Manchester. For much of this period 207 and 97 Squadrons were engaged on operations and there is no record of any feathering failure in the course of operational flying. In December 1941 Pilot Officer Dave Green was to have an engine failure at low level over the Severn Estuary in L7432. In this case the feathering mechanism remained operational and a safe single engine landing was carried out. Moves towards rectification had obviously been made, but quite what and when this was achieved is not established.

With Manchester airframe development finally reaching its ultimate expression and Vulture engine development terminated, in mid-September 1941 the story of the aircraft itself reaches an end. Production had ceased and the Manchester was no more than a stopgap awaiting the Lancaster. Many Manchesters remained engineless and ineffective and it would be the end of the year before enough aircraft were serviceable to begin the task of re-equipping more 5 Group squadrons. It would be early December before 61 Squadron returned to operations, followed in quick succession by 83 and 106 Squadrons.

With many 61 Squadron crews attached to 97 and 207 Squadrons for further training, the remainder of September was principally taken up with testing new aircraft and training new crews. Despite this there were adventures and tragedies aplenty for Manchester crews during the month.

Top: Captain L. D, Gammans MP (suited) visited Coningsby on 21 September 1941, representing the Association of British Malay at the naming of 97 Squadron as the 'Straits Settlements' squadron. Top row, left to right: Flying Officer D. S. Mims; Flight Lieutenant J. Truman; Flight Lieutenant C. E. Rolfe; Pilot Officer W. G. Noble; Flying Officer H. S. Blakeman DFM. Bottom row, left to right: Flight Lieutenant C. P. D. Price DFC; Wing Commander D. F. Balsdon; Squadron Leader J. S. Sherwood DFC, Flight Lieutenant L. Hinds. (Imperial War Museum CH4055) Bottom: Twelve pilots and a 97 Squadron Manchester pose on 21 September 1941 on the occasion of the linking of the unit with the Association of British Malay. (Imperial War Museum CH4056)

On 13 September Sergeant 'Jammy' Hartley and crew of 97 Squadron had a lucky escape when a main wheel tyre burst on L7306 just before lift off. The undercarriage collapsed and the aircraft spun round and caught fire. L7306 was a write-off. That night Pilot Officer D. E. Fox of 97 Squadron ran out of fuel on a cross-country flight in L7383. The aircraft crashed in an attempted forced landing at West Wickhouse, two miles south of the village of North Walsham in Norfolk. One crew member died.

Training of 207 Squadron 'B' Flight crews was progressing over this period and various exercises and night cross-country flights took the aircraft long distances from Waddington. On one such navigation exercise, on 14 September 1941, a 'B' Flight Manchester made a scheduled landing at Millom (or Haverigg) in Cumberland. It appears that when this Manchester later took off from Millom to continue the exercise a thin paper washer in a hydraulic component in the fuselage failed, causing the fluid under pressure to spurt out in a dense spray. The hydraulic system was of relatively low pressure, in large diameter pipes, involving large volumes of fluid. Such was the suddenness of the rupture and the severity of the leak that the wireless operator incorrectly presumed that the aircraft had hit the sea and was ditching. Quickly recognising the true source of the fluid, the wireless operator, who was nearest to the leak, called the pilot, who completed a circuit and landed before all the fluid drained out of the system.

The captain telephoned Waddington to tell them of his plight and another aircraft was quickly made ready and Eric McCabe and a small team of fitters flew up to Millom. When McCabe inspected the unserviceable aircraft the cause of the leak was quickly established, but as the necessary spare parts were not available, the aircraft and fitters returned to Waddington that night.

Next day, with the necessary spares, Pilot Officer Crump took off in L7318 for Millom. Eric McCabe was due to accompany Crump, but at the last moment a Senior Rolls-Royce representative arrived to discuss engine problems. McCabe handed his flying kit to a Senior NCO who took his place. Later, on 15 September, with the repair completed the two aircraft flew back to Waddington where the repaired Manchester landed safely in the early evening.

An Op was planned for 'A' Flight for that night. Six Manchesters were to attack Hamburg, the total force being 169 aircraft. At around 18.30 hours the crews were out on the airfield carrying out their pre-flight checks. Pilot Officer Paskell and crew were busy 'washing down' the tail wheel of their Manchester when Crump appeared in the circuit in L7318. There was just time for him to land before the Manchester force took off.

Hamburg – 15 September 1941:

Serial	Code	Squadron	Captain
L7300	EM-S	207	Fg Off. W. G. Gardiner
L7455	EM-G	207	Plt Off. A. W. Hills
L7378	EM-A	207	Plt Off. D. A. Green
L7373	EM-*	207	Plt Off. W. S. Herring
L7317	EM-C	207	Plt Off. P. C. Birch
?	EM-*	207	Plt Off. L. A. Paskell

'Penny' Beauchamp, the 'B' Flight Commander, was on the airfield awaiting the return of his charges. He watched L7318 as it flew past the airfield at about 1,000 feet on the downwind leg prior to landing. Suddenly, without any warning or radio call from the aircraft, it put its nose straight down and dived vertically into the ground. There was a large explosion as the aircraft plunged into a field at South Hykeham, five miles west of Waddington. The crash and explosion left a large smoking crater and scattered wreckage far and wide. The aircraft was carrying a total of ten air and ground crew and there were no survivors.

A member of the ground crew party sent to the scene soon afterwards, Corporal Terry Flatt, described the horrific sights at the crash site: 'Near one crumpled section of airframe he came upon the torso of a crew member still strapped in his seat, the head was missing and only the stumps of his four limbs remained. It was a gruesome and tragic loss'.

The crash investigation by the Accident Investigation Branch (AIB) proved inconclusive, no defects in the airframe or engines could be found. In the absence of any positive evidence and in view of the timing and position when the crash occurred the AIB inspector hypothesised that, since an extra crew complement was being carried, one or more of them were more than likely travelling in the nose compartment. There was a rule that the aircraft were not to land with any crew members in the nose except on operations. It was suggested that after Crump had lowered the wheels prior to landing he would have called those in the nose to get back into the rear of the aircraft for landing, thus shifting the centre of gravity aft. When the flaps were lowered the centre of gravity would suddenly shift further aft. At such a slow speed lift would disappear, with the result that the nose would drop and the aircraft would crash before control could be recovered. This conjecture was later tested at a safe height in a simulation of the crash. It was found that the aircraft did indeed nose down and lost at least 1,000 feet before level flight could be regained.

Despite the shock at witnessing L7318 going straight-in directly in front of their eyes, the 'A' Flight operation had to proceed. Whilst crash crews and ambulances went out to try and find survivors from Crump's aircraft, the six Manchesters completed their pre-flight checks and trundled out for take-off. Pilot Officer Len Paskell's Manchester, with Sergeant 'Eddy' Edmonds on board, became unserviceable with mechanical trouble before take-off; it is thought the rear tyre burst. Thus, only five Manchesters departed in a tight bunch between 18.49 and 18.52 hours.

On the outward journey they encountered dense cloud which became more broken towards the target, allowing details on the ground to be discerned. At this stage of their operational career, the aircraft were reaching more respectable flying heights, ranging from 13,000 to 17,500 feet in the target area, where they encountered ferocious opposition whilst searchlights and intense flak interfered with bombing accuracy. The aircraft attacked between 21.33 and 21.57 hours. Flying Officer Gardiner's observer watched his bombs burst in a line across a railway junction within one mile of Aiming point 'B', whilst Pilot Officer Herring's bombs, which were a mixture of a 'Cookie', and 4-lb incendiaries, burst one mile north of the railway junction. The intense opposition resulted in a number of casualties in the attacking force. Gardiner recorded a bomber crashing in flames at 21.33 hours. Hills also observed an aircraft in the target area illuminated by searchlights and shot down. Herring saw an aircraft shot down by fighters and another by flak as it was passing over Sylt.

Pilot Officer Dave Green was flying that night with an inexperienced second pilot, Sergeant Thomas. Thomas was to become a capable pilot before being tragically killed with Sergeant Wescombe and crew on 14 January 1942. Sergeant 'Goldie' Goldstraw, the observer in the aircraft, recalls Thomas as a big gangling lad who wore his full Irving jacket and trousers in the cockpit.

On the return flight, when Dave Green judged they were beyond the zone in which German night fighter attacks might be encountered, he suggested that the second pilot should exchange seats with him and obtain some operational experience behind a full set of blind flying instruments. Owing to his size and the cumbersome flying suit, Thomas had some difficulty in making the switch and in doing so unknowingly kicked the flap lever forward, dropping the flaps fully down. At the same time his left elbow inadvertently knocked the autopilot, which was disengaged, to the 'on' position. The autopilot had not been trimmed to fly the aircraft 'hands off' and consequently the aircraft immediately began a vicious climb, which became progressively steeper until, as the speed fell away, the Manchester stalled. Green and Thomas naturally were in a difficult position, not yet strapped in and disconnected from the intercom. As the aircraft reared up both were pushing desperately forward on the control column fighting the autopilot and flaps. Meanwhile the mid-upper gunner was shouting down the intercom: 'The flaps are down. The flaps are down'. It was pandemonium as the shouted comments were deafening everyone other than the only two who had the means to rectify the situation. The aircraft performed several other manoeuvres it was not designed to do before Dave Green had the chance to slip back into the left hand seat.

In the complete darkness, operating by touch only, Green quickly established which of the many potential combination of variables was not as it should be, pulled up the flaps again and disengaged the autopilot. Slowly they calmed down and breathed again, not for nothing would Dave Green receive an assessment of 'Above Average' as a multi-engine pilot on leaving the squadron. His superb qualities of airmanship had undoubtedly saved the aircraft in circumstances where a less experienced pilot may have been unable to diagnose the combination of changes which was causing the control difficulties.

Pilot Officer Birch had a frustrating experience. Having reached the target area his aircraft, L7317, experienced a bomb release failure. Perhaps whilst stooging around trying to release them his aircraft was coned by searchlights and held. He evaded them by gliding. One 1,000-lb bomb was eventually jettisoned in the sea and the remainder brought all the way back. On return he found the hydraulics unserviceable, as did Hills. Both pilots managed to pull off safe landings at Waddington, presumably following the use of the emergency systems to lower the flaps and undercarriage.

They landed back between 00.45 and 01.30 hours. Hamburg was a heavily defended, hard nut of a target. Throughout his tour, Bill Hills had a premonition he was going to be shot down over Hamburg. He did have some narrow escapes but was ultimately one of those to complete a tour.

On this occasion 207 Squadron's modest effort was marred only by the persistent malfunctions of the aircraft and all had returned safely. A great deal of damage occurred in Hamburg in this attack. There were twenty-six fires, seven of them large; eighty-two civilians were killed and 229 injured. The worst incident occurred in Wielandstrasse where a 'Cookie' fell on a large apartment block which was still occupied, sixty-six civilians were killed and 171 injured in this single incident.

Later in September there was more excitement at Waddington. The very first Metropolitan Vickers built Manchester delivered to the RAF, R5782, had just been received by the squadron, which by then was also using Bottesford for flying training.

On 27 September 1941 'Penny' Beauchamp was given the job of air testing this completely new aircraft from Bottesford. The test completed, Beauchamp headed R5782 back. They made their circuit prior to landing but on lowering the undercart the port leg failed to lock down. Overshooting the airfield, Beauchamp decided to divert to Waddington, which had no concrete runways and therefore offered more scope for drifting off-line on landing. On approaching Waddington the undercarriage was lowered again and still the port undercarriage warning light remained a baleful red. There appeared to have been a hydraulic failure on one side. Beauchamp had still not run out of options and activated the auxiliary pneumatic system. Still the red light remained illuminated. They toyed with the possibility that the wheel was indeed locked but that there was an electrical fault. Whatever the reason, Beauchamp had to meet the moment of truth.

The aircraft made a careful approach to Waddington, where Beauchamp touched down the starboard wheel first before gently allowing the port wheel to settle onto the grass as the speed died away. The port undercarriage leg slowly collapsed, dropping the wing and spinning the aircraft round with little damage. It was a textbook emergency landing.

Inspections revealed that the hydraulic supply to the undercarriage had failed, but the reason for the non-operation of the pneumatic system was more of a surprise. Following propeller icing problems, a de-icing system was developed and installed. This involved a 'slinger ring' installed within the airscrew boss. When activated, de-icing fluid was pumped out through the slinger ring and spun outward by centrifugal force along the blades. In this instance they discovered that the emergency compressed air actuating mechanism had been inadvertently connected to the slinger ring instead of the undercart, venting the air uselessly through the slinger ring instead of locking the wheels.

In addition to the Metrovick Manchesters and the new Woodford built Mk.1As arriving, September was a good month for 207 Squadron in that on the 29th 'B' Flight became operational, doubling at a stroke the number of serviceable aircraft generally available for operations, and on the 30th another list of modifications to be incorporated into Manchester and Lancaster aircraft was issued. This time none related to merely keeping the aircraft serviceable and few appear to have been actually installed.

Manchester and Lancaster Modification List – 30 September 1941:
1. Parachutist dropping
2. Multi-flare chute
3. Conversion to glider tug
4. Dual control
5. Special armour protection
6. Arrester Gear
7. AD Type H

Of these, the most interesting was probably item six and arrested landing trials were later carried out by both aircraft types, as described in a later chapter. During October 61 Squadron began flying from North Luffenham's satellite, Woolfox Lodge. When the squadron returned to operational flying in December it flew all its remaining Manchester operations from this base.

On 4, 5 and 9 October 1941 the largest force of serviceable Manchesters yet assembled by 207 Squadron were prepared for operations to Emden (twice), Nuremberg and Karlsruhe, each in turn being cancelled for unspecified reasons. On the 10th another operation was set up but due either to weather problems or uncertainties at Group the planned target was changed from Stuttgart to Karlsruhe and later to Essen. Later still an amendment standing down two of the original force of twelve was received. The actual target finally agreed was the Krupps Works. The 207 Squadron Manchester force joined sixty-eight other Bomber Command aircraft in the Essen force and a further sixty-nine aircraft were sent to Cologne. This was the first operation to involve Manchester Mk.1As. The aircraft took off between 00.26 and 00.45 hours carrying either a 4,000-lb 'Cookie' and incendiaries or 1,000-lb GP bombs and incendiaries.

10 October 1941, Essen – 207 Squadron's biggest yet:

Serial	Code	Squadron	Captain
L7378	EM-A	207	Plt Off. L. A. Paskell
L7454	EM-M	207	Fg Off. P. C. Birch
L7483	EM-H	207	Sqn Ldr K. H. P. Beauchamp
L7485	EM-O	207	Flt Lt W. G. Gardiner
L7419	EM-Y	207	Plt Off. B. D. Bowes-Cavanagh
L7317	EM-C	207	Plt Off. L. F. Kneil
L7309	EM-J	207	FS G. B. Dawkin*
L7486	EM-P	207	Flt Lt P. C. Ward-Hunt
L7484	EM-F	207	Fg Off. J. Wooldridge*
L7373	EM-T	207	Fg Off. W. S. Herring

* First Op of second tour

On the outward flight bad weather was encountered with dense cloud and icing conditions. Pilot Officer Bowes-Cavanagh had crossed the Dutch coast at 12,000 feet when flames were seen issuing from the port engine, accompanied by a rise in engine temperature. He located an airfield below and, arming the bombs, dropped his five 1,000 pounders and incendiaries on it. He made an early return, the fire apparently having died down. Later the airfield was estimated to be Haamstede.

As they continued their penetration to the Ruhr, both Pilot Officer Paskell and Flight Sergeant Dawkins had their air speed indicators (ASI) freeze up. With the ground invisible due to cloud and no ASIs it was impossible to plot time and speed for dead reckoning navigation. As a consequence they soon had only the vaguest idea of their location and instead of the Krupp Works reported later that they had bombed the 'Ruhr area'. Dawkins' ASI remained frozen for two hours. On return nobody could be confident they had found the target, although six crews believed they had bombed near Essen. Dense cloud and haze had protected the city as so often in the past.

Perhaps most indicative of all of the severity of the navigation problems and of how far off course a crew could wander inadvertently in a five hour flight at this stage of the war with no adequate navigational aids is the story

Sergeant Observers Jack Cheesman (moustached) and John Leahy. Cheesman was the sole survivor from Pilot Officer Derek Bowes-Cavanagh's aircraft. Leahy was killed with this entire crew on 24/25 July 1942 in the Lancaster of Pilot Officer J. J. N. McCarthy RNZAF. (Wim Govaerts)

of Flying Officer Birch's return flight. After blind flying all the operation, Sergeant Stead, the observer, had calculated their estimated time of arrival to descend on approaching the English coast to obtain a pinpoint for the last leg to Waddington. They descended to less than 1,000 feet before breaking cloud, only to discover they were still over Holland! Consternation ensued, a check on the fuel situation indicated around 105 gallons still available, which was very marginal to reach base. They continued westwards at the most economical speed and as they progressed it became likely they would have to ditch. All the necessary preparations were therefore made for a sea landing. To their profound relief Birch had eked out their modest remaining fuel so that they just reached East Anglia, landing on the first approach to Horsham St Faith with the fuel gauges reading zero.

Afterwards the crew were able to tease their observer, christening this operation 'Stead's Folly'. Underneath the frivolity it had been a tense and desperate episode, as well as a stark example of the navigational problems facing Bomber Command at this time. The first aircraft back at Waddington landed at 05.37 hours, whilst Peter Birch touched down at Horsham at 07.21 hours. Dawkins, with ASI problems, got back at 06.55 hours, whilst Paskell landed at 07.32 hours.

For an operation on 12 October 207 Squadron put up the previously unattainable number of fourteen serviceable Manchesters. The target was the synthetic rubber factory at Huls in the Ruhr. Three aircraft were later cancelled by Group. Once more the bomber force was split, Command dispatching 152 aircraft to Nuremberg, ninety-nine to Bremen and ninety to Huls. The eleven aircraft took off between 01.30 and 02.00 hours.

Huls – 11/12 October 1941:

Serial	Code	Squadron	Captain
L7486	EM-P	207	Flt Lt P. C. Ward-Hunt
L7378	EM-A	207	Plt Off. L. A. Paskell
L7309	EM-J	207	FS G. B. Dawkins
L7454	EM-M	207	Fg Off. P. C. Birch
L7485	EM-O	207	Flt Lt W. G. Gardiner
L7487	EM-N	207	Sqn Ldr K. H. P. Beauchamp
L7322	EM-B	207	Plt Off. G. R. Bayley
L7422	EM-V	207	Sgt J. C. Atkinson*
L7373	EM-T	207	Fg Off. W. S. Herring
L7484	EM-F	207	Fg Off. J. Wooldridge
L7312	EM-L	207	Plt Off. B. D. Bowes-Cavanagh

* First Op

Pilot Officer Derek Bowes-Cavanagh carried out his pre-flight checks. In his case this included hanging his personal good luck charm – a pair of his girlfriend's French knickers – in the cockpit beside him. As with all such charms and superstitions its function was to ward off evil and keep him safe. So far it had worked it seemed.

Bowes-Cavanagh's observer, Sergeant Jack Cheesman, had laid out a course which picked up a pinpoint on the North Sea coast of Holland close to the Belgian border and thence on across Belgium to the Ruhr. They crossed over the estuary of the Scheldt and were making their way unobtrusively into Belgian airspace. All was calm on board. Quite suddenly and without any forewarning on the intercom, L7312 was riddled from nose to tail by gun fire. Oberfeldwebel Paul Gildner in a Messerschmitt Bf110 of II/NJGI at Leeuwarden had completed a classic night fighter stalk from below and behind in the dark part of the sky.

Before any assessment of the extent of the damage or casualties could be made, although clearly the aircraft was seriously damaged and on fire, Cheesman was contacted on the intercom by Bowes-Cavanagh and instructed to go forward to the bomb aiming position and jettison the bombs.

Cheesman achieved this within a short time period, which was certainly less than a minute, but by then it had become clear to him that the conditions within the aircraft had deteriorated to such an extent that it was irredeemably doomed. With his parachute already on, Cheesman opened the front escape hatch and baled out. He was the only crew member to survive. The blazing Manchester plummeted down and exploded on the ground beneath. Derek Bowes-Cavanagh's lucky talisman had proved no protection against cannon and machine gun bullets.

In his combat report Gildner claimed the aircraft was a Whitley and gave the time of the attack as 04.08 hours. Gildner himself was killed on 24 February 1943 by which time he had 44 victories to this credit. Cheesman himself reached the ground only a short time later near the blazing wreck.

L7312 crashed in a field beside the farm of Fons Van de Keybus at Horendonk in northern Belgium only a few miles from Roosendaal on the border with Holland. Jack Cheesman landed nearby in the garden of the 'Schamhoeve' of Frans Vrients. Ahead Cheesman vaguely discerned moving figures silhouetted in the glow of the fire from the burning Manchester. Heading off in the opposite direction to escape the commotion he encountered others heading for the scene. He tried his schoolboy German and then French on them but they did not understand him and he could not follow their responses. Possibly these were Flemish speaking members of the local population. Lost and confused, Cheesman was soon captured.

According to local residents, the experiences of the next few hours were to prey on Cheesman's mind for the rest of his life. Jack was taken to the crash site, being horrified to witness a German Shepherd dog running around with part of an airman's limb in its mouth. At first only a single body was found, identified from a leather name tag on his uniform as Sergeant Ian Passy. Dismembered remains of other crew members were also soon identified. The Germans then returned with their captive to the village putting him in the sidecar of a motor cycle combination and ordering out onto the street the local people. Then they repeatedly drove the wounded

Rear Gunner Sergeant Ian H. D. Passy. Jack Cheesman's inability to address the desperate need of Passy's parents for details of their son's last operation was to haunt the latter years of his life. (Wim Govaerts)

airman around, laughing and humiliating him in front of these villagers, telling them this was what happened to those resisting German superiority. Finally, he was handed over briefly to Dr Janssens, the local GP, who bathed and dressed his wounds. In a reversal of this atrocity, next day the occupiers conducted and paid for a funeral for the dead crew with full military honours. Two coffins with remains of the six British airmen were interred. By this time it is thought that Jack Cheesman had already been escorted, possibly in a motorcycle combination, to a Luftwaffe night fighter station near Antwerp, and later moved by car to Brussels, and thence by train sent to Dulag Luft for interrogation.

The rest of the aircraft were due on target at 03.15 to 04.00 hours, where 10/10ths cloud made target identification problematical. Fires were reported in the target area. The remaining ten aircraft returned safely.

Whilst Jack Cheesman was experiencing his first day of four years in captivity and wondering why he alone had been picked out to survive, back at Waddington plans for another operation on the 13th were proceeding apace. A sixty-strong aircraft raid on Dusseldorf was planned, together with a thirty-nine aircraft raid on Cologne. Ten Manchesters were detailed for the operation to Cologne, although one was later cancelled in an amendment order from Group.

Top: German personnel standing on the edge of a crater with wreckage of L7312 at Horendonk/Essen 14 October 1941. Bottom: Crash site of L7312 on 14 October 1941. Note parachute in middle ground. (Both Wim Govaerts)

Left: Pilot Officer Lionel A. Paskell, who lost his life on 13 October 1941 in Manchester L7373 keeping the aircraft under control whilst Sergeants Arthur Smith and Ken Houghton baled out, the latter becoming an evader. (Wim Govaerts) Right: Sergeant Ken Houghton, Observer in L7373 and Evader, KIA 2 August 1945, piloting a B-24 Liberator in Palestine. (Tony Sherwin)

Cologne – 13 October 1941:

Serial	Code	Squadron	Captain
L7317	EM-C	207	Plt Off. L. F. Kneil
L7485	EM-O	207	Sqn Ldr T. C. Murray
L7484	EM-F	207	Flt Lt W. G. Gardiner
L7486	EM-P	207	Fg Off. D. A. Green
L7483	EM-H	207	Plt Off. G. R. Bayley
L7487	EM-N	207	Plt Off. J. C. L. Ruck-Keene*
L7300	EM-S	207	Fg Off. P. C. Bitch
L7373	EM-T	207	Plt Off. L. A. Paskell
L7321	EM-D	207	Fg Off. J. Unsworth

* First Op as captain.

13 October 1941 was a Sunday and Pilot Officer 'Jock' Paskell's crew were already advanced in preparations for the forthcoming operation. Sergeant 'Eddy' Edmonds, his rear gunner, was busy in the hangar when Paskell came in to pass on the good news that Edmonds' posting at the end of his tour had just come through. Edmonds had been with the unit since the time of inception at Boscombe Down. The following Thursday Edmonds was to go to Manby on an Air Gunnery Instructors Course. Edmonds told Paskell that he was willing to continue flying in the crew until the day of his posting. Paskell there and then determined that he would personally ensure that Edmonds lived to go to Manby and during the day insisted on making out a leave pass that would carry Edmonds from that day until the next Thursday. Paskell felt strongly that Edmonds had done his bit and there was no way

Oblt. Griese's Messerschmitt Bf110 'G9+KH' of I/NJG1 at St Trond, Belgium, in 1941. (H. Griese)

he would fly with 207 Squadron again. Neither knew, nor could possibly know, that by this action Paskell had saved Edmonds' life, albeit inadvertently, at the expense of another. Such are the laws of chance in wartime.

Another highly experienced member of Paskell's crew at this time was the observer, Flight Sergeant Ken Houghton, who had already completed one tour with 83 Squadron (Handley Page Hampdens) and won the DFM. He had also had his fair share of narrow scrapes. Whilst returning from operations in a Hampden they overflew Britain in bad weather and were forced to ditch in Cardigan Bay. The pilot, Sergeant Farmer, and wireless operator were drowned but Houghton and the rear gunner managed to stay afloat on the partially inflated dinghy and miraculously survived.

In one of those rare flukes of history Ken survived this night, became an evader, returning to Britain and wrote both an account of the events, together with his M19 and AI(k)/Most Secret Evaders Report dated 25 July 1942. He remustered as a pilot but was killed later in the war. Both diary and Evaders Report survive (see Appendix One).

Following the loss of Pilot Officer Bowes-Cavanagh's aircraft the night before, 13/14 October was to be another tragic night for 207 Squadron. For the second consecutive night Bomber Command was bound for the Ruhr, the route traversing Belgian airspace. The aircraft took off between 01.25 and 01.55 hours and almost immediately the over-laden bombers experienced problems, several finding it impossible to reach sufficient height to make a safe traverse of the North Sea. Flight Lieutenant Gardiner jettisoned a 1,000-lb bomb safe off Orfordness. Flying Officer Birch similarly released a 1,000-lb bomb forty miles from the Dutch coast to permit a safe crossing of the enemy coast.

On reaching the anti-aircraft searchlight belt, Pilot Officer Ruck-Keene was coned by the lights near Liège and held. Evasive action was taken and at the same time an enemy fighter, believed to have been a Bf109, was caught in the glare of the lights for a few seconds. L7487 slipped the lights and no fighter attack materialised, the fighter pilot possibly having been temporarily blinded.

Rising along with the Bf109 were a small group of black painted Bf110Cs of I/NJG1 from St Trond in Belgium. The Bf110s carried no airborne radar at this stage and were not even connected to the ground radar stations, relying entirely on visual interceptions and co-operation with the searchlights. Oberleutnant Heinrich Griese had taken off in 'G9+KH' at 03.43 hours local time (02.43 hours GMT) with Unteroffizier Scherke as his radio operator and was now patrolling his assigned 'box' in the Himmelbett system over Liège.

Amongst the mixed bomber force strung out across Belgium and the North Sea was Manchester L7321 EM-D, being flown by Flying Officer Joe Unsworth on the first operation of his second tour. He carried a scratch crew with little experience of flying together, although the wireless operator, Flight Sergeant Moulding, was experienced and also starting his second tour. For this crew the operation had been unusually quiet so far. Suddenly the searchlights surrounding Liège found their second victim within a few minutes, L7321. This time Griese was nearest the aircraft and closed with his quarry, taking pains to remain in the dark part of the sky and not be blinded by the lights. As he came within range Griese identified the triple tail unit of an RAF Manchester. In the last few seconds he dived to approach from below and then pulled up under the tail of Unsworth's aircraft until he was within 25 m (30 yards) and certain of a decisive strike. At 04.43 hours Griese entered the searchlight beams fleetingly and opened fire with his fixed nose cannon on a still unsuspecting prey. His first burst struck home with, it seemed to him, devastating effect.

In L7321 Tom Cox, the second wireless operator/air gunner, was occupying the front turret that night and has no recollection of the aircraft being detected by searchlights. The first intimation he had of an attack was when air fired tracer began to fly past his turret on the right hand side. The next few seconds passed in a blur. Unsworth immediately called the rear gunner, Sergeant Dickson, for information on what was happening. Dickson replied that he had been firing at a night fighter for the last ten minutes. If this was the case nobody in the aircraft had been aware of it and Dickson had not informed Unsworth of the developing attack or suggested any evasive action. Perhaps unprepared for this response, Unsworth instructed the experienced Moulding to discover what was happening at the rear of the aircraft.

Within seconds of the attack and before Moulding could take any action the second pilot, Pilot Officer 'Eddie' Carroll, interjected on the intercom to report that clouds of sparks and a few flames were issuing from the starboard Vulture. Unsworth immediately ordered Carroll to press the fire extinguisher button. Carroll carried out the order but coincident with him hitting the button the entire starboard wing burst into flame. Whether the two facts were in any way linked could not be ascertained.

In the Bf110 Griese had seen the Manchester catch fire within a few seconds of his attack and it is likely that his shells hit more than just the starboard wing. He has no recollection of any return fire from either of the rear defence positions in the aircraft. Recognising that the Manchester was mortally hit he refrained from mounting a follow-up attack to give the crew a chance to use their parachutes. Griese landed back at St Trond at 06.24 hours to learn that the Anti-Aircraft Searchlight Regiment had confirmed his kill.

The intensity and scale of the fire left Unsworth in no doubt that they had only a few seconds before the fuel tanks or bomb load exploded and he immediately ordered the crew to bale out. Receiving the order, Tom Cox climbed out of the front turret, donned his parachute, jettisoned the forward escape hatch and baled out. Carroll was able to follow shortly after Cox. Once his parachute had deployed, Cox was able to watch the blazing Manchester maintain a steady course ahead of him for quite a while before it dived into the ground and exploded on impact at 04.44 hours local time (03.44 hours GMT). The aircraft fell in a small wood at Horion-Hozemont 4 km (2½ miles) east of Comblain-au-Pont 17 km south of Liège carrying the five remaining airmen to their deaths. Cox found it difficult to understand what had prevented the remaining crew members escaping.

As he approached the ground in the clear, dark, moonless night, Cox realised he was drifting backwards. Shortly afterwards he felt the movement arrested as he, too, fell into a small tree on the edge of a wood. Looking down he saw he was only about two feet off the ground and so punched his quick release and dropped free to the earth below. He was unable to disentangle the 'chute initially, but as it became a little lighter and he could make out more detail of what was snagging the canopy he made a fresh attempt to release it. As he was doing so he became aware that he was being approached by two young men close to his own age in civilian clothes. They challenged Cox in English and his first contact with the underground group 'Comète' was made. Together they dragged the parachute down and hid it, along with Cox's flying suit. A raincoat to cover his uniform was produced and together they walked to a safe house at Comblain-au-pont.

Pilot Officer Howard Carroll had also been picked up by the underground and joined a small party of escapers, Larry Birk (RMF), Jack Newton (MF) and a Belgian, Gerard Waucquez. This band formed the fourth group of airmen guided to Spain by 'Comète'. They were conveyed across occupied Europe by an eighteen-year-old girl, Andrée de Jongh, passing the Pyrenees on 10 December 1941. Carroll eventually reached England, only to be lost flying over Germany later in the war (see Appendix One).

Sergeant Tom Cox was passed along the chain of safe houses to Liège, where he was hidden by Monsieur and Madam Debaerts at 82 Rue de Cocq, before moving on to Brussels, Amiens, Paris, Biarritz, San Sebastian, Madrid and Gibraltar. He was joined by Albert Daye (RCAF), Leonard Warburton and John Hutton, forming the fifth group guided by 'Comète' in the capable hands of de Jongh. They reached the Pyrenees on Christmas Day having a party at Anglet near Bayonne before trekking across the mountains. Cox was embarked on a Polish ship, the *Sobieski* and landed back in Britain in March 1942. He remustered as a pilot and saw out the war training glider pilots. The remainder of the crew are now buried at Haverlee War Cemetery near Louvain (see Appendix One).

In the target area a ground haze made target identification difficult and the problems were increased by the persistent and accurate searchlight activity. On his bomb run, in L7484, Flight Lieutenant Gardiner was coned by searchlights and hit several times by heavy flak, fortunately without damage to vital parts. Immediately the bomb load was released violent evasive action shook off the flak and the lights, saving them from further damage. Observation of the result of the bombing was impossible.

Flying Officer Dave Green experienced a similar intense and accurate flak barrage on his run up on board L7486. One box barrage of six heavy flak shells burst only 50 yards ahead and directly at their flying height. They were lucky to escape undamaged. Searchlights and flak also troubled Pilot Officer Ruck-Keene and Flying Officer Birch.

Oblt. Heinrich Griese photographed whilst serving with I/NJGI in 1940. Griese's tit-for-tat engagements with Pilot Officer Unsworth's and Flight Sergeant Pendrill's Manchesters are recounted in the narrative. (H. Griese)

Crews at this era of the war had developed and widely held a belief that their identification, friend or foe (IFF) sets could be used to jam the radar guidance system of the master searchlight. There was no logic behind this belief and indeed it was not simply ineffective but later positively dangerous, when German night fighters were able to home directly onto the IFF transmissions. On this night, crews used their IFF sets to try and mislead the radar and not surprisingly reported variable success on return. When Pilot Officer Paskell in L7373 reached Cologne the crew were untroubled by the haze encountered by others, finding their target in the north-east sector of the town illuminated by bright moonlight. Ken Houghton released their 4,000-lb bomb but they were soon aware that the starboard Vulture was overheating. Following a quick conference they elected to take a direct route home via Rotterdam. En route, whilst at 16,000 feet over the German/Belgian border, Houghton was pouring a cup of coffee from his flask when they were suddenly illuminated by about a dozen searchlights. Len Paskell immediately commenced violent evasive action in an attempt to escape the clinging beams, knowing that these were a magnet for night fighters. Alert in his rear turret, Pilot Officer 'Jock' Paskell had decided to replace the posted 'Eddy' Edmonds in the rear turret with the second wireless operator/air gunner, Sergeant Arthur Smith, who had more experience operating with the crew. The two new gunners, Sergeants Walters and Compton, occupied the mid-upper and front turrets.

At close to 04.10 hours (05.10 hours local time) whilst flying at a height of 14,000 feet in the vicinity of Louvain, Smith observed a Bf110 night fighter approaching from the starboard quarter at about five o'clock. Unbeknown to them, this was Gefreiter Bruhnke of III/NJG1 based at Twente in Holland. The Bf110 bored in at a fast closing speed and as Smith traversed his turret and called a warning Bruhnke opened fire with his cannon from long range. As Smith responded with his four 0.303-inch guns, he could already feel the impacts of the shells on the aircraft structure around him, testifying to the accuracy of Bruhnke's initial burst. Almost immediately the traversing mechanism in the rear turret failed, presumably as a result of a hit in the hydraulic system supplying the power. Smith was still able to fire but could not follow the flight line of the attacking fighter and his return fire was falling short. Paskell continued to take evasive action and the turret guns swung towards the fighter but Smith was unable to draw a bead. As Bruhnke closed in, still firing, Smith heard a call on the intercom: 'We're on fire'.

Ken Houghton remembered the final moments of their fight:

After the first attack the wireless operator, Sergeant Roberts, my best friend in the RAF, tapped me on the shoulder and pointed downwards, where a spiral of smoke was coming up through the floor. Paskell, realising they would be attacked again before they could escape the beams gave the order: 'Prepare to bale out'. I had been dreading such a call and my heart sank. Immediately on the intercom we heard a yell from the rear gunner: 'Turn port', but before any action was possible we felt the aircraft shudder under impact of shells and bullets of a second attack. Fire from the first attack suddenly flared throughout the Manchester, all lights were extinguished and the cockpit filled with acrid fumes. The second pilot, Sergeant Dennis Chant, left his seat, coming back to get his parachute from the rack near my table. I pulled out my intercom and oxygen connectors, and was instantly assaulted by the fumes and began being repeatedly sick.

The aircraft had begun diving out of control in a mass of flames whilst terrible sensations of suffocation, my greatest fear, came over me. I headed for the bomb aimers compartment, squeezing past Sergeant Chant, seeking my parachute and the escape hatch. In my haste my parachute harness seemed to snag on every projection. Once reaching the nose I grabbed my parachute but in total darkness and in view of my physical and mental condition, I had the greatest difficulty clipping it on. Then I hastily threw the cushions covering the escape hatch to one side, pulled the release handle and after a frantic struggle cleared this, too, to one side. Once clear, a thought filled my mind of the story of an airman's body found with his unopened 'chute the nails of his right hand bloody and with a hole worn in the right side of his parachute bag. It was found that his 'chute was upside down with the rip-cord on the left instead of the right side, such that the airman had not been able to locate it. So I checked mine finding it, too, on the left so, taking it in my left hand, I toppled head first out of the aircraft. Fearing we had already lost much of our height, I counted a quick three and pulled the rip cord.

I watched the aircraft, now a mass of flames, diving down like a meteor in a long curve and wondered how many of my friends had been unable to bale out. In my semi-conscious state I realised that I had retained my helmet with its intercom and oxygen leads, which I should have left in the aircraft. This might have been a fatal mistake as I might have got hung up as I tried to leave the aircraft. I think I must have lost consciousness during my descent because when I looked down once I saw the tops of the trees coming up to meet me. I just had time to swing myself round before I crashed into trees backwards. Fortunately for me they were pine saplings only about 10 feet high and they made a perfect cushion for my fall. I lay among those trees for about a quarter of an hour without moving a muscle except to vomit. Whilst lying there I pondered my position. It was a peculiar sensation to realise I was suddenly in enemy territory whilst only an hours flying time from England. Whilst I was descending I felt that it was inevitable that I would very soon be a prisoner of war, but whilst lying among the trees I gradually realised that there might be a possibility of evading capture and escaping to England. (See Appendix One – author).

Meanwhile, immediately after the second devastating attack, Arthur Smith, too, disconnected himself from his intercom and oxygen leads and concentrated on his own survival. The rear turret was jammed to starboard such that only the port turret door provided access to the fuselage. With a struggle, he squeezed through this narrow space and reached into the parachute stowage rack. Whilst clipping the 'chute on in preparation to moving forward to the lower hatch in the nose, Smith tried to push open the draught doors behind his turret but found these jammed. Possibly the doors had been distorted by the ferocity of the attack.

Intensifying his efforts, Smith was able to burst quickly through the draught doors. He was greeted by a veritable Dante's inferno of fire within the fuselage. All thought of reaching the forward hatch disappeared and as the flames enveloped Smith himself he just had time to register the immobile figure of the mid-upper gunner totally ablaze. Later Smith was to speculate that the gunner may have been hit during the first attack as there had been no word on the intercom or return fire from his turret.

Smith could not afford to hesitate. Pulling open the side entry door he dived out, missing the tailplane and then yanking the ripcord. The aircraft flew on for a short while and Smith could see the extent of the flames. Suddenly the blazing wreck nosed forward and plummeted into the ground like a flaming comet, crashing south-west of Lommel and near Louvain.

Unbeknown to Smith, both he and the dying crew were to play vital, if inadvertent, roles in the escape of Ken Houghton. For 45 years Smith was to believe he was the sole survivor and to puzzle why, when the aircraft had flown on straight and level for a spell, no one up front had escaped. In fact they did. Apparently his escape was either much earlier or much later than that of Smith.

Within a short interval, the groping searchlights picked up Smith's parachute and held it in their glare as he gently drifted earthwards. Houghton must have been sufficiently separated along the track of the aircraft that he descended undetected. Smith was taking centre stage and holding the Germans' entire attention. Amidst the excitement and enveloped in the covering darkness, Houghton reached the ground unnoticed. A German patrol with dogs was waiting for Smith on landing but even without his reception committee it is unlikely that Smith could have escaped. His face was blackened and severely burnt, the skin hanging in strips in places.

Smith was treated with great tenderness and dedication by his captors. He was taken to a first aid post where, at 08.00 hours, two German medical attendants and the victorious Bruhnke arrived to care for him and convey him to hospital. The medical orderlies told Smith they had come directly from the wreckage of his aircraft where they had located the remains of the six other crew members. In death the crew had provided a service to their comrade: with Smith in captivity and six aircrew apparently dead, there would be no search for Houghton, the Germans believing him already dead. So it was that Smith had covered Houghton's descent and his fellow crew members presented the opportunity for his escape.

The small party caring for Smith set out and took most of the day getting to a hospital in Brussels. Towards the latter part of the day, Smith lost his sight completely, apparently through shock, and had to rely entirely on his captors for guidance, Smith spent two months being treated by a German burns specialist with the rank of General, who proved most kind and attentive. After five days his sight returned and eventually the skill of this doctor saved him from facial disfigurement.

On reaching Lisbon Ken Houghton flew back to the UK on one of the regular flights across the Bay of Biscay. He was later to comment ruefully that his journey to Portugal took six months, whereas his return took six hours. On reaching this country his first move was to seek out his fellow aircrew in 207 Squadron, walking into the mess at Bottesford unannounced to great rejoicing. A contemporary, 'Scotty' Scott, remembers his arrival well.

Houghton had designs on piloting himself and arranging a transfer to a pilot's training course in Canada. During the course he was to encounter both Jim Duncan and Bob Storey, former 207 Squadron wireless operators, then instructing in Canada. Having qualified as a pilot, Houghton was delegated a Lend-Lease aircraft to fly back to Britain on delivery, only to have it disintegrate around him during a heavy landing in Iceland.

Eventually hitching a ride on another aircraft, he landed up at Prestwick, coming face to face within hours with his ex-fellow crew member 'Eddy' Edmonds. Their greeting was joyous and mutual: 'You lucky bugger!' they called to each other delightedly - Edmonds for missing the fateful operation and Houghton for escaping. With great joy they exchanged experiences since their wartime careers had diverged. Houghton was champing at the bit to get back to operations a third time. Regrettably, for that irrepressible man, it was not to be 'third time lucky', for Ken Houghton was killed soon after in the war.

The 'Grim Reaper' had struck at 207 Squadron with a vengeance in the last 24 hours, resulting in three Manchesters being lost to night fighters. 'Jock' Paskell was on the eighth operation of his second tour, whilst Joe Unsworth was on the first operation of his second. In both cases the aircraft had been over-whelmed in a devastating assault, leaving no time to send a radio message to base of their predicament. All the squadron could record was a bald: 'Nothing further heard since take-off'.

After the initial months, in which the major threat to the squadrons had been the flak defences in the immediate target area on a particular city, the pendulum had now swung towards the night fighter as the main threat. At a time when the squadrons still had no target finding devices of any kind, the ground and airborne radars now being deployed by the Germans were stripping away their protective cover of darkness to a marked degree. Only the small number of fighters available and early problems with equipment serviceability lessened the impact.

In return for these severe losses the achievements had been minimal. The bombing was scattered at Huls on 12 October 1941, and at Cologne on the 13th only a few bombs landed in the city damaging seventeen houses, killing six civilians and injuring five. The high level of pressure on 207 Squadron continued with operations for four and ten Manchesters to Cologne and Emden respectively on the 15th and 18th being requested, but later cancelled due to the weather. Finally, on the 20th, the weather improved somewhat and four 207 Squadron Manchesters were required for mine-laying operations off Sassnitz in the Baltic. This was a minor diversionary operation in support of air force attacks on four targets. It was decided that the aircraft would take-off from and return to Horsham St Faith to shorten the range. The aircraft departed between 18.32 and 18.45 hours.

On this night 97 Squadron returned to operations with its training of new crews complete. It continued to operate the Manchester for only another two months but was to have a fateful re-encounter with operational flying. 97 Squadron supplied eight Manchesters to attack Bremen. At this time the unit's aircraft had begun to carry individual names under their cockpits on the port side to mark their naming as the 'Straits Settlement' Squadron.

Baltic minelaying and Bremen – 20 October 1941:

Serial	Code	Squadron	Captain
L7490	OF-U	97	WO D. H. Rowlands
L7463	OF-P	97	FS R. A. Fletcher
L7461	OF-R	97	FS G. E. A. Pendrill
L7453	OF-X	97	Sqn Ldr J. Dugdale
L7489	OF-T	97	WO T. J. Mycock
L7464	OF-N	97	Sgt C. G. Hughes
R5783	OF-V	97	Sgt C. H. Hartley
L7462	OF-Z	97	Plt Off. W. G. Noble
L7432	EM-O	207	FS G. B. Dawkins
L7422	EM-V	207	Flt Lt W. G. Gardiner
L7322	EM-Q	207	Plt Off. G. R. Bayley
L7487	EM-N	207	Plt Off. J. C. L. Ruck-Keene

In L7422 EM-V Flight Lieutenant Gardiner took off from Horsham St Faith at 18.32 hours in good visibility. Sassnitz was at the limit of their range. It turned out that the crew had failed to take account of a small intense depression shown on the Met. Chart at briefing, which pushed them south of the target. The wind strength locally reached 90mph and cloud and darkness caused them to become lost. Eventually finding a pinpoint near Kiel, their remaining fuel load prevented them returning in the direction of the dropping area. The mines were released fused from 10,000 feet into Kiel Bay and they aborted the operation, reaching Horsham on virtually dry tanks after being airborne for seven hours and fifty-five minutes.

Two 207 Squadron aircraft 'planted' their 'VEGETABLES' in the allocated position, whilst Manchester Mk.1A, L7487, failed to return. It is presumed the aircraft laid its mines and was heading for Horsham St Faith on the return leg. It came down in the North Sea approximately eighteen miles off the Norfolk coast with the loss of the entire crew. There is no information on the circumstances leading to the ditching of this aircraft. Its reported position presumably results from a radio message or homing obtained by a ground station. It has been suggested that the loss of this aircraft was associated with the continued rash of propeller feathering and engine failures still being experienced on the aircraft at this time, but the aircraft could easily have run out of fuel. From Met. reports for the North Sea it can be anticipated that sea conditions for alighting in the water were unfavourable. The last few hours in the lives of Pilot Officer Ruck-Keene and his crew, the fears, failure and final tragedy, remain known only to God.

The eight Manchesters of 97 Squadron took off in a tight bunch headed for Bremen just before 18.30 hours. All appear to have reached the Bremen area where target identification was made difficult by cloud and ground haze. The defences were ferocious, including many searchlight cones involving nineteen or twenty individual lights with intense and accurate flak. Warrant Officer Rowlands' crew also sighted a patrolling Bf110 as they ran in to the target, but it apparently failed to see them. Squadron Leader Dugdale's aircraft, L7453, was slightly damaged by flak in the target area. Following bomb release, Flight Sergeant Pendrill put the nose of L7461 down and dived seawards, pulling out at 1,000 feet and crossing the coast over a five ship convoy near Cuxhaven. Shortly afterwards they were engaged by an enemy warship. Sergeant Bob Gross had been teamed up with Flight Sergeant Gordon Hartley and his crew three weeks earlier, being allocated the mid-upper turret position. Both Hartley's crew and Gross already had operational experience. After the usual familiarisation flights they had embarked on their first Manchester sortie on this night. R5783 OF-V became airborne from Coningsby at 18.20 hours with its load of six 1,000-lb GP for the shallow penetration raid on Bremen.

After an uneventful outward flight to the target they encountered only moderate searchlight and flak activity on their approach. In good weather with some low cloud and haze, they identified Bremen from sightings of the Weser River. Over the target some heavy shells burst nearby, though none seemed to damage their aircraft.

The official sortie report is extremely sketchy and more has been deduced from the personal recollection of Sergeant Gross. Problems began on their return flight when first the elevator trimming wheel was found to be jammed. Far more seriously, the second pilot, Sergeant Appleyard, began expressing concern in respect of their remaining fuel. No mention is made of any need to transfer fuel from a leaking wing tank. Evidently this must have been yet another nail-biting, seemingly interminable return with seven minds focussed on the engine note and the pilots doing everything possible to lean the fuel mixture and eke out their remaining supplies. When they were down to 1,000 feet and still over water, the wireless operator, Sergeant Dean, was instructed to broadcast an SOS. The tension was finally relieved when those up front reported seeing the English coast below, though they still needed to get down safely. Being unable to resolve any features of the darkened landscape to the west, Hartley elected to make a forced-landing on the flat-lying coast itself, sending Gross and Sergeant Mayland, the rear gunner, to brace themselves against the mainspar. Suddenly the engines spluttered and stopped and Hartley put the nose down to maintain flying speed. The aircraft hit the ground tail first and bounced then immediately bellied-in again through a shower of seawater, stopping suddenly with little damage and no serious injuries. It was 00.30 hours on 21 October. Gross and Mayland were alarmed once more when seawater began flooding into the floor of the Manchester and made haste to the upper escape hatch. This was already open with the observer, Sergeant Canham, calling from the starboard wing that their aircraft couldn't sink as he could see grass poking through the water surface. Thus emboldened, Canham jumped down into what he anticipated must be shallow water, plunging instead up to his waist in icy water close to high tide covering the saltmarsh at Friskney near Wainfleet on the coast fronting Boston in Lincolnshire. Canham climbed frantically back up onto the wing.

The aircraft dinghy had not released but R5783 showed no sign of settling into the underlying mud. After six hours flying it had been a very close call. Once the crew had recovered their composure, they were able to take stock. It was very dark and quiet; they couldn't even see land and had no idea of their position. They began firing off their recognition flares from their Very pistol, via the light of these seeing a low shoreline not far to one side with barbed wire entanglements nearby.

As the flares had failed to alert any local inhabitants and though now cold and wet, they had little option but to sit it out and wait for daylight. By this time the water level had fallen and Hartley took the decision to wade ashore. Eventually, after a further wait, voices were heard from behind the earth embankment forming high water

Consistent with everything about the Manchester's performance being marginal Sergeant Hartley of 97 Squadron in R5783 OF-V ran out of fuel in sight of the Lincolnshire coast returning from Bremen on 20/21 October 1941 and just managed to reach the coastal saltmarsh fringe near Friskney. (Author's collection

mark and the remainder of the crew left their aircraft and waded ashore. Hartley had returned with transport and they returned to Coningsby finding that their SOS had not been received, but neither had they been reported missing. Subsequently 58 MU from Newton used its ingenuity resorting to one of the steam traction cultivating machines usually used in pairs, one at each side of a field, pulling ploughs on long steel cables to winch the aircraft across the soft mud to the embankment where it could be dismantled.

A message was received at 00.30 hours from the crew of Pilot Officer Noble in L7462 on his first operation stating that the wireless telegraphy receiver was unserviceable. The aircraft failed to return and it is presumed to have crashed in the sea due to unknown causes on its return flight. Some days later the bodies of two crew members were washed up on the East Anglian coast, possibly indicating that L7462 was also close to home when it crashed. No German night fighter claims were made for this operation.

The Air Sea Rescue service carried out a sweep searching for possible survivors from L7487 and L7462 with no result. Pressure of further operations prevented 207 Squadron from participating, but on the 22nd and 23rd two and three Manchesters respectively carried out a desperate and fruitless search for a dinghy from Ruck-Keene's aircraft. So from this operation the aircraft of Pilot Officers Noble and Ruck-Keene, together with that of Sergeant Hartley had all come down in the North Sea or in the latter case, its very edge.

This was a period when engine reliability was slightly improved, although the propeller feathering problems remained to be solved. Progress was being made with these and aircraft were to be test flown on 26 October 1941. On the same day a party of Air Training Corps (ATC) cadets paid a visit to Waddington and amongst the day's instruction for them was an air experience flight in a Manchester.

The two flight commanders, Squadron Leaders Beauchamp and Murray, divided the group of cadets between them with a view to taking them aloft in the course of the planned air tests for the day. Murray took off on a fifty-five minute test flight in L7419, with his crew amplified by eleven cadets, a massive complement for a Manchester. Beauchamp got aloft in L7422 EM-V with a crew including a new sergeant pilot and a similar number of cadets. L7422 had recently been returned from repair following the serious damage to its tail assembly after the night fighter attack of 31 August 1941.

The object of the test was to obtain sufficient height so that the new second pilot could practice propeller feathering. They soon reached the 1,500 feet height deemed necessary to carry out the test. The designated engine was stopped and the propeller feathered. Having accomplished this successfully the restart procedure was initiated. The rpm and boost increased on the engine and the propeller was unfeathered. However, the engine was giving no thrust, and with the propeller now in coarse pitch, the drag built-up rapidly. A quick check confirmed the rpm and boost readings, suggesting the engine was running, but the drag of the 16-feet diameter propeller and weight of the engine was actually causing an extremely rapid height loss.

A desperate look around the cockpit failed to provide any information on why the engine was not, in fact, producing any thrust and a forced landing became imminent. The crew and cadets were called to take up crash positions and Beauchamp turned his attention to finding a suitable forced landing field. None appeared large enough, but they had no alternative. Beauchamp turned into wind with the last available height and speed, lowered the flaps but kept the undercarriage up. L7422 bellied into an unobstructed small field, bounced, demolished the boundary hedge, careered on into a second field and ground to a halt. As soon as the aircraft stopped all the hatches were thrown open and crew and ATC cadets scattered in all directions. Figures seemed to appear everywhere, feet running before they hit the ground. Fortunately the wreck did not catch fire. They had come down at Linwood, near Market Rasen in Lincolnshire.

A roll call showed the whole crew were uninjured. A crew member was dispatched to find a telephone and as their jangled nerves recovered and the aircraft steadfastly refused to burn Beauchamp finally felt it to be safe to return. He climbed into the pilot's seat and carefully repeated the restart procedure to try and establish the reason for the engine failure. To his dismay he saw that the fuel taps to the engine they had feathered were still off. He hesitated, if the taps were moved to the 'on' position the accident could be blamed on an aircraft malfunction. In view of the many hours spent recently trying to rectify the persistent propeller feathering failures nobody was likely to doubt him. A moment's reflection was enough to convince him that honesty was the best policy, thereby saving the crash investigators and perhaps Avro and de Havilland many hours work chasing red herrings.

At the time of the crash L2422 had a new direction finding (DF) device fitted in the cockpit immediately above the fuel taps and partly obscuring them. The presence of this was the most likely reason for both pilots failing to detect that the taps had not been put on again after shutting down. Thus L7422 crashed due to pilot error, as opposed to propeller feathering mechanism malfunction. The aircraft never flew again and was struck off charge and scrapped soon afterwards.

Flying Officer Bob Fletcher at his captain's seat after his Manchester was named Sri Gajah (Elephant) in commemoration of the association with the Straits Settlement States of Malaya. All the aircraft were named after land animals or birds. Jill was named after Fletcher's niece and goddaughter, not a pin-up. L7463 OF-P was photographed soon after its fourth operation on 8 November 1941. (R. A. Fletcher)

On 31 October 1941 Avro passed a milestone when the first production Lancaster, L7527, made its maiden test flight from Woodford. From then onwards the assembly lines were fully devoted to the new type. Bomber Command's next major operation, on 7 November, proved a watershed in its fortunes for some time to come. Impatient following a prolonged period of bad weather and poor bombing results, the Air Officer Commanding, Sir Richard Pierse, proposed a maximum effort on Berlin. The weather forecast was most unfavourable with thick storm clouds, icing and hail, especially over the North Sea.

Air Vice-Marshal Slessor, the 5 Group Commander, was vehemently opposed to the attack and finally obtained a partial relief for his crews, being permitted to attack Cologne instead. This proved the salvation of many 5 Group crews. The 392 aircraft dispatched was a record for the Command with 169 allocated to Berlin, seventy-five to Cologne and fifty-five to Mannheim. Smaller groups carried out minor operations to Essen, Ostend, Boulogne and various mining areas.

A total of seventeen Manchesters were dispatched from 207 and 97 Squadrons, which were still the only two units operating the type in 5 Group. The raid turned into a disaster, although Slessor's judgement was to safeguard the Manchester force. Ten 207 Squadron Manchesters with experienced crews were detailed to attack Cologne with the main railway station as the Aiming Point. One Manchester was later cancelled by Group. This Manchester, with an inexperienced crew, was prepared instead for the raid on the docks at Boulogne. The Cologne force departed between 19.20 and 19.55 hours to make their way individually to the target.

Sergeant Atkinson experienced a burst hydraulic pipe over the North Sea in R5791 which rendered the front and mid-upper turrets unserviceable. The intercom was also unreliable. The aircraft returned early with bomb load intact. Similarly, Pilot Officer Bayley in L7322 had the rear turret and second pilot's intercom fail some fifteen miles north-east of Brussels. The captain elected to return and a search for an enemy aerodrome as an alternative target was unsuccessful. L7322 landed at base at 23.50 hours.

Cologne – 7 November 1941:

Serial	Code	Squadron	Captain
L7453	OF-X	97	Sqn Ldr J. Dugdale
L7489	OF-F	97	Flt Lt E. Coton
L7522	OF-V	97	FS G. E. A. Pendrill
L7463	OF-P	97	FS L. H. Adams
L7423	OF-S	97	Sgt G. H. Hartley
R5791	EM-V	207	Sgt J. C. Atkinson
L7322	EM-Q	207	Plt Off. G. R. Bayley
L7432	EM-J	207	Fg Off. P. C. Birch
L7455	EM-G	207	Fg Off. W. S. Herring DSO, DFM
L7486	EM-B	207	Flt Lt P. C. Ward-Hunt DFC
L7300	EM-F	207	Plt Off. A. W. Hills DFM
L7485	EM-D	207	Sqn Ldr T. C. Murray DFC
L7484	EM-P	207	Fg Off. J. Wooldridge DFM
L7319	EM-X	207	FS G. H. Coles

*Boulogne – November 7th 1941:

Serial	Code	Squadron	Captain
L7491	OF-C	97	Fg Off. J. G. McKid
L7492	OF-A	97	Plt Off. E. E. Rodley
L7382	OF-D	97	FS S. E. Harrison
?	EM-	207	?

Flight Sergeant Stan Harrison in L7382 OF-D took his new inexperienced crew on a gentle initiation to Boulogne. As they approached the French coast, Harrison had to stifle the chattering from these apprehensive new comers. They saw the target clearly and released their ten 500-lb GP bombs onto wharfs and barges in the harbour. Harrison then turned steeply to starboard carrying them safely out across the Channel and back to Coningsby. The main force attacked the target under cloud from heights ranging from 12,000 to 14,000 feet, generally between 21.18 and 21.50 hours, although Squadron Leader Murray was an hour later at 22.50 hours. Fires were observed burning in the town. All five of the 97 Squadron Cologne force attacked successfully, although Squadron Leader Dugdale's aircraft was peppered by a flak shell bursting beneath it. The port wing tank was badly holed and lost 200 gallons of fuel before the self-sealing closed across the gash.

Flak gunners near-missed L7319, piloted by Flight Sergeant Coles. A hydraulic line was fractured over the target by a shrapnel fragment. The aircraft experienced a hydraulic failure, the bomb doors fell open, and the rear turret became unserviceable. The intercom also failed at about the same time, whether by coincidence or not is unreported. Coles brought L7319 back to base and effected a safe landing after the compressed air system had been used to lock the undercart in the down position.

Flight Sergeant Pendrill and crew had an eventful night. As the Manchester force headed for Cologne Oberleutnant Heinrich Griese and his fellow NJG2 pilots were rising from St Trond and other airfields to do battle with Bomber Command. For once the boot was on the other foot and the night saw the revenge of the Manchesters.

Pendrill had trained his crew into a well-disciplined and experienced team. Following take-off at 18.52 hours, they proceeded to Cologne where they bombed but were unable to observe any results due to low cloud. Turning for their return they were soon trapped in the searchlight belt in the vicinity of Liège. Patrolling nearby, as usual, in 'G9+AH', Griese and his wireless operator, Scherke, spotted L7522, gave the tally-ho radio signal to the ground and advanced the throttles in their Bf110 to maximum. As they approached, Pendrill was vigorously corkscrewing the lightened Manchester and managed to escape the clinging lights.

Now the odds were more even with both crews equally free to search in the darkened sky. Unknown to Greise he had already been spotted and reported by Sergeant Jones, the rear gunner in L7522. This time any attack would be less one-sided than when Joe Unsworth had been brought down. After a few minutes, Griese spotted the Manchester ahead of him, still corkscrewing as it increased its distance from the searchlight belt. Jones kept up a steady commentary and, as Griese went into his well-tried attack pattern, trained his four Brownings on the area of sky the Bf110 had to fly through. Griese entered a steep dive to build up speed and get beneath the weaving bomber. Then, when he judged the instant exactly right, he pulled back hard on the stick to point the nose directly at the Manchester when it passed through his gunsight as he hung on the point of the stall a few metres beneath. Both Griese and Jones judged the interception well, but this time it was the Englishman who was a split second faster, ordering a break from George Pendrill.

As Griese opened fire, the massive black Manchester filling his vision drifted out of the firing line and from a mere 20 m (22 yards) his tracers flew over the top of the bomber. Jones in turn had been following the track of the fighter for some time and had now depressed his Brownings fully, as the Manchester jinked aside he was presented with the perfect shot looking down onto the top of the attacker suspended, apparently stationary, at the apex of his near-vertical climb. Anticipating the direction of the manoeuvre, Jones opened fire at point blank range and saw tracers entering the crew cockpit and both wing roots. The withering fire killed Scherke outright and badly wounded Griese, the cockpit was devastated and the armoured windshield crazed into opaqueness by direct hits. The port engine burst into flames.

'G9+AH' fell away out of control in its death throes. Griese knew he was weakening fast, but managed to haul back the shattered canopy. In his enfeebled state he was unable to jump clear and in clawing his way out found his parachute entangled in the cockpit framing. With his last remaining strength he finally managed to break free and clear the aircraft, pulling the ripcord sharply before fainting from loss of blood.

In L7522 the crew observed a jet of flame shoot up from the ground as 'G9+AH' went in. Griese drifted a short distance from the crash site before hitting the ground unconscious. Unable to control his landing, Griese sustained further injury when the impact broke his left femur. Griese was quickly located and given medical treatment, but it was 1943 before he was sufficiently recovered to return to flying.

Pendrill and his victorious crew landed back at Coningsby at 00.19 hours. Honours that night had been won by the Manchesters, but in the relentless butchery of the bomber war Pendrill and crew had themselves only six weeks to live before they too met the 'Grim Reaper'.

From the Berlin force twenty-one aircraft failed to return, 12.4% of those dispatched. The bombing was very scattered with only fourteen buildings destroyed and eleven civilians killed. The returning crews from the Cologne force reported many fires, but in fact only eight high explosive and sixty incendiaries fell in the town killing five and injuring five more.

The worst results of all related to Mannheim where a specific request to the authorities revealed that no bombs had fallen within the city limits that night. In all thirty-seven aircraft failed to return, more than twice the previous loss rate for night operations. Many casualties were believed to have come down in the North Sea due to fuel exhaustion and icing and a massive air/sea rescue (ASR) was mounted. As a result of this failure, Berlin was not raided in force again until January 1943 and orders were given to conserve aircraft and reduce the scale of the bombing offensive.

These events shaped the immediate operational future of the Manchester squadrons. For 207 Squadron the prospect of a move to a new base, and for the Manchesters the temporary winding down in the scale of operations and the bad winter weather combined to provide a respite. Before this an ASR, a shallow penetration raid and one final main force attack were to be carried out.

Following the catastrophic losses from the Berlin force on the night of 7/8 November 1941, 97 Squadron was called upon next day to provide two aircraft for ASR operations over the North Sea. L7466 OF-N flown by Flight Lieutenant Price and L7488 OF-F, Flying Officer Blakeman, neither of whom had operated the previous night, took off together close to 13.20 hours in the afternoon. The cloud base was still low with poor visibility and intermittent rain. Both aircraft reached their search areas and began flying overlapping search patterns at only 200 feet. Neither aircraft reported any sightings. Blakeman's crew encountered Price's aircraft on six occasions, the last being timed at 16.00 hours and shortly before the search was called off. They landed back at Coningsby close to 18.00 hours. No further sign of Price or his aircraft were ever seen again. Bearing in mind the weather conditions, flying height and falling darkness it is possibly unlikely that L7466 was brought down by the Germans.

Whilst Price and Blakeman were still out searching, three freshmen from 'A' Flight of 97 Squadron and two from 207 Squadron were being prepared for a gentle shallow penetration introductory raid on the docks at Dunkirk, to gain experience. The aircraft departed around 18.00 hours.

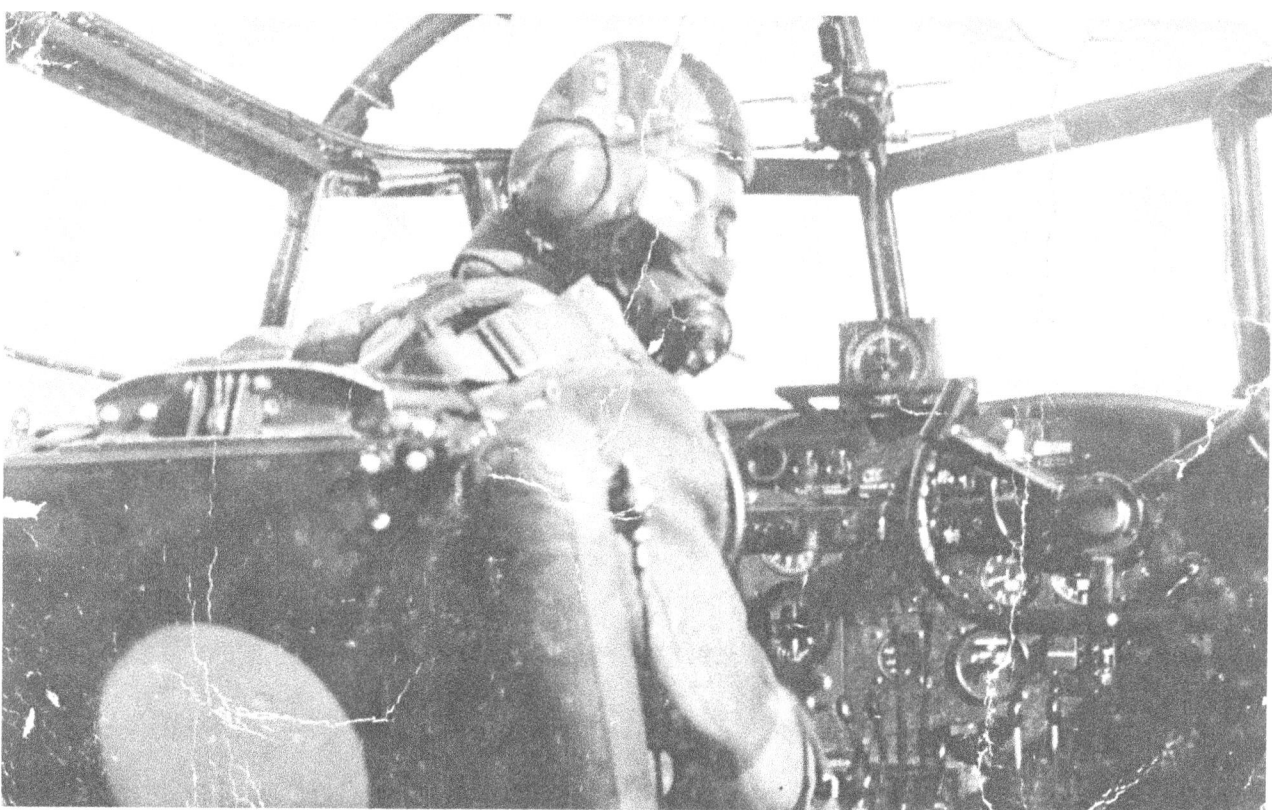

Flight Sergeant George E. A. Pendrill in the captain's seat of his Manchester Mk.1A L7522 OF-V after it was named Sri Garuda. The swastika identifies the victory over Oberleutnant Griese on the night of 7/8 November 1941. (Imperial War Museum CH4157)

Manchester Mk.1 L7455 EM-G of 207 Squadron at Bottesford. Delivered on 10 September 1941, the aircraft was dispatched on 26 sorties by three squadrons. Left to right: Sergeant J. Duncan (first wireless operator); Sergeant S. Allen (second wireless operator); Sergeant A. Hall (observer); Flying Officer P. C. Birch (captain); Sergeant N. A. Lingard (second pilot); Sergeant A. P. Cullerne (mid-upper gunner); Sergeant Boldy (rear gunner). (J. M. Duncan).

Dunkirk, a freshman's run – 8 November 1941:

Serial	Code	Squadron	Captain
L7491	OF-C	97	Sqn Ldr J. S. Sherwood
L7476	OF-K	97	Plt Off. E. A. Deverill
L7475	OF-B	97	Plt Off. E. E. Rodley
L7300	EM-F	207	FS G. H. Hathersich
L7322	EM-Q	207	Fg Off. J. H. Leland

Squadron Leader Sherwood was unable to attack due to the glare from the searchlight batteries; Pilot Officer Rodley attacked successfully with ten 500-lb bombs. Pilot Officer Deverill's crew had a harrowing experience. Their aircraft was heavily engaged by flak batteries whilst running up to bomb at 17,000 feet. The aircraft was very severely damaged by a near miss and plunged to 4,000 feet with the mortally wounded second pilot, Pilot Officer Hodge, obstructing the controls. Deverill was able to level out and jettison part of the bomb load and the remaining four 500-lb bombs were dumped in the North Sea. With the second pilot being cared for on the rest couch, Deverill took stock. All exterior lights were illuminated on the aircraft and could not be extinguished due to a short in the electrical system. The bomb doors were jammed open owing to the failure of the hydraulic system. Deverill was able to return to Coningsby where the emergency system had to be used to lower the undercarriage. Don Hodge, a Rhodesian straight from the Operational Training Unit, was taken to the station sick bay at 20.38 hours but died of his wounds at 23.00 hours the same night. So much for shallow penetration operational experience raids!

Finally, early on 9 November 1941 the experienced main force crews of 207 Squadron were called to provide six Manchesters for a raid on the Hamburg shipyards. Finding no respite, Flight Sergeant Hathersich was again called upon to continue his transition to a fully fledged member of the squadron by taking L7300 to Ostend. The whole force took off between 17.40 and 17.55 hours, Hathersich amongst them.

Hamburg / Ostend* - 9 November 1941:

Serial	Code	Squadron	Captain
L7309	EM-R	207	Sqn Ldr K. H. P. Beauchamp DFC
L7322	EM-Q	207	Plt Off. G. R. Bayley
L7455	EM-G	207	Fg Off. P. C. Birch
L7485	EM-D	207	Plt Off. A. W. Hills DFM
R5791	EM-V	207	FS J. C. Atkinson
L7319	EX-X	207	Fg Off. J. Wooldridge
L7300	EM-F	207	FS G. H Hathersich*

The usual spate of 'Manchester' problems began to descend upon the unfortunate crews. L7319 was by this time becoming rather long in the tooth for an operational aircraft and Flying Officer Wooldridge, who was taking it on operations for the first time, was appalled by its flying performance. He reported it was extremely slow and would not climb. Squadron Leader Beauchamp also had similar difficulties persuading another of the older aircraft, L7309, to climb. Eventually he had no alternative but to jettison one of the four 1,000-lb GPs into the North Sea. He eventually coaxed L7309 up to a height of 14,500 feet as he approached Hamburg.

Other aircraft were experiencing different problems. In L7322, Pilot Officer Bayley encountered rear turret failure, whilst one of the two Brownings in the dorsal FN7A turret went unserviceable. The rear turret in L7455 also packed up and Flying Officer Birch's problems were compounded by hydraulic trouble. Pilot Officer Hills also reported turret failure in L7485. Beauchamp approached the shipyards at about 20.12 hours, impeded by the intense glare of searchlights. Heavy flak was also intense and accurate causing slight damage to L7309. Flight Sergeant Atkinson was similarly impeded by the glare at 13,000 feet as he threaded his way inland keeping the Elbe in sight twenty-five miles to one side. He could only report that his four 1,000-lb GPs had fallen somewhere in the built-up area of Hamburg. Hills was unable to reach the main target owing to the several cones of searchlights, although L7485 was not held or hit by flak. His 4,000-lb 'Cookie' fell in the south-eastern part of the built-up area from 16,000 feet. Hills must have felt very vulnerable with his turret problems.

These were the only three Manchesters to reach Hamburg. In L7322 Pilot Officer Bayley chose to attack Borkum as a last resort target. His aircraft had only one Browning gun capable of being brought to bear in the event of a rear attack from a night fighter and he would have been justified in aborting the operation. Instead, his bombs were aimed at the seaplane base from a height of 15,000 feet.

In the struggling L7319, Flying Officer Wooldridge had eventually reached 12,000 feet. His observer mistook Jade Bay for the mouth of the Elbe and Wooldridge elected to attack Wilhelmshaven docks as a last resort target instead of pressing on to the hot bed of flak and fighters over Hamburg. Wooldridge carried out one of the diving glide attacks he favoured. The searchlight and flak defences were intense as he dived from 12,000 feet, releasing his bomb load before reaching 10,000 feet. The defences were sufficiently ferocious that Wooldridge kept the nose down all the way down to the coast, crossing out at only 1,000 feet.

The remaining disabled Manchester, L7455, captained by Flying Officer Birch, with both turret and hydraulic problems might well, with justification, have returned to Waddington. But Birch was determined to leave some mark on the enemy and diverted to Calais, dropping four 1,000-lb GPs on the docks from 14,000 feet at 20.40 hours. Birch's problems were further compounded when the Lorenz homing device failed. Nevertheless, base was reached and a successful landing made in an aircraft in which the port under-carriage leg refused to lock and with no brakes. L7455 had a lot to answer for that night. Of the Hamburg force, only R5791 had not had mechanical or aerodynamic problems of some kind.

Meanwhile, Flight Sergeant Hathersich with his 'freshman' crew reached Ostend docks at 19.45 hours and dropped twelve 500-lb GPs from 8,000 feet. He was undeterred by searchlights and intense light flak but was unable to see the results of his attack.

The Manchester airframe and colour scheme shown in their final form on Mk.1A L7515 EM-S. The aircraft was delivered to 207 Squadron on 10 October 1941 and photographed during November. It undertook fourteen sorties with 207 Squadron, a further ten with 106 Squadron and was not struck off charge until November 1943. (via British Aerospace)

All in all it had been an extremely unsuccessful operation and a stark indication, if one were needed, that the many problems were far from solved. In military terms such limited results from a relatively major effort was unacceptable. The crews themselves were intensely frustrated. Despite their most determined efforts, the Manchesters still seemed to prevent them making a significant contribution to the war effort, with the Germans hardly needing to enter the arena. Bomber command's successes as a whole were only a little better than those of the Manchesters. From the Hamburg operation on 9/10 November 1941 the recorders on the ground established that from the seventy-one aircraft claiming to attack, three large fires were started. Thirteen civilians were killed and fifty six injured.

From this time the level of operational activity declined for a while. 207 Squadron stood down on 11 November to receive 19 Air Ministry Press representatives. The interviews and photographs appeared in the November 1941 edition of 'The Aeroplane'. Stories of determined efforts against great odds by the crews, which were true, were interspersed with claims for the complete reliability of the Vulture power-plants, which were not. Despite the heavy censorship, a hint that all was not well was the first admission that in its introduction to operations the Vulture had had its fair share of problems. The crews must have regarded this as the understatement of the century.

Emden – 15 November 1941:

Serial	Code	Squadron	Captain
L7432	EM-J	207	FS B. O. Wescombe
L7322	EM-Q	207	Flt Lt W. D. B. Ruth DFC

A 'new crew' operation on 12 November was also cancelled due to bad weather, but on the 15th two such crews were briefed for an attack on Emden. They took off at 17.50 to 17.55 hours in reasonable weather and when the aircraft encountered an occluded front this quickly deteriorated. There was 10/10ths cloud, total darkness and dense fog with no prospect of locating the target with the equipment then available. To make matters worse, Flight Lieutenant Ruth experienced heavy icing. The autopilot and then the hydraulic system in the aircraft failed. Ruth abandoned the operation and bombed Den Helder with four 1,000 pounders from 8,000 feet on the way home.

The observer in L7322, Sergeant Wheatley, was soon unsure of their position and as the ice built-up on the airframe the aircraft began to lose height rapidly. Lost over the North Sea and with a sink rate which would take them into the water within a short period, they were clearly in a desperate position. Only a rapid change in their fortunes could prevent a disaster. Sergeant 'Scotty' Scott, the wireless operator, had lost first one and then the second trailing aerial owing to the weight of ice and was consequently unable to get a fix to help the observer in locating their position. In desperation Scott played his final card and deployed his spare aerial. Before he could contact the various stations this too carried away.

The last prospect of contact with the outside world had disappeared. As ice accumulated on the airframe the turrets and cockpit perspex iced over with a white crystalline hoar frost. Not only had they lost their ears, but with the fog and ice their eyes as well. For the moment the engines and ASI were unaffected but the steadily unwinding altimeter indicated the seriousness of their plight.

Whilst Ruth flew the aircraft, the second pilot, Pilot Officer Gerry Ings, slid open the cockpit window and stuck his head out sufficiently to see ahead. A mid-air conference developed and with visions of flying headlong into the ground within a very short timescale, Ruth and others advocated baling out immediately, whereas Scott and the remainder, unaware of what lay below, preferred to hang on until the last minute in the forlorn hope that something would turn up. Ings was soon sufficiently frozen at his post that it was necessary for him to change places as look out with Scott. The aircraft continued to sink and still they could not be confident whether they had crossed the UK coast. Scott rapidly became chilled to the bone and they were approaching 1,000 feet with still no break in the curtain of fog.

Quite suddenly and to his delight Scott saw a hole in the murk with, amazingly, a lighted flarepath at the bottom. Without hesitation, Scott grabbed the second pilot's control column in front of him and shoved it forward, not taking his eyes off the one prospect of salvation for a second. Feeling the stick move in his hand, Ruth shot Scott a startled glance exclaiming: 'What the hell are you doing?' 'Scotty' replied with increasing confidence: 'There's a flarepath down there'. As the nose dropped Ruth could see it too. 'Good God, so there is' cried Ruth, galvanised into action. With no more ado, Ruth dropped the flaps and wheels, thankful that at least the emergency systems were working and, lining up on the runway closest to their approach direction, trimmed the aircraft and put the propellers into fine pitch. They would go straight in without the customary circuit. As a result of the steepness of their approach, combined with his restricted vision and the weight of the aircraft, Ruth put L7322 down with a jarring crash, but they were down safely and taxied to the indicated dispersal. As they did so the fog closed in around them again and they were to be marooned for three days.

For Scott, who might, given different circumstances, have been in L7310 with Squadron Leader Kydd on the fateful 21 June night flying test, it was the second escape from the jaws of death. Did he but know it, a further two narrow squeaks would follow in the two years he was with 207 Squadron. Such flukes of chance could and did separate the survivors from the victims of wartime flying. On leaving the aircraft and being de-briefed they learned first of all that they had landed at Docking in North Norfolk. In conversation with those on the ground they learned that the sound of their engines, as they approached, had alerted the residents who had illuminated the airfield in the hope that the airmen would see them through the murk. Onlookers had seen their Manchester, ghostly white and festooned with ice, appear as though from a solid wall of fog. The touch-down was even more dramatic when, as Ruth dropped the aircraft onto the tarmac, the shock caused the airframe to shed its mantle of ice in a huge shower, which in the glare of the Chance Light produced a dramatic halo effect, momentarily enveloping the entire aircraft. It was a spectacular and unforgettable arrival. For the crew, however, it was sufficient to find their feet once more on solid ground. It must have been an unwelcome introduction to Manchester operations for Flight Lieutenant Ruth.

On 16 November 1941 207 Squadron moved to Bottesford where it continued to operate its mixture of triple-finned Mk.1 and twin-finned Mk.1A Manchesters. New Manchesters delivered to the Squadron as and when required were Mk.1As and these invariably had the division between the upper shadow shading and the lower black forming the now standard straight line at the top of the fuselage decking. In all cases the black lower colour continued to sweep up over the rear fuselage in line with the leading edge of the position where the third fin would have been. This should not be taken to imply that the third, central, fin had once been fitted and later removed. These Mk.1As were built as such in the factory and no-one had apparently thought to alter the colouring instructions. All these aircraft continued to be delivered with a mid-upper FN7A turret.

At the same time the squadron continued to soldier on with some of its early Mk.1s. These notably included L7300, L7309, L7317 and L7319. In several cases these Manchesters, despite the authorised change in colour schemes to a straight demarcation, continued to operate with the earlier wavy demarcation unchanged. In the case of L7300, the aircraft continued to operate without the FN7A mid-upper turret in the condition it was first delivered back in February. Crews appreciated the lack of fin flutter and the decrease in weight which arose from its absence. This provided an additional safety margin which might make the difference between keeping the aircraft aloft in the event of losing an engine. It is known that L7309 did have a mid-upper turret when lost in January 1942 and photographs of L7319 show it to be so fitted.

The first trickle of Metropolitan Vickers-built Manchesters was starting to arrive, R5791, R5782 and R5796 being on strength. No evidence as to whether these were delivered as Mk.1 or Mk.1As has come to light although it is believed all were originally built as Mk.1s.

Meanwhile, 5 Group had become reconciled to soldiering on with its ageing Hampdens and still only 207, 97 and 61 Squadrons were equipped with Manchesters. 44 Squadron at Waddington had been evaluating the prototype Lancaster, BT308/G, since September 1941 and was due to receive the first production aircraft in late December 1941. Next in line was 97 Squadron. In the meantime the Halifax and Stirling squadrons were receiving the bulk of the press, public and, apparently, RAF attention. After all their fervent endeavours with the Manchester, 207 and 97 Squadrons felt themselves to be on the sidelines.

October and November 1941 saw a further resurgence in pressure to develop cannon armed, power operated turrets for the Manchester and Lancaster. A 5 Group Minute dated 19 November identified the increased number of interceptions by German night fighters, the trend for German night fighters to mount cannon armament themselves and the possible use of the bombers for daylight operations as the main justification for renewed pressure to acquire the heavier armaments.

At various meetings the prospect of two 20-mm cannon in power operated turrets was re-examined, with an alternative interim solution of two 0.5-inch Hispano short-barrelled cannon in the semi-manual installation first offered by Rose Brothers in April/May 1941. In respect of the 20-mm cannon, the power increase, weight increase and size remained unchanged, whilst structural increases arising from the drag and recoil of the weapons was a major problem. Expulsion of cordite fumes was also a severe constraint. A FN4A four gun Browning turret with 2,000 rounds per gun weighed in at 726 lbs. In comparison, two 20-mm Hispano guns with 200 rounds per gun, belt fed, weighed 400 lb on their own, without any turret. Avro had by this time designed a two 20-mm belt fed power operated turret with 550 rounds per gun, but it was likely to weigh in at a massive 2,000 lb. In the event, for whatever reasons, neither the two 20-mm power turret nor the lighter Rose concept attained production status on the Manchester or any other British bomber.

Mid-November spelt the beginning of a miserable period for the personnel of 207 Squadron, coinciding with its move to a new station. Bottesford was a completely new airfield with concrete runways and rapidly constructed, dispersed facilities. A period of settling in was called for and the squadron stood down between the 18th and the 21st to allow for this. Many squadron personnel never forgot the transition. Bill 'Goldie' Goldstraw, first wireless operator to Flying Officer Dave Green, has indelible memories which probably parallel those of many of his compatriots. He recalls that:

Waddington, being a permanent pre-war station, had all the comforts of a well run establishment, brick built accommodation blocks with central heating, dry and warm, with plenty of washing facilities and hot water, everything to hand. There was relatively limited dispersal of the dwelling and operational facilities, which were separated by made-up roads. On the social side, when stood down from flying Lincoln was a couple of miles down the road with convenient public transport. On non-operational nights the pubs and cinemas were packed with aircrew from all the airfields around Lincoln. Entertainment of all description and, in short – tastes – was available.

Bottesford was quite, quite different. For a start virtually the entire site was a sea of mud, still being in the final stages of completion. Wellington boots were the permanent order of the day. The buildings were well dispersed, temporary Nissen huts, often unheated and they leaked. It was cold, damp, muddy and uncomfortable. Goldstraw shared a small room with a rear gunner. The roof leaked, the floor was wet, as were the bedclothes.

They found that the sleeping accommodation was in one area of the airfield, whilst the washing, shaving and feeding facilities were in a communal site with cookhouse, ablutions, messes etc. half a mile distant.

Each morning they had to leave their damp beds, don damp clothes and Wellingtons and walk across the muddy fields to wash, shave and have breakfast. Next they had to walk a mile or so to the operational area where the duty office, briefing rooms and hangars were dispersed. To add to the extreme domestic inconvenience, aircraft operations posed particular hazards since although the perimeter track, taxiways, dispersals and runways were concrete their recently completed nature meant that they were edged with deep soft mud. Taxiing called for extreme caution as immediately a wheel ran off the tarmac it sank axle deep, immobilising the aircraft itself and frequently the remainder of the squadron aircraft snaking and waddling along behind.

The winter of 1941/422 was therefore spent in acute discomfort by the squadron and illness reached epidemic proportions at times. In addition to their immediate domestic and flying problems, Bottesford was a very isolated spot miles from any entertainment. Without public transport and so far from a major centre of population they initially felt trapped and abandoned.

Left to their own devices, they eventually established a system which Bill Goldstraw admits did have its compensations. They organised their entertainment on a squadron basis and, since 207 Squadron had Bottesford entirely to themselves, all the personnel got to know each other far better than at Waddington, where all facilities were shared with another squadron. Moreover, they had another unifying influence – the discomforts and difficulties, which were common to all. After the initial plunge, morale in the unit rose higher than it ever was at Waddington – but this was some time in the future.

Occasionally, on stand-downs from operations, most of the squadron 'decamped' to Nottingham to drink at 'The Airborne Nag' (Flying Horse) or the 'Trip to Jerusalem'. They reassembled at the 'Palais de Dance' where they sang squadron songs and enjoyed themselves. Eventually they congregated on the milk train next morning back to Bottesford.

Another long serving squadron wireless operator, Sergeant Jim Duncan, has additional memories of Bottesford. The crews were interested to discover large concrete structures to either side of the main runway and repeated at either end. Inspection and further enquiry revealed these to be the anchorage points for an arrested landing system for heavy bombers. Such a system had been designed and tested at the Royal Aircraft Establishment, Farnborough. The system involved taut arrester wires stretched transverse to the runway and a large retractable arrester hook mounted in the bomber. In the event no aircraft were fitted with the system.

During the afternoon of 22 November 1941 Pilot Officer Bill Hills took off from Bottesford to fly to Waddington in one of the longest serving Manchesters, L7300 EM-F. Nine persons were on board. These were the regular crew, Bill Hills (captain), Flight Sergeant Plaistowe (second pilot), Sergeants Jackson (observer), Smith (wireless operator), van Puyenbroek (front gunner) and Ward (rear gunner), together with Flying Officer Pattinson who was going off on a course and two air traffic controllers hitching a ride to Waddington. Pattinson's suitcase with personal effects and logbooks were stowed in the bomb bay.

Having raised the undercarriage, Bill Hills then followed a familiar route and adopted a well-established routine. For part of the flight they followed the Lincoln to Boston canal which ran alongside a high embankment carrying the Lincoln to London main railway line. The crews at times got a kick out of flying along the canal at the same height as the bank waving to surprised engine drivers as they overtook them at the same level.

On this occasion they were flying at 500 feet along the route when, with a loud rumble and clatter, the port engine suddenly failed. Hills immediately pressed the button to feather the port propeller. The feathering mechanism initially engaged but failed before the blades had fully rotated parallel to the airflow, leaving the propeller windmilling and creating additional drag. Hills raised the wireless operator on the intercom and instructed him to inform the tower at Waddington that they would be 'coming in on one'. He next advanced the throttle of the starboard engine which would enable them to climb to a safer height. Opening the throttle failed to

Beautifully proportioned lines of Mk.1A L7515 EM-S from below. (Philip Jarrett)

produce any increase in power. Instead, a severe vibration in the engine and airframe was followed by this engine packing up too.

At low altitude with two dead engines and little excess speed there was minimal time to prepare for and no option regarding the site of the inevitable forced landing. They simply had to go more or less straight in dead ahead. By great good fortune there was flat open ground bordering a small tree-lined lake slightly to their left. Hills suddenly remembered that he was not strapped into his seat, but in these few final seconds was unable to take his hands off the controls. A thought flashed into his mind recalling a fellow 49 Squadron Hampden pilot during his first tour who had survived a crash landing in similar circumstances by bracing his feet on the dashboard at the instant of impact.

Accordingly, Hills shouted: 'Hold on' to warn the crew, raised his feet from the rudder bars, bracing them on the instrument panel, and yanked hard back on the stick just before the aircraft hit the ground. The nose rose sharply and the tail hit the ground first. The severity of the impact resulted in the rear fuselage and tail unit breaking off immediately forward of the crew entry door. The triple fin tail unit, fortunately unoccupied, tumbled away and come to rest on the edge of the lake.

Twenty tons of uncontrollable, disintegrating, screeching Manchester slithering on its belly was bearing down on the lake at almost 100 mph. The scene in the flooded disused quarry now known as Fiskerton Lake could not have provided a more marked contrast – a fishing match was in progress. Competitors were distributed around its margin and one of the organisers was out on the lake in a flat bottomed punt. For this group the afternoon epitomised peace, solitude and an escape from war work.

In an instant the careering Manchester appeared over the bank and pitched forwards into perhaps 10 feet of water, throwing up a massive tidal wave as it did so. Fishermen turned and ran as the wave broke upon the bank, whilst the unfortunate occupant of the punt had a grandstand view before the advancing wall of water swept over his craft, rocking it violently and sending cascades of water over its gunwales. Within a few seconds the Manchester had settled and the waves were dissipating, leaving the boatman standing unscathed, soaking wet and transfixed with fear, ankle-deep in water, his sandwiches bobbing gently around him.

On impact, Hills must have catapulted over the top of the control column and then down into the nose, as his next recollection is lying in the nose section with water, mud and gravel spurting in on him. They were all shocked and not reacting rationally. Lying beside him was Pattinson who, on feeling the liquid on him, shouted: 'Look out, petrol!' 'No, it's only water' replied Hills who, finding he could stand, returned to the cockpit, climbed out of his side window and thence onto the wing.

Moans and groans coming from the rear of the aircraft brought the sudden vivid and irrational thought that he had killed the remainder of his crew. To discover their condition and come to their assistance he then released the aircraft dinghy and was relieved to see it inflate undamaged. Climbing in, he paddled the dinghy round to the gaping hole where the rear fuselage had broken off. As he did so he heard a scream of pain from inside: 'Ah! My back. Leave me alone', as one shocked crew member tried to help another.

In his haste and anxiety to help, Hills pulled the dinghy in too firmly against the jagged metal, puncturing it. Despite their injuries the crew came running hell for leather down the fuselage towards him through the water, by now rising inside the rear fuselage. This aircraft was not fitted with a mid-upper turret so that the progress of the crew was unimpeded. As the Manchester settled, the last escaper, van Puyenbroek, found himself completely submerged, but with scrabbling fingers he managed to pull himself clear of the fuselage with the last of his remaining breath.

Although the outer cover punctured and the dinghy partly deflated, the inner skin remained intact and Hills was able to ferry the survivors in groups to the wing of the Manchester, which was still above the water. A head count then established that the entire crew had survived. There were various injuries which were relatively minor in the circumstances; these included van Puyenbroek with a broken arm and skinned fingers and Pattinson with a severely bruised backside. Plaistowe had a cut head and was concussed. They then ferried themselves in stages to the shore. Latterly, the lone sentinel frozen and open mouthed in the punt was galvanised into action and helped them ashore in his swamped vessel.

Bill Hills was left standing on the wing in true captain's style, the last to leave the aircraft, and he found the time to reach inside his soaking clothing and pull out his cigarettes. Finding one still dry he lit it up as he waited his turn to be ferried ashore.

The whole crew was finally assembled on the shore and as they waited for transport to arrive, in their wet clothes began to feel the effects of the extreme November cold. To keep the cold at bay they broached the emergency rations and found seven small bottles of rum. Only Hills and one other crew member liked rum and it certainly did warm them, especially the last bottle.

By this time a private car and ambulance had been rustled up from somewhere and they were ferried to hospital for a check up. The worst injured, including Plaistowe, were stripped of their wet clothes and wrapped in dry blankets.

By now Hills was high on the combined relief from the anxiety of their crash and the effects of the alcohol and insisted in riding up front with the (female) ambulance driver. En route to the hospital the car stopped at a turning and Plaistowe leaped out and raced naked down the street before his compatriots recaptured him. The effects of the concussion were still apparent.

When Hills and the other group arrived in the ambulance at Lincoln hospital those with injuries were taken to the wards, whilst Hills was not only unhurt, but a liability. Suffering from shock, extreme cold and alcohol, he was immediately bundled into blankets and transferred to the medical wing at Waddington. Here the doctor soaked him in a hot bath and the effects of cold and rum slowly abated. That night he appeared in the mess at Waddington resplendent in a uniform loaned by the squadron doctor.

In early December L7300 was recovered from the lake by 58 Maintenance Unit, assisted by a naval diving team and consigned to the scrap heap. The aircraft still carried its early style wavy demarcation between the black undersides and the disruptive brown and green upper surfaces and never had a mid-upper turret.

An internal Rolls-Royce Minute of 26 November 1941 specifies what was possibly the last large scale Vulture problem, although by now it was a problem of more modest proportions. The Minute, entitled 'Vulture Progress' remarks on the epidemic of exhaust manifolds failing at 25 OTU Finningley. All the failures occurred at around 60 hours of life. It was suggested that the trouble was accelerated by the large number of take-offs carried out at the OTU. There were also failures at Coningsby and Bottesford.

The Minute went on that the troubles stressed the need for large quantities of 18-SWG manifolds for retrospective fitting. At that time service replacements consisted of reconditioned 20-SWG manifolds returned after ninety hours. In early December 207 Squadron was stood down for several days to permit all the exhaust manifolds to be changed, presumably they were changed sequentially on each unit.

A rider to the Minute provides a contemporary check on the status of Vulture deliveries at this date; thirty-seven engines were awaiting Mod. No.44, the correction of the con-rod assembly. There were 116 more new engines to deliver to complete the contract. The implication that it was considered that Avro were now responsible for any delay in delivery of completed aircraft is found in the claim that Avro still had more engines than they could cope with, and that it had been possible to supply two spare engines to all the stations (a whole two!) This was mute testimony to the perpetual and desperate shortage of all Vulture spares, which reduced squadrons at times to desperate measures.

On checking Vultures returned for inspection after 120 hours, it became apparent that several examples of excessive barrel wear were coming to light, especially of the master-rod cylinder. In an attempt to reduce barrel wear several engines were modified to take nitrided liners which had a greater wear resistance. Vultures Nos. 682, 694, 696 and 698 were fitted to two Metrovick aircraft, R5793 and R5794, and delivered to 25 OTU at Finningley. It appears this modification was not proceeded with.

A further return to Hamburg was planned for the last night of November.

Hamburg* and GARDENING Willows Area 30 November - 1 December 1941:

Serial	Code	Squadron	Captain
L7382	OF-D	97	FS S. F. Harrison*
R5795	OF-P	97	FS L. H. Adams*
L7495	OF-N	97	FS G. H. Hartley*
L7474	OF-Z	97	Sgt C. G. Hughes*
L7489	OF-T	97	Flt Lt E. Coton
L7522	OF-V	97	FS G. E. A. Pendrill
L7457	OF-Y	97	WO D. H. Rowlands
L7423	OF-S	97	WO T. J. Mycock

The aircraft took off close around 17.00 hours, the Hamburg force mostly returning soon before midnight and the GARDENING force soon after. The GARDENING force found good conditions and all planted their VEGETABLES successfully, though one could only find the alternative drop zone. Three of the Hamburg force attacked the target

L7300 EM-F of 207 Squadron during recovery operations by a naval diving team at Fiskerton Lake, Lincolnshire. The aircraft crashed on 23 November 1941 when Pilot Officer Hills had a double engine failure. (via N. Franklin)

successfully in good weather. Flight Sergeant Harrison had a more eventful abortive trip. In L7382 the crew followed a different route, crossing the enemy coast of Denmark, turning south and encountering severe icing on the approach to Hamburg. Harrison was forced to descend to 6,000 feet to avoid it. As they approached the north bank of the Elbe they encountered heavy flak. Already struggling with a heavily iced aircraft and driven down to low level, the further complication from the flak led Harrison to abandon his attack and reverse his course, jettisoning his bomb load over the Danish coast. On taking this action, a further severe problem manifested itself. As so many times before, their Manchesters seemed more likely to kill them than the Germans.

For the first time L7382 was carrying a vertical looking camera to record the bomb impact point. As the bombs were dumped, George Farara, the bomb aimer, tried to release the photo flash too. They had been warned at briefing that these were liable to jam in the flare chute. Such was the concern that Sergeant George Preston, the wireless operator, was standing-by to make sure this had discharged successfully. To his dismay he found it had not. The flashes were fused to discharge just as the bombs hit the ground and contained 10 lb of very explosive material - sufficient to blow a large hole in the fuselage. George shouted a warning and while he and Bill Townsley, the air gunner, struggled to eject the flash, using a kitchen broom (presumed to be a long-handled sweeping brush - author) for the purpose. Harrison put the aircraft into a steep dive, followed by an equally steep climb in a panic-stricken effort to dislodge it before it exploded. He had just repeated the manoeuvre when a very relieved George called to say their joint efforts had been successful. The crew picked themselves off the floor or fuselage top or wherever else Harrison's ham-fisted jinking had hurled them and they thankfully made our way back to Coningsby. To complete an eventful, though wasted, mission, they were fired on by an Allied vessel as they approached the English coast. Harrison adds: 'thereafter, a kitchen broom became an essential part of our operational equipment'.

In respect of the engine problems, the pilots were still complaining on return from operations that they had been unable to climb above about 7,000 feet. The power available from the twin Vultures was very low but even so they should have been able to reach 15,000 feet. Rolls-Royce engineers once again examined the engines and on the 5 December 1941 Flying Officer Dave Green was ordered to undertake a full warload climb in L7486 to simulate the operational problems. Green took off from Bottesford and on this occasion managed to lift the aircraft to about 17,000 feet. Before reaching the aircraft's ultimate ceiling Green made one of his periodic visual checks on the aircraft and noticed that the wire clipped around the engine cowlings to keep them in place was loose and flapping in the slipstream. Assessing the situation, Green checked all the engine control instruments and found them normal. He believed the most likely explanation for this to be that the clasp had become detached or the cable worn through due to the vibration.

Nevertheless, Green decided to make a precautionary landing to establish the true explanation. It was a wise decision. Green throttled back and spiralled down to the airfield beneath. As they descended into the denser, bumpy air closer to the ground his regular checks appeared to indicate that the entire engine was actually loose on its mountings. In the circuit the suspicions were confirmed as the engine was by this time rising and falling to an alarming degree. They were pleased to land and shut down the engines as soon as possible.

Inspection revealed that the aircraft was indeed closer to disaster than the tell-tale clamping wire had initially indicated. The supercharger cooler mounted on the outboard side of the Vulture engine, where it could not be seen by the crew, was mounted too close to the alloy engine bearers. The supercharger commonly overheated and in this case the heat was sufficiently intense that the bearer had begun to melt. Had Green continued for only a short period, it is certain that the engine would either have caught fire or the entire engine would have fallen out of the airframe completely, with disastrous consequences. Once more the skill and experience of 207 Squadron's aircrews had saved an aircraft and the crew itself from imminent disaster.

Chapter Six: Against the Battlecruisers

Major repairs had been in progress on the *Gneisenau* in Brest since she was severely damaged in early April 1941. *Prinz Eugen* had been released by *Bismarck* in its final hours on 25 May but she in turn was forced to seek shelter in Brest on 1 June due to engine trouble. Dry-docked, on 1 July a bomb hit the cruiser destroying the radio amplifier and compass rooms, as well as the gunnery switching centre and bridge causing deaths amongst the crew.

Repairs to *Scharnhorst* had been completed in May and the vessel was immediately sent south to what was hoped would be a safer berth at the Normandy Dry Dock at St-Nazaire. She sailed on the afternoon of 21 July, calling at La Pallice for gunnery and torpedo trials. Here, on the afternoon of the 24th, when Bomber Command raided Brest in daylight, fifteen aircraft by-passed the port and caught *Scharnhorst* alongside the mole. For heavy losses amongst the attackers, five bombs hit the vessel, again doing enormous damage. That evening she headed back to Brest, fighting off an attack by British carrier-borne aircraft with her own flak defences and arriving with a heavy list. The flooding caused comprehensive damage, most notably to the ship's cabling, which was estimated to require eight months of work. This rendered all three major warships non-operational together. Meanwhile, the *Admiral* S*cheer* and *Admiral Hipper* were refitting in their home ports.

From the German perspective the situation was quite the reverse of what had been intended. Instead of being continually poised to sail at short notice to attack Allied convoys, bombing had kept the ships holed up in Brest, damaged, unserviceable and under repair. Bomber Command had turned the port into a prison. After nine months without any offensive action, Hitler ordered their return via the Channel as soon as possible to free the vessels up for the defence of Norway. Failing this, he demanded that the vessels be decommissioned in Brest and their guns and crews redeployed to reinforce Norwegian coastal defences. It was a humiliating reverse. Now in early December 1941 all three ships were finally sufficiently repaired that plans were adopted to return all three to their home ports whilst opportunity permitted. Very little of this was known to the British.

As December 1941 began, Manchester serviceability problems continued to dog the force. Combined with Bomber Command policy to conserve resources following the severe losses of the 7/8 November 1941 raid, this largely neutralised the Manchester units. Notwithstanding these limitations, pressure was beginning to increase from intelligence sources for further and even more vigorous attempts to take out the *Scharnhorst, Gneisenau* and *Prinz Eugen*. Reports had revealed that the *Scharnhorst* would soon be seaworthy again following lengthy repairs necessitated by the bomb damage suffered back on 24 July. Soon this potent force could be rampaging around the Atlantic once more, at a time when Britain's fortunes and resources were at a low ebb throughout the world. The campaign against the German capital ships waged over the next three months was to witness a variety of unusual and desperate measures, a daylight raid on the ships at Brest, numerous night attacks including the use of a novel anti-shipping weapon, widespread mining operations, including an unprecedented daylight attack in Dutch and German coastal shipping lanes when the intended breakout route was appreciated and finally the chaotic daylight bombing attack on the ships *en passage* in the southern North Sea.

All this lay in front of the Manchester squadrons as December 1941 began. Amongst a plethora of continuing problems at this time there were a few bright spots. 61 Squadron was preparing to return its Manchesters to operations after a three-month work-up and had finally relinquished its Handley Page Hampdens. As this new phase began a glance at the Manchesters which would participate will set the scene.

Whilst the remainder of 5 Group squadrons continued to soldier on with their obsolescent Hampdens, now six to nine months overdue for replacement, the Manchester was sidelined with all eyes on the Avro Lancaster. In the meantime, in early December 83 Squadron at Scampton was designated to be the fourth unit to receive Manchesters. Conversion began during the month to a unit enviously aware of its more favoured cousins receiving Lancasters at nearby Waddington.

In September and October a rush of the latest factory-fresh Mk.1As from L7483 onward had reached 207 Squadron at Waddington, with the main batch in October setting up 61 Squadron, still working up at North Luffenham. A few also reached 97 Squadron at Coningsby. Similarly, the first trickle of Metropolitan Vickers-built Manchesters reached the three units in October, 61 Squadron again taking the bulk of deliveries. These Metrovick aircraft had been built earlier in the year as Mk.1s but whether they had been retrofitted as Mk.1As prior to delivery has not been established. 61 Squadron found that not all deliveries were fitted with an Elsan, but those that had included a privacy curtain which was rapidly dispensed with as a fire risk.

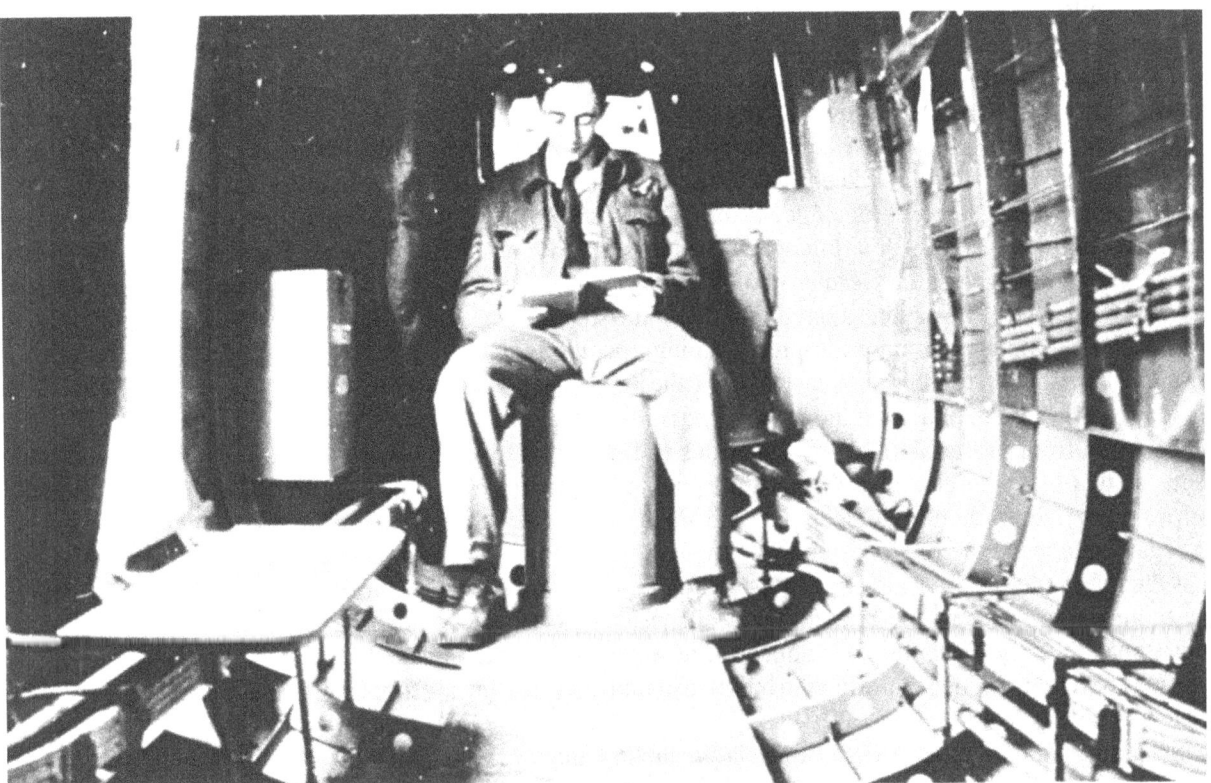

Top: Sergeant Morton (sitting) and Flying Officer Neath in the doorway of Mk.1A L7494 during 61 Squadron's third work up period on the Manchester c. November 1941. L7494 exploded in mid-air running up to Boulogne on its first operation on 7/8 December 1941. The 'A' Flight commander, Squadron Leader Riley, and his crew were killed. Bottom: Ken Leyshon on Ops! Allegedly one of the few Manchesters on 61 Squadron fitted with an Elsan. (Both L. Boot)

Alongside these latest aircraft, the earlier Mk.1s, often retaining their wavy camouflage demarcation, continued in service. In 207 Squadron L7309, L7317 and L7319 were still active. Despite a Bomber Command directive in late June to fit or refit the FN7A to existing Manchesters, a number remained lacking this facility. L7300, just recently written-off, had never had the turret and L7309 and L7322 had lacked the turret initially, although L7309 at least had it installed when it was eventually lost in January. Despite the continuing Rolls-Royce Vulture problems and in an attempt to maintain pressure on the Germans, Bomber Command laid on a main force operation on 7/8 December 1941 to Aachen which was to involve Manchesters from both 207 and 97 Squadrons. Also returning to operating Manchesters after their three-month absence was 61 Squadron, which was to attack Boulogne docks as a gentle re-introduction to operations but, as with 97 Squadron's return in mid-October, things did not proceed very smoothly. These aircraft joined with 124 others allocated to Boulogne. Take-off was unusually late, ranging from 02.12 to 02.24 hours.

Aachen and Boulogne* - 7/8 December 1941:

Serial	Code	Squadron	Captain
L7519	QR-	61*	Wg Cdr T. C. Weir
L7494	QR-	61*	Flt Lt J. L. Riley
L7496	QR-	61*	Flt Lt P. G. Sooby
L7472	QR-	61*	Flt Lt R. A. V. Gascoyne-Cecil
L7491	OF-C	97	Flt Lt J. G. Mackid
L7488	OF-F	97	Fg Off. H. S. Blakeman
L7473	OF-H	97	Fg Off. E. A. Deverill
L7475	OF-B	97	Plt Off. Keir
L7492	OF-A	97	Plt Off. E. E. Rodley
L7476	OF-K	97	FS S. E. Harrison
L7523	EM-M	207	Flt Lt P. C. Ward-Hunt
L7432	EM-J	207	Fg Off. P. C. Birch
L7480	EM-L	207	Fg Off. D. A. Green
R5796	EM-S	207	Sqn Ldr K. H. P. Beauchamp
L7468	EM-Z	207	Plt Off. G. R. Bayley
L7484	EM-P	207	FS G. H. Coles

Of the six aircraft dispatched by 207 Squadron, three bombed what they believed to be the general target area on the estimated time of arrival (ETA) without any results being observed. A Messerschmitt Bf109 passed a mere fifty feet beneath L7523 as Flight Lieutenant Ward Hunt returned.

In R5796 Squadron Leader Beauchamp was unable to find the primary or any suitable alternative target and brought his bombs back, releasing only his load of leaflets in the Aachen area. Flight Sergeant Coles similarly failed to locate the primary owing to 10/10th cloud and severe icing in the target area and released his five 1,000-lb bombs on Dunkirk docks at 05.40 hours on the return flight.

In L7432 Flying Officer Peter Birch was encountering almost insuperable serviceability problems, but with irrepressible spirit carried on towards Aachen. First the rear turret went unserviceable, then the intercom to the front turret failed and finally the dorsal turret guns jammed after a test burst of fire. L7432 was defenceless, but incredibly Peter Birch elected to continue. North of Lille the almost inevitable happened and they were intercepted by a Bf109. By skilful use of cloud and evasive tactics, Birch and his crew kept the fighter at bay for a full thirty minutes before it was seen to break off the engagement to attack a nearby Vickers Wellington.

Finally, bowing to the inevitable and with the added complication of engine trouble, Birch diverted to an alternative target. At 04.15 hours the aircraft was down to 3,800 feet when it attacked the docks at Calais with five 1,000-lb bombs. As a final act of defiance Birch dived to 800 feet to permit the front gunner to shoot out searchlights around the town.

From the 97 Squadron force Pilot Officer Deverill returned when both front and rear turrets proved unserviceable when tested over the North Sea. None of the remaining aircraft located Aachen, which was under deep cloud, and most bombed dock areas on the Belgian and French coast as a last resort. 61 Squadron had equal difficulty locating Boulogne and Flight Lieutenant Riley, the 'A' Flight commander, failed to return. An attacking

Aircrew of 61 Squadron photographed in front of one of their Manchesters, c. December 1941. The commanding officer, Wing Commander Weir, is flanked by his two flight commanders. (via H. Scott)

aircraft had been seen to explode in mid-air on the run up to the target. Since Riley was the only casualty of the night it must have been his aircraft hit by a flak shell. The aircraft crashed into the sea with no survivors.

Of those dispatched, only sixty-four aircraft claimed to attack, whereas the Aachen daily report specifies an attack force of sixteen. Most of the bombs dropped fell in open country to the north of the city and only five high explosive (HE) bombs, two of them duds, and nine incendiaries fell in the city. There were no casualties. A further operation on 8 December was cancelled owing to continued inclement weather and on 10 December the Manchester squadrons were stood down for four days in order to change all manifolds on the Vultures.

The crews returned from a welcome break to find that they were to retrain for daylight formation flying and bombing. At this time, Bomber Command had been plugging away at the *Scharnhorst* and the *Gneisenau* in Brest in the dark for months, seemingly with limited effect. Now it seemed from intelligence reports they may have been on the point of breaking out to ravage the Atlantic convoys, as the *Bismarck* had done in May. Since the first horrific unescorted bombing raids of the war, fighter defences had been provided for shallow penetration raids. Short Stirlings and Handley Page Halifaxes had participated in some of the earliest 'Circus' attacks in France and the Low Countries. Manchesters had been spared this ordeal and were grounded during the summer daylight attacks on La Pallice and St Nazaire.

Now desperation seemed to dictate that the Manchester force could be thrown in with the hope of striking a decisive blow against the capital ships before they lost themselves in the wide expanses of the ocean. The prospect of daylight operations in the Manchester must have filled their hearts with trepidation, but the urgency was such that training began forthwith. In the case of 207 Squadron, formation flying practice commenced on 14 December. It was obvious there was a lot to learn and great care was needed both on the ground and in the air. Groups of nine aircraft at a time participated. The need for a rapid take-off sequence was paramount, but if a single 207 Squadron aircraft snaking along the narrow perimeter track to the active runway put a wheel off the tarmac it immediately sank up to the axle in Bottesford mud and immobilised those aircraft behind. Such aircraft could only be removed by being towed tail first back to the hard standings. However rapid the take-off sequence achieved, the lead aircraft would be fifteen miles ahead by the time the last one took off. Such a distance could never be made up by the heavily laden Manchesters. During practice on 14, 15, 16 and 17 December a system evolved in which the two wingmen of a vic would take-off and join up and then pick up the leader when he took off afterwards.

At the crunch it was 97 Squadron which drew the short straw and was chosen to join the mixed force led by Halifaxes from 76 Squadron, followed by nine Stirlings each from 7 and 15 Squadrons, accompanied by the 97 Squadron force. The operation was planned for 18 December 1941, its urgency heightened by ULTRA intercepts indicating the imminence of the two capital ships breaking out of Brest.

The 97 Squadron force consisted of eleven Manchesters led by the commanding officer, Wing Commander D. F. Balsdon, one of which was intended as a spare in case any aircraft should drop out through unserviceability on the flight across England. Wing Commander Balsdon decided to take the crew of Flight Sergeant George Pendrill, still accompanied as rear gunner by Sergeant Les Jones, who had out-fought Heinrich Griese back in early November. This brought the crew complement to eight. Other crew carried were Sergeant Gibson, the squadron navigation leader, and Flight Lieutenant Wright, the squadron bombing leader. Take-off was close to 09.30 hours.

Port nacelle and undercarriage dwarfing a 207 Squadron crew at Bottesford, early 1942. The aircraft is possibly L7317 EM-C. Left to right: 'Ginger' Hathersich (second pilot); Bob Storey (wireless operator/air gunner); Ken Ferris (air gunner); Frank Belfitt (observer); Jimmy Kneil (captain) and Bob Elliott (air gunner). (K. Ferris)

Brest in daylight – 18 December 1941:

Serial	Code	Squadron	Captain
L7490	OF-U	97	Wg Cdr D. F. Balsdon
L7453	OF-X	97	WO D. H. Rowlands
L7489	OF-K	97	FS C. G. Hughes
L7463	OF-P	97	FS R. A. Fletcher*
L7492	OF-A	97	Sqn Ldr J. S. Sherwood DFC
R5795	OF-W	97	Plt Off. N. G. Stokes
L7460	OF-J	97	Fg Off. H. S. Blakeman
L7525	OF-D	97	Fg Off. B. R. W. Hallows
L7491	OF-C	97	Flt Lt J. G. Mackid
L7425	OF-G	97	Fg Off. E. E. Rodley
L7488	OF-F	97	Fg Off. E. A. Deverill

* operational spare

The six Halifaxes from 76 Squadron, led by their new commanding officer, Wing Commander D. Young, rendezvoused over Linton-on-Ouse with a further five from 10 Squadron and six from 35 Squadron to make up a seventeen-aircraft force. The commanding officer of 10 Squadron, Wing Commander Marks, had already aborted with a jammed starboard undercarriage.

In misty weather, course was set for Lundy Island in the Bristol Channel, where the remainder of the bomber force, including aircraft from the Stirling squadrons and the Manchesters, were to join forces. The rendezvous was achieved successfully, close to the briefed time of 11.20 hours, although a further Halifax aborted and diverted to Boscombe Down with engine trouble. The entire force then headed for the Lizard Peninsula with eighteen Stirlings leading the Halifaxes and the eleven Manchesters at the rear.

Over the Lizard the mist cleared and it became sunny with only occasional wisps of cloud. As all the Manchesters remained serviceable, Flight Sergeant Bob Fletcher, the spare, was able to peel away and return to base. Later Flying Officer Deverill had to return owing to a malfunction in the aircraft, reducing the force to nine.

Ahead, a force of Spitfires and Hurricanes had carried out a fighter sweep of the area with a view to bringing up the German day fighters and using up their fuel. Approaching the French coast, as the Manchesters steeled themselves and bunched up even closer for mutual protection, a jar and roar sent a shock through the tensed up members of Pilot Officer Stokes' crew in R5795 OF-W, on their first operation. The upper escape hatch had flown off and hit the tail fin. The rushing airstream at 17,000 feet brought in the outside air at a temperature of minus 17 degrees Fahrenheit.

As the first clouds from the smoke pots began to drift across Brest harbour the intense flak defences opened up in greeting. At around 12.30 hours Wing Commander Graham led his 7 and 15 Squadron Stirlings over the target, harried all the way by Bf109 fighters, who ignored the dense flak barrage. Next Wing Commander Young led his Halifax force across the French coast in the run up to the target. By the time the Halifax group made their final

L7475 QR-D of 61 Squadron during daylight formation practice, possibly December 1941. (L. Boot)

bomb run, fighter attacks had temporarily abated and they only had the flak to contend with. It appeared that the fighter sweeps had been successful in drawing off much of the Luftwaffe whilst the RAF close escort remained in attendance. Good bombing results seemed to be achieved. Several Halifaxes were damaged by flak and one later ditched in the Channel.

Finally it was the turn of the Manchesters to brave the cauldron of flak over the harbour. As they bored in, maintaining their disciplined three-vic formation, the RAF fighter cover finally had to withdraw, short of fuel, whilst refuelled and armed Bf109s began to reach their height. The Manchesters were on their own.

The flak defences were already having a field day. First, a heavy calibre shell burst close to the left side of Flight Sergeant Hughes in L7489, knocking out the port Vulture, which had to be feathered. Hughes was able to maintain his course and, despite dropping back, released his bomb load. Next, and only a few seconds prior to bomb release, a savage flak burst on the port side of Stokes' R5795 OF-W damaged the port wing and caused the aircraft to yaw to the left, lose speed and fall behind the formation. Sergeant Tom Wade, the observer, released the bombs soon afterwards, but nobody in his crew had the opportunity to observe their fall. Then, a heavy burst exploded beneath L7490 OF-U, buffeting the aircraft, damaging the rear fuselage and tail and wounding the rear gunner, Sergeant Les Jones. The flak intensity and accuracy was hellish for the clumsy Manchesters committed to their straight and level bombing attack and several other aircraft were damaged.

Flying Officer Dave Green in the cockpit of his 207 Squadron Manchester 'Dopey' at Bottesford, c. December 1941. The aircraft is probably L7419 EM-Y. (D. Green)

As they cleared the target, Hughes put L7489 into a dive to put distance between himself and the flak gunners as quickly as possible. Lagging behind the remainder of the force they were set on by a gaggle of Bf109s, which commenced a series of ferocious attacks from astern. Sergeant Gerry McMahon, the rear gunner in L7489, maintained spirited and accurate return fire. Despite being a straggler and being hit repeatedly by the '109s, no vital services were damaged. McMahon claimed hits on four attacking fighters on his return.

Clearing the target, Sergeant Wade closed the bomb doors of R5795 and Stokes put the nose down and turned for home. Ahead the Manchesters streamed out in shallow dives in an attempt to evade the returning Luftwaffe fighters. The straggling Stokes, along with Hughes, last over Brittany and with their escorts already well out in the Channel, was one of the first to feel the savage onslaught from the Bf109s. Sergeants Fell in the rear turret and Heinish in the mid upper gave urgent instructions to Stokes to take evasive action as R5795 was rapidly overtaken. Regrettably, at no time after the flak hit did Stokes reply to instructions or take any evasive action. Either Stokes was badly wounded or he was fully occupied in flying the damaged Manchester. Sergeant Ike Hewitt was sitting impotent, but prepared, in the front turret as R5795 crossed the coast. At least two Bf109s were able to approach from port and starboard quarters and pound the Manchester on its predictable straight and level flight path from long range with their cannon. Fell and Heinish were unable to respond effectively and the first few bursts of cannon fire riddled the rear of the aircraft, incapacitating or killing both gunners. The straggling Manchester was now defenceless to the rear and the Bf109s closed in remorselessly, maintaining steady bursts of fire. R5795 was set on fire amidships and the final order was given to bale out. The observer, Sergeant Tom Wade, second pilot Sergeant Thomas and wireless operator, Sergeant Conn got away through the front escape hatch.

Hewitt made a vain attempt to reach the rear gunner in the hope that he was still alive. Fire quickly drove him back and he then became entangled in the front escape hatch as he tried to follow his three crew mates. Finally breaking free, the last to escape, Hewitt pulled the rip cord to see that his parachute had burnt through in one area. His descent was consequently faster than normal. Stokes had remained at the controls and the Manchester continued to descend on an even keel before plunging into the sea. Hewitt splashed in shortly afterwards. His watch stopped at 13.04 hours and he found that a heavy sea was running. The crash locality is given as four miles off Brest, whereas when he was picked up just before dark at soon after 17.00 hours, Hewitt was told he was 20 miles out and lucky to be found. Along with Thomas and Wade he became a prisoner, but Conn was never found.

German fighters also continued to harry L7489, limping along behind on its remaining starboard engine. Eventually the attacks petered out and the Bf109s withdrew, giving Gerry McMahon in the rear turret more time to take in the happenings around him. As L7489, the last bomber to return from the Brest force, traversed the designated route back, McMahon was struck by the incongruous thought that if he had been a giant he could have walked back to England using the series of floating ditched bombers they passed over en route as stepping stones. Flight Sergeant Hughes could have elected to land soon after crossing the coast but L7489 was flying well on one and all engine instruments read normal. He decided to press on to Coningsby following the rest.

As they plodded on, slowly falling even further behind, it appears that Wing Commander Balsdon too had radioed ahead his intention to return to Coningsby, despite reporting damage to the rear fuselage, tailplanes and elevators of L7490. Flying Officer Blakeman's aircraft had been hit in the starboard oil tank and the two pilots agreed to monitor the engine closely. Blakeman closed in, resuming his position behind and to one side, formating with the commanding officer's aircraft. His crew could see daylight through L7490's rear fuselage, the rear turret was turned on the beam, its guns elevated. Les Jones was motionless in the cramped seat. Fabric was flapping from the shredded elevators. As Blakeman crossed the Channel his crew monitored the rising engine temperature with growing concern. He wisely decided on a precautionary landing at Colerne in Wiltshire where the engine cut out on the runway.

At Coningsby the returning Manchester force arrived back in the late afternoon with a little evening mist but generally favourable weather. Several Manchesters had already landed when the damaged L7490 made its approach. It is not known whether Flight Sergeant Pendrill or Wing Commander Balsdon was flying. The aircraft made a safe and normal circuit and approach, other than that as it let down it was observed to be slightly above the glide path. When the aircraft was on finals and already over the boundary fence its pilot apparently elected to overshoot, as the engines were heard to open up to full power. Regrettably and for unknown reasons, instead of increasing speed and climbing away steadily to make another approach, the nose of the aircraft began to rise steadily and uncontrollably. The nose angle steepened and speed dropped off until the aircraft was almost vertical, a few hundred feet above the airfield. It stalled and flicked over until it was pointing nose down, whereupon it crashed in the centre of the field under the horrified gaze of the control tower staff and wives of several crew members.

On impact the fuselage broke in half at the mid-upper turret, the rear half of the fuselage folding forward over the front. The aircraft was consumed in a ball of flame from which there could be no survivors. The wreckage continued to burn for some time. Indeed by the time Flight Sergeant Hughes arrived in

Cheery ground crew of 61 Squadron digging out the starboard main wheel of a Manchester which strayed off the peritrack on return from an air test, December 1941. (L. Boot)

the circuit some time later it was quite foggy and the fires in the burning wreckage helped him to judge his single-engined landing alongside.

It was next day before the wreck of L7490 had cooled down sufficiently for the debris to be sorted and removed. Personnel found that the only recognisable debris amongst the ashes were the two wing tips and the propellers. The force of the impact had driven the heavy engines down into the ground and all six blades were bent vertically upwards so that their tips projected from the ground. Bob Fletcher, who was billeted with George Pendrill and Les Jones out at Woodhall Spa, returned next day and walked over to the crash site to pay his last respects to his two friends. All that remained was a heap of black ash which Fletcher walked through, numbed into incomprehension by the thought that George and Les were part of those very ashes. The raid itself had achieved little and all 5 Group Manchester airfields were closed by fog for the next four days. On the other side of the coin German sources show that a single hit breached the outer hull of *Gneisenau* but the flooding was minor and the damage was quickly repaired.

Wing Commander Kynoch arrived to take command and 97 Squadron only undertook a few more Manchester operations in early January before they were stood down to convert to the Lancaster. Formation flying by the three Manchester squadrons continued in expectation of a follow-up attack. To their disgust they were even called on to continue their preparations, with a formation flying practice, on Christmas Day.

In the meantime, on 27 December, Group cancelled daylight formation flying and instead specified 207 Squadron to prepare twelve Manchesters for a night operation to Dusseldorf in what was only the third Manchester operation of the month. Later in the day Group cancelled five of the twelve. These seven joined a total force of 132 aircraft.

Dusseldorf – 27 December 1941:

Serial	Code	Squadron	Captain
L7522	EM-M	207	Flt Lt P. C. Ward-Hunt
L7455	EM-G	207	FO P. C. Birch
L7432	EM-J	207	FS B. O. Wescombe
L7484	EM-P	207	Flt Lt W. D. B. Ruth
L7483	EM-O	207	Sqn Ldr K. H. P. Beauchamp
L7322	EM-Q	207	FS G. B. Dawkins
R5791	EM-V	207	FS J. C. Atkinson

On this occasion take-off was well spaced out. Ruth took off at 17.01 hours and Atkinson was last away at 17.47 hours. Take-off and climb performance were marginal, as the crews had come to accept with the Manchester. 'Penny' Beauchamp had undertaken a night flying test in the RAF's first Manchester Mk.1A, L7483, and found it to perform adequately. Close to 17.50 hours, whilst outward bound over Orfordness, the aircraft had struggled to a height of 4,000 feet when the starboard engine lost power and failed. Beauchamp feathered the starboard propeller, put the nose down to maintain airspeed and continued out to sea. The aircraft was unable to maintain height on one engine with the heavy fuel load, 4,000-lb 'Cookie', and two 500-lb general purpose (GP) bombs. Reducing their all-up weight was an urgent necessity but directly in their path ahead to seaward could be one of our coastal convoys, which had been mentioned at briefing. The thin cased 'Cookies' often detonated on impact even when dropped safe. As a precautionary measure Beauchamp continued east to clear the supposed route of the convoy before the bombs were jettisoned. In the event the 4,000-lb bomb did not explode and neither were they troubled by anti-aircraft fire from any convoy which may have been nearby.

By this time L7483 had lost much of what little height had been in hand and was immediately turned inland to return. Despite Beauchamp's best efforts they continued to lose height even without the bomb load. If they were to save the aircraft they would have to find an airfield quickly. Ahead they recognised a single letter flashing PUNDIT beacon showing the coded signal for Martlesham Heath, at this time still a grass airfield. These beacons were mobile and placed at various positions around an airfield. On take-off the crew were given a 'flimsy' showing the chosen codes and the range and bearing of the airfields they marked for that particular night.

Top: 97 Squadron aircrew relax in the crewroom at Coningsby. Sergeant Gordon Hartley is slumped in the chair beneath the dartboard with, to his right, Sergeant 'Fluffy' Berridge, second pilot to Bob Fletcher. Bottom: Manchester Mk.1 L7459 OF-N of 97 Squadron following a forced-landing when a practice bomb detonated as Sergeant 'Jammy' Hartley was taking off from Coningsby on 8 January 1942. Dense smoke blinded and choked the crew. (Both R. A. Fletcher)

Beauchamp called Martlesham on the radio and got a reply from the airman in charge of the flarepath. The airman authorised Beauchamp to land and turned on the flarepath lights. Seeing the position of the airfield for the first time, Beauchamp shaped to make a circuit at around 1,000 feet. On their downwind leg the lights were suddenly extinguished and they completely lost sight of the airfield. It turned out that the airman in charge of the flarepath was 25 miles from his headquarters. He had telephoned his headquarters and informed them he had lit the flarepath for an aircraft which had fired the colours of the day and identified itself as friendly. Headquarters had insisted the aircraft was a hostile and that the flarepath must be extinguished.

The aircraft was continuing to lose height and there was little time left if they were to get down safely. An irate Beauchamp called the airfield again; by now he was on the base leg of the circuit. The lights came on again. By the lights Beauchamp was able to line up on the runway for finals. By then their height was 500 feet, the undercarriage and flaps were down, and they were committed to the landing with no prospect of a second attempt. Without warning the flarepath lights were extinguished yet again. The airfield disappeared, the whole surrounding countryside was blacked out and in the clear half moonlight Beauchamp could vaguely and indistinctly see an open space ahead. Judging height and distance in these circumstances was virtually impossible. Beauchamp continued the approach and when finally down to 50 feet suddenly saw houses coming up on the far side of the airfield. They were overshooting.

Beauchamp had run out of options. At the last moment the lights came on for a third time but too late to help. He rammed the stick forward, the nose dropped and they dived into the ground with the wheels still down. The aircraft hit and the airframe crunched, groaned and ground itself into the turf. There was no significant shock of the impact or deceleration since the enormous forces were mainly taken up by the crushing of the airframe.

The undercarriage legs were driven up through the wings and the aircraft slithered across the grass on its belly, finally coming to a halt with a wingtip against a pill box and the tail against a dispersed Spitfire on the aerodrome boundary. When the noises of the aircraft tearing itself apart finally stopped the only sound was of gurgling, rushing liquid – petrol! To a man the crew abandoned the wreck as fast as their legs would carry them. The ruptured fuel tanks were emptying their contents and the crew ran through a big pool of petrol almost ankle deep in places spreading all round the aircraft. Fortunately it did not catch fire. The time was 18.07 hours.

The entire crew had escaped uninjured, but L7483 was a sorry sight. Although initially categorised as repairable, it never flew again. It was dismantled by 39 Maintenance Unit and passed to 12 School of Technical Training as an instructional airframe.

Unaware of the drama that had befallen Beauchamp and his crew, the remaining pilots nursed their Vulture engines and continued towards Dusseldorf. Soon another Manchester, L7523 flown by Peter Ward-Hunt, had to abandon its attempt to reach the target when the aircraft experienced first a failure of the electrical supply to the rear turret and later an intercom failure. Ward-Hunt diverted to Ostend, releasing five 1,000-lb bombs from 11,000 feet at 18.37 hours. Receiving a diversionary signal, Ward-Hunt returned to Horsham St Faith.

The remaining five aircraft in the depleted force reached what they took to be the target area, where their effectiveness was further reduced when Ruth had his 4,000-lb bomb hang up and Atkinson was unable to release two of his four 1,000-lb bombs. In the target area visibility was good, although one crew had difficulties navigating across the snow covered countryside. Dawkins' aircraft swung at the instant of bomb release with the result that the bombs fell slightly east of the aiming point. Searchlight and flak activity prevented the bomb bursts being observed. In his personalised Manchester, L7455, Peter Birch made a determined attack on the primary at 20.10 hours from 14,000 feet, releasing five 1,000-lb bombs. The bursts could not be distinguished owing to those from other aircraft bursting at the same time, but were estimated to have fallen in the town centre.

Closing the bomb doors Birch then dived to a roof-top height of 150 feet to try his hand as a night intruder. As they proceeded westwards the gunners fired on two factories at Büderich, a train at Heimoud-Masshese and two small towns. All aircraft landed at Horsham St Faith, the hydraulic system in Wescombe's aircraft failing in the process. Although ninety-six aircraft claimed to attack the city, the records reveal that only 32 HE and three cans of incendiaries fell in the built-up area. These caused very slight damage and no casualties.

On 30 December a second daylight attack was mounted on *Scharnhorst* and *Gneisenau,* but the three Manchester squadrons were not required. It is clear that Bomber Command still considered the Manchesters fair game for daylight operations as 207 Squadron was stood by for a daylight attack on 31 December. On this occasion the weather resulted in both this and night flying training being cancelled. As 1942 began 207 Squadron was still shouldering the lion's share of Manchester operations.

On 2 January Warrant Officer Whitehead was in the process of bringing another Manchester crew to the end of their training at 25 OTU at Finningley and had learned that they were posted to 83 Squadron at Scampton to begin operations on these aircraft. On this day the crew was allocated to another second-tour pilot instructor, Flying Officer C. G. Hughes, and aircraft serial L7431. They were to undertake further practice night landings with the new high intensity sodium vapour flares for which the pilot wore very dark goggles to block out the daylight. The crew would have precious little to do and went along for the ride and to rack up the hours in their logbooks. In his 1972 biography *'Gunner's Moon'*, rear gunner Sergeant John Bushby records:

After the first two or three landings Jack Ross-Hoff, Geordie and I settled down on the main spar casing to continue our game of three-handed cribbage. After half an hour or so I rose to stretch my legs and eased forward past the radio position and into the cockpit. Dick Williams was now in the left hand, captain's seat with the instructor, Flying Officer Hughes, beside him in the second pilot's position monitoring his approach. Ahead through the windscreen I could see the bright orange pinpoints of light, brilliant even in daylight, marking the flarepath. Taking this in, I glanced idly out of the port windows at the wing tip.

At this precise moment a sudden sharp explosion, audible above the engine roar, occurred in the port Vulture and I saw something fly off the top of the nacelle and whirl back in the slipstream. Everything seemed to happen at once. Dick tore off the dark goggles and began flicking engine switches and pressing the black propeller feathering button. Meanwhile, Flying Officer Hughes was frantically twirling the rudder trim control wheel and, as the port prop blades slowed and then stopped, began pounding on Dick's shoulder, yelling at him to swap seats. I backed away to allow them to slide and wriggle past each other. However, once this was accomplished the instructor quickly yelled over his shoulder: 'Can't hold her! Got to crash land. Get back and warn the others. Hang on'.

I high tailed it back to the relative safety of the main spar, gasping to the others what was happening as we braced ourselves against any rigid fitting. I dived for the angle between the fuselage and the bulkhead to the wireless compartment and wrapped my arms around a strut. My eyes were glued, hypnotised by a small porthole through which I saw fields and trees sweep underneath ever closer. A small wood, a hedge and then everything tossed, heaved and whirled around me in a crescendo of crashing noise and tearing metal.

We suddenly stopped and it fell silent. I realised I was still in the same position but then a loud hissing sound began which I couldn't recognise. Coming to my senses more, I saw Jack Ross-Hoff back down the fuselage wrestling with the rear entry door. It opened and daylight flooded in. He disappeared through the door and I half ran, half stumbled after him, jumping down onto soft wet earth. Raising my head and turning, I saw that the nose of the Manchester was concertinaed against a large oak tree in a hedge. Behind, across the ploughed furrows, a long swathe scraped in the ground showed our decelerating path across the field. Damage must have been confined to the extreme nose where the front turret had been empty. The cockpit emergency hatch was already open and Sergeant Williams and Flying Officer Hughes were clambering out. 'You alright?' 'Yeah, All OK here. You OK?' 'Think so'.

The loud hissing persisted and after an initial panic they realised this wasn't aviation spirit but instead coolant fluid from a broken pipe dripping onto a hot engine and evaporating. Sergeant Williams and Flying Officer Hughes retreated a few steps into the field and surveyed the aircraft from the rear, lighting a welcome cigarette. 'Reckon they'll send me back on ops for this' was pretty much the instructor's only comment. Even with no bombs and a minimal fuel load the experienced Hughes had been unable to stretch their approach and reach Finningley aerodrome. L7431 was recovered and repaired, its Accident Card giving no further information on the reason for the Vulture failure. It had been a sobering experience for the inexperienced crew on their last flight at 25 OTU. Next day they left Finningley by train for RAF Scampton and 83 Squadron. On 2/3 January 1942 207 Squadron dispatched ten aircraft to St Nazaire and on 5th ten aircraft returned to Brest, followed by a further raid on Brest on 8th/9th.

Brest - 9 January 1942:

Serial	Code	Squadron	Captain
L7486	EM-B	207	FS G. H. Hathersich
L7419	EM-H	207	Fg Off. D. A. Green
L7317	EM-C	207	Plt Off. L. F. Kneil
L7455	EM-G	207	Fg Off. P. C. Birch
L7432	EM-J	207	FS G. H. Coles
L7515	EM-S	207	Fg Off. J. H. Leland
L7322	EM-Q	207	Plt Off. G. R. Bayley
L7468	EM-Z	207	Plt Off. G. B. Dawkins
R5791	EM-V	207	Plt Off. M. E. Doble*
L7453	OF-X	97	FS R. A. Fletcher
L7522	OF-V	97	FS C. G. Hughes

* Freshman to Cherbourg

97 Squadron was able to raise two Manchesters on this date to join the force. All these operations were rendered completely ineffective by exceptionally bad weather with dense unbroken cloud. This resulted in navigation and target location problems. In the absence of any sight of the ground or any aids to navigation, crews were reduced to pinpointing the general area of Brest naval base by the flak bursts in the sky. Even searchlights were unable to penetrate the gloom. Many crews jettisoned bomb loads offshore but a few 'area bombed' the flak activity in the vain hope of a hit with their AP and semi-armour-piercing (SAP) bombs.

In these conditions the weather provided the best protection for the vessels berthed in Brest and Bomber Command blundered around impotently. On this night Pilot Officer Doble in R5791, EM-V, was to include Sergeant John McCarthy as second pilot on his first operation, a 'freshman', for the docks at Cherbourg.

Sergeant McCarthy's account in his own words written within hours of the raid carries all the immediacy and to him excitement, of the occasion:

In the morning (8 January) we do a 'Night Flying Test'. However, it's not our 'kite' and at this stage we don't know just how we stand. At lunch-time the crew list is published and once again we're on it. Guess the afternoon couldn't pass quickly enough for me. Had the whole of the afternoon off and came down to the billet where I did nothing apart from writing a letter. Have an early tea and then down to 'briefing' and it's just as I imagined it. All the crews present seated at long tables littered with maps, target maps and charts. The commanding officer, Wing Commander C. Fothergill, is there with the Intelligence Officer, the Signals Officer, the Armament Officer and almost anyone who has anything to do with the Ops in any way. We inspect a photo of our target area and learn that we are carrying a load of twelve 500-lb GP bombs to be 'unloaded' on the dock area at Cherbourg. Take-off is not until 04.30 hours tomorrow morning for us. I get some of my gear ready and then retire to the billet where I decide to catch a couple of hours sleep before we have a meal in the Mess prior to take-off. Fall asleep wondering what it will be like and hoping like h... that we'll be able to come back and say that we've unloaded right on the target. Reports say that it's easy but we'll have to wait and find out for ourselves.

(Friday 9 January 1942) It's been a 'red-letter' day in my life. I've been over enemy territory and have come back to tell the tale - not that there is anything of note to record. 01.30 hours and out of bed. It's the earliest 'reveille' I've ever known. However, I'm so excited I don't mind in the least bit. I dress and collect a few odds and ends I will need on the trip, empty my pockets and then away to the Mess. This is full of other fellows belonging to other crews. Eight other 'kites' are going over to Brest to give the Scharnhorst and Gneisenau a few more bumps - we hope. They're due away earlier than we are but will be following the same route to the coast of England. We have one fried egg each and a piece of fried bread to go with it, lots of hot tea and bread and butter but it's not a sumptuous or filling meal on which to die.

Transport calls for us at the Mess at 02.40 hours. The night is pretty dark and cloudy and there have been some moderate rain showers in the run up to briefing. I heard a shower of rain when I woke and was dead scared that the whole show would be 'scrubbed'. My keenness is still the wonder of the Squadron.

On arrival at the Crew Room I draw new 'chutes and crew's rations and then it's just a matter of waiting around until 04.08 hours, which is zero hour for us to be in our 'kite'. We're in the 'kite' slightly before time, which is a good thing, and I suddenly find that in my excitement I've forgotten my oxygen tube. It's a mad dash back to the locker room to collect it but I'm back in the 'kite' with time to spare before they start up the engines.

I check petrol contents and find that according to the gauges we're short of the 800 gallons we are supposed to have by over 100 gallons. However, we don't want to say anything in case we are held back, so decide to go on with what we have aboard. We have enough for about five and a half hours flying - maybe. After a pretty good take-off we fly low over England and its good flying. Aerial beacons and lighthouses make our navigation a cinch and we're pretty much on track most of the way to the coast. Nearing the coast we have good visibility so 'Dodo' decides to climb. We get up to 8,000 feet and it's 'oxygen on'. The 'kite' is making fairly good speed and is climbing well. We get up to 16,000 feet with no effort. However, at that height we are well above ten-tenths cloud and have no visibility to the ground. There's a bright moon, or what's left of it, and we would make a pretty good target for any enterprising fighter, but apparently there's no more of the enterprising type left in the German Luftwaffe for we don't meet any opposition. We 'stooge' along in calm unruffled serenity with me working like the devil to keep a good log of engine performance.

Then suddenly I sight some flak away ahead on our s'board side. I've never seen flak before but know that it can be nothing else. We get nearer and see some searchlights trying to nose around under the clouds. They can't pierce the clouds to pick us up. The flak is intermittent and not unduly heavy. It's my first experience and definitely not a bad one.

'Dodo' decides to go and take a look at the locality about which the flak and searchlights are centred. It's obvious that it must be Cherbourg – our 'target for tonight'. We're ahead of our ETA (estimated time of arrival) and we're slightly to left of our track. We move in on the fireworks but 'Dodo' has the wrong approach for he just flies in, steering as though he were helping the navigator to get an astral sight. Then all of a sudden it caught us. It was a combination of a bang and a wham and a boom and a bump, which to my mind would be more aptly described as a 'Whoomff'. It caught us right for-ard near the bomb compartment and for a minute I thought we'd been hit. However, the 'plane kept on going and I yelled to 'Dodo' over the intercom to 'jink' for so-and-so's sake. He then woke up to the fact that we weren't on a picnic and commenced weaving, with the result that we avoided further trouble.

If I'd had the 'kite', I'd have been tempted to go down under the cloud to 'have a lash' but apparently the Skipper had other ideas. Can't say that I blame him for he's a married man with a recently born youngster. It doesn't seem worthwhile wasting time over Cherbourg as there's not a gap in the clouds within a hundred miles.

We see other 'kites' drop flares but what they were doing it for puzzled me. We set course for our alternative – Le Havre. Here again our luck is right out. We stooge along over ten-tenths cloud the whole way and with petrol running low we can't take too many chances. On our ETA we unload our leaflets in the hopes that they will be blown in on French territory. We then set a course to bring us back to England.

It takes us a long time to sight the English coast for we have to cross at the same position as we did on the way out. We can't pinpoint ourselves and its rather uncanny stooging along at about 1,000 feet not knowing where one is or what one is likely to fly into. We finally pick up the landmark beacon at Boscombe Down and we decide to put down there as we've only about enough petrol for an hour's flying – at the outside – if the gauges can be trusted. We land without mishap and duly report to the Watch Office. Base is notified. We inspect the 'kite' but can see no signs of damage from our little 'incident'. It's been quite a good trip, slightly different from the way I would have done it had I been captain, but the experience has given me my first taste of 'things to come'.

A Handley Page Hampden from 144 Squadron at North Luffenham crashed near Boscombe Down about an hour and a half earlier. Two of the crew tried to bale out without success and both were killed. The 'kite' crashed in flames with its bombload on board. All the crew were killed and an hour later three medical orderlies and a transport driver, on guard at the wreckage, were killed when a delayed action bomb blew up. A Scampton 'kite' also crashed near Base but we don't know how the crew fared. For ourselves, we're on the ground and as disappointed at h... that we didn't drop our bombs. Still, maybe the next time ...

We have breakfast and then 'Dodo' and I go along to see how the 'kite' is coming along. We'll be able to take-off at 12.15 hours so we spend the rest of the morning inspecting some of the many types of aircraft they have at this experimental station.

In one morning I see more planes than a layman would see in a lifetime. They included Liberators, Halifaxes, Stirlings, Whitleys, Lancasters, Manchesters, Wellingtons, a special high-altitude Wellington fitted with a pressure sealed cabin, Warwicks, which are a development of the Wellington, Blenheims, both short and long nosed, Lockheed Hudson, Walrus amphibian, Lysander, Douglas Boston and Havoc, Hurricanes and Spitfires, Airacobras equipped as both day and night fighters and the tops of the lot - the D.H. Mosquito, which is the fastest they have and which is used as a day bomber, for photographic reconnaissance, or a night fighter. There were also a collection of other light civil types and some of the usual Oxfords and Ansons, etc. What a marvellous collection. Next to the Mosquito in my opinion came the Liberator which seemed a marvellous job and really luxurious and roomy compared with the old Manchester. There's not the slightest doubt that the Yanks have us well taped for finish and lay-out.

We then have dinner, a swell meal, for the food here is much better than at Bottesford. They have WAAFs working in the Mess here which is strange after having the boys waiting on us back at Base. We get airborne for Base shortly after 13.00 hours and almost immediately 'Dodo' hands over to me. Only did fifteen minutes on the trip this morning so am keen to have some time at the controls. Use 'George' quite a lot on the way home and get myself thoroughly conversant with his manipulation. Am allowed to land the crate and do so with much distinction for I manage to pull off the best landing I've ever been in – by anyone – in a Manchester. Taxi to dispersal and then pile out, back to the crew room, get rid of our gear and on to the final stage – interrogation.

And so it's all over bar the shouting. Once again too lazy to do any correspondence in the evening so go to a movie on camp and see quite a good show – 'Western Union'. And so to bed hoping that we'll be operating again tomorrow.

Amongst the force briefed to attack Brest on 8/9 January, Manchester L7322 EM-Q, captained by Flying Officer G. R. Bayley, took off at 03.59 hours, carrying three 2,000-lb AP bombs, but nothing was heard after take-off. The bodies of Flying Officer Bayley and air gunners Sergeants Goldie RAAF and Seymour RAAF are buried in Crozon Cemetery in Brittany, but the rest of the crew have no known graves. In recent years it has emerged that there were eyewitnesses to the loss of this aircraft, as well as records from the aircrew recovery teams who toured Europe after the war consolidating graves of allied aircrews into approved burial sites.

Once in the target area, one can postulate that Flying Officer Bayley may have used the altimeter to descend through cloud to seaward of where he judged, from flak and searchlight activity, Brest to be. Having broken cloud at low altitude, he made an attacking approach from the north-west. Once Brest harbour entrance had been penetrated, he made landfall on the tip of Ile Longue.

The peninsula of Ile Longue was heavily fortified. In addition to old Vauban forts built as defences against possible earlier British and Spanish invasions, further emplacements were added during the 1914 to 1918 war – forts, pillboxes, etc. Similarly, at the head of the peninsula, a large coastal torpedo test facility, including a harbour with breakwaters was constructed. The Germans had set up their own searchlight and flak batteries on the former French defence works. Having made landfall actually within Brest harbour, Flying Officer Bayley and crew were, likely, trying to identify a pinpoint with a view to altering course and homing in on their target, the battlecruisers holed up in Brest naval dockyard itself. In doing so, they encountered the peninsula defences making their local contribution to the fearsome reputation of the defences of the port.

An eyewitness to the subsequent events was Monsieur Eugène Marzin, a member of a four-man crew of a dredger waiting for the tide in the adjacent small work harbour of Le Fret. The vessel and its crew were engaged in winning sand and gravel on behalf of the Germans for construction of the defences of the Atlantic Wall. Eugène Marzin remembers that they were standing in the rain. Although the loss of L7322 is formally timed at 06.00 hours, he recalls the timing of its penetration of the harbour as coinciding with first light at daybreak, visibility possibly being supplemented by the glow of searchlights reflected back from the base of the cloud layer.

As the opposing forces saw each other, both opened fire. Marzin could clearly see that the aircraft was flying lower than the 15 m height of the peninsula. The Manchester was heading south down the eastern side of Ile Longue searching for an identifiable landmark from which it could head off towards the target ships. The air gunners had trained their turrets to starboard in order to engage the German defences. They, in turn, would have had to depress the angle of their weapons below horizontal in order to fire down on the attacking aircraft. Having reached the low spit of land linking Ile Longue to the mainland, Bayley climbed and banked over it to return northwards up the west coast of the peninsula. In doing so, the Manchester flew at such a low altitude that Eugène Marzin lost sight of it. Marzin formed the view that the aircraft captain was deliberately keeping as low as possible in order to use the landscape features to shelter the aircraft from defensive anti-aircraft fire. As an awestruck Eugène Marzin watched, the Manchester circled the peninsula twice more, the gunners firing each time on the same flak and searchlight batteries. On each circuit it passed close to the transfixed dredger crew.

Flying Officer Bayley would have been acutely aware of his dilemma. If he was to sight and attack the ships with his three 2,000-lb Armour-Piercing bombs from such low altitude, he knew full well they would be unable to reach the terminal velocity necessary for the bombs to penetrate the ships armour. On the other hand, were he to sight the ships and try to climb to a suitable attack height, he would inevitably lose sight of his target in the ground haze and dense cloud plaguing the target area. The aircrew's charmed life could not be expected to last. On their third circuit Eugène Marzin saw the aircraft take a flak hit and catch fire. Bowing to the inevitable, Bayley shifted in an instant from attack to self-preservation mode. He levelled the wings and very likely lowered the flaps and chopped the throttles. For a moment Marzin's heart came into his mouth as he thought the Manchester would hit him and his fellow crew members. However, Bayley successfully ditched the aircraft a few metres from the east coast of the peninsula, 150 m south of the torpedo test launching installation, the fire on board being immediately extinguished.

The aircraft remained afloat for ten to fifteen minutes but, to the horror of the watching French dredger crew, the Germans then opened fire on the stationary wallowing machine. The surviving crew were no longer any possible threat to the defenders, having their entire focus on trying to save themselves. As the aircraft settled and the firing continued, the wind blowing directly towards the eyewitnesses carried the final panic-stricken cries of those of the crew still trapped in the aircraft. The four-man dredger crew couldn't put to sea with a view to trying to help the ditched aircrew as the Germans continued firing at the foundering aircraft.

None of the crew survived. Three bodies were recovered but the remaining four are presumed to have gone down with their aircraft. Later in the day Eugène Marzin saw one body on the shore at Le Zorn immediately south of the ditching site. The soon-to-be Mrs Marzin also saw a body, though it is unclear whether this was that of the same or a different person. Another body was found on the island coast (Ile Longue) about eight days later by a Mrs Carlos, a cousin of the future Mrs Marzin.

Fearing for their lives and being witness at such close quarters to brutal deaths would inevitably have a traumatic impact on these eyewitnesses. Even 60 years later they clearly remember it occurring in the earliest days of 1942. No other Allied bomber loss of the period matches these circumstances – the date and location both appear to fit, as does the fate of the aircrew members. However, there remain residual doubts. For example, Monsieur Marzin is adamant that the twin-engined aircraft he saw was 'not a bomber'. He believes it would have carried four or five crew at most. There were no Allied intruder operations that night.

After the war Wing Commander J. W. Bayley, and former Engineering Officer of 61 Squadron, the brother of Flying Officer G. R. Bayley, was able to gain access to information gleaned by the aircrew recovery and identification team and contained in a letter to him dated 13 May 1947 signed by a D. Bent of the Air Ministry in London. This was the officer who personally visited Ile Longue near Crozon. In respect of this loss, given as occurring at 06.00 hours on 9 January 1942, he laments the reported absence of survivors as confirmed to him by local farmers. However, in a variation he reports that he interviewed a French woman identified as Marcelle Largentau of Ile Longue (probably Langenton, but evidently a local resident), who was employed by the Germans and 'present when a crew member from this aircraft died in the hospital at Ile Longue'.

German servicemen pose alongside a mainwheel from L7322, which appears to have been mounted as a grim trophy. The image of the Germans looking pleased with their handiwork belies the fact that the Manchester's crew were murdered by the defenders..

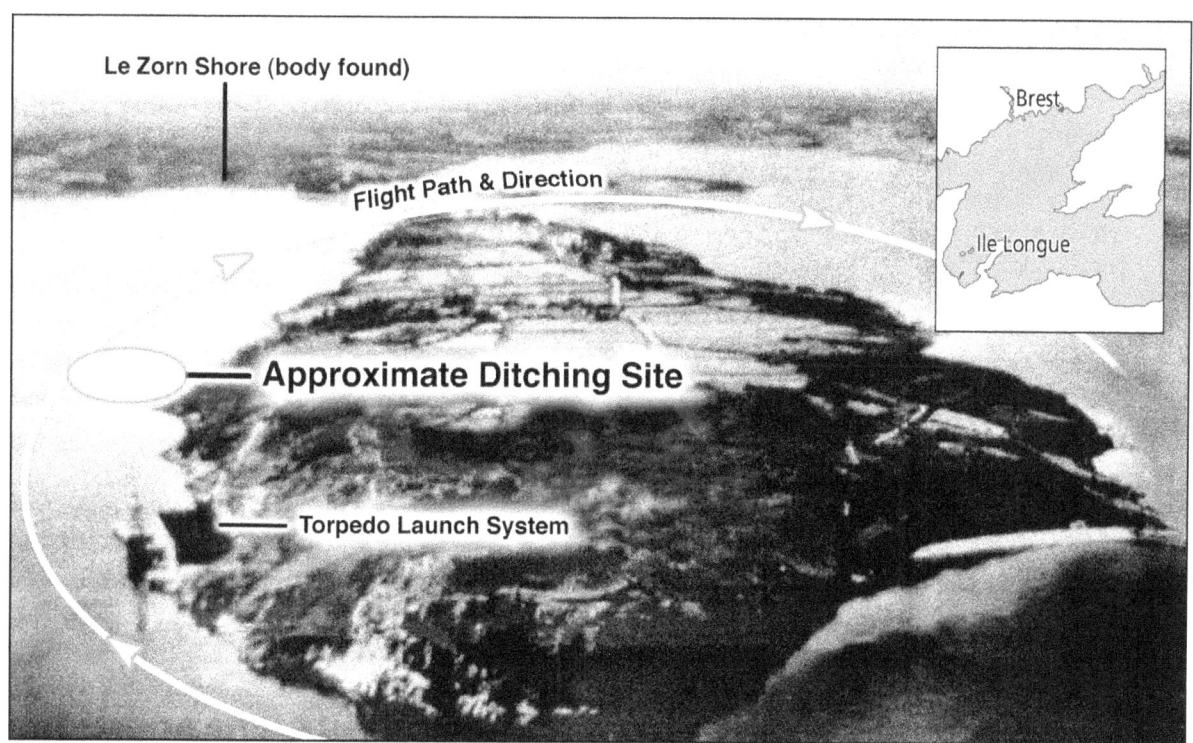

Contemporary oblique aerial photograph looking south of south shore of Brest harbour showing flight path and ditching site of Pilot Officer G. R. Bayley and crew in L7322 on 8/9 January 1942. The defenders made sure there were no survivors. (via Gildas Saouzanet)

One suspects the woman must have been on the hospital staff in some capacity, likely a nurse. The airman, thought to be the Captain, Flying Officer Bayley, had been buried in the cemetery at Crozon but grave records were lost. The local mayor had eliminated all but two options for the British airman's grave and authorised the exhumation of both bodies. One contained a male body in RAF battledress with RAF wings and Flying Officer gold braid on the tunic sleeves. On grounds that Flying Officer Bayley was the only RAF pilot on board (Sergeants Toohill and Seymour were RAAF) and also the only Flying Officer in the crew, Bent considered his identify confirmed. Bent further volunteered that the widow of Flying Officer Bayley had been officially informed that he had died in hospital. Wing Commander J. C. Bayley was advised to show discretion should he approach Marcelle Largentau for further details in a personal capacity.

Eugène Marzin, his wife, and the reports from the mysterious Marcelle Largentau are the closest we are likely to get to a contemporary account. If Flying Officer Bayley was initially recovered alive, we may never find out how he came to reach the shore and how he came to die so soon afterwards.

70 years after the event, it is humbling to finally place on record these events which show a bravery and sense of duty in keeping with the best traditions of the RAF. It had been another frustrating night for the Manchester units. None of the aircraft which returned had anything positive to report. For this date John Justin McCarthy adds in his journal:

Learn with regret that Bill Bayley and his crew are missing after going to Brest. He was a very decent fellow and had given me my 'conversion dual' on to Manchesters. The irony of it was that I was originally crewed with him but later changed to Doble's crew. Toohill, the Aussie, who was my second at Kinloss, was then given to Bayley and had made two other trips with him. It's a bad show. It's the first 'kite' the Squadron has lost since I joined it at Waddington.

In continued bad weather, on 9/10 January 207 Squadron produced a further two Manchesters and 97 Squadron four for a further desperate assault on Brest. Although nominally a squadron equipped with Manchesters since early March 1941, by this date 61 Squadron had accomplished a mere twenty-three sorties in total in the 9-month period. This had been achieved at the expense of three aircraft lost on operations and a further two in training! It was hardly an auspicious record. On this night the squadron was to contribute a further six Manchesters, although the force was restricted to the docks at Cherbourg. However, from this time onwards, under Wing Commander Weir, the squadron was to shoulder a major proportion of Manchester operations.

Brest / Cherbourg* - 9/10 January 1942:

Serial	Code	Squadron	Captain
L7518	QR-	61	Sqn Ldr A. M. Paape*
L7472	QR-	61	Plt Off. G. L. Tofield*
R5789	QR-	61	Plt Off. D. S. Matthews*
L7495	QR-	61	Plt Off. G. W. Gilpin*
R5787	QR-	61	Plt Off. J. R. Hubbard*
R5785	QR-	61	Sgt P. H. G. Webster*
L7457	OF-Y	97	Fg Off. E. A. Deverill
L7475	OF-B	97	Fg Off. B. R. W. Hallows
L7455	OF-X	97	WO D. H. Rowlands
L7476	OF-K	97	WO T. J. Mycock
L7468	EM-Z	207	Sqn Ldr T. C. Murray
L7515	EM-S	207	Fg Off. J. H. Leland

Note: Pilot Officer Gunter of 61 Squadron undertook a NICKELS Op on Rennes in R5786, but his sortie is not in any official record.

The six aircraft of the Brest force departed soon after midnight but encountered insuperable difficulties. The ground and sky were obscured, severely inhibiting prospects for accurate navigation. Leland jettisoned his bombs offshore from Brest whilst Murray jettisoned his load in the target area. His aircraft became hopelessly lost on the return flight and he was lucky to reach base. 97 Squadron crews were similarly impeded. A compass fault in Deverill's aircraft sent them off on a reciprocal course. By the time this was recognised it was too late to reach

Manchester Mk.1 of 207 Squadron in the snow at Bottesford in the winter of 1941/1942. Former groundcrew will recognise the almost inevitable trestle erected around the starboard Vulture. (207 Squadron archives)

Brest. Neither 'Darky' Hallows, nor Rowlands were able to locate a worthwhile target and returned with their bombs.

The best effort of the night was made by Tommy Mycock in L7476 (shades of Pilot Officer Bayley the night before). They had also located the general dockyard area from the various calibres of flak shell bursting in the vicinity. After fruitless circling and searching at ever dwindling altitude, Mycock finally made a diving bomb run from only 1,500 feet. Breaking out of the cloud at almost masthead height, bombs were released when the target area was in the sight, but no ships could be discerned. The crew later attributed this to effective camouflaging of the vessels. Mycock made his escape at a suicidal 200 feet, hotly pursued by light flak bursts. Possibly the defenders were concentrating on higher levels, as Mycock was able to escape unscathed. On his return Tommy was awarded an immediate DFC for his efforts. Despite this desperate tactic *Scharnhorst* and *Gneisenau* suffered no damage.

As the Brest force began to withdraw the feint by 61 Squadron began to come in. Possibly the delayed take-off times of between 04.35 and 05.00 hours were intended to divert the German defences. For the third consecutive operation (2/3 September and 7/8 December 1941 and 9/10 January 1942) 61 Squadron was to lose a Manchester. Two of the squadron aircraft carried passengers on this night and for one it was to be a brief and harrowing experience. Two Regional Control Officers (RCOs), Pilot Officer Butler in Tofield's aircraft, L7472, and Pilot Officer Lancaster in Matthews' aircraft, R5789, were to accompany the raiders. Matthews was setting out on his first operation in a Manchester. 61 Squadron's problems began at base. An aircraft had crashed at Woolfox Lodge rendering the airfield unserviceable and the aircraft had to take-off from North Luffenham instead.

F/Sgt Basil Courtney Wescombe served with 207 Squadron from 15th November 1941 to 14th January 1942. He carried out eight operations, but died in a crash in North Yorkshire, possibly turning back from a nickelling raid after an engine had caught fire.

It was a pitch black night with the same weather restrictions as the Brest force had encountered. The underpowered and overloaded 61 Squadron Manchesters laboured imperceptibly upward. By 06.00 hours Matthews, with Pilot Officer Wilson as his second pilot, and Lancaster, the RCO, as passenger, had reached a few thousand feet over the Wiltshire/Hampshire border when the starboard engine lost power and caught fire. The propeller was feathered and the fire extinguished, but their position was immediately desperate.

With full bomb load and most of the fuel still remaining, their height loss was rapid and irreversible. In the pitch darkness Matthews had no idea of their precise position and bravely elected not to jettison the bomb load for fear of killing innocent civilians. The captain first steadied the aircraft whilst six of the crew baled out. Having safely accomplished this, the two pilots maintained their discipline and attempted a blind forced landing. Like Derek Pinchbeck and John Nunn before and Jim Wilkie afterwards, they were in the hands of fate.

Regrettably, on this cruel night fate was against them and as Matthews flared for landing the aircraft crashed at a shallow angle into a belt of trees at Tidworth, near Wiltshire Cross. Both pilots were killed and the aircraft burnt and later the bomb load exploded. To their eternal credit, in forfeiting their own lives the two pilots saved six more in the crew and avoided any casualties on the ground. Crash investigators were later unable to pinpoint the specific cause of the engine failure and speculated that icing may have been a contributory cause. Lancaster and the remainder of the crew escaped with minor injuries.

Of the remainder of the attack force, Gilpin, Hubbard and Webster were all unable to locate Cherbourg and returned with their bombs. By descending to low level Paape and Tofield were able to get below the cloud base and attack. All five returned to base, landing close to 09.00 hours.

Maritime targets were again the priority on 10/11 January 1942, but for a change Wilhelmshaven was specified to receive the attention of 61, 97 and 207 Squadrons. The aiming point was the main railway station, but with the intention of causing resultant damage in the port area.

Wilhelmshaven – 10/11 January 1942:

Serial	Code	Squadron	Captain
L7497	QR-	61	FS E. W. Noble
L7488	OF-F	97	Fg Off. H. S. Blakeman
L7475	OF-B	97	Fg Off. Keir
L7489	OF-T	97	Flt Lt E. Coton
L7522	OF-V	97	Flt Lt D. J. Penman
L7309	EM-O	207	Sqn Ldr K. H. P. Beauchamp
R5796	EM-W	207	Fg Off. J. de Lacey Wooldridge
L7515	EM-S	207	FS G. H. Coles
L7432	EM-J	207	Fg Off. D. A. Green
L7378	EM-A	207	FS B. O. Wescombe

97 Squadron's aircraft carried one 4,000-lb and four 500-lb GPs, whilst three 207 Squadron aircraft carried 4,000-lb 'Cookies' and four 500-lb GPs, the remaining two carrying six 1,000-lb GPs. A quarter of the latter are recorded as being fitted with 'Screamers' (presumably devices to produce a piercing whistle on the way down). The Germans had taught this lesson well. Take-off was in the late afternoon between 16.44 and 16.58 hours.

The town of Wilhelmshaven should have been an easy target to locate in good weather, lying as it does on the shores of the Jade Bay. Flying Officer Green experienced severe visibility problems when the windscreen of L7432 iced up for the entire operation at heights above 8,000 feet. His debriefing report specifies that the aircraft approached the primary target, the main railway station, by following the railway tracks from the west into the town. His load of six 1,000-lb bombs was believed to have fallen in the target area. Flight Sergeant Wescombe flew down the Jade Bay coastline to release his bombs from 16,000 feet at 19.30 hours. He pinpointed the impact position at one mile north-east of the railway station and his crew saw the 4,000-lb 'Cookie' explode. Squadron Leader Beauchamp attacked a clearly distinguished target and both Wooldridge and Coles reported that many fires were burning in the target area stoked up by their own bombs. Three 97 Squadron aircraft bombed the primary, whilst the fourth hit Emden. Flight Sergeant Noble had high oil temperature in the port engine and so bombed a seaplane base at Terschelling instead.

Whilst the remainder of the aircraft turned for home, 'Dim' Wooldridge made a slight diversion to the German barrier island of Norderney. Descending to 600 feet so the crew could distinguish individual objects on the ground, they first dispatched seven bundles of NICKELS. The flak defences of the Frisians were still engaging incoming bombers and Wooldridge and crew proceeded to disrupt these as much as possible. The Manchester was being used once more by 207 Squadron in the improbable role of low level night intruder. Wooldridge guided R5796 around various nests of searchlight and flak emplacements, where the gunners took the opportunity to interfere with the defences. The gunners claimed four searchlights doused and one heavy calibre flak gun put out of action on Norderney.

Inevitably, as Wooldridge circled to pick out his targets, the action was not all one-sided and a flak burst spattered the aircraft, damaging the hydraulic system. As the precious hydraulic fluid leaked away the bomb doors began to gape and one main wheel leg flopped down: the intercom had also been put out of action. The flak and searchlight suppression was continued for a while but crew co-ordination, speed and manoeuvrability had been impaired. Reluctantly Wooldridge was forced to abandon the interdiction and retrace his route across the North Sea with bomb doors now completely open and the main wheel still down. Fortunately the emergency undercarriage lowering system operated successfully at 22.39 hours.

Whatever the limitations of the Manchester, there was certainly no lack of determination in many of its crews. The bombing results from Wilhelmshaven bore little resemblance to the optimistic claims of returning crews. Although a total of 124 aircraft were dispatched, the German defenders recognised this as only a light attack with only six civilians injured.

Operations planned for 12 and 13 January were cancelled but, following a light snowfall, were on again on 14th. Since the year end 207 and 97 Squadrons had been called to operate virtually every night and now 61 Squadron had joined in, such were the stakes being played for at Brest and in the war in general. This time eight 207 Squadron Manchesters were to go to the Blohm und Voss shipyards at Hamburg, together with two from 61 Squadron. Following night flying tests the aircraft were bombed up.

Hamburg – 14 January 1942:

Serial	Code	Squadron	Captain
R5785	QR-	61	Sqn Ldr P. G. Sooby
L7458	QR-	61	Flt Lt A. M. Paape
L7468	EM-Z	207	Fg Off. J. de Lacey Wooldridge
L7515	EN-S	207	Fg Off. J. H. Leland
L7309	EM-O	207	Plt Off. G. B. Dawkins
L7319	EM-X	207	FS G. H. Coles
L7455	EM-G	207	Fg Off. P. C. Birch
L7485	EM-D	207	Fg Off. D. A. Green
L7523	EM-M	207	FS B. O. Wescombe
L7486	EM-B	207	FS G. H. Hathersich

Manchester Mk.1A L7516 QR-F of 61 Squadron at Woolfox Lodge provides a backdrop for its crew. Left to right: Flight Sergeant G. E. Williams RCAF (captain); second pilot; first wireless operator/air gunner, observer, wireless operator, front gunner, spare gunner, second wireless operator/air gunner. Flight Sergeant Williams was later the sole survivor from a squadron Lancaster. (G. E. Williams)

At briefing the crews were informed of a new tactic to be employed for the first time. Instead of taking off at irregular intervals and making their own way to the target by whatever route captain and navigator favoured, the aircraft were to take-off in a close spaced procession and fly exactly the same route and speed, joining up with other units to form what came to be known as the bomber stream. The object of reversing the previous tactics was to try and concentrate the attack in space and time and so overwhelm the flak and night fighter defences. The new arrangement would be particularly effective against the German night fighter defences in which only one fighter could be controlled in a box 45 km wide and 22 km deep at any one time. The condensed take-off sequence went smoothly until the last aircraft in line – Wooldridge 17.07hours, Birch 17.08 hours, Dawkins 17.09 hours, Hathersich 17.10 hours, Coles 17.11 hours, Leland 17.12 hours, Green 17.18 hours and Wescombe 17.35 hours.

The reason for the delayed take-off of Flight Sergeant Basil Wescombe is unknown. Nothing further was heard from this aircraft until it mysteriously crashed at Cliff House Farm, Holmpton, near Withernsea in Yorkshire at 20.45 hours killing the entire crew, after it had been airborne for three hours ten minutes. With it having been airborne for such a short time it seems unlikely that enemy action caused its early return. The eldest of the three Miss Walkers, who with their brother ran Cliff House Farm for more than fifty years, heard a loud popping sound of a throttled back aero engine at low altitude and rushed outside to see L7523 pass low to the south with flames apparently issuing from the rear. Almost immediately afterwards it hit the ground and exploded. The source of the fire is unknown, but possibly an uncontrollable fire in the port Vulture would have given the same appearance to a ground observer. If attempting to return to Bottesford, the aircraft was way off course.

Only a few days earlier on return from an operation to Brest, the crew had similarly got off course and blundered into the balloon barrage surrounding Southampton. Only the quick action of the second pilot, Sergeant Thomas, had saved them on that occasion. Sadly, on 14 January 1942 they were beyond help. Next morning farm workers found a sorry sight. Soldiers were already guarding the impact point and the tail unit had been thrown over a nearby hedge. Small fragments of airframe were spread over a wide area, the bodies of the crew awaiting collection in a farm building. Apparently the bomb load had already been jettisoned. A freezing rain was falling from a leaden sky and within a short period the farm workers' clothes were frozen stiff. Despite having crashed in Yorkshire, no Aircraft Accident Card summarising results of an investigation has been traced. Flight Lieutenant Paape experienced engine trouble and also had to make an early return, landing back at Woolfox at 18.55 hours.

Meanwhile, the remaining seven Manchesters held identical courses, a few minutes apart, as they traversed the North Sea. The route involved crossing the English coast near Orfordness and flying a 400-mile leg passing between Heligoland and the Frisians to hit the enemy coast in the centre of the mouth of the Elbe estuary. Here they were to turn south-east with a view to flying in, parallel to the Elbe, but 20 miles away from the flak defences lining the river. The penalty of being only slightly off track to the south would be to pass directly over the flak defences of Cuxhaven.

It was a bitterly cold night with continuous overcast over the North Sea. Unusually for the period, both Flying Officer Leland and Pilot Officer 'Gerry' Dawkins carried only six man crews, lacking a front gunner. Dawkins' regular navigator, Flight Sergeant Nisbet, was sick and Flying Officer P. J. Edwards was standing in. L7309 toiled slowly upwards on this eastward leg with Dawkins instrument-flying in the 'clag'. Shortly after passing between Heligoland and the mainland coast they finally began to clear the top of the cloud layer. Edwards immediately took the opportunity of climbing into the astrodome to try and check the drift so they could adjust their course and ETA to the turning point at the German coast.

Before Edwards had time to take any readings, Sergeant Bestel, the Canadian rear gunner, called out a sighting of an aircraft closing from astern. Before he had finished speaking tracer fire started to fly past on the starboard side. The call and tracer fire, coming as it did so quickly after they breasted the cloud layer, galvanised Dawkins into action. Closing the throttle of the port engine he slammed the stick forward and hard left. As he did so the familiar roar and vibration of the four 0.303-inch Brownings in the rear turret could be heard and felt as Bestel, swinging his turret, loosed off a scaring burst. Dawkins' manoeuvre was not one in the flying regulations, but the pilots had found that it was the only way of jinking a large, slow and overloaded Manchester out of the firing line of a night fighter. The Manchester slewed violently to port, slowed down and dropped like a stone, being swallowed up in the cloud almost immediately. The fighter overshot and as they sank back into the cloud layer Bestel was heard to complain that his return fire had missed the target. Once they were in the cloud the fighter was unable to relocate them.

The fighter had only been glimpsed for a few seconds and was not identified. It is likely that its pilot was, in fact, Oberleutnant Rudolf Schoenert of II/NJG2 and that his aircraft had been guided into the bomber stream by ground radar and made a final visual interception. It was Schoenert who, in July 1942, got the blessing of General Kammhuber to test his ideas for fixed obliquely firing armaments in the upper fuselage of a night fighter. Eventually, following his promotion to commanding officer of the Messerschmitt Bf110 equipped II/NJG5, Schoenert had such armament fitted to one of the unit's aircraft and in May 1943 made the Luftwaffe's first kill with what became the widely used 'Schrage Musik' installation. Schoenert went on to make 64 confirmed kills and survived the war.

Gerry Dawkins opened the throttle on the port engine and an immediate check on the cockpit instruments showed all apparently normal. Both engines were running at climbing revs, but it soon became clear that all was far from well with the starboard engine, which was producing no power. The drag from the starboard propeller, still at climbing pitch, was causing the aircraft to slew to the right and the altimeter showed they were sinking instead of maintaining altitude.

Recognising their dilemma, Dawkins ordered the bomb load to be jettisoned and meanwhile reached across to feather the starboard propeller. They felt a reassuring lurch as the bombs fell away, but the propeller steadfastly refused to feather. It became clear that the brief burst of fire from the night fighter had damaged the controls to the starboard engine, which was out of action and with the propeller now windmilling and jammed in fine pitch.

Dawkins turned onto a course of 270 degrees and tried to trim the aircraft to fly home. By experimenting with the engine settings of the port Vulture he found that at maximum power the airspeed hovered close to 165 mph, but that the aircraft lost height at between 100 and 200 feet/min. By slowing down to 145 mph he found they could maintain height but the starboard wing dropped and they slowly swung to starboard due to the drag of the starboard propeller. It seemed to be a no win situation. Meanwhile the crew began ditching every heavy item readily detachable from the airframe. In desperation they tried to train the twin Brownings of the mid-upper turret onto the starboard propeller blades and shoot them off. However, the guns could not depress far enough and they were unable to disconnect the externally mounted deflector installed to prevent that very thing happening by accident.

By this time they had descended to 8,000 feet and the prospects of getting home on one engine, even if it kept going, with the drag of the starboard propeller disc, were zero. Edwards calculated that they had rather less than one hour of flying time before reaching ground level and Dawkins judged that even if they all survived a ditching they would be unlikely to last more than 20 minutes in an open dinghy in the North Sea. The facts left no room for doubt and having thus exhausted all the options Dawkins reluctantly altered course again, turning due south to hit the nearest point on the German coast. They could but hope that the port Vulture, running at full throttle, would prove equal to the task.

Dawkins then directed the wireless operator, Sergeant Mercer, to break radio silence and relay a message to base informing them of his decision. Mercer tried several times to establish contact but was completely unsuccessful, so they pressed the radio destruct knobs and destroyed the set. Edwards, meanwhile, threw overboard all code books and navigation documents.

They continued south for some 40 minutes and mercifully the remaining motor kept turning. At this point, when they had descended to about 4,000 feet and were still enveloped in the blanket of cloud, they were relieved to find themselves on the receiving end of inaccurate light flak. This gave them the satisfaction of knowing they must be traversing the Frisian Islands. As they did so the cloud cover finally started to become more broken and a few minutes later, as they inexorably descended, they reached 3,500 feet and came out of cloud just as they crossed the shore of mainland Germany. Dawkins had flown for 45 minutes with the control column held hard over to the left to lift the starboard wing and there was clearly no chance of making a forced landing in these conditions, they could merely fly straight ahead and would be unable to avoid any obstacle on the ground which appeared in their path.

That being so they had prepared to bale out as quickly as possible after crossing the coast. Bestel left his turret and tried to open the rear entry door in anticipation of baling out, but found it to be frozen solid. Sergeant Cadman then moved forward from the mid-upper turret to jettison the forward escape hatch. Clearly they would all have to get out the same way. As he did so for some inexplicable reason his parachute fell through the open hatch and was lost. More precious time was lost in debating how this problem could be overcome and eventually Sergeant Allen, the second pilot, offered to attempt a double descent with Cadman. Sergeant Mercer helped them to get away first with Cadman piggy backing on Allen. Mercer and Flying Officer Edwards then followed in quick succession. Dawkins still had no hands free and Bestel buckled his parachute on for him before following the crew through the hatch.

Gerry Dawkins was left alone, he only had a single chance to escape because as soon as he released the control column the aircraft would roll onto its back and go out of control. Time was now of the essence. The aircraft was correctly trimmed fore and aft but the stick still had to be held hard left to keep the wings level. Dawkins grabbed the second pilot's stick and held it as he moved first into the right hand seat. Next, having loosed all his intercom leads and straps, he positioned himself to dive through the beckoning hatch. He released the stick and dived straight through, fortunately without getting himself entangled in the process.

As soon as he was clear of the aircraft he pulled the D-ring and breathed a sigh of relief at the jerk of the parachute as it arrested his descent. He was only suspended for a short period but time enough to feel the piercing, numbing cold. The cockpit of the Manchester was very warm and comfortable and he was only wearing his flying jacket and boots on top of normal battle dress in the aircraft. He landed awkwardly, straining himself with the unexpected direction of the deceleration. Close by, the aircraft crashed and exploded.

Dawkins found he could stand and his first action was to collect his parachute and walk across to the blazing wreck and throw the mass of silk into the flames. Turning away he began to formulate an evasion plan, but the extreme cold and pain from his fall quickly overtook such issues and with the last of his remaining stamina he approached an isolated farm and gave himself up.

Sergeant Cadman was not so lucky: during the descent he slipped off Allen's back and fell to his death. The remainder of the crew landed safely and, having been tracked across the coast by the German radar, were soon captured. They had come down at Sandel Moens near Jever, close to Wilhelmshaven in Germany at about 21.00 hours, the last Manchester to be lost by 207 Squadron in the course of air operations. Ironically, but fittingly, it was the result of the loss of an engine and the inability of the remaining Vulture to keep them airborne.

Peter Birch had encountered the same 10/10th cloud with heavy icing conditions over the sea. Having breasted the cloud layer he took to skirting the higher cumulus to cut down ice accretion on the airframe. Darkness and haze led to difficulties in target identification but several crews located and followed the Elbe River. Hamburg was picked out by large searchlight concentrations. 'Dim' Wooldridge reported heavy searchlight clusters co-operating with night fighters and his rear gunner spotted several, although no attacks materialised. Over the town itself the searchlight and flak batteries were working closely together and the crews received a rousing reception. These prevented Bill Goldstraw, observer to Pilot Officer Dave Green, from observing the fall of bombs.

Wooldridge carried out his customary fast diving attack. Having circled to the east of Hamburg at 12,000 feet he dived across the city on a westerly heading planning to release the bomb load at about 8,000 feet. Shortly after commencing the bombing run the aircraft was coned and held by searchlights, which blinded the crew to the extent that the bombs were released prematurely and undershot the designated aiming point. Within a few seconds of bomb release the aircraft was hit by shrapnel from a heavy flak shell bursting nearby, which slightly wounded the front gunner. Soon the speed of the descending aircraft took it clear of the barrage to escape into the enveloping protective darkness and a third loss from the small force was narrowly avoided.

Flight Lieutenant Sooby also found the German flak defences thoroughly roused. He tried approaches from the north, east and south before finally releasing his incendiaries from 13,000 feet on an easterly heading and then turning away northwards to escape the clinging searchlights and insistent flak. Good fires were starting from the combined high explosive and incendiary bombs as the aircraft left the target.

As Pilot Officer Green departed from the target area a loud explosion was heard and felt immediately aft of the bulkhead doors, followed by a prolonged hissing. When the startled crew investigated it was found that an oxygen connection had parted due to metal fatigue. The aircraft was undamaged and the only inconvenience arising was that Dave Green had to land at Coningsby without the assistance of brakes. On inspection next morning the bomb doors of Birch's and Green's aircraft were both found to be damaged by flak. The Germans' own report detailed twelve fires, seven of them large, with six civilians killed and twenty-two injured in Hamburg.

No major raids were planned by Bomber Command during the following week but 97 and 61 Squadrons attacked Hamburg again on 15th/16th and then Bremen on 17th/18th. The latter date was the last night on which 97 Squadron operated Manchesters. The squadron was already working up on Lancasters and became the first RAF unit to relinquish the aircraft. 97 Squadron provided six Manchesters for its penultimate operation with the type on 15 January 1942.

Hamburg – 15 January 1942:

Serial	Code	Squadron	Captain
L7491	OF-C	97	Flt Lt J. G. Mackid
L7473	OF-H	97	Fg Off. B. R. W. Hallows
L7489	OF-T	97	Plt Off. D. H. Maltby
L7476	OF-K	97	FS S. E. Harrison
L7453	OF-X	97	FS R. A. Fletcher
L7522	OF-V	97	FS L. H. Adams

This may have been another experimental attack. Seemingly all six aircraft carried fourteen Small Bomb Containers loaded with cans of incendiaries. All aircraft seem to have located a target believed to be Hamburg and late arrivals were guided by sticks of incendiaries burning on the ground. Searchlight and flak activity was experienced. Flight Sergeant Stan Harrison in L7476 followed the Elbe, releasing his load on the north-west suburbs. So far it had all seemed routine. His homeward leg took them north-west, bisecting the Cuxhaven-Bremerhaven line and then the long North Sea crossing aiming for a landfall at Skegness. Soon after embarking on this final leg, Sergeant George Farara, the bomb aimer/front gunner, drew Harrison's attention to the fact that the starboard engine exhausts seemed to be glowing more fiercely than usual and Sergeant Jack Oates, in the rear turret, reported this engine was shedding incandescent sparks, which trailed behind the aircraft. Harrison had already noticed this and had considered what he could do to reduce the strain on this labouring Vulture. In view of the abysmal single engine performance and the fact that it seemed moment by moment about to catch fire, the level of tension rose noticeably. Harrison elected to nurse the motor as best he could but to press on, hoping for the best. After a seemingly interminable sea crossing they traversed the coast just south of Skegness and requested permission for an immediate landing, omitting the usual circuit.

As the main wheels touched down a brisk fire broke out in the engine. With the main fuel supply turned off, Harrison taxied at speed towards the crash fire tender, which smothered the engine in foam. Their ground crew and flight sergeant arrived running from their dispersal. With the fire quenched the flight sergeant opened the engine cowling with an asbestos-gloved hand in order to examine the engine. He reached out and touched the main fuel line, only to see it disintegrate under his finger! So this had been a very near thing. If the line had fractured whilst they were airborne, the engine would have gone up in a ball of flame.

Two days later, on 17 January 1942, and again in L7476, Harrison flew on 97 Squadron's final Manchester operation. They were already working up on Lancasters and looking forward to the security of four reliable Merlins and a much improved altitude performance. Five crews went to Bremen. In L7476 a hydraulic pipe to the rear turret burst on the outward flight incapacitating this vital key to their defence. Undeterred, they carried on, encountering accurate flak over Bremen and releasing their bombs on ETA. Harrison and crew gladly made the transition to their improved sibling type.

Reports of the 25 Operational Training Unit (OTU) Bombing Section fact-finding tour of the Manchester squadrons in late January 1942 provide a fascinating insight into Bomber Command methods. The OTU were trying to ensure that their teaching was as up to date as possible. The disparate findings of the survey were surprising. No uniformity in bombing tactics was demanded either by Command or 5 Group. Each squadron formulated its own method, or a variation on methods taught at the OTU. 97, 83 and 207 Squadrons adopted a jinking level approach with the fixed bomb sight, generally in the height range 12,000 to 18,000 feet. With few exceptions, glide bombing was not used as the jinking level run up was considered safer and sufficiently accurate. Crews appreciated the need to maintain height in the Manchester, perhaps on account of engine reliability.

In complete contrast, 61 Squadron invariably adopted glide bombing with the tachometric sight, as taught at 25 OTU. For this tactic the glide was commenced at heights between 14,000 to 16,000 feet and the bombs released at heights between 7,000 and 9,000 feet. After commencing the glide a turn of at least forty-five degrees to port was invariably made onto the bomb run. Gliding Manchesters that were picked up by searchlights abandoned the glide. As ground speed increased bombs were released in the target area permitting the attacking aircraft to escape.

Ultra-low level bombing was not liked and seldom done, although reports of very low level attacks were gathered from a number of bomb aimers. When a mixed load of a 4,000-lb high capacity (HC) and 250-lb GP or SAP bombs were carried the normal practice was to aim the HC and allow the GPs or SAPs to follow 'as they will', of course resulting in an overshoot. Bomber Command tactics still had a great way to go before the rigid control in height, time and approach direction essential when aircraft began attacking as a tightly bunched stream.

The winter weather was exceptionally severe, presenting constraints on the ground and aircrews alike. At Bottesford it caused Flight Sergeant McCarthy to miss out on his fourth Manchester operation, still acting as second pilot, as he confides in his diary on 20 January:

The whole 'drome has been under snow since Monday 19th. I've seen snow but never as much as we have had here during the past few days. The wind is bitterly cold and life is fairly miserable. The runways are completely covered over and the only way they can possibly keep this 'drome 'serviceable' is by utilising the available 'manpower' to form clearing parties to shovel and sweep the snow from the runways. It takes about thirty hours to open up the two necessary runways and of that I had to do one shift from 17.30 until 21.30 hours in the evening. No light was available so our task wasn't made any easier. It amazes me that on a 'drome of this size we have no mechanical facilities for snow-clearing such as snow-sweeps or snow-ploughs. Something of that nature would do the job in a tenth of the time and we'd have a serviceable 'drome all the time. Managed to get another 90 minutes of 'solo' flying, included in which was a trip back from Coningsby where I was sent to bring back our own 'kite' – '96 which had been diverted there when returning from Ops. Have managed to get the approaches and landings pretty well 'taped' and am liking the planes more every time I fly them'.

On Wednesday 21 January he again writes:

Quite a good day for 'yours truly' from all points of view. This morning learned we were due for yet another 'trip'. At the same time I received back my application for an interview with the CO re. my Commission and he has minuted it to be re-submitted on completion of six operational trips. More than satisfactory from my point of view as it gives me the impression that - if I last that long, I'll probably be recommended. In a good frame of mind so went out to the 'kite' with Robbie Carr and Alec Boyne, our two gunners, when they went out to do their D.Is (Daily Inspections). The rear turret is full of snow and things don't look too good. I take a dim view of it and feel like using the ground crew as 'pull-through' to clean the guns. We do lots of rushing round to get things serviceable in time for the N.F.T. which 'Dodo' very decently lets me do so that I get a little more time in the 'First Pilot' column. Do a good take-off – straight as a die – and then have the extreme good luck to be able to lay it on the ground without the slightest bump. However, the rear turret is still u/s and we don't know if we'll be able to make it. Still, there's always the reserve aircraft. Briefing right after the N.F.T. and it's us for Emden again. We catch a quick tea and then down to the crew-room for an early take-off. However, we find that the reserve plane is not wired for a camera and once again the rear turret in '96 is u/s. Too bad, but we've 'had it'. Would have liked to have gotten in that trip as it would have been number four, and then number six wouldn't have seemed so far off. However, it just wasn't to be so it would be silly to stick one's neck out. Maybe we weren't meant to go tonight.

Five aircraft joined in a forty-seven aircraft raid to Emden. The designated target was the main post office and bomb loads included 4,000-lb HC, 500 and 1,000-lb GP bombs with a number of aircraft required to drop leaflets in the target area. The weather remained cold and Flying Officers Green and Wooldridge reported the town to be clearly visible from some distance away outlined in the snow. None of the crews found target identification difficult, little or no opposition was encountered by most aircraft, with large fires reported in the vicinity of the railway station, and all returned safely before midnight without damage. The next night Munster was the target.

Munster – 22/23 January 1942:

Serial	Code	Squadron	Captain
L7515	EM-S	207	Sqn Ldr K. H. P. Beauchamp
R5796	EM-W	207	Fg Off. J. de Lacey Wooldridge
L7468	EM-Z	207	Flt Lt W. D. B. Ruth
L7319	EM-X	207	FS G. H. Coles
L7419	EM-H	207	Fg Off. D. A. Green

A contemporary report, coupled with comments in the ORB, is available from the diary of Flight Sergeant John McCarthy in Flying Officer Wooldridge's aircraft. The operation doubtless left a vivid impression in the minds of all the crew.

Another good day. By the CO's instructions I'm to go on a 'big do' this evening and I'm to fly as 'stooge' to Flying Officer 'Dim' Wooldridge. He's supposed to be one of the 'ace' pilots of the squadron and I'm to go along for the experience.

He very decently let's me do the N.F.T. in the morning. We're taking '96 for which I am very glad. It's one swell old crate for operational flying – bags of height if height is wanted, and plenty of speed if we need to have that, too. Do a really good N.F.T. and am tickled about my take-off and landing which are both right up to standard. Had some of Wooldridge's crew with me on the N.F.T. and also one of the ground crew so gave them a thrill with a couple of steep turns and some hedgehopping. Briefing at 14.30 hours and we find we're going in to Munster which means that we've got to go right through the 'fighter zones' and also the famed 'searchlight belt'.

Arrive at the 'Kite' to find that the damned thing isn't completely bombed up despite the fact that it's been on 'top line' since 13.00 hours. Hence we are a couple of minutes late off the ground and are the last but one to get off. Commence climbing right away and get some good pinpoints on the way to the coast. Get clear of cloud by the time we reach the Dutch coast and find we're right on track and that despite the screwy met. winds. Have a little fun going through the searchlight belt and I'm just a little disappointed for I had imagined it to be something rather terrifying. It's a marvellous moonlit night – ideal for the fighter 'wallas' but we don't see any and the searchlights only touched us a couple of times on the entire trip in.

We 'jeered' at the Huns when they missed us with their famed searchlights but practically the whole of the time I wouldn't have been the least surprised if they had picked us out for they seemed to be all over the place. However, Wooldridge told me later that they were not nearly as thick as they used to be. The ground was covered with snow and made pinpointing fairly straightforward with the result that when we sailed smack over the target I had no difficulty in picking it out. There wasn't the slightest bit of activity over the target area when we did our first run over it although away to one side, some miles south-west of the target, there was quite a bit of flak and many searchlights. We weren't 'moths to a candle' and couldn't be tempted away from the target. Apparently the Jerry ground-crews saw through it for they suddenly opened up on us with almost everything they had – seemed that they fired everything at us but the damned guns themselves. We did evasive action losing about 5,000 feet in doing so, when Wooldridge suddenly told boys to watch out: we're going down. At this time I was in the rear of the fuselage shoving out the 'NICKELS' just as fast as I could go. The loss of height didn't trouble me and I didn't know just where we were until suddenly I heard the chatter of machine guns. First thought was that we were 'being followed' but on coming to the front I saw that we flying at about 200 feet and the boys were peppering hell out of what looked like a railway goods train'. (The ORB records this as Bergstein Fort, fifteen miles north-west of Munster - author).

On the way back the boys in the three turrets fired off most of the ammunition shooting up searchlights and also a small town just inside the German border – we hope (Gronau, east of Enschede). At one stage we shot up a searchlight but apparently missed it. The beam was immediately swung to try and pick us up and although it was lined up dead on our track it wasn't able to focus on us because we were flying too low. All this time Wooldridge had his T.R.9 switched on to 'transmit' and he was calling up the Huns and asking them: 'Who are the masters of the air, you German bastards?' (The ORB records the need to take evasive action to avoid hitting radio masts at Apeldoorn - author). Our trip out from the target was done at the same height all the way home – between 150 and 200 feet. Was a great trip and I thoroughly enjoyed myself. It's really the life – let's hope it's a long one. We arrived back at base after having been up only about four and a half hours. All the other boys arrived back safely.

207 Squadron alone had dropped eighteen bombs, three of which were 4,000-lb 'Cookies', and the remaining forty-two aircraft dropped many more. Target identification had been simplicity itself and there was almost no opposition to deter the attackers. In a reflection of Bomber Command's capabilities at this time, contemporary German records note the deaths of five people with no other details. One Wellington was lost.

January 1942 was to end with a return to Brest and three raids spaced four days apart, largely made possible by an improvement in the weather. On 25/26 January 1942 207 Squadron contributed seven and 61 Squadron eight Manchesters to the sixty-one strong aircraft attack. On this night the squadrons were to find only partial cloud cover and apparently enhanced prospects for successful precision bomb aiming. However, their arrival must have been anticipated well in advance because the Germans had plenty of time to activate the smoke screen. Smoke spread in the wind and blanketed the target at ground level. Flying Officer McNaughton had already returned early in R5785 when the dinghy released itself on take-off and Sergeant Underwood returned soon afterwards with low oil pressure, but the remaining thirteen Manchesters were able to attack. All had to aim at the general dock area as an alternative when smoke obscured the ships. Several aircraft were engaged by intense and accurate flak defences, which were especially effective around Brest. Crews believed naval flak gunners had been drafted in from Kiel to bolster the defences. All of the Manchesters involved returned safely.

On 28/29 January 83 Squadron at Scampton made its operational debut in the Manchester when four crews, including the commanding officer, Wing Commander Tudor, in Squadron Leader Rainford's aircraft, were briefed for Boulogne. 61 Squadron provided four Manchesters, two for Boulogne and the remaining two for Brest. 207 Squadron provided a single Manchester to strike Boulogne.

Boulogne, 83 Squadron's debut and Brest* - 28/29 January 1942:

Serial	Code	Squadron	Captain
L7521	QR-	61*	Plt Off. J. R. Hubbard
L7396	QR-	61*	Fg Off. G. A. McNaughton
L7396	QR-	61	Plt Off. L. Gunter
L7470	QR-	61	FS J. B. Underwood
L7427	OL-	83	Sqn Ldr J. R. Rainford
L7453	OL-	83	Plt Off. J. H. Morpett
L7565	OL-	83	Plt Off. R. G. W. Oakley
L7423	OL-	83	WO H. H. Whitehead
R5791	EM-V	207	WO C. Wathey

Whilst each of these sorties took place during the 24-hour period covered by 28 January, they really constitute two operations. The Brest raid involved take-off soon after midnight and a return still in the dark after 18.00 hours. This was followed by the introductory raid on Boulogne the same evening. L7396 thus became the only Manchester to undertake two missions within this timescale. After the extended work up period of the type during 1941 perhaps this indicates eventual improved reliability? In the early hours both Hubbard and McNaughton made low level diving attacks on Brest from 9,000 and 7,500 feet respectively.

All seven Manchesters returned safely having attacked Boulogne, but Warrant Officer Whitehead's introduction was eventful. His autopilot, directional gyro and hydraulics all became unserviceable and the undercarriage had to be lowered by the pneumatic emergency system. Warrant Officer Wathey also attacked, experiencing fierce opposition from flak.

After false starts on the two previous nights, the last day of the month, 31 January/1 February, shaped up to be the biggest Manchester effort since June 1941 and the largest force of Manchesters ever sent out – nineteen in all. Spurred on by persistent intelligence warning of the breakout of the battlecruisers from Brest, Bomber Command put together a major operation. After 300 separate RAF raids on the two capital ships in Brest harbour, and with these imminent ULTRA warnings of their break out from the port, Bomber Command was making a maximum effort and trying every option to cripple the vessels.

61 Squadron contributed nine Manchesters, 83 Squadron six and 207 Squadron four. Bomber Command split its effort and its Manchester force between Brest, where seventy-two aircraft in all were dispatched, and a smaller diversionary raid on St Nazaire. All the 61 Squadron aircraft and two from 207 Squadron were briefed for Brest. The six 83 Squadron aircraft and one from 207 Squadron went to St Nazaire, whilst Flying Officer Pattinson of 207 Squadron carried out a NICKEL raid on Rennes, acting both as a diversion and training flight.

At briefing at Woolfox Lodge it was clear that the operation was to be out of the ordinary and that the Royal Navy had 'Got the wind up'. First of all a Naval Sub-Lieutenant was in attendance to give the crews a pep talk. He told them of official concern that the *Scharnhorst*, *Gneisenau* and, *Prinz Eugen* were about to break out of Brest, when they might cause untold havoc with the Atlantic convoys.

Furthermore the Admiralty did not rule out the possibility that they might be heading for the Mediterranean. 'Should that happen', the Naval Sub-Lieutenant said with emphasis, 'it might tip the balance and we could lose the Mediterranean to the enemy. The importance of crippling the ships could not be over-emphasised'.

In another unusual, but by no means unique, departure from normal, an extra crew member, Squadron Leader Burrough from Headquarters 5 Group, was to accompany Flight Lieutenant Page as an observer: for what purpose has not been established because sadly for Burrough and the entire crew it was to be a one-way trip. Regrettably, the 61 Squadron Operational Record Book (ORB) records nothing about the bomb loads of the aircraft involved. It is likely that most carried three 2,000-lb AP bombs in the hope of hitting the battlecruisers and certainly this was the load carried by the two 207 Squadron Manchesters in the Brest force.

For one 61 Squadron Manchester crew the operation was to prove unique in more ways than one. Pilot Officer Fraser and crew had been selected to introduce a new anti-shipping weapon to RAF service. Fraser and his crew had a separate briefing after the main event in which the 'boffin' who had designed the new bomb explained its operation and how it should be dropped for maximum effect. The bomb is recalled by the surviving crew as a 4,000-lb armour-piercing weapon with a double charge designed to first blast a hole in the armoured deck of a battlecruiser before exploding below The only weapon which bears any resemblance to this description is the 5,000-lb CS or 'Capital Ship' bomb, of which little seems to be known.

The raid was planned to start at 20.00 hours, with a large proportion of the force set to cross the target close to 20.32 hours, creating a diversion under which Fraser would attack with the special weapon from 2,000 feet below the remainder of the attackers. For this special operation Fraser carried, in addition to his normal crew, the squadron bombing leader, Flight Lieutenant Hannigan, whose job it was to aim and release the weapon.
Following the briefing the bomb designer spent some time chatting to Fraser and Hannigan, ironing out last minute details and then accompanied the eight-man crew out to their aircraft. Amongst the superstitious crew this intrusion was greeted with the utmost foreboding. Events were to prove their premonitions well founded.

At Scampton and Bottesford the briefings for 83 and 207 Squadrons were more routine. The six 83 Squadron and one 207 Squadron Manchesters took off first, starting at 17.32 hours to permit them to travel the extra distance to St Nazaire. This force carried 500 or 1,000-lb GP bomb loads.

Right from the start the carefully planned operation began to go awry for Fraser. Whilst the bulk of the force lifted off close to 18.00 hours, L7472, despite being on song during its night flying test earlier in the day, developed engine trouble which delayed its take-off until 18.45 hours. They would have to attack without the cover of their colleagues.

Top: 61 Squadron crew members pose in front of one of their Manchesters. Left to right: Sergeant Furby (second pilot); Sergeant Boot (wireless operator); Sergeant Smart (observer); Sergeant Tomlinson (second wireless operator/air gunner); Sergeant Crawford (rear gunner); Flying Officer Gunter (captain). Bottom: Flight Lieutenant Fraser of 61 Squadron running up L7472 at Woolfox Lodge on 31 January 1942, prior to Ops to Brest from which the aircraft failed to return. (Both L. Boot)

A 2000-lb armour-piercing bomb being checked in the cavernous bomb bay of a Manchester. Wire rope around bomb is believed to be the hoist cable. The crude hand of the censor can be seen inside the bomb bay door. (via Aerospace Publishing)

Manchester maximum effort – 31 January/1 February 1942, Brest, St Nazaire‡ & Rennes*:

Serial	Code	Squadron	Captain
L7396	QR-	61	Flt Lt H. C. S. Page
L7470	QR-	61	Plt Off. L. Gunter
L7458	QR-	61	Fg Off. R. E. Archibald
L7516	QR-	61	FS E. W. Noble
L7492	QR-	61	Plt Off. A. L. Searby
R5787	QR-M	61	Fg Off. J. R. B. Parsons
L7521	QR-	61	Fg Off. I. G. A. McNaughton
L7477	QR-	61	Plt Off. R. E. S. Smith
L7472	QR-	61	Fg Off. R. D. Fraser
R5831	OL-	83	Sqn Ldr O. Altmann‡
R5790	OL-	83	Flt Lt K. Cook‡
R5779	OL-	83	FS P. A. Mackenzie‡
L7327	OL-	83	Plt Off. R. G. W. Oakley‡
L7423	OL-	83	Flt Lt D. A. McClure‡
L7453	OL-	83	Fg Off. M. A. Smith‡
R5796	EM-W	207	Plt Off. M. E. Doble
R5791	EM-V	207	FS G. H. Hathersich
L7491	EM-C	207	WO C. Wathey‡
L7515	EM-S	207	Fg Off. S. E. Pattinson*

Capital Ships beware! Preparing to load a 2,000-lb armour-piercing bomb into an unidentified Manchester of 83 Squadron. (Philip Jarrett)

On the outward flight R5791 of 207 Squadron was labouring heavily, unable to climb. At 20.25 hours, two hours twenty minutes after take-off and whilst off the French coast near Plouescat, the aircraft had staggered to a mere 8,000 feet. Flight Sergeant Hathersich dropped a 2,000-lb AP bomb 'safe' into the sea to permit a climb to a more respectable height. Events proved this to be a wise precaution for as the two squadron Manchesters in the attack force approached Brest they found the town laid out before them like a map, with unlimited visibility. Sergeant Clitheroe, bomb aimer in Pilot Officer Doble's aircraft, R5796, released three 2,000-lb AP bombs from 16,500 feet, but as R5791 started its bomb run, still some thousands of feet below Doble, it was singled out and heavily engaged by the flak defences. A good run up was made and the remaining two 2,000-lb APs released in the target area. Immediately following bomb release the aircraft shuddered from a near miss from a heavy calibre flak shell. The aircraft was extensively damaged, taking hits in the centre fin, the bomb doors, throttle box and front turret. None of the crew was injured but the bomb aimer was temporarily blinded by the spray of oil shooting from the hydraulic lines to the turret. As a result the fall of bombs was not observed.

Both Flying Officer McNaughton and Pilot Officer Smith carried out glide bombing attacks on Brest harbour from a low 7,000 feet. Both were held for long periods in the intense searchlight concentrations illuminating the clear sky and subjected to heavy and intense ground opposition, fortunately without damage to either aircraft.

Pilot Officer Searby was not so fortunate. He also skirted the French coast and eventually attacked from the south-east, gliding down from 12,000 to 6,000 feet before releasing his armour-piercing bombs on dry docks eight and nine. No results could be observed because in the later stages of its bomb run the aircraft was enmeshed in a blinding searchlight battery and ravaged by the ruthlessly efficient flak defences. Their aircraft experienced several near misses, being holed in mid-fuselage and rear turret. The IFF, hydraulics and pneumatic systems to operate the flaps, undercarriage and brakes were all put out of action.

Also en route to Brest that night from 61 Squadron were Flying Officer Archibald RCAF and his crew, including Sergeant Peter Holmes as his second pilot. Holmes was engaged on his first operation after leaving the crew of the 'A' Flight Commander, Squadron Leader Peter West. For this 'baptism' West had loaned Archibald and Holmes his personal Manchester, L7458 QR-A, a special aircraft of exceptionally fine flying characteristics. West cherished and guarded the aircraft, to the extent of keeping a careful check of the serial numbers of its two Vulture engines to ensure these were not swapped during maintenance.

Archibald had carried out a long and patient climb en route to the target, eventually reaching 15,000 feet, a height with which he felt well satisfied. The only problem experienced on the way out occurred when they inadvertently overflew Guernsey and Jersey and drew some ineffective flak from the alert defences. As they approached the French coast visibility was good. They had been briefed to expect that the *Gneisenau*, sown into the quay wall by camouflage nets, would be difficult to locate, but that the *Scharnhorst* was towed out every night onto a mooring and would be easier to spot.

Archibald was to fly the aircraft during the actual attack and when they reached the target area three circuits of the harbour were made whilst all members searched vainly for the *Scharnhorst*. Fortunately they were not caught by the probing searchlights, although these contributed in no small part to their difficulty in locating their targets. Eventually, they decided to make a bombing run from the west across the length of Brest harbour hoping to spot a target at the last minute. Archibald had become very animated in the last few tense minutes prior to bomb release, even though they had, by chance, still not been illuminated.

On feeling the lift in the aircraft following release of the bombs, he ordered bomb doors closed and pulled the nose up sharply and to the left intending a climbing turn onto a nor-north-east homeward course. Unfortunately, in his excitement he pulled up too sharply, causing the Manchester to stall and wing over to the left. Soon they were plunging back down in a near vertical dive heading west, with Archibald fighting to regain control and Holmes, his seat folded to permit the observer access to the nose, standing beside him hanging on for grim death as the aircraft went down like a lift. Balloon cables were foremost in their minds as they shot out westwards through the harbour entrance at an altitude of a few hundred feet. It had been a nerve chilling thirty seconds, but once clear of the harbour they calmed down and made an uneventful return to Woolfox Lodge.

Sergeant Louis 'Gus' Gunter was captain of L7470 that night. He had managed to drag the aircraft up to 15,000 to 16,000 feet and headed into the maelstrom over Brest from nor-north-east. During the run up to the target they were quickly coned by the searchlights and flak shells began to burst close by. Boxed in by the intense and accurate barrage it seemed that it could only be a matter of seconds before they were hit. In any case the glare of the lights made target location quite impossible. Gunter began throwing L7470 around the sky in an attempt to shake off the lights and guns, but to no avail. In a desperate ploy to evade the remorseless defences Gunter ordered the bombs jettisoned and then dived away, turning to starboard, chancing that they would miss the balloon cables and pulling out at 500 feet, by which time the lights were searching for another victim. Once the sheltering cover of darkness was regained they took stock, finding L7470 miraculously unscathed and with all instruments reading normally. Gunter immediately turned for home and began to climb back to regain a safe height for the sea crossing. As they skirted the French coast they suddenly remembered that leaflets remained on board and nipped back over land whilst these were dispatched. They returned safely to Woolfox Lodge.

Flying Officer Parsons and crew in R5787 QR-M experienced loss of power in one engine soon after take-off which restricted the height they could attain to only 9,000 feet. Parsons nevertheless elected to continue with the dangerous mission. The crew found the night so bright and clear that navigation was simple. Following a southerly course they found the Brest peninsula stark and clear beneath a light dusting of snow. The whole countryside below was laid out like a map. As they lined up for their final approach they were immediately coned by searchlights and heavily engaged by the flak defences. Convinced that they would not survive the murderous flak at such low level, Parsons turned away westwards and headed out over the Atlantic west of Brest. Here, in consultation with the observer, Sergeant Holmes, they agreed to circle round to the south-east of Brest and make a second run in from that direction.

On their second approach from 8,000 feet the defences on the south-eastern approaches to Brest were just as vigilant and, before the target came into view, they were again coned and engaged by the flak batteries. After a particularly close burst had jarred the aircraft Sergeant Wright looked out from his position in the mid-upper turret and saw that oil was escaping from the starboard engine and streaming back to smother the fin and tailplane. Wright reported this and Parsons feathered the starboard propeller and shut down the engine, meanwhile continuing spirited evasive manoeuvres. Still they were coned and unable to identify any target owing to the glare. Again Parsons turned away from the city to take stock, this time to the west and then north-west. By now all hope of attack had evaporated and their main preoccupation was their own survival. Parsons instructed Holmes to jettison the bombs to reduce their rapid descent rate. Despite his efforts, Holmes could not achieve this at first, possibly due to flak damage to his bomb aiming panel, but suddenly they felt the bucking of the load dropping away. It was too late to save 'M-Mother'.

Parsons ordered the crew to prepare to bale out because the aircraft was still losing height rapidly on the remaining port engine. The lights finally left them as they headed out north-westwards away from the city. By the time the hatches were released and all crew members ready to abandon the aircraft they were down to 600 feet and already too low for a safe escape. Parsons altered his orders and instead sent the crew to their crash positions. The Brittany landscape they descended into was one of low relief but with many small fields, surrounded by earth embankments topped by hedgerows. They hit the ground in a series of bone jarring crashes in which the front fuselage of the aircraft concertina-ed and the remainder tore itself apart.

The entire front section of the aircraft was telescoped and on fire, Flying Officer Parsons, Sergeants Holmes, McCaskill and Butterworth already dead. Sergeant Kindred, the second pilot, had been thrown from the wreck with multiple injuries including a badly mangled leg, but was alive. In the rear of the fuselage Wright was badly bruised but still functioning, whilst the rear gunner Sergeant Griffiths, was lying nearby with a broken leg. After burning his hand badly trying to release the jammed top escape hatch Wright transferred his attention to the main crew door, which swung inwards easily. A series of loud explosions from the mid-section of the aircraft startled them, but Griffiths recognised them as the oxygen bottles.

Wright was then able to half carry and half drag Griffiths from the blazing wreckage, reaching some 50 yards from the aircraft before both collapsed, exhausted. They were both aware that the blazing wreck and exploding oxygen bottles and ammunition would soon bring the searching Germans and suddenly the sound of a dog barking nearby was clearly audible. Cutting short the farewells and making Griffiths as comfortable as possible, Wright hurried to the blazing wreck, flinging his Mae West, parachute etc. deep into the flames. Then he made off across the fields still unaware of his other crew colleague, Kindred, lying nearby. Wright himself became one of the Manchester evaders (see Appendix One), whilst both Kindred and Griffiths were picked up by the Germans, made prisoners, and survived the war.

In L7472 Flight Lieutenant Fraser and his crew encountered a moonlit sky, with 50% broken cumulus, very suited to locating small targets on the water. Very soon after take-off the troublesome starboard Vulture began overheating and with the prospect of further delay some consideration was given to aborting the operation. Fortified by the exhortations of the naval sub-lieutenant they agreed to proceed and by nursing the starboard engine they steadily hauled the aircraft to 10,000 feet at which height it stubbornly refused to climb higher. Traversing the murderous flak defences of Brest in clear weather at less than 10,000 feet was a suicidal risk, but one which the crew resolutely accepted.

L7472 made landfall on the Brittany coast at Plouguerneau and headed due south across the narrow peninsula towards Brest. As they steered a steady course onwards, Sergeant Bill Shorrock, the observer in L7472, got the feeling he would be happier if Fraser 'threw her about a bit' and as if to reinforce the feeling a battery of six to eight flak guns out in the countryside loosed off a single salvo in their direction. At his seat directly over the bomb Shorrock flinched as a burst close beneath opened up several small holes in the fuselage to his right. Another shell had burst directly ahead and the smell of cordite filled the cockpit area. There was no indication of any damage to the vital systems of the aircraft.

As Shorrock conned them south towards their target the time came for Flight Lieutenant Hannigan to descend to the bomb aiming position in the nose. All was peaceful in the aircraft for several minutes, until, as the bight of Brest harbour came into view and Fraser throttled back for the gliding attack, the lights and heavy flak guns began to seek them out. It was a novelty for Shorrock to be a passenger at this vital stage of the operation, but with Hannigan at the bomb sight he took up a standing position behind the pilot to watch the proceedings.

Suddenly the lights flashed across them and locked on. It was bright enough in the cockpit for the crew to have read a newspaper. Next, all hell broke loose as L7472 struck a balloon cable inboard of the starboard engine, which caused a violent yaw to the right. Fraser, briefly unsighted, wrenched the stick over to counteract the yaw, but at the same moment they heard and felt the detonation of the cable cutter and were freed from its drag. Fraser resumed his course, although his visibility outside was restricted by the glare of the searchlights. All the flak guns in Brest harbour seemed to have concentrated their attention on L7472, but so far there were no more hits. Hannigan called that he could not identify the ships owing to the glare, which was mainly coming from batteries of lights to their right. Over to the left Shorrock could clearly see the inner harbour and the two capital ships. He called: 'I see them hard-a-port' and Fraser banked round sharply eastward towards the target. Having identified the ships, Hannigan requested slight heading adjustments shortly afterwards before calling: 'Bomb away!'

All the while flak had continued to explode, but now as Fraser pushed both throttles wide open to climb away eastward and began to take evasive action the starboard engine immediately burst into flames and cut out. Fraser was frantically pushing the buttons of the fire extinguisher and propeller feathering mechanism. Neither the extinguishers nor feathering mechanism appeared to be operating and their short and long term situation soon looked desperate. To add to the problems, another balloon cable caught L7472 in exactly the same position as the first and again slewed the aircraft violently to the right. This time it was more serious because the cable cutters were a one-time device. Their forward motion caused the cable to shear simultaneously at the ground below and the balloon above. The drag of the heavy steel cable compounded that of the windmilling propeller on the dead starboard engine and the aircraft began to shake and vibrate like a cart crossing cobblestones as it steered once more on a southerly heading. By this time they had crossed out over the water of Brest harbour and were heading for the Plougastel peninsula.

Now the flak finally left them alone, but their situation remained perilous. To counter the drag of the windmilling propeller and cable on the right side, Fraser was flying with full port rudder, his left knee against his chest. The control column was also hard over to keep the starboard wing from dropping. Very little aileron control remained. A ribbon of flame still stretched out past the tail from the starboard engine and they were losing height quickly. Despite the desperate odds there was still plenty of fight left in Fraser, who called for a course for home. Shorrock switched on his intercom and replied: 'Coming up in a minute'.

In their remorseless and rapid descent they had crossed the wide southern expanse of Brest harbour and reached the low lying Crozon peninsula. As they did so the trailing balloon cable finally shook itself loose and fell away, but did little to ease their descent rate. At the sight of land the second pilot, Sergeant Marshall, decided to take his chance and quickly descended to the nose and baled out by the bottom hatch. By this time they were down to 300 feet and to the right the land rose higher than their flying height. They crossed the Crozon peninsula at its narrowest point and at this moment the south shore of the bay at Morgat appeared directly ahead. They were so low that a row of houses along the sea front barred their way, but Fraser raised the nose just sufficiently to halt their descent momentarily and they floated over the chimney pots a few feet below. A few seconds later the port engine failed and Fraser carried out an immediate copy book dead stick landing on the water of the bay.

Jettisoning the top hatch, Shorrock observed with relief that the dinghy had already released. He jumped out to attend to it but was called back by Fraser. Sergeant Mclean, the new gunner on his first trip, had remained in the nose throughout the entire incident but now, as he struggled to climb up into the cockpit, his parachute harness snagged on some projection, trapping him in the rising water. Fraser and Shorrock heaved with all their strength but could not tear him free. They implored him to go back and release himself but the youngster was too frightened to duck back under the water and disentangle himself. Quickly the water rose up over him and they had to vacate the cockpit and join the remainder of the crew in the dinghy.

Still the fast moving series of events was not over. It was about 21.30 hours when they bellied in and a steady ffifteen to twenty knot wind was blowing down from the north. Knowing their heading and the general lie of the land they were concerned that if they cut the 50-fathom line tethering them to the aircraft they would be blown out into the Bay of Biscay and rapidly die of exposure. With this in mind, as L7472 sank under them, they paid out the painter until the aircraft settled onto the seabed below and remained moored to it.

They spent a cold night in the dinghy, but at daybreak they discerned that they were more or less landlocked and moreover the wind had steadily backed to the west. They cut the painter and were driven eastward by the wind parallel to the shore. The crew came ashore at a low rocky peninsula about 50 feet high and all six survivors were able to climb the cliffs into the hands of the waiting Luftwaffe.

61 Squadron was not finished with its adventures for the night even now. In L7516, Flight Sergeant Eric Noble and co-pilot Sergeant Don Macsporran had circled around the Brest peninsula before attacking the harbour from the south in a glide attack down to 7,000 feet. Immediately the course was reversed and the dive continued down to 3,000 feet. As the engines were opened up they were suddenly engaged by the ferocious flak defences, but fortunately escaped damage.

As they tracked back over England on the return flight, they were startled by a loud bang and on checking the instruments found that the pneumatic pressure was zero. A sealing gland had cracked and flown apart on the compressed air bottle and they would now have no brakes for landing. Considering the implications, Noble decided to land at the parent station, North Luffenham, with its longer runway, rather than at Woolfox Lodge. Making a careful approach at the slowest safe airspeed, Noble put L7516 down as near the runway threshold as possible and immediately cut the ignition, leaving the windmilling propellers to create the maximum air resistance and slow them down as much as possible. Steering was only possible early in the landing run when the airflow over the rudders remained sufficient for them to turn the aircraft. The quietness within the aircraft was a strange sensation with only the rumbling of the undercarriage to be heard. Noble sat poised to whip up the undercarriage and drop L7516 onto its belly if an obstruction appeared ahead. Just as they were rolling to a halt they ran through a Hampden dispersal near the perimeter, the Manchester's port wing passing directly over the parked aircraft. As they finally stopped an 'erk' jumped into the aircraft and told them they had just scared the hell out of him as he had been inside the Hampden, trying to start it at the very moment the Manchester loomed silently out of the darkness.

The final sequel occurred next day when Eric Noble was called into the commanding officer's office to explain why he had brought his bombs back. In the excitement the back up jettison action had not been carried out and no-one had noticed that the bombs had hung up.

Fortunately for Pilot Officer Searby in the damaged L7492, neither of the vulnerable Vulture engines was damaged and they limped slowly back, also electing to land at North Luffenham owing to the absence of flaps and brakes. A fast but safe landing was executed, although on shutting down they found themselves to be at Wittering instead! L7492 had been holed in fifty-eight places.

Most poignant of all from the Brest force was the fate of Flight Lieutenant Page and his crew in L7396. Possibly delayed by a malfunction, this aircraft took off late, at 18.50 hours, but the captain bravely pressed on to the target. By the time he arrived the flak gunners would have few potential victims to divide their attention and it seems the belated Manchester must have been damaged during its attack. Page pressed on, determined to reach the British coast and safety, but L7396 was failing and losing height all the while. Soon his wireless operator, Sergeant Turner, was sending out SOS messages indicating the imminence of alighting in the sea. Shore stations fixed the last position of the aircraft 50 miles south of Plymouth and two destroyers were detached from a nearby Channel convoy in an attempt to locate the crew. Both vessels searched all night, but abandoned the task the following morning when signs of neither the crew nor wreckage had been seen. The entire crew, including their passenger from 5 Group, were drowned. The final sad chapter came when the body of Flight Lieutenant Page was washed ashore on the Scilly lslands.

From the eleven Manchesters sent to Brest, all had received a savage reception and found the greatest difficulty penetrating the heavily defended port area. Most had hairy experiences and were lucky to escape. Two returned seriously damaged by flak and three failed to return. Several had experienced losses of engine power, making the initial approach to the target hazardous and all the 61 Squadron aircraft, mindful of the importance of the attack explained at the briefing, attacked from very low level. No results were available of the effects of the special weapon, but it seems this night Brest's defences had very much the upper hand.

The St Nazaire Manchester force was completely thwarted by 10/10th cloud, which began at the coastline. Pilot Officer Oakley had experienced a hydraulic failure on the outward trip and was also seriously concerned at the high fuel consumption in L7427. When the port was completely socked-in at the time over target he wisely jettisoned his bombs and returned. Two aircraft brought their bombs back, whilst two others attacked last resort targets. Flying Officer Smith had only released three bombs but on the return trip his port tank was down to 100 gallons and he jettisoned the remaining five 500 pounders to enable him to reach base. Only Flight Sergeant Mackenzie of 83 Squadron and Warrant Officer Wathey of 207 Squadron thought they had bombed the primary target. Wathey attacked St Nazaire successfully in L7491, although cloud cover prevented the bursts being recorded accurately. During the operation the general services generator in the starboard engine failed, whilst potentially terminal for the crew if it had happened earlier, the starboard Vulture cut on landing at Colerne in Wiltshire. Flight Sergeant Hathersich brought the damaged R5791 back safely, diverting to Coningsby.

Such humour as was to be had in 1941/1942 was often of the black variety. Following the loss of one of 61 Squadron's Manchesters, the 'A' Flight Commander, Squadron Leader Peter West, received a distraught telephone call from a wife whose husband had failed to return from an operation. Before the good lady could be placated she announced her intention of travelling up to Woolfox to obtain such first hand information as was available and hung up. The effect on crew morale of a distressed wife on the station was only too apparent and West immediately dispatched his trusted second pilot, Sergeant Peter Holmes, in an attempt to intercept the widow at one of the train changes en route. Holmes was to try and soothe and offer what little consolation and optimistic prospects could be summoned up in the circumstances. En route, the onerous task ahead weighed heavily on the teenage Holmes who had never been faced with a very probably bereaved wife before. Much practising of appropriate sentiments was rehearsed before he had the good fortune to encounter the upset wife.

L7378 EM-A in the snow at Boscombe Down on 1 February 1942. As it completed more operations than any other Manchester – twenty-five with 207 Squadron and a further eight with 106 Squadron – it might well be called the 'King of Manchesters'. (via N. Franklin)

Taking the lady to one side and sitting her down on a seat on the platform, Holmes chose his most upbeat prospects, emphasising the short period which had elapsed since the loss, the possibilities of baling out, evading and being made a prisoner etc. Only slowly did it dawn on the nervous teenager that the erstwhile partner was actually more concerned with finding evidence for the husband's death, having for some time been involved with someone else! Holmes' entreaties remained equally reassuring: no, no, the chances of survival were remarkably poor, etc. Reassured, the lady returned home, as did a bemused Sergeant Holmes!

As February 1942 began and intelligence reports continued to reveal the imminence of the break out of the battle fleet from Brest, Bomber Command applied itself progressively more single-mindedly to thwarting German efforts. Despite increasingly desperate measures the whole of Bomber and Coastal Commands had little to show for a major effort of long duration. The daylight attack of 18 December by the mixed Halifax, Stirling and Manchester formation had achieved nothing. Repeated attacks in January had met with no success and on the infrequent occasions when clear weather permitted a good sight of the target in night attacks, as on 31 January/1 February 1942, the formidable flak and search-light defences of the naval base proved more than a match. Even the new secret anti-shipping weapon had not, it seemed, got near its target.

During February Bomber Command switched tactics. The Manchesters had not undertaken any GARDENING sorties in January, but in a change heralding the breakout, sixty-eight were to be attempted in February. Less spectacular for the aircrews because they would never hope to see the ships in the cross hairs of a bomb sight and in many respects just as hazardous with the cloud and now the icing of this bitter month, it was none the less to prove more effective in the longer run.

In line with the desperate urgency to parry the breakout, Manchesters were kept bombed up during the first days of February, with experienced 61, 83 and 207 Squadron crews standing by in daylight hours. Naturally, this

L7378 EM-A, carrying its name beneath the cockpit, surrounded by a flock of Westland Lysanders, at Boscombe Down on 1 February 1942. The almost indistinguishable word below the cockpit has been suggested to be the Welsh 'Daran' (Thunder Clap). (via N. Franklin)

largely neutralised the force for other activities and Bomber Command had to play a guessing game, trying as it must to use its force with maximum efficiency. Various bomb loads came on and off the aircraft and from time to time mines were loaded instead. In a new departure, on both 2 and 4 February, 207 Squadron attempted their first daylight operations in the Manchester period. On the 2nd three aircraft were prepared in the early afternoon for daylight mining operations, largely thwarted by the weather. One was scrubbed prior to take-off, a second returned immediately and the third was recalled soon afterwards.

Despite its inherent dangers, a further daylight unescorted mining operation was set up for 61, 83 and 207 Squadrons on 6 February as part of a forty-six aircraft force. Fourteen Manchesters were to take-off soon after 10.45 hours and take advantage of the expected cloud cover to evade searching day fighters. Flying Officer Leland from 207 Squadron was scrubbed in L7515 EM-S when his port engine became unserviceable prior to take-off, but the remaining crews proceeded. The designated drop zones for the four mines in each aircraft were the shipping lanes of the NECTARINE area along the Dutch barrier island coast. All three squadrons recognised it as a maximum effort with the commanding officers of both 61 and 207 Squadrons participating.

GARDENING off Holland in daylight – 6 February 1942:

Serial	Code	Squadron	Captain
L7433	QR-	61	Wg Cdr T. C. Weir
L7477	QR-	61	Sqn Ldr A. M. Paape
L7518	QR-	61	Fg Off. G. W. Gilpin
L7516	QR-	61	Fg Off. S. J. Beard
L7454	QR-	61	Plt Off. J. R. Hubbard
R5831	OL-I	83	Plt Off. C. R. Frost
R5833	OL-N	83	Flt Lt D. A. McClure
R5779	OL-G	83	Fg Off. N. A. J. Mackie

L7480	EM-L	207	Sqn Ldr K. H. P. Beauchamp
L7476	EM-K	207	Fg Off. J. de Lacey Wooldridge
R5782	EM-R	207	Wg Cdr C. Fothergill
L7485	EM-D	207	Fg Off. D. A. Green
L7468	EM-Z	207	Fg Off. L. F. Kneil
L7515	EM-S	207	Fg Off. J. H. Leland

Once airborne, visibility was initially bad, with 10/10th cloud at 1,400 feet. In accordance with orders, Squadron Leader Beauchamp returned to base after two hours flying when he ran into clear skies en route.

The remainder of the force continued in unaccustomed daylight. Flying Officer Wooldridge formated with a Hampden and a Manchester whilst en route to the release area. Wooldridge made landfall at Borkum before turning seaward for a timed run on a compass bearing to the drop site. L7476's load of four mines was released from a height of 500 feet.

On his first operation, Wing Commander Fothergill flew a course to the ETA on the enemy coast. From there he located the west end of Schiermonnikoog, turning seaward for a timed run to the designated area. He was fired on by a heavy flak barrage on Schiermonnikoog which holed the port wing, necessitating a quick jink into cloud. Later an enemy aircraft was seen and Fothergill again sought the sanctuary of the cloud.

Flying Officer Green pinpointed his landfall site on the south-west end of Terschelling and flew a timed course at 600 feet to the spot where his four mines were laid. On completion, he formated on two other Manchesters in the area forming a tight mutual protection group with gunners scanning the skies anxiously for German day fighters. Flying Officer Kneil also placed his four mines accurately in position. Aerial activity around him was intense and off on the beam two Bf109s were seen following a Hampden into cloud. As L7468 headed homewards it was intercepted by a Bf110 at 13.42 hours, which was shaken off by dodging up into the murk above.

83 Squadron seem to have had less eventful operations. Flying Officer Mackie had the frustrating experience of reaching the drop zone only to have all four 'VEGETABLES' hang up, whilst Pilot Officer Frost's aircraft had some kind of hydraulic failure. Two of 61 Squadron's contingent had vision problems caused by icing. Squadron Leader Paape was engaged by light flak and machine gun fire when he made landfall on the Dutch coast to make his timed run, his gunners silencing two machine guns.

Wing Commander Weir had the most unnerving experience when a burst hydraulic pipe in the port engine put the rear turret out of action. Undeterred, Weir pressed on, only to encounter first flak on two barrier islands and a Dornier Do215 on the return journey. All of these were evaded and all the Manchesters returned safely, most having sown their 'VEGETABLES' in the allotted position. Within a few days perhaps these very 5 Group mines were to play a vital role in marring the escape of the *Scharnhorst* and *Gneisenau* to their German home ports.

Immediately on return the aircraft were refuelled and armed to standby once more for attacks on the *Scharnhorst* and *Gneisenau*, and later stood down. The Manchesters were next stood by for operations against the battlecruisers on 8 and 9 February, which were subsequently cancelled.

In an attempt to maintain pressure on mainland targets, on 10/11 February 1942 four 83 Squadron Manchesters were sent in a mixed force to bomb marshalling yards at Bremen. Severe icing of seas and rivers made navigation very difficult, whilst visibility and operation of vital systems in the aircraft were impaired. The Manchesters bombed alternative targets in Bremen, Emden and near the mouth of the Weser. Sergeant John Bushby recalls his own experiences on this operation in his book *'Gunner's Moon'*:

Flying only our second Manchester sortie in R5833, OL-N, I felt our aircraft seeming to wallow and sway through the night sky. I picked up tense exchanges between the two pilots: 'Look at that, Dick'. 'Yeah. Temperature's up. Chop back a bit'. A continual shower of fiery red sparks streamed astern, not only indicating all was not well with the Vulture in question but, incidentally, illuminating our passage to any prowling night fighter. 'Any better?' 'Nope, Bitch won't have it'. By releasing a 1,000 lb GP live over Texel, Whitehead dragged R5833 up to 10,000 feet. However, the demands on the struggling Vulture weren't eased and excess fuel consumption also became an issue. Reluctantly, but wisely, Whitehead diverted to Wilhelmshaven but later to Emden, where they jettisoned the load before nervously nursing the ailing port Vulture all the way back to Scampton. Such unreliability was extremely wearing on the mind.

Squadron Leader Thos Murray accelerating L7378, EM-A for take-off from Boscombe Down on 1 February 1942 en route to Weston-super-Mare for experimental mine trials on behalf of the Torpedo Development Unit. (via Aerospace Publishing)

Frustrated by the general lack of activity, Bomber Command laid on a forty-nine aircraft operation to Mannheim and a second force to Bremen on 11 February, an operation which was to be a tactical mistake. 61 Squadron provided six Manchesters. In addition, eighteen Wellingtons raided Brest, five dropped leaflets and one 207 Squadron aircraft was sent on a mining operation. Six 207 Squadron aircraft were delegated for the Mannheim operation, whilst the seventh aircraft, manned by the trainee crew of Flying Officer Pattinson, was briefed to mine an area off the Frisian Islands.

Mannheim and Bremen* - 11/12 February 1942:

Serial	Code	Squadron	Captain
L7433	QR-	61*	Fg Off. R. E. Archibald
L7474	QR-	61*	Plt Off. G. L. Tofield
L7518	QR-	61*	Plt Off. R. E. S. Smith
R5834	QR-	61*	FS J. B. Underwood
L7473	QR-	61*	Fg Off. I. G. A. McNaughton
L7521	QR-	61*	FS P. H. G. Webster
L7432	EM-J	207‡	Fg Off. S. E. Pattinson
L7491	EM-O	207	Sqn Ldr K. H. P. Beauchamp
L7515	EM-S	207	Fg Off. J. H. Leland
L7484	EM-P	207	Fg Off. J. Wooldridge
R5796	EM-W	207	Plt Off. M. E. Doble
L7391	EM-Y	207	FS J. C. Atkinson
L7486	EM-B	207	FS G. H. Hathersich

‡ GARDENING sortie off the Frisian Islands

Flying Officer Pattinson took off separately from the rest of the force at 18.00hours and was followed by the main group. Over the English coast en route to the target, Flying Officer Wooldridge lost coolant from the port Vulture in L7484 leading to the engine overheating and spewing long exhaust flames. The maximum height he could reach was only 8,000 feet. As a result, he wisely diverted to Dunkirk as a last resort target, dropping six 1,000 lb GPs at 19.45 hours from 7,000 feet before returning to Manston at 20.21 hours.

Pilot Officer Doble had to jettison two 1,000 lb bombs to cross the enemy coast at a safe height. Flight Sergeant Atkinson was unable to locate Mannheim and bombed a built-up area, believed to have been Saarbrücken, as a last resort.

Two aircraft attacked the primary, whilst the remaining two also had to make do with alternative targets. On return all aircraft landed safely, although the weather was so adverse that Beauchamp and Leland diverted to Horsham St Faith, Atkinson found Manston and joined 'Dim' Wooldridge. Doble landed at Boscombe Down, whilst Hathersich returned to West Malling.

The 61 Squadron force took off much later than the Mannheim raiders, leaving at intervals of a few minutes between 01.55 and 02.20 hours. The 61 Squadron Manchesters also experienced serviceability problems and as usual it was the Vulture engines which let down Pilot Officer Tofield. Soon after take-off he noted low oil pressure in his starboard Vulture and shortly afterwards a hydraulic pipe burst in the same engine. He landed back at base after only 20 minutes.

On taking off from Woolfox, L7518 steadfastly refused to climb. As they headed eastward Pilot Officer Smith was unable to coax any additional lift for the underpowered and struggling bomber. Nearing the Dutch coast he had found L7518 quite unable to climb above its ceiling of 9,000 feet and reluctantly diverted to Terschelling to release his bombs before returning.

Flying Officer Archibald also experienced engine trouble on the outward journey in the heavily loaded aircraft. He pressed on to the target, searching for thirty-five minutes for the aiming point and being held in searchlight cones for long periods. His aircraft, L7433, was holed by flak in several places but he finally made a gliding attack from 12,000 feet down to 7,500 feet to release his bombs before returning. Flying Officer McNaughton and Flight Sergeant Webster made similar gliding attacks and turned for home.

That night Warrant Officer H A Scott was flying his eighth and final Manchester operation and his third in the crew of Flight Sergeant Underwood. Scott had been with 61 Squadron from its very earliest days with a few Manchesters back in March 1941. He had at first been in the crew of the commanding officer, Wing Commander Valentine, but on 30 July 1941 had been the sole survivor from a 61 Squadron Hampden when Pilot Officer Adshead crashed returning from a raid on Cologne. Scott's injuries kept him in hospital until early September, thus causing him to be unavailable for Valentine's fateful final operation to Berlin on 2/3 September. Scott was to have yet another brush with fate on 11/12 February 1942. This night Underwood flew in a Manchester with a very small number of flying hours, R5834, being joined in his crew by Sergeant Usher (second pilot), Warrant Officer Scott (observer), Sergeant Bithell (wireless operator/air gunner), Sergeant Anderson (front gunner), Pilot Officer Bluett (mid-upper gunner) and Sergeant Patey (rear gunner).

As R5834 settled on its outward course across the North Sea, Scott put in some practice with a sextant and soon began to suspect that the Met. forecast of a wind from a northerly direction was out by 180 degrees. Most aircraft probably drifted off course to the south but Scott was able to correct Underwood's course to such effect that they became one of the first aircraft in the target area, where they accordingly received more than their fair share of the flak. A gliding attack was made with bombs being released at 9,000 feet. At this stage they remained unscathed, turning to a course which would take them back out to sea, passing to one side of Wilhelmshaven. Soon after establishing this return course and whilst in the vicinity of Wilhelmshaven they were coned by searchlights and engaged by a furious flak barrage. They suffered a very near miss from a heavy flak shell just off the starboard wing.

Underwood called the crew on the intercom, informing them of his intention to dive down the search-light beams in an attempt to escape the flak, but Scott immediately counselled him to keep what height he had and alter course with a view to upsetting the gunners' aim. Underwood swung the nose away from the greatest concentration of lights and they soon escaped into the darkened sky without further near misses, the pilot immediately climbing up to 12,000 feet. Close scrutiny soon showed Scott that they had not escaped unscathed.

The starboard engine temperature steadily rose until it passed the danger point. The crew expected it to seize and catch fire at any moment. Accordingly, to preclude this eventuality, Underwood shut it down and feathered the propeller. In this configuration Underwood found he was unable to maintain height and the wisdom of making the extra height after the flak engagement became apparent. By experimentation, Underwood found that he could reduce the rate of height loss to a few feet per minute only at airspeeds of 105 mph or less, a whisker above stalling speed. Soon Underwood crossed the German coast between Bremerhaven and Wilhelmshaven.

Despite being determined to try their best to regain the English coast, they were reluctant to strike out due east away from land and turned instead south-westwards to fly parallel to the Frisian Islands. They had reached as far as Texel, a few miles to port, when speed momentarily dropped to 100 mph and R5834 suddenly stalled and fell into a spin. Underwood worked hard, closing the throttle to permit spin recovery before re-opening the port engine as they resumed a generally level flight. Almost immediately they fell into a second spin, made worse on this occasion by the port engine cutting. Closing the throttle with the wheels still retracted caused the undercarriage warning klaxon to sound, increasing their sense of foreboding. Fortunately the engine picked up again. Underwood had to set the aircraft up at a crazy angle with the starboard wing high and a lot of right hand rudder to minimise height loss. The height loss did not seem terminal in the short term and the crew slowly began to recover from the shock of almost spinning straight down into the North Sea.

Off on the port beam the wide sandy beaches of Texel were clearly visible in the rising dawn and Underwood offered the crew the choice of an immediate forced landing on the beach or of continuing their attempt to reach the English coast. They unanimously elected to make for home. Efforts were redoubled to trim the aircraft and reduce the rate of height loss. Attempts were made to open the balance cock to transfer fuel from the starboard tank to the port engine. The control was stiff and although it opened eventually Scott was unable to ascertain whether much fuel was transferred.

Sergeant Bithell sent a message to base indicating their predicament and was gratified to receive an acknowledgement. The spin had toppled the gyro in the master unit of the dead reckoning compass, whilst the crabwise, wing high attitude of the aircraft led Scott to be dissatisfied with the headings shown on the P4 compass. Scott asked Bithell to obtain a series of radio fixes as they made their ponderous way westwards.

Despite their best efforts R5834 continued to lose height and it looked progressively more certain that they would have to ditch. The gunners were set to work stripping out and dumping the guns, ammunition, armour plate and any other readily detachable item. Only two guns and a small quantity of ammunition were retained in the rear turret. Thus lightened, they reasoned that they might get a few miles closer to the English coast before ditching.

The aircraft slowly ate up the miles towards the coast, sinking steadily as it did so. With the rising sun they could see the sea surface more clearly and were soon gratified to recognise the bow wave of an air sea rescue launch heading directly towards them. It appeared to have been sent out in response to their earlier radio call for, having passed it, Sergeant Patey called to say it had reversed course and was now following them back westwards.

To their intense relief it began to appear that they would reach the English coast, and soon afterwards they crossed the coast south of Yarmouth, still heading steadfastly towards Woolfox Lodge. This happy situation did not continue for long because, en route to Norwich, the port engine spluttered and stopped, apparently short of

Manchesters returning from the ill-timed Mannheim raid on 11/12 February 1942 were scattered to the four winds. Flight Sergeant Hathersich brought L7486 EM-B down at West Malling, Kent. It is pictured being refuelled prior to return to base. (207 Squadron archives)

fuel. With little height in hand there was no prospect of baling out and Underwood rapidly called all crew members to take up their crash positions. The pilot shaped up to force land in a flattish field directly in their path.

Scott had hastened to sit facing rearwards, his back braced against the main spar. He found he had a good view aft as Sergeant Patey had left the rear turret doors wide open. As they bellied in, turf, earth, divots and pieces of aeroplane flew in all directions and they lurched violently to a halt, the aircraft more or less in one piece. Nobody had been seriously hurt, although Underwood had been thrown forward in his straps by the deceleration and was thus unable to avoid being badly bruised across the chest by the thrashing control column.

As all scrambled out to survey the damage and feel solid ground under their feet, Usher had the misfortune to fall through the ice covering a deep ditch which the Manchester was straddling. Despite their ordeal humour had not eluded the crew and Underwood berated him, recalling his two hour struggle to keep Usher's feet dry only for him to fall into the ditch the moment he left the aircraft!

Luckily a farm was nearby and the undersized Ben Usher was soon warmly dressed in decidedly oversized farmer's clothes. Later that day the crew were transported to Horsham St Faith from where they flew back to Woolfox Lodge. The week-old R5834 was a write-off, but at least it had survived long enough to deliver its precious crew back home.

In mid-February Warrant Officer Scott was posted to Manby on a bombing leaders' course and in his absence Flight Sergeant Underwood and crew flew yet another Manchester operation, returning this time with a number of bricks embedded in the leading edge of a wing after colliding with a high chimney stack during a low level escape from the target. Having converted onto Lancasters, Underwood and his crew failed to return from a subsequent operation with the loss of all on board. Warrant Officer Scott was still at Manby. Yet another brave 61 Squadron crew had made the ultimate sacrifice.

Underwood had bellied in at 07.55 hours but two 61 Squadron Manchesters were still airborne. Flying Officer Archibald reached Woolfox and landed safely at 08.10 hours, whereas Flying Officer McNaughton's crew had left the enemy coast at daybreak but were unable to pinpoint their landfall on the English coast. They flew up and down for two hours until they picked up a course to base, where they landed at 09.15 hours with marginal fuel reserves. Bomber Command's forces were, accordingly, scattered and exhausted when the Germans finally made their audacious breakout.

The next day witnessed one of the RAF's and the nation's most ignominious encounters. Early on 12 February 1942 the *Scharnhorst* and the *Gneisenau*, together with the cruiser *Prinz Eugen* and with a strong destroyer escort, finally broke out of Brest with the intention of forcing a route through the English Channel, trailing their coats across the very doorstep of the most powerful navy in the world. The Germans had chosen the weather for the sortie with the utmost care. It was atrocious, severe gales, low cloud, poor visibility, snow, sleet and rain all served to shroud the racing ships. Right from the beginning, however, luck was on the German side. Coastal Command had been patrolling the harbour approaches for weeks, both day and night, with air-to-surface vessel (ASV) radar equipped search aircraft to provide forewarning of just such an escape. Irrespective of the weather and unbeknown to the Germans, who had no inkling that our aircraft were so equipped, the patrolling Hudson should have detected the ships. By a cruel quirk of fate the ASV set in the Lockheed Hudson chose this particular moment to fail, and to compound matters the standby aircraft also became unserviceable. The game of hide and seek was on with a vengeance.

For days on end, like other 5 Group Squadrons, 207 Squadron had maintained six Manchesters at permanent readiness, armed with 2,000-lb AP bombs. Bomber Command was put on a four-hour standby to attack the ships during the morning, but serious logistic difficulties manifested themselves. In addition to Coastal Command, the Germans had caught Bomber Command on the hop too. Six 207 Squadron aircraft from the previous night's operation were spread the length and breadth of Britain, their crews sleeping-in after getting away from debriefing later than 01.00 hours that morning.

A further difficulty was that the cloud base was so low that there was no prospect of using AP and SAP bombs on the ships. If the aircraft flew at the height sufficient for the bombs to reach the terminal velocity needed to penetrate the deck armour the bomb aimers would have no chance of seeing their target. After months of preparation it looked to be a fudge right from the beginning.

Following frantic telephone calls during the morning the aircraft engaged on the Mannheim raid returned in dribs and drabs to Bottesford. Flying Officer Leland took off from Horsham at 11.25 hours and landed at base at 12.10 hours, where ground crews descended on this and other aircraft to refuel, rearm and load them each in turn with twelve 500-lb GP bombs. Such weapons would be almost totally ineffective against the heavily armoured battlecruisers, but there was a faint chance a near miss below the water line might damage the more vulnerable undersides of the vessels. It was a thousand to one chance, but in this weather and with the equipment then at its disposal it was the only option open to Bomber Command.

The aircraft eventually assembled included five Manchesters from both 61 and 83 Squadrons and six from 207 Squadron. 61 and 207 Squadrons provided their commanding officers and both flight commanders. All aircraft carried twelve 500-lb bombs. For Pilot Officer Leland and his crew it was the second of three operations in less than 36 hours. From 207 Squadron L7455 and L7486 were allocated from the Con Flight, L7488 and L7432 which had been on standby, and L7432 and L7515 returned from their diversionary airfields.

Channel Breakout. Operation FULLER – 12 February 1942: German Operation Cerberus)

Serial	Code	Squadron	Captain
L7458	QR-	61	Wg Cdr T. C. Weir
L7477	QR-N	61	Sqn Ldr A. M. Paape
L7475	QR-D	61	Sqn Ldr P. W. M. West
L7521	QR-	61	Fg Off. G. W. Gilpin
L7473	QR-	61	Plt Off. J. R. Hubbard
R5831	OL-I	83	Plt Off. C. R. Frost
L7465	OL-H	83	FS P. A. Mackenzie
L7525	OL-O	83	Fg Off. M. A. Smith
L7427	OL-J	83	Flt Lt D. A. McClure
L7385	OL-C	83	Fg Off. R. W. Cooper
L7432	EM-J	207	Wg Cdr C. Fothergill
17468	EM-Z	207	Flt Lt P. C. Ward-Hunt
L75I5	EM-S	207	Fg Off. J. H. Leland
L7485	EM-D	207	Sqn Ldr T. C. Murray
L7455	EM-G	207	Fg Off. P. C. Birch
L7488	EM-Q	207	FS J. C. Atkinson

After the heroic attack by Lieutenant Commander Esmonde and the six Swordfish of 815 Squadron, the German ships were once more enveloped in low cloud and squalls. Attempts to shadow the fleet were made difficult by the terrible visibility, the escorting German fighter umbrella and the E-boat and destroyer screen. The obvious intention of the Manchesters was to make a concerted attack on the ships and so divide the ferocious German flak defences. 83 Squadron's Manchesters took off between 13.49 and 15.02 hours, whilst 61 and 207 Squadron aircraft were due off at 15.00 hours or soon afterwards. The hastily contrived operation began to go seriously wrong from the very first.

Whilst running up for take-off two 207 Squadron aircraft from the previous night's raid, L7432, Wing Commander Fothergill, and L7515, Flying Officer Leland, became unserviceable and were cancelled. There were no reserves for the crews to transfer to. The remaining four Manchesters took off between 14.59 and 15.25 hours. L7485, which was last away, experienced a hydraulic failure on take-off in the hands of Squadron Leader Thos Murray, who completed a circuit and immediately landed back at Bottesford.

A force born out of desperation and with little hope of locating their targets, of hitting or of damaging them had thus been reduced by half before the operation started. Despite the most determined efforts by air and ground crew alike, the unreliability of the Manchester was their undoing yet again. Small wonder those involved felt frustrated.

Out over the North Sea a motley collection of RAF aircraft searched blindly and in totally un-coordinated fashion for the fast escaping battlecruisers. Halifaxes, Stirlings, Wellingtons, Whitleys and Hampdens milled around with the Manchesters on the off chance of locating the ships upon which they could unload their totally ineffective bombs.

In the air aircraft had to contend with visibility of only 500 to 1,000 yards and a cloud base as low as 500 feet. They had to fly and search at low level to maintain any contact with the sea surface. Flight Lieutenant Ward-Hunt and Flying Officer Birch were both experienced captains from the Con Flight. Peter Ward-Hunt searched for three hours, constantly asking his wireless operator, Sergeant Gibson, whether news of any sightings had been broadcast, but to no avail. He returned with bomb load intact. In L7455 Peter Birch had an equally uneventful search before bombing small vessels at the Hook of Holland from 500 feet at 16.35 hours as a last resort.

The operation carried out by Flight Sergeant Johnnie Atkinson has been reconstructed from the official record. His aircraft, L7488 EM-Q, was one of the few Bomber Command aircraft which did sight the battlecruisers. The visibility was only 700 yards and Atkinson was almost on top of the alerted fleet before his lookouts spotted them. Having stumbled across the racing fleet, he noted the position of the capital ships before rising up to 800 feet and entering cloud. As he circled to a more advantageous position the bomb doors were opened and Sergeant Worthington, the observer, got down into the nose and fused the bombs. As they dived to attack, heavy rain and mist still impeded their bomb run, but they were immediately engaged by the flak defences of escorts and capital ships alike. All twelve 500-lb GP bombs were dropped from 700 feet at 16.16 hours and are thought to have straddled a cruiser. As they entered a climbing turn to regain the sanctuary of the cloud, the rear gunner, Sergeant Blair, saw five bomb bursts near the starboard side of the vessel but no sign of a hit or damage. At this very instant the aircraft was hit in the tail by a flak burst. No vital damage was done and Atkinson was able to return safely to Bottesford. He was later awarded the DFC for this attack.

Further light can now be shed on this sortie following the emergence in recent years of John McCarthy's diary. This was to be his seventh and penultimate Manchester operation and his last as second pilot before qualifying as a Freshman Captain. McCarthy writes:

Thursday afternoon 12 February. When we received the news the ships were then about sixteen miles due west of Hook of Holland. When they were actually discovered, the RAF threw in lots of planes but these were hampered by the weather and the fact we didn't have the correct type of planes to do the job. Most of our crews had operated the previous night and some landed elsewhere, with the result that we were short of both crews and aircraft. I managed to squeeze myself and the crew into a trip with Johnnie Atkinson. Took a bit of wangling, but we were all tickled pink to be going on a 'daylight' instead of waiting around to do an 'infra-red' on some bally jam factory. (Presumed to be a reference to Bomber Command night target-finding problems - author). We took off at 15.08 hours loaded with twelve 500-lb GPs. Visibility was the most 'duff' I've ever encountered. At no time did we reach a height in excess of 1,200 to 1,400 feet. When we found them, the ships made one of the finest sights I've seen in my lifetime. The big 'un had a screen of rather neat looking destroyers in a semi-circle in front of her as though steaming along in 'review order', and they certainly did a good job. Ceiling was so low that there was no fighter protection as there had been earlier in the day. We were the only plane on the target at the time and we naturally came in for all the '....' they had to throw.

Johnnie Atkinson made a very daring low-level attack at a height of just over 600 feet. The run-up to bomb was made in an almost casual fashion by 'Mike' Leahy, my navigator, who continued to give 'Left', 'Left', etc. despite the intense barrage of flak. We failed to bomb the battlecruiser because Mike did not locate it until we had 'run-up' on the escorting destroyer, which looked almost as big seeing that we were so low. We were taking quite a lot from those ships but I was so damned excited I just couldn't be worried about it. Had my 'inter-com' switched on and kept up a continual chatter to myself and all the boys which, they later informed me, ran something like this: 'There they are! You German B...! Look! Over there! There she is! The big B...! You German B...!' etc. (Shades of 'Dim' Wooldridge. McCarthy makes no mention of seeing the actual bomb release or of the moment they were hit by flak – author).

He carries on:

I've never seen flak so intense. None of the crew were hit and I was greatly amused with Bill Blair, our tail gunner (having found the sanctuary of cloud) who came up to the front turret and kept up a running chatter with Barnett, our second wireless operator, who had been in this turret. Barney had opened up on the ships as we did our 'run-up' but we don't know if he did any damage. Small chance.

We were hit pretty badly in the tail assembly. On landing back at Bottesford we inspected the damage and discovered that the shell apparently exploded inside the tailplane and the shrapnel burst out making holes all over the rear of the fuselage. Bill Blair was really lucky for some fragments went through the fuselage within 2 feet of his turret. The rudder trim control wire was shot half through, the elevator control wire was shot half through, and the shrapnel burst put a huge hole and bend in the main spar of the elevator. The hole in the underside of the tailplane was large enough for me to put my fist right inside the plane. A couple more such hits and we may not have come back. This was my first experience of a 'daylight' and also low level and it certainly is one of the greatest thrills possible to experience. I still think that I'd prefer to be doing low level work. Trip took three hours five minutes. Think Johnnie and Mike deserve some recognition for their work. Looks like I've got a winner for a navigator in Mike. Pilot Officer Price, the Squadron Navigation Officer, says that I'm a 'Jammy so-and-so' in getting Mike as my nav. Marvellous trip. Think I'll remember it to my dying day.

Wing Commander Weir headed off individually at low level for the estimated position of the racing German naval units. Although visibility was poor, L7458 was followed twice en route to the target area, first by a Junkers JU88 and later a Messerschmitt Bf110. These were evaded by dodging into the plentiful cloud cover. On ETA a square search was carried out without any sighting being made. Eventually one track led them onto the Dutch coast at Zandvoort. Weir flew down the coast to Den Haag (The Hague) before turning west and flying out to sea at low level for fifteen miles to commence a second search. Almost immediately the rear gunner, Flying Officer Bluett, spotted the German ships at close range just astern.

Weir advanced the throttles and made a climbing turn up into the enveloping cloud cover. Opening the bomb doors and preparing for the attack, Weir then turned on a reciprocal and headed into a diving attack with all members keeping a sharp look out. On breaking cloud at 400 feet the pilot and bomb aimer, Pilot Officer Beach, found themselves running between and in the same direction as the two columns of ships. Beach began directing Weir to a ship in the right hand column calling: 'Right!' then 'Hard right!' as they overtook their target. At the same time an intense and ferocious barrage of light and medium flak was opened up on them. Weir had banked right and was tightening the turn when a large calibre shell went through the port wing, outboard of the fuel tank, damaging the aileron, which jammed in the up position. Airflow over the port wing then threw L7458 into a steep left hand banked turn, which Weir was fully occupied stopping tightening into a fatal spin.

Pandemonium had broken out with flak bursts all round them, air gunners replying and Beach calling: 'Right, right!' in frustration as Weir, unbeknown to them, strove with might and main just to keep them airborne. A less experienced pilot might have gone straight into the sea there and then, but Weir had an Above Average rating and used all his experience to bring the crippled Manchester under control, still engaged by the German escorts. They had turned sharply left towards the port column of vessels and Weir was still unable to raise the left wing. Quickly closing the throttle of the port engine to half power, he finally managed to get the wings level at about 200 feet. Abandoning any prospect of attack, Weir ordered the bombs jettisoned and bomb doors closed, meanwhile descending to sea level for maximum safety. No further flak hits had occurred and as they passed through the left hand column fire became erratic and ineffective. It seemed the poor visibility and risk of hitting their own ships was deterring the enemy gunners. Weir now zig-zagged his way through the convoy, his crew doing all they could to keep the flak gunners heads down as they passed each ship.

Eventually they were clear and Weir was able to climb into the sanctuary of cloud, relaxing slightly after the last hectic few minutes and their close brush with death. In turn he began calling each crew position to check whether anyone had been injured. Last of all was Flying Officer Bluett who replied: 'OK sir, that was great. Let's go back and do it again!' It raised a wry smile from Weir who was the only one to appreciate how close they had been to death, and the tension in the aircraft dropped perceptibly. They were able to regain base without further incident.

The 'A' Flight Commander, Squadron Leader Peter West, had set out from Woolfox Lodge in L7475 at about the same time as the remainder of 61 Squadron's Manchesters. Heading out from the English coast, as they climbed out through 2,500 feet in bad visibility they met a JU88 head on over Great Yarmouth. Neither crew had any time to respond. They flew on at 3,000 feet over a thick and continuous cloud layer. In the howling gale near ground level the air was very turbulent and L7475 was lurching violently. Soon all the gunners were very airsick.

On ETA, West let down to carry out a square search at 500 feet just below the cloud base. Three Bf109s were seen shortly afterwards, but West popped up into cloud and evaded them. West reached the Dutch coast, where he obtained a fix on one of the radio transmitters before heading off seawards to resume the search. Suddenly they came across a destroyer screen, indicating the German capital ships were nearby and West began a search of the neighbourhood. Intense and accurate flak was encountered whenever they ventured out of cloud. However, the larger units could not be located and cloud base was now locally so low that it would be impossible to release bombs without destroying the aircraft.

Thus thwarted, West gave up the struggle and steadily climbed up through the cloud layer with the intention of returning to base. As they breasted the cloud layer they were shocked to immobility to find they were right alongside a Bf110! The German fighter crew were equally taken off guard, staring across with raised eyebrows. Peter West was the first to galvanise himself into action, stuffing the nose back down and calling out irritably to the gunners: 'Well, fire at the b.....d, someone!'

As both aircraft sheared away the fighter passed through the sights of the mid-upper gunner, who was still too startled to respond, but Pilot Officer Komiski loosed off a quick burst from the rear turret from close range. Komiski believed he had disabled the rear gunner in the aircraft. Following this adventure they set course for base, landing with the bomb load intact.

Squadron Leader Paape flew directly to the Dutch coast, locating it at 400 feet and obtaining a pinpoint. He then returned offshore to make two runs up and down about ten miles out in the hope of locating the German ships. Having no success, he flew to a distance of thirty miles offshore and recommenced his search, locating the convoy shortly afterwards. His aircraft was immediately engaged by flak and sustained two hits. Climbing through cloud Paape skirted the convoy and made a bombing run on one of the battlecruisers from 450 feet. In the excitement his bombs undershot and straddled an escort destroyer.

The anti-aircraft defences may have upset Flight Sergeant Halls' aim and as Paape broke for sea level L7477 was hit several more times. The hydraulic lines were severed, brakes and trimming gear shot away, turrets put out of service and starboard fin, tailplane and petrol tank holed. Loss of hydraulic power prevented the bomb doors from being closed. In this precarious condition Paape limped back to base, where a successful 'wheeler' landing was accomplished.

Neither Flying Officer Gilpin nor Pilot Officer Hubbard located the enemy ships and the disconsolate force returned to base with nothing to show for their efforts. It was 61 Squadron's second and last daylight operation in Manchesters.

83 Squadron remained in the search area until nightfall. All aircraft carried out square searches but in the low cloud, mist and rain four of the five brought their bombs back. Flying Officer Smith's crew sighted the double column of ships briefly, but as they manoeuvred to attack the poor visibility impeded bomb aiming. As they ran in they were spotted by enemy escort fighters which closed in to attack the rear gunner. Sergeant Duff put up a spirited defence, later claiming two 'Heinkels' shot down. He in turn was wounded. The Form 540 details Pilot Officer McFarlane's rear gunner, Sergeant L B Whibley, being killed but there is no record of his operation in the Form 541.

It had been a frenetic and frustrating spell for all concerned. Many ground and aircrew had been on duty for virtually forty-eight hours, grabbing a few hours sleep when they could. For the armourers aircraft had been loaded with alternative weapons three times in less than twenty-four hours. On 207 Squadron, mechanical faults on L7485 and L7515 meant these had been loaded, unloaded, reloaded and then unloaded again all in less than twelve hours!

At the time it seemed that the Royal Navy and the RAF had been entirely non-effective in preventing the escape of the capital ships. Indeed, it was a frustrating and humiliating day, with none of the aircraft having anything to show for their strenuous efforts. Perhaps the most surprising outcome in the swirling mass of British and German aircraft was that there were no collisions. All the Manchesters returned.

Whilst this drama was being acted out unseen, all three squadrons were preparing for the final desperate throw of the dice. At Bottesford the ground crews had worked constantly on L7485 and L7515 to make them serviceable and they were joined by two others for a mining operation to a sea area at the mouth of the Elbe, coded NECTARINE, where the German battlecruisers were believed to be headed. The aircraft each carried four 1,500-lb mines.

GARDENING – 12/13 February 1942:

Serial	Code	Squadron	Captain
L7475	QR-	61	Plt Off. G. L. Tofield
L7519	QR-	61	Fg Off. L. Gunter
L7465	OL-H	83	WO H. H. Whitehead
R5831	OL-I	83	Plt Off. H. G. Hazelden
L7427	OL-J	83	Plt Off. J. H. Morphett
L7391	EM-	207	Sqn Ldr K. H. P. Beauchamp
L7515	EM-S	207	Fg Off. J. H. Leland
R5796	EM-W	207	Plt Off. M. E. Doble
L7485	EM-D	207	Sqn Ldr T. C. Murray

Repairs in progress on Manchester L7477 QR-N of 61 Squadron at Woolfox Lodge, following Squadron Leader Paape's brave attack on the Scharnhorst and the Gneisenau off the Dutch coast on 12 February 1942. Near misses by several flak shells disabled the hydraulics, putting the turrets and brakes out of action. The trimming gear, starboard fin, tailplane, petrol tank and bomb doors were all holed. Paape and crew were very fortunate to return. (via Chaz Bowyer)

Despite the participation of the two flight commanders from 207 Squadron, this operation, too, was an unmitigated disaster. The aircraft took off in a group between 22.50 and 22.58 hours to make their way individually to their designated areas. Flying Officer Leland returned at 02.26 hours with mines intact after encountering severe icing in nimbus stratus cloud. Squadron Leader Murray in L7485, with hydraulics repaired following his aborted operation in the same aircraft the previous afternoon, located the dropping zone but was unable to release his mines due to another hydraulic failure, which prevented the bomb doors opening.

Squadron Leader 'Penny' Beauchamp's logbook records him flying the operation in Manchester Mk.1A L7491 to the Frisian Isles, where the bomb doors failed to open. The manual release also failed, necessitating the four mines being returned to base. By 11 February Sergeant H. E. 'Pip' Parrott had flown five operations as a Wireless Operator in 207 Squadron and settled into the crew of Pilot Officer Doble. He records himself as liking flying in Manchesters and that in his time with the unit 207 Squadron was twice awarded top bomber squadron in Bomber Command. This night Pilot Officer Doble, in R5796 EM-W, had attacked Mannheim (18.29 to 00.08 hours) but landed back at Boscombe Down. They returned to Bottesford next day to discover the flap concerning the escape of the three German capital ships. Their aircraft was descended upon and loaded with four sea mines, taking off for the NECTARINE area in Heligoland Bight at 22.55 hours. Adrenalin, possibly boosted by tablets, kept them alert and, maintaining a low altitude just below the cloud base, they made haste to get ahead of the racing German ships and place their mines. Unfavourable weather with severe icing was encountered. After maybe an hour, Parrott suddenly felt his ankle being kicked hard by the navigator, Sergeant Clitheroe. The crewman was shouting above the engine noise with some urgency: 'How do you send "period" in Morse on the Aldis?'

They were interrupted by the second pilot, George Hawes, who was wielding the Aldis lamp calling: 'What's "N" in Morse?' 'Dash Dit' replied Parrott. Wondering what could have raised this level of urgency, Parrott left his position, made his way forward into the cockpit and looked down. He got a clear view of the sea surface finding himself gazing down seemingly very close to what he thought to be a battleship with all its guns trained directly on them. As he watched, a racing destroyer suddenly appeared around the stern of the capital ship sending by Aldis 'the colloquial two-word English phrase meaning "Go Away"'. It was an RN naval unit also seeking the same prey. They were only too happy to shear away. On reaching the enemy coast, they identified one pinpoint on the north German coast and another on the Danish, making an accurate timed run at 600 feet to the release position at 02.05 hours, still ahead of their potential target. What might otherwise have been a successful attack was marred by the sudden realisation that in his tiredness and excitement the navigator had neglected to fuse the mines prior to release. Disappointment and exhaustion consumed them as they returned to Bottesford in silence.

In exceptionally bad weather, Pilot Officer Tofield took off and climbed to 8,000 feet where he experienced acute icing conditions. Ice built-up on the airscrew blades and was shed in lumps which dented the fuselage and burst through the perspex of the cockpit. The weight caused the aircraft to steadily lose height to a mere 600 feet! Next they flew into a severe snow storm and Tofield had no alternative but to abandon the operation. In contrast, Pilot Officer Gunter elected to fly at 1,500 feet but at this height found conditions very bumpy and visibility nil. At 00.50 hours he calculated that he could not reach the drop zone by the stipulated time and turned for home.

At Scampton 83 Squadron had recovered its Manchesters in the late afternoon. On that chaotic day the remaining crews, who had been on standby at their bombed-up aircraft awaiting orders, were released when soon afterwards a tannoy announcement rang out: 'Stand down. Definitely no take-off'. No sooner had they returned to the Mess when another reversal was announced by the same means: 'Flight Sergeant Whitehead and crew to the crew room immediately!' There they were joined by two other crews. 'You're on!' ordered the commanding officer, Wing Commander 'Mary' Tudor. 'Loading you up with sea mines now'. His finger traced an area on the chart off the Frisian Islands. 'This is where the Fish Heads estimate the ships will be at about 01.00 hours. Your mines are proximity fused. If you see the ships, keep out of their way and drop your mines out of sight and ahead of them. Then, let's hope one of the bastards runs over one. Good Luck!' This wasn't much of a briefing, but the best that could be mustered in the circumstances. Having loaded the aircraft, all three departed close to 23.30 hours. John Bushby records:

As we climbed out over the Lincolnshire coast the weather seemed to have improved. Patches of clear sky were now more frequent and below, the cloud shadows dappled the dark grey shimmer of the North Sea. In their imaginations every shadow looked like the black form of an enemy ship. Wireless Operator Whitehead knew time was against them, explaining to Sergeant Williams on the intercom: 'All this height and speed, we're using a lot of fuel. If the ships are due at the briefed position at 01.00 hours, we've got to get a move on to get there first. No gallivanting about all over the North Sea with this consumption. So I'm keeping the revs up and, Bill (Baines, front gunner) keep your eyes peeled ahead. You, too, Geordie (Pilot Officer Billing, navigator). You won't get any pinpoint check on your D/R until we can see one of the Frisian Islands – ought to be Texel or Den Helder. Gunners, I don't think you need worry about night fighters, but watch out for ships. Report everything you see'.

Bushby recalls:

We roared on eastwards through the night. A dozen times I opened my mouth to sound an alarm but each time realised it was another cloud shadow. Reckon ten miles off Texel, now. Bill's voice broke a long silence. I scrabbled to see my watch under my gloves and fur cuff - ten minutes to one. I could see by the long stream of sparks being thrown out from the exhausts that Whitey must be really pouring on the coal. Up ahead! **(This was Dick William's superior night vision again – author).** *'See that landfall? A gap and another coast further south? Den Helder! Nice work Bill' called Whitehead, a landfall spot-on after two hours in the dark on nothing but D/R. 'OK now. Any sign of anything?' 'Not a thing Skip' called someone. 'OK, turning port now. Check zero-one-zero Bill?' 'Zero-one-zero it is'. 'Going up front now' replied the navigator heading for the bomb-aiming position.*

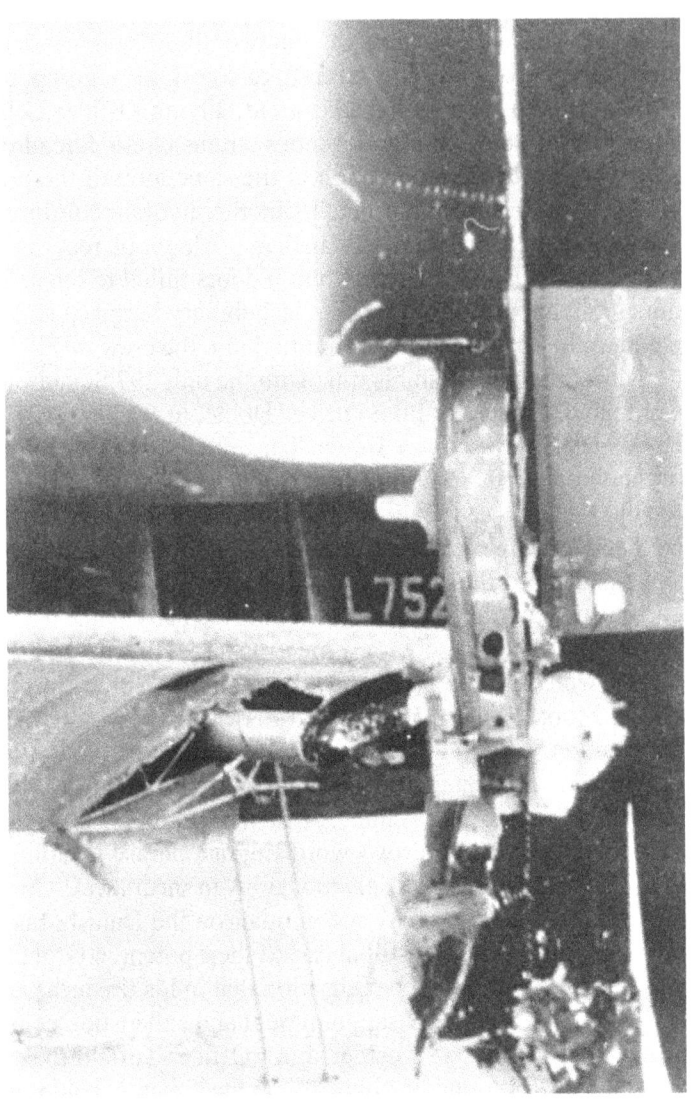

Damaged fin and elevator of an 83 Squadron Manchester (L752?). Two 83 Squadron Manchesters were damaged in the tail area on 12 February 1942 while engaged in Operation FULLER. Flying Officer Smith's rear gunner was injured in L7525 OL-O. Flying Officer McFarlane's rear gunner was reported killed, but his operation is not listed in the squadron records. (via Chaz Bowyer)

The trail of engine sparks and engine note diminished as Whitey throttled back and dropped the nose into a gentle dive. '200 feet, Whitey?' 'OK. Take her up a bit, Dick'. 'Speed about one-twenty'. The engine note rose and L7465 OL-H flew on slowly above the steely water. 'Bomb doors open. Bomb doors open'. 'OK'. A pause, then: 'First's gone'. The remaining three mines fell away fused at ten second intervals and our job was done. To starboard, the Dutch coast remained dark and quiet. 'Right, now let's get the hell out of here!'

They turned and settled on a westerly course for home, climbing as we did so. Silence returned to the crew. There was little danger now. Suddenly Whitehead called: 'Take over a minute, Dick. Going to the Elsan'. It was unusual for Whitehead to leave his seat on an operation but he evidently plugged-in his intercom at the socket provided on his arrival, calling: 'All right, Dick?' An inexperienced and anxious Sergeant Williams called back: 'That you, Whitey? Can you get back as soon as you can?' Whitehead rapidly recovered his left hand seat. 'What's up?' 'Look at that rev counter!' 'Jesus! What's she flying like?' 'Seems alright. I've checked the boost and temperatures. Everything seems OK'. Whitehead tried to sound reassuring: 'Looks like a duff rev counter. Let's hope it is!'

The significance of this last remark was lost on no-one, especially with their recent personal experiences of the Finningley prang. A fluctuating rev counter might indicate an engine about to fail, taking them down into the stormy freezing waters of the North Sea from their low altitude before the Captain could re-trim the aircraft in an attempt at holding height on a single engine. 'Bleeding thing's almost off the clock now'. Williams was doing nothing to improve their peace of mind. 'Must be the gauge itself' replied Whitehead more confidently. They flew on westwards with six pairs of ears intently tuned to the note of their twin Vultures. By the time they reached Scampton and landed the engine sounded as strong as when they began, but all seven in the crew felt dry-mouthed and tense.

The unit ORB records good visibility below 10/10th cloud with a base variously at 1,000 to 1,200 feet. It records Warrant Officer Whitehead as being unable to find the aiming point and returning with his 'VEGETABLES' at 04.16 hours. With few exceptions the crews went to bed exhausted and burning with anguish and frustration. Despite many being continuously awake for more than 36 hours and making a Herculean effort, the Manchester had let them down again. Three out of six from 207 Squadron became unserviceable on the daylight raid and two out of four on the night mining mission.

The weather had conspired to nullify the efforts of the remainder of the force. They were left feeling that, even if the weather had been better, their chances of dealing the Germans a decisive blow were negligible, whilst the chances of the unescorted Manchesters evading the German fighter screen would have been slight. All in all it was a typical, if somewhat extreme, example of the continuing operational limitations of the Manchester.

As the night wore on it had become increasingly obvious that the battlecruisers would make good their escape. The only silver lining to the whole endeavour was that, unseen by the attackers, the *Scharnhorst* had hit and exploded mines on two separate occasions and limped into Wilhelmshaven for repair. The *Gneisenau* had also hit a mine but was less seriously damaged and reached the intended destination, the Elbe, in company with the *Prinz Eugen*. These mines had been laid in the previous few days by the Hampdens and Manchesters of 5 Group, so perhaps 61, 83 and 207 Squadrons did make a significant contribution after all. Indeed, before February was over Bomber Command did draw a line under the activities of one of the German capital ships – the *Gneisenau* had limped on to Kiel and a floating dock for repair of the damage caused by the mine explosion.

A fateful photograph of R5779 OL-G of 83 Squadron at Scampton on 7 March 1942. The aircraft failed to return from Essen the next night. Left to right: Sergeants Rex, Broad, Dalby, Flying Officer Cooper, Sergeants Cross, Key and Mowatt. (G. Rex)

As if the continuing Manchester serviceability problems needed any further emphasis, as February 1942 progressed 83 Squadron, along with the others, continued its attempt to maintain a high level of readiness. A series of remarkable failures impeded their efforts. After their Manchester conversion was severely impeded by repeated heavy snow throughout January, the ORB reports a range of failures on operations. Several aircraft encountered hydraulic failures during February. Aircraft also reported autopilot and Directional Gyro failures – one records:

Leaflets could not be dropped as photo flash jammed in flare chute; two 500-lb GP hung up for unknown reasons. In R5779: radio aerial post broke-off in the course of evading two night fighters; returned due to excessive fuel consumption. L7427 and R5833 two 1000-lb GP jettisoned live at German coast due to inability to climb, returned with bad oil leak, oil cooler burst en route for daylight mining off Terschelling.

Sergeant John Bushby records:

Each day after the Scharnhorst and Gneisenau 'flap', operations were called, but cancelled due to the weather. We still carried out night flying tests prior to each cancellation. Our Manchesters were a mixture of Mk.1s and Mk.1As. On landing after one of these NFTs in a Mk.1, I was first out of the aircraft, glancing as I did so towards my turret in order to check that I had left my guns in the approved manner in the fully depressed position. In doing so, I was shocked to see that the entire fabric covering from the centre fin had been stripped away, leaving only the duralumin skeleton. Our Captain had not commented on any change to the stability of the aircraft. Next day, whilst many air and ground crew were about their various tasks out on the aerodrome and with various Manchesters making leisurely circuits and bumps, one aircraft suddenly shed its entire port fin and rudder. Nevertheless it completed its circuit, landing safely but somewhat asymmetrically and evidently with both pilots holding on full rudder and juggling with throttles to maintain direction.

The very next day Warrant Officer Whitehead and crew had yet another unnerving experience when, on landing normally from another NFT, they taxied to their dispersal, swung the aircraft onto its circular concrete pad, and shut down the engines. As the port propeller flicked over its last dying revolutions a strange and ominous metallic tinkling from the propeller spinner reached their ears. Investigation revealed that, just as the engines had been cut, a complete seizure of the propeller reduction gear had occurred with the retaining bolts shearing neatly off and making a metallic ringing sound inside the propeller spinner. The most succinct summary from these incidents emerged from the 'B' Flight Engineer, 'Chiefy' Whittaker, confronted with this latest failure who expressed himself emphatically: 'F…ing Manchesters!' Had this failure happened five minutes earlier whilst they were airborne in the circuit, their chances of escaping with their lives would have been negligible. All in all, after barely two months experience with their Manchesters, to say that 83 Squadron had 'begun to lose confidence' was something of an understatement.

Still not a month into his operational career in Manchesters, Sergeant John Bushby endured a further traumatic experience in late February. On 21/22 February another German naval flotilla including the *Prinz Eugen* made a foray up the Norwegian coast. The British submarine HMS *Trident* had managed to put a torpedo into *Prinz Eugen* and she diverted to a fjord near Trondheim for shelter. A hasty plan was drawn up for a Swordfish strike from HMS *Victorious*. On grounds of the close proximity to Luftwaffe day fighter airfields, Bomber Command was called up hastily to make a diversionary and unescorted daylight strike on four airfields and six Halifaxes, five Manchesters and four Stirlings were hurriedly assembled. 83 Squadron was allocated Sola aerodrome at the extreme of the Manchester's range. In the event, neither the Swordfish strike nor the diversions were successful. Such was the perilous nature of our military situation that these aircraft, the unreliable Manchesters in particular, were still considered fair game for unescorted daylight intruder work. John Bushby takes up the story:

After the fourth consecutive 'scrub' in as many days, a number of us had descended on Lincoln, it being a happy coincidence of cancelled operations and pay night. Each to his own inclinations, and for me it was a corner of the lounge bar in The Crown, relatively uncrowded at that early hour of the evening. The beer was good, a cheerful fire blazed in the hearth, and in half an hour my 'date' was due to appear. I had hardly taken a second swallow when the door opened and a Military Police corporal, red-cap and all, burst in. All chatter was instantly silenced. From a paper in this hand he shouted out: 'Any of the following aircrew here?' He began calling names all from 83 Squadron, mine amongst them. I stood up. 'What's up, Corp'?' 'Report back to your station immediately'. 'Here we go again' thought Bushby. 'What's on?' 'No idea, look lively. Know where any of these others are'? I suggested one or two other places, including the little music hall across the road. 'OK. Transport's outside'. A three-tonner was there with its engine running. Half a dozen other aircrew sergeants were in the back as I clambered in over the tailboard.

At Scampton we hastened to the crew room. The round-up must have gone well for the crew room was more than half full as, breathless and wondering, we arrived. 'Mary' Tudor was pacing up and down at the end of the room. He looked exasperated. 'Right, chaps. This is a big one. Believe it or not, but those bloody ships are out again!' It was the Scharnhorst and the Gneisenau again! A Coastal Command reconnaissance aircraft had reported them off Stavanger (in fact Prinz Eugen - see above – author). Tudor quickly outlined the plan. 'The Navy are going in with everything they can scrape up. The reported position is close inshore so there'll be lots of fighter cover. That's our job. We prang the airfield at Stavanger to stop the Bf109s taking off at dawn. Give the Swordfish boys a chance'. He quickly added details of weather and the route. The navigators did quick mental arithmetic and voiced their apprehensions. 'I know. It's a hell of a long way, but watch your cruise consumption and you'll make it. I've insisted on one thing with Group though, and this is important. If you calculate you will not reach Stavanger before first light, you are not, and I repeat not, to carry on. In no circumstances is any damned idiot to try and attack a fighter airfield in broad daylight and without cloud cover. Got that?' It was a sensible decision. At extreme range, with an aircraft of inadequate performance, and a front-line Luftwaffe base swarming with fighters, it would have been needlessly throwing away lives and aircraft to have decided otherwise.

'One more thing, chaps. This is to be a scratch crew effort. We've had to make up crews as they've checked in and you're all mixed up. Some crews are already away. Just sort yourselves out into crews and as soon as you're ready get down to the flights and pick yourselves an aircraft. It's that kind of a shambles, I'm afraid'. Immediately the room was alive with chatter and milling aircrew. Squadron Leader Rainford from 'A' Flight was by the door. 'One more gunner! Come on! Shake a leg!' I reached him at the same moment as Sergeant 'Rocky' Taylor, who had originally crewed up with Dick, Geordie and the rest of us at OTU. Since then, through some administrative quirk, he had not flown with us or any other crew, and was champing at the bit to get onto operations. He grabbed my arm. 'Give us a break, mate. You've got some in already. I'll go'. I hesitated. Rainford broke in: 'Make your minds up! I don't care which of you it is'. 'Toss your for it' I said, on a sudden impulse. 'OK. Heads it is'. I spun the coin and it came down heads. Rocky grinned. 'That'll teach you not to gamble', he cheerily called over his shoulder as he ran off for his parachute and flying helmet. I had already found out that Whitey and Dick, not having left camp, had taken off half an hour earlier with a cobbled-together crew (if so, not in unit ORB - author). Squadron Leader Rainford and crew in L7522 OL-N with a load of six 1,000-lb GP bombs took off at 03.48 hours. All crews bar this one returned in full daylight. Dawn had broken whilst they were still an hour from Stavanger and they were on the limit of their remaining fuel. It seemed that Squadron Leader Rainford had ignored orders and pressed on, his aircraft being shot down by Bf109s. The crew, including young Rocky Taylor on his first and last operation, were initially buried on the edge of Sola airfield. However, but for reaching Squadron Leader's Rainford's side simultaneously and the fateful toss of a coin, it would have been me. I kept that penny for years afterwards

On the night of 26/27 February, only two weeks after Operation Cerberus/FULLER, the final scene in the year-long battle between Bomber Command and the *Scharnhorst, Gneisenau* and *Prinz Eugen* was played out, though now over the German home ports. In an operation to Kiel in which Manchesters, for once, didn't take part, 49 bombers attacked the floating dock now holding the mine-damaged *Gneisenau*. Once more immobilised, though relatively slightly damaged, and in view of the small time the vessel would be unavoidably out of action, senior German naval supervisors had made the risky value judgement to leave the entire ships company on board, along with leaving untouched ammunition in one or more 11 inch main gun turret magazines sited just below the armoured deck. Removing to safe storage, followed by restocking, would otherwise have added significantly to the time when the vessel was out of action. This turned out to be a fateful decision. In clear weather a single armour piercing bomb scored a direct hit just ahead of "Anton" turret, penetrated down into its magazine and detonated. The enormous explosion lifted the heavy turret off its bearings, devastating the entire forward section of the ship, killing 112 of the crew as well as causing other extensive damage. The unlucky vessel was decommissioned, her guns being redeployed in bunkers for coastal defence work, whilst the hulk itself was towed to Gdynia but never repaired.

In an extreme though by no means exceptional sign of the time, the same night several aircraft got so far off their intended course that their bombs fell on several settlements in the Baltic islands and on the Danish mainland. At Odense one civilian was killed and seven more injured, whereas at Vijle three died and six more were injured. Vejle lies 100 miles north of Kiel!

Scharnhorst, too, never again became a Bomber Command target. Repaired following the two submerged mine explosions en route to her home ports, in October 1942 she was sent north to 'protect the Norwegian coast'. In an attack on an allied convoy off the North Cape on 26 December she was hunted down and mercilessly destroyed by British naval forces. This was to be looked back on in German circles as another operation of questionable military wisdom.

The Admiralty had pressed Bomber Command to an extreme degree to subject the vessels at Brest to increasing air attack. Whatever the difficulty, finding and attacking these vessels in harbour was infinitely more desirable compared to when they were rampaging at full speed in the open sea. Over the year February 1941 to February 1942 Bomber Command contributed 3,299 sorties against the port. Of these, the Manchester force undertook 212 sorties, losing six of their number. These targets frequently seemed impossible and certainly frustrating to bomber crews. German perceptions provide a contrasted view. During their year in Brest, *Gneisenau* had been damaged by an aerial torpedo, an air-sewn mine and five bombs and *Scharnhorst* was damaged by five bombs on its brief excursion to La Pallice, as well as later by two air-sewn mines. Officers from both vessels were allegedly killed when the Continental Hotel in Brest was hit. *Admiral Hipper* and *Prinz Eugen* also suffered bomb hits resulting in severe damage and all were rarely available for offensive use. The Commander-in-Chief of the Kriegsmarine, Grossadmiral Raeder, stated in interviews after the war: 'Unfortunately it turned out that the possibilities of defending Brest against Allied air attacks did not meet the requirement, to the extent that the ships were damaged repeatedly and extensive repairs became necessary'. The ambition of a forward operating base directly on the Atlantic coast was never achieved.

Manchesters contributed night and daylight bombing and night and daylight mine laying to this long drawn out campaign, though other types contributed a numerically greater effort. This was the bludgeon rather than the rapier and was accompanied by wasteful and undesirable collateral damage. Nevertheless, the first damage in February 1941 was inflicted three years and nine months before Lancasters, aided by SABS, and carrying Tallboy bombs in daylight, could destroy the *Tirpitz* at her moorings in Tromso Fjord. As pointed out, British frustration was not entirely matched by German experience. Similarly, it needs emphasis that this success coincided in time with Bomber Command's lowest ebb in early August 1941, as laid out in the Butt Report.

A further irony for Britain and its armed forces was that through ULTRA intercepts we knew of the mine damage, disabling and decommissioning of *Gneisenau*, but were quite unable to defend ourselves against a barrage of criticism. Perhaps just a few 'in the know' allowed themselves a wry smile? We do know who to credit with the air-launched torpedo hit on *Gneisenau*, but it can't ever be know whether, throughout the year, the Manchester force was responsible for any of the bomb hits for damage due to air-sewn mines on *Scharnhorst* or *Gneisenau*. From recent German sources, this is an early Bomber Command success not previously sufficiently highlighted.

Chapter Seven: New Tactics, New Owners

Up to the end of February 1942 the greatest number of Manchesters dispatched on an operation on a single night was nineteen. The reader would be excused for drawing the conclusion, based on the groundings and delays of May to August 1941, that the Manchester had already been eclipsed, numerically at least, by the contemporary Handley Page Halifaxes and Short Stirlings. However, daily Bomber Command returns indicate that until late February 1942 the average number of serviceable Manchesters never exceeded thirty-one, whilst of Stirlings and Halifaxes there were never more than twenty-one and twenty-three respectively! Throughout much of 1941 and early 1942 the Manchester was, thus, the major heavy type in service. Cast in the light of these statistics it is easier to appreciate why Bomber Command strove so determinedly to persist with such an obviously unsuitable aircraft. Stirlings and Halifaxes also had their share of production delays and serviceability problems. A mark of the rapid expansion of heavy bomber units is evident, though greatly exaggerated, by the landmark first '1,000 Bomber' raid on Cologne exactly three months later, when eight-eight Stirlings, 131 Halifaxes, and seventy-three Lancasters participated in addition to forty-five Manchesters.

The end of February 1942 had marked another sharp change in Bomber Command priorities and is reflected in the deployment of its Manchester forces. Air Chief Marshal Sir Arthur Harris had become commander-in-chief on 22 February. He held strong views on the employment of bomber aircraft and inherited a force poised on the brink of grasping a range of new aids and techniques. Concentration in space and time, use of incendiaries, application of target finding devices and marking techniques, all were in the offing.

For the Manchester, too, it was a period of change. Lancaster production was accelerating rapidly and 5 Group squadrons would finally acquire an aircraft capable of making a significant contribution to the war effort. After almost eighteen months of service, twelve of them operational, 207 Squadron would rejoice in passing the torch to other units. A short burst of activity in early March was all that remained to it. In turn 106, 50 and 49 Squadrons respectively were to re-equip with Manchesters for only a two-month period. By mid-April, 61 and 83 Squadrons passed their Manchesters on to their Conversion Flights and these would only re-appear fleetingly during operations in the all-risks, maximum effort, 1,000 bomber raids of late May and June.

Despite their rapidly approaching obsolescence, Manchester availability did not tail away. Indeed, more aircraft were serviceable in March and April than at any previous time. For a very short time in early April, four squadrons were operational at once. For the first time units would regularly dispatch strengths of eight, nine and ten Manchesters on a single operation. Previous policy and availability had prevented this. The objective of the new tactics was to greatly enhance the effectiveness and striking power of the bomber force and one corollary – of bunching the aircraft into a tightly packed stream – was to locally overwhelm defences and reduce losses. It is possibly surprising and a reflection of enhanced German defensive capability that Manchester losses increased sharply over this period. Roy Chadwick's 1940 prophecy was to be written in blood by the tragic losses in the final three months of operations.

Billancourt – 2/3 March 1942:

Serial	Code	Squadron	Captain
L7519	QR-*	61	Sqn Ldr A. M. Paape
L7473	QR-*	61	Flt Lt I. G. A. McNaughton
L7518	QR-*	61	FS J. B. Underwood
L7480	QR-*	61	Plt Off. R. E. S. Smith
R5832	QR-*	61	Fg Off. L. Gunter
L7521	QR-*	61	Fg Off. S. J. Beard
L7516	QR-*	61	Flt Lt R. A. V. Gascoyne-Cecil
L7497	QR-*	61	FS E. W. Noble
L7464	QR-*	61	Plt Off. G. L. Tofield
R5831	OL-I	83	Fg Off. H. G. Hazelden
L7427	OL-*	83	Plt Off. R. G. W. Oakley
R5838	OL-*	83	Fg Off. M. A. Smith
R5775	OL-*	83	Flt Lt K. Cook
L7453	OL-*	83	Plt Off. R. McFarlane
L7423	OL-*	83	Sqn Ldr D. A. McClure

R5837	OL-*	83	Plt Off. J. H. Mophett
R5780	OL-*	83	Plt Off. P. A. Mackenzie
L7426	OL-*	83	Plt Off. C. R. Frost
L7387	OL-*	83	Plt Off. R. W. Cooper
L7455	EM-G	207	Fg Off. L. F. Kneil DFM
R5782	EM-R	207	Flt Lt P. Ward-Hunt
L7319	EM-X	207	FS G. H. Coles
L7486	EM-B	207	Sqn Ldr T. C. Murray
L7491	EM-O	207	Flt Lt W. D. B. Ruth
L7378	EM-A	207	Fg Off. J. H. Leland
L7488	EM-Q	207	FS J. C. Atkinson

* Individual aircraft letter unknown

On the night of 2/3 March Bomber Command planned an experimental maximum effort to take out a precision target. Command required a significant target in good weather where only modest defences could be expected and chose the Renault factory at Billancourt near Paris. Renault were producing 18,000 lorries a year for the German Army. The briefing called for the attack to be made in three waves, with 235 aircraft to cross the target area in only 1 hour 50 min. The first wave was to be made up of the most experienced crews who, by using massed flares and incendiaries, would light and mark the way for following aircraft. To further ensure concentration on the factory area, aircraft were to go in at very low level. The objective was not only to ensure maximum damage but to avoid hitting French civilians in the adjacent suburbs. The three Manchester squadrons raised a total of twenty-six aircraft, the largest number since the aircraft began operating. 61 Squadron contributed nine, 83 Squadron ten and 207 Squadron seven.

Soon after take-off, 'Jimmy' Kneil in L7455 of 207 Squadron encountered engine trouble and returned. The remaining twenty-five pressed home their attacks. Flight Lieutenant Ward-Hunt and Flight Sergeant Coles of 207 Squadron located the target by the bright moonlight and flares and attacked in the first wave around 20.30 hours, Coles from a mere 1,600 feet. 83 Squadron provided seven aircraft for the first wave, all carrying 1,000-lb general purpose (GP) bombs. Pilot Officer Mackenzie went in at 1,000 feet to make sure his bombs hit the works, his aircraft being shaken by the blast waves of his own bombs and Pilot Officer Morphett and Squadron Leader McClure came down to 2,000 feet to release their bombs. The coloured Target Indicator (TI) bombs used later were not available at this time and these two crews circled after bombing to release the flares intended to mark the target for subsequent waves. Both Pilot Officers Frost and Cooper claimed to have hit and exploded a gasometer.

The remaining four 207 Squadron Manchesters attacked in the second wave around 22.00 hours. By this time the target was ablaze from end to end and readily identifiable. All four Manchesters carried a 4,000-lb 'Cookie' plus four 500-lb GP bombs and attacked at heights ranging from 3,000 to 5,000 feet. Squadron Leader Murray reported that his bomb load detonated in the motor vehicle park. On his bomb run a Vickers Wellington following immediately behind and only 100 feet above hit the same spot at the same time.

The remaining three Manchesters from 83 Squadron also attacked in the second wave. Crews reported flares visible at the target when

F/L Peter Ward-Hunt DFC flew ten Manchester ops with 207 Squadron, and a further one with 49 Squadron. He survived the war.

they were still crossing the Channel and that the target was already a mass of flames. Their 4,000-lb 'Cookies' demanded a higher safe bombing height, but they came in at 5,000 to 6,000 feet.

The nine 61 Squadron crews joined in the third wave. These aircraft reached the target up to thirty-five minutes early and had to orbit until their allotted time. Squadron Leader Paape saw his bombs shatter several buildings in the works and red hot metal flew up to 4,000 feet. Flight Sergeant Noble reported bricks and rooftops flying up to 1,500 feet into the air under the onslaught of their 4,000- lb 'Cookies' and the factory area seemed ablaze from end to end. Whilst the two earlier waves had encountered little opposition, and this from searchlights and the few flak guns, German night fighters began to arrive as this third wave withdrew. Pilot Officer Smith in L7480 was approached by a Junkers JU88, which did not attack. Both Paape and Pilot Officer Tofield observed Messerschmitt Bf110s searching the sky, but neither were attacked and Tofield also passed a single-engined night fighter head on but evaded it. Flight Lieutenant Gascoyne-Cecil's aircraft, L7516, was intercepted and attacked near Paris by an unidentified twin-engined fighter. The rear gunner, Flight Sergeant Say, replied as the fighter closed in and it turned away at close range and disappeared. There were no casualties amongst the Manchesters and on return all the crews who had reached the target were able to give graphic accounts of the point-blank attack on the virtually undefended objective.

The Billancourt factory records confirmed what crews and photoreconnaissance had suggested, namely that the new tactics were enormously successful. A total of 300 bombs fell on the factory, destroying 40% of the buildings. Of the estimated output, direct destruction or loss of production resulted in a loss of at least 2,300 lorries. Unfortunately the toll of French civilian casualties was grievously high and more than double that occasioned in one night on a German target up till that time – 367 civilians were killed and 341 injured. A major contributory factor to this high casualty figure was that the population had received false air raid alerts on countless previous occasions and had consequently failed to take shelter when a real need arose.

The raid broke many of Bomber Command's records. The 235-strong force was the largest number of aircraft sent to a single target, the concentration of aircraft over the target, at 121 aircraft per hour, was the highest yet achieved and a record tonnage of bombs was dropped. The raid consequently represented a major milestone for Bomber Command and a marked contrast with its efforts over Kiel only a week earlier, when sixty-eight aircraft were so far wide of the mark that city authorities recorded engine noises only in their diary of events.

The Air Staff had been evaluating techniques for some months and a series of recent directives greeted Harris on his appointment. Notwithstanding Billancourt, Harris was instructed 'the primary object of your operations should now be focused on the morale of the enemy civilian population and, in particular, of the industrial workers'. To renew this assault the radio navigation aid GEE was released for use on 14 February. It had a projected lifespan of six months and was to be employed in conjunction with 'concentrated incendiary attacks'. A cardinal principle in the use of GEE was to be 'concentration on one target until its destruction has been achieved'. The initial attack was to be on Essen – 'the supreme target'. Harris did not dissent. During March and April eight large scale raids on Essen were to be dispatched. On grounds that the strategic air weapon was not yet fully honed, the results were a great disappointment.

The offensive against the Ruhr, with Essen as the focus, began on 8/9 March 1942. To gain the maximum benefit from GEE, Harris had been directed not to take on the enemy and the weather at the same time. For these attacks the SHAKER technique had been developed. For this the bomber force was divided in three groups – first the target illuminators, next the target markers and close- spaced behind, the followers. The Pathfinder force was presaged in this approach, which in all its essential elements mimicked German techniques of eighteen months earlier on Coventry and elsewhere.

The twenty GEE-equipped illuminators would arrive in five waves at three minute intervals. Each illuminator would carry twelve bundles of triple flares and was to run along the up-wind side of the target, releasing flares at ten-second intervals. Thus it was intended to sky mark the target for twelve minutes with lanes of flares six miles long to assist visual bombing by the target markers. The target markers, also carrying GEE, would release the maximum load of incendiaries to create an unmistakable concentrated area of fire for the high explosive-carrying and non-GEE equipped followers. It required careful timing and discipline from crews in respect of courses, approach direction and belief in their new equipment. Initially this was not to prove evident.

The forthcoming three consecutive nights were to prove an unsatisfactory finale to 207 Squadron's long involvement with the Manchester. 61 and 83 Squadrons also contributed. On 8/9 March 1942 Bomber Command dispatched 211 aircraft to Essen, eight-two of them equipped with GEE. The designated aiming point was the Krupps works. The total Manchester force was twenty-five, of which three were sent mining off Lorient and the remainder joined the followers carrying loads, largely of high explosive. Clearly the Manchesters could not have been GEE-equipped.

Essen – 8/9 March 1942:

Serial	Code	Squadron	Captain
L7518	QR-	61	Sqn Ldr A. M. Paape
L7458	QR-	61	Flt Lt R. A. V. Gascoyne-Cecil
L7521	QR-	61	Fg Off. S. J. Beard
L7471	QR-	61	Fg Off. L. Gunter
L7497	QR-	61	Fg Off. R. E. Archibald
L7464	QR-	61	Plt Off. G. L. Tofield
L7519	QR-	61	Plt Off. A. L. Searby
L7473	QR-	61	Plt Off. R. E. S. Smith
R5786	QR-	61	Plt Off. R. E. Clarke*
L7475	QR-	61	Sgt C. G. Furby*
R5831	OL-	83	Sqn Ldr D. A. McClure
R5838	OL-	83	Fg Off. M. A. Smith
L7465	OL-	83	Plt Off. P. A. Mackenzie
L7387	OL-	83	Fg Off. H. G. Hazeldene
L7423	OL-	83	Plt Off. J. H. Morphett
L7453	OL-	83	Flt Lt D. A. J. Mackie
L7427	OL-	83	Plt Off. R. G. W. Oakley
R5830	OL-	83	WO H. H. Whitehead
L7426	OL-	83	Plt Off. C. R. Frost
R5779	OL-G	83	Fg Off. R. W. Cooper
L7378	EM-A	207	Sqn Ldr T. C. Murray
L7491	EM-O	207	Flt Lt W. D. B. Ruth
L7455	EM-G	207	Flt Lt P. C. Birch
L7484	EM-P	207	FS G. H. Hathersich
L7391	EM-Y	207	Plt Off. F. A. Roper*

* Sent on mining sortie to Lorient

On this night Flight Lieutenant Peter Birch in L7455 EM-G was carrying the redoubtable Group Captain 'Ferdie' Swain OBE AFC, the officer commanding Bottesford, as an eighth crew member. Regrettably it was this crew which had the misfortune to experience troubles with the starboard Vulture, exhaust manifold, autopilot etc. which necessitated an early return from the region of the Dutch coast. The emergency air bottle had also to be used to lower the undercarriage at base.

For two 83 Squadron crews, those of Pilot Officer Chris Frost DFM and Flying Officer Bob Cooper, it was to be their last briefing of the war. They felt the same grim tightening of the stomach when the target for the night, Essen, was announced. Frost was into his second tour and was allocated L7426. Cooper, about to fly his twenty-second Op, was allocated in turn R5779 OL-G. Bob Cooper was twenty-four years old, whereas his second pilot, Sergeant Mowat, was still only eighteen, having lied about his age to join up. Sergeant Cross was the observer, Sergeant George Dalby the wireless operator/air gunner, Sergeant George Rex the second wireless op/air gunner (whose turn it was to fly in the front turret that night), Sergeant Alfred Key the mid-upper gunner and Sergeant Charles Broad the rear gunner.

It was about 01.15 hours when Cooper finally took off on a bright moonlight night with good visibility. When the German defences were alerted to the forthcoming raid, amongst the night fighters scrambled to meet the threat were Bf110s of II/NJG2 at Leeuwarden. Patrolling the coastline searching for incoming bombers was the night fighter ace, Oberleutnant Ludwig Becker. He soon latched onto a bomber, identifying it as a Manchester, and swiftly brought it down to earth in flames. It was Chris Frost in L7426. The blazing wreck plummeted down two miles north-east of Enkhuizen onto the ice-covered Ijsselmeer, which at the time was 80 cm thick. The entire crew were killed outright. The attack has been timed at 00.32 hours, but this seems doubtful.

Following behind and some thirty miles to the north-east was Bob Cooper in R5779. Some prolonged discussion had arisen between the captain and observer when they were unable to pick up any pinpoint on crossing the enemy coast. Eventually they identified a landmark showing them off track to the north. Unbeknown to them the 'FREYA' ground radar was already tracking them and Oberfeldwebel Paul Gildner was in the final moments of a classic night fighter stalk in the dark sky beneath their tail. Now Gildner was formating beneath the big black silhouette of the Manchester. Suddenly, when he judged the moment right, Gildner pulled back on the stick, raising the nose and raking the underside of R5779 with his nose guns as the Manchester flew through his sights. The first inkling the seven man crew had was when tracer lanced up through the airframe from stem to stern with a shattering series of explosions. A confusion of voices rang out on the intercom: 'We've been hit!, We're on fire!', then the strangely detached voice of eighteen-year-old Mowat reporting incredulously that the rear section of the aircraft was on fire.

Cooper was the first to take practical steps to try and save them. He ordered Cross to put the bombs on safe and jettison them. The bomb doors were opened and a few moments later Cross confirmed: 'Bombs away safe'. Whilst Cross was busy down in the nose, Cooper did his best to keep R5779 straight and level, and Rex searched vainly for their assailant. In any case, with Cross blocking the nose compartment he wasn't going anywhere. As soon as Cross turned to recover his seat in the cockpit, Rex climbed out of the front turret with a view to helping fight the fire. He was about to climb up into the cockpit when a second attack, more devastating than the first, enveloped the aircraft. Rex could feel hits nearby in the bomb bay.

As Rex continued to climb he found his head suddenly jerked violently to one side and he fell back into the floor of the nose compartment. In his haste he had forgotten to detach his intercom lead. On his knees he raised his head and saw that the space beneath the cockpit floor was a raging inferno, fanned to a blow torch by jets of air entering through the many shrapnel tears. The floor of the cockpit was already curling like paper. The hydraulic fluid had possibly sprayed from the piping and caught fire. Suddenly the fire flashed over and enveloped the entire cockpit and nose compartment. Engulfed by fire, Bob Cooper just had time to shout his last order: 'Oh hell! Bale out! Bale out!' Rex moved swiftly to obey, yanking out the intercom lead, buckling on his parachute, jettisoning the hatch and diving after it to escape the raging inferno. The transition from noise and fire to cold and silence was such a relief that Rex allowed himself to free fall 2,000 to 3,000 feet before pulling the ripcord. Thanks to his leather flying suit and helmet his burns were confined to his eyebrows and hands. He landed at 02.20 hours in a clump of young fir trees west of Smilde.

After the second onslaught, Sergeant Alf Key in the rear of the aircraft had decided to leave his turret and try to aid Sergeant Broad, the rear gunner. As he dropped to the floor he found that Gildner's cannon fire had blasted away sections of the flaming lower fuselage, through which Key inadvertently tumbled into the night sky. His rapid departure, coupled with the fact that he was already wearing his parachute, saved him from the conflagration and he was able to pull the ripcord and descend. They were the only crew members to survive. Witnesses on the ground watched horrified as 'G-George', burning fiercely, came spinning and sideslipping down on them to crash in a field in the small hamlet of Oranji in the district of Smilde. Key injured his foot and was soon captured. Although Rex attempted to escape and had some help from local residents he, too, was eventually captured.

The rest of the force went on to Essen, but within a few miles of the enemy coast 83 Squadron had already lost twelve men that night. Also from 83 Squadron, Pilot Officer Morphett had to release two of his six 1,000-lb bombs into the sea when L7423 steadfastly refused to climb. He pressed on to the target although the aircraft still only reached 9,500 feet.

All three of the 207 Squadron Manchesters still airborne ran into heavy and intense flak over the Ruhr and were further inconvenienced by searchlights. Flight Lieutenant Ruth was only able to attack the last resort target. Squadron Leader Murray's aircraft was hit in the tail by flak leaving the target whilst L7484, piloted by Flight Sergeant Hathersich, was seriously damaged by a large calibre flak shell which fortunately passed through the fuselage without exploding. Nevertheless, the shell started a fire amongst the ammunition chutes to the mid-upper turret, rounds in which began popping off. With great presence of mind, Sergeant Everett, the wireless operator, beat the fires out with his hands before they got out of control.

The remaining force from 83 Squadron experienced similar savage searchlight and flak defences. R5831 with Squadron Leader McClure was slightly damaged by flak, whilst only Flying Officer Hazelden believed he had hit the Krupps works themselves. The 61 Squadron crews were unable to identify the intended concentrated mass of burning incendiaries dropped by the target markers and had great difficulty identifying any target. On the return flight Pilot Officer Smith dived to low level where his gunners could range onto ground targets. They particularly concentrated their attention on searchlights, several of which were extinguished.

The surviving 20 Manchesters from the Essen force returned to base. All had experienced the effects of the ferocious flak barrage, but two had been fatally stalked and brought down by the rapidly expanding German night fighter force. The results of the new technique were a great disappointment. GEE showed itself to be a navigation aid but not a blind-bombing aid. Many crews still had difficulty operating the set, and of the twenty illuminators it later transpired that only eleven dropped their flares on the GEE fix.

Out of forty-three identifiable photographs, none showed any recognisable feature of the target area. The aiming point, the Krupp factory, was not hit at all and only a few bombs fell on the southern part of Essen. Only a few houses were destroyed; ten civilians were reported killed and nineteen missing. The Essen authorities classified it as a light raid. The raid was a great disappointment and a major contrast with Billancourt only a few days earlier. In many respects the raids were a rehearsal for the full-blooded Battle of the Ruhr which began almost a year later on 5/6 March 1943. Then, as in March 1942, Bomber Command was to find the Ruhr a very hard nut to crack.

The nights of 9/10 and 10/11 March 1942 were in many respects repetitions of the first assault. Ten and thirteen Manchesters respectively were dispatched and there were no casualties. On 9th/10th two of 207 Squadron's six Manchesters were scrubbed prior to take-off and a third returned with an engine over-heating after jettisoning its bombs near the Dutch coast. Two of the remaining three aircraft were damaged by flak. All six Manchesters of 83 Squadron attacked.

The next night 207 Squadron mustered six aircraft. One failed to take-off and three returned early due to engine troubles and inability to climb. One of the two aircraft which did participate was damaged by flak over Essen. All eight 61 Squadron aircraft dispatched attacked Essen and, with fire in their bellies, two crews, those of Flying Officer Archibald, L7497, and Pilot Officer Smith, L7518, dived to low level for the return flight and engaged themselves in the increasingly popular searchlight suppression activities. Crews felt safer from both heavy flak and night fighters at ground level and could participate in some offensive activity. On this latter night, cloud cover presented target location difficulties, but still sixty-two aircraft from the 126 aircraft force claimed to have attacked Essen.

These claims are at marked variance with actual experiences of the residents of Essen. Only two bombs hit industrial targets – the railway lines near the Krupp factory. There was minimal damage in the town – one house destroyed, five civilians killed and twelve injured. Even in this small group not all casualties were a direct consequence of bombing as one of those killed was a Polish immigrant worker who was hit by a descending unexploded 88-mm flak shell whilst standing outside an air raid shelter! Failures hardly come more total.

With this operation 207 Squadron completed it's almost eighteen months of active service with the Manchester and gladly moved on to Lancasters. Right to the bitter end engine problems had dogged the unit and continually conspired, despite everyone's best efforts, to reduce the effective striking power of the unit.

For ten days in March front line Manchester strength had fallen to two squadrons, but by now a fifth, 106 Squadron, was working up to operations on the type at Coningsby. 106's involvement with the Manchester was to be deployed mainly over the short six week period between 20 March and 10 May, although it did supply Manchesters for each of the 1,000 bomber raids. During that period, 106 Squadron concentrated to a large extent on mining activities, in which sphere it became expert.

Whilst Bomber Command concentrated on the development and refinement of its new techniques, Manchester losses began to increase perceptibly in proportion to the force dispatched. Just how harrowing bomber operations could be for an unlucky crew can be demonstrated from the final three operations of Pilot Officer Hubbard and his crew over just a two week period. How crews could continue to fly and carry out their orders with such fortitude and bravery almost defies comprehension.

On 10/11 March Hubbard and his crew in L7473 joined the bomber force attacking Essen. They flew through heavy flak to bomb the target and soon after turning for home sustained a very near miss from a flak burst just below the bomb bay which jolted the aircraft skywards momentarily and peppered it with splinters. A check of all instruments revealed no sign of damage and they returned safely to England, where an undercarriage check prior to landing produced two reassuring 'greens'. However, unbeknown to them the starboard main wheel was punctured, but in the pitch darkness of 00.45 hours this was not apparent to any of the crew until L7473 touched down when, before any speed was lost, the aircraft fell onto its starboard undercarriage legs, slewed violently to the right and sheared off the undercart. L7473 was severely damaged but did not catch fire. Hubbard and his crew were shaken and unnerved but suffered only minor physical injury.

On the 13th/14th, 61 and 83 Squadrons rostered sixteen Manchesters to attack Cologne and Hubbard was down to fly again, this time in L7395. Once again two of the sixteen-strong force were lost. Outward bound over the North Sea, Hubbard began to experience serious control difficulties and L7395 continually stalled at 150 mph as he attempted to climb. In a desperate attempt to save the aircraft and crew, Hubbard jettisoned the bomb load safe fifty miles offshore and turned for home. Control difficulties eased but immediately after establishing the return course a coolant leak developed in the port engine, which overheated and began smoking badly. Hubbard shut down the engine to prevent it catching alight and feathered the propeller. They flew in over The Wash and located one of the homing beacons, but were unable to contact base. On one engine, unable to locate a safe landing strip and with only marginal control, Hubbard ordered the crew to bale out at 4,000 feet. The pilot himself managed to escape when the aircraft had descended to 2,000 feet, the starboard engine catching fire shortly afterwards. The aircraft crashed in flames near Wittering with all the crew descending safely – Sergeant Tom Stanley landing in a tree.

Sergeant J. P. Dowd, W/op AG to Pilot Officer Bromiley of 83 Squadron, shot down 13/14 March 1942 and became an Evader. (Author's collection)

The second Manchester lost that night was L7423 OL-S from 83 Squadron, flown by Pilot Officer Bromiley, which had taken off from Scampton at 20.30 hours. Regretably this and the records of other Manchesters lost by 83 Squadron are omitted from its ORB. Two crew members escaped by parachute, the captain and wireless operator Flight Sergeant James Dowd, but neither could be located in the course of research for this book. Pilot Officer Bromiley, who, unusually, may have escaped from the top escape hatch in the cockpit, was captured and made a POW. Although also initially captured, Sergeant Dowd became a thorn in the German's flesh, a persistent escaper, and ultimately an evader. His MI9 interrogation report made soon after getting back to the UK, plus recent Luftwaffe night fighter/Bomber Command combat tie-ups give limited information. Similarly, his escapades in occupied Europe are set out in the dedicated chapter *'The Women Who Took a Hand'* in the 1952 book *Escape or Die* by Paul Brickhill (see Appendix One). Dowd was an exceptionally tough Glaswegian who had joined the RAF in 1939. Having trained as a wireless operator/air gunner, he completed his first tour on Hampdens with 83 Squadron. Returning to the unit after a rest, he was shot down on the first trip of his second tour. In his Escape Account, dated 26 to 28 September 1943, MI9 was mainly concerned with his evasion tactics with the result that his description of this final sortie is very perfunctory. He says: 'On the way in to the target we were attacked at 22.40 hours over the Dutch-German frontier by a JU88 and were ordered to bale out. In fact it has now been established that the Bf110 of Oberleutnant Reinhold Knacke of 2/NJG1 based at Venlo shot down their aircraft. It crashed 1.5 km north-west of Brockhuizen near Nijmegen in Holland. Flight Sergeant Dowd may well have been blown eastwards as he descended in his parachute. On landing, mistakenly thinking he was in Holland, he found a house and knocked on the door. Unfortunately he was in Germany!

Amongst sixteen aircraft from 61 and 83 Squadrons on this Cologne raid on 13/14 March the usual range of Manchester problems occurred. To gain height Pilot Officer McFarlane of 83 Squadron jettisoned two 1000-lb GP bombs live along the coast between Ostend and Dunkirk, whilst Sergeant Markides jettisoned his bomb load safe over the North Sea following a power failure. From the 61 Squadron force the Manchesters of Pilot Officers 'Pranger' Tofield, Searby and Smith all returned early with serviceability problems. Only two aircraft from 61 Squadron and five from 83 Squadron made successful attacks, only ten out of the sixteen dispatched. Middlebrook and Everitt record this as the first successful raid aided by GEE navigation. On a moonless night leading crews illuminated the target with flares and incendiaries and succeeding aircraft made an attack five times more accurate than average recent raids on the city. Much industrial damage and disruption was caused, with more than 1,500 houses damaged or destroyed and sixty-two citizens killed. Forty-six of the dead were attributed to collapse of apartment blocks due to explosion of 4,000-lb 'Cookies'. According to this record the Manchester of Pilot Officer

Bromiley was the sole casualty. Five crew members from L7423 lost their lives, whilst Pilot Officer Hubbard and crew had endured a second consecutive dreadful experience.

The night of 25/26 March 1942 was an integral part of the most tragic 24 hours in the entire lifespan of the Manchester, with five aircraft written off and many crew members killed. At this time the sixth squadron, 50, was taking delivery of Manchesters at Skellingthorpe at the start of its re-equipment programme. Mk.1A L7486 was a newly arrived aircraft recently taken over from 207 Squadron and became the first casualty. In the evening of 25 March Sergeant Atkinson and his crew were engaged in circuits and landings to familiarise themselves with the type. At 19.15 hours, on one of his first approaches, Atkinson held off, ballooned once and stalled the aircraft onto the runway on one wheel from 20 feet, collapsing the undercarriage. The aircraft caught fire, but the crew managed to escape with minor injuries. The local fire-fighting facilities were inadequate to prevent the aircraft burning out.

The three operational squadrons, 61, 83 and 106, were briefed to follow up operations to Essen that night, with an additional Manchester from 106 Squadron delegated to 'GARDENING'. 61 Squadron produced the major contribution of ten aircraft, 83 Squadron produced five, whilst 106 Squadron sent four bombers and the 'GARDENER'. The raid was part of Bomber Command's developing experiments with target location and marking. Bomber Command dispatched 254 aircraft – Wellingtons, Stirlings, Hampdens, twenty Manchesters and seven Lancasters – the force taking off soon after 20.00 hours. On crossing the enemy coast inbound, the crew of Warrant Officer Whitehead's 83 Squadron Manchester could clearly distinguish sky marking flares over a target ahead, but these had burnt out by the time they arrived. Despite the flak defences being relatively subdued, night fighters were apparently active and engagements were reported by several aircraft.

At 22.28 hours Flight Lieutenant Dunlop-Mackenzie in L7390 of 106 Squadron was intercepted by Oberleutnant Ludwig Becker of 6/II/NJG2 at Leeuwarden, shot down and crashed on the ice of the ljsselmeer near Kornwerderzand in Holland. Dunlop-Mackenzie was on his first operation in a Manchester. Sergeant Markides, in Manchester L7465 OL-H of 83 Squadron, was shot down at 23.44 hours. The aircraft crashed at Lichtaert in Belgium with the loss of the entire crew. It is likely they were victims of Leutnant Kurt Loos of 2/NJG1.

Air and ground crew of 83 Squadron at Scampton in front of OL-B, including Pilot Officer J. Rowe (fourth from left). (via Chaz Bowyer)

)fficer J. Rowe (left) and Flight Sergeant K. Cook DFC (right) of 83 Squadron in front of one of t} 1esters at Scampton. (via Chaz Bowyer

From 106 Squadron the 'GARDENING' Manchester returned to base when the front and rear turrets both developed hydraulic leaks. It was a typical Manchester operation in many respects, with Pilot Officer Lumb of 83 Squadron having to release a 1,000-lb bomb over the North Sea to ensure a safe inbound crossing of the enemy coast. Warrant Officer Whitehead followed another aircraft into the target area, which released a load of incendiaries and flares. He backed up and bombed onto these, but his navigator doubted they had fallen on the primary target. As usual, the Ruhr was hazy, which made target location problematical and most aircraft chose to bomb on the flares. Anti-aircraft opposition was not heavy on this occasion but Warrant Officer Merralls' 106 Squadron Manchester was damaged by flak.

Several 61 Squadron crews found the flares useful in locating the target and employed their customary gliding or diving attacks. On the return journey Flying Officer Gilpin dived to 4,000 feet near the Ijsselmeer to fire at four troublesome searchlights. One light was dowsed and in reply the attack attracted light tracer which failed to find the swooping Manchester. Squadron Leader McClure of 83 Squadron had already witnessed an aircraft shot down at 52°43'N 04°56'E, from which one parachute was seen to open and then be held in searchlights. Flying Officer Gunter of 61 Squadron observed an aircraft shot down in flames at the Dutch coast on his return flight. This was possibly Dunlop-Mackenzie or, more likely, his fellow squadron member Pilot Officer Hubbard. 61 Squadron lost two Manchesters. In L7497 Sergeant Furby fell with his entire crew at Werterbruch near Bolholt on the Dutch/German border, following attack by Oberleutnant Woltersdorf of 7/NJG1 and, again, there were no survivors. Hubbard's aircraft did have two survivors and from them the story of their ruthless and pitiless destruction has been reconstructed. On this night, John Hubbard was allocated Manchester Mk.1A, L7518 QR-O. In addition to himself, his crew were Pilot Officer Buchan RCAF (second pilot, on his first operation), Pilot Officer Heggie (navigator), Flight Sergeant Clelland (wireless operator), Sergeant Baker (front gunner), Sergeant P. Jones (mid-upper gunner) and Sergeant T. Stanley (rear gunner).

On a bright moonlit evening Hubbard took off early and headed east for the familiar maelstrom of 'Happy Valley'. Despite their recent close shaves, a grim humour supported the well-drilled crew. The Dutch coast slid beneath them and at 21.55 hours they got their first sight of the target, burning, ahead and in the distance. Jones felt the familiar tightening of his stomach as the well practised exchanges between the crew commenced. So far they had traversed the searchlight belt undetected, but as they commenced their bombing run they began to be heavily engaged by flak.

Bob Heggie moved down to the bomb aiming position and after some minutes announced over the intercom that he was 'all set for business'. Hubbard steadied the Manchester as they ran in to the aiming point. Scanning the sky around them Jones took in a Handley Page Hampden to port trapped in a cone of searchlights having the living daylights pasted out of it by the flak gunners. To starboard and below the same thing was happening to a Wellington. In turn, both burst into flames and plunged earthwards. The gunners were knocking seven bells out of L7518 too, but Hubbard's approach was unswerving and so far nothing vital had been hit. The release of tension when the bombs dropped free was almost audible. Someone voiced the feelings of all of them: 'Let's get the hell out of here!' and another: 'Put the nose down Johnny and let's go home'. The bomb doors closed, Hubbard was only too happy to comply.

Flak continued to pound them, but as they eventually drew clear Hubbard gave a reassuring call to keep up crew morale: 'OK lads, we'll make it'. As they continued to weave and corkscrew back towards the Dutch coast both Jones and Stanley became aware of a new threat. Searchlights were pointing up on either side, forming a lighted avenue down which they were forced to fly. As they moved out of range, other lights ahead took over. They took this as a sure signal that night fighter attacks were imminent and immediately redoubled their vigilance. However, there was to be no escape for L7518 that night and their 'charmed life' was approaching a brutal end. Long, tense minutes passed with no sighting of any incoming attack and they had reached as far as the Dutch coastal zone. They began to hope that attention had passed to other home-coming bombers behind.

Suddenly Jones spotted a twin-engined aircraft closing fast and from the lower port quarter. Jones yelled a warning as he traversed his turret and began a disciplined defence, firing off short bursts one after another as the Bf110 bored in. At almost the same instant the fighter opened up, raking them with a devastatingly accurate volley of cannon and machine gun fire. Tracking the Bf110 as it rose up over them, Jones was momentarily distracted by a burst of firing from another source. A hasty glance revealed that Tom Stanley, in turn, had opened up on a second stalking Bf110, his tracer crossing with that of the additional assailant dead astern. They certainly had their hands full.

The first Bf110 broke off above, receiving a parting burst from Jones' twin Brownings, whilst the second dived down beneath, overtaking them. Immediately the guns fell silent, Jones was shocked to smell smoke and traversing his turret saw that the front of the aircraft was on fire. Finding the intercom u/s, both gunners vacated their turrets and one elected to go forward for instructions. Pushing open the armoured doors a scene of utter devastation met his eyes. The inside of the fuselage was a shambles, with holes everywhere. To his left the wireless operator, Flight Sergeant Jock Clelland, was crouched unhurt, conscientiously sending out news of their attack to base. Beyond, the observer was slumped over his table apparently lifeless. Stepping forward the gunner discerned the second pilot sprawled dead in the gangway. The pilot was hanging in his straps, head lolling to one side, seriously wounded but doggedly fighting with his remaining consciousness to hold the stick and maintain some control. Flames were leaping up in places and one long glance was enough to convince the gunner that the aircraft and part of the crew were doomed.

He began his retreat aft from the flames and heat, tapping Jock Clelland urgently on the back as he did so. Clelland nodded and rose to follow him, but suddenly turned on his heel and bent to his set to accomplish some final task. As he did so a further fighter attack developed, unannounced and uncontested from dead ahead. As before, the attack had pinpoint accuracy and devastating effect. Tracer and exploding cannon shells ripped through the cockpit area again and Clelland folded up onto his set and lay still. The pilot, too, must have been hit again, because the nose went down and the aircraft entered a shallow spiral dive. In a last valiant act the trusty Hubbard summoned his fast draining strength, raised his head and signalled the gunner to bale out.

Flames of renewed intensity flared in the cockpit and there could clearly be little time left. Returning aft the gunner assisted his companion to don his parachute before opening the rear entry door. Sergeant Jones dived out of the gyrating aircraft followed later by Sergeant Stanley. Peter Jones felt a terrific jerk that drove virtually every breath from his body as his 'chute opened, but came round in the cool, sweet, peaceful air in time to see L7518 spiralling down beneath, outlined in fire with both engines still roaring. Tom Stanley was not so fortunate. His jump took him face first into the tailplane as it swung to the right in front of him. The impact broke his nose and almost rendered him unconscious. Racked by pain from his wounds and the injuries received in his collision with the tail, Stanley expended precious seconds before he regained his senses sufficiently to wrench the D-ring of his parachute. There was a merciful explosion of silk above him, but before the 'chute deployed fully and his downward speed was completely arrested, he plunged into the water and mud of what turned out to be a small canal.

Manchester L7518, with its remaining five crew members, had crashed to earth nearby only a few seconds earlier, erupting in a fireball as the flames found the remaining fuel load. Stanley must have taken some time to collect and orientate himself and disentangle himself from his 'chute. He dragged himself painfully up the bank and, seeing figures outlined in the glare from the blazing aircraft, found his emergency whistle and blew it. One figure swung towards him, turning out to be not the expected Sergeant Jones, but the village doctor, Rein Posthuma, from Warmenhuizen, a village between Alkmaar and Schagen. In addition to his broken nose and bruised face, Tom Stanley's injuries included a bullet in the right shoulder, a second in the side and a third in his right thigh, plus numerous shrapnel splinters.

Jones had baled out higher and opened his parachute earlier, resulting in him reaching ground level last of all. As he drifted lower he distinguished an expanse of water beneath him and had no more time than to think 'out of the fire and into the kettle' before plunging into it. Although he had clearly seen the aircraft crash on land, Jones was gripped by the fear of the limitless size of the North Sea into which he had the misfortune to descend. He inflated his Mae West, unbuckled his parachute harness and struck out for a group of three or four searchlights on the shore some distance away. He took care to check his watch, being surprised to find it still ticking. Noting the time at 22.35 hours, he took it off his wrist and placed it in the special pocket in his Mae West. The cold was numbing and he rested every ten minutes or so to regain his strength. He was at the limit of his endurance with his wounds, exhaustion and hypothermia when he reached a muddy shoreline about three hours later.

He lay in a ploughed field sleeping in fits and starts till daybreak when he awoke to find his flying suit frozen solid. Having engaged in vigorous exercise to get the circulation going, he struck off inland, crossing fields and swimming or wading the many canals. Whilst crossing one of these he had no time to hide when a barge rowed by four Dutchmen and with two armed German soldiers appeared. The first soldier raised his machine pistol and with a grin gestured for Jones to put his hands on his head and join them in the barge.

Marched a mile and a half across country to the nearby village, Jones and his guards were met by a car which took them to the nearby airfield. Here he queue-jumped the usual group crowded outside the medical officer's office and could not resist a rueful smile at their shocked response to seeing 'a victim of operational flying' at first hand. He was freezing cold, soaking wet, plastered in mud, his hair matted with dried blood and his body

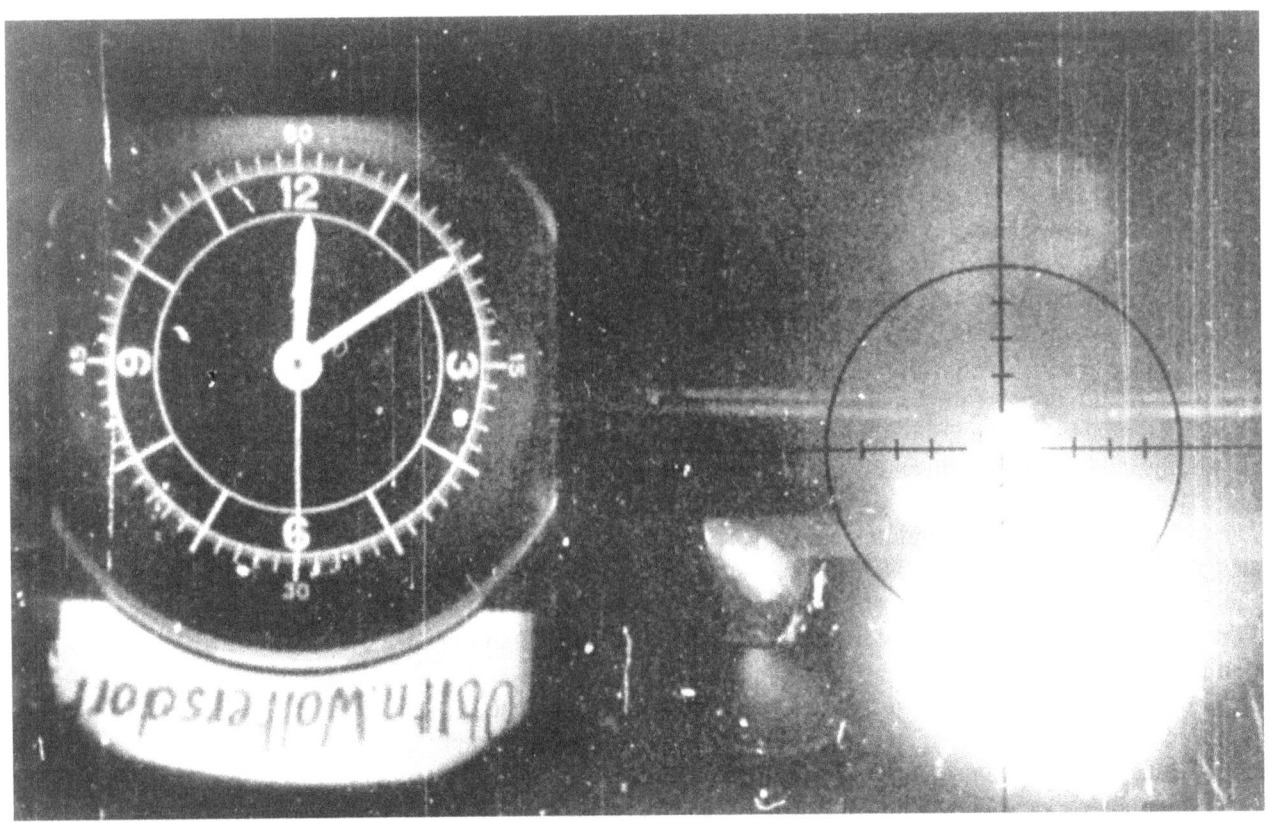

This photograph, together with reports from survivors from Flying Officer Hubbard's aircraft which was also lost on the night of 25/26 March 1942, vividly portrays the awesome destructive power of German night fighters. Here L7497 of 61 Squadron is already disintegrating whilst Oberleutnant Woltersdorf still has his finger on the firing button. Sergeant Furby and his crew fell at Wertherbruch, near Bolholt on the Dutch/German border. Oberleutnant Woltersdorf was in turn killed on 6 June 1942. (Aders/Rapp)

peppered with shrapnel splinters. The station doctor cleaned him up and dressed his wounds before he was permitted to sleep.

He was later transported to Amsterdam jail where, after a couple of days, he received a visit from the German night fighter pilot who claimed to have shot them down. German records attribute the victory to the rising fighter ace Hauptmann Helmut Lent of II/NJG2 at Leeuwarden in Holland and the time of the engagement to 00.32 hours. The discrepancy in time may be accounted for by the difference in British local time and that in Europe over the war period. The visitor expressed his sympathy to Jones for the loss of five of his crew mates whose bodies had been found in the wreckage. Sergeant Stanley was being held in Amsterdam hospital he was told. Their destruction had been ruthlessly efficient and merciless. No quarter had been asked or given and Jones learned that return fire from the rear or mid-upper turret guns had killed the radio operator/gunner in the night fighter. In their last three operations, 10 March to Essen, 13 March to Cologne, and now 25 March to Essen, Pilot Officer Hubbard and his crew had crashed each time. Now they finally had their ultimate disaster.

On this one night four Manchesters had been lost in quick succession, all to night fighters, and from the twenty-eight crew members only two survived. The Manchester loss rate for the night was four out of twenty or 20%. Deflected from the Ruhr by its lack of success, Command considered other targets within GEE range. Target location was always easier for coastal sites and if these proved to be only lightly defended they would be all the more appropriate at this stage in the development of area bombing techniques. Eyes fell on Lubeck on the Baltic coast, a medieval town containing a warren of ancient wooden houses. The Bomber Command Operational Research Station appraised it as 'a particularly suitable target for testing the effect of a very heavy attack with incendiary bombs'. Harris' own evaluation was more emotive. It was 'built more like a fire lighter than a human habitation'. Lubeck thus became a target principally on grounds of its operational vulnerability.

On the night of 28/29 March 234 bombers, guided by GEE for much of the outward leg, attacked Lubeck using the SHAKER technique. Twenty-one Manchesters from 61, 83 and 106 Squadrons were involved. Attacking aircraft released some 300 tons of bombs, almost half of which incendiaries, in a devastating attack. The old town burned like tinder and the firefighters below were totally over-whelmed. Afterwards some 45 to 50% of the whole

Left to right: Neville Patton (rear gunner); unknown; Peter Kent (second pilot); Ken Leyshon (wireless operator); Eric Noble (captain) in front of Mk.1A L7497 QR-? of 61 Squadron at Woolfox Lodge, 1942. L7497 was lost with Sergeant Furby and his crew on the night of 25/26 March 1942. Flight Sergeant Noble and his crew were killed on the night of 6/7 April 1942. (D. H. MacSporran)

city, 190 acres, were judged destroyed; 1,425 houses were demolished, 1,976 heavily damaged and 8,000 to a lesser extent. More than 300 citizens were killed and 780 injured, making it the heaviest death toll inflicted on a German population to date.

Bomber Command had finally shown that it could wreak major devastation from the air and the Command itself and Britain in general in these darkest of days celebrated the achievement with considerable satisfaction. In truth it had required the combined effects of GEE, excellent visibility including a full moon, negligible defences in the target area and an attack from as little as 2,000 feet on the wooden fabric, but it had been done. Bomber Command never raided Lubeck again in strength. One Manchester, that of Flying Officer Lumb of 83 Squadron, was lost together with its entire crew. In the seventy years since this tragic loss little further information has emerged. The crew were buried in Kiel, indicating that R5781 probably came down on land. The weather was clear with a full moon and all night fighter/bomber claims have been confidently linked. The attack itself was made at low level. Possibly this aircraft was brought down by flak?

Next night the three serving Manchester squadrons dispatched only eight aircraft between them for mining operations to the NECTARINE area off Terschelling on the Dutch coast. Flight Sergeant Dimond of 106 Squadron and Pilot Officer Churchill of 61 Squadron, both on their first full operation as Manchester captains, failed to return. There were no survivors from either aircraft. This represented 25% of the Manchester force dispatched.

It is now known that L7394 of 106 Squadron was brought down at 22.00 hours in the North Sea north of Terschelling by Oberleutnant Helmut Lent of Stab. II/NJG2 – his thirty-fourth victory. Soon after, at 22.31 hours, Oberleutnant Reinhold Knack accounted for L7454 of 61 Squadron. The Manchester fell into the sea north-west of Vlieland. Both nightfighter crews flew Bf110s. Though nothing other than the enigmatic 'Nothing heard following take-off' would ever appear in Bomber Command records for Lent's thirty-fourth victory, it became a mystical *cause célèbre* in Nachtjagd folklore as 'The Battle of Helmut's Glove'.

A staged photograph of Lent standing next to the tailfin of his Bf110 marked up with thirty-four victories and with an RAF airman's heated glove jammed between the fin and rudder was published in the Berliner Illustrierte Zeitung. The photograph's caption, attributed to Lent, is typical of propaganda at the time:

I crept up on a Tommy from above and positioning myself astern opened fire. I see my tracer disappearing into his fuselage, then the Tommy explodes like a shell. Pieces of aeroplane rain around my aircraft. I dive away thinking I have incurred fatal damage but my machine flies bravely on, though my rudder control feels jammed and is pulling hard to one side. When I land I inspect the damage. Like a dead man's hand there is a heavy English electrically heated glove rammed in the slot and hanging where the fin and rudder meet. Some bizarre twist of fate has torn it from the pilot's hand when the bomber exploded and whirled it into my rudder.

However, as with much propaganda, Lent identifies the type he attacked as a Stirling, though his first and last victory over this type occurred around 4 to 5 May 1943. Lent's achievement awards and the tail marking put the date between September 1941 and June 1942. The extent to which this incident was embellished or even invented by Joseph Goebbel's Ministry of Propaganda can't now be established. Whatever the truth, Flight Sergeant Dimond and his crew, as with Pilot Officer Hubbard and his only a few days earlier, had stood no chance against such a consummate professional as Lent.

As April 1942 began, for the first and virtually only time, four Manchester squadrons were operational together. At Skellingthorpe 50 Squadron had been the sixth squadron to receive Manchesters and had been working up for some time. The overlap only lasted a few days because 61 and 83 Squadrons were both at an advanced stage in converting to Lancasters. Not surprisingly, squadrons could not get rid of their Manchesters quickly enough. On 8/9 April 1942, eighteen Manchesters from amongst the four squadrons were raised for operations. 50 Squadron dispatched its first operation, when three aircraft carried out a leaflet raid, being joined by a further two from 83 Squadron. In addition 61, 83 and 106 Squadrons raised in turn three, five and five bombers respectively to attack Hamburg. Sadly for 83 Squadron they were to lose two more aircraft that night, a total of 11% of the force.

Hpt. Helmut Lent, Kommandeur of II/NJG2 at Leeuwarden, poses stoically holding his dog, Peter, for the photographer from the Ministry of Propaganda with the port fin and rudder of his Bf110 showing thirty-four kill markings. At 22.00 hours on 25 March 1942 he shot down Fight Sergeant Dimond of 106 Squadron flying Manchester L7394. Note silk glove claimed to be from his victim jammed between fin and rudder. The resulting account became widely known in Luftwaffe folklore as 'The Battle of Helmut's Glove'. (Tina Delavre, née Lent)

Pilot Officer Hedley Hazelden was one of seven Manchester pilots briefed for Hamburg. His usual co-pilot, Sergeant Zaleschuk, was replaced by Wing Commander Crighton-Biggie ('CB') who had been posted to command 83 Squadron from a desk job at Air Ministry. Crighton-Biggie was one of the giants of Bomber Command, well-known to everyone in 5 Group, but who never became a household name like some of his peers. Crighton-Biggie commenced by doing a few trips with second tour captains to gain operational experience. Later he went on to fly operations with every crew in the squadron and was a real tower of strength. His second operational trip was on 8/9 April 1942. Their aircraft that night was L7484, a Mk.1A and the bomb load six 1,000-lb GP.

All went normally on the outward leg. The target was attacked and Hazelden turned L7484 towards home. As they settled down on the homeward leg they soon began experiencing over-heating of the starboard Vulture. By the time they crossed the German coast at 9,000 feet, heading out into the Heligoland Bight, they observed wide and rapid radiator temperature fluctuations on the engine. Their initial diagnosis was a faulty gauge, but this theory was hastily abandoned when the engine began throwing trails of sparks from the exhausts, which turned into a long tongue of flame.

In the darkened cockpit both 'CB' and Hazelden went for the feathering button, each unaware of the other's action (shades of Bill Hills and Derek Bowes-Cavanagh in 207 Squadron – author). The feathering buttons were located near the bottom of the instrument panel towards the right hand side. Hazelden leaned across from the pilot's seat, felt what he thought was the port button and pressed the next on the right, which should have been the starboard. Looking over his right shoulder he watched the propeller wind down and stop. The flames disappeared. As Hazelden tried to retrim the aircraft he was surprised to find little change considering the asymmetry of the thrust.

A casual, if somewhat strained, remark from the wireless operator, Flight Sergeant C. J. Taylor, on the intercom drew his attention: 'Seems a trifle quiet in here, Skip', and made him glance round at the port engine. That, too, was feathered and stopped! Hazelden's first thought was that somehow both circuits had operated from the single button, but to unfeather the port engine was now urgent and imperative. A torch was produced and used to illuminate the pitch dark cockpit, alerting night fighters by so doing being a lesser risk.

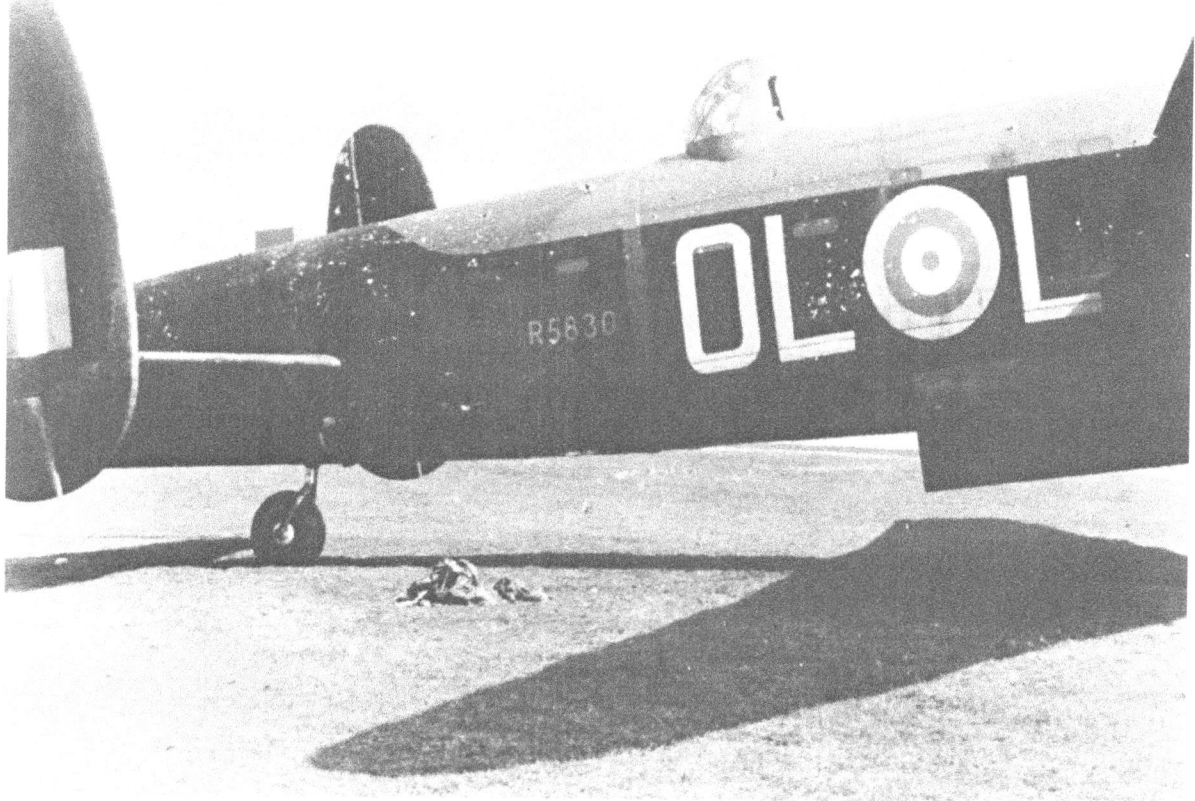

Rear of Mk.1A R5830 OL-L of 83 Squadron following early return by Squadron Leader McClure on the night of 28/29 March 1942. The aircraft was seriously damaged by a night fighter and equipment had to be jettisoned to remain airborne on the return flight, a frequent Manchester problem. (Chaz Bowyer)

Feathering and unfeathering was achieved by depressing the same button, with separate buttons for each engine. Pressing once and holding-in resulted in feathering. Repress and hold unfeathered the propeller. On unfeathering, the point at which to release the hold was difficult to judge, to release too soon meant that the propeller would not have reached the blade angular range for constant speeding, whereas holding too long could easily result in the blade passing straight through the constant speeding range towards full fine pitch, with resultant over-speed. Hazelden was determined to avoid this last eventuality at all costs, with the result that he twice released the button too soon and had to go back to the feathered position and start again. There was much bated breath all round. On the third attempt he was successful and power was restored on the port engine at 4,500 feet, exactly half the altitude at which the emergency had occurred.

Using full rated power, Hazelden then set about discovering how to fly the aircraft to maintain height. Strange to say by present standards, they had no information on speeds, heights, weights, power settings etc for single engine flying. Over the next half hour or so they lost a further 500 feet and discovered by trial and error that in their condition a speed of 137 knots IAS was best, since at both 140 and 135 knots the rate of descent was greater. Hazelden reckoned this rate of descent was tolerable as they would reach UK territory before running out of atmosphere. In fact they were able to maintain 4,000 feet, probably due to using up fuel, and after running the port Vulture at full throttle for an hour and a half they reached Horsham St Faith and, thankfully, landed.

The subsequent inquest revealed that in the original emergency 'CB' and Hazelden were both feeling in the dark for the feathering button on the starboard engine. 'CB' found the first button, which was indeed the starboard, and pressed it. Hazelden found what he took to be the port and pressed the next one on the right. This turned out to be the port engine feathering button because what he had found first was the brake pressure gauge.

Pilot Officer Hazelden and crew were consequently more fortunate than two of their fellow crews. Pilot Officer Morphett in L7427 OL-Q was one of those who failed to return. His rear gunner was the sole survivor, but

Capturing the essential spirit of the aircraft – L7427 OL-Q of 83 Squadron taken from a sister aircraft in March 1942. Released for press publication on 21 April 1942, by which time the aircraft had been lost on 8/9 April on a raid to Hamburg on its sixteenth Op with Pilot Officer Morphett and his crew. (Central Press CP5338A)

unfortunately died whilst a prisoner of war. We now know that this aircraft was brought down at 00.49 hours as the first victory of Feldwebel Gerhard Goerke of I/NJG3 falling west of Lastrup south-east of Cloppenburg

Manchesters were now highly vulnerable even during the shallowest penetration introductory Freshman raids, as evident from the loss of the second 83 Squadron aircraft on the night of 8/9 April and a 61 Squadron machine two nights later. Pilot Officer Sproule was on an introductory NICKEL raid on Paris in R5837 prior to commencing his operational career with 83 Squadron. On the 8th/9th he was carrying an eight man crew, with an Intelligence Officer (IO) along to gain operational experience. Unfortunately R5837 was hit by flak near Calais, which stopped one of the engines. Sproule tried to return on the remaining one but was unable to maintain height, eventually alighting on the sea near Margate. An SOS had been sent out but the aircraft settled so swiftly that only Sproule was able to locate the dinghy. The pilot spent fourteen hours afloat before being picked up by the Air Sea Rescue Service. A grim sidelight on this tragedy was that when the unfortunate widow of the Intelligence Officer tried to claim a pension on her loss she was told she was not eligible because her man was officially AWOL (absent without leave)!

On 10/11 April 1942 the main force operated to Essen. At this time 61 Squadron had about double the number of aircrews as Manchesters. Sergeant Don MacSporran was waiting to fly his first operation as a captain with his own crew. Accordingly, he was rostered to take Manchester R5785 QR-M, on a 'NURSERY' raid to Le Havre.

Wing Commander Weir briefed MacSporran carefully, explaining that R5785 was the squadron's worst Manchester. It was badly in need of a 'ring job' and, as a result, the engines did not produce as much power as they should, which severely restricted the take-off and altitude performance. Weir made it quite clear that if it became evident that the aircraft was letting them down they were not to hesitate to turn back.

As they droned southwards across England, MacSporran tried to coax the best ceiling he could from the struggling Manchester, but eventually found that 9,000 feet was the maximum possible. He had decided to cross the French coast west of Deauville before turning left and carrying out the bombing run on a northerly track, which would carry them out across the Channel and towards home. Having crossed the enemy coast he turned and, heading northwards, entered a gentle dive to let down to 8,000 feet at the point of bomb release.

Three quarter rear and below shot of L7427 OL-Q. (Philip Jarrett)

Immediately the bombs fell away the aircraft was enveloped by an intense accurate flak barrage. Shrapnel was slashing through the airframe in many places and the pilot felt a distinctive twitch in the control column as fragments perforated the ailerons.

MacSporran had expected to come out of the flak within a short period but, when he looked round for any reason why they were still suffering the unabated fury of the defenders, he was shocked to find the aircraft had turned back and was heading inland again. The starboard engine had failed, with the result that the aircraft had yawed to the right and swung back on a southerly heading.

The pilot then feathered the starboard propeller and turned left again towards the good engine and finally made it out to sea. By this time they were down to 4,000 feet, their speed had fallen to 120 mph and they were descending at 400 feet per minute. Just before crossing the coast, MacSporran called the crew and gave them all the option of baling out over land, but all decided to stay aboard in the hope of making the English coast.

Regrettably, even with the throttle of the port Vulture fully open, MacSporran could do nothing to prevent them descending into the sea about 20 miles off the French coast. He barely had time to pull back on the stick before they wallowed into the sea at a mere 100 mph. The aircraft neither bounced nor skated on the surface, but dug its nose in and stopped abruptly. R5785 sank very quickly under them and they all got soaked escaping from the hatches. As they cast off, the tail swung up, towering over them, and 'M-Mother' plunged vertically to the bottom. All seven crew had reached the dinghy safely.

They remained at sea undetected until the afternoon of 16 April when, in a weakened condition, they finally fetched up on rocks on the Cherbourg peninsula only 50 feet offshore. Four of the crew tried to swim the last few feet but it was at this point that the wireless operator, Sergeant Dave Meikle, finally used up the remainder of his strength, his head dropped forward into the water and he drowned. The dinghy itself finally floated into the shore and the remaining crew were able to disembark to captivity. As Manchester activity diminished from mid-April onwards, with only 50 and 106 Squadrons still active on the aircraft, losses thus remained high. A total of nine Manchesters were lost during April.

Consistent with the continuation and development of its area bombing techniques, Bomber Command had been planning a series of hammer blows on Rostock on the Baltic coast. These fell on four consecutive nights between 23 and 26 April. Only six, nine, five and nine Manchesters respectively could be mustered for this assault, the aircraft consequently playing only a minor role. Unlike Lubeck, Rostock contained a number of important industries - shipbuilding, an Arado aircraft factory and the Heinkel works at Marienehe in the suburbs. It, too, was lightly defended and easy to locate. Bomber Command was at this time simultaneously striving to test the twin tactics of a concentrated incendiary area attack combined with a precision high explosive attack. The precision attack was entrusted to the 5 Group squadrons, which had strived to perfect navigational and bombing accuracy.

The first two attacks went in on 23/24 April (161 aircraft) and 24/25 April (125 aircraft) and both were disappointing. Despite clear skies and a bright moon, the Heinkel factory was not hit and most of the bombs fell two to six miles wide. 106 Squadron lost Pilot Officer Stoffer in the first attack. It is reported that an engine overheated and caught fire. Six of the crew baled out, but the main spar burnt through and the aircraft shed a wing, carrying Stoffer to his death near Tinglev in Denmark.

On the third night of the series of raids on Rostock (25/26 April) 128 aircraft were dispatched including sixteen from 5 Group. Only 106 Squadron operated Manchesters that night, Wing Commander Guy Gibson leading five. One aircraft made an early return, but the remainder overflew the factory from only 5,000 feet. Of seventy-one night photographs taken, thirty showed the centre of Rostock, a further thirty-five were within five miles of the centre, and three showed the factory itself. The operation was a triumph. Finally, on the last night (26/27 April), 107 aircraft were dispatched, with both 5 and 3 Groups going for the Heinkel factory.

Pilot Officer Harold Southgate captained one of the four 50 Squadron aircraft briefed for this final raid on Rostock. Only two days previously he had attacked the same target from 7,000 feet, rejoicing in the almost total lack of opposition. This night, in L7432, he viewed the seven and a half to eight hour operation as a 'piece of cake'. The aircraft carried six 1,000-lb GP and Southgate was sufficiently emboldened by his recent experience to elect to attack Rostock from 4,000 feet. The outward flight was uneventful and Southgate's observer, Sergeant Shirley, brought them onto Rostock from the agreed approach direction. On the final approach at 4,000 feet, with the bomb doors open, all hell broke loose from the hastily reinforced flak defences below.

Guns of all calibres ranged on them, shells burst all round and the aircraft jolted steadily as it took a series of hits. In desperation and with little height in hand, Southgate nosed forward to increase their speed in the hope of escaping the defences. Eventually, close to what they believed was the Aiming Point, the observer released the load from an almost fatal 2,000 feet. Shortly afterwards the aircraft was punched skyward, as if by enormous fists, as the bombs detonated only a little to the rear. Within a short period numerous other crushing jolts from bombs released by aircraft overhead at a safer height buffeted the aircraft.

Neither the explosions nor the flak had damaged L7432 fatally and Southgate and his second pilot, Flight Sergeant Morgan, working in unison, were able to regain some semblance of control. They had taken several hits. The rudder had clearly been distorted by a near miss, although none of the other vital systems of the aircraft had been damaged. Lateral control forces had become extreme and the two pilots had to use all their combined strength to steady the aircraft. Meanwhile, the flak gunners appeared to have transferred their attention elsewhere and the two pilots were able to steer a course by bracing one leg locked straight on the rudder bars.

In this condition and without any relief from the extreme physical effort they endured the three hour return to Skellingthorpe.

Once in the vicinity of base they radioed ahead for a priority landing, which was safely accomplished after further Herculean effort. Southgate vowed never again to under-estimate the Germans' capability to reorganise and redeploy their defences.

On this night, the *piece de resistance*, ninety-two aircraft reached the target and of the fifty-two photographs taken every one showed the target area. Thirteen showed the factory itself, where most 5 Group aircraft had attacked from 2,000 feet. Subsequent reconnaissance showed widespread devastation and a second great victory for Bomber Command so soon after the attack on Lubeck. Furthermore, from the four-night, 521-sortie attack, only twelve aircraft were lost. 60% of the built-up area (130 acres) was destroyed, 204 citizens were killed and eight-nine injured.

Reinforcing this success further, Gneisenau had now been transferred to a floating dry dock in Kiel to rectify its recent mine damage. Also on 26th-27th April, 49 aircraft, none Manchesters, attacked this now immobilised vessel. Weighing up the desirability of an expected quick return to operational status, the Germans chose not to carry out the always desirable, but time-consuming, task of discharging the vessels 11inch gun ammunition from "ready to use" magazines immediately beneath each turret. By chance this understandable expediency proved the ships undoing. A single armour-piercing bomb hit the armoured deck just forward of the vessels "Anton" turret, penetrating through into the full magazine. The subsequent massive explosion lifted the turret off its bearings and devastated the entire forward section of the ship, killing 112 of the crew, along with causing other extensive damage. It never returned to operational status. Its main guns were removed and used in coastal defence installations.

At Skellingthorpe, whilst preparing for conversion to the Lancaster, 50 Squadron had now been operating Manchesters for three weeks of a desultory eight week period. Despite the rather short period and relatively restricted numbers of aircraft generally dispatched on operations, 50 Squadron were to lose ten Manchesters on operations and another two in training. Also by this time at Scampton 49 Squadron was working up on Manchesters to become the seventh and final squadron to receive the aircraft with a view to undertaking operational flying. 49 Squadron operated the aircraft on a small scale basis for less than a month but were still to lose six Manchesters. Whilst Bomber Command had room to rejoice at the relatively modest casualty list from this period of shallow penetration operations, the Manchester crews were finally reaping the whirlwind for hanging on so long with a vulnerable and obsolescent type.

From late March onwards, 61, 83 and 106 Squadrons and then 50 and 106 Squadrons had invested a major effort in mining operations in the North Sea and beyond. 106 Squadron lost four of its seven operational casualties in mine-laying operations. Frequently, the Manchesters lost during mining operations crashed at sea with no survivors. Just occasionally there were survivors to tell the tale, as was the case on 29/30 April 1942 when 50 Squadron sent five Manchesters to lay their 'VEGETABLES' in the FORGET-ME-NOT, QUINCE, ENDIVE and RADISH marine areas. One aircraft returned early with violent buffeting of the rudders and three others were successful.

The experiences of Flight Sergeant Willett and crew in the fifth aircraft were every bit as harrowing as those of crews lost on attacks on land targets. They were allocated a former 61 Squadron Mk.1A, L7516 VN-N, to attack Kiel Bay. For wireless operator Hector Macdonald this was to be his seventh Manchester operation in just twelve days. L7516 took off from Skellingthorpe at 23.30 hours and all went to plan until they were over Denmark on the return flight. Willett had just initiated a climb to give them some height in hand and the aircraft had reached 10,000 feet, when the observer, Pilot Officer Hannah, reported his suspicion that one of their four mines had hung up. Macdonald took a torch to the observation port at the rear end of the bomb bay and shone it for Hannah, at the forward observation port, to confirm his suspicions. At this moment and without warning they were attacked from behind by a Bf110 night fighter.

Manchester Mk.1A R5833 OL-N of 'B' Flight 83 Squadron at Scampton, 8 April 1942. From left to right the crew are Sergeant J. Bushby; Pilot Officer Billings; Sergeants Dodsworth, Baines, and Williams and their captain, Warrant Officer Whitehead. The moon and stars crescent is inscribed in Welsh, Ar hyd y nos (All through the night). (via R. Low/F. Harper, 83 Squadron archives)

Converted Mk.1A R5837 OL-R (some sources quote it as OL-J – author) allegedly waiting to be bombed up at Scampton on 8 April 1942. That night the aircraft ditched near Margate with flak damage after aborting a NICKEL raid on Paris. The pilot, Pilot Officer Sproule, was the sole survivor. (via R. Low/F. Harper, 83 Squadron archives)

The Manchester shook under the impact of a number of 20-mm shells, following which the fighter broke away. Willett called the rear gunner for a situation report, but being unable to raise him, sent Macdonald from his intercom position aft of the bomb bay. As Macdonald approached he could see that the turret was fully traversed on the port beam and Sergeant Williams slumped over his guns, probably already dead. He was about to operate the 'dead man's handle' to rotate the turret and extricate the inert figure, when a second and devastating attack materialised. Macdonald was enveloped in tracer and in Willett's violent evasive manoeuvres was tossed around the rear fuselage.

In this follow-up attack the aircraft was fatally damaged. Both engines caught fire, the wing tanks were punctured, the fuselage riddled. A stray round shorted out the lighting circuit turning all the lights on, including the landing lights. L7516 was now lit up like a Christmas tree. With the severe bumps and bruises he had sustained, Macdonald did not immediately realise that a shell sprinter had severed several fingers on his left hand, which were left hanging by the skin. To add to the cacophony of noise, Sergeant Miners, the mid-upper gunner, loosed off a burst at the fighter as it closed in for the kill. Still plugged in to the intercom and still unaware of his wounds, Macdonald was the first to react when Willett, fighting to control the gyrating bomber, cried out: 'Put those bloody lights off'. Macdonald returned to the fuse box. Speed was the essence, and without taking the time to consult the list of fuse positions, began removing every fuse in turn until he found one which doused the lights.

During the course of the attacks L7516 had lost much of the height it had gained and was now a fire trap. Macdonald heard Willett give an order to bale out, clearly indicating them to be over land. Moments later Willett called again, cancelling the order and saying they were back over water. An immediate ditching was inevitable. The fighter pilot must have recognised that the aircraft was doomed for no further attacks developed. With the mine still on board and with time for only minimal preparation of the aircraft by Willett, they bellied onto the water between Rantum and Morsum on Sylt. Instead of skating across the compliant surface they found that the aircraft hit a shallow submerged sand bank beneath, which brought them to an abrupt halt. Fortunately Macdonald did not receive any further serious injuries in the ditching. However, the front gunner, Sergeant Scott, and second pilot, Flight Sergeant Packard, were not so fortunate.

L7289, a late starter from the initial production batch of twenty, went initially into store at 37 Maintenance Unit, Burtonwood before being reworked at Avro and reaching 83 Squadron on 11 April 1942, where it became OL-Q. It only undertook one sortie before being passed to 50 Squadron, when it failed to return from its first operation with Sergeant Roy. (Chaz Bowyer)

It transpired that when the order came to bale out both got down into the nose compartment and jettisoned the lower hatch. What happened next is unclear, but it appears Scott left the aircraft, without his parachute, at too low a height. After Scott vacated the hatch, Packard, already cut off from the intercom, took his place sitting with his legs dangling in space prior to baling out. He was caught in this posture when L7516 bellied in, being thrown forward and trapped by the legs when the aircraft settled onto the sand beneath.

The captain, navigator, mid-upper gunner and Macdonald himself all scrambled out of the upper hatch. By now L7516 had settled in only 2 or 3 feet of water, but both engines continued to blaze and the oxygen bottles began to explode sporadically. With the mine still nestling in the wrecked bomb bay, petrol spewing out and 0.303-inches ammunition nearby, the four survivors hastened to leave the scene. The aircraft dinghy had failed to deploy. At this moment and before they could gather themselves together a splash and gasp from the water revealed the head of Flight Sergeant Packard bobbing to the surface. They dragged him onto the wing, alive but badly injured in his legs.

The bright moonlight, combined with the fact that a searchlight was trained on them across the water, allowed the crew to see the coast. Bearing in mind the risk of explosion they decided to wade to the shore. However, they rapidly discovered that the sand bank was deeply dissected by tidal channels, which were precarious to cross, especially now that they were assisting the wounded Packard. Eventually they agreed to return to the burning wreck of L7516, but not before Hector Macdonald had come across the body of the front gunner floating in a tidal channel, his Mae West inflated. Back at the wreck they perched on the wingtip, keeping as far from the flames as possible.

Soon an inflatable boat appeared and they were taken prisoner, Macdonald and Packard being conveyed straight to hospital on the island of Sylt where they had come down. They had ditched at close to 03.00 hours. Within days they received a stream of visitors, including Oberleutnant Günter Köberich, the pilot of the Bf110 of Stab. II/NJG3 based at Westerland, who had shot them down. From him they learned that return fire from their mid-upper gunner had killed the rear gunner in the Messerschmitt, Unteroffizier Walter Schubert.

When Macdonald and Packard were sufficiently recovered from their injuries they were interrogated. Possibly from the markings on their ditched aircraft, it was apparent that the Germans had learned that they were assigned to 50 Squadron. Not only did they know the base at Skellingthorpe and the previous history of their aircraft, but questioned them in detail about their CO, Wing Commander 'Beetle' Oxley, and his regular pep talks to the crews in which he urged them to whip up what he called 'Hun-hate'. They had little doubt that Oxley would be high on the Gestapo wanted list should he ever be captured.

On 2/3 May 1942 49 Squadron dispatched a single preparatory NICKELLING sortie as a gentle introduction to Manchester operations and 50 Squadron dispatched a further three. That same night Bomber Command had laid on an exclusively minelaying operation involving ninety-six aircraft of 3 and 5 Groups with release positions extending from the Baltic to Brittany. As the specialist minelaying unit, 106 Squadron was called upon to make a maximum effort, recording in its ORB (Form 540) that it had achieved a new unit record of dispatching without a hitch eight Manchesters each carrying four mines to the FORGET-ME-NOT and WALLFLOWER sea areas. The weather was recorded as 'Fine' with no cloud, some haze and good visibility at the Danish coast. Expectations were high and returning crews were all confident of a good outcome after encountering little opposition. Pilot Officer Picken and crew in L7378 overflew a coastal convoy in the target area with which they exchanged fire, Flight Sergeant Appleyard had L7391 damaged and the rear gunner injured by light flak from Esbjerg, whereas Pilot Officer Aytoun in L7305 reported encountering a JU88 over Fano, which was shaken off. Two aircraft had laid 'VEGETABLES' in the alternative Hawthorn 'GARDEN'.

Regrettably, and as outlined in Form 540, this operation proved an 'inexplicable misfortune, if not a disaster' for 106 Squadron. Manchesters R5840 (Flight Sergeant Hurd) and L7399 ZN-X (Flight Sergeant Young) took off at 22.20 and 22.25 hours and were both lost, an unsupportable 25% casualty rate. In view of the easy time reported by returning crews the unit could find no explanation, nor had it intercepted any distress calls. It later transpired that both aircraft came down onshore. Two crewmen escaped when L7399 came down 14 km west of Hadersley in Denmark and the entire crew survived when R5840 was 'shot down' at Pellworm Island in Germany. None of these nine former POWs has ever been located in order to describe events. All we can be sure of is that no German night fighter claims were made for this night.

Finally, on 8/9 May 1942, eleven Manchesters from 50 and 106 Squadrons were dispatched on operations. Two 50 Squadron aircraft went GARDENING and the remaining nine bombing at Warnemunde. Of the three aircraft element from 50 Squadron, Sergeant Wilkie's aircraft was so badly damaged by flak that it had to be written-off on return to base.

Mk.1 Manchester, L7385 OL-C, of 83 Squadron being bombed up with three 2,000-lb armour-piercers at Scampton in March/April 1942. L7385 met a gruesome fate with 207 Con Flight on the evening of 6 August 1942 when Lancaster R5550 taxied head on into it as it flared for landing at Bottesford. (via Chaz Bowyer)

Light flak hits in the target area prevented the bomb doors being closed on Sergeant Maurice Gruber's aircraft. Despite use of full throttle, the aircraft could not be lifted above 6,000 feet and a decision was made to divert to neutral Sweden. By now they were losing height and approaching the Danish Island of Møn difficulties multiplied when the starboard engine and wing burst into flames. Sergeant Gruber used all his skills to keep L7489 aloft and all but the captain baled out over the island and survived. Sergeant Gruber was killed in the ensuring crash.

From this time onwards Manchester operational activity all but ceased. Lancasters were coming in to replace them and Bomber Command was conserving all aircraft in the risky attempt to capture the political and military high ground by committing every operational aircraft and all reserves under advanced training to a cataclysmic thousand bomber raid. At a stroke this would almost quadruple the bomber force from its current 250 to 350 maximum. Manchesters still equipped 49 and 50 Squadrons as well as the Conversion Flights of many Lancaster Squadrons in 5 Group. They had been issued to 44 and 408 (RCAF) Squadron Con Flights and were already working up on 420 (RCAF) Squadron. Despite mounting losses, Manchesters were still considered fair game for a last ditch and desperate maximum effort.

The distinctive tail unit of a 106 Squadron Manchester, probably L7399 ZN-X, amongst other wreckage after it crashed at Lilholt near Haderslev, Denmark, with Flight Sergeant Young, whilst engaged on a 'GARDENING' operation. Only two crew survived. (Berger Hansen)

Chapter Eight: The Thousand Raids

By early May 1942, the Manchester was slipping unnoticed and unmourned into oblivion. 61 and 83 Squadrons had both converted to Avro Lancasters, carrying out their final flurry of Manchester operations in early April, save for a brief 83 Squadron effort on 5 May. Manchesters had passed to their Con. Flights. 97 and 207 Squadrons were both well established on Lancasters, with Manchester Con. Flights, 44 Squadron on Lancasters and 408 and 420 Squadrons on Handley Page Hampdens also had Manchester training flights. Starting from 17 April 49 Squadron had been converted to Manchesters with a view to gaining experience in the dual cockpits before they, too, moved on to Lancasters. As a result of the fact that there was initially no intention to carry out operations with the Manchester, 49 Squadron received mainly 'the halt' and 'the lame' – Manchesters from the initial non-operationally fit batch. Many were still without their mid-upper FN7A turret. They were almost without exception the original, triple fin Mk.1 variety. This left 50 and 106 Squadrons. 106 Squadron was at an advanced stage in converting to Lancasters, its Manchesters passing to a recently formed Con. Flight, whilst 50 Squadron, too, had begun the conversion process, although still largely Manchester equipped.

In addition to their obsolescence, Manchesters were now experiencing disproportionate casualties. Whilst crews still tried to get the most out of often very ancient, ill-equipped aircraft, both RAF aircraft performance and the German defences had rapidly outstripped their capability. To heighten the mismatch, worn out engines and lack of spares served to degrade still further Manchester performance.

It was ironic then that the thousand bomber raids ordered by Harris on 30/31 May 1942 to Cologne and 1/2 June to Essen were to result in the deployment of the largest Manchester forces ever dispatched. On 25/26 June the third and last thousand raid of the series, on Bremen, was the final Manchester operation, although by then four squadrons scraped together just nineteen aircraft. Ironic, too, that the Manchester, which had been around during the darkest days for Bomber Command in mid-1941, and itself contributing in no small way to that poor performance, should hang on to see Bomber Command finally demonstrate the enormous striking force of a strategic area offensive.

Following its protracted and inauspicious introduction, the Manchester was to make a timely exit, with Bomber Command as a whole on a high note. Yet for the aircraft involved and their crews it was to be very much the recipe as before. In the short period of his tenure as Air Officer Commanding (AOC) Bomber Command Air Vice-Marshal Harris had grasped the new technology just becoming available and rapidly improved the tactics for area bombing. Now he recognised the need to demonstrate the awesome power of the modern bomber. The concept of the mass attack with the 'magic' figure of 1,000 aircraft was born.

In order to strike such a blow, Harris needed to both conserve and assemble his forces. He needed good weather and a full moon period. The last few days in May were earmarked. Thus, from 9/10 May Manchester operations were heavily curtailed.

In anticipation of the operation, work-up and training continued. On the night of 19/20 May a new crew, captained by Flight Sergeant Freeman of 49 Squadron in L7287 EA-G, were engaged, along with others, in a searchlight co-operation exercise to London. At about 22.20 hours they were in collision over Grantham with another unseen Scampton aircraft, the 83 Squadron Lancaster of Squadron Leader Hinton. The underside of the starboard wing of the Manchester lost several square feet of skin, whereas the Lancaster lost its starboard wing tip and the starboard outer engine stopped. Both aircraft returned safely to Scampton after 40 minutes flying, but it had been a lucky escape. L7287 required a new mainplane. Corporal Trevor Simpson remembers:

Whilst we were changing the outer wing the aircraft was being cannibalised for other items. Fortunately, as it subsequently turned out, as parts were removed they were replaced by the duff item with a label stating that it was unserviceable. The aircraft was serviceable again in time for the Cologne raid.

The planning and build up to the raid needs no repetition here, other than the reminder that as the last few days in May loomed it seemed the weather might thwart the carefully laid plans. Much inter-changing of aircraft and crews, accompanied by the drawing together of scratch crews composed partly of instructors and partly of pupils at advanced stages in their operational training, had to occur. The weather reports were unfavourable for the nights of Wednesday/Thursday 27/28 May and the 28th/29th, as were those for the 29th/30th. All crews were confined to base and the appreciation that 'something big' was afoot was unmistakable. The weather was unusually bad for late May with thundery outbreaks and heavy cloud both over the home bases and over the potential German targets – Hamburg and Cologne.

Wherever possible, flying training, especially by those crews too inexperienced even to be contemplated as potential participants, continued. On the night of 29/30 May this was to remove two potential Manchester participants from inclusion in the big raid. A number of 'Fresher' crews were dispatched on training details from 50 Con. Flight at Skellingthorpe.

Weather conditions were variable with heavy cloud patches, within and below which visibility was poor and rain was very heavy. Sergeant Eyres had been out in Manchester L7492 on a night cross-country, during the course of which a TR9 radio failure occurred. He arrived in the vicinity of the airfield soon after midnight in a heavy rain squall. Air Traffic Control tried to contact the aircraft to advise the captain to hold off until the rain abated but were unable to do so. The poor visibility and heavy rain led to the airfield being very difficult to identify. Not having developed the experience and judgement to handle these conditions, Eyres held off too high and stalled on one wheel, causing the undercarriage to collapse and the aircraft to be left blocking the runway. There were no casualties in the crew. Efforts commenced to move the damaged aircraft, but in the meantime other returning crews diverted to Waddington.

The weather had turned worse than forecasted and was now too difficult for the inexperienced crews. Pilot Officer D. W. Garland arrived in the circuit at Waddington in R5786 in continuing poor visibility and heavy rain. He

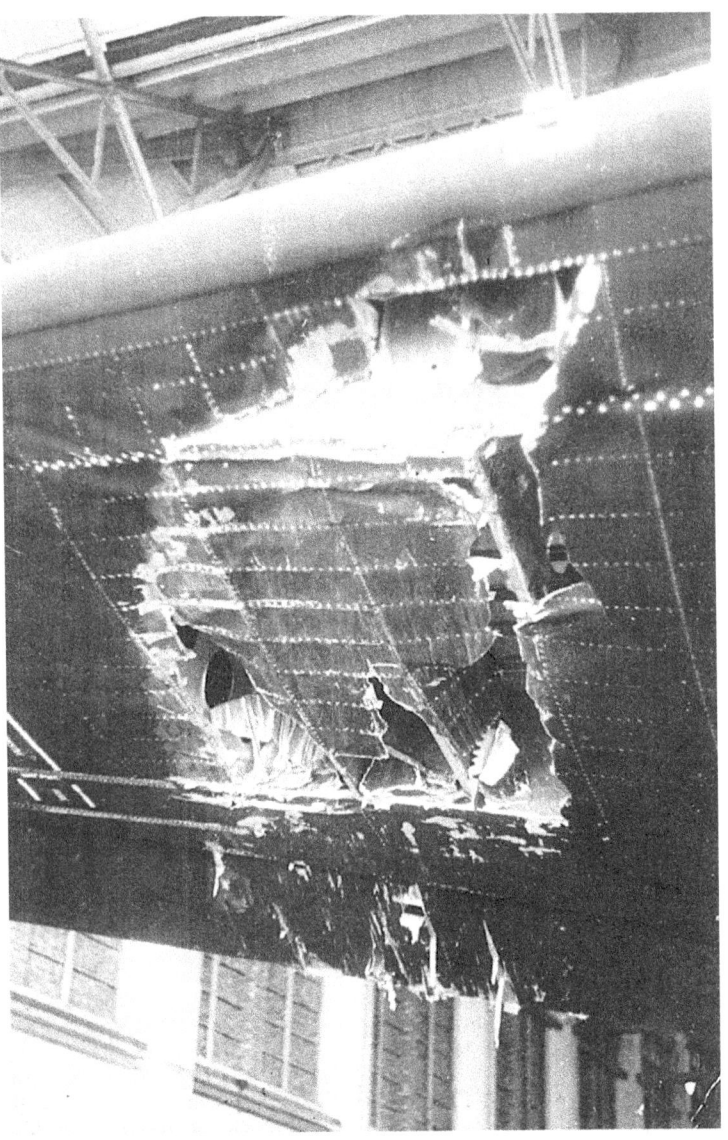

Lucky escape. Damage to the underside of the starboard wing of L7287 EA-G of 49 Squadron after Flight Sergeant Freeman and crew were in collision over Grantham with another, unseen, Scampton aircraft on 19/29 May 1942. This was a Lancaster of 83 Squadron flown by Squadron Leader Hinton. (via P. Gaunt)

touched down well along the grass runway, but the aircraft failed to slow, even when full brake was applied in the later part of the landing run. The aircraft overshot, breaking through the airfield boundary, crossing a road and falling into a field beyond, below the aerodrome level, where the undercarriage collapsed. R5786 was more seriously damaged and two crew members were injured.

At 09.20 hours on Saturday 30 May, the weather forecast put before Air Chief Marshal Harris proved decisive. The local thundery showers and convection cloud over the home bases which had undone Sergeant Eyres and Pilot Officer Garland the night before were decreasing. Thundery cloud was likely to be heavy over north-west Germany but it would break and decrease south during the night. Hamburg was out of the question, but Cologne looked possible. Harris gave the orders and Operation MILLENNIUM was underway.

Whilst 97 and 207 Conversion Flights were not to produce any Manchesters and none of the crews of 420 (RCAF) Squadron at Waddington was proficient in their Manchesters, seven other units did cobble together a major force. In all, forty-five Manchesters were mustered to take part in MILLENNIUM.

Mk.1 L7425 EM-C of 207 Conversion Flight at Bottesford in February 1942. It retains the older, wavy, demarcation of colours and has the white areas of its national markings darkened. L7425 was first delivered to 97 Squadron on 19 June 1941, passed to 207 Squadron on 21 January 1942 and moved on to 50 Con Flight on 18 March 1942. The six personnel were armourers of 207 Squadron. (207 Squadron archives)

Cologne, Operation MILLENNIUM – 30/31 May 1942:

Serial	Code	Squadron	Captain
Balderton - along with nineteen Hampdens			
L7401	EQ-Ā	408 CF	Sqn Ldr L. B. B. Price
Coningsby - along with eleven Lancasters			
L7434	ZN-	106	Plt Off. J. Aytoun
R5796	ZN-	106	Plt Off. S. Cockbain
R5780	ZN-	106	Plt Off. M. Duff
L7391	ZN-	106	Plt Off. R. G. Churcher
L7488	ZN-	106	FS G. Appleyard
Scampton - along with thirteen Lancasters			
L7287	EA-G	49	Flt Lt R. E. R. Paramore
L7479	EA-	49	Plt Off. S. T. Farrington
L7290	EA-	49	Plt Off. P. W. Floyd
L7389	EA-L	49	Sgt H. G. Burton
L7429	EA-	49	FS J. P. Carter
L7526	EA-V	49	Sqn Ldr P. D. S. Bennett
R5775	EA-	49	Plt Off. G. S. Jeffreys
L7524	EA-	49	Plt Off. A. S. Perry
R5794	EA-	49	Plt Off. W. C. Shackleton

L7421	EA-	49	FS R. G. Lewis
L7493	EA-F	49 CF	Sqn Ldr P. C. Ward-Hunt
L7398	EA-	49 CF	FS D. H. Rowlands
L7293*	OL-	83	FS J. Marchant
L7397	OL-	83	Sgt R. N. Williams
L7293*	OL-	83	Plt Off. J. Hodgson
L7308	EA-	49 CF‡	Sgt T. G. Irvine
?	EA-	49 CF‡	Plt Off. A. J. F. Rayment
R5768	EA-	49 CF‡	Plt Off. J. G. MacDonald

Skellingthorpe - along with two Lancasters

R5784	VN-	50	FS E. J. Morgan
L7471	VN-	50	Sgt A. Weber
R5769	VN-	50	Plt Off. H. B. Martin
L7319	VN-	50	Plt Off. D. A. Atkinson
L7468	VN-	50	Plt Off. J. S. Bunbury
L7432	VN-	50	Fg Off. H. W. Southgate
L7525	VN-	50	Plt Off. R. O. Calvert
L7491	VN-	50	Flt Lt P. J. Stone
L7476	VN-Z?	50	Plt Off. T. Cole
L7460	VN-	50	Sgt P. M. Crampton
L7475	VN-	50	Fg Off. J. T. Heaton
L7419	VN-	50	Sgt E. Dampier-Crossley
R5833	VN-	50	Sgt D. Gray
L7301	ZN-D	106CF§	Plt Off. L. T. Manser
L7456	ZN-	106CF§	Sgt J. B. Wilkie

Syerston - along with fifteen Lancasters

L7425*	QR-	61	FS N. Turner
L7425*	QR-	61	Sgt T. A. Stewart
L7473	QR-	61	Fg Off. R. E. Archibald
L7477	QR-	61	Fg Off. L. Gunter

Waddington - along with ten Lancasters

L7430	KM-N̄	44 CF	Fg Off. H. E. Maudslay
L7480	KM-Ā	44 CF	Sqn Ldr W. S. Herring

* identity as given in the ORB, one or the other in error
Letter and log book of Sergeant Jack Berry, bomb aimer to Sergeant T. A. Stewart of 61 Squadron identify his aircraft as L7425. No information reference the 83 Squadron duplication
‡ on loan to 83 Squadron
§ on loan to 50 Squadron
Not included are two Manchesters one each from 49 and 61 Squadrons which became unserviceable just before take-off

Metropolitan Vickers built Mk.1 R5771 assembled 10 June 1941 at Woodford, but stored until late March 1942. After brief periods at 25 Operational Training Unit and 83 Squadron it was passed to 49 Squadron and undertook three sorties. (G. A. Jenks collection)

A new-looking R5771 in final colour scheme, possibly photographed at Woodford. The FN5 front turret is fully slewed to the left. (J. Simpson)

On this night, despite their increasing vulnerability, it was believed that the Manchesters could take advantage of the swamping of the anti-aircraft defences around Cologne and not unduly expose their crews to risk. However, the whole operation was a risk, involving as it did so many inexperienced crews.

Many of the Conversion Flight aircraft were old, having in some cases a large number of airframe hours (for a Manchester), whilst a surprising number were from the initial production batch of twenty and not considered fit for operations. These had originally been issued to 207 Squadron for crew training and development flying and then handed on successively to 97 and 61 Squadrons and the other units in turn for training purposes. They had flown occasional operations but many had been withdrawn from service and held in store at maintenance units (MUs) for prolonged periods. Amongst this early batch were L7287, L7289, L7290 and L7301.

Arising from their languishing in MUs or being issued to Conversion Flights for second line duties, most remained unmodified to the latest standard. For example, most if not all still retained the triple fins and short span tail of the first twenty Mk.1s, whilst most also had no mid-upper turret fitted. Indeed, in the case of at least one aircraft, L7287, which had been the trials aircraft for the FN7A mid-upper turret, by the time of the MILLENNIUM raid its turret had been removed. Squadron Leader Peter Ward-Hunt had recently been appointed to command 49 Squadron Con. Flight. In spite of being rested from operations, he elected to participate, taking along with him as second pilot, the 49 Squadron Commanding Officer Wing Commander Leonard C. Slee.

Prior to Operation MILLENNIUM there had been little flying at Skellingthorpe. All sorts of rumours had been 'doing the rounds'. 50 Squadron were in the final days of operating their Manchesters.

Leslie Baveystock, a second pilot under training, had just commenced a weekend leave. His wife was already on the train from London to Lincoln to join him when he heard his leave was cancelled and that he was operating that night. He learned he was to join the crew of Pilot Officer Leslie Manser, with whom he had not previously flown. Manser informed him that they had orders to fly over to Coningsby that afternoon to collect one of the 106 Conversion Flight aircraft, which was used only for circuits and bumps. Baveystock obtained Manser's agreement to at least meet his wife from the railway station and install her in the 'Station Hotel' before returning to base. A scratch crew collected the aircraft and flew it back to Skellingthorpe, arriving in the late afternoon.

They found they had acquired one of the earliest Manchesters, L7301, now coded ZN-D, of 106 Squadron. Despite being received by the RAF on 21 December 1940, L7301 had done very little flying, possibly being one of the initial, non-operationally fit 'pre-production' aircraft. First it had been stored at 27MU, Shawbury. Later, in March 1941, it was sent back to Avro at Ringway ostensibly for an engine change and held there until April, when it was finally reworked to later production standards. Which modifications were incorporated is not recorded. It was issued to 106 Squadron Conversion Flight on 28 April 1942. On arrival at Skellingthorpe on 30 May the ground crews found the mid-upper turret had still not been fitted and that the lower escape hatch, where the mid-under turret would originally have been, was sealed by a series of permanently mounted metal plates. Consistent with this early batch of aircraft, no autopilot was fitted.

Time at Skellingthorpe only permitted the barest checking and topping up of oil and coolant levels as the aircraft was hurriedly refuelled and bombed up with 1,260 4-lb incendiaries in fourteen containers. Following briefing and a meal the crew were driven out to the aircraft. Manser had discussed his attack plan with Baveystock and informed him of his intention to bomb from 7,000 feet instead of their briefed height of 12,000 feet. The prospect of all the light and medium flak at that height, not to mention the falling bombs and incendiaries caused Baveystock an inward shudder.

When they reached the aircraft and got down from their transport Baveystock saw L7301 for the first time, taking in amongst other things that it lacked a mid-upper turret. Why then need they carry Sergeant Stanley King, the second wireless operator/air gunner, who would be a mere passenger with nowhere to sit and nothing to do? At least someone had given some thought to this problem and Baveystock was surprised to see a young Corporal Armourer waiting to greet them. He told Manser and King that he had drawn a pair of Vickers Gas Operated (VGO) machine guns and several pans of 0.303-inches ammunition from the armoury in lieu of the mid-upper turret and suggested that if they were attacked from the beam Sergeant King might like to 'poke' a hole in the side of the fuselage and fire at the attacker. Of course the entire concept was ludicrous. There was no rack in the aircraft to store the guns or 0.303-inches pans, no bracket to mount the VGO, no aperture to point the gun through or even windows to sight and aim it. Possibly pre-occupied with more serious and immediate issues, Manser allowed the extra weight of the VGOs, their ammunition and the useless gunner to be loaded in the aircraft. In

Aircrew of 106 Squadron pose in front of one of the unit's Manchesters at Coningsby. (D. Richards/106 Squadron Association)

addition to expending Sergeant King needlessly in the next few hours even more was at stake that night because L7301 carried not just two but a third pilot. Flying Officer Richard Barnes, the observer, was also a pilot.

1,043 crews took off between 22.19 and 00.30 hours with a view to concentrating the attack in a 90 min. period. The 5 Group crews were given a fifteen minute period between seventy and ninety minutes after the start of the attack in which to bomb. 'Z' hour was 00.55 hours. Most 5 Group Manchesters took off soon after 23.00 hours.

Over at Scampton 83 and 49 Squadrons both put up Manchesters for the operation. The aircraft were carefully marshalled to permit a streamed take-off. The twelve Manchesters of 49 Squadron were away first between 22.50 and 23.31 hours, followed by the 83 Squadron Manchesters between 23.29 and 23.47 hours and finally the Lancasters of 83 Squadron.

The Manchester force soon began to experience problems. As Pilot Officer Perry of 49 Squadron tried to make height in L7524 the aircraft began to vibrate and lose altitude. He had no alternative but to land at Docking after forty-five minutes in the air. Sergeant Weber in L7471 of 50 Squadron had the intercom to the rear turret fail at the Dutch coast and returned early. From 83 Squadron, Flight Sergeant Marchant in L7293 experienced intercom and a rear turret failure and returned to base with his bombs.

Pilot Officer Hodgson of 83 Squadron lost engine power in his aircraft and had to jettison the bomb load to remain under control. He, too, returned early. Pilot Officer Rayment in one of the 49 Squadron Con. Flight Manchesters loaned to 83 Squadron also lost power and had to release his bomb load over the North Sea. Squadron Leader Price was delayed taking off in the sole 408 Squadron Con. Flight Manchester, L7401, possibly due to technical problems. It was to no avail because the aircraft experienced a hydraulic failure and had to return with its incendiaries still on board. So, six Manchesters dropped out from the initial force of forty-five aircraft, leaving the remaining thirty-nine to attack Cologne.

Flight Sergeant Carter took off in 49 Squadron L7429 from Scampton early in the take-off sequence at 23.00 hours local time. Nothing further was heard from this aircraft after take-off, but several bodies from this crew were recovered from the North Sea the next day. Seventy years later correlation of RAF and Luftwaffe records makes clear that ground-based radar had begun tracking the incoming raiders. The defending night fighter force was directed seawards. Guided by controllers and relying on close range visual identification and interception, at 01.36 hours. Oberleutnant Heinrich Prinz zu Sayn-Wittgenstein of 9/NJG2 homed-in on the unsuspecting cumbersome L7429, shooting it down into the sea and claiming his third victory. Carter thus became the first

Manchester loss of the night. The Prinz went on to become a leading ace, claiming 83 victories before being killed in action on 20/21 January 1944.

Pilot Officer Roy Calvert was flying L7525 of 50 Squadron and had had an uneventful outward flight, other than the unusual experience of all hands keeping a careful watch for other aircraft in the bomber stream. Both the number of aircraft involved and their proximity in space and time was still a novelty to the crews. On their bomb run they had traversed Cologne at 9,000 feet and the bomb aimer had just called: 'Bombs away!' when the aircraft was struck by a flak burst in the starboard engine. The similarities with Pilot Officer Manser's experiences later that night, other than the outcome, are astounding. Calvert's starboard engine burst into flame. Calmly, but quickly, Calvert closed the bomb doors, shut off the fuel supply to the starboard Vulture, pressed the extinguisher button and feathered the propeller.

The crew were relieved when the fire diminished and went out and the feathering mechanism worked satisfactorily. Calvert advanced the throttle of the port Vulture and pushed forward the stick, diving to clear the searchlights in the target area as quickly as possible. They cleared the lights at about 7,000 feet and levelled out on a westerly heading. As the speed built-up in the dive ebbed away Calvert, having trimmed the aircraft to fly on one engine, found to his dismay that L7525 was still inexorably sinking. It seemed the inevitable Manchester problem would be their undoing too.

Evaluating their options, Calvert chanced opening the fuel tap on the starboard Vulture and unfeathered the prop to restart the engine, hoping for a little help from it. The engine started, but promptly burst into flames again. Now the situation was potentially terminal because Calvert knew the Graviner bottle would be empty. He refeathered the propeller and turned off the fuel. To his immense relief the fire died down of its own accord. Next he instructed the crew to prepare to abandon the aircraft, but in the meantime to jettison any moveable items on board. The crew turned to with a will and their rate of descent steadily decreased. However, after 45 minutes flying they were approaching the Dutch coast, still without a sign that the aircraft would maintain its altitude.

By now they were down to a critical altitude of 200 feet. Soon after crossing the coast they encountered low filmy cloud at sea level and Calvert judged them to be completely safe from attack by night fighters. Thus assured, he ordered the gunners to strip out all guns and ammunition and ditch these through the open hatches. Still they sank inexorably lower. The port throttle was fully advanced and, at 100 feet, Calvert tried another ploy. He closed the radiator flap under the port nacelle, which reduced the drag, increased the speed and lift and permitted a climb to 200 feet. Then he quickly reopened the flap to let the engine cool down, gradually losing height to 100 feet again. Still they flew on.

This procedure was repeated several times until the crew finally recognised the approaches to the Thames Estuary ahead. By this time, too, more fuel had been burned off and having reached the coast they found there seemed to be fractionally more lift over the land. They were then able to climb to a few hundred feet without overheating. The first airfield they came to was Tempsford, where a precautionary landing was thankfully carried out. Next day inspection revealed a sliver of shrapnel in the coolant pipe of the starboard engine which had led to the fire.

The story of Pilot Officer Manser's brave and selfless attack on Cologne has been recorded many times. The run across the target was prolonged by his determination to bomb on the edge of a dark patch in the flaming city. In so doing they were trapped in the searchlights and shortly after the incendiaries were released, with the experienced navigator, Richard Barnes, in the bomb aimer's position calling: 'Hold for the photograph. Steady', the aircraft was jolted from beneath by a flak hit. Manser immediately thrust the stick forward in an attempt to shake off the lights, but despite their twisting flight path they continued to be held and peppered by a hail of light 20 mm flak, until they finally slid out of range of the lights at 700 feet. Manser then hauled back on the stick and began climbing to provide the additional height necessary if they needed to bale out.

Meanwhile, the crew assessed the damage around their crew stations. The rear gunner, Sergeant Ben Naylor, reported that he had been hit by shrapnel from the flak bursts, which had also seriously damaged the tail and rear fuselage, leading to control difficulties for asymmetric single-engine flying.

Mk.1 R5784 VN-? of 50 Squadron is said to be at Hinton-in-the-Hedges, not its home base, Skellingthorpe. (50 Squadron archives via Peter Green)

Few photographs of 50 Squadron's short association with the Manchester have emerged. This one is of a Mk.1 VN-Z, possibly L7476, of 50 Squadron at Skellingthorpe, April-June 1942. (50 Squadron archives)

Rear section of Mk.1 L7434 ZN-J of 106 Squadron, Coningsby, c. May 1942. It undertook nine operations before being passed to 1656 Conversion Unit. (D. Richards/106 Squadron Association)

At 2,000 feet there was an explosion and roar from the port engine, which burst into flame. Manser instructed Baveystock to operate the extinguisher and feather the propeller. The extinguisher seemed to have no effect and indeed the fire was trailing aft of the wing and beyond the tail unit. With the threat of the fuel tank exploding or the main spar burning through the crew expected the order to bale out any moment. Manser remained supremely calm and instructed them to wait and see if the fire went out. He obtained a course for Manston in Kent, his determination to reach and bomb the target now replaced by an equal determination to get them home. Sergeant Bob Horsley, the W/op AG, was on his last operation before the end of his tour. By this time he recalled walking away from 3 Manchester forced landings.

Horsley called the under-employed Sergeant Stanley King, instructing him to make his way aft, extract the wounded Ben Naylor and dress his wounds. However, shock, fear and inexperience had paralysed the supernumary Second W/op AG Horsley then left his set, grabbed King and examined him, finding no sign of physical injury. He led King to the wireless station, sat him down and instructed him to send a damage report back to base. He then turned, put the internal lights on and made his way aft to drag Ben Naylor from the rear turret. Horsley saw blood everywhere from wounds to the bridge of the gunner's nose, his left shoulder and foot. He opened the gunner's clothing, put a field dressing over the shoulder wound beneath his parachute harness and gave him a shot of morphine to dull the pain, laying him down near the rear entry door, ready to bale out should it become necessary. At the same time he plugged Naylor into the intercom again and kept calling Sergeant King to send the damage report.

Fortunately, at least the feathering mechanism worked, and in the next few minutes the fierce fire in the nacelle gradually burnt itself out. The short term emergency was replaced by a longer term concern, for they were gradually losing height on the remaining Vulture. As with Pilot Officer Calvert's aircraft in similar straits nearby, the crew set about jettisoning everything removable from the airframe to reduce weight. One of the first items Baveystock ditched was the two useless VGOs and their ammunition from the mid-section.

In the case of L7301, bravery and discipline proved more enduring than the aircraft for, as they crossed into Belgian airspace, the starboard engine began to overheat from the strain, speed dropped away further and Manser began to have control difficulties as the port wing kept dropping, causing the aircraft to bank and yaw off course. With the starboard engine temperature rising off the clock and the engine likely to seize and catch fire at any moment and, moreover, with their steady descent unabated, Manser made his final and perfectly timed judgement. In doing so he saved six lives and forfeited his own. 'Parachutes on. Prepare to abandon aircraft!' called Manser. Horsley, Naylor and King, the wireless operator and rear and 'mid-upper' gunners, stood by the rear entry door, whilst Barnes, the observer, and Mills, the front gunner jettisoned the lower escape hatch in the nose.

'Bale out! Bale out!' Mills jumped followed by Barnes, but Baveystock remained behind with the intention of helping Manser into his 'chute. The aircraft was shuddering on the point of the stall and would fall out of control at any moment. Manser thrust Baveystock away. 'For God's sake, get out! We're going down!' Recognising that he could do no more, Baveystock doubled himself up and dropped through the hatch. His tumbling body was arrested partly by his half-open parachute and partly by the 4 to 5 feet of water in the ditch into which he immediately fell.

Meanwhile, Horsley had acknowledged the bale-out call, opened the rear entry door and sat on the step before rolling out. Naylor and King had been unwilling to go first but did then follow him. Horsley realised they were already down to about 1,000 feet and pulled his rip-cord as soon as the tail flashed by, landing a few seconds later in a soft, wet marshy area. King and Naylor reached the ground safely close-by. Of these survivors, Richard Barnes, the navigator, handed himself in to a Belgian civilian who immediately passed him on to the Germans. Les Baveystock, Bob Horsley, Stanley King, Alan Mills and the wounded Ben Naylor found each other and stayed together.

Ahead, Manser had finally lost control and the Manchester rolled over and plunged into the ground, killing him instantly. They had come down in farmland near Bree in eastern Belgium. Next day the wreck was visited and photographed by a German night fighter pilot, Oberleutnant Baake of II/NJGI, who mistakenly claimed to have shot the aircraft down at 02.14 hours European Time. Baveystock and the remainder of the crew had a remarkable escape and by chance four of them evaded capture and were eventually able to return to England. On the basis of their report Leslie Manser received a posthumous Victoria Cross. Never was an award more appropriate, but it was also awarded on behalf of the other Manchester crews who had shown equal bravery but whose self-sacrifice had gone unreported.

At least one other 50 Squadron Manchester had an adventurous night over Cologne, from which it also failed to return. Sergeant Jim Wilkie had also flown over to Coningsby to collect another machine from 106 Con. Flight, L7456. His second pilot was Sergeant Cyril Tobias. With sixteen operations to his credit, Tobias had been posted from 455 Squadron RAAF for conversion onto Lancasters as these became available. In the meantime he would do a few Manchester operations. Nineteen year old Wilkie was approaching Cologne at 9,000 feet, having tried every ploy to coax the Manchester to a safer height. On the run-up searchlights and flak brought down a bomber ahead of them and he swung north to get around this hot spot, only to run into one of his own. The flak defences were fully alerted and the low flying Manchesters were easy meat. His aircraft was coned and heavily engaged by accurate anti-aircraft fire. He threw the over-laden aircraft around in a vain attempt to shake off the lights and tried diving. As he did so a flak burst disabled his port engine, which began running rough and spitting fire. Wilkie feathered the engine and operated the fire extinguisher. The deliberate height loss became inadvertent and try as he might Wilkie could not prevent the aircraft from sinking under its heavy load. All hope of reaching the inner city was gone and their entire efforts turned now to survival. The bomb load was jettisoned in the suburbs of Cologne and Wilkie turned away, still enmeshed in the blinding searchlights.

Despite releasing the bombs the aircraft was still unable to maintain height. Wilkie was unsure of his heading and his manoeuvres trying to evade the lights cost further precious height, which he could not claw back. Suddenly they passed out of range of the lights, but their height was now critically low and he immediately ordered the crew to bale out. He judged their chances of survival at this low level better than his own in the forthcoming forced landing into the dark unknown ahead.

Top and Bottom: The sorry remains of L7301 ZN-D which carried Flying Officer Leslie Manser to his death and a posthumous Victoria Cross on the night of 30/31 May 1942. Photographs attributed to Oberleutnant Baake of II/NJG1, who mistakenly claimed the Manchester destroyed at Kimroy at 02.14 hours. (via P. Loncke)

Jim Wilkie was holding on full left rudder to counteract the asymmetrical thrust of the starboard Vulture and knew that the instant he released it the aircraft would flip over on its back and crash. Like Derek Pinchbeck, John Nunn and other Manchester pilots who had to force land blind in the dark before him, Wilkie had no option but to sit there and accept the inevitable, whatever that turned out to be.

In a desperate attempt to see something in the total darkness ahead, Wilkie, alone now except for second pilot Tobias, flipped on the switch of the landing light. He was shocked to see trees illuminated and flashing by just beneath them. Bowing to the inevitable and hoping for some cushioning by the pine tree tops, Wilkie hauled back on the stick and cut the throttle to belly in into the forest. Instead they felt a jolt and rapid deceleration and dust and grass flew into the cockpit. By pure chance they had carried out a perfect belly landing, but a much greater coincidence was soon to become apparent. Both engines were now burning fiercely and by the glow of the still illuminated landing light, shining across the ground, they made out a fence with houses and gardens beyond. Wilkie and Tobias hurried back down the fuselage, both to escape the flames and check that all crew members had departed. They jumped down and began to flee the blaze, but were almost immediately surrounded by Luftwaffe personnel and captured. Miraculously L7456 had chosen to return to earth in the middle of Dusseldorf airfield!

The veteran L7319 allocated to Pilot Officer Atkinson of 50 Squadron resolutely refused to climb. He released part of his incendiary load approaching the Dutch coast. Flying Officer Heaton encountered enemy fighters on three occasions but managed to escape detection and attack successfully. All 50 Squadron Manchester crews, other than the early return, found Cologne alight from end to end. The river, cathedral and streets were clearly visible through the dense smoke already beginning to rise. Crews bombed from heights ranging between 5,000 and 10,500 feet.

Flying Officer L. T. Manser, who was posthumously awarded the Victoria Cross for his sacrifice on 30/31 May 1942 in a 106 Squadron Con Flight aircraft allocated to 50 Squadron. (Peter Green collection via Andy Thomas)

Australian Pilot Officer H. M. 'Micky' Martin, later to achieve fame in 617 Squadron, allocated R5769 of 50 Squadron, participated in the operation with three other Australians – Sergeants Leggo (observer), Foxlee (front gunner) and Simpson (rear gunner) – who were to remain in his crew for much of the war. In 5 Group Martin was greatly respected for his piloting skills, but at this time was not known for his respect for discipline or dress. He still proudly wore his dark blue battledress jacket even though it was faded and worn out at the elbows. He attacked Cologne from 7,400 feet noting the ineffective flak and stoking up the raging fires. Amongst the 49 Squadron aircraft heading for Cologne was the elderly L7290, being flown that night by Pilot Officer Phillip Floyd with Sergeant J. R. M. Valentine as observer. L7290 also lacked a mid-upper turret but, as with the similar aircraft sent out by 50 Squadron that night, they still carried a seven man crew. In this case Sergeant Randall flew as a passenger, curtaining himself off in the rest bed reading a novel until the action began to get out of hand. What a ridiculous waste to sacrifice a fully trained airman to the enemy for no possible benefit! Fortunately Randall was to escape with his life.

A vic of Manchester Mk.1s of 49 Squadron, EA-N, EA-G and EA-T, airborne from Scampton c. May 1942. EA-G, leading, has no mid-upper turret and is probably L7287. (Imperial War Museum, FLM2005.)

Manchester Mk.1A L7493 EA-F of 49 Squadron taxiing at Scampton c. May 1942. Initially delivered to 25 Operational Training Unit, L7493 reached 49 Squadron in May 1942 and undertook two operations. (Imperial War Museum, FLM2006)

L7290 was desperately slow, fully loaded they barely made 150 knots, and Floyd had the familiar fight to gain altitude. Eventually they nursed the aircraft up to 8,000 feet, a dangerously low altitude for the well-defended targets of the Ruhr. Urged on by the briefing, Floyd continued across Belgium, seeing Cologne from many miles distant. By the time they arrived, the defenders had recognised the approach direction of the bomber stream and in their run up to the target they were caught in a mammoth cone of searchlights. Floyd began to weave and corkscrew in an attempt to shake off the lights, always anxious not to lose the precious height they had fought for two hours to gain. Searchlights seemed to extend to the horizon in all directions and the flak gunners appeared to be concentrating on their aircraft, at what was, for them, point blank range. They took a number of hits, one of which knicked the hydraulic lines in several places. Valentine was drenched by the high pressure fluid, the front and rear turrets were put out of commission and the fuselage floor was flooded with the slippery oil.

Floyd recognised the imminence of their destruction if they remained at this height and dived for lower levels to restrict the field of fire of the guns and to throw off the lights. Speed built-up and at 3,000 feet they left the lighted arena and plunged temporarily into the anonymity of the night. Doggedly, Floyd headed on in towards Cologne and the aiming point, but now a new danger manifested itself for they had come within range of the rapid firing light flak guns. L7290 was raked with tracer.

Monitoring his instruments and still in control of the fast moving train of events, Floyd suddenly noticed that the oil temperature on the starboard engine was rising rapidly. A quick glance from the astrodome revealed that coolant was rippling back across the wing and streaming back in the slipstream. Moments later the engine caught fire. Floyd stopped it and feathered the propeller.

With the bomb load still on board and their descent rate increasing on the remaining engine, Floyd gave the inevitable order to bale out before they descended too low. Whilst Floyd stamped on full right rudder to counteract the pull of the port engine and held the stick hard over to keep up the starboard wing the crew hurried to the exits. Like Calvert, Manser, Wilkie and Carter faced with identical situations that same night in their Manchesters, Floyd knew the odds. As the crew tumbled out, Valentine gave Floyd a last few words of encouragement and thanks: 'You've done bloody well, Phillip. I'm going out in a second – I hope you'll follow me'. Floyd reached out and shook Valentine's hand before the latter flung himself down to the forward hatch. He was almost his own undoing when he prematurely pulled his D-ring and his 'chute spilled inside the aircraft. He bundled it up before it billowed out too far and lunged through the hatch. Sergeant Smith, the front gunner, was still waiting in the nose too afraid to jump, but Valentine could do nothing for him.[1]

The overloaded Manchester was sinking like a stone. The next second the faltering aircraft rolled onto its back, possibly as Floyd made his own attempt to bale out. It plunged nose down vertically into the ground, its bomb load exploding in the crash. Floyd and Smith were still on board and died instantly. The remaining five in the crew descended safely at Mulheim-Oberhausen and were taken prisoner.

Of the 49 Squadron aircr Fraft which evaded the rapacious night fighters over the North Sea, all made successful attacks. Sergeant Burton turned in an excellent performance, bombing the target despite engine and airframe trouble and an intercom failure. Flight Lieutenant Paramore's aircraft was fired on by an unidentified aircraft but not damaged, whilst Flight Sergeant Rowland's aircraft was approached by a Junkers JU88 which closed in twice but broke away on each occasion as soon as evasive action was taken. Most of the night fighters seemed unusually hesitant, although Flight Sergeant Lewis did report an aircraft engaged by a night fighter followed shortly afterwards by an explosion on the ground. All attacked from similar heights to 50 Squadron crews and reported the same extensive area of fires.

83 Squadron had already had three early returns from its force of six and in the target area its problems continued. The crew of R5768, captained by Pilot Officer MacDonald, saw their bombs straddle a factory, but soon afterwards they were engaged by flak which knocked out the hydraulics, shot away the fixed aerial and put the rear turret out of commission. Only Sergeant Williams had an uneventful operation.

Sergeant T. G. Irvine of 83 Squadron had taken the old 49 Conversion Flight Manchester, L7308. The fact that 49 Conversion Flight may not have had much time for the aircraft may be indicated by the fact that they never

---

[1] Frances Zagni (nee Valentine) set down the experiences of her father JRM Valentine and mother Ursula in her book *Gepruft – The Remarkable Second World War letters of Prisoner of War John Valentine and his wife Ursula (Fighting High, 2018)*. Gepruft is German for 'Checked'.

Triple fin Manchester 1 L7389 EA-L of 49 Squadron aloft from Scampton, c. June 1942. The aircraft served sequentially with 61, 207, 83 (as OL-M?) 49 Squadrons and 106 Squadron 'Con' Flight. A year earlier, on 30 June 1941, as QR-J of 61 Squadron, whilst engaged overnight on intensive engine trials in the hands of Pilot Officer Stevens, the starboard engine failed. In the dark the second pilot inadvertently feathered the port propeller and a dead stick belly landing was accomplished at Fowlmere. (via P. Gaunt)

tried to operate it. In fact it had been through a major rebuild following a serious accident with 97 Squadron back in September 1941.

Despite its vintage, Irvine managed to bomb the primary target at a late stage in the raid from 12,000 feet, although his bomb bursts could not be distinguished amongst the many fires. Having turned for the return leg, concern soon arose due to excessive fuel consumption. Thirty-two minutes prior to landfall checks revealed 120 gallons remaining in the port tank and only 100 in the starboard. Irvine tried to nurse the aircraft towards Scampton, but on approach his difficulties were accentuated by recognition of a hydraulic failure, which necessitated the undercarriage and flaps being lowered by the emergency system. Soon after this one shot system had been activated their problems escalated sharply, when the starboard engine failed as they turned in on approach to the first available aerodrome, which turned out to be Ingham in Lincolnshire. By this time the Manchester was losing height rapidly and the inexperienced captain felt powerless to stretch the glide. In the final moments the port Vulture began to splutter through lack of fuel. L7308 hit the ground ten yards short of the aerodrome boundary, descending like a lift, and the undercarriage collapsed. It slid through the boundary fence and came to a halt. All the crew escaped without injury.

Meanwhile, in Manchester R5268 pilot Officer MacDonald also had problems. On return it was found that the undercarriage could not be lowered with the emergency system. MacDonald then carried out a successful belly landing at Scampton, causing only slight damage to the aircraft. 83 Squadron had had a rough night, but at least all its Manchesters returned.

61 Squadron had a less eventful night with all four of its Manchesters bombing Cologne. Flying Officer Archibald released his load from only 7,000 feet and then dived to ground level for the return. His gunners fired on factories and a gasometer on the return flight. Sergeant Turner climbed to 15,000 feet approaching the target and released his bombs in a power dive from 14,000 feet.

Aircrews of 106 Squadron, Coningsby, looking exuberant, as well they might, on the morning of 31 May 1942. The previous night's 'thousand bomber' raid had been a stunning success and the unit suffered no casualties. A Mk.1 and a Mk.1A are at rest in the background. Wing Commander Guy Gibson in centre foreground and Flight Lieutenant John Wooldridge is second row, third from right. (via Aerospace Publishing)

Likewise, all five of 106 Squadron's aircraft attacked with minimal interference and returned. Squadron Leader Herring reached 17,000 feet in his Manchester, L7480, bombing the target at 02.05 hours. Flying Officer Henry Maudslay was late taking off in the second 44 Conversion Flight aircraft, L7430. By the time he arrived the target was well alight and the enemy defences had been overwhelmed. He released his load of incendiaries from 6,800 feet at 02.13 hours to add to the conflagration.

In the analysis the raid proved the wisdom of Roy Chadwick's concern for the Manchester. At least four of the aircraft whose experiences are related here had reached the target area and attacked at suicidally low level. Most had proved incapable of climbing above 10,000 feet. Amongst the survivors many were less seriously damaged only because their numbers had overwhelmed the defences and prevented them concentrating on individual targets for long.

In the case of these four, and excepting the fifth flown by Flight Sergeant Carter, it was flak not night fighters that did the damage. In all cases once one engine was put out of action the other had proved inadequate, or in the case of Pilot Officer Calvert, just adequate to the task. So Bomber Command's maximum effort coincided with that of the Manchester.

Following their return, the 'Thousand Force' was kept together in the hope that a second, telling, blow could be delivered on Hamburg. Crews were dog-tired and greatly relieved when weather led to the operation being cancelled that night. However, they were on again on 1/2 June 1942 and, although Hamburg remained cloud-covered, Harris went for Essen with 956 aircraft. The same seven squadrons were involved, this time supplying thirty-three Manchesters. However, the raid was to be a total failure with bad weather causing bombs to be scattered far and wide.

Essen, a near MILLENNIUM – 1/2 June 1942:

Serial   Code   Squadron   Captain

Balderton - also sixteen Hampdens
?   EQ-N̄   408   Sqn Ldr L. B. B. Price

Coningsby - also nine Lancasters
Serial	Code	Squadron	Captain
L7434	ZN-	106	Plt Off. J. Aytoun
R5796	ZN-	106	Plt Off. S. Cockbain
L7457	ZN-	106	Plt Off. G. Cooke
L7488	ZN-	106	FS G. Appleyard
L7391	ZN-	106	Plt Off. R. G. Churcher
R5780	ZN-	106	Plt Off. M. Duff

Scampton - also ? Lancasters
Serial	Code	Squadron	Captain
L7389	EA-L	49	Sqn Ldr P. M. de Mestre
L7493	EA-F	49	Sgt H. G. Burton
L7398	EA-	49	Plt Off. A. S. Perry
L7526	EA-V	49	Plt Off. G. S. Jeffreys
L7479	EA	49	Plt Off. S. T. Farrington
R5775	EA-	49	Flt Lt R. E. R. Paramore
L7421	EA-	49	FS R. G. Lewis
R5794	EA-	49	Plt Off. W. C. Shackleton
L7397	OL-	83	Plt Off. J. Hodgson

Skellingthorpe
Serial	Code	Squadron	Captain
L7476	VN-	50	Plt Off. T. Cole
L7319	VN-	50	Plt Off. D. A. Atkinson
L7432	VN-	50	Fg Off. H. W. Southgate
L7471	VN-	50	Sgt A. Weber
L7419	VN-	50	FS E. J. Morgan
R5769	VN-	50	Plt Off. H. B. Martin
L7460	VN-	50	Sgt P. M. Crampton
R5833	KM-	44 CF§	FS D. Gray
?	ZN-G	106 CF§	Plt Off. Q. D. Beatty

Syerston - also eleven Lancasters
Serial	Code	Squadron	Captain
L7477	QR-	61	Plt Off. E. R. Seibold
L7401	QR-	61	FS P. W. Gregory
L7415	QR-	61	FS J. G. Stewart
L7491	QR-	61	Sqn Ldr R. A. V. Gascoyne-Cecil
L7458	QR	61	FS N. R. Meyer
L7425	QR-	61	Sqn Ldr A. M. Paape

Waddington - also eleven Lancasters
L7480   KM-Ā   44   Fg Off. Maudsley

§ on loan to 50 Squadron

At Scampton 49 Squadron ground crews had a battle to get the Manchesters airborne. Seven of the force got away close either side of midnight. Pilot Officer Farrington did not take-off until 00.50 hours owing to unspecified problems, whilst Squadron Leader de Mestre was delayed until 00.56 hours with engine trouble. Both returned from the Dutch coast, having insufficient time to reach the target. R5794 with Pilot Officer Shackleton failed to return. An SOS was received at 02.19 hours reporting that the starboard engine had failed but nothing more was heard. Shortly after that the aircraft was shot down by a night fighter flown by Feldwebel Heinz Pähler of 2/NJGI crashing at Voorheide, 12 km east-northeast of Turnhout, Belgium. The two survivors were taken prisoner. The remaining crews claimed to attack the primary target.

All 50 Squadron aircraft attacked what they believed to be the primary target and reported very little response from the defences. A flak hit injured Flight Sergeant Stevens, the observer in Pilot Officer Cole's aircraft, and a Messerschmitt Bf109 followed Sergeant Crampton's aircraft for a while on return, but did not attack.

Three of the 61 Squadron Manchesters returned early. Flight Sergeant Stewart was delayed taking off by intercom failure and returned when it became clear he could not reach the target by the time ordered. Squadron Leader Paape experienced excessive tail shudder, which led him to return early as a precaution. It is not clear why Pilot Officer Seibold returned early. Flying Officer Gregory bombed fires on the ground, having had problems locating the target. Squadron Leader Gascoyne-Cecil claimed a visual on the aiming point and Flight Sergeant Meyer made a good effort. His port rev counter went u/s 150 miles out but be carried on and bombed the target from 10,000 feet. On 61 Squadron's last Manchester operation Pilot Officer Hodgson was unable to locate the primary and believed he hit Oberhausen instead.

All 106 Squadron crews reported attacking the primary, although target identification had been problematical. Flying Officer Maudslay in the 44 Conversion Flight aircraft had to attack an alternate target from 8,000 feet when he was unable to locate Essen. Similarly, Squadron Leader Price in the 408 Conversion Flight aircraft had target identification problems and bombed a built-up area he believed to be Essen. In fact the raid was widely dispersed. Some damage was caused to Oberhausen, Mulheim and Duisburg.

On 3/4 June 1942 Bomber Command dispatched 170 aircraft to attack Bremen. Amongst the force of six Manchesters from 50 Squadron, two went NICKELLING to Le Mans and the remaining four to the principal target. 106 Squadron also sent two Manchesters. 49 Squadron sent two inexperienced Manchester crews NICKELLING to Lille. Flying Officer J. F. Heaton took off from Skellingthorpe in Manchester Mk.1 L7432 VN-Z of 50 Squadron at 21.10 hours but was intercepted and the aircraft was damaged by Oberleutnant Viktor Bauer of III/NJGI. Four of the crew were killed as a result of the engagement, which was recalled by the Wireless Operator, Sergeant Ken Gaulton:

We flew across Northern Holland and made our briefed attack on Bremen. I immediately called the captain (02.30 hours) to advise that we were cleared to return to base. On our homeward flight over Holland we were attacked by a Bf110. His tracer caused our starboard wing to catch fire. Heaton called that he was going to dive in an attempt to extinguish the flames, but the blaze was fierce and this action failed to staunch the fire. Deciding that our aircraft was fatally damaged (true) and we were defenceless (untrue), Oberleutnant Bauer then performed a victory roll at the rear of our aircraft. Our hydraulics, intercom, etc. remained serviceable and the crew still at their posts. Our tail gunner, Sergeant P. Buttigieg, drew a bead on the night fighter and from close range shot him down. I was amazed to hear the gunner yelling with delight at his success.

After another failed attempt at diving to extinguish the fire and several thousand feet lower, I requested Heaton's permission for the rear and mid-upper gunners (Buttigeig and Farquher) to join me and prepare the rear entry door for evacuation. This was approved and the three of us jumped in turn, me being last out. I left the aircraft when it was slightly under 1,000 feet, quickly pulled the ripcord and was promptly knocked unconscious by my chest parachute jerking upwards and striking me under the jaw. Meanwhile, the aircraft never pulled out of its dive and crashed, killing Heaton, Pilot Officer J. Steen, the second pilot, Pilot Officer A. Sheen, the navigator, and Sergeant S. Thomas, the front gunner - all of whom were grouped in the forward part of the aircraft. In my dazed condition I was unprepared for what came next. I speared up to my chest in mud on an ebbing tide in a shallow part of the Zuider Zee. I was revived in due course by an Alsatian dog licking my face and its owner eventually extricated me and took me to visit a doctor at about 05.30 hours. I was unable to walk. It became evident from their exchanges that the man who brought me in was a collaborator and the doctor could do no more than clean me up and check me for any injuries. I was then taken by car to Arnhem, where the Gestapo interrogated me, and then by train to Amsterdam, where I was locked up in the watchtower for four days. While I was there a senior Luftwaffe officer from the night fighter unit which had shot us down visited me (about 6 June). He told me that L7432 had crashed on a hunting lodge near Apeldoorn owned by the Dutch Royal family. He also told me that the two-man crew of the night fighter had been killed but as we had lost four dead in our aircraft they were two ahead.

Manchester Mk.1 L7287 EA-G running up at Scampton, probably in May 1942. L7287 was from the pre-production batch and had been used as the FN7A trials aircraft. The turret had been removed by the time it was issued to 49 Squadron for operations. It was lost on 6/7 June 1942 with Flight Lieutenant Paramore and crew. (Imperial War Museum. FLM2004)

German records for Bremen which became available post-war record this as the third heaviest casualty toll of the war. Eighty-three people were killed, twenty-nine seriously and 229 slightly injured. The raid missed the U-boat construction yards and Focke-Wulf factory but the harbour area, including the destroyer Z-26, were hit together with residential areas.

On 5/6 June 50 Squadron lost another Manchester captained by Pilot Officer D. Garland in R5833. They took off from Skellingthorpe at 22.27 hours to lay mines in the GORSE region. Only the mid-upper gunner, Pilot Officer R. Gill, survived to become a prisoner of war. He reports "Our aircraft was intercepted by enemy fighters whilst inward-bound to the drop zone at low level. We were close to Ile de Quiberone, near Lorient. Aircraft hit the sea and I remember nothing until I came up to the surface and found blazing petrol on the water. No-one else was to be seen. Germans told me I was the sole survivor". Wing Commander Slee took L7469 of 49 Squadron on a NICKELLING raid on Rennes. En route he had reached 15,000 feet when a photoflash went off, rendering all W/T equipment unserviceable. Crew members eventually got the IFF working. They returned safely to base.

On 6/7 June 1942 the Manchester force of seven, two from 50 Squadron and five from 49 Squadron, joined a 233 aircraft attack on Emden – the first major raid on this town since November 1941. It was a terrible night for the Manchesters. The highly decorated Squadron Leader P. de Mestre DSO, DFC and crew in L7469 of 49 Squadron were shot down into the North Sea from 17,500 feet by the experienced Oberleutnant Ludwig Becker of 6/NJG2 at a location 20 km north-west of Borkum. Four bodies were eventually washed ashore on the coast of mainland Europe. Squadron Leader de Mestre and two others have no known graves. Flight Lieutenant R. E. R. Paramore, another decorated Captain in 49 Squadron, had the misfortune to be allocated one of the earliest non-operationally-fit Manchesters, L7287. Its modification status is unknown. They took off from Scampton at 23.19 hours and were lost without trace. The seven crew members have no known graves and they must also have

Mixed gaggle of Lancasters and Manchesters taxiing to take off from Scampton on 25/26 June 1942 for Ops to Bremen, 'MILLENIUM TWO', and the last Manchester operation of the war. From the Manchesters L7453 EA-T captained by Sergeant J. W. Heard and R5788 EA-K captained by Sergeant T. V. Webster both attacked and returned successfully. (Peter Green collection)

come down in the North Sea. No night fighter claim is linked to this loss and, other than being a victim of flak defences, this loss might be another consequence of engine failure. Pilot Officer A. D. 'Don' Beatty of 50 Squadron in L7471 and his all RAAF crew took off from Skellingthorpe at 23.16 hours, sending a message asking for help from close to the Dutch coast. They did not acknowledge the response and ditched their Manchester off the Dutch Frisian Islands after their aircraft also developed engine problems. Pilot Officer Beatty died in captivity from his injuries three months later and his second pilot, Sergeant Burton, was lost at sea, having no known grave. The remaining five in the crew somehow made it to shore but were captured and made prisoners for the duration. The North Sea reaped a high and tragic harvest from the two squadrons in a few pitiless days. 300 houses were destroyed and a further 200 seriously damaged in the Emden attack. Seventeen people were killed and forty-nine injured. Some damage was caused in the docks area.

Finally, during the next full moon period, on 25/26 June 1942, the force again reassembled for another attempt to achieve the results of the Cologne raid a month earlier. This time the target was Bremen and approaching 100 Coastal Command Hudsons joined Bomber Command in raising a force of 1,006 aircraft. It was the last operation of the war flown by Manchesters, but by now only twenty serviceable aircraft could be raised, mostly from 50 Squadron. The operation was code-named MILLENNIUM TWO. The aircraft raised were:

Bremen, MILLENNIUM TWO and Manchester bow out – 25/26 June 1942:

Serial	Code	Squadron	Captain

Coningsby - also seventeen Lancasters

| R5839 | ZN- | 106 | Sgt T. B. Crowfoot |
| R5780 | ZN- | 106 | Sgt S. E. J. Jones |

Scampton - also one Lancaster

R5772	EA-	49	Plt Off. R. F. Elliott
L7453	EA-T	49	Sgt J. W. Heard
R5788	EA-	49	Sgt T. V. Webster

Skellingthorpe - also two Lancasters

| L7455 | VN- | 50 | FS J. F. Taylor |
| L7289 | VN- | 50 | Sgt J. C. Roy |

L7415	VN-	50	FS E. J. Morgan
R5835	VN-	50	Sgt R. C. Wiseman
L7496	VN-	50	Plt Off. T. Cole
L7277	VN-	50	Sgt D. Gray
L7521	VN-	50	FS A. Weber
L7416	VN-	50	Plt Off. R. O. Calvert
L7464	VN-	50	Flt Lt P. J. Stone
L7401	VN-	50	Plt Off. J. S. Bunbury
L7294	VN-	50	Fg Off. H. W. Southgate
R5769	VN-	50	Plt Off. H. B. Martin

Syerston - also ? Lancasters
R5835	QR-	61	FS F. Hobson
L7477	QR-	61	FS C. P. Shriner

Waddington - also eleven Lancasters
L7430	KM-N̄	44	Plt Off. S. T. Farrington*

*on loan from 49 Squadron

The specific 5 Group target in Bremen was the Focke-Wulf factory. However, as at Essen, the large amount of cloud cover prevented a concentrated attack. The three 49 Squadron Manchesters attacked what they believed was the built-up area of Bremen instead. From the 50 Squadron force only one aircraft, that of Flying Officer Southgate which came down to 2,500 feet, managed to bomb the factory. Flight Sergeant Taylor had a rear turret failure after being airborne for an hour. He turned north out of the bomber stream, jettisoned his incendiaries and returned to base. Pilot Officer Martin had the intercom to the rear turret fail and bombed Alkmaar airfield as a last resort target before returning. Flight Sergeant Roy and his crew became the last operational Manchester casualty of the war when his aircraft failed to return. It was brought down in a field at Grembke with the loss of the entire crew. No further details have come to hand, nor can any night fighter claims be linked to this loss. Both Manchesters from 61 Squadron aborted and reports from the two 106 Squadron flight crews are unavailable.

Sadly the recently converted 49 Squadron had suffered the highest percentage Manchester loss rate in Bomber Command. During the last three months the loss rate on Manchesters seemed to be increasing beyond that experienced earlier:

Manchester Losses March-June 1942:

Date	Dispatched	FTR	Loss Rate %
8/9 March	25	2	8.0
13/14 March	16	2	12.5
25/26 March	20	4	20.0
28/29 March	21	1	4,8
29/30 March	8	2	5.0
8/9 April	18	2	11.0
10/11 April	16	1	6.3
2/3 May	17	2	11.8
8/9 May	11	2	18.0
30/31 May	45	4	8.8
6/7 June	7	3	42.9

Naturally, with such small sample numbers, the variability is high, but clearly the loss rate was sufficiently high to trigger an inquiry within Bomber Command. The report, No.44 from the Operational Research Section (ORS), apparently assessed various possible reasons for the high losses. It did not have the information available presented in this history and amongst other suggestions a possible problem with the fuel system was considered and dismissed. The only common feature was the low operating height of the Manchester, but Bomber Command responded by pointing out that there was no technical reason why the Manchester should be operated at a lower average height than other 'heavies', especially the Stirling, which had a more favourable loss rate. The operational

An appropriate photograph upon which to close the operational career of the Avro Manchester - armourers loading 0.303-inch ammunition into the rear turret of Mk.1A L7526 EA-V of 49 Squadron at Scampton. L7526 was the last Avro-built Manchester and had initially been with 25 Operational Training Unit. (Imperial War Museum, FLM2003)

ceiling was stated to be almost 3,000 feet higher than the Stirling. Any tendency for crews to operate the Manchester at lower heights was considered to be due to a disinclination of crews to overtax their engines. Loss rates were regularly reaching double figure percentages and at times 25% and above. At this rate a Manchester crew would not survive a tour of thirty operations but perhaps four instead.

This seems to be an altogether shallower and unsympathetic dismissal of the Manchester crews by Bomber Command. At a time when operational squadrons, as shown by entries in aircrew logbooks and ORBs, were still sanctioned to release part of their bomb load at the enemy coast in order to permit a climb to a safe height to cross the Kammhuber Line, when they were attacking within range of a wider calibre of anti-aircraft guns and could be quickly reached by night fighters taking off late following feints by the attacking force, few would deliberately chose to fly at such low levels. Added to this, on their bomb runs in the emerging bomber streams, to fly through a shower of bombs released by their much-envied fellow crews in the sibling Lancasters 10,000 feet above them was additionally unwelcome.

A look at the fates of operational Manchesters in the Appendix plus the accounts related here highlights the perpetual concern with engines which had proved the Achilles heel of the type from the beginning. A factor largely absent from the loss statistics of other aircraft is this risk of loss following one of the Vulture engines being put out of service by enemy action, or even at this late stage the direct risk of an unprovoked engine failure. Indeed, minutes circulating in late 1941 and early 1942 had examined the concerns over burning out of exhaust manifolds and of weaknesses in the hydraulic piping in the Vulture engines. This was to worsen as the spares situation deteriorated for aircraft in second line duties.

In the event the ORS report only became available on 10 June 1942, by which time the Manchesters had only one more mission to undertake before being withdrawn. Consequently the matter was not pursued further. The loss statistics served only to reinforce the obvious obsolescence of the Manchester, which could no longer survive in the night skies over occupied Europe.

Chapter Nine: Second Line Service

As described in earlier chapters, during the initial development stages various roles, such as dive bombing, torpedo dropping and transport were allowed to fall by the wayside. Attention focussed instead on engine, airframe and defensive armament rationalisation, including the so-called Manchester armament development aircraft with four cannon turrets. All these were in respect of defining an ideal front line operational machine. As serviceable aircraft became available, even during the 18-month operational period, other urgent war trials and development roles were thrust to the fore. From mid-1942, as Bomber Command expanded, when Manchesters were withdrawn from squadron service, the remaining aircraft found a new and equally vital training role in support of the squadrons now operating four-engined Lancasters.

As the clouds of war had darkened a welter of technological demands spiralled. During the 1930s and 1940s as aircraft weights and sizes increased, concerns arose as to whether the small grassy airfields of the time could adequately cope with the increased loads. The difficulties encountered by Sam Brown flying the prototype Manchester, together with test flights on new Ansons and Blenheims coming off the Woodford production lines with both flooding and bogging down of aircraft outlined early in this book highlight this starkly. This was to find expression in the late 1930s and 1940s in what was ultimately to prove a stillborn scheme, the Direction Controlled Take-Off (DCTO). Various other technical limitations of designs of the time and visions for the future included undercarriage wheel tyre pressures and propeller design. In the event more desirable options, including metalling of runways, almost unimaginable increases in engine power and development of variable pitch propellers were to nullify the need for these other options. Manchester L7246 became the sole trials aircraft for this system, with the consequence that the installation at Farnborough has sometimes been referred to as the 'Manchester Railway'.

At the end of the 1920s a requirement was drawn up to accelerate an aircraft weighing 18,000 lb to a speed of sixty mph within 300 feet. The Head of the Design Department at RAE in the early 1930s, Percy Salmon, initially came up with a winch and cable system powered by two compressed air engines. The winch drum was securely anchored to the ground and the aircraft located ahead of it standing on its main wheels with its tail raised into the flying position on a wheeled trolley. It seems that a winch wire ran forward from the drum close to the ground, passing on under the trolley, between the undercarriage legs and ahead the necessary few hundred feet to a firmly anchored sheeve and pulley. The wire then ran back under the aircraft again being attached to the trolley. Acceleration of the trolley with its low-placed wire avoiding any whirling propeller resulted in the aircraft lifting out of the trolley at the take-off point. At the 1931 RAF Pageant at Hendon the system was demonstrated using a Vickers Virginia, the siting of the twin propellers on which avoided proximity to the tow wire. However, accelerating any device from such an aft-mounted attachment point induced inherent lateral instability and a strong yawing moment. The scheme was soon abandoned.

By 1936 when the specifications for the 55,000-lb B12/36 and the 45,000-lb P13/36 were drawn up, the requirement had escalated to one of accelerating a 60,000-lb weight to 110 mph for take-off. Both the B12/36 and P13/36 were to be stressed to cope with catapult take-off. Once more the catapult section at RAE was involved. This time they came up with a multi-ram hydro-pneumatic catapult. In anticipation of the requirement for much larger aircraft Mr Salmon had already commenced design of this system possibly called the Mark III catapult. Its design was based on experience in developing catapults for various shipboard applications.

Development continued in parallel with that of the Short Stirling, Handley Page Halifax and Manchester aircraft themselves. Installation of the heavy aircraft catapult was scheduled for a number of bomber airfields and had commenced at Harwell during 1938. Development snags were experienced, and RAF bomber policy was shifting to favour three metalled runways laid out at 120 degrees and the concept was abandoned in the late 1939.

From 1938, and overlapping with the Mark III Catapult, the DCTO system was beginning its development, the original drawings being dated 25 November 1938. In addition to the limitations driving the various devices in the early 1930s another may have been that the system could be laid out over rough ground, or that it might have had tactical overtures capable of being deployed in future theatres such as that in Norway or Greece – countries having little flat ground. This latter suggestion can't be allowed much weight as launching from rough ground ignores the issue of subsequent safe recovery and the events of the military campaigns in the above countries were beyond the worst imaginings of the late 1930s. Furthermore, in its ultimate complexity any such prefabricated kit would have required a nearby port, good transport links and some weeks to assemble. An inherent limitation would have been that once in-situ, aligned into the prevailing wind, no account could be taken of varying wind directions at any particular moment. For this reason researchers have perhaps given undue weight to hints at the ability to slew the aircraft out of parallel with the track in order to accommodate angular offsets in wind direction. Avro papers from June 1940 requesting funding for a modification to the 'Direction Controlled Trolley' have been taken to imply this, but it now seems that this title related to work for the scheme described below. The words 'Direction Controlled' seem more likely to relate to an intrinsic limitation, namely that once installed there was no option as to the take-off direction. Similarly, it has also been speculated that in order to minimise drag, consideration was given to mounting the aircraft in such a manner that it could take-off with main wheels retracted. There is no evidence for this. Finally it has been suggested that some form of amplifying acceleration device, rockets, a winch or catapult must have been involved. This, too, seems not to be the case. Instead the device relied on the power from the aircraft's own engines to reach flying speed. With this in mind and without the drag on an undercarriage provided by soft muddy ground, the DCTO installation has sometimes been referred to as a 'Frictionless Take-Off' device.

The installation on Cove Common, Farnborough involved a loading turntable located on the catapult trials site at Jersey Brow. A carriage to support the aircraft was mounted on an extended twin steel track 1472 yards (1.3 km) long laid in a shallow trench and supported on concrete bases cast into the ground with a spacing between the rails of 22 feet 9 inches (6.9 m) the centre line spacing of the Manchester under-carriage and wheel units. This was laid out with an initial and providential downhill slope along what had been known as the 'Mile Straight' into Laffan's Plain. A carriage braking system occupied the final 100 yards (90 m) or so of the track.

Each 'rail' was fabricated as a pair of rolled steel channels with the flanges inward facing. The joints with adjacent rails were carefully finished to maintain a smooth-running surface. The carriage itself involved a robust steel tube welded to an upturned steel box above which steel guides held the main wheels and within which three tapered wheels were sited running within the inward-facing flanges of the track. The leading wheel or bogie, of heavy construction, within this upturned box carried the weight of the aircraft. The rear bogie provided the support for the rear fuselage of the aircraft. This took the form of an inverted V-frame terminating at its apex in a spherical cup. Each of the splayed legs was fixed to the rear bogie. A spherical hitch was fitted beneath the strengthened rear fuselage of L7246 behind the bomb bay.

In use a turntable provided for the purpose was rotated through 90 degrees and the aircraft towed backwards onto the front bogies using a large handwinch sited to one side. Once in place a small rectangular platform perhaps on a hydraulic ram would raise the tail of the aircraft into flying attitude permitting the V-frame to be connected. In anticipation of flight, the platform would then be lowered and the turntable rotated to align the aircraft with the track. Only the power from the engines was used for take-off. During the run the tail-up position was maintained until flying speed had been attained when a trigger at a pre-determined point along the track released the V-frame at the ball-joint, allowing the frame to fall forward, away from the fuselage. The centre-mounted pair of bogies along the carriage carried a wire net spanning the width of the track into which the V-frame fell in order to prevent it touching the ground. When the aircraft reached take-off speed it lifted off the trolley and was free, the carriage then free-wheeling into the braking system. This finally comprised a separate, free-running carriage stationed ahead of the braking zone and being propelled by impact of the take-off carriage towards the end of its run. This braking carriage carried a set of two dozen horizontally opposed hydraulic rams about six inches apart in which the outer, free ends faced inwards. A longitudinal series of upstanding steel plates was laid between the tracks. Rollers fixed onto the ram ends ran over these plates providing the retardation mechanism, the rams 'pumping' as the rollers ran over the axial set of plates.

When this installation was initially tested it was first hand-pushed down the gentle starting incline of the rails. Subsequently, a rope hauling system and later, it is claimed, a package of small cordite motors was used to proof-test the carriage and braking system. The first two runs with an aircraft mounted involved a Handley Page Heyford lashed to the trolley, purely for a final proof of concept prior to the Manchester test. Amongst other things, this evaluated the V-frame and braking system. Naturally, the aircraft was unable to fly.

Thin gauge spoked wheels seen ahead of and behind the front bogie on photographs were suggested to be for some accelerometer or other test device and are not part of the installation. The tapered steel wheels of the support bogie were about 5 inches (130 mm) in diameter and fitted with large diameter ball-races. With a Manchester taking off at about eighty mph these wheels would be spinning at about 5,000 rpm. Depending on the part of the launch sequence, these might be bearing on the upper or lower flanges of the track. After only three runs, including the only flight with the Manchester, these wheels were found to be damaged with flats burned into the wheel circumferences.

The date of this Manchester test flight is believed to have been a Sunday morning in July 1941. It is said the aircraft weighed 38,000 lb. Dates on RAE photographs of 5 and 8 September 1942 are certainly printing dates of the images, this being standard practice. As L7246 was damaged in arrested landing trials on 1 August 1942 and the prints show no sign of airframe damage, the earlier date seems more likely. The timing of the actual photographs could alternatively have been solely for a photo-call to get the events on record many months after the trial flight.

As remarked on earlier, loading an aircraft onto its carriage on the turntable proved time-consuming. Were the project to have developed into an operational method for Bomber Command aerodromes with recognition of need for much reduced intervals between take-offs, the intension was for the braking system to be extended to create a 'race track' or 'merry-go-round' of track. The carriage unit would freewheel into the braking area after each take-off and be hauled back along the reverse leg while the next aircraft was being launched. The turntable loading bay, possibly several, was to be shifted into a 'siding' and each aircraft already on its carriage wheeled out onto the main track ready for launching. The service requirement for such installations had ceased to exist with the advent of metalled runways at RAF airfields. It remains an anachronism and blind-alley in which the Manchester, coincidentally, played a part.

Direction Controlled Take-Off trials on the accelerator at Farnborough dated 5 September 1942, though the only flight was undertaken in July 1941. L7246 was aligned perpendicular to the rails and hauled tail first on to the turntable, using the hand winch directly behind it. A ram beneath the tail wheel then raised the aircraft into flying attitude. (Crown Copyright 42278)

The ventral V-strut was fixed to a spherical hitch beneath the fuselage and the tail wheel ram then retracted. Horizontal rams resting on the rails slid the V-frame rearwards when it passed the trigger along the track and it then fell forwards into a steel net. The 1,470-yards, initially downhill, track can be seen beneath the belly of the aircraft. (Crown Copyright 42276)

The turntable has been rotated through ninety degrees and L7246 towed on to the track ready to accelerate itself from Jersey Brow dated 8 September 1942, though the only trial launch took place fourteen months earlier. (Crown Copyright 42322)

L7246 was painted with white photo-calibration and yellow prototype 'P' markings prior to the frictionless take-off trials at Farnborough. Photograph dated 8 September 1942. The arrester hook has been removed since the earlier photograph, but the fin guards are retained. (Crown Copyright 42321)

Close-up of the V-strut and undercarriage 'bogies'. (via Author)

Early type of heavy bomber arrester hook fitted to Manchester L7246 for trials with the arrested landing system at Farnborough, 6 August 1941. (Crown Copyright 36562)

At the same time as the frictionless take-off experiments were in progress, operational experience with night bombers landing on small, muddy, poorly lit aerodromes revealed a significant number of accidents arising from aircraft overshooting runways. As a possible palliative, consideration was given to fitting arrester systems comparable in principal to these in use on carrier-based aircraft. Consideration had been given to the concept extending back as early as 1938. The initial RAE drawing from 25 November 1938 shows both the accelerator rails and the arrester system installed alongside. In late 1940 and early 1941 development of this system was speeded up.

The scheme proposed installing arrester gear at each end of the three runways at a bomber base. The equipment needed to be simple in construction and operation and had to be made available quickly. The working parameters involved a nominal 60,000-lb aircraft at a maximum approach speed of 72 mph and bringing it to a halt within a distance of 450 feet (130 m) at a maximum deceleration rate not to exceed with the 0.5G. This differed from the carrier-borne system which involved aircraft entering the arrester at flying speed and being brought to a halt within 156 feet (47 m) at a peak deceleration of less than 2G.

The scheme had crystallised by late 1940 to involve a pair of steel wires stretched across the runway about 200 yards (180 m) from each end (see diagram). The wires were supported by V-frames pre-tensioned to stand about four inches above runway level, running through deck sheaves to a braking system built underground. The braking system consisted of a pair of Mather and Platt mine shaft winches carrying a pair of grooved rope drums some 6 feet in diameter and with a horizontal axis. One rope end was fixed to each drum and the wire wound on as a single layer. This involved the 'fleeting wire' system of rope rigging, in other words when one rope is being extended under load the return wire to the second, idle leg would also be moving through its
sheaves. It is asserted that the steel ropes had a hydraulic retardation system to decelerate the aircraft at the specified rate.

Each rope drum would incorporate a brake drum having a pair of heavy duty 'Ferodo' friction pads which bore down on the outer circumference. The drums spanned 4 feet in diameter with the pads about one foot in width. Large springs held the machinery in tension and a separate Ford V8 petrol engine was used to recover the extended rope after it was dragged out by an overshooting aircraft. These twin winches were sited in a substantially built concrete underground pit and incorporated a heavy-duty roof to permit aircraft to taxi over it. The arrester was manually controlled by an operator and one can readily imagine that, on a cold snowy winter's night with the potential for a high speed pull on the large tensioned wire, this would have been one of the least favourite ground crew assignments.

A refinement incorporated on the brake assembly involved means to vary the retardation capability in some way. A quadrant allowed settings of this mechanism to be displayed to the operator. One arc is marked 'Normal Landing Load' and itemises in order Stirling, Lancaster, Halifax and Warwick. On an arc beneath it another sequence, 'Maximum Landing Load' with a higher retardation and the same sequence of aircraft is marked.

Manchester prototype L7246 was also used for this trials programme. Much strengthening of the under fuselage skin aft of the bomb bay and ahead of the tail wheel, presumably accompanied by significant beefing-up of the hook attachment point, was necessary. A number of 'sting-type' arrester hooks were evaluated. One is reported as being made from preformed steel plates in a welded configuration, another featured a large radius beak or spoon to assist cable entry. A third contained a roller whose axle lay in the plane of the hook itself. The purpose of this latter was to permit the wire to run over it smoothly were it to engage a wire close to one of the pick-up points, implying uneven payout. It is further suggested that an extra heavy duty naval hook was also adapted for Manchester experiments. In parallel, rudimentary experiments were undertaken to damp vertical and lateral movements as the hook trailed along the runway.

For the tests themselves the Manchester would be ranged at the end of the runway and taxied into the wires at varying approach speeds, when both the system and the test hooks were evaluated. A number of photographs

L7246 with yellow under surfaces and the final arrester hook lowered during the trials programme at Farnborough, 8 November 1941. Note what appear to be cable deflectors under both fins. Two Hurricanes and a Spitfire in the background. (Crown Copyright 37963)

illustrating these trials are published here, including a number of stills from a cine film discovered in an unmarked can at the Imperial War Museum in the early 1990s. In the latter, L7246 is seen flaring for landing with its arrester hook extended. Later in the sequence the hook is seen to engage an arrester wire, though the distance of the landing run and aircraft speed at the moment of catching the wire can't easily be determined. Following a series of tests the system was sufficiently developed that a demonstration is said to have been set-up for 1 August 1942 in front of a distinguished group including Air Chief Marshal Sir Arthur Harris. What wasn't revealed in anticipation of this was that a few days earlier a torrential rain storm had flooded the arrester machinery pit, the sump drainage pump being unable to cope with the volume of water. It was decided to proceed with the demonstration and the RAF fire service was called in to pump out the pit. There was time only to dry out and check the cable recovery/pre-tensioning motor. No attention could be given in the short time period available to checking of the winch drums. L7246 was positioned on the runway and picked up the appropriate speed until it entered the experimental area, the aircraft shuddering as it snagged a wire. The wire rope stretched and twanged, the aircraft tail lifted high off the runway and then parted, viciously flailing ends whipping across the runway in opposite directions, one allegedly close to the distinguished observers. The tail then crashed down damaging the aircraft. The winch drums had seized solid due to water ingress including across the full width of the brake shoes so increasing their frictional retardation by a large amount.

The operational deployment concept is said to have initially required installation of this Brake Drum Arrester Gear at RAF Elsham Wolds, Lakenheath, Linton-on-Ouse, Middleton St George, Swinderby and Waterbeach, whilst another source states that some 120 sets were on contract for placement on twenty Bomber command airfields. This very list implies that wider uptake of the concept beyond 5 Group was involved, to include, maybe, 1, 3, 4 and 6 Groups with Stirlings, Halifaxes and Lancasters in the frame. Other than L7246, the only other photographic proof for testing in other bomber aircraft is that in Lancasteer L7529 at RAE. Other recordsmaintain that a set of six units were delivered to RAF Woodhall Spa in August 1941 and tested by L7246 with five arrested landings as late as 22 October 1942.

In letters home to his family, George Hawes, an Australian pilot in 207 Squadron writes that on 15 June 1942 there was no flying at RAF Bottesford whilst contractors undertook installation of arrester gear. He pondered whether this would ever be used and sure enough, over the months, aircrews watched the concrete pits and hard points for mounting sheaves tilt and settle into the soft ground. By the 1990s, when historians quartered the site of the former base, five of the pits were found to be flooded and a sixth still dry. When the telephone was lifted, eerily, it still worked, though its controllers at the other end had long since departed.

Manchester L7246 was withdrawn from use on 20 November 1942, became a maintenance airframe and played no further part but by then the system was considered fully evolved and developed. In November 1942, Bomber Command decided that all its operational airfields, heavy OTUs and major diversion airfields should be equipped with arrester units. However, with the bomber offensive in full swing, Command began to have reservations about the weight penalty of the hook installation, which was said to prejudice fuel and bomb-carrying capacity in aircraft. Equally, with plans advancing urgently for mid-under defensive armament, plus competition of this space for the H_2S radar target-finding device, the arrester system fell out of favour. Moreover, pilot training and aircraft development, coupled with metalling of runways, had refined such that over-shooting of runways became somewhat less of a problem. In July 1943 Bomber command finally decided it had no further requirement for the system and by November all the units were 'mothballed' and abandoned in-situ.

RAE evaluated the hooks in a series of static load trials and one source claims that, after several failures, a hook which maintained its integrity at 60,000 lb and failed at 72,000 lb was eventually developed. These values appear exceptionally close together. Possibly more than one type of aircraft mounting was evaluated because RAE records refer to both arrester hooks and also 'pulley-type' arrester hooks. The trials programme itself did not progress entirely without incident. Again, according to the unsubstantiated memories of Group Captain Wilson, the earliest tests were conducted prior to metalled runways being installed at Farnborough. The size of the concrete anchor blocks had been carefully calculated to permit them to take the deceleration loads induced. A trials observation group was assembled to witness the first 'live' arrest. Wilson recalls flaring perfectly to catch a wire, whereupon the weights of the buried foundation blocks proved only a fraction of that necessary and a number of wires and blocks were jerked free, to be catapulted in the vicinity of the rapidly departing observers once more. Again, if any damage to the aircraft ensued, this is not evident in the accident cards. This story may be in degree or in its entirety apocryphal as the system wasn't designed to retard heavy aircraft from flying speed.

What is documented is that on 1 August 1941 during ground trials at high speed an arrester gear failure resulted in the tail of L7246 rising high in the air before crashing with great force back onto the runway. The tail plane spar extensions into the fuselage, fuselage bottom skin and fuselage former in this neighbourhood were damaged. Avro working parties attended at Farnborough to effect repairs, which included a new tail plane. The trials programme then continued. Full scale trials progressed satisfactorily, the aircraft flying with the hook retracted against the outer skin of the aircraft and being lowered onto the runway when it was necessary to engage an arrester wire. The fully loaded Manchester was arrested from 72 mph in 460 yards during the course of the trials programme.

Still from a trials film dated 14 February 1942, showing the Manchester prototype L7246 engaged in arrested landing trials. The aircraft is taxiing at high speed with the hook lowered. The first wire is mounted on a low V-frame (extreme left). (Imperial War Museum, FLM2143)

A few seconds later, the hook has engaged the first wire. Short white sections of the wire were a visibility aid to the pilot. (Imperial War Museum, FLM2148)

Belly shot looking aft, showing the hook just engaging the wire – tail wheel behind. Note the spoon shape of the hook with what may be a locking bar ahead to retain the wire. (Imperial War Museum, FLM2146)

L7246 flares for landing with the arrester hook lowered, 14 April 1942. First wire may be adjacent to the blurred figure ahead, beside the runway. If so, this was not the operating mode for which the system was designed. (Imperial War Museum, FLM2145)

Two teenage cyclists, later RAF aircrew, photographed a large, and no doubt highly secret, aircraft out in the meadows bordering Farnborough in the winter of 1941/1942. Close inspection reveals it to be Manchester L7246, complete with lowered arrester hook. (207 Squadron archives)

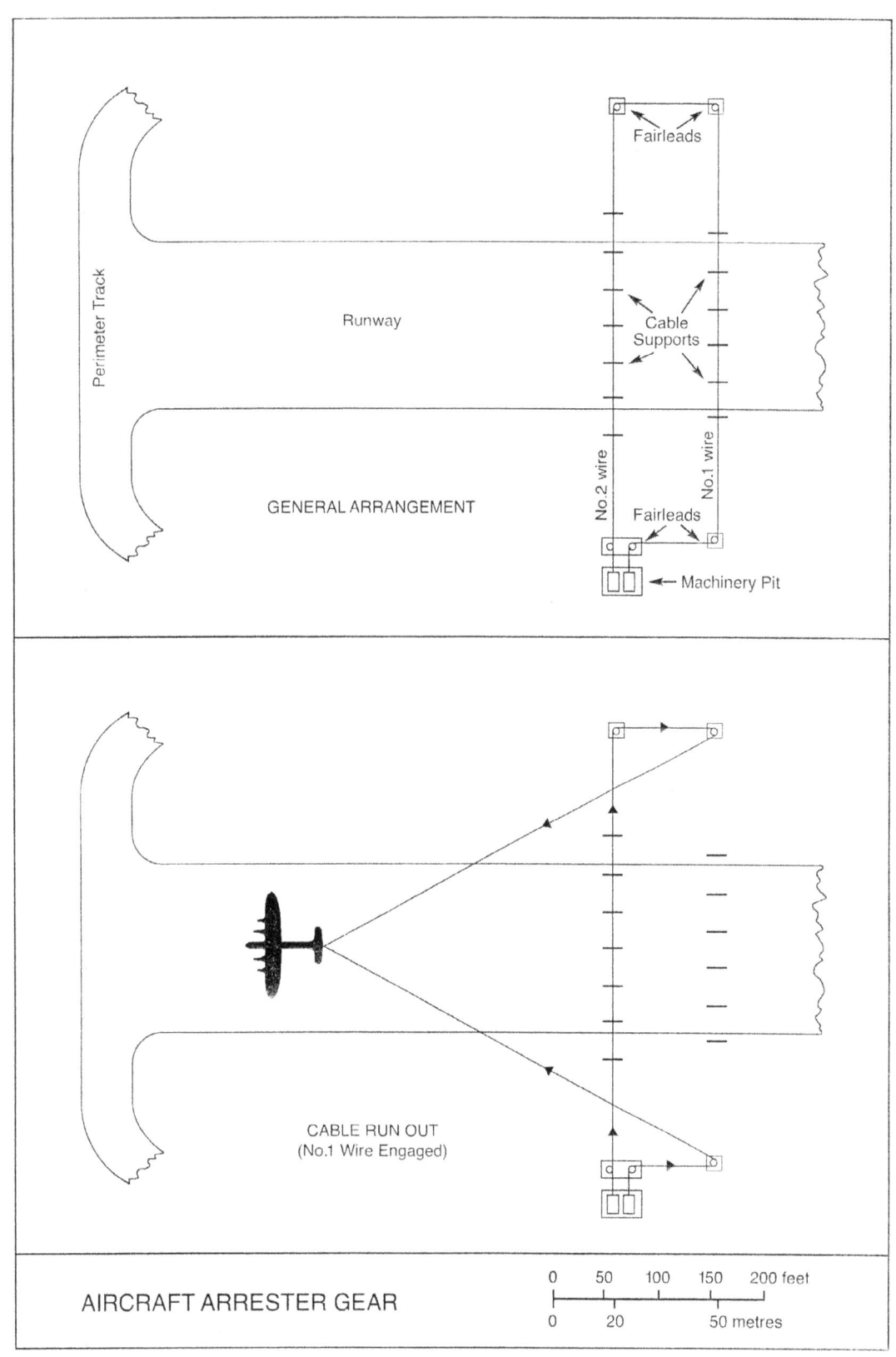

Installation drawings of Aircraft Arrester Gear showing set and extended positions. (Author's collection)

Whereas extensive testing of accelerated take-off and arrested landing systems were undertaken, other projects were stillborn. Amongst the few surviving Avro drawings for the Type 679, one dated 3 December 1940 specifies all the plant for tanker and receiver installations for in-flight refuelling, in conjunction with Flight Refuelling Ltd. The project involved a 1,000 gallon transfer tank in the bomb bay of the tanker aircraft. A large diameter hose drum suspended horizontally from trunnions ahead of the tank projected into the airstream. In this respect the installation presaged the later UPKEEP installation of the bouncing bomb. The hose itself was led from the drum aft to the mid-under position from which it was trailed aft and below to mate with the receiver. Presumably the eventual aim was to install receiver equipment in operational Manchesters.

The intention was for the receiver aircraft to formate beneath the tanker. The reception coupling was to be mounted beneath the rear turret, a windlass on the rear floor was to deploy a hauling device with some form of grapnel to snag and recover the trailing hose. Union was to be effected at the coupling beneath the rear turret, from which point twin lines led forward to the two wing tanks. There is no information as to whether this project proceeded any further than the paper stage. Other problems with the Manchester were of a more immediate nature.

In early August 1941, in pursuance of the centre fin vibration problems, which had bedevilled the Manchester since the FN7A mid-upper turrets began to be fitted in March, L7320, the trials aircraft, arrived at the Aeroplane & Armament Experiment Establishment (A&AEE) Boscombe Down. Presumably arising from wind tunnel tests, it had been recognised that the most severe eddies were shed from the turret apex. An inverted 'dishplate' or cap was fitted to the turret top to smooth the airflow and so decrease fin buffeting.

In an unusual test arrangement L7320 was not only fitted with the enlarged Lancaster-type twin fins and rudders but also the Mk.1 Manchester central fin. Flight tests were carried out at 185, 225, 250 and finally 310 mph with various turret angles. Only at the highest air speed did centre fin vibration become severe. It was concluded that the 'dishplate' would provide a major benefit, but by this time a decision had been made to adopt the twin fin arrangement thereby eliminating centre fin vibration problems. An unexpected secondary benefit was that the 'dishplate' also reduced vibration in the FN7A, making it a more stable gun platform even at speeds up to 310 mph. On these grounds A&AEE recommended that despite elimination of the centre fin, incorporation of the 'dishplate' was recommended for all aircraft fitted with the FN7A. This recommendation was not acted upon.

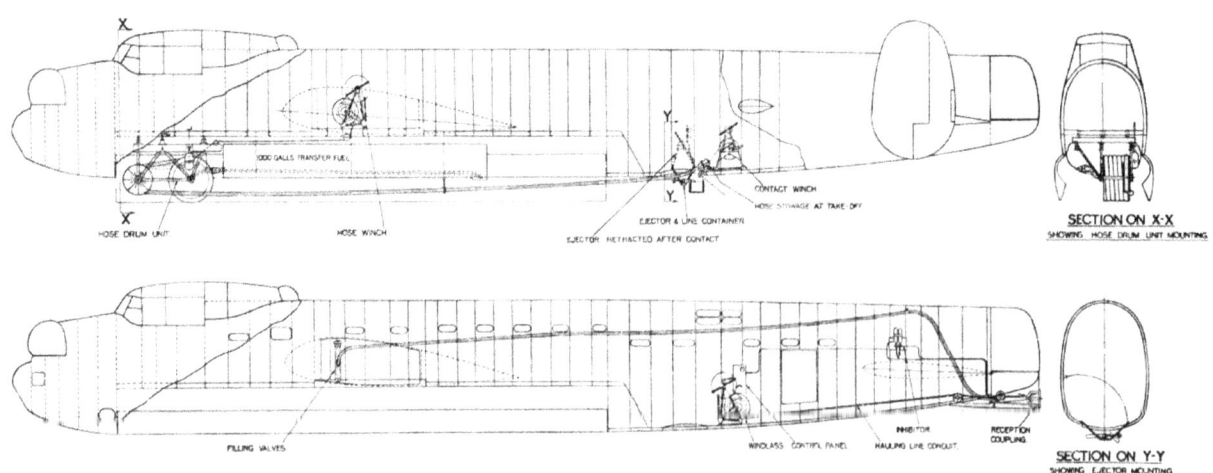

Avro drawings of the Type 679, tanker (upper) and receiver (lower) Manchesters. Drawing A.1611 prepared by Flight Refuelling Ltd at Malvern, dated 3 December 1940. (via Chaz Bowyer)

Top and Bottom: Head on and side view of the trials aircraft, L7320, dispersed at Boscombe Down. (A&AEE HA447-3)

At the end of the trial L7320 was dived to 320 mph and the turret slewed to the port beam. Vibration in the centre fin increased and the pilot could feel this in the rudder pedals despite the centre fin not being connected to the controls. This was due to the 'panting' of the fabric cover to the fin. As speed increased the fabric cover ballooned on either side of the fin. Suddenly the fabric on the port side split vertically and tore away, followed rapidly by the ribs and fabric breaking away and detaching. As L7320 was eased out of the dive only the leading edge, spar and their adjacent fabric remained in place. With this front section only remaining, L7320 returned to Boscombe Down having tested the modification to destruction.

Novel and fascinating as these various special trials may be, the main non-operational uses of the Manchester were more mundane and involved crew training during 1942 and 1943. Initially training was carried out on the squadrons. It was closely interwoven with early trials and has been discussed earlier. As 1941 drew on and the delays and engine problems increased it became apparent that operational squadrons had more than enough to contend with without the additional burden of crew training.

In a Minute from Headquarters Bomber Command, High Wycombe, dated 9 May 1941 concerning modification to early Manchesters, a policy decision to establish 25 Operational Training Unit (OTU) for crew training was stipulated. As such aircraft would not be used for operational flying, only four major modifications had to be incorporated - modified engines, 33 feet tailplane, Avro-fixed olive couplings in the hydraulic system and, if possible, de-icing equipment. Balloon barrage cutters and auto-pilots were not required. The Minute specified that twelve Manchesters were to be allotted, but later lists an Initial Establishment of six with three in reserve. It was recommended that a total of fourteen aircraft should be modified to this status with those unallocated being held in reserve to replace any wastage. L7280, L7283, L7286, L7276, L7279, L7284, L7291, L7292, L7294, L7282, L7288, L7290, L7298 and L7299 were earmarked. The aircraft listed above were disposed at the time at Waddington (three), Hemswell (six), and Coningsby (five). This would leave two aircraft from this initial batch, L7281 and L7295, to be modified at some later date.

The twin fin (AVRO MOD NO.390) trials aircraft, L7320, airborne from Boscombe Down. This view emphasises the bulk of the Rolls-Royce Vulture engine. (via Chaz Bowyer)

'Dishplate' fitted to the apex of the FN7A 'Botha' turret for trials in L7320, aimed at reducing turret/centre fin interactions. Unusually, L7320 had the enlarged twin 'Lancaster' fins and also the standard centre fin for this trial. The 'dishplate' reduced both turret and centre fin vibration, but the switch to twin fin configuration led to the abandonment of the 'dishplate'. (A&AEE HA447-1)

At various times L7320 evaluated tail vibration induced by the rotation of the FN7A turret, the twin fin installation and the erosion of climbing performance caused by the oil cooler lips installed on the upper wing surface outboard of the engines. Close inspection shows the FN7A is fitted with the 'dishplate' but the aircraft is not equipped with the centre fin. L7320 finally met the same fate as many other Manchesters – forced landing and being written-off after engine failure. (via Chaz Bowyer)

25 OTU began to receive these Manchesters at Finningley as early as June 1941. It is suggested aircraft may have been coded 'PP-', but no proof of this is available. In addition to flying from Finningley, night circuits and landing practice was carried out from the nearby grass satellite, Bircotes. 25 OTU had the same problems with their Manchesters as the operational squadrons, although they at least were not over the North Sea or enemy-held territory.

In November 1941 the unit lost its first Manchester when the port engine of L7428 caught fire in flight. Flight Sergeant Adams was possibly in the company of several other pilots relieving each other taking off and landing, and delayed feathering the propeller, with the result that the aircraft lost height rapidly and struck the ground through a hedge, killing three and injuring the remaining two on board. The crash occurred at Scaftworth near Bawtry. It is not known when 25 OTU finally gave up its Manchesters, but if the aircraft accident cards are any indicator this could have been soon after March 1942.

In November and December 1941 Manchesters finally began to receive their modified engines and in rapid succession 83, 106, 50 and 49 Squadrons re-equipped. Insufficient aircraft were available for both the squadrons and the OTU. With the increase of Manchester squadrons it was decided in late 1941 that a number of formal Conversion ('Con') Flights would be attached, replacing the earlier and rather haphazard conversion training on the squadrons. In each case the initial complement would be four Manchesters, often from the earlier pre-production batches. On 6 January 1942 formal authority was given for such establishments manned by tour-expired aircrews from the squadrons themselves and by the end of the month 44, 97 and 207 Squadrons all had Manchester Conversion Flights.

Manchesters were semi-ideal Lancaster conversion aircraft, having identical instrumentation and layouts and comparable flying characteristics. When lightly loaded the Manchesters flew well and, unlike the Lancasters, were equipped with a second seat and extensions for all flying controls. Aircraft instruments were not, however, duplicated.

61 and 83 Squadrons may have had Manchester Conversion Flights soon after, but certainly by 27 March 1942, when 61 Squadron at Woolfox Lodge was ordered to re-equip immediately with Lancasters, a Conversion Flight

establishment of two Manchesters and two Lancasters was specified. Soon after this both Squadron and Conversion Flight moved to Syerston. Two weeks later a Conversion Flight was attached to 83 Squadron at Scampton, similarly equipped with two Manchesters and two Lancasters. Plans to re-equip 83 Squadron were also in hand. 97 and 207 Squadrons had already re-equipped, their Manchester complements being retained in their Conversion Flights or transferred to other squadrons and Conversion Flights. 106, 50 and 49 Squadrons were in the process of re-equipment.

Early 1942 was truly a period of rapid interchanges of Handley Page Hampden, Manchester and Lancaster aircraft. By early May, Manchesters had already been superseded by Lancasters in 106 Squadron and a number of Lancasters also reached its Conversion Flight. In many cases Conversion Flights continued to train from the operational parent base, causing unnecessary congestion and loss of sleep to the operational crews. All this suggested the need for a further re-organisation, facilitated by the rapid introduction of the Lancaster, which in turn released more Manchesters for training. The operational life of the Manchester was rapidly drawing to a close, albeit after a period of almost eighteen months – a long time for an under-developed and unsuccessful aircraft.

On 19 May 1942, 1654 Conversion Unit (CU) came into existence at Swinderby to standardise and provide badly needed conversion facilities for 5 Group. The new CU received eight Manchesters and eight Lancasters. In the same month both 49 and 50 Conversion Flights began to receive Lancasters to commence their respective conversions to this type. In turn 408 and 420 Squadron Conversion Flights formed with Manchesters. Five weeks later these two flights were both subject to cancellation due to a decision to retain Hampdens on the parent squadrons for the time being.

On 18 May 1942, Squadron Leader Dave Penman found himself posted to Waddington as the sole instructor to convert 420 (RCAF) Squadron to Manchesters. L7386, L7400, L7402, L7416 and R5771 were allocated. Squadron crews continued to fly Hampden operations over the next few weeks with the result that conversion was a protracted business. The first five pilots commenced dual instruction on 23 May but, with other squadrons receiving Lancasters directly, 420 Squadron were somewhat reluctant to embrace the Manchesters.

Matters came to a head on the night of 11 June when Penman was giving dual to Flight Sergeant Hiley in L7402, with three other crew members. It was a clear dark night with no wind and the aircraft was taking off and landing towards the east across the grass, slightly downhill, towards the Lincoln road. The flare path was a mere four or five goose-neck flares. Sitting in the Manchester's right hand seat the goose-necks disappeared on the final approach as the tail came down for each landing. A number of successful landings were accomplished until, with the goose-necks out of view on one more circuit, as Hiley cut the throttles, Penman had the feeling that L7402 was a little high.

Over-riding Hiley's action, Penman opened both throttles just as the Manchester began to sink. Such action would have saved a Lancaster, but the two Vultures were simply not responsive enough and L7402 dropped so hard onto the grass that both undercarriage legs collapsed and the aircraft skidded to a halt in a cloud of dust. The retaining leg of the second pilot's canvas, fold-up chair jumped out of its seating with the impact, projecting Penman and the seat forwards and down into the bomb aiming position. Fortunately the aircraft did not catch fire and all five crew members scrambled out safely. The accident seemed to settle matters as far as the Canadians were concerned and they retained their Hampdens until August, when they transferred to 4 Group and converted to Vickers Wellingtons instead.

On 20 May 1942, Sergeant A. J. McHardy and the crew of 106 Conversion Flight were nearing the end of their training and undertook a long cross country flight from Coningsby. The five man crew made a routine radio transmission as they crossed the Pembrokeshire coast en route for a turning point at the Scilly Isles and were never heard of again.

In late May it became clear something unprecedented was in the offing, with no operations, all leave cancelled and a maximum effort in prospect. Not only operational but training unit aircraft were required. Indeed it was aircraft availability as opposed to aircrews which presented the major problem. All Conversion Flights provided their aircraft, often with scratch crews, combinations of experienced captains with other crew members at an advanced stage in their training. Much interchanging of aircraft took place to optimise aircrew and aircraft availability. The participation of Conversion Flight Manchesters in the 'thousand' bomber raids on Cologne and Essen has been outlined in the previous chapter.

R5797 at Tollerton early in 1942, with members of a wireless fitting party from West Drayton who had uprated the wireless by installing a new Marconi T1154/R1155. Used only as a trials installation aircraft, including work on the Mk.XIV bomb sight, R5797 has nevertheless been modified to Mk.1A status and is fully armed. (S. Hall)

Air and ground crew pose in front of the fifth production aircraft, L7280 OL-X of 83 'Con' Flight at Scampton. Built with a FN21A mid-under and 28-feet span tail, the aircraft was reworked but still did not operate after being allocated to 83 Squadron on 2 April 1942. Note the C1 type roundels. (via R. Low/F. Harper, 83 Squadron archives)

Following these two nights, Conversion Flight Manchesters never operated again but reverted to their true role of training. This included all aspects of operational flying. Circuits and landings to train the pilots were followed by air-to-air firing for the gunners, bombing for the pilots and navigators at various nearby ranges and later extended navigation training on a variety of routes around the coast of the United Kingdom. Finally, crews carried out a simulated raid on a blacked out British City, later called a BULLSEYE, as a final dress rehearsal for operations.

One day a Westland Lysander target tug approached Waddington and landed hesitantly. After a short run, it stopped in the centre of the airfield, its engine running and impeding any further aircraft movements. Attempts to contact the pilot by radio failed, and a vehicle was sent out. Its driver found the Lysander pilot dead from bullet wounds incurred from wayward fire from a Manchester mid-upper gunner under training.

By the end of June the Manchesters were withdrawn from first line service and made generally available to the many Conversion Flights and to 1654 CU at Swinderby. Manchesters also went to 9 and 57 Squadrons' Conversion Flights. On 5 June 1654 CU moved to 'Wicked' Wigsley – the most desolate and depressing station in 5 Group and the only station without a pub in striking distance. There were, however, moments of excitement. At about 18.00 hours on 3 July two Junkers JU88 intruders appeared unannounced at low level over the airfield and fired on one of the Manchesters at its dispersal point. No one was hurt and only slight damage was done to the aircraft.

On 6 August 1942 a tragic accident occurred at the 207 Squadron airfield at Bottesford, when Manchester L7385 collided on the runway with Lancaster R5550 causing four fatalities. Only ten days later Flight Sergeant Dickenson in a 50 Squadron Conversion Flight aircraft, L7475, encountered what was to become a frequent Manchester accident, one which mirrored the squadron losses with relentless precision. Following a landing at Talbenny near Cardigan, Dickenson took off again at 15.30 hours to continue his exercise. At 150 feet, at a critical stage after take-off, the starboard engine caught fire. It was shut down and the propeller feathered, but Dickenson was unable to maintain height on the port engine alone. The captain was fortunate in carrying out a belly landing in a field at nearby Narloes. The aircraft was totally burnt out but only one crew member was injured. After questioning the crew and inspecting the wreckage, accident investigators concluded a fuel line had cracked and the high octane had ignited.

On 21 August 50 and 83 Conversion Flights were both posted from their parent units and sent to Wigsley, whilst on the 22nd 61 Conversion Flight moved into Swinderby, being joined next day by 207 Conversion Flight from Bottesford. The way was open to merge the various Conversion Flights into more effective training echelons. On the 24th authority was given in principle for a build-up of all Conversion Flights to an establishment of eight aircraft – four Manchesters and four Lancasters. This was not an adequate solution to training problems.

By October 1942 it was recognised that the policy of having most of the heavy bomber training undertaken by small sub-units attached to each squadron was becoming increasingly impracticable. It was decided that the future policy would be that the conversion of aircrew to heavy bombers would take place entirely on dedicated Conversion Units – to be known as Heavy Conversion Units. The normal establishment would be thirty-two aircraft in four Flights – sixteen Manchesters and sixteen Lancasters.

1654 HCU was already in being, but 1656 HCU was soon established with three Flights at Breighton, soon moving to Lindholme. 1660 HCU was established at Swinderby and 1661 HCU at Skellingthorpe with four and three Flights respectively.

At the CFs and HCUs some of 5 Group's most senior and experienced tour-expired pilots were responsible for crew training. These were the fortunate few who had already survived two tours of operations with 5 Group – men like 'Kipper' Herring, Peter Ward-Hunt, Micky Martin, etc. Some, like Wing Commander 'Junior' Gardiner and Charles Stenner, were regulars, having joined the RAF at Halton as Aero Engine/Motor Transport Apprentices in the early 1930s. Stenner had completed sixty-eight operations by this time and had learnt from his earliest training to nurse his engines. To him the two big Vultures were like sewing machines and although he had to take-off at maximum power he always climbed and ran the engines at less than the stipulated maximum settings. Few can have flown more Manchesters than Gardiner. As stated earlier, he flew sixty-two of the 202 aircraft built, starting with L7300 on 15 February 1941 and finishing with L7307 on 12 September 1943 – a total of 337 hours operationally and in training.

Together, these experienced pilots tried to instil discipline and confidence into their fledgling crews on the CFs and HCUs. The reputation for engine fires and alleged inability to fly on one engine were well known and the Manchester still retained its fearsome reputation. To try to counteract this Stenner would frequently shut down one engine with trainees on board and circle the airfield demonstrating the single engine performance. Gardiner, similarly, appreciated the giant bomber's flying characteristics, likening it to a big Avro Anson with no vices and very responsive in the roll.

Despite their best efforts the Manchesters continued to live up to their reputation, even when flown lightly loaded at the training units. Again it was almost invariably engine failures, often leading to fires in the air, which led to crashes. By now though component shortages, fatigue failures and burn outs of components long overdue for replacement were a contributory factor. Acute spares shortages were to finally lead to the aircraft being declared obsolete. The aircraft crash cards and resulting inquiry summaries of findings itemise large numbers of such failures, whilst the Appendix lists numbers of Manchesters from 1654, 1660, 1661 HCU, 57 CF and 1485 Bombing & Gunnery Flights written-off in crashes following engine failures or fires.

In mid-December 1942 changes occurred to the equipment of the four HCUs – Nos. 1654, 1656, 1660 and 166. Hitherto all had operated sixteen Lancasters and sixteen Manchesters but now the Lancaster complement was reduced to twelve and the Manchester increased to twenty. As 1942 drew to a close and 1943 began the spares situation, especially for the Rolls-Royce Vulture engines, became steadily more acute. Even in 1941 certain components were in such critical short supply that squadron ground crews were want to cannibalise usable engine components from crashed aircraft before the accident investigators arrived on the scene. By the time the aircraft reached the CUs components were having their lives extended well beyond normal just to keep aircraft flying. Thus, small components began to burn out, often leading to major engine fires and accidents.

On 10 September 1942 Squadron Leader Long was conducting flying training in R5784 of 57 Conversion Flight at Scampton when the starboard engine caught fire in the circuit. The aircraft made a normal landing and the station fire service extinguished the blaze. Investigation revealed the fire to have been caused by the 'D' block engine exhaust pipe burning out. The loss of L7386 of 57 CF on 5 October 1942 was later found to have its primary cause in the cracking of a light alloy hydraulic pipe which then sprayed inflammable fluid onto the red hot exhaust manifold.

When 1654 CU lost R5772 on 26 January 1943 the investigators found that the primary cause of the engine fire was the failure of No. 3 exhaust valve on the port engine due to burning through of the valve head. This in turn led to the flame traps burning through and igniting the engine itself. On 14 February 1943 L7286 of 1660 CU belly-landed at Waddington after the starboard Vulture caught fire at 1,000 feet. The flame traps in 'A' and 'B' blocks were burnt through. A similar incident at Swinderby on 24 March 1943 led to L7453 making a belly-landing. In this case the fire started from the burning through of the exhaust manifold of 'A' block on the port engine.

Only three weeks later a fire in the vicinity of 'B' block on the starboard Vulture of R5841 of 1660 CU at Swinderby led to a serious crash, with three killed and three injured in the crew. Further incidents involved L7468 of 1660 CU at Swinderby on 1 May 1943 and L7297 of 1661 CU at Winthorpe on the 19th. In both cases fires in the flame traps were the primary cause. Despite all that the experienced flying instructors tried in order to instil confidence in their fledgling crews, the Vultures continued to warrant their evil reputation.

On 1 January 1943 1661 HCU moved from Skellingthorpe to Winthorpe and on 16 March 1943 the aircraft complements were further adjusted. Later still, further movement and expansion ensued and in September 1943 the move to 'Group Stations' was formalised and each Group allotted either two or three numbered bases, each consisting initially of either three or four stations. Swinderby housed 51 Base in 5 Group and had 1660 HCU in occupation, this base also controlling 1654 HCU at Wigsley and 1661 HCU at Winthorpe. 1656 HCU was transferred to 11 Base in 1 Group.

However, by then the Manchesters had virtually disappeared from RAF second line service. Declared obsolete at the end of June 1943 due to severe spares shortages, a few soldiered on into the early autumn. Rows of Manchesters at each unit stood forlornly as spares aircraft, steadily being cannibalised. The Manchester era had ended but the child it spawned was on the way to becoming a war-winner. An anachronism before it even entered service the Manchester had nevertheless served the RAF during three years of war (autumn 1940 to autumn 1943). By the time it went out of service it was unnoticed, by-passed by the great advances in bomber design it had in part contributed to. Its demise was, nonetheless, a marked contrast to the expectations attendant on its specification, design and early development.

Manchesters also served with the Torpedo Development Unit (TDU) at Gosport although the name itself was something of a misnomer because the unit was responsible for developing and testing almost all the air-dropped weapons used by Coastal Command. The TDU comprised a Headquarters Section, the Torpedo Development Flight and a Torpedo, Mine and Bomb Section, all controlled by the Ministry of Aircraft Production. The unit regularly sent detachments for trials at Pembrey and Weston-super-Mare. Each of these three aerodromes was adjacent to a particular trials area.

In the case of Weston-super-Mare the attraction was the high tidal range of the Severn Estuary. At high water on spring tides coastal sites at Sand Bay and nearby Pawlett Hams would be covered by 40 feet of water which drained completely at the next low tide only six hours later. This allowed the performance of various weapons to be tested in relatively deep waters, as well as readily retrieved from the seabed for examination. In October 1941 the unit had a range of aircraft allocated for trials purposes including Bristol Beauforts, Blackburn Bothas, Westland Lysanders, Fairey Albacores and Swordfishes, Handley Page Herefords and Hampdens.

At various times requirements developed for other trials aircraft and Manchesters were detached on an 'as available' basis for specific trials from the operational squadrons. The TDU Operational Record Book (ORB) and Appendices specify Manchester aircraft being involved from as early as November 1941 and continuing until July 1943, by which time an Albacore and Manchester were at last supplemented by a Lancaster. From late 1941 to April 1942 TDU relied entirely on Manchesters seconded from the operational squadrons. In that month the unit received two aircraft of its own from the previously unconverted Metropolitan Vickers batch, R5773 and R5774 being allocated.

Manchesters seem to have been used almost exclusively from Weston-super-Mare and occasionally from nearby Lulsgate Bottom, both a short distance from the Sand Bay and Pawlett Hams ranges. In the main, serial numbers of aircraft used at TDU are not recorded in its ORB, whereas for such second line duties little or nothing is recorded in squadron ORBs.

The TDU ORB entries are a laconic recitation of the various trials mainly conducted fortnightly to coincide with the spring tides. Were it not for aircrew flying logbooks and personal recollections of the aircrew, little would remain discoverable on this aspect of Manchester service.

As a general rule it appears that squadron air and ground crew were detached with all necessary tools and spares, whilst TDU detached a working party of six men to provide weapon loading and dropping facilities to Weston. The range of weapons tested during the period November 1941 to July 1943 included depth charges of many marks, a wide range of mines with various fuses and the parachutes used to deploy them, as well as a variety of anti-submarine bombs, ranging from thirty to 600 lb. Tests varied from air photography of ballistics to ricocheting behaviour off water and the seabed. More uncommon devices included anti-surface vessel buoys, JW Bombs, flame floats, Schermully 'water snowflakes' and the mysterious and enigmatic 'Special Stores'.

The only hint of events untoward is the record for 28 August 1942 revealing that the TDU Manchester flown to Weston by Sergeant Thornton on the 24th had become unserviceable and he returned by train to collect the reserve Manchester. This presumably relates to R5773 and R5774. However, like everything concerning the Manchester, all was not as routine as the records imply.

On 31 January 1942, Squadron Leader Thos Murray's 207 Squadron crew were detached to Weston for a week's mining trials with the unit. Murray and crew, plus twelve ground crew members and all their equipment and personal kit took off from Bottesford in L7378 and flew to Boscombe Down to prepare for the trials. Next day they flew from Boscombe to Weston to be briefed and for L7378 to be got ready for the trials programme. Finally all was ready and on 3 February L7378 took off from Weston loaded with the experimental mines. After 1 hour 40 min flying the aircraft had to make an emergency landing at Chipping Warden, fortunately without injury to the crew or damage to the aircraft. The ground crew at Weston were alerted and four fitters travelled to Chipping Warden, where repairs were effected. It was not until 5 February 1942 that L7378, complete with air and ground crew, could return to Weston. The mining trials were resumed with flights on the 5th and 7th before the aircraft, crew and twelve ground crew returned to Bottesford on the 8th.

Following the slight hiccup during this trials programme, Flying Officer Dave Green was the pilot on a second detachment to Weston on 8 March 1942. This time the aircraft was L7432 EM-J, still reverently referred to on 207 Squadron as 'Kipper's Aircraft', it being the Manchester Herring had successfully brought back from Berlin on one engine on 7/8 September 1941. Aircraft, air crew and the necessary supporting ground crew were detached for a week to be at the disposal of the naval commander for the purpose of undertaking a series of trials with small, 30-lb anti-submarine bombs. The objective was to release the weapons at various low levels, below 1,000 feet, and speeds, to study their ballistics, trajectory and how they survived impact with the water. The drops would be made at high water at Sand Bay and the fragments collected for examination at low water.

At Bottesford L7432 was loaded with everything necessary for detached duty for a week. In addition to personal gear, this included trestles, tool boxes, bomb loading winches, armaments and the ten engine and airframe fitters who would accompany the seven aircrew. The aircraft was consequently very heavily loaded on take-off from Bottesford and, moreover, the overload weight could not be jettisoned in an emergency.

They flew down to Weston in daylight with clear instructions of how to signal the airfield defences to lower the defensive balloon barrage around the airfield to permit them to effect a safe landing. The Manchester was to announce its presence to the naval unit by diving at 500 feet over the observation post on the end of Weston Pier. The duty officer would then telephone the airfield and instruct them to lower the balloons. Accordingly, they made a pass over the pier, which produced no response. A second pass was made with the same result. On the third overpass from the land, running along the length of the pier, they dived to 200 feet and finally received a flashing light response as they headed out across the Severn Estuary towards Cardiff.

At this precise moment the constant speed unit of the starboard propeller disintegrated with a loud bang, followed by a louder howl as the propeller ran away out of control. By chance, sitting right by the engine controls with Green in the cockpit was one of the best engine fitters on the squadron. Taking instant action without having to be instructed, the fitter immediately pressed the feathering button and turned off the fuel supply. Miraculously the feathering mechanism worked and the windmilling blades began to turn to present their edges to the airflow, slowing down as they did so. To be able to feather the propeller on the dead engine was a significant element in their favour, but the immediate situation was extremely grim. They were at 200 feet over the turbulent, unforgiving waters of the Severn in an overloaded Manchester on one engine with a seventeen-man crew.

Many Manchesters would not even maintain height on one engine whilst lightly loaded. At 200 feet they had neither the time nor the capability to lighten the load they were carrying. Dave Green acted immediately, advancing the port throttle and working quickly and efficiently to set the aircraft up to fly on one engine. As a precaution against the inevitable, Green ordered the entire crew to ditching stations. As they held their breath L7432 responded wonderfully once more to the challenge – not only were they not losing height but they were almost imperceptibly climbing.

For a Manchester to maintain height on one engine was unusual, to be able to climb was exceptional, but to be able to climb in such an overloaded condition must have been virtually unique. Suddenly the situation did not seem quite so grave and Dave Green was even able to think in terms of attempting a return to Weston. By now they were some seven to eight miles north of the airfield. If only they could reach 1,000 feet, and if only the port Vulture would keep turning, they might make it.

Dave Green began a gentle turn back towards the airfield and eventually levelled off at 1,200 feet. This gave him enough of a safety margin of height to ease back a little on the port throttle and nurse the engine home. When they got within sight of the aerodrome again they were relieved to see that the signal had got through and the balloons had been lowered. The approach had to be right, they would have only one chance. Green did a normal circuit, lined up onto the active runway and made a successful landing without damaging the aircraft. Switching off they all tumbled out, breathing immense sighs of relief. Dave Green's superb airmanship had got them down safely once more and the reputation of 'Kipper's Aircraft' increased.

There was, of course, no prospect of carrying out the proposed trials programme. The naval unit must have wondered at the bravery of young men who daily flew around in aircraft which, with so little provocation and at such frequency, fell out of the sky. On 9 March 1942 Flight Lieutenant Huntley-Wood flew down to Weston in L7515 then returned to Bottesford with the two aircrews and part of the ground crew, leaving the engine fitters to replace the engine on L7432. Dave Green and crew eventually returned to Weston in R5835 on 14 March and undertook the anti-submarine bombing trials during twelve flights lasting until the 23rd. A small boat was moored close to the target buoy filming the drops – Sergeant 'Goldie' Goldstraw marvelled at the film crew's confidence in his bomb aiming.

The only other unit to make significant use of the Manchester was 1485 Bombing & Gunnery Flight (B&GF) at Dunholme Lodge, which mainly used the aircraft for air gunnery, fighter affiliation and bombing training in the period August 1942 to February 1943. L7484, L7473 and R5791 were amongst aircraft used.

It has been suggested that Manchesters were allocated to Lancaster Finishing and Air Gunnery Schools. Study of Aircraft Movement Cards confirms that the final allocation of a number of Manchesters was one of a range of Air Observer Schools, Air Gunnery Schools and Schools of Technical Training. When aircraft flew with a unit for any significant period minor and major accidents would lead to them quickly appearing in Aircraft Accident Cards and no accidents are recorded for any of these latter units. It would appear they were allocated as ground instruction airframes.

In early June 1943 one of the last and, as it turned out stillborn, twists in the Manchester saga is an Air Ministry directive dated 9 June 1943 specifying that Manchester aircraft had been earmarked for transfer to the Americans and they were not to be broken up when the type was declared obsolete at the end of the month.

It turns out a small number of expendable aircraft had been requested for 1478 Flight as flying wireless telegraphy stations. The aircraft were required for a special United States operation with the Tactical Air Force in North Africa. Aircraft were to be ferried to North Africa, where the nature of the operation required a good duration but a flying life of only 80 hours per airframe.

Initially two specially-equipped Manchesters were considered, but their rapidly approaching obsolescence and critical shortage of all spares demanded a substantial number of airframes to be allocated for possible cannibalisation. Furthermore, concern was focused on the lack of provision for tropicalisation of the Vulture engines. The Air Ministry minute affirms that it was lack of spares which had forced the RAF to declare the aircraft obsolete. After a few days of deliberation it was suggested to the Americans that they were more likely to obtain the results they needed in North Africa by providing two of their own Douglas Dakotas. The final record is a telegram confirming that 'The Americans do not, repeat not, want Manchesters'. Possibly someone had tipped them the wink on what they might be letting themselves in for?

Wing Commander W. G. (Junior) Gardiner later served as the Chief Instructor at 5 Lancaster Finishing School at Syerston. The unit operated its Lancasters in addition to using the fuselage section of L7307 which Gardiner himself had delivered from Swinderby to Syerston on 12 October 1943 for use as a ground instruction airframe. Air Vice Marshal Sir Ralph Cochrane was 5 Group Commander and most determined, among his many other obligations, that crews coming to Syerston to convert to Lancasters flew nineteen hours on the type and made best possible use of their course. On his frequent visits, accompanied by Gardiner, he routinely checked training standards in this dummy fuselage. On one occasion he grabbed the nearest pilot in the room, told him to get in the cockpit, and that he would put him through the drills. Gardiner immediately attempted to chip in, but was silenced by the AVM. The pilot in the cockpit performed the ordered actions to perfection, earning praise from Cochrane for his efficiency. No-one dared so much as to permit themselves the slightest snigger until the great man was out of earshot as everyone knew that, by chance, Cochran had randomly selected not a pupil but the fuselage instructor! Such courses lasted well into 1944 and it is appropriate to reflect that the Captain flying most individual aircraft and most sorties on type for that crew position was also one of the last to have any involvement with the Manchester. Indeed, it is an opportune point to leave the history of Avros first contribution to strategic bombing.

Chapter Ten: Reckoning

Not unnaturally, history has tended to judge the Manchester harshly. Together with the crews and their endeavours over eighteen months official histories dismiss the aircraft in a few words as a failure and a disappointment. To many of the crews who flew the aircraft and lived with the constant and high risk of failure of the Rolls-Royce Vultures, the aircraft, too, is best forgotten. Its achievements were indeed eclipsed by the Handley Page Halifax, the Short Stirling and, ultimately, by its offspring, the Avro Lancaster.

Like all human activity, performance in war tends to be judged on attainment with little recognition for those who, despite giving all, have little tangible to show for their skill, fortitude and dedication. As a result, the efforts of the Manchester crews have been neglected and the crews have been assigned to the role of peripheral bystanders in the mainstream of war which passed them by and consigned their efforts to obscurity, along with their aircraft.

A judgement on the aircraft itself depends upon perspectives. Those regular and auxiliary aircrews flying at the time of the Munich Crisis in 1938, who faced the prospect of war with a well-armed Germany in single-engined Hawker Hart and Hind bi-planes and gained their operational experience in Handley Page Hampdens, saw some salvation in the Manchester, with all its foibles. Technology had made giant strides for them in two short years.

In contrast, for the aircrews who initially served in Manchesters and later progressed to the Lancaster, their trepidation over the Vulture provided a marked contrast to the confidence they had in their four Merlins. The same airframe was transformed from rating only a few lines in the official history, to the machine which fulfilled the military strategists' dream.

Despite the years of frustration and failure, the Manchester did at least ease the transition to operational status of the Lancaster. The Manchester, and in turn its aircrew, were simply a victim of circumstances. By all reasonable standards an aircraft as advanced and untried as this should never have been expected to fly operationally before all its developmental problems had been overcome. However, the Manchester was introduced at the Allies' blackest time of the war. Britain and its far-flung Empire stood alone, its army virtually disarmed at Dunkirk and its navy heavily committed in all the oceans of the world. Notwithstanding the severe limitations of the Vulture engines, production and operational flying continued. What the RAF needed was aircraft, any and every aircraft, as soon as it could get its hands on them. Thus, despite being reduced to the role of a stop-gap type until the more capable Lancaster became available, the aircrews had no alternative but to get what they could from the Manchester.

Almost all the problems with the Manchester can be laid at the feet of the Rolls-Royce Vulture. Yet it was that same wartime expediency that forced the Manchester to centre stage before it was halfway ready, which in turn, killed off the Vulture before its capabilities could be proved and extended. Only enough effort was available in Rolls-Royce to cater for the Merlin and to prepare for its offspring, the Griffon. By brilliant design, power output from the Merlin was increasing monthly, whilst the Vulture was ultimately pegged back by the Achilles' heel of its star-rod design. Had Rolls-Royce had equivalent skill and manpower to lavish on the Vulture, for which a superior con-rod design and split crank-case was already at an advanced stage, then it, too, could well have followed the pathway of steadily increasing power output, keyed to the reliability which attended its stable-mates. Viewed with hindsight, it must be clear that far too much was being expected of Rolls-Royce and of an engine at the start of its development life.

When Vulture problems became critical, Avros turned initially to the Napier Sabre and Bristol Centaurus of equivalent power. Two Centaurus engines were reportedly installed in an airframe but never test flown. Viewed in the perspective of these two engines it is hardly surprising that the Vulture proved unequal to the task in 1940. The Sabre was not available in the Hawker Typhoon until 1942 and then gave untold trouble during the first year, whilst the Bristol Centaurus did not appear in the Hawker Tempest until after the end of the war in 1945.

Nor can Vulture output be considered wasteful. In addition to the Hawker Tornado, Vickers Warwick, Blackburn B20 and Hawker Henley test installations, a bare minimum of 404 Vultures were required to equip the 202 Manchesters produced. In this context it is remarkable that Vulture production terminated at 538 units. With such a small engine change capacity it was little wonder that Vulture spares were perpetually so critically limited.

In many respects the evil reputation the Vulture earned for unreliability and catching fire was richly deserved and in the circumstances it is perhaps not surprising, compounded as it was by the secrecy of the Air Ministry, that this reputation should at times get out of hand. In September 1941, when 61 Squadron temporarily relinquished its troubled Manchesters, the crews were convinced amongst themselves that the official reason was that Manchesters spontaneously caught fire over the target area. At the development stage at which it was abandoned the Vulture was still to all intents and purposes an experimental engine, even though it was to remain operational in the Manchester for a total of eighteen months. At this distance in time the faults and mistakes with the Vulture seem obvious and its premature service use can only be understood and appreciated from the standpoint of the extreme and desperate situation in which Britain found itself in the early war.

One elementary mistake in the Vulture not readily explained, was the omission of the balance pipe between the two coolant pumps and the prolonged delay before this was appreciated and rectified. More fundamental and equally difficult to explain was the designer's choice of the low ductility, high Brinell steel for the con-rod bolts. Many engineers in Rolls-Royce were to reflect that this was the real killer, which finally doomed the engine. The choice of this material was dictated by the unusual star-rod design and the forces on the con-rod bolts arising from the four pistons. Seventy years ago the metallurgical properties of this material were poorly understood. To this major step in the dark in materials and their properties must be added the fact that for many months Manchesters flew on operations with uneven and arbitrary tensions on the con-rod bolts. Only when multiple failures and write-offs occurred were con-rod bolt loads recalculated and the need for even and lower bolt tensions to withstand the extensions of normal use brought forcibly home.

Finally, it was this recognition of excessive bolt loads and how close they perpetually came to failure that led Lovesey to take the wholly exceptional step of ordering that bolt loadings must be substantially reduced by decreasing maximum rpm from the initial 3,200 to a safer 2,850. For an engine designer this was an admission of defeat. In truth the bolt head loads had simply been wrongly calculated. With bolt loads at the very limit of safety, even at 2,850 rpm, it is easy to see why the engine was not capable of achieving enhanced output without the major redesign of the con-rod finally recognised as essential.

The use of the two long and two very short con-rod bolts was the inevitable consequence of the unusual design adopted for the star-rod assembly in the engine. The odd combination of a master and one subsidiary rod on one side and a cap with the remaining two rods had dictated the diagonal split line and in turn the untried combination of short and long bolts in a strong material of dubious ductility. All these were the undoing of the Vulture and insurmountable obstacles to further development without the sweeping redesign outlined earlier. Although serious problems had been experienced with the bearings these had been overcome by the development and adoption of LA4 silver materials by the time the engine was abandoned. It was not considered that the four con-rods on a single bearing resulted in an excessive or unreasonable load. Indeed radial engines employed large numbers of con-rods to a single bearing. The prolonged problems with bearing materials in the Vulture had other origins. So the Vulture passed into history with none of its systems being perpetuated through into other engines. It was a dead end.

It is an oft repeated 'fact' that more Manchesters were lost on operations due to engine failures than to enemy action. Modern analysis of losses can at least lay this ghost. Although in the period up to August 1941, 207 and 97 Squadrons did lose a number of Manchesters due to engine failure, from this time onwards such operational losses became remarkably few, as is apparent from the Appendix. The efforts of Rolls-Royce to improve the reliability of the Vulture, especially in the critical May to August 1941 period, are well reflected in the loss statistics.

Although far fewer Manchesters were lost due to engine failures than wartime rumour suggested, it is equally apparent that many Manchesters continued to be lost following often quite superficial damage to just one engine. This exposes to scrutiny yet another of the popular myths of the aircraft, which has continued to be debated with some vehemence by those directly involved, as to whether the Manchester could maintain height on one engine. Again the answer seems clear. Some aircraft could and others decidedly could not, whereas some highly skilled and experienced pilots could and others, less proficient, could not. With the possible permutations of aircraft and pilots this breaks down to a ratio of one in four chances of remaining airborne. This, naturally, is an indication of the odds, not of the statistical chances, because aircraft and aircrew performance cannot be retrospectively established.

Top and Bottom: Following its withdrawal from active service, L7420 was used by both the RAF and USAAF for dinghy and ditching training. On 13 June 1956 it was salvaged from a flooded gravel pit of the Lincolnshire Sand and Gravel Company on the Burton Estate by aircrews from USAF Sturgate. The longest surviving Manchester, it is assumed to have been scrapped following recovery. L7420 was struck off charge on 19 November 1943, and never undertook Ops. (Lincolnshire Echo via Peter Green)

A feature of this history which perhaps stands out above others is the many examples of the most determined and desperate attempts at bringing home Manchesters on a single engine. In this respect, amongst others, we find examples of the increased stress factors which Manchester aircrews faced. In addition to the numerous examples presented in the narrative where crews baled out of, crash-landed or ditched their failing Manchesters, it is not surprising too that numerous other examples of successful single engine returns have come to light.

It is clear that on 7 September 1941 'Kipper' Herring and his crew were by no means alone in their experiences. Examples of Manchesters returning successfully from well out in the North Sea, from the German coast, from Brest and the Ruhr are on record. What still endures is that Herring did complete the longest single engine return. His gallantry award was richly deserved, but the experiences of his peers in equivalent circumstances lead one to wonder if, as was suggested, anyone who flew Manchesters on operations against such odds was equally eligible.

Possibly a further manifestation of the success of Rolls-Royce efforts to improve engine reliability, albeit within the narrow limits of the serious under-powering, was that almost all the successful single engine returns took place after the May to August 1941 spate of engine modifications. As with 'Kipper' Herring's achievements, those of Leslie Manser have several parallels. Many equally courageous and selfless endeavours and sacrifices in Manchesters went unrecognised and unrewarded and are recorded in this account for the first time. However, in this the Manchester was no different from other wartime aircraft.

Avro themselves had started with problems equally as serious as Rolls-Royce with their 'side of the deal'. The initial flying surfaces had all been ridiculously undersized and all had been extended. The original predictions of speed for the Manchester, at 341 mph maximum, had been way above what was realistic and the weight had risen alarmingly. The airframe weight, fixed military load and crew complement had all spiralled upwards. Even the weight of a pair of Vulture engines was more than one ton greater than that initially forecast by Rolls-Royce. Small wonder then that Chadwick was worried and had so soon turned to the four-Merlin alternative concept. Despite these weight increases, power output from the Vulture remained much as originally envisaged. By sheer hard work, Avro had overcome their problems and indeed, in the main, had done so much earlier than Rolls-Royce had come to grips with theirs. Chadwick was later to recognise and accept that his initial forecast of twelve months between the start of the design and the first flight was over-optimistic.

However, during this phase he had many, often stillborn, changes foisted on him by the Air Ministry. In turn the unrealistic ancillary roles of dive bombing, torpedo bombing and troop carrying were abandoned, but not before months of precious time and effort had been squandered on them. Not just basic problems, but also ancillary problems like the hydraulic system were solved. All this was undertaken at the same time as major constructional innovations were being proven.

These problems had largely been ironed out in the Manchester, which nevertheless was perpetually handicapped by its catastrophic under-powering. Yet, behind this failure, something quite outstanding was waiting to emerge. Thankfully that occasional combination of far sightedness and good fortune came together. The Manchester was basically an aircraft with outstanding stability and flying characteristics, which reached their peak in the perfectly proportioned Mk.1A. It was easy to fly and possessed of light, well harmonised controls, and gave unequalled manoeuvrability for such a heavy aircraft.

On the production line the Manchester had evolved rapidly. Only nine, ten or eleven airframes had the unsatisfactory FN21A mid-under turret and these were removed before operations began. Only the first twenty had the short span 28-feet tail. This was replaced by the 33-feet tail from the twenty-first aircraft onwards. The twin fin 'Lancaster' tail replaced the triple fin on the 133rd aircraft. By this time, other than in respect of its shorter span and greater leading and trailing edge taper of its main planes, the aircraft was to all intents and purposes a Lancaster in appearance. However, much additional restressing and beefing up of the structure internally was necessary to create the Lancaster.

Total production came to 202 Manchesters – two prototypes, followed by 157 production aircraft by Avro and forty-three by Metropolitan Vickers – before output transferred to the Lancaster. Its operational roles were confined to bombing, mining and leaflet dropping, in which capacity a little over 1,260 sorties were dispatched. Seven operational squadrons and two conversion flights undertook operations. 207 Squadron contributed the lion's share of Manchester operations, followed by 61 Squadron.

The prototype Avro 683 Lancaster, BT308/G. First flown at Woodford 9 January 1941 possibly with 28-feet tail. Lacking the weight of increased structural strength, it leapt off the runways and climbed like an angel. (Peter Green collection)

In spite of early engine failures in service, the loss statistics show a pronounced trend in which the earliest squadrons have the best and the later squadrons a sequentially worse loss record. The Manchester's vulnerability, largely due to the inadequate power and unreliability of its Vulture engines, was soon appreciated. This did not prevent a number of audacious and desperate daylight bombing and mining operations, the latter at low level, being attempted. By the same token, throughout 1941 and early 1942, as the role of the strategic bomber was just emerging and before the regimented flying heights' times and courses were specified, the more determined crews did not think it out of the ordinary to descend to ground level and become night intruders on homeward operational flights.

Shipping convoys, trains, airfields and anti-aircraft installations were all considered fair game in this informal aggressiveness. Latterly, low level searchlight suppression operations were officially sanctioned for the returning bombers. Determined, yes, but foolhardy, never, these often experienced second tour crews had a clear perception of how dire their plight would be if return fire caused a Vulture failure at such low altitude.

With 202 Manchesters contributing just over 1,260 sorties, the average attempted sorties lies close to six per aircraft. However, fifteen Manchesters were dispatched on twenty or more occasions, of which L7378 is the clear leader having attempted thirty-three operations. At least forty Manchester pilots undertook ten or more operations as aircraft captains. No captain completed a thirty Ops tour exclusively on Manchesters, but Pilot Officer W. G. Gardiner holds the record for setting out on twenty-seven occasions.

Given the small number of Manchesters built, and its acknowledged limited military achievements, it should be pointed out that the aircraft was in squadron service for twenty months, operational for seventeen of these, and that throughout 1941 and the first part of 1942 remained, on average, the heavy bomber most numerically abundant (not most commonly available but in highest number) for operations in Bomber Command. All war is wasteful of materials, but it is suggested that the FN7A mid-upper turrets used in the Manchesters were diverted from production for the unsuccessful Blackburn Botha, whereas the unsatisfactory FN21A mid-under turrets were later re-engineered into Leigh Light installations for Coastal Command. Engine serviceability notwithstanding, of the total Manchesters built, details of total airframe hours for slightly less than 30% have survived. If this group is considered to be representative of the whole, then 66% of aircraft completed more than 100 hours flying. Five aircraft, 9%, completed more than 400 hours, whilst R5835 achieved the highest airframe total – 471¼ hours. Judged on these grounds, Bomber Command derived commendably efficient service from the Manchesters.

Of the 200 production Manchesters built the operational squadrons lost seventy-seven on operations and twenty more in accidents prior to the aircraft's withdrawal from first line service at the end of June 1942. A further twenty-four were lost in non-operational flying accidents by second line units, making a total of 121 in all. The operational squadrons lost twelve of their aircraft as a direct consequence of engine failure, whilst the non-operational units lost a further twenty-one. The circumstances of a number of other losses on operations could be not established. In addition, there were an unknown number of engine failures following which aircraft landed on one engine or were damaged to various degrees but not destroyed.

For the most part Manchesters were well served by their aircrews, amongst whom were highly experienced regulars, second tour crewmen and a significant number of the small percentage of pilots with 'Above Average' ratings. Peter Burton-Gyles, Charles Kydd, 'Kipper' Herring and Guy Gibson were amongst the Manchester 'giants' who served with exceptional distinction but who failed to survive the war.

Another pilot, who also went on to become a leading night intruder on de Havilland Mosquitos, was John de Lacey Wooldridge. Not only was he an exceptionally audacious pilot but also an author, composer and musician! He wrote *'Low Attack'*, describing his Mosquito experiences, and the script for *'Appointment in London'* which was made into a play and film. His music was performed by the New York Philharmonic Orchestra conducted by Leonard Bernstein.

Above all, 'Dim' Wooldridge was a larger than life character. The opposite of dim, he had earned his nickname for allegedly getting lost returning from a raid and landing in Germany to ask the way! Visiting a hotel on a rare spell of leave, he registered and was approached by the hotel porter who asked if there was luggage to be carried to his room. 'Yes', replied 'Dim', rifling through his pockets until he came across his toothbrush, which he presented to the startled porter before following him up the staircase! During part of his Manchester tour an integral part of 'Dim's' pre-flight operational procedures was to open the upper cockpit hatch, reach back and tie a by-then grubby lady's bra to the wireless mast. This streamed out in flight for all the world like the paying off pennant flown by a naval vessel returning to its home port after a long foreign assignment. 'Dim' explained that this lucky mascot was a trophy won 'in a fair fight during the Battle of Scunthorpe'.

Exceptional qualities were not only to be found amongst the pilots but also amongst the other trades. A number of the air gunners and gunnery leaders were of the highest quality and several had multiple claims for German fighters to their credit. More outstanding individuals came from the other ranks. None can represent the calibre of these better than wireless operator/air gunner Sergeant Maxwell Riddell. Known universally in 207 Squadron as 'Mad Max', he not only stood foursquare and flew his Manchester operations with distinction, but was perpetually to be found hanging about the crew room door when Ops were pending, hoping to scrounge spare trips over and above his commitment.

For the crews involved, flying bomber operations was perpetually stressful, frightening and occasionally harrowing. For the Manchester crews it was arguably worst of all. They were flying operations in a general wartime climate of successive military reverses. It seemed that Germany and Japan were becoming stronger by the day. In their immediate sphere, experienced crews detected a perceptible stiffening of German defences. Whatever the target, they were forced to steel themselves for a double crossing of the searchlight belt in Holland. This was often more dangerous than the bombing raid itself. Flak defences, especially the highly mobile light guns, were increasing rapidly in numbers and efficiency.

The night fighters, too, were beginning to get going and presented an ever more serious threat. Targets, too, were becoming better defended and radar prediction of guns and searchlights further increased the risk. On top of this, there was frequently Northern Europe's inclement weather!

Whereas the earlier Hampden crews enjoyed the benefit of their reliable Bristol Pegasus engines, flying with relative impunity night after night across blacked out Germany, generally able to keep below cloud to ease navigational difficulties, and with the satisfaction of seeing and hitting their targets, it was quite different for the Manchesters, who had to fly higher and take to the clouds for their own self-protection. Now the frustration increased. Manchester crews could rarely find their targets, had no navigational aids and spent long, dangerous periods quartering the sky looking for gaps in the cloud to pinpoint their position. Only very rarely did they have the satisfaction of seeing their bombs explode on the designated aiming point. However, in all these respects the Manchester crews were in no worse a position than other RAF night bomber crews.

Operating the Manchester imposed enormous stresses upon the aircrews. Whereas a tour on Hampdens would be completed in as little as four months, some 207 Squadron aircrews joined the unit in November 1940 and did not complete their tours until March or April 1942 – after the Manchesters were replaced by the Lancaster. The many engine failures during the work up period made it a dangerous time for the crews, a lot of whom had been operational for over a year.

The extremely unreliable nature of the Vulture engines contributed another major additional stress. Even when not directly threatened by the enemy in the air, the many possible sources of engine failure were a cause of profound worry. Unlike other aircraft, which could take a lot of punishment, crews knew that just one flak or fighter hit, or even a spontaneous leak in any of the cooling or lubricating lines to one engine, meant the almost inevitable loss of the aircraft. Manchesters carried abundant threats from within!

All Bomber Command aircrews went through the same process in the lead up to an operation and this took its toll irrespective of whether the operation was carried out or cancelled at some time before take-off. Weather and other operational reasons led to cancellations. 207 Squadron embarked upon ninety-four separate operations during its Manchester era, whilst at least a further fifty-nine were briefed but cancelled prior to the squadron becoming airborne. Military or weather problems frequently led to crews being at readiness for five or six consecutive days.

Even when operations were mounted, a crew often went through the entire physical and mental preparation only for their aircraft to become unserviceable in the hours prior to take-off or soon after becoming airborne. This induced an extreme frustration and anger in the crews, who naturally felt their aircraft was letting them down, whilst they had precious little to show in military terms in return for their efforts. Commonly such failures resulted in a sufficiently serious hazard to the aircraft that they were as dangerous as any enemy action.

A further factor which preyed on the minds of aircrew through much of 1941, although this was common throughout Bomber Command, was that the concept of a tour of a predetermined number of operations had yet to be introduced. The crews went on flying until they were lost on operations or their squadron or station commanders decided they had earned, or more likely needed, a rest. Not surprisingly the crews felt they were on a treadmill with only one possible escape.

Bob Fletcher, a 97 Squadron Manchester pilot, was caught up in this 'never ending treadmill feeling' along with the rest. He managed to get in eleven Manchester operations in nearly twelve months of a seemingly nightmarish prolonged torture. Fletcher likened the experience to walking in a dark tunnel with no light at the end and could never envisage himself completing one tour, let alone his eventual two. His happiest recollection was of seeing the last of them and moving onto the Lancaster.

As the war progressed, Chadwick's visionary design achieved its full potential. Not only was the Lancaster superior in performance to the Halifax and Stirling but, just as importantly, it was a production triumph for Avros. Construction as major sub-assemblies not only eased transport but also repair. The Air Ministry was so impressed

The second prototype Lancaster, DG595. It carried the definitive oval shaped tailfin, dispensing with the middle fin. The tailplane had a 33-feet span. It had a mid-under turret and bulged bomb bay doors. (Peter Green collection)

by the superiority of the type that the Ministry of Supply decided to evaluate Avro's production techniques with a view to making them standards throughout the aircraft industry. On 6 January 1944, Mr R. Lubbock and Professor Postan visited Chadwick at the Chadderton works for an extensive interview. In respect of the design, Chadwick emphasised the early importance he had attributed to the bomb compartment and bomb gear, followed closely in his judgement by the undercarriage. By concentrating all fuel in the wings and bombs in the fuselage this was certainly one major area in which his design surpassed the Halifax and Stirling. Furthermore, his undercarriage was lighter than that in the Halifax and far superior to the terrible contraption used in the Stirling.

His long, slim, low set Merlin installations contrasted with the short and high-set engine mountings in the Halifax. As a consequence the propellers in the latter were located in the up-current of air rising over the wing leading edge. Each blade rotation took it alternately through the upstream airflow on one arc and the downstream airflow on the other. Engine and airframe vibration resulted. Although Chadwick may not have itemised it to Lubbock and Postan, Alec Harvey-Bailey Jnr. of Rolls-Royce recalls that in one three month period he had ninety-five reduction gear failures from Merlin Halifaxes through his hands, seventy-five of which were from the port outer engine. To counteract this, Merlin Halifaxes were seen with four-bladed propellers, often fitted to the port outer only from this time.

By now the cautious comments of Type 679 and Lancaster supporters in November 1940, that there seemed no reason to suppose that the 'Manchester III' should not at least match the Halifax in performance, were in the past. In respect of production, Professor Postan mentioned that Sir Frederick Handley Page had also tried to cater for the split assembly methods, perfected by Chadwick, but had clearly been less successful. Unusually for him, Chadwick's response included the gentle jibe that Sir Frederick's principal contribution to the war effort had been to try to convince Lord Beaverbrook that there should be only one heavy bomber - the Halifax - and that the Lancaster was no good.

So, from the modest and humble beginnings of 'Hettie' Hyde and a few others in the pre-production Manchesters, a mighty strike force of Lancasters was created. Avros had given birth to a line of bomber aircraft which developed sequentially into the Lancaster, the York, the Lincoln, and the Shackleton. It was a distinguished family line which served the RAF for 50 years. Clearly, once released from the burden of its under-developed and unreliable engines, the airframe justified all the aspirations of its makers, the aircrew and the RAF. Even 50 years later the Shackleton had bomb bay components constructed from Type 679 drawings.

Historians have evaluated the extent to which unreasonable restrictions and reparations imposed on Germany after the First World War, Hitler and his henchmen, the Peace League, public opinion in Britain and the politicians in general contributed to the outbreak of the Second World War. Wherever responsibility lies, it was the staff of Avro and Rolls-Royce who paid the price in exhaustion arising from seven day a week, 18-hour days in bringing the premature Manchester and its Vultures into service. Uniquely though, the 5 Group aircrews, operating their engine test-beds into the very heart of enemy airspace on more than 1,200 occasions, paid their price in blood.

The least we can offer is to remember them.

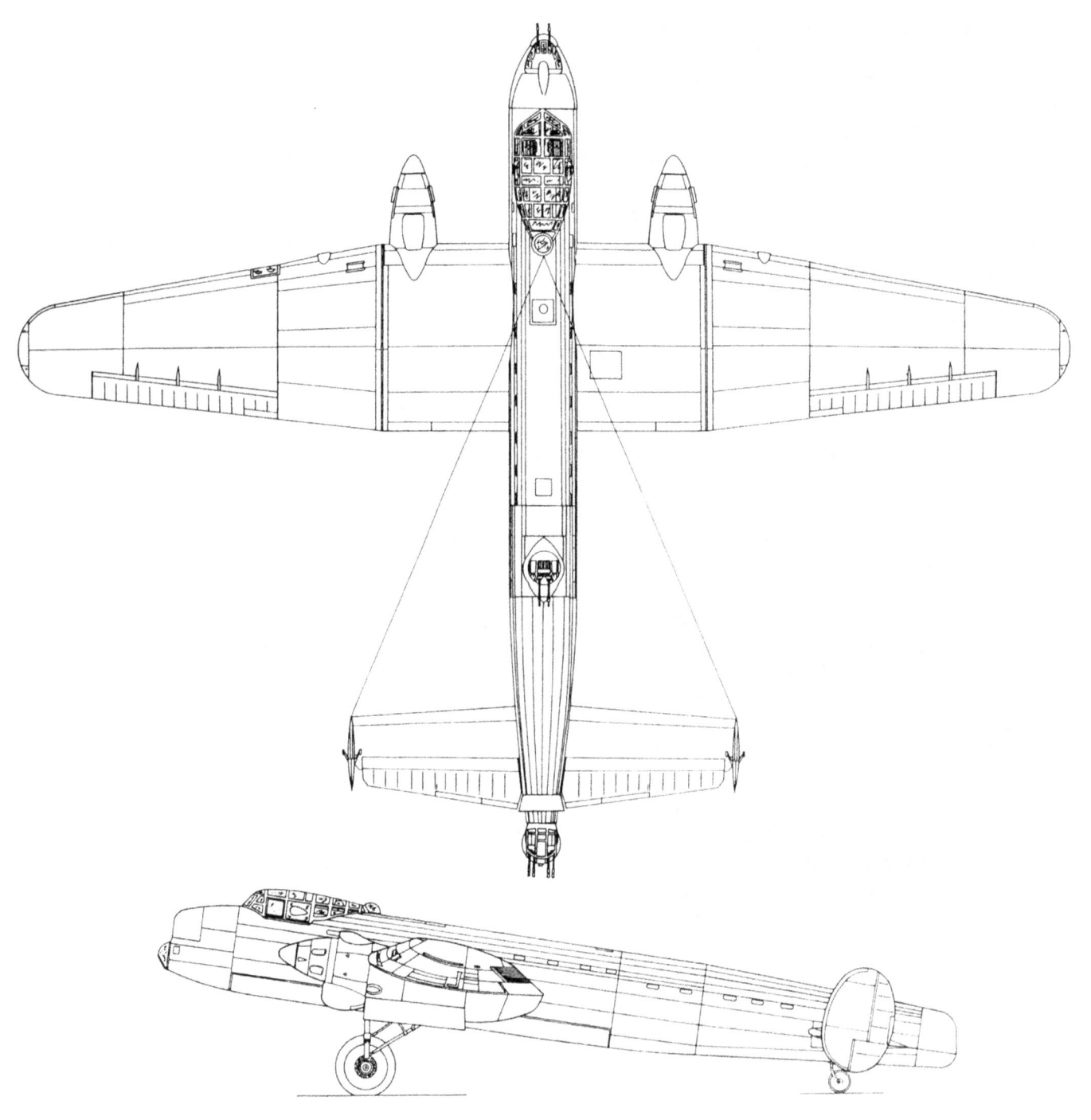

General Arrangement Drawings. Top: Definitive Manchester Mk.1A. This configuration applied from L7483 to L7526 and many of the later Mk.1 conversions. Bottom: The unarmed first prototype with 80-feet 2-inch span wings. All of the flying surfaces proved too small and were enlarged during development.

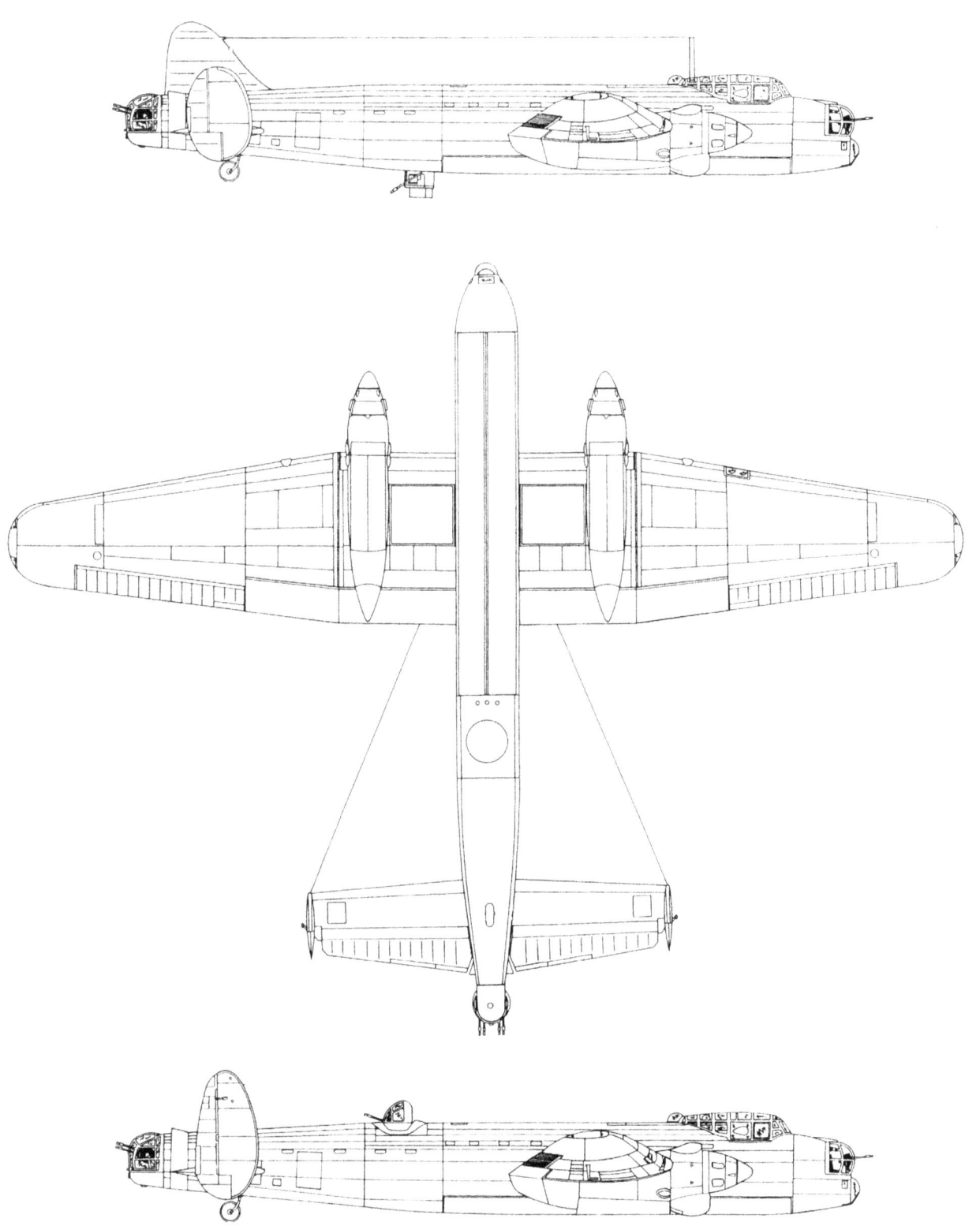

Top: The first nine, ten or eleven pre-production airframes (records vary) were delivered with the Fraser Nash FN21A 'low-drag' mid-under turret. These aircraft also had the original short span 28-feet tailplane and flat-bottomed bomb doors. The FN21As were removed before operations commenced. Bottom: Underside of a Mk.1 or Mk.1A and side view of a Mk.1A.

Appendix One: Manchester Evaders Reports

MOST SECRET - M.I.9 INTERROGATION – EVADERS REPORT
Manchester L7321 of 207 Squadron. Captain, Pilot Officer J. Unsworth. Ops to Cologne. Took off 00.35 hours 14 October 1941, shot down at approx. 02.00 hours inward-bound to the target. Two survivors: Pilot Officer H. B. Carroll, Second Pilot, and Sergeant G. T. Cox, W/op AG. Both became evaders.

Statement by 68806 Pilot Officer CARROLL H. B. 207 Squadron Bomber Command, RAF.

I was second pilot of a Manchester Mk.1 which took off from Waddington (Lincs.) at 00.35 hours on 14 October 1941, our objective being Cologne railway station. Just north of Liège we were caught in a cone of searchlights and attacked by four enemy fighters, the starboard engine being hit. (Two of the enemy fighters were, I think, shot down). One engine caught fire, and we were ordered to bale out. The second wireless operator went first and I followed. I came down at approx. 02.00 hours on 14 October at Comblain-au-Pont, south of Liège. I do not know if the others got out, but I heard an explosion before I reached the ground and later I saw blazing wreckage. The other members of the crew were:

Pilot Officer UNSWORTH, DFM, First Pilot and Captain (believed dead);
Pilot Officer SIMPSON, RCAF, Observer (believed dead);
Flight Sergeant MOULDING, Wireless Operator (believed dead);
Sergeant COX, Second Wireless Operator (in MADRID);
Sergeant DICKSON, RCAF, Rear-Gunner (believed dead);
Sergeant MASON, Mid-Upper-Gunner (believed dead).

I came down in a wood and after burying my parachute and Mae West got away as quickly as possible to the edge of another wood about half a mile away and remained in hiding till about 16.00 hours. I did not then know whether I was in Germany or Belgium. I began walking westwards along a road, hoping to hitch-hike. After about an hour I met a Belgian who turned out to be a Brussels gendarme home on leave at Comblain-au-Pont. I told him who I was and he immediately took me to his home in Comblain-au-Pont, gave me food, clothes, and 150 francs, and took me the same night (14 October) to Brussels via Liège. I stayed the night at a tobacconist's shop, and was taken next morning to the house of a friend of the gendarme. Although a poor man – I believe he earned only 800 francs a month – my host supplied me plentifully with food and clothes, being assisted by three gendarmes.

Friends of my original helper got in touch with the ORGANISATION, and on 20 November I was taken to another address in Brussels, where Sergeant Cox (of my crew) was already staying. On 5 December I left Brussels with Sergeant Jack H. Newton (S/PG, (-) 649), Sergeant Larry Birk (in Gibraltar), and a Belgian who acted as guide. At Valenciennes, where we crossed the frontier, the German guards on the Belgian side could not speak French and did not notice that I did not speak it very well. On the French side I pretended to the French gendarme that I was Flemish. At Valenciennes we were met by a young Belgian girl, Dédée, and crossed the River Somme at the usual point near Corbie before catching the train to Paris and on to Jean-de-Luz via Bayonne and Biarritz. Details of the journey are best described in Sergeant Newton's report. From the De Greefs' house at Anglet, we went to Francia Usandizaga's farmhouse, where preparations were made for the crossing of the mountains. Florentino Goïcocchea led the three of us and Dédée over the Pyrenees and into Spain, but first we had to cross the Bidassoa.

This rock-strewn river, which for the last dozen kilometres of its journey into the Atlantic between Hendaye (France) and Inin (Spain) marks the Franco-Spanish border, has its source deep in the Pyrenees. Swollen now by recent heavy rain, we found that it was in spate and too dangerous to ford in the dark. Disappointed, we could only retrace our steps to Urrugne. Four days later we decided to try to cross the river again. It was still in spate, but Florentino remembered a wooden rope-bridge that we might be able to use, though it would be guarded. Finding the Spanish guards as expected, we waited until they were asleep before crossing safely into Spain on 10 December 1941. Dédée then led us to the British Consulate at Bilbao.

Joined Comet Group 8. Reached Spain 10 December 1941, reached Gibraltar 4 January 1942. Flown back to Plymouth from Gibraltar on the night of 20/21 January 1942. Mentioned in Dispatches 1 April 1943. Killed in accident 19 November 1945.

MOST SECRET - M.I.9 INTERROGATION – EVADERS REPORT

Manchester L7321 of 207 Squadron. Captain, Pilot Officer J. Unsworth. Ops to Cologne. Took off 00.35 hours 14 October 1941, shot down at approx. 02.00 hours inward-bound to the target. Two survivors: Pilot Officer H. B. Carroll, Second Pilot, and Sergeant G. T. Cox, W/op AG. Both became evaders.

Statement by 1251523 Sergeant G. T. COX, Second W/op AG, RAF in Pilot Officer Unsworth's crew, 207 Squadron, Bottesford

We left Waddington 14 October 1941 to bomb Cologne. We were caught by searchlights and attacked by fighters north of Liège. We shot down two but the aircraft was set on fire. We baled out at 02.00 hours. The rest of the crew were:

Pilot Officer UNSWORTH, First Pilot (believed dead)
Pilot Officer CARROLL (S/P.G.(-)666)
Pilot Officer SIMPSON, Observer, (believed dead)
Flight Sergeant MOULDING, Wireless Operator, (believed dead)
Sergeant DIXON, Rear Gunner, (believed dead)
Sergeant MASON, Dorsal Gunner, (believed dead).

I was told later that the aircraft was completely destroyed.

I came down in a tree near Comblain-Au-Pont south of Liège. I left my parachute in the tree and hurried away from the locality. At 06.00 hours I was found by some Belgians who had followed my tracks from the place of the crash. They gave me a coat and boots and took me to St. Roc where I was hidden in the school. On 17 October I was taken to Liège where I stayed alternate weeks with two families for six weeks. These people got in touch with the organisation in Brussels and I was taken there at the end of November to a house where I was given an Identity Card. I stayed in Brussels for two weeks and there met Pilot Officer Carroll, Second Pilot of my crew. Pilot Officer Carroll left for Spain on the 5 December and I returned to Liège for two weeks. I was taken back to Brussels on the 21 December, where I met Sergeant Day (S/P,.G.(-)693), Sergeant Warburton (S/P.G.(-)687), and Sergeant Hutton (S/P/G.(-)688). My narrative corresponds with that of Warburton from this point onwards.

Sergeants Hutton and Warburton were Air Gunners in a Wellington shot down on the night of 31 August/1 September 1941 and immediately picked up by Flemish peasants. They were taken to Brussels on 6 September and two days later were separated. The Resistance reunited them on 23 September and they remained together until 21 December. On this day, I (Cox), and my travelling companion, A. C. Day, were brought from Liège and left for Spain immediately in our group of four with Hutton and Warburton. We reached Spain on Christmas Day 1941. We travelled on together to Gibraltar, reaching there on 4 January 1942, though it was another eight weeks before we sailed for home, arriving Gourock on 10 March 1942.

Joined Comet Group II.
Mentioned in Dispatches 1 January 1943.

MOST SECRET - M.I.9 INTERROGATION – EVADERS REPORT
Manchester L7373 of 207 Squadron. Captain, Pilot Officer L. Paskell. Ops to Cologne. Took off 01.00 hours 14 October 1941, shot down at approx. 05.00 hours whilst homeward-bound. Two survivors: Flight Sergeant K. H. L. Houghton, Observer, and Sergeant A. Smith, Rear Gunner. Houghton evaded whilst Smith was captured, becoming a POW.

Statement by 580451 Flight Sergeant HOUGHTON K. H. L. 207 (Bomber) Squadron, RAF.

(What follows below is Ken Houghton's M.I.9 Evaders Report merged with, and amplified by, a journal account of his experiences he began on his return, but which remained incomplete on his death in 1945. It has been preserved by his nephew, Tony Sherwin – author)

I was a Flight Sergeant Observer, stationed at Waddington on the First Manchester Heavy Bomber Squadron. From the beginning of the war I had been very lucky and had completed 48 night operations over enemy territory. My story begins on 13 October 1941.

The other members of the crew whose names I remember were:
Pilot Officer PASKELL (pilot) and Sergeant ROBERTS (wireless operator), who I heard from the Red Cross in Switzerland were killed and buried in Belgium.
Sergeant SMITH (rear-gunner). I do not know what happened to Sergeant Smith and the other members of the crew.

The previous night I had been on my second operation in three nights and was, therefore, due for a night off duty. At 15.00 hours I was detailed for another raid that night. I was rather disappointed at this, as I had made arrangements to meet my girlfriend that evening. However, on finding that briefing was not until 20.00 hours. I was able to slip down into Lincoln, collect a couple of tyres for my car and explain to my girlfriend that I was on duty

Although I had never stated what sort of duty I was on, my girlfriend naturally assumed that I was going on another raid and with womanly superstition said she felt very worried about me, as her two previous boyfriends had both been reported missing, and she wondered if she was a bit of a jinx. I lightly informed her that only the good die young, so there was no need to be anxious about me as I always got back safely.

At 21.00 hours I arrived back at the camp and wandered into the mess where most of the flying crews were gathered and at 01.30 hours on 13 October I took off in a Manchester from Waddington – Target: Cologne, Route: Orfordness, Furness, Charleroi, Cologne.

Bright moonlight illuminated the target north-east of the town and I dropped my 4000-lb bomb. Observing the starboard engine overheating, I decided to s/c for Rotterdam taking a more direct route home.

Crossing the German/Belgium frontier at about 05.00 hours, I was getting out a cup of coffee when we were caught by a dozen searchlights which were part of a great belt of searchlights extending from the Franco-Belgium frontier to the north of Hamburg. At this time we were at 16,000 feet. We tried violent evasive action to escape these searchlights but to no avail. Suddenly, without warning, we felt shells and bullets ripping into us. We realised we were being attacked by a night fighter invisible to us from outside the cone. After the first attack my W/op., Sergeant Roberts, who was my best friend in the RAF, tapped me on the shoulder and pointed downwards, where I observed a spiral of smoke coming up through the floor. My pilot, realising that we would be attacked again before we got out of the searchlights gave the order, 'Prepare to bail out'. Hearing this, my heart sank as this was one of the things I had been dreading. Then on the intercom we heard the rear gunner yell, 'Turn port', but before we could do this we felt the aircraft shudder from the impact of shells and bullets of the second attack. The aircraft burst into flames, all lights were extinguished and the cabin became full of acrid fumes. Immediately the second pilot came back to get his parachute from near my table.

I pulled out my intercom and oxygen plugs and on breathing in the fumes, I was repeatedly sick. This was horrible suffocation, which was my greatest horror in life. This put me into rather a panic with the aircraft diving down in a mass of flames out of control. I managed to squeeze past the second pilot making for the Bomb Aimer's compartment where my parachute and the escape hatch were.

In the scramble my parachute harness seemed to catch on every projection. Having reached the compartment I grabbed by parachute. Owing to my condition and total darkness I had the greatest difficulty in putting it on. The next thing I did was to hastily throw the cushions covering the escape hatch to one side, pull the escape hatch release and after frantic struggles I managed to clear the hatch on one side. Now that the way was clear for me to leave the aircraft across my mind passed the story of a man who had baled out and was picked up dead with his right hand bleeding at the finger nails and a hole worn in the right side of his parachute cover. He had put his parachute on upside down and the rip cord release was on the left hand side instead of the right. So I checked mine and sure enough my release was on the left, so putting my left hand on the rip cord I toppled head first out of the aircraft, fearful as to whether we had lost too much height to allow time for a parachute to open before I hit the ground. In view of this I counted a rather quick three and pulled my rip cord.

I opened my eyes and saw a fire above me and I gathered the horrible impression that my 'chute was on fire. Then I felt a jerk as my parachute opened and as my descent arrested I realised that the fire was the burning aircraft above me. I then found myself floating in the moonlight about 8,000 feet above the ground. This was an amazing sensation, hanging there on the end of a parachute in utter lonely silence of the cool night air, after my recent frantic semi-conscious struggles in that roaring inferno a few seconds ago, and effected on me an indescribable reaction.

I watched the aircraft, now in a mass of flames, diving down in a long curve like a meteor and I wondered how many of my friends had been unable to bale out. In my semi-conscious state I realised that I still retained my helmet with its intercom and oxygen leads, which I should have left in the aircraft. This might have been a fatal mistake as I might have got hung up as I left the aircraft. I think I must have lost consciousness during my descent because when I looked down once I saw the tops of the trees coming up to meet me. I just had time to swing myself round before I crashed into the trees backwards. Fortunately for me they were pine saplings only about 10 feet high and they made a perfect cushion for my fall.

I lay among those trees for about quarter of an hour without moving a muscle except to vomit. During this time I pondered my position. It was rather a peculiar sensation to realise myself suddenly in the middle of enemy territory whilst only an hour's flying time from England. Whilst I was descending by parachute I felt that it was inevitable that I should very soon become a prisoner of war, but lying among the trees I gradually realised that there might be a possibility of eluding capture and escaping back to England.

I then tried to think of the best way to get home but realised that it would be much too dangerous to try and make for the Channel, so I decided straight away to head south for Spain. It seemed a devil of a long way to go and I did not cherish much hope of success but I was determined to try.

I realised it was hopeless to look round to see if any of my pals had descended by parachute and it was imperative if I was to elude capture to get as far away from the scene of the crash at once.

I got up and divested myself of my flying equipment. It was impossible to hide my chute as it was strung across the trees. The saplings were very close together so that I had to crawl for several hundred yards to the edge of the wood. The surrounding district consisted of masses of these saplings intersected by cart tracks. Taking my bearings from the stars I headed south along the cart tracks keeping near to the edge of the woods so that I could quickly duck in if I came across a 'Jerry' as I could hear them about searching.

After an hour's walking I came upon a peasant's cottage at the edge of a wood. By this time it was 06.00 hours and another hour before daylight, so I hid at the wood's edge waiting to see some activity at the cottage as I suspected the possibility of a searchlight detachment billeted there.

When it was just getting light an old peasant came out and lit a small fire in a shed, so I emerged from the wood and went up to him. He was very surprised to see me and called for his wife who came from the cottage. By my uniform and actions I indicated that I was a survivor from a bomber that had crashed during the night and that I needed help. After more explaining by signs he indicated that he was pro-British and that he would help me as much as he could. Giving me a blanket, he showed me to a pile of hay where I could sleep, indicating he would send one of his sons to keep an eye on the Germans and warn me of any danger. Being absolutely exhausted I slept until 11.00 hours.

On awakening I went into the cottage where they gave me food which I had great difficulty in eating as the food was unpalatable and also the fumes had upset my system. I requested if they could give me any clothes as I obviously could not wander around in uniform. One of the sons went away and half an hour later came back with a pair of trousers, jacket and a very old cap. I donned these clothes but they were too small for me to wear under my uniform so I decided to go without my uniform and risk being shot as a spy if captured, knowing that it was shit or bust. I then realised that I had gone flying without my escape outfit, which consisted of two silk maps, a compass and a hacksaw blade. All I had was about 13s 6d in English money. Luckily for me, sometime before I had lost my flying boots so was wearing my ordinary boots.

At this time the boy who had been watching the Germans came back and said that the Germans had found my chute and were still looking for me in the woods behind the cottage so I decided that it was time I made tracks. I realised that I must find some sort of a map. On the windowsill I found a school atlas and I ripped out a page which showed Belgium and Holland. By diligent enquiry I at last decided that I must be about thirty km north-north-east of Hassalt. I wasn't absolutely certain of my position as the people didn't seem to know themselves. Straight away I decided that I would travel by daylight acting the part of a poor peasant so I deliberately made myself dirty even down to my finger nails which I tore and ingrained with dirt. I put my watch in my pocket and did my best to obliterate the mark it had made on my wrist. Fortunately I wore an old roll neck blue pullover. I told the people if they wanted to keep my uniform to hide same as it would be very dangerous.

All the time I was at the cottage one of the sons was posted outside on watch to inform me of any impending danger.

These Flemish peasants, being well out in the wilds away from any centre of habitation, were very ignorant of how the war was progressing, only knowing that Belgium was still occupied by the Germans but, always having been very poor, they were hardly affected in any way by the war and the Germans, which probably accounted for the fact that they did not seem unduly worried at the risk they were taking in sheltering me.

At 14.00 hours I set out from the cottage having said thank you to these brave people but having no way of recompensing them for what they had done for me. Immediately south of the cottage I could hear machine gun fire so I headed west hoping to strike a road running south. This I did after about half an hour and had my first experience of walking along under the eyes of German soldiers of whom there were plenty about. At the first sight of them I felt like hiding behind a hedge but I overcame this urge and carried on as I thought an ordinary peasant would and everything passed off OK.

After walking among the German soldiers in the village for some time I gradually gained confidence which became greater as time went by and they soon gave me no qualms at all. I carried on in this way until about 4pm when I came to the outskirts of a small town. By this time I was lame from blisters and I decided that in some way I must obtain a bicycle. I saw one leaning up against the side of a shop so I leant against a house on the opposite side of the road for about ten minutes to see if anyone would come for this bicycle. Finally I plucked up courage, strolled across and took the bicycle. In Belgium most of the roads are cobbled and as I jumped on the cycle I realised, with a sinking feeling in my stomach, that the back tyre was flat, and, as I was bumping along over the cobbles with a crowd of children jeering at me, I realised straight away that it was impossible to take the cycle back to the shop and also that I hadn't time to pump up the tyre and that I could not very well go along as I was attracting too much attention. Luckily about 200 yards further along the road there was a short hump back bridge, on getting over this and out of sight I chucked the bike in the ditch and walked on. At about 18.00 hours it began to get dark and started to rain hard. By this time I was very lame with the blisters on my feet so I thought I better start looking round for some place to sleep.

The country around was very flat consisting of fields and one or two small farmhouses. I went to the nearest one of these which, like the rest, was practically a brand new ugly little house with perhaps one little wooden shed. I knocked on the front door and someone shouted 'Entrez'. I opened the door and stepped straight into a kitchen which appeared to be the living room, the furniture consisting of a stove, wooden table, two or three wooden chairs and a pile of sticks in one corner, also there was a prevailing odour of manure every-where. The people in the room seemed very poor and were sitting on the chairs or on the floor around the stove. In my best French, which was not very good, I explained who I was and asked to be allowed to stay under their roof for the night. The man of the house looked around with a rather vacant expression, muttered a few words, which I believe were in Flemish, then turned back to the stove. This was all I could get out of them. There was an air of apathy about them all. This happened at about six of these farmhouses which I visited in turn. By this time I was wet through and shivering having no coat, very lame and not being able to see in which direction I was going the night being pitch black. I regained the road and trudged on, soon coming to the outskirts of a small town.

By this time I was becoming rather desperate, feeling terribly lonely and hardly caring whether I was caught or not. I wandered up a drive leading to the back of a large house hoping to find a wood shed where I could shelter and sleep. I found a little shed and sat down on a log of wood inside and tried to get some sleep, but this I found was impossible being absolutely drenched through and frozen, so in the end I decided to try the house. I knocked on the door of a verandah at the back of the house for about ten minutes without getting any answer. Through the window I could see a light coming from beneath another door. The verandah door opened at my touch so I knocked on the inner door with the same result. I opened this door and found myself looking into a kitchen where I saw a large range and a roaring fire which was so inviting that I went in and sat down beside it. After about half an hour the owner of the house came in. The first thing he said in French on seeing me was: 'Where is my wife?' I said I had not seen her whereas he opened another door and called for her and after a few moments she came down. It appeared that on hearing me knocking she had been too afraid to come down. After I had explained who I was he fixed me up with something to eat. I then asked him if I could stay in the kitchen for the night. He explained that I had been very lucky in selecting his house as both his neighbours were pro-Nazi. He said that he would like to help me but he could not risk it on account of having a wife and child and there being so many Germans about. So at about 21.00 hours he led me down to the end of the drive and left me. It was still pitch black and pelting down with rain so I crept back to the wood shed again and managed to get to sleep. I woke up at about midnight to find him looking at me through the door. I got up believing that he would insist on my departure and feeling very peeved I said 'alright' and started walking down the drive once more. At this he called me back and took me into the kitchen and rigged up a couch for me near the fire where I fell asleep once more.

In the morning of 14 October he woke me up at about 05.00 hours and after thanking him I started off once more before it was light. I still had in my mind the idea of stealing a bike. Along the road there were several little farms with small outhouses which I investigated one after the other in search of a bike, without success and often being scared off by the bark of the owner's dogs.

At about 10.00 hours I came to a town called Diest. I passed right through the town still looking for a bike. It was amazing how difficult it was to find a bicycle when one wants to steal one. I was determined to find one in this town so I returned to the centre, and as it had started raining I stood in a shop doorway under cover. After a few moments a man came along on a bike which he left outside a shop practically opposite me. I waited about five minutes to see if the man came out again and also hoping that by this time anyone who had seen him leave the bike and go in the shop had gone out of sight. I then walked across, took the bicycle and rode at an ordinary pace down the street, turned a corner, then peddled as fast as I could out of the town. I might say whilst waiting I had had a blinking good look to see that it hadn't got a flat tyre.

Still heading south and taking this easily I soon covered a good distance, blessing the man who had invented the bicycle, it being the fastest and most inconspicuous form of travel on a journey of this kind.

At about midday I stopped at a little country pub where they gave me a little bread and cheese. During the afternoon I turned a corner of the road and found myself riding slap into a German patrol.

They were checking everyone who passed for the identification cards. Realising it was too late to turn and go back I kept on. A man on a bicycle in front of me was stopped so I did not see much hope for me getting through. Cycling at a very slow pace, showing a straw in my mouth and the cap on the side of my head, I looked into the face of the nearest German with an absolute vacant expression on my face, trying my best to give them the impression that I was a farm labourer going to work in one of the fields further up the road. The patrol looked at me suspiciously, but allowed me to pass through without being stopped at which I heaved a big sigh.

That evening I passed through Charleroi, and when night fell I found some sheaves of corn under a sloping roof at the side of a farmhouse. I chucked my bike in a ditch to hide it and made a bed for myself in the sheaves. Just as I was retiring one of our bombers was going over at about 16,000 feet and he was caught in many searchlights. I wished him the best of luck. I for one knew the terrible hazard of that searchlight belt for our bombers.

At some time about midnight I got up and picked my bike out of the ditch and started riding down the road. Realising I was going in the wrong direction I turned round and went the other way. After cycling for some time I suddenly woke up to the fact that I had done all this unconsciously, as it had been my intention to sleep throughout the night. I then realised that it must have been the strain of the last few days working on my subconscious mind which had made me travel on although I was still asleep. Having defined a new place to sleep, I came across a big brick barn with a big archway in the centre in which was standing a threshing machine. Looking around inside for a cosy place to sleep I was accosted by a man who came through a door. I explained who I was and what I wanted, whereupon he took me into a room adjoining the barn and sat me down in a comfortable chair beside a stove where I slept for the rest of the night. It appeared that he and his wife were working all night making bread. In the early morning about 05.00 hours on 15 October they gave me something to eat and after having thanked them I continued on my way.

Passing through Phillipville and Chimay I then left the main road, as I was coming near the French Frontier, and took to some minor roads. Coming within a few miles of the frontier during the afternoon I came across a small farmhouse, and after having done a reconnaissance of the place, as I always did before accosting any house, I asked the lady of the house, who at that time was the only occupant, whether she could tell me the best way to cross frontier, and she thereupon asked me inside for some tea. I left there having been supplied with my desired information and left the road carrying along on a cart track which led up through the woods across the frontier. On the frontier I noticed some men dismantling some pill boxes and tank traps. By this time I had gained complete confidence that I could pass off anywhere as a peasant, and so I decided that I would pass through Paris on my way south, and whilst I was in Paris I would try to look up a French girl whom I had known before the War and whose address I still remembered. So after crossing the frontier I turned and went, hoping soon to strike a main road south to Paris. The school map which I had on me ended at the French Frontier, so I threw it away, it being of no more use to me, and which might prove embarrassing if at any time I were to be searched. At this juncture, I realised that I had better tear off the Belgium registration plate attached to the front end of the bike as if someone in France noticed it there might be some awkward questions asked.

Carrying along on a minor road I passed several small cemeteries in which I observed a large number of German soldiers' graves.

Coming into a small village I found myself riding beside a young boy of whom I asked the best way to get to Paris. After having some difficulty making myself understood he told me to carry on to a town called Hirson where I would find a main road heading south. I arrived at Hirson just as it was beginning to get dark so I decided to start looking around for another place to sleep. A few miles to the other side of Hirson I came across a large farm where I noticed there was a big Dutch barn with a stack of straw underneath which I thought would be an ideal place to sleep. Still feeling hungry, however, I decided to go to the farmhouse and ask permission that I might sleep under the Dutch barn in the hope that they would offer me food without me having to ask for it, which I did after having made my usual reconnaissance of the place and the people.

The lady of the house, on my accosting her, invited me in for some food. While I was eating my meal the farmer and a friend of his came in from the out-buildings and we were introduced. The old man, the friend of the farmer, on hearing that I was a member of the RAF, absolutely insisted on me coming along with him to stay at his little cottage in the village. As by this time it was pitch dark we left the farm together and went to his home where he introduced me to his wife, small daughter and his father who I later learned was ninety-three years old. These good people were highly delighted and excited at being able to help me since they were vehemently pro-English. With great difficulty we managed to hold a conversation which lasted far into the night. Finally they showed me into their best bedroom at which I remonstrated but they assured me that they only kept this room for their friends.

The next morning, 17 October, after having slept well in a very comfortable bed, I was woken up by the old man who lent me his shaving tackle as by this time I had not shaved for three days. After having had a very good but plain breakfast, I asked him how it was that he managed to get so much food that he was able to give me all that he had. He told me that he was in the fortunate position of being great friends of the farmer up the road, and he was able to get quite a nice amount of butter, cheese, eggs and bread. Telling me that he knew a lady who could speak a little English, he went off and came back later in the morning with this lady who, it seemed, was a great friend of the family. It turned out, however, that I could speak French as well as she could speak English, but between us we got along famously. After having explained all about myself I said that I was trying to make for Spain and hoping to pass through Paris and look up an old girlfriend of mine on the way. At which she agreed with me about making for Spain but said that it would be much too dangerous for me to go to Paris, and also that Paris was chock full of Germans. She then suggested that they put me and my bike on a train at Hirson and supplied me with a ticket that would take me down through Nancy to Epinal. At first I did not care much for this idea as I deemed it much safer to travel by bicycle than incurring all the risks that would beset me if I travelled by public conveyance. In the end they persuaded me, making me realise how many days travelling I should save going by train than on a bike. After this she left us assuring me that she would be back later with the tickets and with maps for my route and also to collect my bicycle to take it to the station and put it on a train, which would save me many complications.

During the afternoon the old man disappeared, saying that he was going to listen to the BBC with some of his friends. While he was away there was a knock at the front door and I was hurriedly shown upstairs to hide. It then struck me how well I was being treated by these people because, having ascended the ladder, I found myself in a bare attic devoid of all furniture except two beds where the family slept.

The walls were just bare brick and the wooden floor had no covering at all. The visitor, however, did not stay very long and I was soon called downstairs again. When the old man came back, he inspected my bike and said that I should have a reflector on the back and also my mudguards should be painted white. He then made an improvised reflector and painted my mudguards to conform with all regulations. He also sent out and bought me a little metal plaque; which was a licence plate for my bicycle. Just before tea time the lady returned with my train tickets, maps and some money which she charged me thirteen shillings for and which I still had on me. Having told her that if I was ever questioned I should act deaf, dumb and daft, she hit on the brilliant idea of writing me out a note in French which translated meant, 'The bearer of the note, Pierre Delmont, is an imbecile. Will anyone who sees this note please have pity on him and direct him to Epinal'. This note, as will be seen later, saved me in a very awkward situation. She also gave me an address of a friend of hers in (location omitted) who would help me and which I had to memorise as it would be too dangerous to put on paper.

A short time after this she left us and I observed her driving away in a car with my bike in the back to take it to the station. I have often wondered since how it was that she managed to get petrol from the Germans to enable her to run a car. The old man tried to persuade me to stay on at his house longer but thanking him I said that I thought they had all been wonderful in taking such risks for me but that I thought it unfair to jeopardise them any longer, so after another night's comfortable sleep in the big double bed I prepared to leave the next morning after breakfast. The lady of the house gave me a small haversack in which were provisions that would last me some time. She then sewed a little plaque depicting the Virgin Mary on the inside of my shirt by which act I was very touched. I then said my farewells and tried to thank them but any thanks, whatever they might have been, were much too inadequate to thank them for what they had done for me.

Just as I was about to leave the house the lady came up and whispered to me that her small daughter would like to kiss me goodbye. This being done I felt both touched and embarrassed.

Leaving the house with the old man leading and myself keeping about 300 yards behind him, he led me for several miles to the station at Hirson.

At the station, armed with the ticket, I found I had to pass a Ticket Inspector and then find my right platform where I could catch the train. The old man, seeing that I might have some difficulty not being able to ask any questions, asked the Inspector if he might show his young friend who was slightly mental on to the right train, and I found myself acting the part of an imbecile for the first time which later was to help me out of many difficulties. The train arrived and my friend showed me into the right carriage and before we parted we shook hands and he gave me an encouraging wink. The train pulled out at 11.00 hours and I found myself sitting in a third class carriage, my neighbours being mostly women, and before very long they were all talking as fast as they could go.

After making several attempts at trying to draw me into the conversation at which I always played deaf and dumb, pretending not to be able to hear them; they finally gave it up in disgust. At lunch time I got out my provisions and, after having watched how the other peasants ate their food, I thought it would be safest to eat in the approved style of the poor French class, as they seemed to have a way of their own of cutting their bread.

They cut off a chunk of bread by pulling the knife towards them. I considered that it would be very easy to make people suspicious if I did not behave in the approved style, especially in a country where no one knew whether he could trust his neighbour.

During the afternoon we arrived at (location omitted or forgotten). By this time I was feeling rather tired and sore, as the seats were wooden, and the carriage seemed to be running on square wheels. In the sidings of some of the stations I had passed through, I noticed on most of the covered trucks words to the effect that in the truck there was room for either eight beasts or thirty men which struck me at the time as being rather poor taste. On the station platform at Nancy there were a large number of German Officials and men waiting to board the train. I didn't like the look of this very much, but after some time in their company I got quite used to the idea. In the carriage I also noticed several young men with the Nazi eagle and Swastika emblem on a band on their arms. These men I took to be French members of a German Labour corps. Arriving at Nancy at about 18.00 hours, just as it was getting dark, I got out of the train, having been told that I would have to change here.

Now I was confronted with the problem of finding the right train in which to complete my journal to Epinal. I noticed several porters in their light blue smocks, running around and gesticulating in every direction as if they had gone off their heads. These porters didn't seem as though they would have time or could be bothered to ask any awkward questions, so, picking out the most excited one I could find, I said in a questioning tone 'Epinal?' He then pointed to a small train at a dead end platform saying 'Voila', and then he turned away and went off with his barrow as fast as he could in another direction.

By this time I had complete confidence in myself, saying to myself as I wandered over to the train indicated, this is dead easy. At the side of the train I found another porter, so just to make sure that this was the correct train, as I couldn't afford to make any mistake, the ceremony was repeated, as with the first porter, and I clambered aboard. I found myself in a dimly lit carriage with shoulder high partitions and the usual wooden seats. I found one compartment vacant and chose a corner seat, hoping that no-one else would get in so that I could stretch my legs along the seat and be more comfortable.

In this I was unfortunate as very soon other people filled up the carriage. First of all a woman and a young girl, then a man, another woman and just before we started, a blind man came in, groping his way and with a suitcase and white stick. Soon they all started talking and the subject came around, as usual, to the war. At this the blind man started laying down the law as to what a mess England was making of things and why didn't we do this and that. I found myself being very tempted to start trying to tell him a few things myself, and I think I would have joined in the conversation, but I could not help but be suspicious of this blind man in his actions. There were several things he did which I could not help but think were just a little curious for a blind man, perhaps I was mistaken so I held my peace, which most probably was the best thing, as I couldn't afford to take any chances.

At last we reached Epinal at about 20.00 hours. It was very dark in the station, as it was blacked out and it took me some time to find the waiting room. Rain was falling again, so I had decided to stay the night in the waiting room. It was quite a large room, very bare and devoid of all comfort. There was a partition halfway up the room, and as I looked around I saw several civilians and about twenty German soldiers. Picking out a seat in the corner on the wooden bench, which ran all the way round the room, I settled down and ate my supper. After this I lay down on the bench, using a loaf as a pillow. Before I managed to get any sleep, I opened my eyes several times to find a pair of jack boots in front of my nose, and I realised that some of the soldiers were coming across to read the timetable which was on the wall above my head. I managed to get to sleep after some time as I was very tired and I put the thought of the Germans out of my head, believing that I should be very unlucky if they accosted me.

At some time during the early hours of the morning I was woken up by a hand roughly shaking my shoulder. I sat up and found two Gendarmes standing near me. They then asked me for my Identification Card, and my heart nearly stood still. Then I suddenly remembered the note which the French woman up near (name omitted) had given me.

Assuming an absolutely vacant expression, with wide open eyes, gaping mouth and shaking my head slowly from side to side, I slowly handed my note to them. While they were reading it, still pretending to be a halfwit, I glanced around the room and saw that most of the Germans were curiously looking in my direction and I then realised I was acting for my life. The two Gendarmes by this time were conferring between themselves and casting suspicious glances in my direction. Still acting as well as I could, I was by this time supremely confident that I could get away with it, which probably accounts for my not showing any nervousness in any way, which could have been disastrous.

After a few minutes the Gendarmes handed me back my note, and, apparently satisfied, left me to go to sleep again which I very soon did. My friends later told me that it was a wonder that the Germans didn't shoot me out of sheer pity, at which I replied that they did not know the meaning of the word pity.

I woke up on 18 October just as the first grey light of dawn came creeping into the station. Feeling cold, bruised and rather miserable, I sat up and ate the remaining food I had in my haversack, for breakfast. Often during my journey my thoughts went home where my Mother must have received a telegram which says: 'We regret to inform you that so and so is reported missing on the night etc.' I could image what she must be thinking, and here was I perfectly safe and still a free man with no means of letting her know.

Picking up my haversack, I wandered out onto the platform, looking for the luggage office to retrieve my bicycle. I found it after a short time and went in, and acting the part of a mute I proffered my ticket to a porter. After looking at it he said something, but perceiving that I was dumb he smiled in a sympathetic way, and finally made me understand that I had to pay a franc. Handing it over, I smiled knowing by this time that a franc was worth less than a penny at the present rate of exchange, and the whole journey for the bike had only cost three francs. I then picked out my bicycle and after the porter had checked it with the ticket I wheeled it out of the station. After having inspected my map, I mounted and rode off down the cobbled street which was practically devoid of people as it was only about 06.30 hours. I turned off onto a side road just outside the town as I wanted to make a short cut. The country in these parts was very hilly and wooded and I would have enjoyed my ride, but soon it began to drizzle and the wind came up from the south. Soon I found it very difficult to make any headway against such a foul wind and I was drenched through in no time.

About ten km south of Epinal, after passing through a village, I came to a very poor peasant's cottage at Donoux. By this time I was utterly miserable, so I stopped and asked a boy who was about eighteen years old who was working on a manure heap whether I could go into the shed, which was part of the cottage, to shelter out of the rain. After being in this shed for a short time, a woman came through a door leading into the living quarters and having been told who I was asked me into the room where she sat me down near the kitchen stove so that I could get warm and try to dry my clothes. Soon they were all putting on their best clothes to go out and I suddenly realised it was Sunday morning and they were going to Church into the village. I had never kept count of the days as it didn't make any difference to me what day it was. I found myself left behind with only a very old woman for company.

I was sitting near the stove, half undressed, trying to get some of my clothes dry. The old woman, whom I took to be the grandmother of the family, was sitting at a table behind me, and from the continuous mutter which came from her, I realised that she must be reading aloud to herself out of a prayer book or Bible. After about half an hour after the others had left, the young man came back and told me that some friends wanted me to accompany him to their house in the village. I protested at this, however, as the fewer the people who knew me, the better for my peace of mind. In the end, however, he persuaded me and after having put my partially dry clothes on again, I followed him on my bicycle back to the village I had passed through previously. We finished up at the back of a Café which we should call a public house.

He took me into the living quarters of the Café and introduced me to the family, who were very friendly indeed. Soon after, the young man left, and after I had told my story to my new friends they made me at home and started off by taking my top garments to get them dried, while the owner lent me his shaving tackle with which I managed to make myself a little more presentable. I stayed there all day and that night I slept in a very comfortable bed. At 05.00 hours the next morning, 19 October, I was woken up and after having a bite to eat, the old lady fixed me up with an overcoat and filled my haversack. Her intention was to put me on a train at the village station. When I left the house in the company of the old lady, the daughter of the house bent out of one of the upper windows and wished me: 'Bon voyage et bon chance'.

It rather surprised me that it was the lady of the house and not the man who was my guide, but it seems that it is often this way on the Continent. It was still dark outside and I followed the woman as quietly as possible through the village to the station, which was about 1km from the Café. I still had my faithful old steed with me. As we quietly slid into the country railway stop, we found the Station Master just coming out of his house. I had been previously told that I could completely trust this man, as on previous occasions they had all assisted ex-

French prisoners of war to escape to 'France Libre'. They fixed me up with a ticket for my bicycle but they would not permit me to buy a ticket for myself, saying that the Guard of the train would look after me when I arrived at my destination, which was Lure. I persisted that I must have a ticket but they would not hear of it. I didn't like this a bit, but I finally allowed myself to be persuaded that I would be OK. The snag was that I did not know enough French to argue with them.

The train arrived at about 06.30 hours and after having said goodbye to my friends I was off on another lap of my journey. Just the other side of Luxveil, I noticed an aerodrome lit up but no signs of activity. Throughout my journey I had been on the lookout for any military information which might be useful to our people at home if I ever got through. So far I had noticed practically nothing. Somewhere about 08.00 hours the train pulled up at Lure and I dismounted, looking round for the guard who was to help me, but I could see no sign of him and my fears about not having a ticket for myself was realised. Now what to do? I could see that all the passengers' tickets were being collected at the barrier. I went along to the luggage van and handed over my ticket in exchange for my bike. With it I crossed over the lines which were between me and the exit, looking around for a way out. Then I hit on the idea of going out via the luggage room, which I did trying my hardest to appear as though I had just collected my bike from there. Everything went off without a hitch and I found myself out in the street without having been stopped.

Going round the corner into a deserted side street, I studied my map to find out the shortest way to Montbellard without having to go round by Belfort. Having imprinted in my mind the route, which went mainly along by-roads, so that I should not have to look at the map again when there were other people about, which would look suspicious, I set out heading south-east through the town. On the outskirts I noticed a German Cavalry barracks. I tried to see what insignia the men were wearing, but I was unable to get close enough to find out.

Leaving the town behind me, I left the main road, taking a smaller road, and I soon found myself in very hilly and wooded country. It was in trying to ride up hills like these that I found that my worthy steed was some relation to a steam roller and I generally found that I had to get off and walk. I also had great difficulty going down steep hills, and in keeping my bicycle under control, as to brake I had to press backwards on the pedals, which meant that if the hill was very steep I had to stand on one pedal while exerting extra force by pulling myself downwards by means of the crossbar.

Eventually I rode into Montbellard at about midday and my next job was to find the house of the Curate of whom my friends near Hirson had told me. Looking around I soon found a big church. Knowing that the Curate's house was very near to the church, I left my bicycle and had a look round. There was a great number of old houses nearby and I couldn't make up my mind which was the right one. Seeing an old man wheeling a barrow I picked him out as a good and safe source of information, as he was old and poor and, therefore, most likely to be trusted not to be in with 'Jerry'. I asked him in my best French, using a phrase I had often rehearsed, if he could show me the house I wanted and he immediately indicated the house, showing no curiosity at my French, much to my relief. Knocking at the door I was informed that the Curate was away but would I like to speak to another Curate. Not knowing whether I was being a fool, I was shown into a room where after a few minutes a young Curate came in and I immediately told him my story. After saying that he was not sure if he could help me, he asked me to return at 14.00 hours when he would ask a certain lady to come along who could speak English.

Leaving him I wondered where it would be best to go to sit down and have a bite to eat. Seeing a steep hill on the very outskirts of the town I thought it would be an ideal place on the top of it as it was a beautiful sunny day. Cycling half way up, I left my bike behind a bush and climbed the rest. On top I had a wonderful view of the surrounding countryside. In the distance I could see a high range of hills, and looking at my maps, having noted that they were to the east by the sun, I saw that they must form the frontier to Switzerland. Then for the first time I thought: 'Why not cross over into Switzerland'. I could rest there, get money, maps and advice.

(The detailed personal account ends here unfinished. Ken Houghton was too busy, lost interest, or was killed. His escape is completed, though in less detail, from his M.I.9 report – author).

I followed one of the priests, both of us on bicycles, to the Swiss frontier, all the priests having advised me to go to Switzerland rather than to try to get to Spain. We passed through the village of Glay on the French side of the border and, after the priest had pointed out the way to me, I crossed the frontier and went to Grandfontaine, where I gave myself up about 19.00 hours (20 October). I said I was a British airman and had not been interned.

I was taken that night to the prison at Forgremtruy, where I was kept for three days. There I made another statement as to who I was and how I had come to Switzerland. I did this without giving away details of my journey. I was then sent to Berne, where I was questioned by a Colonel of the Swiss Intelligence Service. He asked me about my journey and about the RAF. I only answered those questions about the RAF where the information was common knowledge.

The colonel told me that I would either be able to stay in a hotel or to continue my journey. but, on the night of 24 October I was sent to the internment camp at Munchenbuchsee, where the Air Attache came to see me next day. I remained in Munchenbuchsee till 26 February 1942.

The men there lived in a wooden house and stables and cooked their meals in a garage and ate them in a room in a hotel. With Flight Sergeant Dunkerley, who was in charge of the internees, I slept in a private house in the village. From 26 February 1942 I worked in the Air Attache's office in Berne for four months. I was still technically interned and was not allowed to leave Berne. I began my return journey to this country on 19 June.

I left Berne on 19 June 1942, having got the Swiss authorities to order me back to the internment camp at Munchenbuchsee on the pretext that I was tired of working in the Legation. I went alone to Geneva by train, where I telephoned Mr Farrell, who took me to the house of a police officer. Next morning (20 June) a car called for the police officer and myself about 04.00 hours and we picked up Flying Officer Szkuta (S/P.G.(-)786), Flying Officer Wasik and a Dutchman.

We were driven to the frontier, walked through a churchyard and round the back, through a stream, and over some barbed wire into France. The police officer left us in the cemetery after pointing out the way. We walked to a crossroads where we met a man on a bicycle smoking a pipe. At 10.00 hours another guide collected us at this man's house and took us to his house in Annemasse by train about 17.30 hours and we arrived in Marseilles at 06.30 hours on 21 June. We went to a café in the main street near the railway station, and a guide took us to a house where we met Mario. I was travelling on Czech identity papers as far as Marseilles, and Mario now supplied me with Polish papers. That same day a guide took us to Nimes, where we remained for a week. On 29 June, again with a guide, we went by train to Toulouse. I remained there with the two Polish officers for three days in the Hotel de Paris. I went on to Osseja with a Frenchman and waited a day there for the Poles.

We all left Osseja on 4 July to cross the Pyrennes with a smuggler and his wife. After walking all night we slept the whole of the day in some woods on the Spanish side and at night the same guide took us to Burga, where we stayed a day and a night in a house above a restaurant. About 02.00 hours on 6 July a Spaniard and his sister took us from Burga to a small railway station about two hours' walk away over some more mountains. The sister then took us by train to Barcelona. We knew her as Senorita Ramona. Her home is in Burga.

In Barcelona (6 July) we were taken to a cafe, whence another guide took us late at night to different houses in the slums. We remained there until 13 July, when we left by train for Madrid. On the train Flying Officer Wasik was caught by the police. Against the advice of the guide he had insisted on wearing an expensive watch he had bought in Switzerland. The policeman who was examining his papers remarked on the watch, speaking in Spanish, to which Flying Officer Wasik could not reply. We had all been provided with Spanish papers. Flying Officer Szkuta's were examined, but mine were not.

Flying Officer Szkuta and I were two days in Madrid, being again hidden in the slums. The guide then took us to Merida, near the Portuguese frontier. We arrived there about 18.00 hours on 20 July. I understood the guide to tell us to get under the arch of a bridge where we would meet us later. We stayed there all day. By sunset the guide had not turned up, but we found him again just as we were about to set out alone. The guide supplied us with some food. He told us to walk towards Badajoz, keeping to the main road. He insisted we should let him go first, giving him half an hour's start, and promised to pick us up again at 06.00 hours. Flying Officer Szkuta and I walked for about forty km, but we did not see the guide again. We waited for several hours beside a river, and about 11.00 hours a man on a horse came up and asked if we were Italian and were going over the frontier. We replied that we were not. The man rode off, and we decided it was best to clear out. We walked across country the whole of that day and all the next night. We forded one river and swam another, carrying our clothes on our backs. We continued until about 05.00 hours and then found some very poor people living in grass huts who gave us coffee and directed us towards the Portuguese frontier. We crossed on 18 July in open country, avoiding a village at which there seemed to be some sort of frontier post.

We walked on to Campo Maior and surrendered to the police. We spent a day and a night in Campo Maior and were then handed to the International Police at Elvas. We lived for two days in the officers' mess in the army barracks at Elvas and were then taken to Lisbon (22 July), where we spent two nights and a day in a filthy jail before being taken by the International Police to the Embassy (23 July). The Embassy supplied us with clothes and arranged for our journey home by British Airways.

While we were in Campo Maior we were visited by a very pro-British civilian. I believe he told the 'Times' correspondent in Lisbon of our arrival in Portugal, and I think the 'Times' correspondent passed the information on to the Embassy, who seemed to be expecting us.

The guide who left us on the way to the frontier had been with us from Barcelona. I understood he was the chief of the organisation in Spain. I had given him my RAF navigator's watch and a Dunhill lighter (worth £2) which I had bought in Switzerland.

Awarded DFM 22 November 1940 on 83 Squadron.

Left Lisbon by Sunderland, landed Poole harbour.

Awarded Bar to DFM 1 November 1942.

Killed 2 August 1945 in Liberator KN826, Middle East.

MOST SECRET - M.I.9 INTERROGATION – EVADERS REPORT
Manchester R5787 of 61 Squadron. Captain, Flying Officer J. R. B. Parsons. Ops to Brest. Took off approx. 18.30 hours 31 January 1042, shot down at approx. 20.30 hours whilst running in to target. Flight Sergeant A. L. Wright, Mid-Upper-Gunner, Sergeants R. Kindred, and Griffiths, both injured, became POWs.

Statement by 548615 Flight Sergeant A. L. WRIGHT, 61 (Bomber) Squadron, RAF

I took off from Woolfox, Rutland, on 31 January 1942 at 18.30 hours to bomb the *Scharnhorst* and *Gneisenau* at Brest. We approached the target twice without bombing but were hit by flak on the second run up. We were obliged to fly for a time on one engine, and finally crash landed north-west of Brest at about 20.30 hours in open country, consisting of fields surrounded by earthen breast-works for irrigation purposes.

The rest of the crew were:
Flying Officer PARSONS
Sergeant MEGASKILL
Sergeant HOLMES
Sergeant GRIFFITHS (rescued from the aircraft, but left by it with a broken leg)
Sergeant BUTTERWORTH
a Second Pilot (author: Sergeant R Kindred)

I saw the aircraft burst into flames and burn fiercely, and I heard the oxygen bottles exploding. I heard later that three of the crew were taken prisoner, two were dead, and that one other had escaped. I think that the two killed must have been Butterworth and Holmes. I have heard no other news about any of them. I found out later on that we had crashed near St Renan (north-west of Brest), close to a road running between Lanildut (on the coast) and Lanrivaoare. At first I did not know exactly where I was; I therefore decided to walk in a north-westerly direction, away from the bursts of flak over Brest, which I could see behind me.

I soon came to a road which I followed through Breles to Lanildut, walking on towards the sea and finally hiding in bushes near the mouth of the river. I noticed a sentry on the far side of the river, but none on my side. This made me cautious and I lay up during the day (1 February 1942).

I intended to walk east after this, but actually went south-east, back through Breles towards St Renan, when two cyclists hailed me. I declared my identity, and found them very friendly. Under their direction I went on to a farm near St Renan. At this time it was raining and I was in need of rest and refreshment. The family at the farm gave me food and clothing and put me up for two nights in a hayloft. During this time Germans came twice to look for 'two men', but without actually searching the place. Meanwhile, my hosts got in touch with a helper in Brest.

On 3 February I went with the farmer in a cart to Brest. We picked up a man and a boy on the way. The cart stopped just before Brest and I continued on foot with these two, who put me in touch with an organisation headed by a French-Canadian, O'Leary, who would soon have me on my way to England by submarine. Unfortunately, the Germans arrested those that were about to help me, and I found myself trapped in Brittany. Continually moving from house to house, in mid-March I went to the Château Tréfry, home of the Comte and Comtesse de Poulpiquet, where I stayed until May, when the countess herself helped me get to Quimper. Another guide, a Jewish psychiatrist, took me as far as the Demarcation Line, where a young girl saw me across. She left me at a pre-arranged point while I walked on alone to a car, the driver of which, waiting to take me to La Haye-Descaries (Indre-et-Loire), was Doctor Voure'h, one of those who had earlier helped me in Brittany. Dr. Voure'h, having had to make good his escape to Vichy France when he learnt that he was a wanted man, now took me to Monthuçon but, failing to make contact with the next human link in the chain, escorted me to the American Consulate in Lyon.

It was still possible at that time, June 1942, for telegrams to be sent between Vichy France and England and, while I was in Lyon I received the wonderful news that my wife had given birth to a son. The US Vice-Consul, George Whittinghill, saw that I was well looked after. Within a few days someone from the PAO line took me and Dr Voure'h to Marseille, where I was introduced to Pat O'Leary himself. Taken to the Nouveaus' apartment, I 'actually arrived wearing a dinner jacket!'

Albert Wright continued to be sheltered by the Resistance until early June 1942, when he was moved in a mixed group from Marseille to Toulouse. After four days at a hotel near the railway station, on 9 June they were all taken to Banyuls where they were soon joined by two further escapees, one a mysterious figure who, Wright learned, was a French Intelligence agent.

Setting off with two Spanish guides it took the group of twelve men, including Wright, two days on foot to reach Spain on 11 June, their guides taking them to within twenty km of Gerona

Sergeant Wright, the last of the group to get back to Britain, and the only one to go by ship, had had the misfortune, along with the four Belgians in the group, to be caught by the Spanish police in a control check on the train to Barcelona. Whether or not they would have got away with their papers, which declared them all to be Czechoslovians, will never be known, because one of the young Belgians, in the heat of the moment, blurted out their true identities. Wright was thrown into a police cell at Barcelona before being transferred to the Cárcel Modelo where, amongst other privations, his hair was shaved off. He was eventually passed on to the notorious concentration camp at Miranda de Ebro. This was a step down even from Barcelona where prisoners were kept six to a cell, without blankets, in flea-ridden conditions and given only one mug of soup when other prisoners got two because, as the Spanish sergeant said: 'they were English'.

In Miranda de Ebro Wright caught up with the original crossing party. He was released from the camp on 23 September, returning to Scotland on HMS *Malaya* a week later.

See *Safe Houses are Dangerous*, p207 and *The Evaders* (Cosgrove) pp 62-108.

Canadian enlisted in RAF 1937.

Guided by Ponzán Network

MOST SECRET - M.I.9 INTERROGATION – EVADERS REPORT

Manchester L7423. Captain, Pilot Officer Bromiley of 83 Squadron. Ops to Cologne. Took off Scampton approx. 20.00 hours 13 March 1942, shot down at 22.40 hours whilst inward-bound to the target. Two survivors: Pilot Officer Bromiley, Pilot and Sergeant J. P. Dowd, Wireless Operator. Both captured, Dowd subsequently escaped and became an evader.

Statement of account of escape of 553789 Flight Sergeant DOWD James Patrick, 83 Squadron, Bomber Command, RAF

Captured: Kranenburg (Germany) 13 March 1942

Escaped: Arbeitskommando E488 Grottkau (Stalag VIII B) 29 August 1943 after two previous attempts.

Left: Stockholm, 24 September 1943.

Arrived: Leuchars, 25 September 1943.

Date of Birth: 25 June 1922

Private Address: 13 Craigmillar, Castle Terrace, Craigmillar, Edinburgh

Peacetime Profession: RAF

RAF Services: since May 1939.

OTU: 14 OTU. (Cottesmore)

Post in crew: First Wireless Operator

Other members of the crew:

Pilot Officer BROMILEY (First Pilot) (POW)

Sergeant FOSTER (Second Pilot) (killed)

Name unknown (J. A. Feim) (Navigator) (killed)

Sergeant DAVIES (Second Wireless Operator) (killed)

Sergeant ROSE (Mid-Upper-Gunner) (killed)

Sergeant THOMPSON, RCAF (Rear Gunner) (believed killed)

and self

Capture

I was a member of the crew of a Manchester aircraft which took off from Scampton on 13 March 1942 at about 20.00 hours to bomb Cologne. On the way in to the target we were shot down over the Dutch-German frontier at 22.40 hours by a JU.88 (actually a Bf110 - author). When ordered to do so I baled out. I am not certain where we were attacked, but it was probably near Nijmegen (north-west Europe 1:250,000, sheet 34). (In this report Dowd makes a mention of Pilot Officer Bromiley. Knowledge of his escape and capture may have reached UK from the International Red Cross - author).

I landed in a small fir wood and after tearing my parachute, harness and Mae West into pieces I buried them in the snow. I got out of the wood and on to a farm track. In a short time I reached a house, at the door of which a man and woman and two children were standing. They were pointing to the aircraft which was burning about two miles away. I heard them talking, and, as I thought I was in Holland, I called the man over and told him I was a British airman. He took me into his house and got me a cup of coffee. I was in the house for about ten minutes and got out my escape maps. Just as the man was pinpointing my position the door opened and two policemen came in. I then realised I was in Germany and that the man had sent his son for the police.

Both the policemen, one of whom was a special constable, were armed. They took me away at once to the police station. As I had injured my knee in landing, they allowed me to ride on the special constable's bicycle. On the way I think I heard one of the policemen mention Kranenburg, and I believe that it was to that village I was taken. The ordinary policeman telephoned, presumably to arrange for a search for the rest of the crew, and more policemen arrived. The policemen all wore badges with the word 'Düsseldorf'.

I was at the police station until 05.00 hours on 14 March, when two Luftwaffe men, one a Feldwebel and the other an Unteroffizier, arrived for me and took me in a car driven by a Luftwaffe Gefreiter to a town which was probably Nijmegen. Here I was kept for about two hours at what appeared to be a Luftwaffe Headquarters, and was given coffee and rolls. I was not interrogated at all here, not being asked even my name, rank and number. The policemen had already taken from me my escape kit and the few coppers I had with me.

The Feldwebel and Unteroffizier then took me by train in a reserved compartment to Utrecht, and thence by electric train to Amsterdam. From Utrecht we travelled with a Luftwaffe Major, who spoke English, and two SS men in army uniform. We arrived in Amsterdam about 17.00 or 18.00 hours.

In Amsterdam I was taken to a Luftwaffe Headquarters off one of the main streets, and put into what appeared to be a detention barracks. In the cell next to me was a Luftwaffe Feldwebel who told me in good English that he had been given a sentence of six months imprisonment for low flying. After the guard commander had gone in the evening, the Feldwebel slipped me some cigarettes.

I was not interrogated until the next morning 15 March when an interpreter, a Gefreiter, asked me my name, rank and number, which I gave him, and the names of rest of the crew, which I did not give him. He gave me three of my own cigarettes. In the afternoon after exercise I was taken to the sick-bay and X-rayed for broken ribs. While exercising on the parade ground I met Pilot Officer McDonald, P.R.U. who had also been shot down on 13 March.

On 16 March, Pilot Offcer McDonald and I, accompanied by a Feldwebel and two Gefreiter, left Amsterdam by train at 07.10 hours and travelled via Cassel to Frankfurt-am-Main, which we reached about 23.30 hours that day. We slept that night in the German Red Cross room in the station.

Dulag Luft

On the morning of 17 March I was taken with Pilot Officer McDonald by train to Dulag Luft at Oberursel (Germany 1:250,000, Sheet 64). On arrival, about 07.00 hours, we were put into separate rooms in a building near the Kommandantur outside the camp proper. I was put in a room upstairs and Pilot Officer McDonald in a room downstairs. I was alone in my room for four days. Meals were adequate by German standards.

When I was first put into my room a Feldwebel took away all my uniform and flying boots, which he returned in about ten minutes, presumably after having searched them. He also took my watch which was returned to me when I went into the main camp.

I was interrogated in my room on the first day by an officer (probably a Leutnant) named Eberhardt, who spoke good English. He gave me a Red Cross form to fill in. I said I would keep it for use when I went to the lavatory, and he said he was only trying to help me. He then tried to persuade me to fill in just my name, and this also I refused to do. He produced a list of names all with the Squadron numbers against them, and rattled off a number of names, some of which I knew. He asked if I knew any of the names, and I said I had been in the RAF for only about two weeks. He asked how I came to be a Flight Sergeant wireless operator after such short service, and I replied that promotion was very quick.

Next day (18 March) Eberhardt returned and said that if I had been only a short time in the RAF, plenty of people seemed to know me, adding: 'I, too, know you. You are from 83 Squadron'. I think he must have discovered my squadron number from someone in the camp who knew me. I refused to speak and he said: 'The Scots have very bad manners'. (He had realised from my accent that I came from Scotland).

On the third day (19 March) a Luftwaffe Major, who appeared to be a radio specialist, visited me and began a discussion about wireless. He produced photographs and circuit drawings of an I.F.F. and I noticed that the most important circuit was missing from the drawings. He also had photographs and circuit drawings of almost every type of radio set that I knew, and of some that I did not know. I did not answer his questions and said that I did not know anything about radio sets beyond how to operate them. He went away disgruntled, but afterwards brought me a book to read.

That afternoon another officer (probably an Oberstleutnant) visited me and began telling me about the new FW 190. He wanted to know from me about the performance of the Lancaster. I said I did not know anything about it, and he did not press the interrogation.

On the fourth day (20 March) Eberhardt returned with a sheaf of Red Cross forms. He filled in particulars on one of my name, rank, number and date of birth, which I had told him, and the number of my squadron and the type of aircraft, which he had got from other sources. He asked me to complete the form, and when I refused he said he would do it for me.

About 15.00 hours that day the Feldwebel took me to be photographed in the same building, after which I was moved to the camp proper. I was not interrogated again. Immediately I arrived in the camp a Flight Lieutenant warned me against talking, because of the existence of microphones and stool-pigeons, and advised me not to trust anyone except people I had known at home, and not to say much even to them. I was put into a room with three Sergeants. There may have been microphones concealed in our room, but we could not locate them.

At the end of March an attempted escape was made by Pilot Officer Key, P.R.U. He hid in the camp as a sergeant to give the Germans the impression that he had escaped. After two days' search the Germans concluded that he had really got away. Only a few sergeants and a few of the permanent staff knew that he was still in the camp. As part of his plan to escape Pilot Officer Key buried himself in a sheep pen in the playing field with only a piece of piping sticking out of the ground to breathe through. He was buried for about two hours. When the guard came to lock the gate of the playing field in the evening he went straight to the sheep pen, which he had never done before, kicked up the earth, and pulled out Pilot Officer Key. I am of the opinion that his plan to escape had been definitely given away to the Germans by someone in the camp.

Stalag VIII B (Lamsdorf) – Arrival

On about 14 April I was moved to Stalag VIII B (Lamsdorf), (Germany 1:100,000, Sheet 11) with a party of seventy or ninety Flight Sergeants and Sergeants. We arrived at Lamsdorf about 17 April and I was put into the main camp. Our flying boots were taken from us, possibly to be sent to the German Army on the Russian front, and we were given wooden clogs.

First Attempted Escape

In June 1942 I planned to escape with Sergeant Gough, RAF, but he was moved to Stalag Luft III, Sagan, before we could carry out our plan. I decided, however, to make the attempt alone, and changed places with Private Bruce, Gordon Highlanders, on a working party of fifteen which was going to join a party of about fifty who were working near Rothfest (Sheet 117) clearing the bed of a canal. We arrived at our billet about 13.00 hours and at 21.00 hours I escaped with a soldier from Newcastle (name unknown) whom I had met for the first time on the working party.

We escaped through the window of our room by bending back the bars. There were three guards in the room next door, but they did not hear us. My plan was to make for Prague, as we had heard in the camp that there were Czechoslovakian organisations there which would help us to get to Switzerland. I had maps, which I had got in the camp from an RAF Sergeant, and a supply of food which would have been enough for one man for about three weeks. I carried the maps, the food and a spare shirt in a small attaché case which Private Moran, Black Watch, had given me. He had got the case while working outside the camp.

After leaving the billet we headed south-west across country, and after passing through Niklasdorf (Sheet 116) we got into the hills on the Czechoslovakian frontier. Unfortunately, my companion lost the homemade compass which we had with us, and on the seventh day our food gave out. We had then crossed the frontier and were somewhere near Freiwaldau. We went to a house and asked for food expecting the people to be Czech. However, the owner of the house was a Sudenten German who, recognising us from our uniform, immediately sent for the police. We were taken to the police station, locked up for the night and next morning sent back to Stalag VIII B by train.

In the camp I was put into the 'Strafblock' (punishment compound) to await my turn to go into the cells, which, as usual, were crowded. In the punishment compound I was visited by Capt. Webster, RAMC, who said he would help me to make another attempt at escape.

In the punishment compound I went at first under the name of Bruce, the name of the soldier whose place I had taken on the working party. One day, however, I was recognised as RAF by Unteroffizier Cissel, a Ukrainian, serving in the German Army. Cissel was in charge of the RAF compound. He reported my true identity to the Gerichtsoffizier, who gave me fourteen days' imprisonment instead of the seven normally given for a first attempted escape.

Second Attempted Escape

While doing this sentence of fourteen days I was put into the cell next to Dvr. Geoffrey Roberts, RASC, who was also being punished for an attempted escape. He had already served ten days in a civilian prison, and was then doing the last four days in the camp cells. He was anxious to make another attempt at escape, but wanted a little time to build up a food supply from Red Cross parcels, and agreed to change cells with me. This we did by climbing over the barbed wire on top of the wooden partition between the cells. I took his place on the last day of his imprisonment. When the Unteroffizier came to release me that night he realised that I was not Roberts. Both Roberts and I had given him a considerable amount of trouble, and this seemed to confuse him, because when I insisted that I was Roberts he eventually signed my release form.

I was then moved to the convalescent compound, Captain Webster having arranged for me to be sent there so as to facilitate another attempt at escape. He certified me as fit for work, and I was sent next morning to the working compound. Here I met two other RAF Sergeants - Sergeant James Paton, RCAF and Sergeant David Moran, RCAF - who, like me, had assumed the identity of soldiers in order to escape. With them I was sent on a working party to a paper factory, Arbeitskommando E42 at Rothfest (Sheet 117).

We spent about a week at Rothfest collecting information for our escape. Our plan was to go to the North first of all, the general direction of the German search for escapers being towards the south, and then head west towards France, or, failing that, towards Holland or Belgium. The Dieppe raid had just taken place, and, believing that the second front had opened, we hoped to join the invading British forces. We decided to cross Germany by following the main roads. We made a collection of food, and both Moran and I had maps, I having managed to retain mine with my attaché case after my first escape.

We made our escape during the first week of August 1942 while working on the night shift at the paper factory. Only about fourteen POWs were employed at night and supervision was not strict. We stole civilian clothes from the German workmen's dining room and bicycles from the factory yard. We left the factory about 23.00 hours and cycled to Deutsch Wette, about two miles north of Rothfest. Here we tried to jump on a goods train, but the train was moving too fast. We continued north to Neisse (Sheet 117). While passing through the town we came to a roundabout, and swung left instead of right. This attracted the attention of two policemen who were standing nearby. They stopped us and asked us for our papers. As we had no papers, we said we were Ukrainian workers. The policemen took us to the police station about 50 yards away so that they could check our names and addresses. We arrived at the station just as the duty Sergeant was taking down particulars of our escape from the camp. We spent the night and the next day in the gaol and were then sent together to Stalag VIII B.

When we reached the gate of the camp Unteroffizier Cissel was standing there speaking to one of the guards. He made a rush at me, but was stopped from attacking me by a German medical officer. Cissel then sent me to the cells, where he visited me later with two guards. He said he was going to knock me down. I took off my battledress blouse and stood up to him. He backed away and produced his pistol. He then called the two guards who held me against the wall while he punched me in the stomach with his fists and hit me with the butt of his pistol. He also hit me across the nose with the butt of his gun, and I fainted. When I woke up I was alone in the cell. I reported this incident next morning to the Gerichtsoffizier, an elderly lawyer who has since been moved from the camp. He was half drunk, as usual, and added seven days to my sentence, making twenty-one days in all. I served the whole of this sentence.

Chaining at Stalag VIII B

After I came out of the cells at the end of September or the beginning of October, the Germans began their chaining 'reprisals', and I was among those shackled. At first we had our hands crossed in front of us and tied. We were tied from 08.00 to 20.30 hours with only a break for soup, between 11.00 and 11.30 hours. After the first month we were put in handcuffs between which there was about a foot of chain. The chaining was still going on when I left Stalag VIII B on 22 June 1943, although about 500 men, all of whom had been prisoners for a long time, had been unchained by then.

At the beginning of the chaining all Red Cross parcels were stopped for six weeks. The Germans then allowed us rations from the parcels, without actually giving us the parcels. Over Christmas 1942 and the New Year 1943, we got about four parcels each.

Hospital

On 6 January 1943 I was sent into the camp hospital with a cold. In hospital I contracted tinea (ringworm/any of several skin diseases caused by fungi) of the arms, and was kept in hospital till the first week of April.

(Third) Escape from Grottkau, Arbeitskommando E.488 (Stalag VIII B) – Preparations

Immediately I came out of hospital I began to prepare for another escape. In hospital I had studied maps brought in by Sergeant Cronie, RAF. From the Escape Committee I also obtained a Bescheinigung (certificate) and an Ausweis (identity card/passport). The photograph for the Bescheinigung was taken by Sergeant Boyle, Gordon Highlanders, with a small camera which he got outside the camp, I think from a German civilian. By bribing the German guard with two tins of cocoa and fifty cigarettes he also obtained a film, developing materials and printing paper. The Bescheinigung and Ausweis were typed documents. The Bescheinigung stated that I was a Belgian worker named Jan Dyke, and that my Arbeitsbuch (work book) was in the Central Registry for stamping. The Ausweis certified that I had been working in Dresden and had to proceed as quickly as possible – this phrase was inserted to cover travel by Schnellzug (fast train) – to Stettin to report to the labour bureau there for further work in a war factory. The Ausweis also stated that my Arbeitsbuch and Lohnzettel (pay book) were following through the usual official channels. Both documents bore what purported to be the stamps and signatures of the Polizie Präsident and the chief of the Labour Bureau, Dresden, and both also stated that I had permission to travel by rail. I collected a considerable store of chocolate for my journey. My plan was to escape from a working party and get to Stettin and from there by ship to Sweden. Before leaving Stalag VIII B I had been given 50 Reichmark by Captain Gorrie. I relied on getting civilian clothes once I had reached the Arbeitskommando which was at Grottkau.

Transfer to Grottkau

I left Stalag VIII B on 22 June 1943 for Arbeitskommando E.488 at the Mende Sägewerk (sawmill) at Grottkau (Sheet 117). I worked here for about two months, going into strict training for my escape. We had first-class food here. Most of it came from Red Cross parcels, and the German civilian butcher gave us pork chops about twice a week. Corporal Taylor, who was captured at St. Nazaire and was in charge of the Arbeitskommando, gave me extra rations to take with me. I was able to get eggs from the Ukrainian and German civilian workers in the sawmill in exchange for articles of civilian clothing that I had received in parcels from home. I also managed to acquire another 100 Reichsmark in exchange for a pair of socks, a packet of tea, and a packet of cocoa.

Escape

I escaped from the billet at Grottkau, a building attached to the house of the Nazi manager of the sawmill, about 19.00 hours on 29 August. I was wearing the following clothes:

Green jacket that I stole at the factory.

Pair of battledress trousers (with turn-ups) dyed brown. (I obtained the dye from a German apprentice in the sawmill for two cigarettes, and dyed the trousers myself in the billet.

Grey shirt from a parcel from home.

Blue pullover, also from a parcel from home.

Blue tie with white and red stripes, obtained from a German by barter.

British Army socks.

Pair of civilian shoes from a parcel from home.

Black peaked cap that I had got from a Ukrainian.

Ukrainian workers had promised me a civilian suit, but in the end did not produce it.

The guard was having supper at the time and I simply walked out. I had arranged to meet L/Sergeant Alexander Todd Wood, Gordon Highlanders, who had escaped from the Arbeitskommando three days before and had returned to a German woman who lived in the old gate house of the sawmill. As she was getting nervous, he had decided to go with me.

I met Todd Wood by the railway adjoining the sawmill and we walked south along the line to Grottkau Station. Todd Wood had been supplied with food by Corporal Taylor, but had no identity papers, although he also proposed to pose as a Belgian worker. At the station Todd Wood bought two railway tickets for Brieg (Sheet 105) and we left Grottkau about 19.15 hours. In Brieg we had to change trains. Here Todd Wood decided that, as he had no papers, he would not go with me, but would go to Oberberg, near Mährisch Ostrau, Czechoslovakia, where he hoped to get shelter and help from a Czech woman.

Brieg to Breslau

After Todd Wood left me I bought a railway ticket for Breslau. I did not need to show my papers here or anywhere else during my journey. The first train from Brieg to Bresslau, which left at about 21.15 hours, turned out to be a special train carrying troops from the Russian front. Almost immediately afterwards the conductress came round and asked what I was doing on a 'Wehrmachtzug' (army train). I said I was a foreign worker, and, without seeing my papers, she said this was a 'Schnellzug' and demanded two Marks additional fare. As she left me she shook her finger at me and said: 'Passt auf!' (look out!)

I was standing in the corridor and was the only civilian there. An SS policeman in black uniform was standing near me, and kept looking at me rather suspiciously. An Unteroffizier of the Bahnhof Polizie then came along. (He was dressed in ordinary infantry uniform, and had round his neck a chain bearing a large metal plate with the word 'Bahnhofwache' and a number on it). When he saw me he went up in the air, but an Oberfeldwebel of the Luftwaffe who was standing between me and the SS policeman, said the conductress had seen me and that I had paid the extra fare. The policeman subsided, and saying: 'Ach so! Gut' passed on. There was no further incident on the journey.

The train arrived at Breslau about 22.00 hours and I got out immediately and off the platform before the troops had left the train. I went into the booking hall, where there were hundreds of people about, there being a Hitler Youth rally in Breslau that day. I hung about the station until 23.30 hours when I got into a queue and bought a ticket for Frankfurt-an-der-Oder.

Breslau to Stettin

At 00.41 hours (30 August) I got a Personenzug (slow train) for Frankfurt-an-der-Oder. I slept all the way, arriving in Frankfurt about 06.30 hours. I had a wash and brush up on the station and went into the waiting room to eat some of my food, and drink a bottle of beer which I had brought. I walked round the town for a little and then returned to the station about 08.30 hours. The station restaurant opened about that time and I waited there till 10.00 hours, when I bought a ticket for Eberswalde, about thirty miles north-east of Berlin. I had decided to avoid Berlin in case of identity controls during air raids.

I arrived in Eberswalde at 14.00 hours. I went into the station restaurant and had coffee and some of the biscuits from my own store. Potatoes were the only food to be had there without a ration card. I then bought a ticket for Stettin. I thought that the girl in the booking office was about to ask me for my papers, but she did not do so. I caught a Schnellzug for Stettin about 15.00 hours, arriving in Stettin about 17.30 hours.

Stettin

(Note: all map references to this section are to Pharus Plan of Stettin)

I left the railway station immediately and walked round the town. During my walk I met a man who called himself a Pole and whom I afterwards discovered to be a Polish-Ukrainian. I told him I was a Swedish sailor, had missed my boat, and wanted to meet some Swedes. He took me to a brothel for foreign workers near the harbour. This place was forbidden to Germans.

I hung about the place from 19.00 till 21.00 hours. As the Pole and I were leaving the house we met two young Dutchmen whom I heard speaking English to a Swede. Thinking they were English, I asked them who they were and told them I was an RAF escaper and that I wanted to get on board a Swedish ship. I left with the two Dutchmen and the Swede to go to the boarding house where one of the Dutchmen was living. On the way the Swede, who was half drunk, jumped on board a tram and I did not see him again. At the boarding house I shared a bed with the Dutchman.

Next day (31 August) one of the Dutchmen took me to see a Dutch friend who shared a room with a German. The two Dutchmen took me to the harbour area in the afternoon and we made a trip round the harbour in a small pleasure steamer called the *Gneisenau*. I stayed that night with the Dutchman.

Each day while I was in Stettin I had lunch in a restaurant on the Bollwerk (G.8), between the Baumbrücke and the Hansabrücke. The staff of the restaurant did not know I was English, but merely that I was a foreigner. I ate unrationed food – soup, red cabbage, and potatoes – every day. The Dutchman went with me there only one day.

On 1 September the Dutchman with whom I had been staying said I could not remain any longer, as the owner of the house was returning that night. That day I had another trip round the harbour, this time alone. At night I returned to the brothel and met the two Dutchmen by arrangement. We found two Swedish sailors, but they would not take me on their ship. While I was in the brothel, the Gestapo arrived. I got hold of a Polish girl, and went upstairs to her room. She spoke German, and I told her I was a British airman. At first she was scared, but I coaxed her round, and she hid me under the bed. She sat down on the bed, and when the Gestapo men came in they merely looked round and walked out. The girl told me to leave at once, but to come back next evening and meet her outside the door before the house closed. She said she would try to find a pro-British Swede. I met my Dutch friend outside after this and returned his passport, which he had lent me. (He also had an identity card and did not require the passport).

I went with the Dutchman to a camp for foreign workers off Alte Vulkanstrasse (J.34) and spent the night (1/2 September) in his dormitory. There were three German ARP (Air Raid Precautions) workers sleeping in the room, and when they went to work in the morning they informed the police at the ship yard nearby that there was one too many in the room. Two policemen came to the camp. They were dressed in dark blue uniforms with black peaked caps. On the caps they wore a badge with an anchor and the word 'Schiffswerft' (Shipyard/Dockyard). The policemen asked me what I was doing in the camp, and I said I was a Swedish seaman, that I had missed the tram the night before, and that I was going to my ship, where I had to start work at 06.00 hours. Fortunately, I was wearing a small Swedish seaman's union badge which one of the Dutchmen had given me. (On the badge was a white lighthouse, with a double beam, and the letters 'S.S.F' all on a red background). One of the Germans recognised this badge and believed my story. They told me to get out and not come back. I left the camp at once.

I went back to the town and sat in the Haken Terrasse (G.7) till 11.00 hours. I had a bar of chocolate and some biscuits for breakfast from the store of food which I carried in the small despatch case. I had lunch in the restaurant in the Bollwerk, and after another trip round the harbour I went to the pictures in the afternoon. In the evening I returned to the brothel and got a Dutchman to tell two Swedish seamen who I was. I offered them money to take me on their ship, but they said I would be caught in the Freihafen (H.J.789) and refused to take me. I saw the Polish girl again, but she said that she had not been able to find a Swede to help me, and could not help me herself. I left the house with my original Dutch friends and travelled with them on the tram car which took them to their camp off the Alte Vulkanstrasse. I continued on the tram to the terminus to the north of the town, and slept the night (2/3 September) in a small copse.

Next morning (3 September) I returned to the town, partly on foot, and partly by tram and went again to the Haken Terrasse. I spoke to three Swedish sailors who came along the Terrasse from a seamen's home nearby. They said it would be impossible for me to get on to a Swedish ship and advised me to give myself up. That afternoon, after lunch in the restaurant on the Bollwerk, I went to the pictures. I tried the brothel again in the evening, but the Swedes there either could not or would not enter into conversation with me.

About 22.00 hours I went to the Freihafen. I crossed the Baumbrücke (G.8) and went along the Am Danzig quay (H.J.78). I climbed a fence running along the railway line on the Viehhof Kai at the Freihafen and got alongside a small Swedish sailing and auxiliary motor ship. I was crossing the plank to the ship when a harbour policeman appeared. (He wore military uniform with an armlet bearing, I think, the word 'Hafenpolizei' in gold letters on a black ground). I staggered, pretending to be drunk. He asked for my 'Ausweis' and I said: 'Ich habe hier zwanzig Ausweise' ('I've got twenty passes here'). At the same time I pulled out a packet of 20 French cigarettes. The policeman looked at the cigarettes and at me and asked what I was. I said I was Swedish and that my ship was the *Vestis*. (This was the name of a ship I had seen lying off the Bollwerk). He said that I was in the wrong harbour. I said I was sorry and offered him a cigarette. He took the whole packet and showed me out through the main gate. To reach the gate we had to pass through a gate house in which there were about five guards, but none of them said anything. Once I had got out I ran off as fast as I could.

I then walked right round the outside of the Freihafen to try to get in at the west side. At the end of the Kaiser Wilhelm Kai there was a small waiting room used by passengers on the ferry which crossed the Freihafen. Two Danish ships were loading near this waiting room. Two searchlight beams were trained on the ships and lit up the wire round the Freihafen just where I had hoped to climb it. There were also two harbour policemen standing near the ships, and it was obvious that I could not hope to climb the fence then. I laid down on a bench in the waiting room and fell asleep, hoping the policemen would be gone by the time I wakened.

I was awakened at 06.00 hours the next day (4 September) by an old German workman who said that the ferry was about to leave. I got on board the ferry and crossed the Freihafen. I then walked back into the town and along the Haken Terrasse, going later to the Parade Plade (E.F.78), where I had a wash at a public lavatory. I went to the restaurant on the Bollwerk for lunch and to the pictures in the afternoon.

From the picture house I went to a pub in Fischerstrasse (G.8) and stayed there from about 16.00 hours till 18.00 hours. I then decided it was 'do or die' and started to go back to the end of the Kaiser Wilheilm Kai. At the Hansabrücke five Danish seamen stopped and asked me the way to the nearest restaurant. I took them into a pub nearby and told them who I was. One of them spoke English.

They agreed to take me back to their ship, the *Margarete*, (2,000 tons) which was lying in the River Oder on the eastern side of the Oder-Danzig Insel (H.7) and which was sailing at 09.30 hours next day. The ship was moored in the river because her sailing had been delayed on account of the riots in Denmark.

We went along the Bollwerk until we were opposite the ship, and the Danes signalled for a small boat. The Danish watchman from the ship came over in the boat and said that the German watchman was still on the ship. The Danes had a half bottle of Schnapps left and we decided to get the German watchman drunk.

We all went to the ship in the rowing boat. On board I found that the German watchman was already half drunk, and gave him the Schnapps. When his relief came on board about an hour later the German watchman left without counting the number of seamen on board. I was put in the forecastle with four of the five sailors who had befriended me. The five seamen, the watchman, three firemen, the cabin boy and the cook knew I was on the ship, but none of the officers knew about me. The cook, who spoke English, gave me a hot meal that night.

Stettin to Sweden

The next day (5 September) the ship sailed at 09.30 hours. At 09.15 hours the ship was searched by the Germans, but as she had already been searched in the Freihafen, they were not very thorough. I was hidden under one of the bunks in the forecastle. The ship was bound for Riga (Latvia) with stone chips, which, I was told, were for making runways in Russia. We arrived in Riga on 8 September and remained there until 15 September. I was hidden in the forecastle all the time.

We left Riga on 15 September and anchored off Dragor (Denmark 1:100,000 Sheet 41) on 18 September. I persuaded five of the Danish seamen, all the seamen in the crew except one, to desert, and at 01.00 hours on 19 September we took one of the ship's life boats, and began rowing across to Limhavn, south-west of Malmo, Sweden. The crossing took five hours. The sailors rowed and I acted as navigator, steering by the stars. We took a compass with us but when we unwrapped it we found it was unserviceable.

We got into the harbour at Limhavn about dawn. A Swedish Customs officer came along and telephoned the police, who took us to the gaol in Malmo. Here the police asked me questions to identify me.

Next morning (20 September) a Swedish Air Force officer tried to interrogate me, but I only gave him the markings of my aircraft and asked him to pass the information to the British Consul. I also told him that I had escaped from Germany. Later that morning the Air Force officer took me to the British Consulate in Malmo. I left that night for Stockholm, arriving next morning (21 September), when I reported to the British Legation, and was interrogated by the Assistant Military Attache.

Returned to UK in bomb bay of BOAC Mosquito.

Account written as Chapter 3 'The Women who took a hand' p71-91 in Paul Brickhill's *Escape – or Die*, Pan Books, 1954.

MOST SECRET - M.I.9 INTERROGATION – EVADERS REPORT

Manchester L7301 of 50 Squadron. Captain, Pilot Officer L. Manser. Ops to Cologne. Took off 22.50 hours from Skellingthorpe 30/31May 1942. Damaged by flak that probably pierced a coolant pipe in port engine which exploded and caught fire. Height could not be maintained. The crew baled out before Manser lost control and crashed. Pilot Officer R. Barnes became a POW. Sergeant L. Baveystock, Pilot Officer Horsley, and Sergeants King, Mills and Naylor all became evaders.

Statement by 1376820 Sergeant BAVEYSTOCK L. H., 50 Squadron, RAF

We left Skellingthorpe at 22.50 hours on 30 May 1942 to bomb Cologne. On the return journey I was forced to bale out over Belgium. The rest of my crew were:

Pilot Officer MANSER, (killed)
Pilot Officer HORSLEY, (S/P.G.(-)771)
Pilot Officer BARNES, (POW)
Sergeant KING, (S/P.G.(-)775)
Sergeant MILLS, (S/P.G.(-)774
Sergeant NAYLOR, (S/P.G.(-)773)

I landed in a dyke in five feet of water, about three miles north-east of Bree on 1 June 1942. I hid my parachute and Mae West in the water under some bushes and set off westwards. I had just stepped into a clearing in the woods when a man appeared on the far side of it. I thought it was all up with me, but as greatly relieved to find it was one of my crew, Sergeant King. We carried on in the direction of Bree and lay in a cornfield for a few hours before dawn. As it was now raining very hard we tried a farmhouse, where we were very well received. We were hidden in an outhouse and given food. The people in this farm were able to put us in touch with an organisation, who arranged for my return to this country with Pilot Officer Horsley.

Having landed in a marshy area of Belgium, a few kilometres north-east of Bree, Bob Horsley was able to dry his wet clothes in a farmhouse, whither taken by the farmer. 'The people told me that in the village of Bree there was an agent of the organisation. The farmer took me by bicycle to the house of a doctor in Tongerloo. There I met Sergeants Naylor and Mills who had been directed separately and by different people to an isolated farmhouse near Bree occupied by Dr and Mme. Grunnen. Only Mme. Grunnen takes an active part in the organisation'. As the organisation was unable to move all three of us together to Liège, Horsley was left behind while Naylor and Mills were taken to the windmill at Dilsen (the 'Moulin rouge', some fifteen kilometres south of the crash site) on the night of 31 May/1 June.

After the departure of Mills and Naylor, Horsley was taken back to Bree where he met Les Baveystock and Stan King. Les had met up with Stan, who had turned an ankle, soon after they had parachuted onto Belgian soil, and they had been 'hidden by some wonderful farming people named Nijskens, who put us in touch with the Underground'. On the night of 1/2 June, we (Horsley, Baveystock and King) left the Nijskens' farm on bicycles 'accompanied by two men and a girl'. Cycling along side roads to Mechelen we had a wash and a rest before continuing to the windmill at Dilsen, reaching it at around 04.00 hours on 2 June. There a Dutchman gave his spare clothes to Bob Horsley, who 'was very disreputable'. We left not long afterwards on 'a sort of tram/train' to Tongres, from where we caught the train to Liège.

Our pre-arranged pick-up point was the church of St Denis, and there we were collected by Commissioner Rademecker, and subsequently 'met up with all of the crew'. Once together, we were subjected to a rigorous examination by our helpers, the usual necessary precaution to ensure that we were not German infiltrators. Having satisfied the cautious Belgians, plans were set in train to get us to Spain, and we left for Brussels on 5 June. We (Les Baveystock and Bob Horsley), having stayed together in a house opposite the Palais de Justice were first to leave for the south. Taken to Paris by Andrée Dumon on the night of 9/10 June, we were handed over to Dédée, who took us to the first floor of a block of flats at 10, rue Oudinot, in the 7th Arrondissement of Paris. Here, I remember, 'a girlfriend of Dédée' lived. This girl was a little older than Dédée, but I did not discover her name'.

Also living in a rented apartment on the fourth floor of 10, rue Oudinot was Elvire Morelle. Having broken her leg in February, she had had to follow a more sedate lifestyle and had rented 'a huge, ugly villa at St Maur, on the outskirts of Paris, during the summer months of 1942. There we could stay in comfort and bask in the sun behind the high garden wall. Elvire was housekeeper and cook, and Charlie, her brother, would often appear at the house, bringing a new group of airmen from Brussels'. As the safe house at St Maur was some distance from the main railway stations, Elvire moved to rue Oudinot in the heart of Paris. Yet a third flat in the block, Aimable Fouquerel's on the fifth floor, was used as an overflow when the situation demanded it. Aimable 'worked as a masseur at a hospital nearby, which necessitated frequent absences at night. This capable, generous and loyal man put his flat at the disposal of the organisation. Sometimes, when there were many airmen waiting to be sent to the frontier, three of them would sleep in his large bed'. So, for 'nearly a year airmen and soldiers were hidden in these three flats, and not a soul in the building, save the old concierge, knew the truth'.

Living conveniently close to the rue Oudinot were Robert Aylé and his wife Germaine, two more Comet helpers, whose apartment on the fourth floor of 37, rue de Babylone was also used as an overflow. Rue de Babylone, near the Hôtel des Invalides, on the south bank of the Seine, 'was a street of sad, grey houses of the Second Empire. A gloomy *maison de repos* for priests overshadowed the apartment house on the other side'.

After an evening meal Dédée took Bob and I to the station for the journey to the south-west. But before doing so, she told us that we would be travelling with a young Belgian, Jean Depraetre, and another airman claiming to be Sergeant H. E. 'Hal' De Mone RCAF. She added that they were sure of Jean's bona fides, but they were not so sure of the airman, who seemed to know nothing of the RAF. He was, frankly, suspected of being a German. It would be up to Bob and I to find out. If we did not get the right answers from the man, then he would be 'eliminated' in the interests of security. From the replies to our questions, however, Bob and I were convinced that the airman was indeed who he claimed to be. In view of what he told us though, it was hardly surprising that Comet had been put on their guard by his lack of RAF knowledge.

Dédée escorted Hal to Paris, where they arrived at around 9 o'clock that evening, and it was then that he met the two of us. Thanks to our 'all clear' he left with us, Dédée and Jean Depraetre for Spain on the overnight train on 10/11 June. At Bayonne, Elvire De Greef and her daughter, Jeanine, got on the train. Hal swapped his ticket with Jeanine as his 'did not go all the way'. In any case, when we got to St Jean-de-Luz, Hal was not asked to produce his identity card, 'probably because I look French and was wearing a cross round my neck'. We then walked together from the station to a flat above a café and stayed the night there.

By various means our group made its way to Francia Usandizaga's farm near Urrugne, and was guided by Florentino Goïcoechea over the Pyrenees on the night of 12/13 June. After a short sleep in a barn, Dédée took

Bob Horsley and Hal de Mone to a café in a nearby village, where they were joined by the rest of our party some two hours later. From San Sebastián we were driven to Madrid.

Joined Comet Group 20. Back to UK on SS *Narkunda*, landed Greenock.

Evasion written up p62-125 in *Wavetops at my wingtips*, L. Baveystock, DSO, DFC, DFM, Airlife, 2001.

MOST SECRET - M.I.9 INTERROGATION – EVADERS REPORT

Statement by 1386637 Sergeant NAYLOR B. W. and 972986 Sergeant MILLS A. M., 50 (Bomber) Squadron, RAF

We were Rear Gunner and Front Gunner, respectively, of an aircraft which left Skellingsthorpe (Lincs.) at 22.50 hours on 30 May 1942 to bomb Cologne. Just after leaving the target an engine caught fire, and we were forced to bale out near the village of Bree (Belgium) about twenty miles north of Maastricht, about 02.00 hours on 31 May 1942.

The First Pilot (Pilot Officer MANSER), who was killed, held the aircraft steady to let the rest of us jump, and it dived into the ground from about 800 feet just as we had left. The other members of the crew were:

Sergeant BAVEYSTOCK (Second Pilot) (S/P.G.(-)772)

Pilot Officer BARNES (Navigator), (captured)

Pilot Officer HORSLEY (First Wireless Operator) (S/P.G.(-)771)

Sergeant KING (Front Gunner) (S/P.G.(-) 775)

Sergeant Naylor

On touching down I hid my parachute and other kit and stayed in a wood till daybreak. I then got in touch with a farmer who bathed my wounds and gave me a clean shirt. I also drank a large bowl of milk, and after that I was able to go to another house, where I had my wounds properly dressed. I then went back into hiding in the wood. After a time I returned to the house and was told I would find Sergeant Mills in the wood.

Sergeant Mills

I baled out first when we were about a mile inside the Belgian frontier. After hiding in a wood, I met a farmer's boy who put me on to a road, on which I met two Flemish civilians. They gave me a civilian suit and boots and directed me to a house (the same one Sergeant Naylor was taken to). The lady of the house said she would go to morning mass and meet another woman who would put me on the right road. After getting some bread to eat, I was sent back to the woods, the lady promising to send a man for me, who would call: 'Jock, Jock'. The man came for me about 16.00 hours and by this time I had met Sergeant Naylor at a cowshed three-quarters of a mile from the house. We sheltered in the shed till the man came. He told us to return to the house about 18.30 hours. We did so and were given bread and coffee – food seemed very scarce – and civilian raincoats. We were sent back to the woods and collected about 23.00 hours.

Sergeants Naylor and Mills

We were then put in the care of an organisation which arranged for our journey home.

Shortly after landing we were both directed separately and by different people to an isolated farmhouse near Bree, occupied by Dr and Mme. Grunnen. Only Mme. Grunnen takes an active part in the organisation. At 23.00 hours on 31 May we returned, by arrangement, to this house, whence two men conducted us on bicycles to a windmill called 'Moulin Rouge', the exact location of which we do not know. The men cycled about 200 yards in front of us, and the arrangement was that if their rear lights went out, we were to put our bicycles in the ditch and get behind a hedge. Once only we were stopped by two civilians with a storm-lamp: for what reason was not clear. At 'Moulin Rouge' we got some cognac and new clothes and were able to wash and shave. The clothes were given us by a Dutchman who was on his way to this country and was splitting up his wardrobe.

We left the windmill about 03.30 hours (1 June) and got a train at 04.00 hours to Tongres, where we changed to an electric train for Liège. We were accompanied by the Dutchman and Mlle. Saul, Villa Aurers, Maeseyck.

At Liège, which we reached about 08.00 hours, we knocked around while Mlle. Saul made contact with the Commissar of Police, IV Group, Liège, Louis Rademecker. She returned alone about 09.00 hours and we went to a church in the main square and sat there. The Commissioner had formed a group known as 'L'Epingle Noir' (The Black Pin) from among his police colleagues and from high civil servants, customs officers, café owners and hoteliers. A branch of this group, 'Jam', functioned specifically to help evading or escaping airmen and French prisoners of war. We were told that in this district RAF personnel should go to the largest church in the town, where someone connected with the organisation goes at 10.00 hours each day. About 10.00 hours we went to a café, where, on the Commissar's arrival, Mlle. Saul and the Dutchman left us to return to the 'Moulin Rouge'. Following the Commissar, we went by back streets for about a mile to a grocer's shop. There the Commissar was joined by an assistant who had been in the Belgian army. One of us (Sergeant Mills) accompanied the Commissar, and the other (Sergeant Naylor) was sent with the assistant.

We met again at a cross roads on the outskirts of the town. There the assistant took the parcels in which we had been carrying part of our uniforms, and the commissar took us to a house in Liège. We believe this was the Commissar's house; two elderly ladies were looking after it. After we had been one night there, we were joined by Pilot Officer Horsley (S/P.G.(-)771), Sergeant Baveystock (S/P.G.(-)772), Sergeant King (S/P.G.(-)775), and the Dutchman.

We all left Liège on 5 June. We were met at the station by two members of the organisation, who provided us with railway tickets for Brussels. In Brussels we split into two parties, and we went with Sergeant King to a flat at 16, Palais de Justice Apartments, where we stayed with M. Van Steenbeek (head of the 'Service LUC'. M. Luclerqu, originator of this organisation, was stated to be in London at 34, Brunswick Square).

We remained in Brussels till 17 June, the three of us confined in a small bedroom all the time. The organisation supplied a doctor for Sergeant Naylor's wounds (shrapnel wounds to shoulder, nose and toe). We were very well fed with 'black market' food. Van Steenbeek's son took our photographs for identity cards.

Sergeant Naylor was well enough for the three of us to leave Brussels on 17 June en route to Louvain, where we got a train for Paris. There were three searches on the way – before, at, and after the frontier – but we were not asked for identity cards. We had a woman guide with us, whose husband, an Englishman, was in St Jean de Luz. Our companion between Louvain and Paris was Andrée Dumon.

In Paris we were met by Frédèric de Jongh, the father of Didi, who took us to his flat where we joined two Polish airmen serving in the RAF – one called Edward Chudyecki. There the party split again. One of us (Sergeant King) and a Pole were taken to Asnieres, where we were sheltered by a Mrs. Thomas (French), who had a grocer's shop. We stayed there till the evening of 22 June. Next, we (Sergeants Naylor and Mills) were taken to a house in a suburb (the street name was rue de Frase) owned by a Captain Violette, a wood fibre merchant, who had been an interpreter in the French army. He was a new member of the organisation and we were the first he had sheltered. We stayed till 22 June.

Sergeant King and the Polish airman met me (Sergeant Mills) again on the evening of 22 June, and we left at 21.15 hours for St Jean de Luz. We had a Pole and two guides with us – Didi (Didi and Dédée de Jonge are one and the same famous Belgian helper – mentioned by others) and another girl, who broke a leg on her last trip over the Pyrenees. We had no trouble on the journey. At Bayonne we were joined by the woman and her husband who had brought us from Brussels to Paris and her husband. They brought us tickets from Bayonne to St Jean de Luz.

From Biarritz one of us (Sergeant Naylor) and the Pole were taken by the English man and his wife along the esplanade on foot to St Jean de Luz. The others (Sergeants Mills and King) remained on the train with the original guides and at St Jean de Luz were taken to the house of a Basque, where I (Naylor) and the Pole joined them.

Next day (24 June) the party left individually with guides for a small farmhouse in the Pyrenees. About 23.00 hours, guided by Didi and a Spanish Basque, the party set off across the mountains. We went to a café in a village on the Spanish side of the frontier and had breakfast (25 June). Didi went about 08.00 hours to San Sebastian and brought back a taxi, which took us to the town. We were sheltered at a flat, where a British Vice-Consul took our personal details and informed the Embassy. At 23.00 hours we were sent to the pictures with the Spanish owner of the flat. When we got out about 00.45 hours (26 June) the Vice-Consul met us and took us to a car in which Major Sir Peter Norton-Griffiths was waiting. We arrived in Madrid about 09.00 hours and were sent to Gibraltar (1 July) for repatriation.

Sergeant Mills joined Comet Group 21.
Sergeant Naylor joined Comet Group 23
Both returned together on SS *Narkunda*.
Both DFM, 6 October 1942.

Appendix Two: Manchester Units

OPERATIONAL SQUADRONS in order of equipping

207 Squadron (Code EM-)
First Manchester taken on charge (toc), L7279, 6.11.40
First Manchester Operation 24/25.2.41
Final Manchester Operation 10/11.3.41
Commanding Officers:
Wg Cdr N. C. Hyde 1.11.40 – 8.4.41
Acting CO Sqn Ldr C. J. F. Kidd (8.4.41 – 30.4.41 and 6.5.41 – 21.5.41)
Wg Cdr J. N. D. Anderson 30.4.41 – 6.5.41
Wg /Cdr K. P. Lewis 21.5.41 – ?.?.41
Wg Cdr C. Fothergill ?.?.41 – 10.3.42
Bases:
Waddington, Lincs. 1.11.40 – 17.11.41
Bottesford, Leics. 17.11.41 – 11.3.42

97 Squadron (Code OF-)
First Manchester toc 25.2.41(various, 8 del'd: L7282 o/c the following day)
First Manchester Operation 8/9.4.41
Final Manchester Operation 17/18.1.42
Commanding Officers:
Wg Cdr D F Balsdon 25.2.41 – 18.12.41
Wg Cdr J H Kynoch 18.12.41 – 17/18.1.42
Bases:
Waddington, Lincs. 25.2.41 – 11.3.41
Coningsby, Lincs. 11.3.41 – 17/18.1.42

61 Squadron (Code QR-)
First Manchester toc L7307, 18.3.41
First Manchester Operation 21/22.6.41
Final Manchester Operation 25/26.6.42 (Con Flt)
Commanding Officers:
Wg Cdr G. E. Valentine 1.3.41 – 2/3.9.41
Wg Cdr T. C. Weir 2/3.9.41 – 25/26.6.42
Bases:
Hemswell, Lincs. 1.3.41 – 17.7.41
North Luffenham, Rutland 17.7.41 – ?.10.41
Woolfox Lodge, Rutland ?.10.41 – 5.5.42
Syerston, Notts. 5.5.42 – 25/26.6.42

83 Squadron (Code OL-)
First Manchester toc L7382, 10.10.41
First Manchester Operation 28/29.1.42
Final Manchester Operation 1/2.6.42 (Con Flt)
Commanding Officers:
Wg Cdr S. O. Tudor
Bases:
Scampton, Lincs. ?.12.41 – 1/2.6.42

106 Squadron (Code ZN-)

First Manchester toc L7390, 20.1.42
First Manchester Operation 20/21.3.42
Final Manchester Operation 25/26.6.42 (Con Flt)
Commanding Officers:
Wg Cdr R. S. Allen
Wg Cdr G. P. Gibson
Base:
Coningsby, Lincs. ?. 2.42 – 25/26.6.42

50 Squadron (Code VN-)
First Manchester toc R5778, *c.* 25.1.42
First Manchester Operation 8/9.4.42
Final Manchester Operation 25/26.6.42 (Con Flt)
Commanding Officers:
Wg Cdr J. M. Southwell 30.3.42 – ?
Wg Cdr Oxley
Bases:
Skellingthorpe, Lincs. 30.3.42 – 20.6.42
Swinderby, Lincs. 20.6.42 – 17.10.42

49 Squadron (Code EA-)
First Manchester toc L7287, 18.4.42
First Manchester Operation 2/3.5.42
Final Manchester Operation 25/26.6.42 (Con Flt)
Commanding Officers:
Wg Cdr L. C. Slee 17.4.42 – ?
Second CO not identified
Base:
Scampton, Lincs. 17.4,2 – ?

44 Squadron Conversion Flight (Code KM-)
First Manchester toc L7382, 26.2.42
First Manchester Operation 30/31.5.42
Final Manchester Operation 1/2.6.42
Commanding Officer:
Wg Cdr Smales
Base:
Waddington, Lincs.
(44 Squadron's first Manchester, L7382, toc 27.12.41. They undertook no operational flying as an all-Manchester unit, however L7430 KM-N̄ captained by Pilot Officer S. T. Farrington on loan from 49 Squadron, undertook the 'MILLENIUM TWO' raid to Bremen on 25/25 June 1942 together with eleven of First Manchester toc L7425, 17.5.4244 Squadron's Lancasters)

408 Squadron RCAF Conversion Flight (Code EQ-)
First Manchester Operation 30/31.5.42
Final Manchester Operation 1/2.6.42
Commanding Officer:
Wg Cdr J. D. Twigg
Base:
Balderton, Notts

CONVERSION FLIGHTS AND UNITS

9 Conversion Flight
Formed 8.8.42 at Waddington. (9 Squadron's first Manchester, R5838, toc 8.8.42 but no operational flying. 9 CF's first Manchester, L7425, toc 13.9.42.) Disbanded by merging into 1661 HCU 7.10.42, L7464 'D'

44 Conversion Flight
Formed ?.1.42 at Waddington, first Manchester toc 26.2.42, L7382. Disbanded by merging into 1661 HCU 7.10.42, L7280

49 Conversion Flight
Formed 16.5.42 at Scampton, first Manchester toc 18.5.4, L7429. Disbanded by merging into 1661 HCU 7.10.42, L7296 'Y'

50 Conversion Flight
Formed 16.5.42 at Skellingthorpe, first Manchester toc 18.5.42, L7521. Moved 17.6.42 to Swinderby and 21.8.42 to Wigsley. Disbanded by merging into 1654 CU 7.10.42, L7521

57 Conversion Flight
Formed ?, first Manchester toc ? No allocation has been traced to 57 CF, however, R5771 and L7386 were issued to 57 Squadron on 6. or 8.9.42 respectively but no operational flying. Disbanded. ? L7386

61 Conversion Flight
Formed 27.3.42 at North Luffenham, first Manchester toc 19.4.42, L7286. Moved 5.5.42 to Syerston and 22.8.42 to Swinderby. Disbanded by merging into 1660 HCU 7.10.42, L7458

83 Conversion Flight
Formed 11.4.42 at Scampton, first Manchester toc 17.4.42, L7280. Moved 21.8.42 to Wigsley. Disbanded L7382 by merging into 1654 HCU 7.10.42, L7382

97 Conversion Flight
Formed ?.1.42 at Coningsby, first Manchester toc 16.2.42, L7457. Moved ?.8.42 to Woodhall Spa and ?.9.42 to Skellingthorpe. Disbanded by merging into 1660 HCU 7.10.42, L7482

106 Conversion Flight
Formed 5.5.42 at Coningsby, first Manchester toc 15.4.42, L7457. Moved 1.10.42 to Skellingthorpe. Disbanded by merging into 1660 HCU 7.10.42, L7301

207 Conversion Flight
Formed ?.1.42 at Bottesford, first Manchester toc 4.5.42, L7385. Moved 23.8.42 to Swinderby. Disbanded by merging into 1660 HCU 7.10.42, L7297

408 Conversion Flight
Formed 16.5.42 at Syerston, first Manchester toc 18.5.42, L7400. Disbanded 19.6.42, L7401

420 Conversion Flight
Formed 16.5.42 at Waddington, first Manchesrter toc 16.5.42, L7400 (erroneous attribution? see above). Disbanded 19.6.42, L7402

460 Conversion Flight
Formed 22.5.42 at Holme-on-Spalding-Moor, first Manchester toc 1.10.42, L7464. Moved 26.9.42 to Breighton. Disbanded by merging into 1656 HCU 7.10.42, L7325.

HEAVY CONVERSION UNITS

1654 HCU

Formed 16.5.42 at Swinderby, first Manchester toc 22.5.42, L7281. Moved ?.6.42 to Wigsley. (Became 1654 HCU on 7.10.42 on absorbing 50 and 83 CFs). Disbanded 1.9.45? at Woolfox Lodge, L7288 UG–J, L7419 UG–B

1656 HCU

Formed 7.10.42 from 103 and 460 CFs at Breighton, first Manchester toc 1.10.42, L7325. Moved 26.10.42 to Lindholme. Disbanded 10.11.45?, L7434 BL–Y

1660 HCU

Formed 7.10.42 from 61, 97, 106 and 207 CFs at Swinderby, first Manchester toc 20.10.42, L7283. Disbanded ?.9.46 into 1653 HCU, R5768 TV–A

1661 HCU

Formed 7.10.42 from 9, 44 and 49 CFs, first Manchester toc 8.11.42, L7425 at Skellingthorpe. Moved 1.1.43 to Winthorpe. Satellite at Scampton 9.11.42–1.1.43. Disbanded 24.8.45, R5839 GP–G

OTHER MANCHESTER UNITS

1485 Bombing and Gunnery Flight

Formed at Skellingthorpe, date unknown, first Manchester toc 13.8.42, L7591. Disbanded ? L7473

25 Operational Training Unit 'D' Flight

Formed 1.3.41 at Finningley, first Manchester toc 7.6.41, L7420. Disbanded 1.2.43, R5829.

Torpedo Development Unit

First Manchester toc 27.4.42, R5774. Formation and disbandment dates unknown.

Appendix Three: Sortie and Despatch Statistics

Manchester Sorties Dispatched by Pilots as Aircraft Captain (Ten or more operations)

Tours of operations on Manchester squadrons often took up to fifteen months to complete. Arising partly from groundings of the aircraft in mid-1941, no pilot is known to have completed a complete tour of exclusively Manchester operations, most being mixed in various proportions with Hampden sorties or completed after conversion to Lancasters. 'Dispatched' is defined as having taken off from base. Rank is given at the time of the service on Manchesters.

Rank and Name	Unit	Notes	Total
Plt Off. W. G. Gardiner	207		27
Plt Off. P. C. Birch	207		25
Plt Off. W. S. Herring	207 (20), 44 (1)	KIA	21
Sqn Ldr T. C. Murray	207		20
Sqn Ldr K. H. P. Beauchamp	207		17
WO W. L. Young	106	FTR 2/3.5.42	17
Fg Off. W. J. Lewis	207	FTR 7/8.9.41	16
FS G. H. Coles	207		16
Fg Off. H. S. Blakeman	97		16
Fg Off. D. A. Green	207		15
Flt Lt A. M. Paape	207 (8), 61 (7)	KIA	15
Fg Off. J. H. Leland	207		14
Fg Off. J. De L. Wooldridge	207		13
Flt Lt W. D. B. Ruth	207		13
Fg Off. C. A. J. Smith	83		13
Plt Off. L. F. Kneil	207		12
Plt Off. H. W. Southgate	50		12
Fg Off. I. G. A. McNaughton	61	KIA	12
FS G. Appleyard	106		12
FS G. H. Hazelden	83		12
FS J. C. Atkinson	207		11
FS G. H. Hathersich	207		11
Fg Off. P. R. Burton-Gyles	207	KIA	11
Flt Lt P. C. Ward-Hunt	207 (10), 49 (1)		11
Flt Lt D. J. French	207 (6), 97 (5)		11
Sgt L. R. Crampton	50		11
Flt Lt D. A. J. McClure	83		11
Fg Off. P. G. W. Oakley	83		11
WO D. H. Rowlands	97		11
Plt Off. G. L. Tofield	61	KIA	11
Plt Off. R. E. S. Smith	61		11
Plt Off. B. J. Gunter	61		11
Plt Off. A. L. Searby	61	KIA	11
Plt Off. G. R. Bayley	207	FTR 8/9.1.42	10
Plt Off. W. N. Whammond	106		10
Fg Off. S. J. Beard	61		10
Fg Off. R. E. Archibald	61	KIA	10
FS E. W. Noble	61	FTR 6/7.4.42	10
WO Whitehead	83		10

FTR – Failed to return, date missing from a Manchester Operation
KIA – Known to have been killed in action during World War II

Sergeant Jim M. Duncan, W/op AG, who served with 207 Squadron between 22.12.40 and 15.7.42 undertook 36 Manchester and 1 Hampden sorties.

Manchester Sorties Dispatched

Unit	Bombing Sorties	Mining Sorties	Other Sorties	Unit Total
44 Con Flt	4	0	0	4
49 Squadron	28	6	14	48
50 Squadron	70	34	22	126
61 Squadron	163	40	6	209
83 Squadron	103	30	12	145
97 Squadron	141	8	2	151
106 Squadron	81	63	5	149
207 Squadron	370	48	12	430
408 Con Flt	2	0	0	2

'Other' sorties refer to NICKELS, ASR, etc.
Grand Total Manchester Ops   1,264

Statistics show a general trend in which loss rate increases in relation to the timing of equipment and inversely with the total number of operations dispatched. The major departure is provided by 106, which flew a larger proportion of mining operations.

Sortie Records

Record	Unit	Sorties
Most Operations	207 Squadron	430
Most Bombing Ops	207 Squadron	370
Most Mining Ops	106 Squadron	63
Most Ops in one month (April 1942)	106 Squadron	74

Most sorties in one operation

Unit	Total	Date
50 Squadron	15	30/31.5.42
49 Squadron	12	30/31.5.42
50 Squadron	12	25/26.6.42
97 Squadron	11	18.12.41
207 Squadron	11	12/13.12.41

Manchester Losses by Unit

Unit	Operation Losses	Per cent Losses	Per cent loss less 'Other'
44 Con Flt	0	-	-
49 Squadron	6	12.5	14.7
50 Squadron	10	7.9	9.6
61 Squadron	16	7.7	7.8
83 Squadron	9	6.2	6.0
97 Squadron	10	6.6	6.0
106 Squadron	7	4.7	4.9
207 Squadron	19	4.4	4.5
408 Con Flt	0	-	-

Loss statistics are affected by the fact that 49, 83 and 97 Squadrons each lost one aircraft during 'other' Ops.

Manchesters dispatched on 20 or more sorties

Serial   Delivered   Squadrons allocated and Total Sorties Dispatched

L7378	13.4.41	207 (25), 106 (8)		33
L7319	6.3.41	207 (22), 106 (4), 50 (5)		31
L7432	4.7.41	207 (18), 50 (8),	FTR 3/4.6.42	26
L7455	10.9.41	207 (15), 97 (1), 50 (10)		26
R5796	18.11.41	207 (14), 106 (12)		26
L7317	25.2.41	207 (17), 106 (7),	FTR 14/15.4.42	24
L7517	10.10.41	207 (14), 106 (10)		24
L7475	28.10.41	97 (5), 61 (9), 50 (9)		23
L7485	12.9.41	207 (15), 106 (7),	FTR 16/17.4.42	22
L7488	15.10.41	207 (4), 97 (6), 106 (12)		22
L7322	17.3.41	207 (20)	FTR 8/9.1.42	20
L7468	9.11.41	207 (15), 50 (5)		20
L7480	9.11.41	207 (5), 61 (8), 50 (5), 44 (2)		20
L7484	10.9.41	207 (15), 83 (2), 49 (3)		20
L7486	12.9.41	207 (19), 61 (1)		20

Appendix Four: Aircraft Losses by Unit

Entries give date, aircraft serial number and the name of the captain. Refer to Appendix Five for greater detail.

49 Squadron
30/31.5.42	L7290	Plt Off. P. W. Floyd
30/31.5.42	L7429	Plt Off. J. P. Carter
1/2.6.42	R5794	Plt Off. Shackleton
6/7.6.42	L7287 EA-G	Flt Lt R. E. R. Paramore
6/7.6.42	L7469	Act Sqn Ldr P. M. De Mestre
20/21.6.42	L7387	Sgt J. H. O'Brien

50 Squadron
25.3.42	L7486	Sgt D. Atkinson
17/18.4.42	R5782	Plt Off. G. Baker
29/30.4.42	L7516 VN-N	FS T. Willett
8/9.5.42	L7489	Sgt M. Gruber
8/9.5.42	R5778	Sgt Wilkie
13.5.42	L7519	FS P. J. W. Blake
30/31.5.42	L7456 ZN-?	Sgt Wilkie
30/31.5.42	L7301 ZN-D	Fg Off. L. Manser
3/4.6.42	L7432	Plt Off. J. F. Heaton
5/6.6.42	R5833	Plt Off. D. W. Garland
6/7.6.42	L7471	Fg Off. A. D. Beatty
25/26.6.42	L7289	Sgt R. G. Roy
16.8.42	L7475	FS Dickenson
5.9.42	L7521	Sqn Ldr Carter

61 Squadron
26/27.6.41	L7304	Fg Off. K. G. Webb
29.6.41	L7315	Plt Off. C. G. Colborne
2/3.9.41	L7388	Wg Cdr G. E. Valentine
2.11.41	L7520	Plt Off. A. L. Searby
7/8.12.41	L7494	Sqn Ldr J. L. Riley
9/10.1.42	R5789	Plt Off. D. S. Matthews
15/16.1.42	L7495	Fg Off. Beard
31.1/1.2.42	R5787 QR-M	Fg Off. J. R. B. Parsons
31.1/1.2.42	L7396	Flt Lt Page
31.1/1.2.42	L7472	Flt Lt R. D. Fraser
10.2.42	R5834	FS J. B. Underwood
16/17.2.42	L7433	FS P. H. G. Webster
13/14.3.42	L7395	Plt Off. J. R. Hubbard
25/26.3.42	L7518 QR-O	Plt Off. J. R. Hubbard
25/26.3.42	L7497	Sgt C. G. Furby
29/30.3.42	L7454	Plt Off. C. S. Churchill
6/7.4.42	L7470	FS E. W. Noble
10/11.4.42	R5785 QR-M	Sgt D. H. MacSporran

83 Squadron
21/22.2.42	L7522 OL-N	Sqn Ldr J. R. Rainford
8/9.3.42	L7426	Plt Off Frost
8/9.3.42	R5779 OL-G	Fg Off. R. W. Cooper
13/14.3.42	L7423 OL-S	Plt Off. J. L. Bromiley

Date	Aircraft	Pilot
24/25.3.42	R5831 OL-S	Sgt E. M. Price
25/26.3.42	L7465 OL-H	Sgt P. Markides
28/29.3.42	R5781 OL-?I	Fg Off. T. A. Lumb
8/9.4.42	L7427 OL-Q	Plt Off. Morphett
8/9.4.42	R5837 OL-J	Plt Off. M. A. Sproule

97 Squadron

Date	Aircraft	Pilot
10/11/5/41	L7323 OF-A	Plt Off. R. S. Ayton
15/16.5.41	L7324	Flt Lt G. O. L. Bird
26/27.6.41	L7374	Fg Off. F. Eustace
12/13.8.41	L7424	Fg Off. J. A. Little
16/17.8.41	L7384	Flt Lt J. Nunn
13.9.41	L7306	Sgt G. H. Hartley
13/14.9.41	L7383 OF-F	Plt Off. D. E. Fox
28.9.41	L7375 OF-B	Fg Off. H. S. Blakeman
20/21.10.41	R5783 OF-V	Fg Off. G. H. Hartley
20/21.10.41	L7462 OF-Z	Fg Off. Noble
8.11.41	L7466 OF-N	Flt Lt C. P. D. Price
24.11.41	R5792	Fg Off. H. T. Hill
18.12.41	R5795 OF-W	Plt Off. N. G. Stokes
18.12.41	L7490 OF-U	Wg Cdr D. F. Balsdon
8..1.42	L7459 OF-N	Sgt G. H. Hartley

106 Squadron

Date	Aircraft	Pilot
12.3.42	L7474	Sgt G. K. Carter
25/26.3.42	L7390	Flt Lt R. J. Dunlop-Mackenzie
29/30.3.42	L7394	FS E. R. Dimond
14/15.4.42	L7317	Plt Off. J. A. Worswick
16/17.4.42	L7485	Plt Off. C. Scatchard
23/24.4.42	L7463 ZN-L	Plt Off. H. M. Stoffer
2/3.5.42	R5840	FS Hurd
2/3.5.42	L7399 ZN-X	FS W. L. Young
20.5.42	L7418	Sgt A. J. McHardy

207 Squadron

Date	Aircraft	Pilot
13/14.3.41	L7313 EM-C	Fg Off. H. V. Matthews
20/21.3.41	L7278 EM-A	Sgt F. B. Harwood
27/28.3.41	L7303 EM-P	Flt Lt J. A. Siebert
8/9.4.41	L7302 EM-R	Wg Cdr N. Hyde
2/3.5.41	L7379 EM-T	Fg Off. D. Pinchbeck
18.5.41	L7393 EM-V	Sqn Ldr J. C. Mackintosh
21.6.41	L7310 EM-H	Sqn Ldr C. J. F. Kydd
21/22.6.41	L7314 EM-Y	Fg Off. J. G. D. Withers
12/13.8.41	L7381 EM-R	Fg Off. M. Smith
12/13.8.41	L7377 EM-G	Sqn Ldr G. R. Taylor
16/17.8.41	L7311 EM-F	Plt Off. Keartland
31.8/1/9.41	L7316 EM-U	Plt Off. Gilkderthorp
7/8.9.41	L7380 EM-W	Flt Lt W. J. Lewis
15.9.41	L7318 EM-K	Plt Off. E. D. G. Crump
12/13.10.41	L7312 EM-L	Plt Off. P. B. Bowes-Cavanagh
13/14.10.41	L7373 EM-T	Plt Off. L. Paskell
13/14.10.41	L7321 EM-D	Plt Off. J. Unsworth
20/21.10.41	L7487 EM-N	Plt Off. J. C. L. Ruck-Keene
26.10.41	L7422 EM-V	Sqn Ldr K. H. P. Beauchamp

Date	Aircraft	Crew
23.11.41	L7300 EM-F	Plt Off. A. W. Hills
27/28.12.41	L7483 EM-O	Sqn Ldr K. H. P. Beauchamp
8/9.1.42	L7322 EM-Q	Plt Off. Bayley
14/15.1.42	L7523 EM-M	FS Wescombe
14/15.1.42	L7309 EM-O	Plt Off. G. Dawkins
6.8.42	L7385	Sgt Pearson

25 OUT

18.11.41	L7428	FS L. H. Adams
10.2.42	L7478	Plt Off. E. R. Siebold

1654 HCU

5.7.42	L7496	FS E. W. Lancey
30.8.42	L7416	Plt Off. W. J. Picken
1.9.42	L7298	Sgt L. G. Knight
24.1.43	L7457	FS Taylor
26.1.43	R5772	FS Schnier
25.2.43	L7400	Sgt Hendry
2.3.43	L7277	Flt Lt P. J. Stone
4.4.43	L7291	??? – see Appendix Five
15.4.43	L7294	Sgt W. H. Eager
17.5.43	L7491	Plt Off. A. Walters

1656 HCU

19.10.42	R5780	Plt Off. R. D. Horner

1660 HCU

2.1.43	L7482	Fg Off. H. C. Goodyear
14.2.43	L7286	Sgt N. C. Keeffe
11.4.43	R5841	Flt Lt J. M. Whitwell
30.5.43	L7389	??? – see Appendix Five
4.7.43	R5770	Plt Off. J. L. Cooper
16.11.43	L7421	??? – see Appendix Five

1661 HCU

½.12.42	R5836	Plt Off. J. M. Desmond
12.3.43	R5838	WO E. Knight
24.3.43	L7453	Sqn Ldr Oakley
19.5.43	L7297	Sgt J. Clifford

MISCELLANEOUS UNITS

Rolls-Royce

26.5.41	L7295	Mr R. Kirlew

Aeroplane and Armament Experimental Establishment

12.12.41	L7320	Sgt F. J. Robinson

Royal Aircraft Establishment

16.4.42	L7285	??? – see Appendix Five

57 Conversion Flight

5.10.42	L7386	Plt Off. M. E. Walsh

1485 Bombing and Gunnery Flight

6.10.42   L7473   FS H. H. Taylor
11.2.43   L7391   FS R. Eyres

Torpedo Development Unit
31.10.43   L7276   ??? – see Appendix Five

Appendix Five: Individual Aircraft Histories

Information culled from Aircraft Movement Cards and Aircraft Accident Cards, cross referenced to Squadron Operational Record Books, Raid Summary Books, Personal Experience Report Files, Flying logbooks and contacts with former air and ground crew. Particular care has been taken to show the entries on the Aircraft Movement Cards in the order they are given. Where date structures are clearly, or quite possibly, wrong this has been denoted by (ce) noting corrupt entry.

Allocation and delivery dates often differ but, for brevity, are not differentiated. Where both are known only the former are listed. They usually differ by a few days.

No attempt is made to append records of internal system failures in aircraft on operational or non-operational flying except where these led in turn to major ensuing damage.

Aircraft Accident Cards are only available up to 26.7.43. A number of known accidents are not in Aircraft Movement Cards. A number of apparent repairs in Aircraft Movement Cards do not have an equivalent Aircraft Accident Card.

Only 28% of aircraft have total airframe hours preserved of which R5835 has the maximum, 471¼ hours (given as 471.15 in the tables). Where known, flying hour totals are given at the end of each entry. Also given at the end of each entry is the total number of operational sorties known to have been undertaken by that aircraft. Where no figures are given, the aircraft in question is not known to have undertaken any Ops.

For accidents a standard approach has been made to note crew circumstances. Beyond details of the loss (often pre-fixed with MFO – missing following Ops) will appear a linked listing of data.

For example: QR-0, Plt Off J. R. Hubbard – 7 – 2 – Essen

This shows aircraft code (where known), captain, number in crew, number of survivors, sortie. In many cases the sortie will be the name of a town or city, eg. Dortmund, in which case that was the duty target for the particular Op. Other examples of sortie may include details of a GARDENING Op. or a training duty, etc.

ABBREVIATIONS

In order that the individual histories do not take up an inordinate amount of space, it has been necessary to use extensive abbreviations. These should present few problems to readers, especially following reference to this section prior to referring to the histories themselves.

Units/Departments

AAEE	Aircraft & Armament Experimental Establishment
AAS	Air Armament School
AFEE	Airborne Forces Experimental Establishment
AFU	Advanced Flying Unit (possibly corrupt attribution?)
AFW	? possibly corrupt
AFG	Air Gunnery School
AMDP	Air Member for Development & Production
AOS	Air Observers School
B&GF	Bombing & Gunnery Flight
CF	(Squadron) Conversion Flight
CU	Conversion Unit
DGRD	Director General of Research & Development
DTD	Director of Technical Development
LFS	Lancaster Finishing School
1 MPRU	Metal Produce & Recovery Unit, Cowley
MU	Maintenance Unit
RAE	Royal Aircraft Establishment
Sqn	Squadron
SofTT	School of Technical Training
TDU	Torpedo Development Unit

Accident Damage Categories & Equivalents

Pre–1941		1941-1942
Cat.U	Undamaged	
Cat.M(u)	Capable of being repaired on site by operating unit	Cat.A
Cat. M(c)	Repair is beyond unit capacity	Cat.Ac
Cat.R(b)	Repair on site not possible. Beyond repair on site. Aircraft must be dismantled and sent to repair facility	Cat.B
--	Allocated to Instructional Airframe duties	Cat.C
Cat.W	Aircraft is a write-off	Cat.E
--	Write-off but considered suitable for component recovery	Cat.E1
--	Write-off, suitable only for scrap	Cat.E2
--	Aircraft is burnt out	Cat.E3
--	Aircraft missing from an operational sortie	Cat.Em

also postscripts, eg:
Cat.E(FA)   Write-off as a result of flying accident
Cat.E (FB) Write-off as a result of flying battle damage
Cat./OR   Category varies. Operational reasons
Cat./AII   Category varies. Major inspection required
Cat./MR   Category normally E. Major repair required

Loss Abbreviations
Country in which aircraft crashed or force-landed:
B – Belgium; D – Denmark; F – France; G – Germany; N – Norway; NL – Netherlands

Operational Abbreviations
In addition to standard RAF examples:
(D) – daylight raid. NF – night fighter

RAF Semi-official
A/c   Aircraft
AC2   Aircraftsman Class 2
AF hours   Airframe flying hours
AP   Aiming Point
ASR   Air Sea Rescue
ATC   Air Traffic Control
Aw/cn   Awaiting Collection
C & L   Circuits & Landings
Dd   Delivered (if Avro, to Flight Shed)
Ff   First Flight
F/G   Front Gunner
F/L   Forced Landing
FTR   Failed to Return
43 GDA   Group Deposit Account (Used to dispose of lost or damaged aircraft from units to salvage and repair organisations. Normally preceded by 43)
GI Airfr   Ground Instruction Airframe
IAS   Indicated Air Speed
IFF   Identification Friend or Foe
MFO   Missing from operations, used to denote dispatched on an Op or lost either en route, over or returning from the target
MUG   Mid-Upper Gunner
NFD   No Further Details
NFT   Night Flying Test
ORB   Operations Record Book (made up of Forms 540 & 541)
Ops   Operations

R/G	Rear Gunner
RIW	Repaired In Works
ROS	Repaired On Site
RPM	Revolutions Per Minute
SAS	Service & Supply (Backup Organisation)
SOC/PSOC	Struck Off Charge/Presumed Struck Off Charge
TA	Target Area
TI	Trial Installation
TO	Take (Took) Off
U/c, u/c	Undercarriage
u/s	Unserviceable
W/op	Wireless Operator

General

BA blister	Bomb Aimer's (perspex) blister
Br	Bracket
Circs	Circumstances
Cl	Closed
Corr	Corrosion
Cr	Crashed
Ct	Caught
Dam	Damaged
Eng	Engine
Exs	Exercises
Fd	Found
Fr	Front
Fter	Fighter
Gd	Ground
Ht	Height
Jett	Jettisoned
ld, ldg	land, landing
Mntn	Maintenance
Nr	Near
Pt	Port
Rec	Recovery
rep'd	Reported
Stbd	Starboard
Twd	towards
Vibr	Vibration
Wt	Weight

NOTES ON PRODUCTION BATCHES

L7246

First prototype, initially unarmed.

L7247

Second prototype. Full turret armament including FN21A mid-under.

L7276 to L7302

Twenty-seven aircraft. All Mk.1s. First nine, ten or eleven aircraft (including L7247 - records vary), delivered with FN21A mid-under turret. Some reached 207 Squadron but all removed prior to first Op. First twenty delivered with early 28-feet span tail and triple fins. Twenty-first and subsequent aircraft fitted with 33-feet span tail and triple fins. First twenty not retrofitted with 33-feet tail until late 1942. Up to L7302 (?) all delivered lacking mid-upper turrets. Last aircraft delivered without mid-positioned turrets unknown. L7309, outside this range, known not to be fitted with FN7A mid-upper turret initially. Some airframes, (ie 7303?), may have had FN7A retrofitted. Early aircraft from this production batch not fully operationally fit and rapidly withdrawn for conversion training and development. All service aircraft had FN7A removed during June/July 1941.

L7303 to L7482 (?)

One hundred and three aircraft (?). All Mk.1s. Early airframes delivered lacking FN7A mid-upper turret which in some (? all) cases was retrofitted. Remainder carried standard three turret armament from factory. All delivered with 33-feet span, triple fin tail. L7313 had first FN7A.

R5768 to R5841

Forty-three aircraft. All delivered to Avro Woodford for assembly as triple fin Mk.1s. Retained at factory and at dispersed sites until September 1941 from which time issued as required fitted with improved Vulture engines. All carried standard three turret armament.

L7483 to L7526

Twenty-seven aircraft. All Mk.1As. Only aircraft delivered direct with twin fin, 33-feet span tailplane. All aircraft carried standard three turret armament.

From the Avro (L-serials) and Metropolitan Vickers (R-serials) production runs a number of airframes were retrofitted with twin fins on their existing 33-feet span tails becoming Mk.1A. No reliable record of those so fitted has come to light. All previous lists have concluded that no more than twenty Mk.1s were built, the remainder being Mk.1As. In fact, only twenty-seven Mk.1As were delivered direct from the factory. Known Mk.1A conversions are noted in italics in the individual histories.

PROTOTYPE & PRODUCTION CONTRACTS

L7246 to L7247

Prototypes to Contract No 624973/37 dated 30 April 1937.

L7276 to L7284

Two hundred aircraft. Contract No 648770/37 dated 1 July 1937. Batches as follows: L7276 to L7325, L7373 to L7402, L7415 to L7434, L7453 to L7497, L7515 to L7526 all completed as Manchester Mk.1s. L7527 onwards completed as Lancaster Mk.1s.

R2671

Contract No 7625/39 dated 25 July 1939 for cannon turret trials aircraft.

R4525 to R4744

One hundred and fifty aircraft. Contract number not recorded, date not traced, but likely early September 1939. Ordered from Fairey but cancelled. Batches as follows: R4525 to R4554, R4572 to R4611, R4630 to R4649, R4670 to R4694, R4710 to R4744.

R5273 to R5477

One hundred and fifty aircraft. Contract No 982865/39, undated. Ordered from Armstrong Whitworth, but cancelled. Batches as follows: R5273 to R5320, R5339 to R5380, R5397 to R5426, R5448 to R5477.

R5482 to R5763

Two hundred aircraft. Contract number and date not recorded. Batch ordered as Manchesters, built as Lancasters.

R5768 to R5917

One hundred aircraft. Contract No 982866/39. By Metropolitan-Vickers. Batches as follows: R5768 to R5797, R5829 to R5841. Specified airframes only (forty-three) completed as Manchester Mk.1s.

W1280 to W1498

One hundred and fifty aircraft. Contract No B.982865.39 shown as placed with the Armstrong Whitworth Group, dated 12 January 1940, valued at £4.5 million. All cancelled. Batches as follows: W1280 to W1299, W1319 to W1350, W1374 to W1410, W1426 to W1475, W1488 to W1498.

Avro 679 Manchester. Two Prototypes ordered to Contract No 624973.37 of 30 April 1937. Built by AVRO at Woodford

L7246
FF 24.7.39; 29.11.39 F/L Charnos Hall, Staffs on deliv AAEE when pt eng stopped after inadvert running on reserve; 12.12.39 F/L after eng failure outside Boscombe Down; 23.12.39 F/L after eng failure outside Boscombe Down; AVRO/RIW 12.4.40; AAEE/AMDP 9.7.40; AVRO/AMDP 24.8.40; AAEE 14.10.40; 43GDA–; RAE Farnborough/DGRD 18.12.40 frictionless take-off & arrested ldg trials at RAE; 1.8.41 A/c dam in arrested ldg trials R0S; To 3422M at 1 SofTT/Halton 20.11.42. **L7247**
FF 26.5.40; AAEE/AMDP 9.7.40; recorded again 13.9.40; AVRO/AMDP 8.10.40; AAEE/AMDP 25.11.40; AVRO 21.2.41; To 2738M at 1 SofTT (allocated 8.10.41), ?.5.42.

Avro 679 Manchester Mk.1s built by Avro at Woodford to Contract No 648770/37 of 1 July 1937. 157 aircraft, delivered between August 1940 and November 1941. L7483 to L7526 (27 aircraft) completed as Mk.1As. Others converted to Mk.1A.

L7276
AAEE 5.8.40; 61 Sqn–; 25 OTU–; AVRO 31.8.41; 39 MU (Colerne) 9.7.42; TDU ?.12.43; CAT.E 31.10.43 No accident card. A/C movement card cites this as date scrapped. 1st Prod., Ops 0.

L7277
AAEE 25.10.40; AVRO/SAS 28.2.41; 1654 CU 1.6.42; 408 Sqn 8.6.42; 1654 CU 16.6.42; 1467 Flt 24.8.42 (Corrupt); 130 Flt 23.9.41 (Corrupt); 1654 CU 10.10.42, CAT.E 15.00 hours 2.3.43 Feathering demo to trainee pilot. Port prop would not unfeather. Undershot 'drome on F/L attempt due to premature lowering of u/c. Attempted belly landing, struck tree at North Searle*, Notts.. A/c ct fire Flt Lt P. J. Stone–6–6–trng. Feathering practice now discontinued on this type. SOC 16.3.43, Ops 1. (*As on history card, perhaps Scarle?).

L7278
27 MU (Shawbury) 31.7.40; AVRO/AMDP 7.10.40; 207 Sqn 10.11.40; CAT.E 20/21.3.41 as MFO EM-A Sgt F. B. Harwood–6–2–Lorient. 0.5% silver bearing failure 15 min after take-off. Cr at Wymondham, Leics. 80 AF hours, Ops 3.

L7279
6 MU (Brize Norton) 22.10.40; 207 Sqn 6.11.40; 61 Sqn 15.4.41; AVRO/SAS 14.7.41; 39 MU (Colerne) 10.8.42; RAE 11.6.43; 39 MU (Colerne) 21.8.43; CAT.E2 11.10.43 No accident card. SOC 11.10.43, Ops 1.

L7280
AVRO/AMDP 4.8.40; 27 MU (Shawbury) 11.11.40; 207 Sqn 2.12.40; AVRO/SAS 13.6.41; 44 CF 6.3.42; 83 Sqn 2.4.42; 83 CF 17.4.42; 1654 CU 10.10.42; CAT.Ac 11.00 hours 19.10.42 Heavy landing at Wigsley; 1654 CU 7.11.42; 10.30 hours 2.1.43 CAT.A R5796 struck by L7280 whilst both taxiing. Both pilots negligent; 1660 CU 11.7.43; ? 22.9.43; CAT.E2 15.10.43; No accident card. SOC 18.10.43, Ops 0.

L7281
AVRO/AMDP 4.9.40; AVRO/DGRD 19.10.40; AAEE/DGRD 2.11.40; 6 MU (Brize Norton) –; AVRO 12.1.42 for Eng. Ch. & conv. to Mk.1A; 1654 CU 22.5.42; 49 Sqn 26.5.42; 49 CF 29.5.42; 49 Sqn –; CAT.B AE? 13.7.42 No accident card ROS 20.7.42; 49 CF 1.8.42; 1661 CU 9.11.42; CAT.E2 undated. No accident card. SOC 14.9.43, 327.05 AF hours, Ops 0.

L7282
6 MU (Brize Norton) 29.10.40; 207 Sqn 21.12.40; 97 Sqn 20.2.41; AVRO/SAS 17.8.41 Eng. Ch & Mk.1A; 39 MU (Colerne) 10.8.42; 12 SofTT 4.6.43. SOC –, Ops 0.

L7283

6 MU (Brize Norton) 29.10.40; 207 Sqn 28.11.40; AVRO/SAS 13.6.41; 25 OTU 27.3.42; 97 CF 15.4.42; 1660 CU 20.10.42; 10 AGS 23.6.43 as instr. airframe 3743M. SOC –, Ops 0.

L7284
27 MU (Shawbury) 29.10.40; 207 Sqn 29.11.40; 24.2.41 u/c failure. F/L ex Ops at Waddington; 43 GDA 25.2.41; 207 Sqn 6.4.41; 61 Sqn 15.4.41; AVRO/SAS 14.7.41; 39 MU (Colerne) 12.9.42. SOC –, Ops 1.

L7285
Unknown allocation 29.10.40; 27 MU (Shawbury) 1.11.40; 37 MU (Burtonwood) 7.7.41; AVRO 29.3.42 for mods.; 83 Sqn 11.4.42; RAE –; CAT. Ac 16.4.42 U/c collapsed on a/c parked at Farnborough; AVRO 16.4.42; RAE 24.4.42; 39 MU (Colerne) 13.10.42. SOC 15.6.43, Ops 0.

L7286
6 MU (Brize Norton) 29.10.40; 207 Sqn 7.12.40; AVRO/SAS 13.6.41; 61 CF 19.4.42; 83 Sq? 20.4.42?; 16.5.42 CAT.Ac at 61 CF Syerston. Hydraulics, then emergency system failed. Stbd wheel only lowered for ldg, ROS –; 83 Sqn 25.7.42; 1660 CU 20.10.42; 11.00 hours 14.2.43 CAT.Ac Stbd eng. ct. fire at 1000'. A/c belly-landed Waddington. Flame traps to A & B blocks burnt through. SOC 7.3.43, 218.05 AF hours, Ops 2.

L7287
AVRO/DGRD 16.8.40; DGRD 11.12.40; AVRO/SAS –; 83 Sqn 16.4.42; 49 Sqn 18.4.42; 19.5.42 Mid-air collision with 83 Sqn Lanc. Not in accident cards; CAT.E 7.6.42 MFO EA-G Flt Lt R. E. R. Paramore –7–0– Emden. Presumed in North Sea. NFD. Ops 5. 88.10 AF hours.

L7288
6 MU (Brize Norton) 17.11.40; 207 Sqn 7.12.40; 97 Sqn 26.2.41; 61 Sqn 22.4.41; AVRO/SAS 24.7.41; 1654 CU 29.6.42; AVRO (Waddington) 12.5.43. Presumed SOC, Ops 2.

L7289
37 MU (Burtonwood) 5.7.41; AVRO 27.3.42; 83 Sqn 11.4.42; 02.50 hours 25.4.42. Heavy landing. Pilot held off too late, a/c bounced & wing touched gd, ROS 27.4.42; 83 Sqn –; 50 Sqn 5.6.42 MFO Sgt R. G. Roy–7–0– Bremen. Shot down by flak. Cr. Grembke, G. Ops 2(?) 110.15 AF hours.

L7290
27 MU (Shawbury) 17.11.40; 207 Sqn 31.12.40; 97 Sqn 26.2.41; AVRO/SAS 11.6.41; 1654 CU 24.5.42; 49 Sqn 25.5.42; CAT.E 30/31.5.42 MFO Plt Off. P. W. Floyd-7-5-Cologne. Hit by flak. Stbd eng. failed. 5 baled out. A/c rolled onto back and cr at Mulheim-Oberhausen, G. Ops 2.

L7291
46 MU (Lossiemouth) 17.11.40; 207 Sqn 3.1.41; 97 Sqn 26.2.41; AVRO/SAS 11.6.42; 106 Sqn 13.5.42; 50 Sqn 14.5.42; 420 CF 17.5.42; 1654 CU ?.7.42; 11.00 hours 19.10.42 CAT.Ac. Heavy landing at Wigsley, ROS 29.10.42; 1654 CU 7.11.42; CAT.E (Burnt) 4.4.43; No accident card. SOC 5.4.43?, Ops 1.

L7292
46 MU (Lossiemouth) 17.11.40; 207 Sqn 3.1.41; 97 Sqn 30.3.41; 61 Sqn 22.4.41; 43 GDA undated –
 AVRO/SAS 28.7.41; 39 MU (Colerne) 25.7.42;TDU 1.12.42; AVRO/MR RIW 7.1.43; AW/CN 6.3.43; 39 MU (Colerne) 15.3.43; CAT.E2 6.11.43 No accident card. SOC 10.11.43, Ops 2.

L7293
37 MU (Burtonwood) 15.7.41; Rolls-Royce (Derby) 10.3.42; AVRO/mods 2.4.42; 83 Sqn 18.4.42; 49 Sqn 11.6.42; 61 CF 2.8.42; 207 CF 22.9.42; 1660 CU 20.10.42; 3773M. SOC 15.10.43, Ops 2.

L7294

27 MU (Shawbury) 24.11.40; 207 Sqn 29.12.40; 97 Sqn 26.2.41; 61 Sqn 27.4.41; AVRO/SAS 24.7.41 Eng Ch & Mk.1A; 1654 CU 11.6.42; 18.50 hours 15.4.43 CAT.E. Eng. misfired & ct. fire. A/c stalled on approach, cr & burnt out. Sgt W. H. Eager-7-trng. SOC 26.4.43, Ops 5.

L7295
Unknown allocation 24.11.40; Rolls-Royce/DGRD 4.12.40; AVRO/DGRD 21.2.41; Rolls-Royce/DGRD 9.3.41; Uncontr. eng fire due to uneven coolant distrib. Undershot. Cr. Ternhill 26.5.41. Mr R. Kirlew-4-3-test. SOC –, Ops 0.

L7296
6 MU (Brize Norton) 24.11.40; AVRO/SAS 28.2.41 Eng. ch & Mk.1A; 49 Sqn 25.6.42; 49 CF 22.7.42; 1661 CU 9.11.42; AVRO/ROS 30.4.43 No accident card; 1661 CU 8.5.43; RAF Benson 5.10.43; 15.10.43 CAT.E2 No accident card. SOC 18.10.43, 404.10 AF hours, Ops 0.

L7297
37 MU (Burtonwood) 15.7.41; Rolls-Royce (Derby) 10.3.42; AVRO 17.4.42; 83 Sqn 28.4.42; 207 CF 7.6.42; 1661 CU 30.10.42; 1.4.43 CAT.A R5769 blown back in gale, damaged L7297 parked at Winthorpe; 12.15 hours 19.5.43 CAT.E Eng fire in flight. Emerg. landing Winthorpe, u/c retracted to stop on overshoot, flametraps in A & D blocks had burnt out. Sgt J. Clifford-?-all trng. SOC 26.5.43, Ops 1.

L7298
6 MU (Brize Norton) 24.11.40; 207 Sqn 24.12.40; 97 Sqn 26.2.41; AVRO/SAS 24.7.41; 1654 CU 29.6.42; 23.15 hours 1.9.42 CAT.E. Eng. failed on landing. Belly-landed outside 'drome. Partial cl. of fuel master cock caused fuel starvation. Sgt L. G. Knight-?-all-trng SOC 9.9.42, 157.50 AF hours, Ops 1.

L7299
46 MU (Lossiemouth) 24.11.40; 207 Sqn 3.1.41; 97 Sqn 26.2.41; AVRO/SAS 9.7.41; 39 MU (Colerne) 11.7.42; 31.10.43 CAT.E2 No accident card. SOC 4.11.43, Ops 0.

L7300
6 MU (Brize Norton) 21.12.40; 207 Sqn 3.2.41; AVRO 10.10.41; 207 Sqn –; undated 23.11.41 CAT.E Double eng. failure. Cr Fiskerton Lake. EM-F Plt Off. A. W. Hills-9-9-trng. SOC ?.12.41, Ops 17.

L7301
27 MU (Shawbury) 21.12.40; AVRO/SAS 18.3.41; 106 Sqn 28.4.42; CAT.E 30/31.5.42 MFO ZN-D Fg Off. L Manser-7-6-Cologne. Cr nr Bree, B 106 CF a/c on loan to 50 Sqn, Ops 2.

L7302
46 MU (Lossiemouth) 21.12.40; 207 Sqn 16.2.41; 8/9.4.41 MFO EM-R Wg Cdr N. C. Hyde-6-6-Kiel, G. Sqn CO. Damaged by flak, eng caught fire. Crew baled out. Cr Hostrup, G. Ops 8. 59 AF hours.

L7303
6 MU (Brize Norton) 22.12.40; 207 Sqn 11.2.41; 27/28.3.41 MFO EM-P Flt Lt J. A. Siebert-6-5-Dusseldorf, G. Encountered flak, eng failure and NF piloted by Oblt Herzog 3/NJG1, Eindhoven. Cr Bakel, NL. Ops 2. 27 AF hours.

L7304
6 MU (Brize Norton) 22.12.40; 207 Sqn 11.2.41; 61 Sqn 15.4.41; 26/27.6.41 MFO Fg Off. K. G. Webb-6-0-Kiel. Shot down by Bf110 Oblt Walter Fenske 3/NJG1. Cr at Marne/Holstein, G. Ops 3.

L7305

27 MU (Shawbury) 22.12.40; AVRO/DGRD 6.1.41; 25 OTU 22.1.42; 106 Sqn 18.4.42; 106 CF 19.5.42; 9.6.42 CAT.A C&L Collided with trestles when turning at downwind end of flarepath; 1660 CU 20.10.42; To 4279M 22.9.43 at 3SofTT. SOC undated, Ops 1.

L7306

27 MU (Shawbury) 22.12.40; 97 Sqn 15.4.41; 26/27.8.41 three bombs fell thro' bomb doors before reaching enemy coast. This & other unserviceabilities caused early return; 13.9.41 CAT.E Tyre burst on TO at Coningsby. U/c coll. & a/c swung to right. Eng. ct. fire, Graviner button pressed but a/c burnt out. Sgt G. H. Hartley-7-7-non.op. SOC undated, Ops 6.

L7307

46 MU (Lossiemouth) 22.12.40; 97 Sqn 18.3.41; 61 Sqn 18.3.41; 207 Sqn 10.9.41; 97 Sqn 15.9.41; 25 OTU 21.10.41; 1654 CU 10.7.42; 1660 CU 11.7.43; (poss incorr seq'd ?), 3 SofTT 22.9.43; 1668 CU 12.10.43; 5 LFS –; 4118 M. SOC 12.9.45, Ops 1.

L7308

46 MU (Lossiemouth) 22.12.40; 97 Sqn 1.3.41; 28.10.41 CAT.B Pt airscrew feathered itself on TO from Woodhall Spa. Unable to mntn ht. F/L in field. Tail torn off, u/c & props dam. SOC 13.11.41; AVRO/RIW 22.11.41; AW/CN 12.5.42; 49 Sqn 25.5.42; 30/31.5.42 CAT.B Loaned to 83 Sq. Stbd eng. failed due to fuel shortage on retn from Ops. F/L at Ingham, ROS 4.6.42; 49 CF 2.8.42; 20.10.42 CAT.Ac damage found on inspection at Wigsley, ?ROS 24.10.42; 49 CF 31.10.42; 1656 CU 1.12.42; 39 MU (Colerne) 14.12.42; ?.5.43 F/L in field adjacent to Woodhall Spa due to both props feathering. No accident card. SOC 26.5.43?, Ops 5.

L7309

6 MU (Brize Norton) 21.1.41; 97 Sqn 1.3.41; 207 Sqn 6.3.41; 8.4.41 CAT.Ac (FB) Flak shell passed thro' mainplane on ops; 29.4.41 Hit mntn trestles at Waddington; 43 GDA –; 10/11.5.41 CAT.Ac (FB) A/c attacked by 2 Bf110s & dam. in fins, elevators, tailplane, pt & stbd wing tanks, mainplanes & u/c doors. Heavy ldg at base; 97 Sqn 22.8.41?; 19.10.41 Hit trestles taxiing to dispersal with 207 Squadron; 9.11.41 Slight flak dam. on Ops; Corrupt? Ca OAC? (sic) 14.11.41 Corrupt? RAAA? 29.12.41; 207 Sqn 31.12.41; 14/15.1.42 MFO EM-O Plt Off. G. Dawkins-6-5-Hamburg. Shot down by Oblt G. Schoenert II/NJG2 cr at Sandel/Moens nr Jever, G. Ops 13.

L7310

27 MU (Shawbury) 21.1.41; 207 Sqn 11.2.41; 26.2.41 Taxiing on muddy ground Waddington. Tail swung into fence; 21.6.41 Eng. failed on take-off. F/L & hit embankment; EM-H Sqn Ldr C. J. F. Kydd-3-1-trng. Loose tappet nut led to valve blockage and eng failure on take-off. Cr at Dunstan Pillar, Lincs. 43 GDA –; AVRO/SAS 7.8.41 SOC –, Ops 5.

L7311

46 MU (Lossiemouth) 21.1.41; 207 Sqn 11.2.41; 16/17.8.41 MFO EM-F Plt Off. Keartland-6-6-Dusseldorf. Shot down by Bf110 of 1/NJG1 Venlo. Pilot Hpt W. Streib, cr at Kruchten, G. Ops 10 119 AF hours.

L7312

6 MU (Brize Norton) 21.1.41; 207 Sqn 11.2.41; 28.2.41 U/c collapsed in 'normal' ldg Waddington; 43 GDA -undated; 207 Sqn 13.6.41; 29.9.41 Flak dam. on Ops; 12/13.10.41 MFO EM-L Plt Off. D. B. Bowes-Cavanagh-7-1-Huls. Shot down at 0408 by Bf110 Obw. P. Gildner of II/NJG1 Leeuwarden, cr Eschen, B. Ops 9.

L7313

6 MU (Brize Norton) 24.1.41; 207 Sqn 11.2.41; 13/14.3.41 MFO EM-C Fg Off. H. V. Matthews-6-1- Hamburg. Shot down by JU88 intruder, pilot Oblt H. Hahn I/NJG2 Gilze-Rijen, G at Whisby, nr Lincoln, Ops 3.

L7314

27 MU (Shawbury) 24.1.41; 97 Sqn 1.3.41; 207 Sqn 17.3.41; 21/22.6.41 MFO EM-Y Fg Off. J. G. D. Withers-7-0-Boulogne. Attacked in error by 25 Sqn Beaufighter, cr at Wollaston, Northants. Ops 4.

L7315

46 MU (Lossiemouth) 24.1.41; 97 Sqn 18.3.41; 61 Sqn 18.3.41; 10.4.41 Held off too late on local night landings. U/c collapsed; 43 GDA –; 61 Sqn – undated; 29.6.41 C & L Eng. failed. A/c aband. on catching fire. Plt Off. C. G. Colborne-2-1-non-op. Con-rod bolt failure led to fire. W/op baled out. pilot killed nr Grantham. SOC – undated, 85.55 AF hours, Ops 3.

L7316

27 MU (Shawbury) 24.1.41; 207 Sqn 13.4.41; 2/3.5.41 Form 540 gives L7317 hit by flak on Ops. Form 541 identifies a/c as L7316; 9/10.5.41 Intercepted by Bf110 & dam. by flak on Ops; 31.8/ 1.9.41 MFO EM-U Plt Off. Gilderthorp-6-2-Cologne. Shot down by Bf110, Oblt Max Thimmig 2/NJG1 cr at Oberkruechen, G. Ops 15. 136 AF hours.

L7317

6 MU (Brize Norton) 23.2.41; 207 Sqn 13.4.41. See L7316 above. Refers to a/c of Fg Off. Romans; 22.1.42 CAT.Ac (FA) Mainwheel ran off peri-track taxiing. Forced back on by burst of eng. power. U/c coll. Bottesford; 207 Sqn 21.2.42; 106 Sqn 12.3.42; 14.4.42 MFO Plt Off. J. A. Worswick-7-7?-Dortmund. Lost, ran out of fuel and ditched in sea one mile north-west of Lee-on-Solent, Ops 24.

L7318

6 MU (Brize Norton) 23.2.41; 97 Sqn 1.3.41; 207 Sqn 6.3.41; 15.9.41 CAT.E 1810 EM-K Plt Off. E. D. C. Crump-10-0-trng. Nosed down in circuit & crashed nr Waddington. SOC – undated, Ops 1.

L7319

27 MU (Shawbury) 23.2.41; 97 Sqn 1.3.41; 207 Sqn 6.3.41; 7.11.41 CAT.Ac (FB) Shrapnel severed hydraulic pipe on Ops causing compl. hydraulic failure; 2/3.1.42 CAT.Ac (FB) A/c dam by flak on Ops; 106 Sqn 12.3.42; 50 Sqn 16.5.42; 50 CF 17.7.42; 1654 CU 10.10.42; 15.00 hours 6.11.42 CAT.Ac damaged oleo taxiing over small trench. ROS; 1654 CU 12.12.42; 25.2.43 CAT.B No accident card. SOC 1.4.43, Ops 31.

L7320

AVRO/DGRD 28.2.41; AAEE/DGRD 23.3.41; 12.12.41 CAT.E (FA) Lost power on stbd. eng. with full bomb load. Lost height. F/L in field; AVRO (Bracebridge Heath) 20.12.41. SOC 1.1.42, 117.3 AF hours, Ops 0.

L7321

97 Sqn 1.3.41; 207 Sqn 17.3.41; 13/14.10.41 MFO EM-D, Plt Off. Unsworth-7-2-Cologne. Shot down by Bf110 'G9+KH', Oblt Griese, 1/NJG1 St Trond. Cr at Hozemont, B Ops 8 146 AF hours.

L7322

207 Sqn 15.3.41; 11.6.41 CAT.Mu Struck mntn trestle & small pile of logs; 11/12.10.41 CAT.Ac (FB) single flak hit on Ops; 207 Sqn -; 8.1.42 MFO Plt Off. G. R. Bayley-7-0-Brest, cr at 0600 in Brest Hbr, nr Ile Longue, Crozon Penin., F, following flak hit . Ops 20.

L7323

97 Sqn 15.3.41; 12.5.41 MFO OF-A Plt Off. R. S. Ayton-6-6-Berlin. Ditched in North Sea after eng. failure. Crew POWs, Ops 4. 32.2 AF hours.

L7324

97 Sqn 15.3.41; 16.5.41 MFO Flt Lt G. O. L. Bird-6-0-Berlin. Ditched nr Borkum in North Sea after failure of both engines, Ops 4. 30.4 AF hours.

L7325

97 Sqn 22.3.41; 22.6.41 Attacked by Defiant night fighter returning from Ops; 43 GDA –; 97 Sqn 26.8.41; 11.10.41 CAT.R Eng. ct. fire landing at Coningsby; 25 OTU 21.10.41; AVRO/RIW 11.11.41 No accident card; RAF Finningley 15.12.41; AVRO 1.2.42; 25 OTU –; 29.1.42 CAT. Mc Heavy ldg, bounced, landed on one wheel, u/c collapsed. Bircotes; 25 OTU 7.3.42; 49 Sqn 20.4.42; 9 CF 12.8.42; 57 CF 11.9.42; 1656 CU 1.10.42; 39 MU (Colerne) 31.12.42; To 12 SofTT 4.6.43 as 3751M. SOC 10.?.45, Ops 2.

L7373
97 Sqn 22.3.41; AAEE/DGRD 13.4.41; 207 Sqn 16.5.41; 26/27.6.41 Many flak hits on Ops none serious, with 97 Squadron (poss mistaken identity?); 13.8.41 Sgt Hall fell on floor in heavy ldg ex-Ops with 207 Sqn; 13/14.10.41 MFO EM-T Plt Off. L. Paskell-7-2-Cologne. Shot down by Gefr Bruhnke III/NJGI Twente. Cr SW of Lommel, B, Ops 13 163 AF hours.

L7374
97 Sqn 22.3.41; 27.6.41 MFO Fg Off. F. Eustace-7-0-Kiel. A/C reported R/G killed by enemy NF fire. Shot down by Bf110, Oblt Walter Fenske, 3/NJG1. Cr in North Sea at Suderkoeg, G. One body washed up at Westerhever, Frisian Is., Ops 4 81.5 AF hours.

L7375
97 Sqn 21.3.41; 43 GDA - undated; 97 Sqn – undated; 26/27.6.41 Many flak hits on Ops none serious; 97 Sqn 9.9.41; 28.9.41 CAT.R(B) Props failed to unfeather during exercise. Ht could not be mntd. Belly-landed E Sibsey. Feath ex's now prohib below 3,000 feet and must be gliding dist from 'drome; AVRO/SAS 3.10.41; NFD. P SOC, Ops 2.

L7376
97 Sqn 21.3.41; 3AGS, -, Prob. incor. seq'd; 25 OTU 24.12.41; 106 Sqn 14.4.42; 1654 CU –; 18.10.42 Collided with gunpit whilst taxiing at Swinderby, u/c damaged, ROS undated; 1654 CU 24.10.42; to 3747M. SOC 11.5.43, Ops 5.

L7377
97 Sqn 21.3.41; 207 Sqn 13.4.41; 12/13.8.41 MFO EM-G Sqn Ldr G. R. Taylor-6-1-Berlin. Shot down by flak. Cr at 0200 nr Gross-Beeren/Teltow nr Berlin, G, Ops 4.

L7378
97 Sqn 21.3.41; 207 Sqn 13.4.41; 2/3.9.41 CAT. Ac (FB) Hit by flak on Ops; 7/8.9.41 CAT.Ac (FB) A/c hit 15 times by flak on Ops; 21/22.10.41 A/c hit by flak on Ops; CAT. Ac 28.10.41 NFD. No accident card; 207 Sqn 11.12.41; 8.3.42 CAT. Ac (FB) A/c hit in tail unit by flak; 106 Sqn 12.3.42; 50 CF 6.7.42; 1654 CU 10.10.42; AVRO 19.10.42; 39 MU (Colerne) 8.12.42; To 12 SofTT 17.6.43 as 3752M. P SOC, Ops 33.

L7379
207 Sqn 9.4.41; 2/3.5.41 MFO EM-T Fg Off. D. Pinchbeck-6-6-Hamburg. Damaged by flak. Crew baled out. Pilot F/L nr Hamburg, G, Ops 1. 10 AF hours.

L7380
207 Sqn 13.4.41; 7/8.9.41 MFO EM-W Flt Lt W. J. Lewis-6-6-Berlin. Dam. By Bf110, Fw Siegfried Ney, IV/NJG1 nr Kiel at 0100. Ditched in surf zone on beach at Ameland Is, Frisians, NL, Ops 5.

L7381
207 Sqn 13.4.41; 12/13.8.41 MFO EM-R Fg Off. M. Smith-6-0-Berlin. Shot down by Do215, pilot Oblt L. Becker IV/NJG1 Leeuwarden, cr 0050 Lange Dijk, Groningen, NL Ops 9.

L7382

97 Sqn 23.4.41; 26/27.6.41 Attacked by Bf110 over North Sea. A/c took several hits. MUG slightly wounded in head; 83 Sqn 10.10.41 (Suspect 10.12.41 more likely); 44 Sqn 25.12.41; 44 CF 26.2.42; 83 Sqn 2.4.42; 83 CF 17.4.42; 1705 hours. 10.8.42 CAT.Ac. A/c thrown into air on touch down & tail bounced twice. Due to rough surf. of 'drome, ROS; 83 CF 22.8.42; AVRO 23.9.42 No accident card, RIW; AW/CN 10.10.42; 39 MU (Colerne) 16.10.42; To 3753M; 6 AOS? - poss corrupt initial allocn?; Reduced to spares 13.3.45. Ops 5.

L7383
61 Sqn 16.4.41; 97 Sqn –; 14/15.8.41 Repeated flak hits on Ops; 14.9.41 CAT.W F/L out of fuel on X country. Both engines cut. OF-F Plt Off. D. E. Fox-6-5-non.op. cr at West Wickhouse, Norfolk. Pilot did not do Ops. SOC 26.9.41, Ops 10.

L7384
97 Sqn 23.4.41; 6.5.41 CAT.Mc Glide approach slightly slow. Landed too high & tail down; 43 GDA –; AVRO (Flight Trials) 25.5.41; 97 Sqn 1.6.41; 14/15.8.41 MFO Flt Lt J. Nunn-7-5-Dusseldorf. Attacked by Hpt W. Strieb I/NJG1 Venlo in Bf110. 5 baled out. F/L at Kimroy, B, Ops 2.

L7385
61 Sqn 16.4.41; AVRO (Mods) 12.10.41; 83 Sqn 9.1.42; 12.2.42 CAT.M(u). Attempted to land on side of runway at Scampton to avoid crashed a/c but wt of a/c with 6,000-lb bombs & slippery surf. made response sluggish & a/c collided with wreck; 83 Sqn –; 20.40 hours 24.3.42 CAT.Ac. Touched down in front of metalled road Xing 'drome. A/c bounced & tail wheel landed heavily. Roadway being removed, ROS 29.3.42; 83 Sqn 7.4.42; 8/9.4.42 Dam. by flak on Ops; 44 CF 30.4.42; 207 CF 4.5.42; 15.15 hours 21.5.42 CAT.Ac. C & Ls. Swung off runway on ldg & evid dam. tail wheel which collapsed after further swing, ROS 27.5.42; 207CF 13.6.42; 0050 6.8.42 CAT.E. Lanc R5550 EM-B taxied onto flarepath & was hit by L7385 EM-Ū landing. Sgt Pearson-5-3-trng at Bottesford. SOC 13.8.42, 112.4 AF hours, Ops 4.

L7386
RAF Cranage 6.5.41 for eng. change; AVRO (Woodford) 5.12.41; 25 OTU 24.12.41; 24.3.42 CAT.A Overshot thro' hedge into field adjoining Bircotes; 49 Sqn 20.4.42; 420 Sqn 23.5.42; 1654 CU 12.7.42; 9 CF 9.8.42; 57 CF 8.9.42; 5.10.42 CAT.E Stbd eng. ct fire in air. Attempted to stretch approach to Scampton but a/c touched outside boundary & bounced onto 'drome. U/c collapsed. Fire due to cracked hyd. pipe. Plt Off. M. E. Walsh-?-all. test SOC 16.10.42, 151.50 AF hours, Ops 2.

L7387
61 Sqn 24.4.41; 207 Sqn 10.9.41; 97 Sqn 15.9.41; 10.10.41 CAT.Ac One wheel bounced in heavy lding, opened thr. too quick & choked engs. U/c leg coll; 97 Sqn 9.11.41; 83 Sqn 4.12.42; 16.15 hours 4.4.42 CAT.Ac Landed diagonally in front of road Xing 'drome which caused a/c to become airborne again. Stbd rudder struck ground, ROS 8.4.42; 83 Sqn 9.5.42; 49 Sqn 7.6.42; 21.6.42 CAT.E MFO Sgt J. H. O'Brien-7-0-search sortie. Cr in sea. One of crew buried in Sweden, another at Schiermonnikoog, NL. 5 not recovered. NFD. SOC 26.6.42, Ops 10 220.30 AF hours.

L7388
61 Sqn 24.4.41; 2/3.9.41 MFO Wg Cdr G. E. Valentine-7-0-Berlin. Sqn CO. Attempted morale-boosting low level raid by senior crew. Shot down by flak and cr nr Berlin, G. Ops 6.

L7389
61 Sqn 24.4.41; 30.6.41 CAT.R (B) Stbd eng. failed in flight. 2nd pilot feathered pt prop in error. Belly landed Fowlmere. Recommend luminous paint on buttons; AVRO/SAS 8.7.41; RAE? 24.10.41; 207 Sqn 25.11.41; 83 Sqn 9.12.41; 12.2.42 CAT.Ac (FB). Presumed a/c of Plt Off. McFarlane. Att. by day fighter. R/G killed. Not in Sqdn ORB, ROS 17.2.42; 83 Sqn 10.4.42; 49 Sqn 23.5.42; 106 CF 19.7.42; 1660 CU 20.10.42; 1 SofTT Halton 30.5.43 as 3763M. SOC?, Ops 6.

L7390

AVRO/SAS 24.4.41 Eng ch. etc; AVRO (Woodford) 21.12.41; 97 Sqn 9.1.42; 106 Sqn 20.1.42; 25/26.3.42 MFO Fg Off. R. J. Dunlop-Mackenzie-7-0-Essen. Shot down by Oblt L. Becker 6 II/NJG2 Leeuwarden. Cr in Ijsselmeer nr Kornwerderzand, NL. Ops 2.

L7391

AVRO/SAS 24.4.41 Eng. ch.; ROS 1.12.41 No accident card; AVRO (mods) 1.1.42; 207 Sqn 17.1.42; 21.1.42 Stationary a/c struck by lorry, AVRO/ROS 24.1.42; 207 Sqn 31.1.42; 9.3.42 Escape hatch blown off & hole made in bomb doors by flak; 10.3.42 Pt. windscreen blown in & many holes in bomb doors by flak; 106 Sqn 12.3.42; 26/27.3.42 Flak dam on Ops; 2/3.5.42 Rear turret dam by flak; 106 CF –; 15.00 hours 11.6.42 CAT.Ac Eng. failed in flight, NFD; 1485 B&GF –; 15.40 hours 11.2.43 Air-air firing ex. Stbd eng. failed at 1200' 1540 hr. Ht could not be mntd. Belly-landed nr Boston. FS R. Eyres-?-all trng. SOC 27.3.43, 160 AF hours, Ops 13.

L7392

AVRO/SAS 24.4.41 Eng. ch.; AFEE (Ringway) 9.2.42; 39 MU (Colerne) 3.9.42; 24.10.43 CAT.E2 No accident card. SOC 26.10.43, Ops 0.

L7393

207 Sqn 27.4.41; 18.5.41 CAT.E2 Stbd eng. failed in flight. F/L Perranporth, retracted u/c to stop; EM-V Sqn Ldr J. C. Mackintosh-5-5-trng, AVRO/SAS 1.6.41; To 2600M GI airfr. ?.8.41 SOC –, Ops 6.

L7394

RAF Cranage 2.5.41, Eng. ch; AVRO (Mods) 7.2.42; 83 Sqn 27.2.42; 106 Sqn 27.2.42; 25/26.3.42 Slight flak dam on Ops; 29/30.3.42 MFO FS E R Dimond-7-0-NECTARINE. Shot down into North Sea, N of Terschelling by Bf110 Oblt Helmut Lent of Stab II/NJG2, Ops 4.

L7395

RAF Cranage 2.5.41, Eng. ch; AVRO (Mods) 28.1.42; 61 Sqn 13.2.42; 13/14.3.42 MFO Plt Off. J. R. Hubbard-7-7-Cologne. Eng failed over Wash on retn. Abandoned. A/c cr 1.5 ml south of Wittering, 1MPRU Cowley 20.3.42. Ops 1?

L7396

RAF Cranage 6.5.41 for Eng ch. 23.12.41; AVRO (Mods) 3.1.42; 61 Sqn 22.1.42; 31.1/1.2.42 MFO Flt Lt Page-8-0-Brest. Cr in Eng Channel, possibly on return. Body of pilot only recovered. NFD. SOC 2.2.42, Ops 3.

L7397

AVRO/DGRD 24.2.41; 2 AFW – , prob incor seq'd & corrupt; AVRO 15.4.41; 83 Sqn 29.4.42; 49 Sqn 3.6.42; 207 CF 2.8.42; 1660 CU 20.10.42; To 3762M NFD on circs. P SOC -, Ops 3.

L7398

RAF Cranage 13.5.41 Eng. Ch 14.12.41; AVRO (Mods) 13.10.41; 97 Sqn 9.1.42; 106 Sqn 20.1.42; 49 Sqn 2.5.42; 20.6.42 CAT.Ac structural defect Frame 35, ROS; 49 Sqn 4.7.42; 97 CF 3.7.42 (Note chronological error); 14.00 hours 23.8.42 CAT.Ac. Overshot, ran over 2 ditches in field. Stbd oleo leg coll. following air firing ex. Pilot error; 97 Sqn 31.10.42; 1661 CU 20.1.43; 1660 CU 28.1.43. SOC 30.4.43, 286.05 AF hours, Ops 8.

L7399

Rolleston Avtn/SAS 14.5.41; Still stored Rolleston 31.12.41 awaiting mods; 106 Sqn 26.4.42; 3/4.5.42 MFO ZN-X FS W. L. Young-7-2-GARDENING. Cr. Lilholt. 14 km W of Haderslev, D. NFD, Ops 1.

L7400

Rolleston Avtn/SAS 15.5.41; Still stored awaiting mods 31.12.41; RAE (Farnborough) 7.5.42; ? CF 18.5.42; 49 Sq? 19.5.42; 1654 CU 25.6.42; 25.2.43 CAT.A Practice bomb exploded in bomb bay prior to TO, Wigsley. Sgt Hendry. Accident not in a/c movement card records. SOC 11.9.43, Ops 0.

L7401

Rolleston Avtn/SAS 17.5.41; Still stored awaiting mods 31.12.41; 408 Sqn 20.5.42; 1654 CU 10.6.42; 1485 B&GF 11.9.42; 1654 CU 25.4.43; 1661 CU 6.5.42; RAF Kidlington? 6.10.43; 15.10.43 CAT.E2 crashed. No accident card; ORBs also give Ops for this aircraft with 50 & 61 Sqdns making up total of 3 if correctly attributed. SOC 16.10.43, 366.45 AF hours, Ops 3?

L7402

Rolleston Avtn/SAS 18.5.41; Still stored awaiting mods 31.12.41; 49 CF 19.5.42; 420 CF –; 12.6.42. CAT.Ac Pilots could not see flarepath. Too high, landed heavily, u/c collapsed, ROS 15.6.42; 420 CF 5.9.42; 1661 CU 7.1.43; CAT.E1 No accident card. SOC 31.3.43, Ops 0.

L7415

Rolleston Avtn/SAS 20.5.41; Still stored awaiting mods 31.12.41; 408 Sqn 27.5?.42; 1654 CU 16.6.42; ? 26.8.42; 1660 CU 6.11.42; 1661 CU 25.2.43; RAF ? 20.9.43; If correctly attributed, ORBs give 3 Ops for this aircraft with 50, 61 & 106 Sqdns. SOC 1.10.43, 207.30 AF hours, Ops 3?

L7416

Rolleston Avtn/SAS 24.5.41; Still stored awaiting mods 31.12.41; 1654 CU 4.6.42; 420 Sqn 6.6.42; 1654 CU 16.6.42; 16.30 hours 30.8.42 CAT.E Landing X wind with no brakes, swung & cr. into trees. Wigsley. Air press. line blown; Plt Off. W. J. Picken-?-all-trng. ORB gives the Op to 50 Sqdn. SOC 5.9.42, 82.25 AF hours, Ops 1.

L7417

RAF Cranage 20.5.41. Eng ch. 28.12.41; AVRO (Mods) 25.2.42; 61 Sq? –; 106 Sqn 19.3.42; 106 CF 19.5.42; 1660 CU 20.10.42; 29.10.42 CAT.B accident card gives 'Cause unknown'. SOC 9.11.42, Ops 5.

L7418

RAF Cranage 20.5.41. Eng. ch.; AVRO (Mods) 13.2.42; 83 Sqn 26.2.42; 106 Sqn 27.3.42; 19.5.42. CAT.E lost in Celtic Sea on X country. Sgt A. J. McHardy-5-0-non op. Last heard of crossing Pembroke coast on nav. ex. prior to going operational SOC 20.5.42, Ops 4.

L7419

AVRO/SAS 22.5.41; 207 Sqn 2.7.41; 2.11.41 CAT.B failed to level out soon enough on approach. Flew into gd & bounced. ROS 10.11.41; 207 Sqn 20.11.41; 27.1.42 CAT.R Heavy ldg on NFT. Iced up windscreen & falling snow made it imposs to see even thro open clear viz panel. U/c collapsed, ROS 29.1.42; 207 Sqn 10.3.42; 50 Sqn 26.3.42; 13.4.42 CAT.Ac Pt eng ct fire when taxiing due to failure of hydraulic pipe to hot air control. Fire temporarily cont. by a/c extinguisher & finally by stn fire tender, ROS 22.4.42; 50 Sqn 25.4.42; 30/31.5.42 Slight dam to bomb door by flak; 408 Sqn 5.6.42; 1654 CU 10.6.42; 21.9.42 CAT Ac damage found on inspection, ROS 22.9.42; 1654 CU 3.10.42; 4 AGS - undated; 3748M, GI airframe. SOC 10.8.44, Ops 14.

L7420

25 OTU 7.6.41; 44 CF 3.5.42; 207 CF 4.5.42; 1660 CU 20.10.42; 1661 CU 25.2.43; 1660 CU 12.10.43; 16.11.43 CAT.E2 MR No accident card. SOC 19.11.43, Ops 0.

L7421

25 OTU 11.6.41; 2.1.42 CAT.Mc Tailwheel collapsed on ldg due to rough surf. at Bircotes. A lighter type of a/c to Op from this newly laid grass 'drome in future. Manchesters to Finningley, ROS 11.1.42; 25 OTU 14.2.42; 29.3.42 CAT.Ac Tailwheel found damaged on inspection. Attrib to fair wear & tear & repeated C&Ls, ROS 2.4.42; 25 OTU 25.4.42; 49 Sqn 2.5.42; 9.6.42 CAT.Ac Frame 35 failure found on insp, ROS –; 49 Sqn 27.6.42; 00.05 hours 7.7.42 CAT.Ac Heavy ldg. Pilot flew into gd, bounced & corrected with throttle. Tail damaged, ROS –; 49 CF 8.7.42; 106 CF 5.8.42; 97 CF 28.8.42; 1660 CU 20.10.42; 17.5.43 CAT.A stabilising fin torn away in flt during bombing practice. Attachmt corroded. Whole structure weakened by vibr & corr; 16.11.43 CAT.E2 No accident card. poss date scrapped? SOC 19.11.43, Ops 4.

L7422

AVRO/SAS 20.3.41; 207 Sqn 26.6.41; 31.8/1.9.41 CAT.Ac (FB) Attacked by night fighter causing loss of control. Bombs jett. Recovered. Made early retn. Severe tail dam; Conv to Mk.1A during repairs. 43 GDA 1.9.41; 207 Sqn –; 26.10.41 CAT.E2 After unfeathering stbd prop pilot failed to switch on ign. Lost ht. Belly-landed. EM-V Sqn Ldr K. H. P. Beauchamp-13?-13?-trng. Cr at Hardings Farm, Linwood, Lincs. ORBs show Ops with 61 & 97 Sqs as well as 207. SOC ?.9.43, 70.00 AF hours, Ops 11.

L7423
97 Sqn 12.6.41; 29/30.10.41 Landed Martlesham Heath with slight dam after aborted Op; 7/8.11.41 holed by flak on Ops; 83 Sqn 22.1.42; 13.3.42 MFO OL-S Plt Off. J. Bromiley-7-2-Cologne. Shot down by Bf110, Oblt Reinhold Knacke of 2/NJG1, Venlo. Cr at Broekhuizen, NL, Ops 12, 22.2 AF hours.

L7424
97 Sqn 1.6.41; 12/13.8.41 MFO Fg Off. J. A. Little-7-7-Berlin. Poss flak splinter pt Vulture, which caught fire on return flight. Signal received 0228. Crew baled out, cr nr Munster, G. Ops 12, 22.2 AF hours.

L7425
AVRO/SAS 10.6.41; 97 Sqn 26.6.41; 207 Sqn 21.1.42; 50 Sqn 18.3.42; 408 Sqn 16.5.42; 408 CF 17.5.42; 9.6.42 CAT.Ac defect discov on inspection, ROS 15.6.42; 408 CF 4.7.42; 1654 CU 12.7.42; 9 CF 9.8.42; 1661 CU 8.11.42; 8 AGS –; 3741M as GI Airframe. SOC 13.2.47?, Ops 3.

L7426
61 Sqn 26.6.41; 4.7.41 CAT.Mc. Eng failed in flt during intensive flight trial. Overshot thro' hedge. Rearsby. U/c collapsed in ditch; 43 GDA 4.7.41; 83 Sqn 10.12.41; Flying accident. No accident card, ROS approx 17.1.42; 83 Sqn 14.2.42; 8/9.3.42 MFO Plt Off. Frost-7-0-Essen. Shot down at 0032 by Oblt L Becker II/NJG2. Ditched off Enkhuizen, NL. SOC 10.3.42, Ops 2.

L7427
AVRO/SAS 14.6.41; 97 Sqn 26.6.41; 3.7.41 CAT.R(B) Stbd eng. failed in flt during intensive eng. trial. Yawed, unable to mntn ht. F/L in field 2 ml E Spalding; 43 GDA 3.7.41; 83 Sqn 9.1.42; no accident card, AVRO/ROS 10.2.42; 83 Sqn 14.2.42; 8/9.4.42 MFO OL-Q Plt Off. Morphett-7-1-Hamburg. Shot down by Bf110 Fw Gerhard Goerke I/NJG3 W of Lastrup, SE of Cloppenburg, G at 0049. R/G died whilst POW. Ops 16.

L7428
25 OTU 11.6.41; 18.11.41 CAT.W Pt eng. failed in flt on NFT. Prop not feathered. Ht lost rapidly. Belly-landed thro hedge. Scaftworth nr Bawtry; FS L. H. Adams-5-2-night trng AVRO (Bracebridge Heath) 4.12.41. SOC 2.1?.42, 56.35 AF hours, Ops 0.

L7429
25 OTU 12.6.41; 97 Sqn 21.10.41; 25 OTU 31.12.41; 49 Sqn 28.4.42; 49 CF 18.5.42; 30/31.5.42 MFO Plt Off. J. P. Carter-7-0-Cologne. Shot down into North Sea by Bf110 Oblt Heinrich Prinz zu Sayn-Wittgenstein. 9/NJG2 at 0136 hr. Several bodies recovered next day. SOC, Ops 1.

L7430
25 OTU 11.6.41; 44 CF 30.4.42; 26.9.42 CAT.? Collided with parked Tiger Moth on landing at Kingstown, Cumb. Error of Judgement; 1661 CU 8.11.42; 27.3.43 CAT.Ac. Frame 46 found damaged at Winthorpe, ROS 31.3.43; 1661 CU 7.4.43; 1654 CU 12.6.43; 1661 CU 16.7.43; RAF ? 22.9.43. SOC 30.9.43, 449.15 AF hours, Ops 1 (no rec'd alloc. to an operational unit).

L7431
25 OTU 11.6.41; 8.11.41 CAT.Ac No accident card; 25 OTU 24.11.41; 2.1.42 CAT.B. Sodium flarepath ldgs. Pt. eng. emitted loud bangs & panel behind air intake blew off. Unable to mntn ht., belly landed, Cotterill Woods Fm, Woodsetts; 25 OTU 8.1.42; 1654 CU 6.7.42; 21.30 hours, 10.8.42 CAT.Ac Heavy ldg. with drift at Coningsby. Stbd u/c collapsed, ROS 15.8.42; 1654 CU 3.10.42; To 3772M GI Airframe. SOC –, Ops 0.

L7432
207 Sqn 13.6.41; 43 GDA –; 207 Sqn –; 7/8.9.41 Flak hit stopped pt eng. over Berlin. Crew jett. loose gear to mntn ht. Single eng. retn W Raynham; 207 Sqn 16.10.41; 50 Sqn 25.3.42; 8/9.4.42 Bird strike thro perspex BA blister on Ops; 26/27.4.42 Sev flak hits in TA. Most serious distorted fins. Landed safely after diffic retn; 4.6.42 MFO VN-Z Plt Off. J. F. Heaton-7-2-Bremen. Shot down by Bf110 Oblt Viktor Bauer III/NJG1 with stbd wing ablaze. Cr 02.33 hours nr Apeldoorn. 3 baled out of rear door, 2 from front hatch. Oblt Bauer shot down and crew killed by R/G. Ops 26s 245.35 AF hours.

L7433
97 Sqn 13.6.41; 6 MU (Brize Norton) 6.7.41; 61 Sqn 13.12.41; 10/11.2.42 CAT.Ac (FB) Holed by flak in several places; 16.2.42 MFO FS P. H. G. Webster-7-0-GARDENING. Hit by flak and cr in North Sea nr Terschelling, NL, Ops 5.

L7434
97 Sqn 13.6.41; 6 MU (Brize Norton) 6.7.41; 25 OTU 13.12.41; 106 CF 15.11.42; 1656 CU 25.11.42; 39 MU (Colerne) 31.12.42; To 4221M GI Airframe; 13.10.43 CAT.E2 No accident card, poss date scrapped? SOC 16.10.43, Ops 10 (with 106 Sq).

L7453
AVRO/SAS Eng Ch 5.7.41; 207 Sqn 29.8.41; 97 Sqn 26.9.41; 20/21.10.42 A/c dam by flak on ops; 7/8.11.41 Pt wing & fuel tank holed by flak. Presumed ROS 11.11.41; 97 Sqn 26.11.41; 83 Sqn 22.1.42; 20.3.42 CAT.Ac (FB) A/c dam by Bf110 night fighter, ROS 29.3.42; 83 Sqn 16.5.42; 49 Sqn 23.5.42; 44 CF 2.8.42; 1661 CU 8.11.42; 15.25 hours 14.3.43 CAT.B Pt eng ct fire shortly after TO Swinderby. Feathered prop & belly-landed. Fire due to burning of exhaust manifold of 'A' block pt eng. Sqn Ldr Oakley-?-all-trng, RIW 5.4.43; ORBs show Ops with 49, 106 & 83 Sqdns. Recat E1 1.5.43, Alternative fate has mid-air collision with Halifax at Winthorpe. SOC 1.5.43, Ops 16.

L7454
AVRO/SAS Eng Ch 5.7.41; 207 Sqn 10.9.41; 31.10.41 CAT M(c) Unable to see ground due to rain & mist at Waddington, heavy ldg with drift. U/c coll. ROS 8.11.41; 207 Sqn 3.1.42; 61 Sqn 24.2.42; 29.3.42 MFO Plt Off. C. S. Churchill-7-0-GARDENING. Pres lost at sea. Ops 7.

L7455
AVRO/SAS Eng Ch 12.7.41; 207 Sqn 10.9.41; 50 Sqn 17.3.42; 9 CF 4.8.42; 1661 CU 8.11.42; 8 AGS 21.5.43; To 3742M as GI Airframe. SOC 23.5.44?, Ops 26.

L7456
AVRO/SAS Eng Ch 12.7.41; 6 MU (Brize Norton) 26.11.41; 25 OTU 16.12.41; 106 Sqn 7.5.42; 30/31.5.42 MFO whilst on loan to 50 Sqn from 106 CF. Sgt Wilkie-7-4-Cologne. Hit by flak, pt eng caught fire. F/L on airfield at Dusseldorf, Ops 1.

L7457
AVRO/SAS Eng Ch 12.7.41; 207 Sqn 13.9.41; 97 Sqn 13.9.41; 4/5.11.41 Dam by flak on ops; 97 CF 16.2.42; 106 Sqn 15.4.42; 21.5.42 CAT.Ac Tailwheel found damaged due to previous heavy landing, ROS 25.5.42; 106 Sqn 15.6.42; 83 CF 11.6.42; 14.9.42 CAT.Ac Coll. with air raid shelter taxiing at Wigsley, ROS 15.9.42; 83 CF 26.9.42; 1654 CU 10.10.42; 15.10 hours 24.1.43 CAT.E. Pt. eng. ct. fire in flight. Crew slow to feather prop. Unable to mntn ht. F/L West Bank, Highfield Farm, Saxilby. FS Taylor-?-all-trng SOC 24.1.43, Ops 13.

L7458
AVRO/SAS Eng Ch, etc 23.7.41; 83 Sqn 10.12.41; 61 Sqn 11.12.41; 12.2.42 Daylight Op. Serious dam to port wing by ships flak caused near loss of control & bombs to be jett; 23.3.42 CAT.Ac. Tail wheel shimmy on ldg caused tail to rise & tail wheel unit then fell out. Attrib. to prev. heavy ldg., ROS 26.3.42; 61 Sqn 9.5.42; 61 CF 17.5.42; 1660 CU 20.10.42; 10.11.42 CAT.Ac. Tailwheel collapsed during ldg run at Swinderby, ROS 10.11.42; 1660 CU 5.12.42; 3 SofTT 22.9.43 as 4280M GI Airfr. PSOC –, Ops 9.

L7459
AVRO/SAS Eng Ch 19.7.41; 97 Sqn 27.9.41; 8.1.42 CAT.E Practice bomb exploded on TO blinding & choking pilot. Throttled back & stalled onto gd at Coningsby. OF-V Sgt G. H. Hartley-7-7-non op. SOC 16.1.42, 78.45 AF hours, Ops 1.

L7460
AVRO/SAS Eng Ch etc 23.7.41; 83 Sqn 10.12.41; 97 Sqn 11.12.41; 18.12.41 CAT.Ac (FB) Hit by flak on daylight Op. Stbd oil tanks holed. Eng. cut on ldg Colerne; 97 Sqn 8.1.42; 97 CF 16.2.42; 83 Sqn 2.4.42; 50 Sqn 16.4.42; 57 CF 8.9.42; 1656 CU 1.10.42. SOC 26.7.43, Ops 8.

L7461
AVRO/SAS 19.7.41; 97 Sqn 19.9.41; 29/30.10.41 Form 540 gives 'Shot up by enemy fighter & jett bomb load. Form 541 gives 'A/c dam by flak & retn with bombs CAT.Ac' ?ROS 1.11.41; 97 Sqn 22.11.41; 10.12.41 CAT.B Hydraulic & emerg system failure led to inability to lower flaps or u/c when ldg at Coningsby, ROS 14.12.41; 97 Sqn 19.2.42; 106 Sqn 2.3.42; 10/11.4.42 CAT.B (FB) A/c severely dam by flak. Crew ordered to bale out. Control regained. F/L at Martlesham Heath, ROS 14.4.42; 106 Sqn -; 1661 CU 8.12.42; 1654 CU 12.6.43; 1660 CU 22.7.43; To 3 SofTT 23.9.43 as 4278M. SOC –, Ops 6.

L7462
AVRO/SAS 26.7.41; 97 Sqn 26.9.41; 20/21.10.41 MFO OF-Z Plt Off. Noble-7-0-Bremen. Cr in sea NFD (Intense and accurate flak rep over target), Ops 1.

L7463
AVRO/SAS 26.7.41; 97 Sqn 26.9.41; 106 Sqn 20.1.42; 23/24.4.42 MFO ZN-L Plt Off. H. M. Stoffer-7-6-Rostock. Eng overheated and caught fire. 6 baled out. Mainplane broke off. Cr at Visgard, 3 km E of Tinglev, G. 1st Op for crew, Ops 1.

L7464
AVRO/SAS Mods & Eng Ch 26.7.41; 97 Sqn 9.1.42; 61 Sqn 23.1.42; 50 Sqn 13.4.42; 13.4.42 CAT.Ac Delivery N Luffenham-Skellingthorpe. Misjudged ht, pt wing dropped & struck gd. Pilot opened throttles to make further circuit but pt eng failed, a/c swung to pt & u/c collapsed. Error of judgment, ROS; 50 Sqn 18.6.42; 57 CF 12.9.42; 460 CF 1.10.42; 1656 CU 2.10.42; 26.3.43 to 1AAS as 3624M GI Airframe. PSOC, Ops 12.

L7465
AVRO/SAS Mods & Eng Ch 26.7.41; AW/CN 22.12.41; 83 Sqn 24.12.41; 25/26.3.42 MFO OL-H Sgt P. Markides-7-0-Essen. Shot down by Kurt Loos 2/NJG1. Cr Lichtaert, B Ops 8, 47.20 hours.

L7466
AVRO/SAS Mods & Eng Ch 26.7.41; AW/CN 22.12.41; 97 Sqn 26.9.41; 23/24.10.41 Dam by Bf109 night fighter on Ops, ROS 30.10.41?; 97 Sqn 3?.11.41; 8.11.41 MFO OF-N Flt Lt C. P. D. Price-7-0-ASR (Daylight) Search for possible survivors from previous night's Berlin Op. Reported six times by sister a/c. Last time at 1600. NFD, Ops 3.

L7467
AVRO/SAS 30.7.41; 25 OTU 10.10.41; 30.10.41 CAT.Ac No accident card; 25 OTU 31.10.41; 97 CF 7.5.42; 1.6.42 An AC2 walked into prop when going to assistance of gd crew member attempting to remove wheel chock; 1660 CU 20.10.42; 1661 CU 25.2.43; 1660 CU 12.6.43; ?50 MU 21.9.43; 25.9.43 CAT.E2 No accident card, rep'd crashed. SOC 25.9.43, Ops 0.

L7468
AVRO/SAS 2.8.41; 207 Sqn 9.11.41; 14/15.1.42 CAT.Ac (FB) F/G slightly wounded by flak burst on Ops; 50 Sqn 28.3.42; 30/31.5.42 CAT.Ac (FB) Hit twice by flak. Bomb release inoperable, ROS; 50 Sqn 20.6.42; 9 CF 9.8.42; 50 CF – undated; 1660 CU 10.11.42; 1.5.43 CAT.Ac Eng. faltered in circuit & failed compl. as turned into wind. Eng ct fire on ldg. Flame trap on 'A' block had failed; To 12 SofTT June 1943 as 3732M GI Airframe. SOC 12.1.4?, Ops 16.

L7469
AVRO/SAS 2.8.41; 25 OTU 10.10.41; 49 Sqn 21.4.42; 6/7.6.42; MFO Act Sqn Ldr P. M. De Mestre-7-0-Emden. 'A' Flt Cdr and crew. Shot down in North Sea at 00.20 hours by Oblt Ludwig Becker of 6/NJG2 20km NW of Borkum G. 4 bodies eventually recovered from European coast. SOC 13.6.42, Ops 3 192.40 AF hours.

L7470
AVRO/SAS 2.8.41; 61 Sqn 11.10.41; 7/8.4.42 MFO FS E. W. Noble-7-0-Essen. Shot down by Oblt von Bonin in Bf110 of II/NJGI St Trond & cr nr St Trond, B, Ops 8.

L7471
AVRO/SAS 9.8.41; 61 Sqn 9.11.41; 50 Sqn 19.4.42; 6/7.6.42 MFO. Beatty-7-6-Emden SOS fix MBQ 4801 01.40 hours 3rd class. Heston. Ditched off Dutch Frisian Is. foll. eng. probs. Ops 16. 59.4 hours.

L7472
AVRO/SAS 9.8.41; 61 Sqn 11.10.41; 31.1/1.2.42; MFO Flt Lt Fraser-8-6-Brest. Set on fire by flak over Brest and snagged balloon cable. One baled out too low. Ditched half mile offshore. Six escaped, one drowned, Ops 4.

L7473
AVRO/SAS 9.8.41; 97 Sqn 28.10.41; 61 Sqn 28.1.42; 10.2.42 CAT.Ac (FB) Ops to Bremen. NFD in ORB. ROS?; 00.45 hours 11.3.42 CAT.Ac Returning from Ops. A/c made heavy lding with glim lamps to stbd, bounced, slewed, tyre burst, u/c collapsed, ROS 15.3.42; 61 CF 9.9.42; 50 CF 3.10.42; 1485 B&GF undated; 14.00 hours 6.10.42 CAT.E Eng failed at 50 ft. Pilot made short circuit & crash landed on 'drome at Dunholme Lodge. SOC 17.10.42, 213 AF hours, Ops 12.

L7474
AVRO/SAS 9.8.41; 97 Sqn 28.10.41; 106 Sqn 26.1.42; 12.3.42. CAT.E Iced up on X country training. U/c damaged in attempted ldg at Coningsby. Crew ordered to point a/c twd N Sea & abandon. Cr Winceby. SOC 18.3.42, Ops 2.

L7475
AVRO 16.8.41; 97 Sqn 28.10.41; 61 Sqn 23.1.42; 50 Sqn 8.4.42; 50 CF 17.7.42; 15.30 hours 16.8.42 CAT.E Stbd eng. ct. fire at 150 feet after take-off. Ht could not be mntd, belly-landed in field & burnt out. SOC 21.8.42, Ops 23.

L7476
AVRO 16.8.41; 97 Sqn 27.9.41; 8.11.41 Ops to Dunkirk. Hit by flak. Bombs jett on run up to AP. 2nd pilot died of wounds on retn; 207 Sqn 29.1.42; 50 Sqn 23.4.42; 13.7.42 (date error) CAT.B Fire on gd during refuelling at Swinderby. Cause obscure; 1/2.6.42 Essen. Hit by flak in TA. Nav wounded; 50 CF 17.8.42; 1654 CU 10.10.42. SOC 26.4.43, Ops 14.

L7477
AVRO 16.8.41; 61 Sqn 12.10.41; 25/26.1.42 Sev. flak hits on Ops; 12.2.42 CAT.Ac (FB) Op FULLER, in daylight. Hit by flak. Bomb doors, brakes, flaps, trimgear, turrets all u/s. Stbd fin, tailplane & fuel tanks hit, ROS 17.2.42; 61 Sqn 25.4.42; 61 CF 29.4.42; No accident card but ROS 30.10.42; 1661 CU 7.11.42; 1485 B&GF 4.3.43; 1654 CU 22.4.43; AVRO (Waddington) 12.5.43. SOC 6.6.44, Ops 8.

L7478
38 MU (Llandau) 16.11.41; 25 OTU 23.12.41; 14.30 hours 10.2.42 CAT.W. Eng failed in flight, A/c yawed & undershot 'drome. Pilot had failed to diagnose fault as RPM & boost indic remained normal & erroneously approached at 120 IAS with u/c and flaps down. 2nd pilot inadvertently cut off fuel to stbd eng instead of closing radiator shutters, Cr N of Bawtry. SOC 16.2.42, Ops 0.

L7479

AVRO 23.8.41; 25 OTU 26.11.41; 49 Sqn 13.5.42; 19.6.42 CAT.Ac Structural defect in Frame 35. ROS 21.6.42; 49 CF 4.7.42; 1656 CU 20.10.42. SOC 15.7.4?, Ops 3.

L7480

AVRO 23.8.41; 207 Sqn 9.11.41; 61 Sqn 16.2.42; 50 Sqn 11.4.42; 44 CF 2.5.42; 1661 CU 8.11.42; No accident card but ROS 2.2.43. SOC 30.4.43, 260.50 AF hours, Ops 20.

L7481

AVRO 23.8.41; 6 MU (Brize Norton) 2.11.41; 46 MU (Lossiemouth)14.11.41; 25 OTU 24.11.41; 15.3.42 Tyre burst on runway. A/c swung, u/c coll, ROS 19.3.42; 25 OTU 16.5.42; 49 Sqn 27.6.42; 44 CF 16.7.42; 1661 CU 3.11.42 CAT.E2 No accident card. SOC 14.9.43, 323.25 AF hours Ops 0.

L7482

AVRO 23.8.41; 25 OTU 26.11.41; 97 CF 7.6.42; 1660 CU 20.10.42; 2.1.43 CAT.E Inadvert. ldg at Coleby. Erroneously tried to fly on to intended destination at Waddington. A/c aband by crew due to severe icing whilst attempting to climb thro snowstorm. SOC 21.1.43, 244.20 AF hours, Ops 0.

L7483

207 Sqn 29.8.41; 27.12.41 CAT.B. Stbd boost & revs dropped & lost ht outwd bound on Ops. Bombs jett offshore. U/c coll in emerg. ldg. Martlesham Heath; AVRO 15.1.42 for repair but recat.E; AW/CN 14.11.42; 39 MU (Colerne) 8.12.42 (dismantled); To 12 SofTT 17.6.43 as 3749M GI Airfr. PSOC, Ops 4.

L7484

207 Sqn 29.8.41; 13/14.10.41 CAT.Ac (FB) sev flak hits on Ops; 8/9.3.42 CAT.Ac (FB) Dud flak shell passed thro fuselage. Ammo exploded & fire started which W/op beat out with hands, RIW 17.3.42; AW/CN 28.3.42; 207 CF 3.4.42; 83 Sqn –; 6/7.4.42 Eng failed due to flak dam on Ops. Single eng retn to Horsham St Faith; 83 Sqn 18.4.42; 49 Sqn 22.4.42; 408 Sqn 27.5.42; 1654 CU 20.7.42; 9 CF 2.8.42; 16.00 hours 9.8.42 CAT. Ac Eng. failed & stbd mainplane dam by oil tank bursting. Invest showed wooden blanking plug not removed from tank vent on installn, ROS 11.8.42; 9 CF 15.8.42; 1485 B&GF 23.9.42; 26.9.42 CAT. Ac During fighter affil ex, severe vibr exp in a/c after evasive action. Landed Dunholme Lodge where rivets on tail fr & rear spars found to be loose, ROS 3.10.42; 1485 B&GF 3.10.42; 1654 CU 22.4.43; 1AGS 17.6.43 as 3776M GI Airfr. SOC 19.10.4?, Ops 20.

L7485

Mk.1A 207 Sqn 12.9.41; 17.45 hours 6.1.42 CAT.Mu Struck bomb trolley on edge of runway at Bottesford taxiing in bad viz; 106 Sqn 12.3.42; 10/11.4.42 Sev flak hits on Ops; 16/17.4.42 MFO Plt Off. Scatchard-7-0-GARDENING Deodars. Presumed lost in Engl. Chan. Crew's 1st Op, Ops 22.

L7486

207 Mk.1A Sqn 12.9.41; 50 Sqn 17.3.42; 19.15 hours 25.3.42 CAT.E Held off, ballooned & stalled a/c onto runway on one wheel from 20 feet. A/c burnt out but could have been saved with more adeq fire fighting facils at Skellingthorpe. SOC 2.4.42, Sgt D. Atkinson-?-all-non op, Ops 20.

L7487

Mk.1A 207 Sqn 12.9.41; 20/21.10.41 MFO EM-N Plt Off. J. C. L. Ruck-Keene-7-0-GARDENING Sassnitz. Ditched off Yarmouth ret from Op, NFD, Ops 4?, 26 hours.

L7488

Mk.1A 97 Sqn 14.9.41; 207 Sqn 21.1.42; 12.2.42 CAT.Ac (FB) Op FULLER in Daylight. Hit in tail by ships flak; 106 Sqn 12.3.42; 50 CF 7.6.42; 1654 CU 10.10.42; AVRO. No accident card but RIW 19.11.42; AW/CN 12.12.42; 39 MU (Colerne) 22.12.42; To 12 SofTT 23.6.43 as 3750M GI Airframe. PSOC, Ops 22.

L7489

Mk.1A 97 Sqn 14.9.41; 50 Sqn 12.2.42; 8/9.4.42 MFO Sgt M. Gruber-7-6-Warnemunde. Dam by flak in TA. Attempted divert to Sweden. Over island of Møn in Baltic stbd eng caught fire. Crew baled out but Captain killed in cr., Ops 14.

L7490

Mk.1A 97 Sqn 24.9.41; 29/30.10.41 Confusion in records. Form 540 says, a/c dam. by flak & retn with bombs. Alt, Form 541 says a/c attacked by enemy fighter & jett bomb load. 18.12.41 MFO OF-U Wg Cdr D. F. Balsdon-8-0-Brest in daylight. Dam by flak. Stalled on overshoot and cr at Coningsby, Ops 7, 89.45 hours.

L7491

Mk.1A 25 OTU 27.9.41; 97 Sqn 21.10.41; 207 Sqn 21.1.42; 9.3.42 CAT.Ac (FB) BA blister blown in & 10 flak hits in fuselage on Ops, ROS 12.3.42; 207 CF 3.4.42; 50 Sqn 16.4.42; 1654 CU 25.10.42; 11.55 hours 17.5.43 CAT.E A/c swung on TO at Wigsley. Attempted to correct but stbd u/c coll. Suspect stbd brake seized. SOC 26.5.43, Ops 19.

L7492

Mk.1A 25 OTU 1.10.41; 97 Sqn 21.10.41; 61 Sqn 22.1.42; 31.1/1.2.42 CAT.Ac (FB) Holed in 58 places by flak esp mid-fus & rear turret. IFF, hydraul & brakes all u/s. ROS 15.2.42; 61 Sqn 4.4.42; 50 Sqn 18.4.42; 00.15 hours 30.5.42 CAT Ac. Ct in heavy rain attempting to ld at Skellingthorpe on retn from night X country. Stalled on one wheel & u/c collapsed. TR9 radio failure in a/c prevented ATC advising a hold. ROS 2.6.42; 50 CF 22.8.42; 1485 B&GF 7.10.42; 1654 CU 22.4.43; To 4AOS 20.7.43 as 3985M GI Airframe. SOC 22.6.4?, Ops 6.

L7493

Mk.1A 25 OTU 1.10.41; No accident card, ROS 19.3.42; 25 OTU 28.3.42; AVRO/MR 20.4.42 No accident card; AW/CN 9.5.42; 49 Sqn 12.6.42; 49 CF 1?.5.42; 1660 CU 9.11.42; RAF B???? 7.10.43; 15.10.43 CAT E2 No accident card. Poss date scrapped. SOC 18.10.43, 397.05 AF hours, Ops 2.

L7494

Mk.1A 61 Sqn 4.10.41; 7/8.12.41 MFO Sqn Ldr J. L. Riley-7-0-Boulogne. 'A' Flt Cdr. An a/c exploded in mid-air & cr in sea in target area. Night's only casualty. NFD, Ops 3.

L7495

Mk.1A 61 Sqn 20.10.41; 14.11.41 CAT.Ac Sqdn Non-opnal. No accident card; 61 Sqn 21.11.41; 16.1.42 CAT.E Made landfall at mouth of Humber lost & short of fuel on return from Ops in bad weather. A/c aband. Fg Off. Beard-7-7-Hamburg. A/c cr at Grimoldby, Lincs, Ops 3.

L7496

Mk.1A 61 Sqn 4.10.41; 8.1.42 CAT.R(B). Undershot & hit step where existing & runway extention meet. U/c collapsed, ROS 11.1.42; 61 Sqn 28.3.42; 50 Sqn 13.4.42; 420 Sqn 22.5.42; 1654 CU 17.6.42; 16.35 hours 5.7.42 CAT.E Stbd eng. failed when throttles opened to carry out overshoot at Wigsley. Landed str. ahead, A/c cr. & ct fire. FS Lancey-?-all-trng. SOC 16.7.42, Ops 3.

L7497

61 Sqn 10.10.41; 25/26.1.42 Rear turret dam & R/G slightly wounded by flak on Ops; 26/27.3.42 MFO Sgt C. G. Furby-7-0-Essen. Shot down at 2209 by Oblt Woltersdorf of 7NJGI & cr. at Wertherbruch on NL/G border. Ops 8.

L7515

Mk.1A 207 Sqn 10.10.41; 22.11.41 CAT M(c) Taxied off runway and became bogged at Bottesford. Dam on recov. ROS 26.11.41?; 207 Sqn 11.12.41; 106 Sqn 11.3.42; 49 CF 2.8.42; 1656 CU 21.11.42; AVRO, No accident card, RIW 30.1.43; AW/CN 6.3.43; 39 MU (Colerne) 15.3.43; 14.11.43 CAT.E2. No accident card. Poss date scrapped. SOC 16.11.43?, Ops 24.

L7516

Mk.1A 61 Sqn 10.10.41; 50 Sqn 13.4.42; 24/25.4.42 Bomb doors dam by light flak on Ops; 30.4.42 MFO VN-N FS T. Willett-7-5-GARDENING Forget-me-nots. Shot down by Bf110 of II/NJG3 Westerland, pilot Oblt G. Koberich. F/L on tidal flats at Sylt, G, Ops 18.

L7517

Mk.1A burnt out in works. Not delivered to service. Contract reduced by one. -----

L7518

Mk.1A 61 Sqn 15.10.41; 25.3.42 MFO QR-O Plt Off. J. R. Hubbard-7-2-Essen. Shot down at 0032 by Hpt Lent II/NJG2 Leeuwarden and cr nr Warmenhuizen, NL, Ops 10.

L7519

Mk.1A 61 Sqn 20.10.41; 50 Sqn 13.4.42; 16.45 hours 13.5.42 CAT.E Dived into gd from 800 feet & ct fire on impact at Thurlby. A/c had been flown by others that day with no problems. Sugg engaged autopilot before gyro was spun. FS P. J. W. Blake-5-0-non.op. SOC 18.5.42, Ops 9.

L7520

Mk.1A 61 Sqn 21.10.41; 2.11.41 CAT.E Port eng. cut. Used incorrect method to feather prop. Unable to mntn ht. F/L in field. Ekinsfield, Colden, Beds. Plt Off. A. L. Searby-?-all-non.op. SOC 9.11.41, Ops 1.

L7521

Mk.1A 61 Sqn 25.10.41; 27.3.42 CAT.Ac (FB) No Ops this day & no accident card, RIW 9.4.42; AW/CN 9.4.42; 61 Sqn 8.4.42; 50 Sqn 11.4.42; 50 CF 18.5.42; 1654 CU –; 12.15 hours 5.9.42 CAT.E Stbd prop failed to unfeather following ex. Emergency approach to Waddington but baulked by an incoming Oxford. A/c turned sharply whilst semi-stalled. Cr short of 'drome & burnt out. Sqn Ldr Carter-?-all non.op SOC 17.9.42, 346.40 AF hours, Ops 19.

L7522

Mk.1A 61 Sqn 25.10.41; 97 Sqn 27.10.41; No accident card, ROS 2.12.41; 21.12.41; 97 Sqn 31.12.41; 83 Sqn 31.1.42; 22.2.42 MFO OL-N Sqn Ldr J. R. Rainford-7-0-Stavanger, N. Daylight, shot down by Bf109 during 5 a/c attack on Stavanger airfield, Ops 8.

L7523

Mk.1A 207 Sqn 31.10.41; 14/15.1.42 MFO EM-M FS Wescombe-7-0-Hamburg. Cr. At Cliff House Farm, Holmpton, nr Withernsea, Yks at 2045. Airborne 3.10 hours, Ops 4.

L7524

Mk.1A 6 MU (Brize Norton) 2.11.41; 46 MU (Lossiemouth) 14.11.41; 25 OTU 11.12.41; 11.12.41 CAT M(c) Undershot practicing flapless ldgs. Dropped heavily on uneven gd at edge of peritrack at Bircotes. U/c coll. ROS 14.12.41; 25 OTU 17.1.42; 49 Sqn 15.4.42; 1485 B&GF 1.10.42; 1661 CU 25.4.43; RAF Kidlington 7.10.43; 15.10.43 CAT.E2, No accident card. Poss date scrapped. SOC 16.10.43, 275.35 AF hours, Ops 2.

L7525

Mk.1A 38 MU (Llandau) 15.4.41; 97 Sqn 10.12.41; 106 Sqn 25.1.42; 83 Sqn –; 12.2.42 Op FULLER. A/c dam & R/G wounded by day fighter. ROS 17.2.42; 83 Sqn 11.?.42; 50 Sqn 13.5.42; 30/31.5.42 Stbd eng. hit by flak in TA & ct fire, jettis. all moveable gear to reach Tempsford; 1485 B&GF 18.8.42;1661 CU 25.4.43. SOC 24.8.43, 423 AF hours, Ops 3.

L7526

Mk.1A 25 OTU 26.11.41; 1.1.42 CAT M(c) Tail wheel fork failed & tyre burst ldg on rough gd at Bircotes, ROS 5.1.42; 25 OTU 30.1.42; 49 Sqn 15.6.42; 207 CF 5.8.42; 15.15 hours 2.9.42 CAT Ac Tailwheel coll twd end of ldg run at Woodhall Spa; 207 Sqn 12.9.42; 1656 CU 22.10.42. SOC 15.7.43, Ops 3.

AVRO MANCHESTER A/C built by Metrovick, Trafford Park for erection at Woodford, Contract No.982866. Forty-three aircraft delivered from March 1941 to March 1942. (First thirteen A/C destroyed by enemy action at Mosely Road Works on 23.12.40. Serials re-allocated).

R5768
AVRO 10.3.41 Retained & conv Mk.1A; 83 Sqn 18.4.42; 30/31.5.42 CAT.B (FB) Badly dam by flak. F/L at base on retn. ROS 4.6.42; 83 CF 26.9.42; 1656 CU 23.4.43; 16.11.43 CAT.E2. No accident card. Poss date scrapped SOC 19.3.43, Ops 2.

R5769
AVRO Cranage 20.3.41 Stored, mods & Eng ch; 25 OTU 27.3.42; 106 Sqn 15.4.42; 50 Sqn 16.5.42; 9 CF 12.8.42; 1661 CU 8.11.42; 1.4.43 CAT.Ac Blown back into L7297 in gale at Winthorpe. ROS 12.4.43; 1661 CU 1.5.43. SOC 2.9.43, 284.45 AF hours, Ops 4.

R5770
AVRO for mods etc. 9.4.41; 25 OTU 8.3.42; 106 Sqn 15.11.42; 1660 CU 3.1.43; 4.7.43 CAT.E. Eng failed on TO. A/c swung. u/c raised to stop. foreign mat. fd in carb. Plt Off. J. L. Cooper-?-all-trng. SOC 13.7.43, 213.50 AF hours, Ops 5.

R5771
AVRO/SAS 10.6.41 for mods etc; 25 OTU 27.3.42; 83 Sqn 13.4.42; 49 Sqn 15.4.42; 420 Sqn 23.5.42; 57 CF 6.9.42; 50 CF 23.9.42; 1654 CU 10.10.42; To 2 AGS 27.5.43 as 3746M GI Airframe. SOC 6.12.4?, Ops 3.

R5772
AVRO for mods etc 27.4.41; 25 OTU 2.4.42; 49 Sqn 16.4.42; 83 CF 26.7.42; 1661 CU 10.10.42; 26.1.43 CAT.E 1st Solo on type. Pt eng cut circling 'drome. On att'd restart it ct fire. F/L in field. Burnt out. Primary cause failure No 3 exhaust valve. FS Schnier-1-1-trng. SOC 8.2.43, Ops 1.

R5773
AVRO/SAS 23.7.41; RAE (Farnborough) 24.4.42; TDU (Gosport) 2.5.42; CAT.B. No accident card. AVRO MR RIW 25.11.42; TDU (Gosport) 24.12.42; NFD on service; To 3892M GI Airframe ?.3.43 SOC 1.11.4?, Ops 0.

R5774
AVRO/SAS 26.7.41; TDU (Gosport) 27.4.42; 14.40 hours 12.9.42 running up stbd eng at Weston-super-Mare. Stbd wheel chock slipped whilst eng at 1500 rpm. A/c lurched fwd & pushed over platform on which Cpl Smith was wking. ROS 5.10.42; TDU 10.10.42; AVRO. CAT.B No accident card. RIW 25.11.42; AW/CN 31.12.42; TDU 2.1.43; To 11 SofTT as 3890M GI Airfr. 30.6.43. Reduced to spares 21.2.4?, Ops 0.

R5775
AVRO 18.6.41, 408 CF 27.3.42; 49 Sqn 28.3.42; 83 CF 26.7.42; 1654 CU 10.10.42; 1660 CU 19.4.43; 3 SofTT as 4281M GI Airfr. 22.9.43. SOC 12.10.44, Ops 3.

R5776
AVRO 18.6.41; 1AGS - Prob. incor seq'd; AVRO 5.8.41; 1654 CU 1.6.42; 408 CF 7.6.42; 1654 CU 16.6.42; 10.8.42 CAT.A collided with armourer's lorry; To ? as 3745M GI Airfr ?.3.43; SOC 14.5.43, Ops 0.

R5777
AVRO 18.7.41; 1654 CU 29.6.42; 00.40 hours 16.7.42 CAT.B Bounced & yawed in heavy ldg. Stbd u/c leg collapsed at Wigsley. RIW; AW/CN 8.5.43; 39 MU (Colerne) 22.5.43; 1654 CU?; 31.10.43 CAT.E2 No accident card. SOC 4.11.43, Ops 0.

R5778
AVRO 18.7.41; 207 Sqn 17.1.42; 50 Sqn 25.1.42; 9.2.42 CAT. Mc Struck concealed gun pit whilst making way for departing a/c & u/c coll. Gun pit hidden by nets & snow. ROS 13.2.42; 50 Sqn 14.3.42; 9.5.42 CAT.E Aborted bombing mission after being hit by flak, knocking out Pt eng. Resulting damage led to a/c being SOC on retn. Sgt Wilkie-7-7-Warnemunde. SOC 15.5.43, Ops 7.

R5779
AVRO for storage, mods & eng ch 1.8.41; 83 Sqn 24.12.41; 8/9.3.42 MFO OL-G Fg Off. R. W. Cooper-7-2-Essen. Shot down at 0329 by Obfw Gildner of II/NJG2. Cr. Nr Smilde, NL, Ops 4.

R5780
AVRO for storage, mods & eng ch 1.8.41; 83 Sqn 27.12.41; 29.3.42 Oil cooler burst on Ops; 23/24.4.42 Dam. by flak on Ops; 106 Sqn 13.11.41 (date error); 49 CF 29.6.42; 15.7.42 CAT.Ac Undershot Scampton, hit mound, bounced, lded heavily tail down. Tailwheel unit collapsed. ROS 16.7.42; 49 CF 8.8.42; 57 CF 7.9.42; 1656 CU 1.10.42; 19.10.42 CAT.E Unauthorised low flight by Australian crew. Hit tree beating up local pub and nosedived into ground, bursting into flames. 2 ml ENE of Lichfield. Plt Off. R. D. Horner-6-0-trng. SOC 9.11.42, Ops 14.

R5781
AVRO 1.8.41; 83 Sqn 9.1.42; 28/29.3.42 MFO OL-I? Fg Off. T. A. Lumb-7-0-Lubeck. Cr Gemeinde, Ploen, G. NFD, Ops 2, 23.45 AF hours.

R5782
AVRO 3.9.41; 207 Sqn 19.9.41; 27.9.41 CAT.B. Both hydr & emerg. pneu system failed after air test. Lded pt u/c locked & stbd semi-retracted. ROS 6.10.41; 207 Sqn 24.10.41; 23.12.41 CAT.Mc. Dam in error during fmn flying pract by Spitfire. ROS 29.12.41; 207 Sqn 15.1.42; 3.3.42 CAT.Ac (FB) Bomb doors slightly dam by flak; 6.2.42 GARDENING in daylight. Top of port wing dam. by flak; 50 Sqn 18.3.42; 17/18.4.42; MFO Plt Off. G. Baker-7-5-Hamburg. Shot down by Flak Batteries 1 & 2/225 at Glashütte, G at 0355, Ops 12, 118.25 hours.

R5783
AVRO 3.9.41; 97 Sqn 23.9.41; 21.10.41 MFO OF-V Plt Off. G. A. Hartley-7-7-Bremen. Ran out of fuel on return and F/L at Friskney, Lincs, Ops 2.

R5784
61 Sqn 4.10.41; 31.1.42 CAT.Ac Failure of Former 35 disc on inspection, app. due to unrep'd heavy ldg. ROS 17.2.42; 61 Sqn 4.3.42; AVRO CAT.B 5.5.42, No accident card, RIW; AW/CN 6.5.42; 50 Sqn 12.5.42; 9 CF 9.8.42; 57 CF 8.9.42; 16.35 hours 10.9.42 Stbd eng ct fire in circuit. A/c made normal ldg. 'D' block exhaust had burnt thro; 1485 B&GF 28.11.42; 1660 CU 9.1.43; AVRO 21.1.43 No accident card. ROS?; 1660 CU 30.1.43; 9? AFU 20.7.43 (prob incorr attrib); 26.7.43 CAT.Ac. Pilot of No 3 Ferry Pool experienced alarming tail flutter in flight. Precautionary ldg at Hawarden. Blamed on faulty construction; Became 3984M GI Airfr ?.7.43. SOC 22.6.4?, Ops 4.

R5785
AVRO 3.9.41; 61 Sqn 12.10.41; 11.4.42 MFO QR-M Sgt D. H. MacSporran-7-6-Le Havre. Stbd eng failed after flak hit over target. Ditched in English Channel twenty miles off south coast. Crew made POWs, 1 drowned, Ops 8.

R5786
AVRO 2.9.41; 61 Sqn 10.10.41; 14.1.42. CAT Ac (FB) Failed to hold off. Flew into gd, bounced, swung. Tyre burst, u/c coll. returning from Ops. Dk night, no floodlts. ROS 18.2.42; 61 Sqn 14.3.42; 1.4.42 Mainplane holed by 20-mm flak shell. A/c persistently stalled on next op & early retn nec.; 50 Sqn 11.4.42; 50 CF 18.5.42; 02.50 hours 30.5.42 CAT.B Overshot in poor vis. & heavy rain. Full brake failed to check. Ran across road & fell into field below 'drome level at Waddington. U/c coll. Had diverted from Skellington due to cr. a/c (L7492). ROS

2.6.42; 1654 CU 18.7.42; unknown allocation. 21.12.42; 25.1.43 CAT.B MR AVRO. No accident card. SOC 28.1.43, Ops 9.

R5787
AVRO 22.9.41; 61 Sqn 20.10.41; 31.1/1.2.42 MFO QR-M Fg Off. R. B. Parsons-7-3-Brest. Hit by flak over Brest. F/L at St Renan, F, Ops 2.

R5788
AVRO for Storage, mods & eng ch 3.10.41; 207 Sqn 31.10.41; 17.11.41 CAT.Mc. Held off too high. Heavy ldg. Tailwheel dam. RIW 24.11.41; 83 Sqn 13.12.41; 49 Sqn 8.6.42; 11.00 hours 6.7.42 CAT.Ac A/c landed, ran 200 yards, u/c lock warning horn sounded & u/c coll. On approach horn silent. ROS; 49 CF 31.10.42; 1660 CU 9.1.43; 1AFU 20.7.43 as 3983M GI Airframe. SOC 1.11.44, Ops 2.

R5789
AVRO 3.10.41; 61 Sqn 20.10.41; 9.1.42 MFO Plt Off. D. S. Matthews-8-6-Brest. Engine ct fire over England. six baled out, two pilots killed in F/L at Wiltshire Cross, Wilts. Captain on 1st Op, Ops 1.

R5790
AVRO 7.10.41; 207 Sqn 22.10.41; 11.11.41 CAT.Ac No accident card; 207 Sqn 10.12.41; 83 Sqn 11.12.41; 6/7.4.42 Dam by flak on Ops, pilot wounded. Control lost. Two baled out. 2nd pilot recovered a/c & retn to Coltishall; 49 Sqn 8.6.42; 44 CF 20.9.42; 1661 CU 8.11.42; 5.12.42 CAT.Ac Tail oleo failed at Waddington. ROS 11.12.42; 1661 CU 19.12.42; Became 3774M GI Airframe. SOC 26.9.45, Ops 16.

R5791
AVRO 8.10.41; 207 Sqn 29.10.41; 31.1/1.2.42 CAT.Ac (FB) A/c took flak hit imm. after bomb release. BA temp blinded by hydraulic fluid from front turret. Centre fin, bomb doors & throttle box also hit. ROS 3.2.42; 207 Sqn 6.3.42; 13.46 hours 21.4.42 CAT.Ac. V heavy ldg Bottesford. Pilot failed to keep a/c straight. Pt wheel ran into ditch at edge of runway. U/c collapsed. ROS 24.4.42; 207 CF 14.7.42; 1485 B&GF 25.8.42; No accident card but ROS 3.10.42; 1485 B&GF 17.10.42; 7.11.42 CAT.B Tailwheel collapsed taxiing at Fulbeck. ROS 13.11.42; 1485 B&GF 12.12.42; 1654 CU 22.4.43; Became 4001M at Squires Gate 26.7.43; To Henlow 27.5.44. Reduced to spares 6.2.45, Ops 10.

R5792
AVRO 10.10.41; 97 Sqn 29.10.41; 24.11.41 No accident card. Mid-air collision with Hurricane. cr. Walpole St Andrew. Fg Off. H. T. Hill-7-0-non.op. Hurricane of 57 OTU unauthorised mock attack. 1MPRU Cowley 5.12.41. SOC 5.12.41, Ops 1.

R5793
AVRO 30.10.41; 25 OTU 16.11.41; 49 Sqn 27.4.42; 16.6.42 CAT.A Eng. sluggish. Tail swung & hit lorry; 83 CF 5.8.42; 1656 CU 17.11.42; 39MU (Colerne) 24.12.42. SOC 26.5.43, Ops 0.

R5794
AVRO 4.11.41; 25 OTU 16.11.41; 49 Sqn 13.5.42; 1/2.6.42 MFO Plt Off. Shackleton-7-2-Essen. SOS received at 01.29 stating stbd eng failure. Fix given THPJ3207. Shortly afterwards a/c shot down by Bf110 Fw Heinz Pähler 2/NJGl & cr. at Voorheide nr. Turnhout, B. Ops 2, 136.45 AF hours.

R5795
AVRO 4.11.41; 97 Sqn 22.11.41; 18.12.41 MFO OF-Z Plt Off. N. G. Stokes-7-3-Brest, F.daylight, shot down by Bf109s and cr in sea four miles offshore Brest. Ops 2, 27.55 hours.

R5796
AVRO 8.11.41; 61 Sqn 18.11.41; 207 Sqn 21.11.41; 10.1.42 CAT.Ac (FB) Embarked on LL interdiction after bombing. Flak dam hydraulics, bomb doors and one wheel lowered. Div'td to Coningsby on retn; 21.50 hours

24.2.42 CAT.Ac (FB) GARDENING. ORB says hit at 500 feet on stbd side by fire from flak ships. Dam rear fus. wing & elevators. Raid Summary Book says attacked by Bf109 at 22.25 hours; 106 Sqn 13.3.42; 30/31.5.42 Dam. by flak on Ops; 57 CF 8.9.42; 50 CF 23.9.42; 1654 CU –; 11.10.42 CAT.Ac Dam discovered on daily insp. Wigsley, ROS 19.10.42; 50 CF 31.10.42; 1654 CU –; 10.30 hours 2.1.43 A/c struck by L7280 whilst taxiing; 1654 CU 16.1.43; 1660 CU 11.7.43; 16.11.43 CAT.E2 MR No accident card. SOC 19.11.43, Ops 26.

R5797
AVRO 11.11.41; DD Flt Shed 19.11.41; AW/CN 23.11.41; To DTD 24.12.41 AVRO Ringway 22.2.42. TI work incl. Mk.XIV bombsight at Finningley; AVRO Ringway, became 3778M 2.7.42 Prop tests GI Airfr ?.6.43. SOC -, Ops 0.

R5829
AVRO 29.11.41; 25 OTU 17.12.41; 12.3.42 CAT.Ac Swung off runway on TO & hit Chance light. ROS 17.3.42; 25 OTU 16.5.42; 1654 CU 4.8.42; 3 AGS 18.6.43. SOC 15.7.43, Ops O.

R5830
AVRO 7.11.41; AAEE (Boscombe Down) 11.1.42; 83 Sqn 13.2.42; 29.3.42 CAT.Ac (FB) Early retn. dam by fighter. Gear jett to mntn ht. ROS 2.4.42; 83 Sqn 25.7.42; 1656 CU 16.11.42; 39 MU (Colerne) 5.2.43; 14.11.43 CAT.E2 No accident card. SOC 16.11.43, Ops 5.

R5831
AVRO 7.11.41; 83 Sqn 9.1.42; 8/9.3.42 Slight dam. by flak on Ops; 25/26.3.42 MFO Gironde. Flew into balloon cable, cr. 02.10 hours Warden Point, Sheppey, Kent, 82 AF hours, Ops 1.

R5832
AVRO 2.12.41; 61 Sqn 28.1.42; 11.2.42 Cat.B (FB) A/c did not operate that night. No accident card, NFD; 61 Sqn –; 01.45 hours 30.3.42 CAT.Ac. Uncertain of position on retn from Ops. Attempted ldg small 'drome at Westwood, Peterboro. Poor viz. Overshot. ROS 4.4.42; 61 Sqn 13.6.42; 61 CF 16.6.42; 1660 CU 20.10.42; 1661 CU 25.2.43; To 3744M GI Airfr, ?.4.43. SOC 30.4.43, 410 AF hours, Ops 7.

R5833
AVRO 2.12.41; 207 Sqn 6.2.42; 83 Sqn 1.4.42; 50 Sqn 15.4.42; 6.6.42 MFO Plt Off. D. W. Garland-7-1-GARDENING. Gorse. Cr nr Ile de Quiberone, F. NFD, Ops 11, 142 AF hours.

R5834
AVRO 2.12.41; 61 Sqn 28.1.42; 11.2.42 CAT.R(B) F/L ex-Ops. Stbd eng knocked out in TA. Fuel transfer problems. Pt eng cut for lack of fuel on finals. Belly-landed & struck ditch. FS J. B. Underwood-7-7-GARDENING. RIW 9.3.42. SOC 15.4.42, Ops 1.

R5835
AVRO 2.12.41; 207 Sqn 6.2.42; 83 Sqn 1.4.42; 49 Sqn 24.4.42; 408 Sqn 23.5.42; 1654 CU 22.6.42; 4.7.42 CAT. Ac Damaged in raid by enemy intruders; 1654 CU –; 26.2.43 CAT. Ac Tail wheel oleo failed whilst on tow ROS 3.3.43; 1654 CU 13.3.43; 1661 CU 11.7.43; RAF Benson 29.9.43. SOC 6.10.43, 471.15 AF hours, Ops 2.

R5836
AVRO 2.12.41; 83 Sqn 13.2.42; 19.3.42 CAT.B (FB) Ops 13/14.3.42 Uneventful. Poss flying accident? No accident card. ReCAT. Ac ROS 19.3.42; 83 Sqn 13.6.42; 49 Sqn 25.6.42; 49 CF 22.7.42; 1661 CU 9.11.42; 1.12.42 CAT.B Came in too high. Failed to take overshoot action promptly. Stalled from 15 feet u/c coll. ReCat.E 2.12.42. Plt Off. J. M. Desmond-all-trng at Scampton. SOC 3.12.42, Ops 2

R5837

AVRO 1.1.42; 83 Sqn 1.3.42; 5/6.4.42 slightly dam by flak on Ops; 8/9.4.42 MFO OL-J Plt Off. M. A. Sproule-8-1-NICKELS. Paris F Ditched in English Channel at Margate, flak dam, Ops 11.

R5838
AVRO 5.2.42; 83 Sqn 13.2.42; No accident card. Poss dam on mining Op 20/21.3.42? ROS 24.3.42; 83 Sqn 1.4.42; 12/13.4.42 CAT. Ac (FB) Badly dam by night fighter, R/G killed. One eng failed at Dutch coast. Ret to Coltishall on one. ROS 15.4.42; 83 CF 25.7.42; 9 CF 8.8.42; 1661 CU 8.11.42; 12.3.43 CAT.B Demo prop feathering at 5,000 feet. Port prop failed to unfeather. Attempted ldg at Wickenby. Overshot into ditch. Stbd u/c coll. WO E. Knight-?-all. ReCAT.E. SOC 24.3.43, Ops 11.

R5839
AVRO 7.2.42; 61 Sqn 28.2.42; 106 Sqn 28.2.42; 20.3.42 Cat. Ac Early retn from Ops. Hydraulics failed after TO. A/c carrying 6,000 lb of mines. Perm given to ld Coningsby. U/c coll after ballooning due to rough surf. of 'drome. ROS 1.4.42; 106 Sqn 18.5.42; 49 Sqn 29.6.42; 1485 B&GF 29.8.42; 1661 CU 25.4.43; RAF Kidlington 6.10.43; Cat.E2 15.10.43. SOC 18.10.43, 298.30 AF hours, Ops 2.

R5840
AVRO 7.2.42; 61 Sqn 28.2.42; 106 Sqn 28.2.42; 6/7.4.42 Dam. by flak on Ops; 2/3.5.42 MFO F/S Hurd-7-7-GARDENING, shot down & cr. Pellworm Is. G, Ops 14.

R5841
AVRO 9.2.42; 61 Sqn 10.3.42; 106 Sqn 10.3.42; 26.3.42 CAT.B Overshot Exeter returning from mining Op. ROS 12.4.42; 106 Sqn 4.7.42; 26.7.42 CAT.Ac No accident card; 106 CF 24.8.42; 1660 CU 30.10.42; 18.50 hours 11.4.43 CAT.E Stbd eng failed & ct fire during circuits & ldgs. A/c cr. Swinderby. Expect fire reached cockpit before ldg. Seat of fire est as 'B' block in stbd eng poss due to hydraulic pipe failure. Flt Lt J. M. Whitwell-6-3-trng, SOC 21.4.43, 189.35 AF hours, Ops 2.

Bibliography

Air Ministry, *The Manchester Aeroplane, Two Vulture Engines* (Air Publication [AP]1660A, 1941)

Barker, R., The Thousand Plan. The Story of the First 1000 Bomber Raid on Cologne (Chatto & Windus, 260pp, 1965)Bending, K., Achieve your aim. The History of 97 (Straits Settlements) Squadron in the Second World War. (Woodfield Publishing, 364pp, 2005)

Bearman. M. "The Other Sound Barrier". (The Aviation Historian. p64-75 2021)

Boiten, T. E. W., The Nachtjagd War Diaries: An Operational History of the German Night Fighter Force in the West. Volume 1 Sept. 1939 - March 1944 (Red Kite, 396pp, 2008)

Bowman, M. W. & Boiten, T. E. W., *Raiders of the Reich: Air Battle Western Europe: 1942-45* (Airlife Classic, 224pp [p16-17 on Manchester loss], 1996)

Bowyer, C., *Avro Manchester* (Profile Publications Ltd, 24pp, 1974)

Bowyer, C., Manchester Moments. In: Bomber Group at War (Ian Allan, p42-50, 1981)

Bowyer, M. J. F., *Bombing Colours. Part 25. The Avro Manchester* (Airfix Magazine, p476-481, 1971)

Brickhill, P., Escape or Die. Authentic Stories of the RAF Escaping Society. Chapter 3: The women who took a hand. [Attempted evasion by Sergeant James Dowd, W/op on 83 Squadron] (Evans Bros. Ltd, London 190pp, also Pan Books Ltd, 1952)

Bushby, J., Gunner's Moon: A memoir of the RAF night assault on Germany [Rear Gunner, 83 Squadron] (Ian Allan, p92-129. 1972)

Chorley, W. R., *RAF Bomber Command Losses of the Second World War. 1941* (Midland Counties Publications, 224pp, 1993)

Chorley, W. R., *RAF Bomber Command Losses of the Second World War. 1942* (Midland Counties Publications, 318pp, 1994)

Clegg, P. V., *Avro Test-Pilots Since 1907. Vol 1, From Alliott Verdon-Roe to 'Sam' Brown* (G. M. Enterprises in association with Aero Book Co., 199pp, 1996)

Finn, S., *Lincolnshire Air War 1939-1945* (Aero Litho Company [Lincoln] Ltd, 115pp, 1973)

Foreman, J., Matthews, J. & Parry, S., *Luftwaffe Night Fighter Combat Claims. 1939-1945* (Red Kite, 248pp, 2004)

Garbett, M. & Goulding, B., Lancaster at War: 3 ['Three Times Down, but Not Out, p12-16] (Ian Allan Ltd, 152pp, 1984)

Green, W. & Swanborough, G., *WWII Aircraft Fact Files. RAF Bombers. Part 1* (MacDonald & Janes, p19-25, 1979)

Gunston, W., *Rolls-Royce Aero Engines* (Patrick Stevens Ltd, 7pp, 1989)

Hall, C. F.,'Missing, Believed Killed'. Personal account of his loss in Manchester L7380 and subsequent experiences as a POW (Hall family private papers, 89pp [unpublished], 2004)

Hamblin, J., Always Prepared: The story of 207 Squadron Royal Air Force (Air-Britain Publication, 232pp, 1999)

Harrison, S. E., A Bomber Command Survivor: The Wartime Reminiscences of a Bomber Command Pilot [97 Squadron - Manchester Ops] (Self-published, 140pp, 1992)

Harvey-Bailey, A., *The Merlin in Perspective - the combat years* (Rolls-Royce Heritage Trust. Historical Series No2, 132pp, 1983)

Harvey-Bailey, A., *Rolls-Royce - Hives. The Quiet Tiger* (Sir Henry Royce Memorial Foundation, Historical Series No 7, 101pp, 1985)

Hellwinkell, L., Hitler's Gateway to the Atlantic. German Naval Bases in France 1940-1945 (Pen & Sword Books Ltd, 234pp, 2014)

Hillier, M., Suitcases, Vultures & Spies. From Bomber Command to Special Ops. The story of Wing Commander Thomas Murray DSO, DFC* (Yellowman Ltd, 143pp, 2014)

Hinchliffe, P., *The Lent Papers. Helmut Lent* (Cerberus, 304pp, 2003)

Holmes, H., *Avro: The Story of Manchester's Aircraft Company* (Published Neil Richardson, 27pp, 1993)

Holmes, H., *Avro: The History of an Aircraft Company* (Airlife Publishing Ltd, 196pp, 1994)

Holyoak, V., *On the Wings of the Morning. RAF Bottesford 1941-1945* (Self published, ISBN 0-9526739-0-8, 144pp. Printed by The Local History Press, 3 Devonshire Promenade, Lenton, Notts 1995)

Jackson, A. J., *Avro Aircraft since 1908* (Putnam, 511pp, 1965)

Kirby, R., Avro Manchester: The Legend Behind the Lancaster (Midland Publications, 208pp, 1995)

Lewis, W. J. (Mike), *Flying the Manchester* (CAHS - Journal of the Canadian Aviation Historical Society, Vol 32, No 2, 1994)

Low, R. G. & Harper, F. E., *83 Squadron 1917-1969* [Privately published by R G Low, 333pp, 1992)

Lumsden, A., *British Piston Aero-Engines and Their Aircraft* (Airlife Publishing Ltd, 322pp [p200-201 on the Rolls-Royce Vulture], 1994)

Mason, F. K., *The Avro Lancaster* (Aston Publications, 437pp, 1989)

McCarthy, J. J. N., (RNZAF), Transcript of a journal kept by the late Fg Off. John Justin Neville McCarthy between August 1941 and July 1942, 141pp (Unpublished family papers of Dwight Blok, 1941/2)

Messenger, C., *Cologne. The First 1000 Bomber Raid* (Ian Allan, 64pp, 1982)

Middlebrook, M. & Everitt, C., The Bomber Command War Diaries. An Operational Reference Book 1939-1945 (Viking, 804pp, 1985)

Minney, C., Manchesters. In: Aeromilitaria, Vol 2, p31-40 (Air Britain, 1990)

Moyes, P. J. R., *Bomber Squadrons of the RAF and Their Aircraft* (MacDonald & Co, 384pp, 1964)

Neale, M. C., (Ed.), An Account of Partnership - Industry, Government and the Aero Engine. The memoirs of George Purvis Bulman (Rolls-Royce Heritage Trust. Historical Series No 31, 376pp, 2002)

Penrose, H., Architect of Wings. A biography of Roy Chadwick - Designer of the Lancaster Bomber (Airlife Publishing Ltd, 246pp, 1985)

Robertson, B., *Lancaster - The Story of a Famous Bomber* (Harleyford Publications Ltd, 216pp, 1964)

Rope, D., For The Duration. Extracts from the diary and letters of F/S W G Hawes [207 Squadron Manchester Second Pilot] (Mackenzie Publications [Australia], 132pp, 1984)

Taylor, E., Operation Millenium. Bomber Harris's Raid on Cologne, May 1942 (Robert Hale, 218pp, 1987)

Walker, N., Strike to Defend. A book about some of the men who served in RAF Bomber Command in World War II [83 Squadron Manchester Ops] (Spearman, 128pp, 1963)

Ward, J., 'Beware of the dog at War'. An Operational Diary of 49 Squadron Spanning 49 years, 1916-1965 (551pp, 1999)

Wood, D. C., *The Design & Development of the Lancaster* (Royal Aeronautical Society, Manchester Branch, 88pp, 1991)

Zagni, F. (nee Valentine)"Gepruft"(="checked" in German) The remarkable Second World War letters of POW John Valentine and his wife, Ursula. Fighting High 232pp 2018

www.ingramcontent.com/pod-product-compliance
Lightning Source LLC
Chambersburg PA
CBHW080237170426
43192CB00014BA/2471